Lecture Notes in Computer Science 7005

Commenced Publication in 1973
Founding and Former Series Editors:
Gerhard Goos, Juris Hartmanis, and Jan van Leeuwen

Marcello Pelillo Edwin R. Hancock (Eds.)

Similarity-Based Pattern Recognition

First International Workshop, SIMBAD 2011
Venice, Italy, September 28-30, 2011
Proceedings

Springer

Volume Editors

Marcello Pelillo
Università Ca' Foscari, DAIS
Via Torino 155, 30172 Venice, Italy
E-mail: pelillo@dsi.unive.it

Edwin R. Hancock
The University of York
Heslington, York YO10 5DD, UK
E-mail: erh@cs.york.ac.uk

ISSN 0302-9743 e-ISSN 1611-3349
ISBN 978-3-642-24470-4 ISBN 978-3-642-24471-1 (eBook)
DOI 10.1007/978-3-642-24471-1
Springer Heidelberg Dordrecht London New York

Library of Congress Control Number: 2011937058

CR Subject Classification (1998): I.4, I.5, I.2.10, H.3, F.1, J.3

LNCS Sublibrary: SL 6 – Image Processing, Computer Vision, Pattern Recognition, and Graphics

Typesetting: Camera-ready by author, data conversion by Scientific Publishing Services, Chennai, India

Printed on acid-free paper

Springer is part of Springer Science+Business Media (www.springer.com)

Preface

Traditional pattern recognition techniques are intimately linked to the notion of "feature spaces." Adopting this view, each object is described in terms of a vector of numerical attributes and is therefore mapped to a point in a Euclidean (geometric) vector space so that the distances between the points reflect the observed (dis)similarities between the respective objects. This kind of representation is attractive because geometric spaces offer powerful analytical as well as computational tools that are simply not available in other representations. Indeed, classical pattern recognition methods are tightly related to geometrical concepts and numerous powerful tools have been developed during the last few decades, starting from the maximal likelihood method in the 1920's, to perceptrons in the 1960's, to kernel machines in the 1990's.

However, the geometric approach suffers from a major intrinsic limitation, which concerns the representational power of vectorial, feature-based descriptions. In fact, there are numerous application domains where either it is not possible to find satisfactory features or they are inefficient for learning purposes. This modeling difficulty typically occurs in cases when experts cannot define features in a straightforward way (e.g., protein descriptors vs. alignments), when data are high dimensional (e.g., images), when features consist of both numerical and categorical variables (e.g., person data, like weight, sex, eye color, etc.), and in the presence of missing or inhomogeneous data. But, probably, this situation arises most commonly when objects are described in terms of structural properties, such as parts and relations between parts, as is the case in shape recognition.

In the last few years, interest around purely similarity-based techniques has grown considerably. For example, within the supervised learning paradigm (where expert-labeled training data is assumed to be available) the well-established kernel-based methods shift the focus from the choice of an appropriate set of features to the choice of a suitable kernel, which is related to object similarities. However, this shift of focus is only partial, as the classical interpretation of the notion of a kernel is that it provides an implicit transformation of the feature space rather than a purely similarity-based representation. Similarly, in the unsupervised domain, there has been an increasing interest around pairwise or even multiway algorithms, such as spectral and graph-theoretic clustering methods, which avoid the use of features altogether.

By departing from vector-space representations one is confronted with the challenging problem of dealing with (dis)similarities that do not necessarily possess the Euclidean behavior or not even obey the requirements of a metric. The lack of the Euclidean and/or metric properties undermines the very foundations of traditional pattern recognition theories and algorithms, and poses totally new theoretical/computational questions and challenges.

This volume contains the papers presented at the First International Workshop on Similarity-Based Pattern Recognition (SIMBAD 2011), held in Venice, Italy, September 28–30, 2011. The aim of this workshop was to consolidate research efforts in the area of similarity-based pattern recognition and machine learning and to provide an informal discussion forum for researchers and practitioners interested in this important yet diverse subject. The workshop marks the end of the EU FP7 Projects SIMBAD (http://simbad-fp7.eu) and is a follow-up of the ICML 2010 Workshop on Learning in non-(geo)metric spaces.

We believe that there are two main themes underpinning this research topic, which correspond to the two fundamental questions that arise when abandoning the realm of vectorial, feature-based representations. These are:

- How can one *obtain* suitable similarity information from data representations that are more powerful than, or simply different from, the vectorial?
- How can one *use* similarity information in order to perform learning and classification tasks?

The call for papers produced 35 submissions, resulting in the 23 papers appearing in this volume, 16 of which presented orally at the workshop and 7 in a poster session. The papers cover a wide range of problems and perspectives, from supervised to unsupervised learning, from generative to discriminative models, and from theoretical issues to real-world practical applications. In addition to the contributed papers, the workshop featured invited keynote talks by Marco Gori, from the University of Siena, Italy, Ulrike Hahn, from Cardiff University, UK, and John Shawe-Taylor, from University College London, UK. All oral presentations were filmed by Videolectures, and will be freely available on-line in due course.

We gratefully acknowledge generous financial support from the PASCAL2 network of excellence, and thank the International Association for Pattern Recognition (IAPR) for its sponsorship. We also acknowledge the Future and Emerging Technology (FET) Programme, of the 7th Framework Programme for Research of the European Commission, which funded the SIMBAD project, within which this workshop was conceived and of which was an outgrowth.

We would also like to take this opportunity to express our gratitude to all those who helped to organize the workshop. First of all, thanks are due to the members of the Scientific Committees and to the additional reviewers. Special thanks are due to the members of the Organizing Committee. In particular, Samuel Rota Bulò and Nicola Rebagliati managed the online review system and were webmasters, Furqan Aziz assembled the proceedings, and Veronica Giove provided administrative support.

Finally, we offer our appreciation to the editorial staff at Springer in producing this book, and for supporting the event through publication in the LNCS series. Finally, we thank all the authors and the invited speakers for helping to make this event a success, and producing a high-quality publication to document the event.

August 2011

Marcello Pelillo
Edwin Hancock

Organization

Program Chairs

Marcello Pelillo	University of Venice, Italy pelillo@dsi.unive.it
Edwin R. Hancock	University of York, UK erh@cs.york.ac.uk

Steering Committee

Joachim Buhmann	ETH Zurich, Switzerland
Robert Duin	Delft University of Technology, The Netherlands
Mario Figueiredo	Technical University of Lisbon, Portugal
Edwin Hancock	University of York, UK
Vittorio Murino	University of Verona, Italy
Marcello Pelillo (Chair)	University of Venice, Italy

Program Committee

Maria-Florina Balcan	Georgia Institute of Technology, USA
Manuele Bicego	Univeristy of Verona, Italy
Joachim Buhmann	ETH Zurich, Switzerland
Horst Bunke	University of Bern, Switzerland
Tiberio Caetano	NICTA, Australia
Umberto Castellani	University of Verona, Italy
Luca Cazzanti	University of Washington, Seattle, USA
Nicol Cesa-Bianchi	University of Milan, Italy
Robert Duin	Delft University of Technology, The Netherlands
Francisco Escolano	University of Alicante, Spain
Mario Figueiredo	Technical University of Lisbon, Portugal
Ana Fred	Technical University of Lisbon, Portugal
Bernard Haasdonk	University of Stuttgart, Germany
Edwin Hancock	University of York, UK
Anil Jain	Michigan State University, USA
Robert Krauthgamer	Weizmann Institute of Science, Israel
Marco Loog	Delft University of Technology, The Netherlands
Vittorio Murino	University of Verona, Italy

Elzbieta Pekalska	University of Manchester, UK
Marcello Pelillo	University of Venice, Italy
Massimiliano Pontil	University College London, UK
Antonio Robles-Kelly	NICTA, Australia
Volker Roth	University of Basel, Switzerland
Amnon Shashua	The Hebrew University of Jerusalem, Israel
Andrea Torsello	University of Venice, Italy
Richard Wilson	University of York, UK

Additional Reviewers

Marco San Biagio
Jaume Gibert Paola Piro
Nicola Rebagliati
Samuel Rota Bulò
Simona Ullo

Organization Committee

Samuel Rota Bulò (Chair)	University of Venice, Italy
Nicola Rebagliati	University of Venice, Italy
Furqan Aziz	University of York, UK
Teresa Scantamburlo	University of Venice, Italy
Luca Rossi	University of Venice, Italy

Table of Contents

Clustering and Dissimilarity Data

Applications

Spectral Methods and Embedding

On the Usefulness of Similarity Based Projection Spaces for Transfer Learning*

Emilie Morvant, Amaury Habrard, and Stéphane Ayache

Laboratoire d'Informatique Fondamentale de Marseille,
Aix-Marseille Université, CNRS UMR 6166, 13453 Marseille cedex 13, France
{emilie.morvant,amaury.habrard,stephane.ayache}@lif.univ-mrs.fr

Abstract. Similarity functions are widely used in many machine learning or pattern recognition tasks. We consider here a recent framework for binary classification, proposed by Balcan et al., allowing to learn in a potentially non geometrical space based on good similarity functions. This framework is a generalization of the notion of kernels used in support vector machines in the sense that allows one to use similarity functions that do not need to be positive semi-definite nor symmetric. The similarities are then used to define an explicit projection space where a linear classifier with good generalization properties can be learned. In this paper, we propose to study experimentally the usefulness of similarity based projection spaces for transfer learning issues. More precisely, we consider the problem of domain adaptation where the distributions generating learning data and test data are somewhat different. We stand in the case where no information on the test labels is available. We show that a simple renormalization of a good similarity function taking into account the test data allows us to learn classifiers more performing on the target distribution for difficult adaptation problems. Moreover, this normalization always helps to improve the model when we try to regularize the similarity based projection space in order to move closer the two distributions. We provide experiments on a toy problem and on a real image annotation task.

Keywords: Good Similarity Functions, Transfer Learning, Domain Adaptation, Image Classification.

1 Introduction

Many machine learning or pattern recognition algorithms are based on similarity functions. Among all of the existing methods, we can cite the famous k-nearest neighbors, k-means or support vector machines (SVM). An important point is

* This work was supported in part by the french project VideoSense ANR-09-CORD-026 of the ANR in part by the IST Programme of the European Community, under the PASCAL2 Network of Excellence, IST-2007-216886. This publication only reflects the authors' views.

M. Pelillo and E.R. Hancock (Eds.): SIMBAD 2011, LNCS 7005, pp. 1–16, 2011.

to choose or adapt the similarity to the problem considered. For example, approaches dealing with numerical vectors are often based on the Mahalanobis distance [12,15,27] and many methods designed for structured data (strings, trees or graphs) exploit the notion of edit distance [7,14,24]. For binary classification with SVM classifiers, the similarity function must often be a valid kernel[1] in order to define a potentially implicit projection space which is an Hilbert space and where data can be more easily separated. In this case, the similarity function must be symmetric and positive semi-definite (PSD), allowing one to define a valid dot product in the implicit projection space. However, these constraints may rule out some natural similarity functions. Recently, a framework proposed by Balcan *et al.* [2,3] considers a notion of *good similarity function* that overcomes these limitations. Intuitively, this notion only requires that a sufficient amount of examples are on average more similar to a set of *reasonable* points of the same class than to *reasonable* points of the opposite class. Then, the similarity can be used to build an explicit (potentially non geometrical) projection space, corresponding to the vector of similarities to the reasonable examples. In this similarity based projection space, a classifier with good generalization capabilities can be learned.

This kind of result holds in a classical machine learning setting, where test data are supposed to have been generated according to the same distribution than the one used for generating labeled learning data. This assumption is in fact very useful to obtain good generalization results, but is not always valid in every application. For example, in an image classification task, if labeled data consist of images extracted from the web and test data images extracted from different videos, the various methods of data acquisition may imply that labeled data are no longer representative of test data and thus of the underlying classification task. This kind of issue is a special case of transfer learning [22] called *domain adaptation* (DA) [18,23]. DA arises when learning and test data are generated according to two different probability distributions: the first one generating learning data is often referred to as the *source domain*, while the second one for test data corresponds to the *target domain*. According to the existing theoretical frameworks of DA [4,20] a classifier can perform well on the target domain if its error relatively to the source distribution and the divergence between the source and target distributions are together low. One possible solution to learn a performing classifier on the target domain is to find a projection space in which the source and target distributions are close while keeping a low error on the source domain. Many approaches have been proposed in the literature to tackle this problem [9,10,11,19].

In this paper, we consider the case where a learning algorithm is provided with labeled data from the source domain and unlabeled data from the target one. Our aim is to investigate the interest of the framework of Balcan *et al.* for domain adaptation problems. More precisely, we propose to study how we can use the lack of geometrical space of this framework to facilitate the adaptation. We consider two aspects. First, the influence of a renormalization of the similarity

[1] Nevertheless there exists some approaches allowing to use indefinite kernels [16].

function according to the unlabeled source and target data. Second, the addition of a regularization term to the optimization problem considered for learning the classifier in order to select reasonable points that are relevant for the adaptation. This approach can be seen as a feature selection for transfer learning aiming at moving closer the two distributions. We show experimentally that these two aspects can help to learn a better classifier for the target domain. Our experiments are based on a synthetic toy problem and on a real image annotation task.

The paper is organized as follows. We introduce some notations in Section 2. Then we present the framework of *good similarity functions* of Balcan *et al.* in Section 3. We next give a brief overview of *domain adaptation* in Section 4. We present in Section 5 the approach considered and we describe our experimental study in Section 6. We conclude in Section 7.

2 Notations

We denote by $X \subseteq \mathbb{R}^d$ the input space. We consider binary classification problems with $Y = \{-1, 1\}$, the label set. A learning task is modeled as a probability distribution P over $X \times Y$, D being the marginal distribution over X. For any labeled sample S drawn from P, we denote by $S_{|X}$ the sample constituted of all the instances of S without the labels. In a classical machine learning setting, the objective is then to learn a classifier $h : X \rightarrow Y$ belonging to a class of hypothesis $\mathcal{H}$ such that h has a low generalization error $\mathrm{err}_P(h)$ over the distribution P. The generalization error $\mathrm{err}_P(h)$ corresponds to the probability that h can commit an error according to the distribution P, which is defined as follows:

$$\forall h \in \mathcal{H},\ \mathrm{err}_P(h) = \mathbb{E}_{(\mathbf{x},y)\sim P} L(h(\mathbf{x}), y)$$

where L corresponds to the loss function modeling the fact that $h(\mathbf{x}) \neq y$. We will see later that in a DA scenario, we consider two probability distributions P_S and P_T corresponding respectively to a source domain and a target one.

We now give a definition about the notion of similarity functions.

Definition 1. *A similarity function over* X *is any pairwise function*

$$K : X \times X \rightarrow [-1, 1].$$

K *is symmetric if for any* $\mathbf{x}, \mathbf{x}' \in X$: $K(\mathbf{x}, \mathbf{x}') = K(\mathbf{x}', \mathbf{x})$.

A similarity function is a valid kernel function if it is positive semi-definite, meaning that there exists a function ϕ from X to an implicit Hilbert space such that K defines a valid dot product in this space, *i.e.* $K(x, x') = \langle \phi(\mathbf{x}), \phi(\mathbf{x}') \rangle$. Using a valid kernel offers the possibility to learn a good classifier into a high dimensional space where the data are supposed to be linearly separable. However, the choice or the definition of a good kernel can be a tricky task in general. We present in the next section a framework that proposes a rather intuitive notion of good similarity function that gets rid of the constraints of a kernel.

3 Learning with Good Similarity Functions

In this section, we present the class $\mathcal{H}$ of linear classifiers considered in this paper. These classifiers are based on a notion of *good similarity function* for a given classification task. A common general idea is that such a similarity function is able to separate examples of the same class from examples of the opposite class with a given confidence $\gamma > 0$. Given two labeled examples $(\mathbf{x}, y)$ and $(\mathbf{x}', y')$ of $X \times Y$, this idea can be formalized as follows: if $y = y'$ then $K(\mathbf{x}, \mathbf{x}') > \gamma$, otherwise we want $K(\mathbf{x}, \mathbf{x}') < -\gamma$. This can be summarized by the following formulation: $yy'K(\mathbf{x}, \mathbf{x}') > \gamma$. The recent learning framework proposed by Balcan *et al.* [2,3], has generalized this idea by requiring the similarity to be good over a set of *reasonable* points.

Definition 2 (Balcan et al. [2]). *A similarity function K is an (ϵ,γ,τ)-***good similarity function** *for a learning problem P if there exists a (random) indicator function $R(\mathbf{x})$ defining a set of reasonable points such that the following conditions hold:*

(i) A $1 - \epsilon$ probability mass of examples $(\mathbf{x}, y)$ satisfy

$$\mathbb{E}_{(\mathbf{x}',y')\sim P}\left[yy'K(\mathbf{x}, \mathbf{x}')|R(\mathbf{x}')\right] \geq \gamma, \tag{1}$$

(ii) $Pr_{\mathbf{x}'}[R(\mathbf{x}')] \geq \tau$.

From this definition, a large proportion of examples must be on average more similar, with respect to the margin γ, to random reasonable examples of the same class than to random reasonable examples of the opposite class. Moreover, at least a proportion τ of examples should be reasonable. Definition 2 includes all valid kernels as well as some non-PSD non symmetric similarity functions [2,3]. The authors have shown that this definition of good similarities allows also to solve problems that can not be handled by classical kernels, which makes the definition a strict generalization of kernels. According to the following theorem, it provides sufficient conditions to learn a good linear classifier in an explicit projection space defined by the reasonable points in the set R.

Theorem 1 (Balcan et al. [2]). *Let K be an* **(ϵ, γ, τ)-good similarity function** *for a learning problem P. Let $S = \{x'_1, \ldots, x'_d\}$ be a sample of $d = \frac{2}{\tau}\big(\log(\frac{2}{\delta}) + 8\frac{\log(2/\delta)}{\gamma^2}\big)$ landmarks (potentially unlabeled) drawn from P. Consider the mapping $\phi^R : X \to \mathbb{R}^d$ defined as follows: $\phi^R_i(x) = K(x, x'_i)$, $i \in \{1, \ldots, d\}$. Then, with probability at least $1 - \delta$ over the random sample R, the induced distribution $\phi^R(P)$ in $\mathbb{R}^d$ has a separator of error at most $\epsilon + \delta$ relative to L_1 margin at least $\gamma/2$.*

Thus, with an (ϵ,γ,τ)-good similarity function for a given learning problem P and enough (unlabeled) landmark examples, there exists with high probability a low-error linear separator in the explicit ϕ^R-space, corresponding to the space of the similarities to the d landmarks. The criterion given by Definition 2 requires to minimize the number of margin violations which is a NP-hard problem generally difficult to approximate. The authors have then proposed to consider an adaptation of Definition 2 with the hinge loss formalized as follows.

Definition 3 (Balcan et al. [2]). *A similarity function K is an* (ϵ, γ, τ)**-good similarity function in hinge loss** *for a learning problem P if there exists a (random) indicator function $R(x)$ defining a (probabilistic) set of "reasonable points" such that the following conditions hold:*

(i) we have

$$\mathbb{E}_{(\mathbf{x},y)\sim P}\Big[[1 - yg(\mathbf{x})/\gamma]_+\Big] \leq \epsilon, \tag{2}$$

where $g(\mathbf{x}) = \mathbb{E}_{(\mathbf{x}',y')\sim P}[y'K(\mathbf{x},\mathbf{x}')|R(\mathbf{x}')]$
and $[1-c]_+ = \max(0, 1-c)$ *is the hinge loss,*

(ii) $Pr_{\mathbf{x}'}[R(\mathbf{x}')] \geq \tau$.

Using the same ϕ^R-space than Theorem 1, the authors have proved a similar theorem for this definition with the hinge loss. This leads to a natural two step algorithm for learning this classifier: select a set of potential landmark points and then learn a linear classifier in the projection space induced by these points. Then, using d_u unlabeled examples for the landmark points and d_l labeled examples, this linear separator $\boldsymbol{\alpha} \in \mathbb{R}^{d_u}$ can be found by solving a linear problem. We give here the formulation based on the hinge loss presented in [2].

$$\min_{\boldsymbol{\alpha}} \sum_{i=1}^{d_l} \left[1 - \sum_{j=1}^{d_u} \alpha_j y_i K(x_i, x'_j)\right]_+ \quad \text{such that} \sum_{j=1}^{d_u} |\alpha_j| \leq 1/\gamma. \tag{3}$$

In fact, we consider a similar formulation based on a 1-norm regularization, weighted by a parameter λ related to the desired margin.

$$\min_{\boldsymbol{\alpha}} \sum_{i=1}^{d_l} \left[1 - \sum_{j=1}^{d_u} \alpha_j y_i K(x_i, x'_j)\right]_+ + \lambda\|\boldsymbol{\alpha}\|_1. \tag{4}$$

In the following, a classifier learned in this framework is called a SF classifier.

4 Domain Adaptation

Domain adaptation (DA) [4,20] arises when the learning data generation is somewhat different from the test data generation. The learning data, generally called the *source domain*, is represented by a distribution P_S over $X \times Y$ and the test data, referred to the *target domain*, is modeled by a distribution P_T. We denote by D_S and D_T the respective marginal distributions over X.

A learning algorithm is generally provided with a *Labeled Source sample* $LS = \{(\mathbf{x}_i, y_i)\}_{i=1}^m$ drawn *i.i.d.* from P_S, and a *Target Sample* which contains a large set of unlabeled target instances $TS = \{\mathbf{x}_j\}_{j=1}^{m'}$ drawn *i.i.d.* from D_T and sometimes a few labeled target data drawn from P_T. The objective of a learning task is then to find a good hypothesis with a low error according to target distribution P_T. In this section, we provide a brief and non-exhaustive overview of some existing DA approaches, note that some surveys can be found in [18,23].

The first theoretical analysis of the DA problem was proposed by Ben-David *et al.* [4,5]. The authors have provided an upper bound on the target domain error err_{P_T} that takes into account the source domain error $\mathrm{err}_{P_S}(h)$ and the divergence $d_{\mathcal{H}}$ between the source and target marginal distributions:

$$\forall h \in \mathcal{H},\ \mathrm{err}_{P_T}(h) \ \leq\ \mathrm{err}_{P_S}(h) + \frac{1}{2} d_{\mathcal{H}}(D_S, D_T) + \nu. \tag{5}$$

The last term corresponds to the optimal joint hypothesis over the two domains $\nu = \mathrm{argmin}_{h\in\mathcal{H}}\, \mathrm{err}_{P_S}(h) + \mathrm{err}_{P_T}(h)$. It can be seen as a quality measure of $\mathcal{H}$ for the DA problem considered. If this best hypothesis performs poorly, it appears then difficult to obtain a good hypothesis for the target domain. This term is then supposed to be small to ensure a successful adaptation.

The other crucial point is the divergence[2] $d_{\mathcal{H}}$ which is called the $\mathcal{H}$-distance. This result suggests that if the two distributions are close, then a low error classifier over the source domain can be a good classifier for the target one. The intuition behind this idea is given in Figure 1. The distance $d_{\mathcal{H}}$ is actually related to $\mathcal{H}$ by measuring a maximum variation divergence over the set of points on which an hypothesis in $\mathcal{H}$ can commit errors:

$$d_{\mathcal{H}}(D_S, D_T) \ =\ 2 \sup_{h\in\mathcal{H}} \left| Pr_{D_S}[I(h)] - Pr_{D_T}[I(h)] \right|$$

where $\mathbf{x} \in I(h) \Leftrightarrow h(\mathbf{x}) = 1$. An interesting point of this theory is that the $\mathcal{H}$-distance can be estimated from finite samples when the VC-dimension of $\mathcal{H}$ is finite. Using a VC-dimension analysis, the authors show that the empirical divergence converges to the true $d_{\mathcal{H}}$ with the size of the samples. Let U_S be a sample *i.i.d.* from D_S and U_T a sample *i.i.d.* from D_T. Consider a labeled sample $U_S \bigcup U_T$ where each instance of U_S is labeled as positive and each one of U_T as negative. The empirical divergence can then be directly estimated by looking for the best classifier able to separate the two samples[3] [4]:

$$\hat{d}_{\mathcal{H}}(U_S, U_T) \ =\ 2\left(1 - \min_{h\in\mathcal{H}} \underset{U_S,U_T}{\hat{err}}(h)\right), \tag{6}$$

with $\underset{U_S,U_T}{\hat{err}}(h) = \frac{1}{m}\left(\sum_{\substack{\mathbf{x}\in U_S\cup U_T,\\ h(\mathbf{x})=-1}} \mathbb{1}_{\mathbf{x}\in U_S} + \sum_{\substack{\mathbf{x}\in U_S\cup U_T,\\ h(\mathbf{x})=1}} \mathbb{1}_{\mathbf{x}\in U_T} \right)$, where $\mathbb{1}_{\mathbf{x}\in U_S} = \begin{cases} 1 \text{ if } \mathbf{x}\in U_S \\ 0 \text{ otherwise.} \end{cases}$

Note that finding the optimal hyperplane is NP-hard in general. However, a good estimation of $\hat{d}_{\mathcal{H}}$ allows us to have an insight of the distance between the two distributions and thus of the difficulty of the DA problem for the class $\mathcal{H}$. We will use this principle to estimate the difficulty of the task considered in our experimental part.

---

[2] The authors consider actually the divergence over $\mathcal{H}\Delta\mathcal{H}$, the space of symmetric difference hypothesis, see [4] for more details.

[3] By considering the 0-1 loss, L_{01}, defined as follows: $L_{01}(h, (\mathbf{x}, y)) = 1$ if $h(\mathbf{x}) \neq y$ and 0 otherwise.

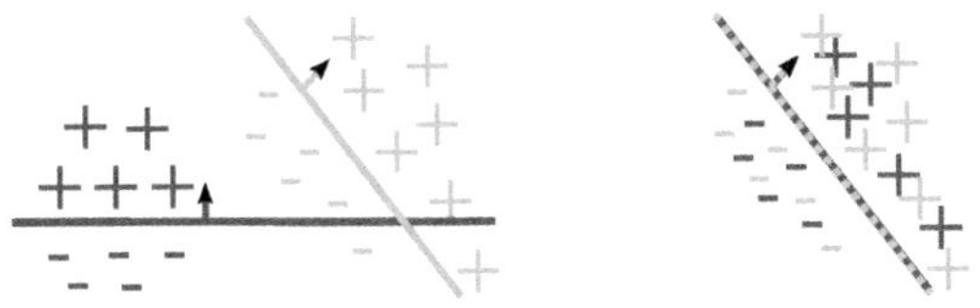

Fig. 1. Intuition behind a successful domain adaptation. Source points are in (dark) green (pos. +, neg. −), target points are in (light) orange. (a) The distance between domains is high: the two samples are easily separable and the classifier learned from source points performs badly on the target sample. (b) The distance between domains is low: The classifier learned from source points performs well on the two domains.

Later, Mansour *et al.* [20] have proposed another discrepancy measure allowing one to generalize the $d_{\mathcal{H}}$ distance to other real valued loss functions. Note that the bound presented in their work is a bit different from the one of Ben-David *et al.*. Moreover, they have also provided an average analysis with interesting Rademacher generalization bounds. These theoretical frameworks show that for a good domain adaptation, the distance between distributions and the source error must be low. According to [6], minimizing these two terms appears even necessary in general.

One key point for DA approaches is thus to be able to move closer the distributions while avoiding a dramatic increase of the error on the source domain. In the literature, some methods have proposed to reweight the source instances in order to get closer to the target distribution. They are often based on some assumptions on the two distributions [8,17,19,20,26]. For example some of these approaches rely on hypothesis like the covariate shift where the marginal distributions over X may be different for the two domains, but the conditional distribution of Y given X are the same, *i.e.* $P_S(y|\mathbf{x}) = P_T(y|\mathbf{x})$ for every $\mathbf{x} \in X$ and $y \in Y$ but $P_S(\mathbf{x}) \neq P_T(\mathbf{x})$ for some $\mathbf{x} \in X$ [26]. Other works are based on iterative self labeling approaches in order to move progressively from one domain to the other one [10]. Another standpoint for moving closer the two distributions is to find a relevant projection space where the two distributions are close. In [9], the authors propose a *structural correspondence learning* approach to identify relevant features by looking for their correspondence in the two domains. Another idea is to use an augmented feature space for both source and target data and use the new input space obtained with classical machine learning algorithms [11]. Some authors have also proposed to use spectral approaches to build a new feature space [21].

The main underlying ideas among the different approaches presented in this section is that a potential good adaptation needs to have the source and target distributions close. One way to achieve this goal is to build a relevant feature space by defining a new projection operator or by choosing relevant features. In the next section, we study the usefulness of the framework of Balcan *et al.*. to deal with domain adaptation problems. More precisely, we propose to investigate how the definition of the similarity function and the construction of the feature space - *i.e.* the ϕ-space of similarities to a set of reasonable points - can help to improve the performance of the classifier in a domain adaptation setting.

5 Modifying the Projection Space for Domain Adaptation

In this section, we present our two approaches for modifying the similarity based projection space in order to facilitate the adaptation to the target distribution. First, we present a simple way for renormalizing a similarity function according to a sample of unlabeled instances. Second, we propose a regularization term that tends to define a projection space where the source and target marginal distributions tend to be closer.

5.1 A Normalization of a Similarity Function

For a particular DA task, we build a new similarity function K_N by normalizing a given similarity function K relatively to a sample N. Recall that, from Definition 2, a similarity must be good relatively to a set of reasonable points. We propose actually to renormalize the set of similarities to these points. Since the real set of reasonable points is unknown *a priori*, we consider a set of candidate landmark points R' and we apply a specific normalization for each instance of $\mathbf{x}'_j \in R'$. The idea is to apply a scaling to mean zero and standard deviation one for the similarities of the instances of N to $\mathbf{x}'$. Our procedure is defined as follows.

Definition 4. *Let K be a similarity function which verifies the Definition 2. Given a data set $N = \{\mathbf{x}_k\}_{k=1}^{p}$ and a set of (potential) reasonable points $R' = \{\mathbf{x}'_j\}_{j=1}^{d_u}$, a normalized similarity function, K_N, is defined by:*

$$\forall \mathbf{x}'_j \in R',\ K_N(.,\mathbf{x}'_j) = \begin{cases} \dfrac{K(.,\mathbf{x}'_j) - \mu_{\mathbf{x}'_j}}{\sigma_{\mathbf{x}'_j}} & \textit{if } -1 \leq \frac{K(.,\mathbf{x}'_j)-\hat{\mu}_{\mathbf{x}'_j}}{\hat{\sigma}_{\mathbf{x}'_j}} \leq 1, \\ -1 & \textit{if } -1 \geq \frac{K(.,\mathbf{x}'_j)-\hat{\mu}_{\mathbf{x}'_j}}{\hat{\sigma}_{\mathbf{x}'_j}}, \\ 1 & \textit{if } \frac{K(.,\mathbf{x}'_j)-\hat{\mu}_{\mathbf{x}'_j}}{\hat{\sigma}_{\mathbf{x}'_j}} \geq 1, \end{cases} \tag{7}$$

where $\hat{\mu}_{\mathbf{x}'_j}$ is the empirical mean of similarities to $\mathbf{x}'_j$ over N:

$$\forall \mathbf{x}'_j \in R',\ \hat{\mu}_{\mathbf{x}'_j} = \frac{1}{|N|}\sum_{\mathbf{x}_k \in N} K(\mathbf{x}_k,\mathbf{x}'_j),$$

and $\hat{\sigma}_{\mathbf{x}'_j}$ is the empirical unbiased estimate of the standard deviation:

$$\forall \mathbf{x}'_j \in R',\ \hat{\sigma}_{\mathbf{x}'_j} = \sqrt{\frac{1}{|N|-1}\sum_{\mathbf{x}_k \in N}\left(K(\mathbf{x}_k,\mathbf{x}'_j) - \hat{\mu}_{\mathbf{x}'_j}\right)^2}.$$

By construction, the similarity K_N is then non symmetric and non PSD. In the following, we will consider that a learning algorithm is provided with two data sets: $LS = \{(\mathbf{x}_i, y_i)\}_{i=1}^{m}$ constituted of labeled source domain data, and $TS = \{\mathbf{x}_i\}_{i=1}^{m'}$ of unlabeled target domain data. According to the theoretical result of domain adaptation of Ben-David *et al.*. recalled in Equation (5), the learned classifier should also perform well on the source domain. We then propose to define our normalized function, denoted by K_{ST}, with $N = LS_{|X} \cup TS$ in order to link the two domains by considering the information of both of them at the same time, for avoiding an increasing of the source error. Our choice is clearly heuristic and our aim is just to evaluate the interest of renormalizing a similarity for domain adaptation problems. In order to study the potential of adaptation, we will only consider candidate landmark points R' from the source domain.

5.2 An Additional Regularization Term for Moving Closer the Two Distributions

As a second contribution, we propose to add a regularization term to the optimization Problem 4 proposed by Balcan *et al.*. The objective is to control the selection of reasonable points leading to a projection space where the two distributions are close. According to the empirical divergence $d_{\mathcal{H}}$ given in Equation 6, the source and the target domains are close if it is difficult to separate source from target examples. Let two subsets $U_S \subseteq LS$ and $U_T \subseteq TS$ of equal size, our idea is then to build a set $\mathcal{C}_{ST}$ of pairs belonging to $U_S \times U_T$. And then, for each pair $(\mathbf{x}_s, \mathbf{x}_t) \in \mathcal{C}_{ST}$, we propose to regularize the learned classifier such that the outputs of the classifier are close for the two instances $\mathbf{x}_s$ and $\mathbf{x}_t$. For any classifier $h(\cdot) = \sum_{i=1}^{|R|} \alpha_i K(\cdot, x'_i)$, this can be expressed as follows:

$$
\begin{aligned}
|h(\mathbf{x}_s) - h(\mathbf{x}_t)| &= \left| \sum_{j=1}^{|R|} \alpha_j K(\mathbf{x}_s, \mathbf{x}'_j) - \sum_{j=1}^{|R|} \alpha_j K(\mathbf{x}_t, \mathbf{x}'_j) \right| \\
&\leq \sum_{j=1}^{|R|} \left| \alpha_j \left(K(\mathbf{x}_s, \mathbf{x}'_j) - K(\mathbf{x}_t, \mathbf{x}'_j) \right) \right| \text{ by using triangle inequality} \\
&= \left\| \left({}^t\phi^R(\mathbf{x}_s) - {}^t\phi^R(\mathbf{x}_t) \right) \operatorname{diag}(\boldsymbol{\alpha}) \right\|_1 . \qquad (8)
\end{aligned}
$$

This leads us to propose a new regularization term which tends to select landmarks with similarities close to both some source and target points, which allows us to define a projection space where source and target examples are closer. Let R be a set of d_u candidate landmark points, our global optimization problem is then defined as follows:

$$
\min_{\boldsymbol{\alpha}} \sum_{i=1}^{d_l} \left[1 - \sum_{j=1}^{d_u} \alpha_j y_i K(x_i, x'_j) \right]_+ + \lambda \|\boldsymbol{\alpha}\|_1 + C \sum_{(\mathbf{x}_s, \mathbf{x}_t) \in \mathcal{C}_{ST}} \left\| \left({}^t\phi^R(\mathbf{x}_s) - {}^t\phi^R(\mathbf{x}_t) \right) \operatorname{diag}(\boldsymbol{\alpha}) \right\|_1 \qquad (9)
$$

The construction of C_{ST} is difficult since we have no information on the target labels. In practice, we build the matching C_{ST} from U_S and U_T by looking for a bipartite matching minimizing the Euclidean distance in the ϕ-space defined by the set of candidate landmarks. This can be done by solving the following problem. Note that in the particular case of bipartite matching, this can be done in polynomial time by linear programming for example.

$$\begin{cases} \min\limits_{\substack{\beta_{st} \\ 1\leq s\leq |U_S| \\ 1\leq t\leq |U_T|}} \sum\limits_{(\mathbf{x}_s,\mathbf{x}_t)\in U_S\times U_T} \beta_{st}\|\phi^R(\mathbf{x}_s)-\phi^R(\mathbf{x}_t)\|_2^2 \\ \text{s.t.: } \forall(\mathbf{x}_s,\mathbf{x}_t)\in U_S\times U_T,\ \beta_{st}\in\{0,1\}, \\ \qquad \forall \mathbf{x}_s\in U_S,\ \sum_{\mathbf{x}_t\in U_T}\beta_{(st)}=1, \\ \qquad \forall \mathbf{x}_t\in U_T,\ \sum_{\mathbf{x}_s\in U_S}\beta_{(st)}\leq 1. \end{cases}$$

Then $\mathcal{C}_{ST}$ corresponds to the pairs of $U_S\times U_T$ such that $\beta_{st}=1$. The choice of the points of U_S and U_T is hard and in an ideal case, we would like to select pairs of points of the same label. But since we suppose that no target label is available, we select the sets U_S and U_T randomly from the source and target samples, from different draws, and we choose the best sets thanks to a reverse validation procedure described in Appendix A.

6 Experiments

We now propose to evaluate the approaches presented in the previous section on a synthetic toy problem and on a real image annotation task. For every problem, we consider to have: a labeled source sample LS drawn from the source domain, a set of potential landmark points R' drawn from the marginal source distribution over X and an unlabeled target sample TS drawn from the marginal target distribution over X.

As a baseline, we choose a similarity based on a classical Gaussian kernel, which is a *good similarity function* according to the framework of Balcan *et al.*:

$$K(\mathbf{x},\mathbf{x}')=\exp\left(-\frac{\|\mathbf{x}-\mathbf{x}'\|_2^2}{D^2}\right).$$

We then consider the normalized similarity K_{ST} which corresponds to the normalization of K according to the instances of the source and target samples $LS_{|X}\cup TS$. For each of the two similarities K and K_{ST}, we compare the models learned by solving Problem (4), corresponding to learning a classical SF-based classifier, to those learned using our regularized formulation in Problem (9). We tune the hyperparameters with a "reverse" validation procedure described in Appendix A. Moreover, in order to evaluate if K_{ST} is a better similarity for the target domain, we propose to study the (ϵ,γ,τ)-guarantees on the target sample according to Definition 3. For this purpose, we estimate empirically ϵ as a function of γ from the target sample (we use here the real labels but only for this evaluation), *i.e.* for a given γ, $\hat{\epsilon}$ is the proportion of examples $\mathbf{x}\in TS$ verifying:

$$\sum_{\mathbf{x}'_j\in R'} y_i y'_j K(\mathbf{x}_i,\mathbf{x}'_j)<\gamma.$$

We also assess the distance $\hat{d}_{\mathcal{H}}$ between the two domains by learning a SF-based classifier with K for separating source from target samples in the original space. From Equation (6), a small value, near 0, indicates close domains while a larger value, near 2, indicates a hard DA task.

6.1 Synthetic Toy Problem

As the source domain, we consider a classical binary problem with two intertwinning moons, each class corresponding to one moon (see Figure 3). We then define 8 different target domains by rotating anticlockwise the source domain according to 8 angles. The higher the angle is, the harder the task becomes. For each domain, we generate 300 instances (150 of each class). Moreover, for studying the influence of the pair set $\mathcal{C}_{ST}$, we evaluate the obtained results when $\mathcal{C}_{ST}$ corresponds to a set of "perfect pairs $(\mathbf{x}_s, \mathbf{x}_t)$" where $\mathbf{x}_t$ is the obtained instance after rotating $\mathbf{x}_s$. These results correspond to an upper bound for our methods. Finally, in order to assess the generalization ability of our approach, we evaluate each method on an independent test set of 1500 examples drawn from the target domain (not provided to the algorithm). Each adaptation problem is repeated 10 times and the average accuracy obtained for each method is reported in Table 1. We can make the following remarks.

- Our new regularization term for minimizing distance between marginal distributions improves significantly the performances on the target domain.
- As long as the problem can be considered as an easy DA task, the normalized similarity does not produce better models. However, when the difficulty increases, using a normalized similarity improves the results.
- Regarding the bipartite matching influence, having perfect pairs leads to the best results and is thus important for the adaption process, which is expected. However, our reverse validation procedure helps us to keep correct results when a set of perfect pairs can not be built.

Figure 2 shows the goodness guarantees of the similarities over each adaptation task. A better similarity has a lower area under the curve, meaning a lower error in average. The $\hat{\epsilon}$ rate is relatively high because we consider only landmarks from the source sample in order to study our adaptation capability. We observe for hardest problems ($\geq 50°$) an improvement of the goodness with the normalized similarity K_{ST}. For easier tasks, this improvement is not significant, justifying the fact that the similarity K can lead to better classifiers. Our normalized similarity seems thus relevant only for hard domain adaptation problems.

6.2 Image Classification

In this section, we experiment our approach on PascalVOC 2007 [13] and TrecVid 2007 [25] corpora. The PascalVOC benchmark is constituted of a set of 5000 training images and a set of 5000 test images. The TrecVid corpus is constituted of images extracted from videos and can be seen also as an image corpus. The goal is to identify visual objects and scenes in images and videos. We choose the

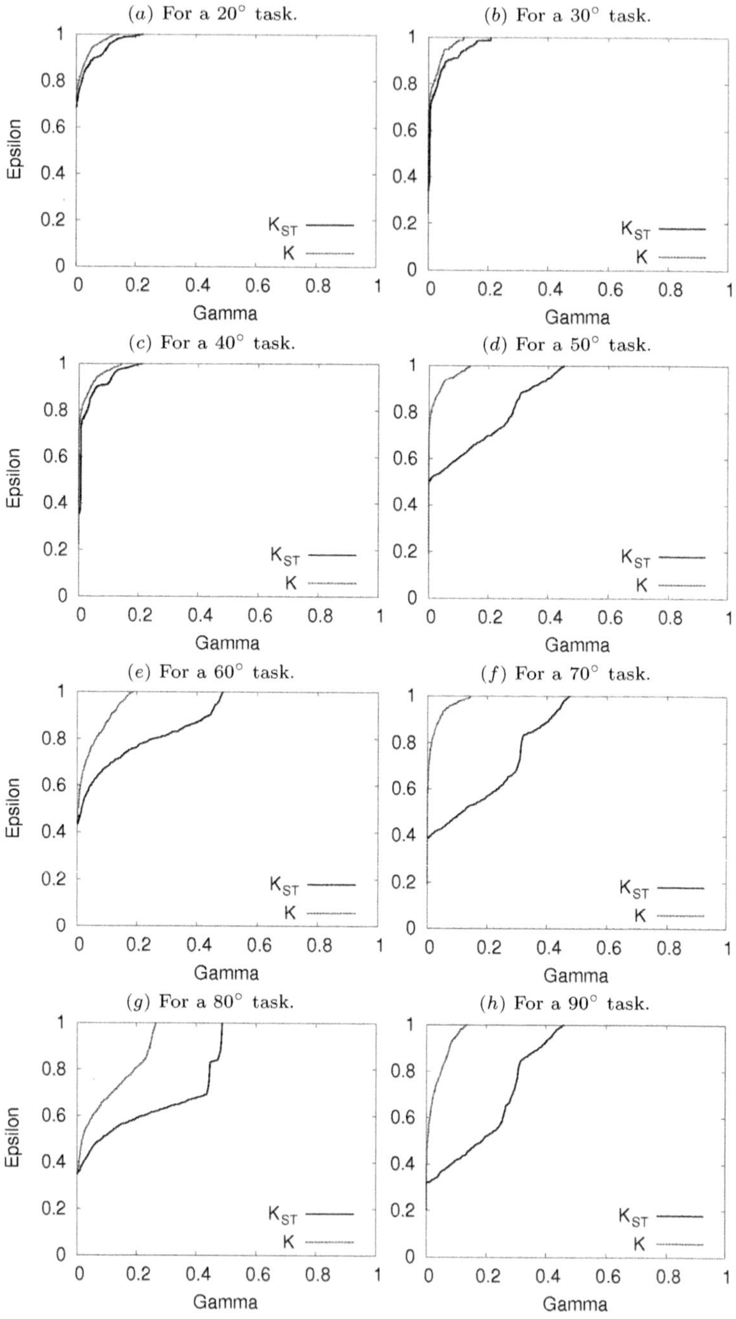

Fig. 2. Goodness of the similarities over the target sample: $\hat{\epsilon}$ as a function of γ

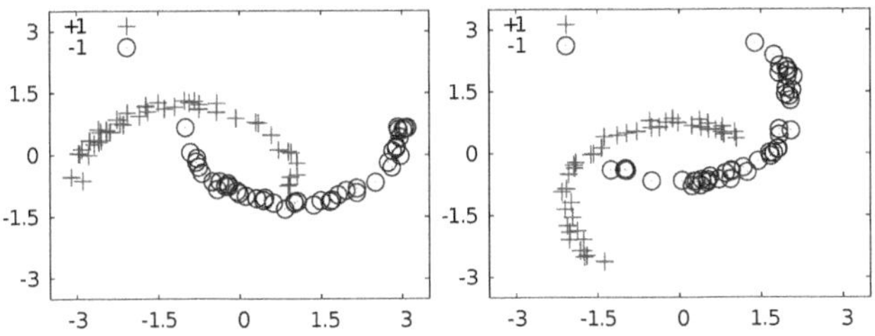

Fig. 3. Left: A source sample. Right: A target sample with a 50° rotation

Table 1. Average results in percentage of accuracy with standard deviation on the toy problem target test sample for each method

ROTATION	20°	30°	40°	50°	60°	70°	80°	90°
$\hat{\mathbf{d}}_{\mathcal{H}}$	0.58	1.16	1.31	1.34	1.34	1.32	1.33	1.31
SF without distance regularization								
WITH K	88 ± 13	70 ± 20	59 ± 23	47 ± 17	34 ± 08	23 ± 01	21 ± 01	19 ± 01
WITH K_{ST}	79 ± 10	56 ± 15	56 ± 10	43 ± 09	41 ± 08	37 ± 10	36 ± 10	40 ± 09
SF with distance regularization								
WITH K	$\mathbf{98} \pm 03$	$\mathbf{92} \pm 07$	$\mathbf{83} \pm 05$	70 ± 09	54 ± 18	43 ± 24	38 ± 23	35 ± 19
WITH K_{ST}	93 ± 05	86 ± 08	72 ± 12	$\mathbf{72} \pm 013$	$\mathbf{69} \pm 10$	$\mathbf{67} \pm 12$	$\mathbf{63} \pm 13$	$\mathbf{58} \pm 09$
SF with distance regularization and perfect matching								
WITH K	***99*** ± 01	***96*** ± 01	***86*** ± 02	73 ± 11	65 ± 23	56 ± 29	47 ± 23	39 ± 19
WITH K_{ST}	97 ± 04	92 ± 06	83 ± 10	***75*** ± 12	***73*** ± 16	***73*** ± 02	***69*** ± 7	***60*** ± 11

concepts that are shared between the two corpora: `Boat`, `Bus`, `Car`, `TV/Monitor`, `Person` and `Plane`. We used visual features extracted as described in [1]. We consider as the source domain, labeled images from the PascalVOC 2007 training set. For each concept, we generated a source sample constituted of all the training positive images and negatives images independently drawn such that the ratio $+/-$ is $\frac{1}{3}/\frac{2}{3}$. As the target domain, we use some images of the TrecVid corpus, we built also a sample containing all the positive examples and drew some negative samples in order to keep the same ration $+/-$ of $\frac{1}{3}/\frac{2}{3}$. In these samples, the number of positive examples may be low and we propose to use the *F-measure*[4] to evaluate the learned models. The results are reported in Table 2. The different nature and ways of acquisition of the images make the problem of adaptation difficult. As an illustration, the empirical $\hat{d}_{\mathcal{H}}$ between the two domains is high for every concept. In this context, for all the tasks, the normalized similarity with distance regularization provides the best results. This is confirmed on Figure 4 where the evaluation of the goodness of the two similarities for two concepts is provided: the normalized similarity is better for difficult tasks.

[4] The F-measure or the balanced F-score is the harmonic mean of precision and recall.

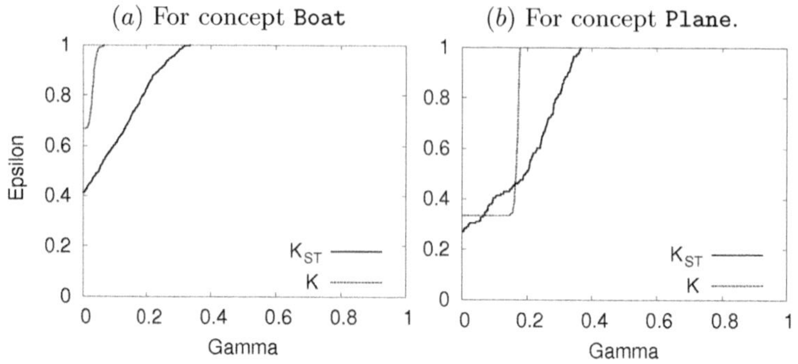

Fig. 4. $\hat{\epsilon}$ on the target domain as a function of γ for 2 concepts

Table 2. Results obtained on TrecVid target domain according to the F-measure

Concept	boat	bus	car	monitor	person	plane	Average
$\hat{\mathbf{d}}_{\mathcal{H}}$	1.93	1.95	1.85	1.86	1.78	1.86	1.86
SF without distance regularization							
with K	0.0279	0.1806	0.5214	0.2477	0.4971	0.5522	0.3378
with K_{ST}	0.4731	0.4632	0.5316	0.3664	0.3776	0.5635	0.4626
SF with distance regularization							
with K	0.2006	0.1739	0.5125	0.2744	0.5037	0.5192	0.3640
with K_{ST}	**0.4857**	**0.4891**	**0.5452**	**0.3989**	**0.5353**	**0.6375**	**0.5153**

7 Conclusion

In this paper, we have proposed a preliminary study on the usefulness of the framework of Balcan *et al.* [2,3] for domain adaptation. We have proposed a normalization of a similarity function according to a test sample based on the fact that a similarity does not need to be PSD or symmetric. We have also proposed a new regularization term that tends to define a projection space of reasonable points where the source and target distributions of the examples are closer. We have provided experiments on a toy problem and on a real image annotation task. Our regularization term generally helps to improve the learned classifier and the normalization proposed seems only relevant for difficult adaptation tasks.

As a future work, we will continue on the idea of normalizing a similarity in order to adapt it to the target domain. Around this idea, many questions remain open like the choice the landmark points, the influence of the test set or avoiding overfitting. The use of some labeled target data may also help to produce a better projection space. From a theoretical standpoint, a perspective would be to consider an extension of the framework of robustness of Xu and Mannor [28] to domain adaptation.

References

1. Ayache, S., Quénot, G., Gensel, J.: Image and video indexing using networks of operators. Journal on Image and Video Processing, 1:1–1:13 (2007)
2. Balcan, M.F., Blum, A., Srebro, N.: Improved guarantees for learning via similarity functions. In: Proceedings of COLT, pp. 287–298 (2008)
3. Balcan, M.F., Blum, A., Srebro, N.: A theory of learning with similarity functions. Machine Learning Journal 72(1-2), 89–112 (2008)
4. Ben-David, S., Blitzer, J., Crammer, K., Kulesza, A., Pereira, F., Vaughan, J.: A theory of learning from different domains. Machine Learning Journal 79(1-2), 151–175 (2010)
5. Ben-David, S., Blitzer, J., Crammer, K., Pereira, F.: Analysis of representations for domain adaptation. In: Proceedings of NIPS 2006, pp. 137–144 (2006)
6. Ben-David, S., Lu, T., Luu, T., Pal, D.: Impossibility theorems for domain adaptation. JMLR W&CP 9, 129–136 (2010)
7. Bernard, M., Boyer, L., Habrard, A., Sebban, M.: Learning probabilistic models of tree edit distance. Pattern Recognition 41(8), 2611–2629 (2008)
8. Bickel, S., Brückner, M., Scheffer, T.: Discriminative learning for differing training and test distributions. In: Proceeding of ICML, pp. 81–88 (2007)
9. Blitzer, J., McDonald, R., Pereira, F.: Domain adaptation with structural correspondence learning. In: Proceedings of EMNLP, pp. 120–128 (2006)
10. Bruzzone, L., Marconcini, M.: Domain adaptation problems: A DASVM classification technique and a circular validation strategy. IEEE Trans. Pattern Anal. Mach. Intell. 32(5), 770–787 (2010)
11. Daumé III, H.: Frustratingly easy domain adaptation. In: Proceedings of the Association for Computational Linguistics, ACL (2007)
12. Davis, J., Kulis, B., Jain, P., Sra, S., Dhillon, I.: Information-theoretic metric learning. In: Proceedings of ICML, pp. 209–216 (2007)
13. Everingham, M., Van Gool, L., Williams, C.K.I., Winn, J., Zisserman, A.: The PASCAL Visual Object Classes Challenge 2007 (VOC 2007) Results (2007), http://www.pascal-network.org/challenges/VOC/voc2007/workshop/
14. Gao, X., Xiao, B., Tao, D., Li, X.: A survey of graph edit distance. Pattern Analysis & Applications 13(1), 113–129 (2010)
15. Goldberger, J., Roweis, S., Hinton, G., Salakhutdinov, R.: Neighbourhood components analysis. In: Proceedings of NIPS, vol. 17, pp. 513–520 (2004)
16. Haasdonk, B.: Feature space interpretation of svms with indefinite kernels. IEEE Trans. Pattern Anal. Mach. Intell. 27(4), 482–492 (2005)
17. Huang, J., Smola, A., Gretton, A., Borgwardt, K., Schölkopf, B.: Correcting sample selection bias by unlabeled data. In: Proceedings of NIPS, pp. 601–608 (2006)
18. Jiang, J.: A literature survey on domain adaptation of statistical classifiers. Tech. rep., Computer Science Department at University of Illinois at Urbana-Champaign (2008), http://sifaka.cs.uiuc.edu/jiang4/domain_adaptation/da_survey.pdf
19. Jiang, J., Zhai, C.: Instance weighting for domain adaptation in NLP. In: Proceedings of ACL (2007)
20. Mansour, Y., Mohri, M., Rostamizadeh, A.: Domain adaptation: Learning bounds and algorithms. In: Proceedings of COLT, pp. 19–30 (2009)
21. Pan, S., Tsang, I., Kwok, J., Yang, Q.: Domain adaptation via transfer component analysis. In: Proceedings of IJCAI, pp. 1187–1192 (2009)

22. Pan, S., Yang, Q.: A survey on transfer learning. IEEE Transactions on Knowledge and Data Engineering 22(10), 1345–1359 (2010)
23. Quionero-Candela, J., Sugiyama, M., Schwaighofer, A., Lawrence, N.: Dataset Shift in Machine Learning. The MIT Press, Cambridge (2009)
24. Ristad, E., Yianilos, P.: Learning string-edit distance. IEEE Trans. on Pattern Analysis and Machine Intelligence 20(5), 522–532 (1998)
25. Smeaton, A., Over, P., Kraaij, W.: High-Level Feature Detection from Video in TRECVid: a 5-Year Retrospective of Achievements. In: Multimedia Content Analysis, Theory and Applications, pp. 151–174. Springer, Berlin (2009)
26. Sugiyama, M., Nakajima, S., Kashima, H., von Bünau, P., Kawanabe, M.: Direct importance estimation with model selection and its application to covariate shift adaptation. In: Proceedings of NIPS (2007)
27. Weinberger, K., Saul, L.: Distance metric learning for large margin nearest neighbor classification. Journal of Machine Learning Research (JMLR) 10, 207–244 (2009)
28. Xu, H., Mannor, S.: Robustness and generalization. In: Proceedings of COLT, pp. 503–515 (2010)
29. Zhong, E., Fan, W., Yang, Q., Verscheure, O., Ren, J.: Cross validation framework to choose amongst models and datasets for transfer learning. In: Balcázar, J.L., Bonchi, F., Gionis, A., Sebag, M. (eds.) ECML PKDD 2010, Part III. LNCS, vol. 6323, pp. 547–562. Springer, Heidelberg (2010)

A Appendix

Given a classifier h, we define the *reverse classifier* h^r as the classifier learned from the target sample self labeled by h : $\{(\mathbf{x}, \text{sign}(h(\mathbf{x})))\}_{\mathbf{x}\in TS}$. According to the idea of Zhong *et al.* [10,29], we evaluate h^r on the source domain (see Fig. 5). Given k-folds on the source labeled sample, we use $k-1$ folds as labeled examples for solving Pb. (9) and we evaluate h^r on the last k^{th} fold. The final error corresponds to the mean of the error over the k-folds: $\hat{\text{err}}_S(h^r) = \frac{1}{k}\sum_{i=1}^{k} \hat{err}_{LS_i}(h^r)$. Among many classifiers h, the one with the lowest $\hat{\text{err}}_S(h^r)$ is chosen.

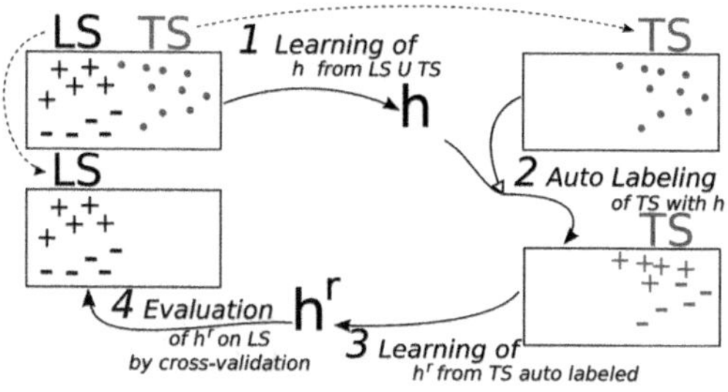

Fig. 5. Reverse validation. Step **1**: *Learning* h with Problem (9). **2**: *Auto-labeling* the target sample with h. **3**: *Learning* h^r on auto-labeled target sample by Problem (4). **4**: *Evaluation* of h^r on LS (with a k-folds process) for validating h.

Metric Anomaly Detection via Asymmetric Risk Minimization

Aryeh Kontorovich[1,2], Danny Hendler[1,2], and Eitan Menahem[1,3]

[1] Deutsche Telekom Laboratories
[2] Department of Computer Science, Ben-Gurion University of the Negev
[3] Department of Information Systems Engineering, Ben-Gurion University of the Negev

Abstract. We propose what appears to be the first anomaly detection framework that learns from positive examples only and is sensitive to substantial differences in the presentation and penalization of normal vs. anomalous points. Our framework introduces a novel type of asymmetry between how *false alarms* (misclassifications of a normal instance as an anomaly) and *missed anomalies* (misclassifications of an anomaly as normal) are penalized: whereas *each* false alarm incurs a unit cost, our model assumes that a high *global cost* is incurred if *one or more* anomalies are missed.

We define a few natural notions of risk along with efficient minimization algorithms. Our framework is applicable to any metric space with a finite doubling dimension. We make minimalistic assumptions that naturally generalize notions such as *margin* in Euclidean spaces. We provide a theoretical analysis of the risk and show that under mild conditions, our classifier is asymptotically consistent. The learning algorithms we propose are computationally and statistically efficient and admit a further tradeoff between running time and precision. Some experimental results on real-world data are provided.

1 Introduction

Cost-sensitive learning [10,38] is an active research area in machine learning. In this framework, different costs are associated with different types of misclassification errors. In general, these costs differ for different types of misclassification. Classifiers are then optimized to minimize the expected cost incurred due to their errors. This is in contrast with cost-insensitive learning, where classification algorithms are optimized to minimize their error rate — the expected fraction of misclassified instances, thus implicitly making the (often unrealistic) assumption that all misclassification errors have the same cost.

Cost-sensitive classification is often useful for binary classification, when the datasets under consideration are highly imbalanced and consist mostly of normal instances and with only a small fraction of anomalous ones [19,23]. Since the terms "false positive" and "false negative" are confusing in the context of

M. Pelillo and E.R. Hancock (Eds.): SIMBAD 2011, LNCS 7005, pp. 17–30, 2011.

anomaly detection, we call a normal instance misclassified as an anomaly a *false alarm* and an anomaly misclassified as normal a *missed anomaly*. Typically, the cost of a missed anomaly is much higher than that of a false alarm.

We consider a cost-sensitive classification framework, in which learning is based on normal instances only and anomalies are never observed during training. Our framework introduces a novel type of asymmetry between how false alarms and missed anomalies are penalized: whereas *each* false alarm incurs a unit cost, our model assumes that a high *global cost* is incurred if *one or more* anomalies are missed.

As a motivating example for our framework, consider a warehouse equipped with a fire alarm system. Each false fire alarm automatically triggers a call to the fire department and incurs a unit cost. On the other hand, *any nonzero number* of missed anomalies (corresponding to one or more fires breaking out in the warehouse) cause a *a single* "catastrophic" cost corresponding to the warehouse burning down one or more times (only the first time "matters").

We define a natural notion of risk and show how to minimize it under various assumptions. Our framework is applicable to any metric space with a finite doubling dimension. We make minimalistic assumptions that naturally generalize notions such as *margin* in Euclidean spaces. We provide a theoretical analysis of the risk and show that under mild conditions, our classifier is asymptotically consistent. The learning algorithms we propose are efficient and admit a further tradeoff between running time and precision — for example, using the techniques of [15] to efficiently estimate the doubling dimension and the spanner-based approach described in [14] to quickly compute approximate nearest neighbors. Some experimental results on real-world data are provided.

Related Work. The majority of published cost-sensitive classification algorithms assume the availability of supervised training data, were all instances are labeled (e.g. [9,12,24,32,35,38,39]).

Some work considers semi-supervised cost-sensitive classification. Qin et al. [29] present cost-sensitive classifiers for training data that consists of a relatively small number of labeled instances and a large number of unlabeled instances. Their implementations are based on the expectation maximization (EM) algorithm [8] as a base semi-supervised classifier. Bennett et al. [4] present ASSEMBLE, an adaptive semi-supervised ensemble scheme that can be used to to make any cost-sensitive classifier semi-supervised. Li et al. [22] recently proposed CS4VM - a semi-supervised cost-sensitive support vector machine classifier. Other cost-sensitive semi-supervised work involves attempts to refine the model using human feedback (see, e.g., [16,25,27]).

Our framework falls within the realm of *one-class classification* [34] since learning is done based on normal instances only. Crammer and Chechik [7] consider the one-class classification problem of identifying a small and coherent subset of data points by finding a ball with a small radius that covers as many data points as possible. Whereas previous approaches to this problem used a cost function that is constant within the ball and grows linearly outside of it [3,30,33], the approach taken by [34] employs a cost function that grows linearly within the ball but is kept constant outside of it. Other papers employing the one-class SVM technique include [18,26]. Also relevant is the approach of [31] for estimating the support of a distribution — although in this paper, the existence of a kernel is assumed, which is a much stronger assumption than that of a metric.

Definitions and Notation. We use standard notation and definitions throughout. A *metric* d on a set $\mathcal{X}$ is a positive symmetric function satisfying the triangle inequality $d(x, y) \le d(x, z) + d(z, y)$; together the two comprise the metric space $(\mathcal{X}, d)$. The diameter of a set $A \subseteq \mathcal{X}$ is defined by $\mathrm{diam}(A) = \sup_{x,y \in A} d(x, y)$. In this paper, we always denote $\mathrm{diam}(\mathcal{X})$ by Δ. For any two subsets $A, B \subset \mathcal{X}$, their "nearest point" distance $d(A, B)$ is defined by $d(A, B) = \inf_{x \in A, y \in B} d(A, B)$. The *Lipschitz constant* of a function $f : \mathcal{X} \to \mathbb{R}$ is defined to be the smallest $L > 0$ that makes $|f(x) - f(y)| \le L d(x, y)$ hold for all $x, y \in \mathcal{X}$. For a metric space (X, d), let λ be the smallest number such that every ball in $\mathcal{X}$ can be covered by λ balls of half the radius. The *doubling dimension* of $\mathcal{X}$ is $\mathrm{ddim}(\mathcal{X}) = \log_2 \lambda$. A metric is *doubling* when its doubling dimension is bounded. Note that while a low Euclidean dimension implies a low doubling dimension (Euclidean metrics of dimension k have doubling dimension $O(k)$ [17]), low doubling dimension is strictly more general than low Euclidean dimension.

Throughout the paper we write $\mathbb{1}_{\{\cdot\}}$ to represent the 0-1 truth value of the subscripted predicate.

Paper Outline. The rest of this paper is organized as follows. In Section 2 we present our theoretical results: first, for the idealized case where the data is well-separated by a known distance, and then for various relaxations of this demand. Some experimental results are provided in Section 3. We close with a discussion and ideas for future work in Section 4.

2 Theoretical Results

2.1 Preliminaries

We define the following model of learning from positive examples only. The metric space $(\mathcal{X}, d)$ is partitioned into two disjoint sets, $\mathcal{X} = \mathcal{X}_+ \cup \mathcal{X}_-$, where $\mathcal{X}_+$ are the "normal" points and $\mathcal{X}_-$ are the "anomalous" ones. The normal set $\mathcal{X}_+$ is endowed with some (unknown) probability distribution P and the training phase consists of the learner being shown n iid draws of $X_i \in \mathcal{X}_+$ according to P. In the testing phase, the learner is asked to classify a new $X \in \mathcal{X}$ as *normal* or *anomalous*. By assumption, normal test points are drawn from P, but no assumption is made on the distribution of anomalous test points.

Further structural assumptions are needed to make the problem statement non-trivial. By analogy with common separability assumptions in supervised learning by hyperplanes, we make the following assumption:

$$d(\mathcal{X}_+, \mathcal{X}_-) \equiv \inf_{x \in \mathcal{X}_+, y \in \mathcal{X}_-} d(x, y) > \gamma \tag{1}$$

for some *separation distance* $\gamma > 0$.

We distinguish the two types of classification error: when a normal point is wrongly labeled as an anomaly, we call this a **false alarm**, and when an anomaly is wrongly classified as normal, we call this an **missed anomaly**.

2.2 Known Separation Distance

When the separation distance γ is known, we propose a simple classification rule $f : \mathcal{X} \to \{-1, 1\}$ as follows: given a sample $S \subset \mathcal{X}_+$, classify a new point x as normal (corresponding to $f(x) = 1$) if $d(x, S) \leq \gamma$ and as anomalous ($f(x) = -1$) if $d(x, S) > \gamma$. Our assumption (1) implies that f will never make a missed anomaly error, and we can use the techniques of [14] to bound the false alarm rate of this classifier. Define the *false alarm rate* of f by

$$\mathrm{FA}(f) = \int_{\mathcal{X}_+} \mathbb{1}_{\{f(x)<0\}} dP(x). \tag{2}$$

Theorem 1. *Given a training set* $S = \{X_1, \ldots, X_n\}$ *drawn from* $\mathcal{X}_+$ *iid under the distribution* P*, define the* proximity classifier $f_{n,\gamma}$ *as above:*

$$f_{n,\gamma}(x) = \mathbb{1}_{\{d(x,S)\leq\gamma\}} - \mathbb{1}_{\{d(x,S)>\gamma\}}. \tag{3}$$

Then, with probability at least $1 - \delta$*, this classifier achieves a false alarm rate that satisfies*

$$\mathrm{FA}(f_{n,\gamma}) \leq \frac{2\left(D \log_2(34en/D) \log_2(578n) + \log_2(4/\delta)\right)}{n}, \tag{4}$$

where

$$D = \lceil 8\Delta/\gamma \rceil^{\mathrm{ddim}(\mathcal{X})+1} \tag{5}$$

and $\mathrm{ddim}(\mathcal{X})$ *is the doubling dimension of* $\mathcal{X}$*.*

Proof. Consider the function $h : \mathcal{X} \to [-1, 1]$ satisfying

(i) $h(x) \geq 1$ for all $x \in S$
(ii) $h(x) < 0$ for all x with $d(x, S) > \gamma$
(iii) h has the smallest Lipschitz constant among all the functions satisfying (i) and (ii).

It is shown in [14,36] that h (a) has Lipschitz constant $1/\gamma$ and (b) the function $x \mapsto \operatorname{sgn} h(x)$ is realized by $f_{n,\gamma}$ defined in (3). Corollary 3 in [14] shows that the collection of real-valued $1/\gamma$-Lipschitz functions defined on a metric space $\mathcal{X}$ with doubling dimension $\mathrm{ddim}(\mathcal{X})$ and diameter Δ has a fat-shattering dimension at scale 1/16 of at most $(8\Delta/\gamma)^{\mathrm{ddim}(\mathcal{X})+1}$. The claim follows from known generalization bounds for function classes with a finite fat-shattering dimension (e.g., Theorem 1.5 in [2]). □

Remark 1. Note that the approach via Rademacher averages in general yields tighter bounds than those obtained from fat-shattering bounds; see [36].

In the sequel, we will find it useful to restate the estimate in Theorem 1 in the following equivalent form.

Corollary 1. *Let $f_{n,\gamma}$ be the proximity classifier defined in Theorem 1, based on a sample of size n. Then, for all $0 \le t \le 1$, we have*

$$P(\mathrm{FA}(f_{n,\gamma}) > t) \le \exp((A_{n,\gamma} - t)/B_n)$$

where

$$A_{n,\gamma} = \left(2D_\gamma \log_2(34en/D_\gamma)\log_2(578n) + 2\log_2 4\right)/n$$

and

$$B_n = 2/(n \ln 2)$$

and $D = D_\gamma$ is defined in (5).

Proof. An equivalent way of stating (4) is that

$$\mathrm{FA}(f_{n,\gamma}) > A_{n,\gamma} - B_n \ln \delta$$

holds with probability less than δ. Putting $t = A_{n,\gamma} - B_n \ln \delta$ and solving for δ yields the claim. □

2.3 Definition of Risk

We define risk in a nonstandard way, but one that is suitable for our particular problem setting. Because of our sampling assumptions — namely, that the distribution is only defined over $\mathcal{X}_+$ — there is a fundamental asymmetry between the false alarm and missed anomaly errors. A false alarm is a well-defined random event with a probability that we are able to control increasingly well with growing sample size. Thus, any classifier f has an associated false alarm rate $\mathrm{FA}(f)$ defined in (2). Since $f_{n,\gamma}$ itself is random (being determined by the random sample), $\mathrm{FA}(f_{n,\gamma})$ is a random variable and it makes sense to speak of $\mathbf{E}[\mathrm{FA}(f_{n,\gamma})]$ — the expected false alarm rate.

A missed anomaly is not a well-defined random event, since we have not defined any distribution over $\mathcal{X}_-$. Instead, we can speak of conditions ensuring that no missed anomaly will ever occur; the assumption of a separation distance is one such condition. If there is uncertainty regarding the separation distance γ, we might be able to describe the latter via a distribution $G(\cdot)$ on $(0, \infty)$, which is either assumed as a prior or somehow estimated empirically.

Having equipped γ with a distribution, our expression for the risk at a given value of γ_0 becomes

$$\mathrm{Risk}(\gamma_0) = \int_{\gamma_0}^{\infty} \mathbf{E}[\mathrm{FA}(f_{n,\gamma})] dG(\gamma) + C \int_0^{\gamma_0} dG(\gamma)$$

which reflects our modeling assumption that we pay a unit cost for each false alarm and a large "catastrophic" cost C for *any* nonzero number of missed anomalies.

2.4 Classification Rule

As before, we assume a unit cost incurred for each false alarm and a cost C for any positive missed anomalies. Let $A_{n,\gamma}$ and B_n be as defined in Corollary 1 and assume in what follows that n is sufficiently large so that $A_{n,\gamma} < 1$ (the bounds are vacuous for smaller values of n).

When γ is known, the only contribution to the risk is from false alarms, and it decays to zero at a rate that we are able to control.

Theorem 2. *Suppose the separation distance γ is known. Let $f_{n,\gamma}$ be the proximity classifier defined in Theorem 1, based on a sample of size n. Then*

$$\mathrm{Risk}(\gamma) \le (A_{n,\gamma} + B_n)$$

where $A_{n,\gamma}$ and B_n are as defined in Corollary 1 and n is assumed large enough so that $A_{n,\gamma} < 1$.

Proof. We compute

$$\begin{aligned}
\mathrm{Risk}(\gamma) &= \mathbf{E}[\mathrm{FA}(f_{n,\gamma})] \\
&= \int_0^\infty P(\mathrm{FA}(f_{n,\gamma}) > t)dt \\
&\le \int_0^1 \min\{1, \exp((A_{n,\gamma} - t)/B_n)\}\, dt \\
&= \left[\int_0^{A_{n,\gamma}} dt + \int_{A_{n,\gamma}}^1 \exp((A_{n,\gamma} - t)/B_n)dt\right] \\
&= [A_{n,\gamma} + B_n - B_n e^{(A_{n,\gamma}-1)/B_n}] \\
&\le (A_{n,\gamma} + B_n),
\end{aligned}$$

where the first inequality is an application of Corollary 1. □

When the exact value of the separation distance γ is unknown, we consider the scenario where our uncertainty regarding γ is captured by some known distribution G (which might be assumed a priori or estimated empirically).

In this case, the risk associated with a given value of γ_0 is:

$$\begin{aligned}
\mathrm{Risk}(\gamma_0) &= \int_{\gamma_0}^\infty \mathbf{E}[\mathrm{FA}(f_{n,\gamma})]dG(\gamma)\gamma + C\int_0^{\gamma_0} dG(\gamma) \\
&\le \int_{\gamma_0}^\infty (A_{n,\gamma} + B_n)dG(\gamma) + C\int_0^{\gamma_0} dG(\gamma) \\
&=: R_n(\gamma_0),
\end{aligned}$$

where the inequality follows immediately from Theorem 2.

Our analysis implies the following classification rule: compute the minimizer γ^* of $R_n(\cdot)$ and use the classifier f_{n,γ^*}. As a sanity check, notice that $A_{n,\gamma}$ grows inversely with γ (at a rate proportional to $1/\gamma^{\mathrm{ddim}(\mathcal{X})+1}$), so γ^* will not be arbitrarily small. Note also that $R_n(\gamma_0) \to 0$ as $n \to \infty$ for any fixed γ_0.

2.5 No Explicit Prior on γ

Instead of assuming a distribution on γ, we can make a weaker assumption. In any discrete metric space $(\mathcal{S}, d)$, define the quantity we call *isolation distance*

$$\rho = \sup_{x \in \mathcal{S}} d(x, \mathcal{S} \setminus \{x\});$$

this is the maximal distance from any point in S to its nearest neighbor. Our additional assumption will be that $\rho < \gamma$ (in words: the isolation distance is less than the separation distance). This means that we can take ρ — a quantity we can estimate empirically — as a proxy for γ.

We estimate $\rho = \rho(\mathcal{X}_+, d)$ as follows. Given the finite sample $X_1, \ldots, X_n$ drawn iid from $\mathcal{X}_+$, define

$$\hat{\rho}_n = \max_{i \in [n]} \min_{j \neq i} d(X_i, X_j). \tag{6}$$

It is obvious that $\hat{\rho}_n \leq \rho$ and for countable $\mathcal{X}$, it is easy to see that $\hat{\rho}_n \to \rho$ almost surely. The convergence rate, however, may be arbitrarily slow, as it depends on the (possibly adversarial) sampling distribution P.

To obtain a distribution-free bound, we will need some additional notions. For $x \in \mathcal{X}$, define $B_\epsilon(x)$ to be the ϵ-ball about x:

$$B_\epsilon(x) = \{y \in \mathcal{X} : d(x, y) \leq \epsilon\}.$$

For $S \subset \mathcal{X}$, define its ϵ-envelope, S_ϵ, to be

$$S_\epsilon = \bigcup_{x \in S} B_\epsilon(x).$$

For $\epsilon > 0$, define the ϵ-covering number, $N(\epsilon)$, of $\mathcal{X}$ as the minimal cardinality of a set $E \subset \mathcal{X}$ such that $\mathcal{X} = E_\epsilon$. Following [5], we define the *ϵ-unseen mass* of the sample $S = \{X_1, \ldots, X_n\}$ as the random variable

$$U_n(\epsilon) = P(\mathcal{X}_+ \setminus S_\epsilon). \tag{7}$$

It is shown in [5] that the expected ϵ-unseen mass may be estimated in terms of the ϵ-covering numbers, uniformly over all distributions.

Theorem 3 ([5]). *Let $\mathcal{X}$ be a metric space equipped with some probability distribution and let $U_n(\epsilon)$ be the ϵ-unseen mass random variable defined in (7). Then for all sampling distributions we have*

$$\mathbf{E}[U_n(\epsilon)] \leq \frac{N(\epsilon)}{en},$$

where $N(\epsilon)$ is the ϵ-covering number of $\mathcal{X}$.

Corollary 2. *Let $U_n(\epsilon)$ be the ϵ-unseen mass random variable defined in (7). Then*

$$\mathbf{E}[U_n(\epsilon)] \leq \frac{1}{en}\left(\frac{\Delta}{\epsilon}\right)^{\mathrm{ddim}(\mathcal{X})+2}.$$

Proof. For doubling spaces, it is an immediate consequence of [21] and [1, Lemma 2.6] that

$$N(\epsilon) \leq \left\lceil \frac{\Delta}{\epsilon} \right\rceil^{\mathrm{ddim}(\mathcal{X})+1} \leq \left(\frac{\Delta}{\epsilon} \right)^{\mathrm{ddim}(\mathcal{X})+2}.$$

Substituting the latter estimate into Theorem 3 yields the claim. □

Our final observation is that for any sample $X_1, \ldots, X_n$ achieving an ϵ-net, the corresponding $\hat{\rho}_n$ satisfies

$$\hat{\rho}_n \leq \rho \leq \hat{\rho}_n + 2\epsilon.$$

We are now in a position to write down an expression for the risk. The false-alarm component is straightforward: taking $\hat{\gamma} = \hat{\rho}_n + 2\epsilon$, the only way a new point X could be misclassified as a false alarm is if it falls outside of the ϵ-envelope of the observed sample. Thus, this component of the risk may be bounded by

$$\frac{1}{en} \left(\frac{\Delta}{\epsilon} \right)^{\mathrm{ddim}(\mathcal{X})+2}.$$

On the other hand a missed anomaly can only occur if $\hat{\gamma} > \gamma$. Unfortunately, even though $\hat{\gamma} = \hat{\rho}_n + 2\epsilon$ is a well-defined random variable, we cannot give a non-trivial bound on $P(\hat{\gamma} > \gamma)$ since we know nothing about how close ρ is to γ. Therefore, we resort to a "flat prior" heuristic (corresponding roughly to the assumption $\Pr[\rho + t\Delta > \gamma] \approx t$), resulting in the missed-anomaly risk term of the form

$$\frac{2C\epsilon}{\Delta}. \tag{8}$$

Combining the two terms, we have

$$R_n(\epsilon) = \frac{1}{en} \left(\frac{\Delta}{\epsilon} \right)^{\mathrm{ddim}(\mathcal{X})+2} + \frac{2C\epsilon}{\Delta}$$

which is minimized at

$$\epsilon_n = \frac{\Delta^{\mathrm{ddim}(\mathcal{X})+3}}{2Cen}.$$

Note that as $n \to \infty$, we have $\epsilon_n \to 0$ and $R_n(\epsilon_n) \to 0$, implying an asymptotic consistency of the classifier $f_{n,\hat{\rho}_n+2\epsilon_n}$ for this type of risk. Observe also that analogous asymptotically consistent estimators are straightforward to derive for risk bounded by

$$R_n(\epsilon) = \frac{1}{en} \left(\frac{\Delta}{\epsilon} \right)^{\mathrm{ddim}(\mathcal{X})+2} + \frac{2C\epsilon^a}{\Delta}$$

for any $a > 0$.

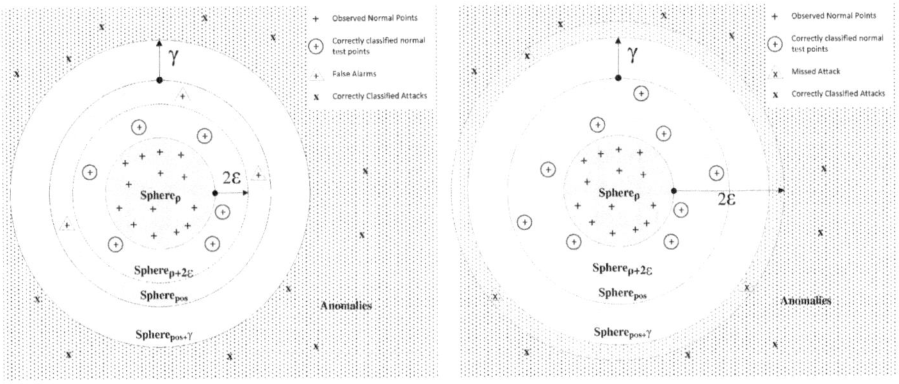

Fig. 1. A schematic presentation of the various quantities defined in Section 2.5. In the left diagram, ϵ is too small, resulting in false alarms. On the right, a too-large value of ϵ leads to missed attacks.

3 Experiments

3.1 Methodology

We experimented with several datasets, both synthetic and real-world. The Euclidean metric $d(x, x') = \|x - x'\| = \sqrt{\sum(x_i - x'_i)^2}$ was used in each case. For each dataset, a false alarm incurs a unit cost and any number of missed anomalies incurs a catastrophic cost C. The value of C is strongly tied to the particular task at hand. In order to obtain a rough estimate in the case of an attack on a computer network, we consulted various figures on the damage caused by such events [13,37] and came up with the rough estimate of $300,000$ for C; this was the value we used in all the experiments. The diameter Δ is estimated as the largest distance between any two sample points and the doubling dimension $\mathrm{ddim}(\mathcal{X})$ is efficiently approximated from the sample via the techniques of [15]. The figures presented are the averages over 10 trials, where the data was randomly split into training and test sets in each trial.

Before we list the classifiers that were tested, a comment is in order. For a fair comparison to our proposed method, we need a classifier that is both (i) cost-sensitive and (ii) able to learn from positive examples only. Since we were not able to locate such a classifier in the literature, we resorted to adapting existing techniques to this task. The following classifiers were trained and tested on each dataset:

- Asymmetric Anomaly Detector (AAD) is the classifier $f_{n,\hat{\rho}_n+2\epsilon_n}$ proposed in Section 2.5 of this paper.
- Peer Group Analysis (PGA) is an unsupervised anomaly detection method proposed by Eskin et al. [11] that identifies the low density regions using nearest neighbors. An anomaly score is computed at a point x as a function of the distances from x to its k nearest neighbors. Although PGA is actually

a ranking technique applied to a clustering problem, we implemented it as a one-class classifier with $k = 1$. Given the training sample S, a test point x is classified as follows. For each $x_i \in S$, we pre-compute the distance to x_i's nearest neighbor in S, given by $d_i = d(x_i, S \setminus \{x_i\})$. To classify x, the distance to the nearest neighbor of x in S, $d_x = d(x, S)$ is computed. The test point x is classified as an anomaly if $d_x = d(x, S)$ appears in a percentile α or higher among the $\{d_i\}$; otherwise it is classified as normal. We set the parameter $\alpha = 0.01$ (obviously, it should depend on the value of C but the dependence is not at all clear).
- Global Density Estimation (GDE), proposed by [20] is also an unsupervised density-estimation technique using nearest neighbors. Given a training sample S and a real value r, one computes the anomaly score of a test point x by comparing the number of training points falling within the r-ball $B_r(x)$ about x to the average of $|B_r(x_i) \cap S|$ over all $x_i \in S$. We set r to be twice the sample average of $d(x_i, S \setminus \{x_i\})$ to ensure that the average number of neighbors is at least one. In order to convert GDE into a classifier, we needed a heuristic for thresholding anomaly scores. We chose the following one, as it seemed to achieve a low classification error on the data: x is classified as normal if $\exp(-((N_r(x) - \bar{N}_r)/\sigma_r) > 1/2$, where N_r is the number of r-neighbors of x in S, $\bar{N}_r$ is the average number of r-neighbors over the training points, and σ_r is the sample standard deviation of the number of r-neighbors.

Each classifier is evaluated based on the cost that it incurred on unseen data: c units were charged for each false alarm and an additional cost of C for one or more missed anomalies. As an additional datum, we also record the cost-insensitive classification error.

3.2 Data Sets

We tested the classifiers on the following three data sets.

2D-Single-Cluster. This is a two-dimensional synthetic data set. As shown in Figure 2, the normal data points are concentrated along a thin, elongated cluster in the middle of a square, with the anomalies spread out uniformly. A total of 363 points were generated, of which 300 were normal with 63 anomalies. For the normal points, the x-coordinate was generated uniformly at random and the y-coordinate was a function of x perturbed by noise. A positive separation distance was enforced during the generation process.

9D-Sphere. This is a 9-dimensional synthetic data set containing 550 instances. The coordinates are drawn independently from mean-zero, variance-35 Gaussians. Points with Euclidean norm under 90 were labeled as "normal" and those whose norm exceeded 141 were labeled "anomalies". Points whose norm fell between these values were discarded, so as to maintain a strong separation distance.

BGU ARP. The abbreviation ARP stands for "Address Resolution Protocol", see [28]. This is a dataset of actual ARP attacks, recorded on the Ben-Gurion

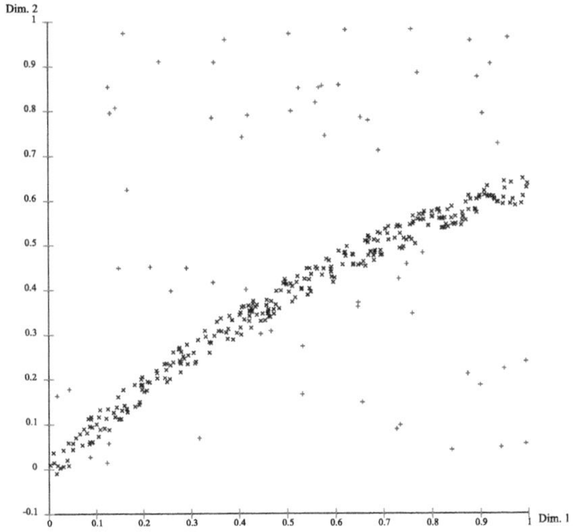

Fig. 2. The 2D-Single-Cluster dataset

University network. The dataset contains 9039 instances and 23 attributes extracted from layer-2 (link-layer) frames. Each instance in the dataset represents a single ARP packet that was sent through the network during the recording time. There were 173 active computers on the network, of which 27 were attacked. The attacker temporarily steals the IPv4 addresses of its victims and as a result, the victim's entire traffic is redirected to the attacker, without the victim's knowledge or consent. Our training data had an anomaly (attack) rate of 3.3%. The training instances were presented in xml format and their numerical fields induced a Euclidean vector representation.

3.3 Results

Our basic quantities of interest are the number of false alarms (FA), the number of missed anomalies (MA), and the number of correctly predicted test points (CP). From these, we derive the classification error

$$\text{err} = \frac{\text{FA} + \text{MA}}{\text{FA} + \text{MA} + \text{CP}}$$

and the incurred cost

$$\text{Cost} = \text{FA} + C \cdot \mathbb{1}_{\{\text{MA}>0\}}.$$

Although in this paper we are mainly interested in the incurred cost, we also keep track of the classification error for comparison. The results are summarized in Figure 3. Notice that our classifier significantly outperforms the others in the incurred cost criterion. Also interesting to note is that a lower classification error does not necessarily imply a lower incurred cost, since even a single missed attack can significantly increase the latter.

Dataset	Classifier	% Classification Error	% False Alarms	% Missed Attacks	Incurred Cost
2D-Single-Cluster	AAD	0.44	0	0.01	24,000.08
	GDE	16.03	0	0.91	273,000.10
	PGA	1.24	0.01	0.03	57,000.24
9D-Sphere	AAD	0.24	0	0	0.13
	GDE	28.45	0.29	0	15.65
	PGA	1.11	0.01	0.07	21,000.54
BGU ARP	AAD	0.18	0	0	0.14
	GDE	59.1	0.61	0	45.57
	PGA	4.55	0.01	1	300,000.90

Fig. 3. The performance of the classifiers on the datasets, averaged over 10 trials

4 Discussion and Future Work

We have presented a novel (and apparently first of its kind) method for learning to detect anomalies in a cost-sensitive framework from positive examples only, along with efficient learning algorithms. We have given some preliminary theoretical results supporting this technique and tested it on data (including real-world), with encouraging results.

Some future directions naturally suggest themselves. One particularly unrealistic assumption is the "isotropic" nature of our classifier, which implicitly assumes that the density has no preferred direction in space. Directionally sensitive metric classifiers already exist [6] and it would be desirable to extend our analysis to these methods. Additionally, one would like to place the heuristic missed-anomaly risk term we proposed in (8) on a more principled theoretical footing. Finally, we look forward to testing our approach on more diverse datasets.

Acknowledgments. We thank Lee-Ad Gottlieb for helpful discussions.

References

1. Alon, N., Ben-David, S., Cesa-Bianchi, N., Haussler, D.: Scale-sensitive dimensions, uniform convergence, and learnability. Journal of the ACM 44(4), 615–631 (1997)
2. Bartlett, P., Shawe-Taylor, J.: Generalization performance of support vector machines and other pattern classifiers. pp. 43–54 (1999)
3. Ben-Hur, A.: Support vector clustering. Scholarpedia 3(6), 5187 (2008)
4. Bennett, K.P., Demiriz, A., Maclin, R.: Exploiting unlabeled data in ensemble methods. In: KDD, pp. 289–296 (2002)
5. Berend, D., Kontorovich, A.: The missing mass problem (in preparation, 2011)

6. Breunig, M.M., Kriegel, H.-P., Ng, R.T., Sander, J.: Lof: identifying density-based local outliers. SIGMOD Rec. 29, 93–104 (2000)
7. Crammer, K., Chechik, G.: A needle in a haystack: local one-class optimization. In: ICML (2004)
8. Dempster, A.P., Laird, N.M., Rubin, D.B.: Maximum likelihood from incomplete data via the EM algorithm. J. Roy. Statist. Soc. Ser. B 39(1), 1–38 (1977) With discussion
9. Domingos, P.: Metacost: A general method for making classifiers cost-sensitive. In: KDD, pp. 155–164 (1999)
10. Elkan, C.: The foundations of cost-sensitive learning. In: IJCAI, pp. 973–978 (2001)
11. Eskin, E., Arnold, A., Prerau, M., Portnoy, L., Stolfo, S.: A geometric framework for unsupervised anomaly detection: Detecting intrusions in unlabeled data. In: Applications of Data Mining in Computer Security. Kluwer, Dordrecht (2002)
12. Fan, W., Stolfo, S.J., Zhang, J., Chan, P.K.: Adacost: Misclassification cost-sensitive boosting. In: ICML, pp. 97–105 (1999)
13. CEI figures: Computer Economics Inc. Security issues: Virus costs are rising again (2003)
14. Gottlieb, L.-A., Kontorovich, L., Krauthgamer, R.: Efficient classification for metric data. In: COLT (2010)
15. Gottlieb, L.-A., Krauthgamer, R.: Proximity algorithms for nearly-doubling spaces. In: Serna, M., et al. (eds.) APPROX and RANDOM 2010. LNCS, vol. 6302, pp. 192–204. Springer, Heidelberg (2010)
16. Greiner, R., Grove, A.J., Roth, D.: Learning cost-sensitive active classifiers. Artif. Intell. 139(2), 137–174 (2002)
17. Gupta, A., Krauthgamer, R., Lee, J.R.: Bounded geometries, fractals, and low-distortion embeddings. In: FOCS, pp. 534–543 (2003)
18. Heller, K.A., Svore, K.M., Keromytis, A.D., Stolfo, S.J.: One class support vector machines for detecting anomalous windows registry accesses. In: ICDM Workshop on Data Mining for Computer Security, DMSEC (2003)
19. Japkowicz, N., Stephen, S.: The class imbalance problem: A systematic study. Intell. Data Anal. 6(5), 429–449 (2002)
20. Knorr, E.M., Ng, R.T.: A unified notion of outliers: Properties and computation. In: KDD, pp. 219–222 (1997)
21. Krauthgamer, R., Lee, J.R.: Navigating nets: Simple algorithms for proximity search. In: 15th Annual ACM-SIAM Symposium on Discrete Algorithms, pp. 791–801 (January 2004)
22. Li, Y.-F., Kwok, J.T., Zhou, Z.-H.: Cost-sensitive semi-supervised support vector machine. In: AAAI (2010)
23. Ling, C.X., Sheng, V.S.: Cost-sensitive learning. In: Encyclopedia of Machine Learning, pp. 231–235 (2010)
24. Ling, C.X., Yang, Q., Wang, J., Zhang, S.: Decision trees with minimal costs. In: ICML (2004)
25. Liu, A., Jun, G., Ghosh, J.: A self-training approach to cost sensitive uncertainty sampling. In: Buntine, W., Grobelnik, M., Mladenić, D., Shawe-Taylor, J. (eds.) ECML PKDD 2009, Part I. LNCS, vol. 5781, pp. 10–10. Springer, Heidelberg (2009)
26. Luo, J., Ding, L., Pan, Z., Ni, G., Hu, G.: Research on cost-sensitive learning in one-class anomaly detection algorithms. In: Xiao, B., Yang, L., Ma, J., Muller-Schloer, C., Hua, Y. (eds.) ATC 2007. LNCS, vol. 4610, pp. 259–268. Springer, Heidelberg (2007)

27. Margineantu, D.D.: Active cost-sensitive learning. In: IJCAI, pp. 1613–1622 (2005)
28. Plummer, D.C.: Rfc 826: An ethernet address resolution protocol – or – converting network protocol addresses to 48.bit ethernet address for transmission on ethernet hardware (1982), Internet Engineering Task Force, Network Working Group
29. Qin, Z., Zhang, S., Liu, L., Wang, T.: Cost-sensitive semi-supervised classification using CS-EM. In: 8th IEEE International Conference on Computer and Information Technology, CIT 2008, pp. 131 –136 (July 2008)
30. Schölkopf, B., Burges, C., Vapnik, V.: Extracting support data for a given task. In: KDD, pp. 252–257 (1995)
31. Schölkopf, B., Platt, J.C., Shawe-Taylor, J., Smola, A.J., Williamson, R.C.: Estimating the support of a high-dimensional distribution. Neural Computation 13(7), 1443–1471 (2001)
32. Sun, Y., Kamel, M.S., Wong, A.K.C., Wang, Y.: Cost-sensitive boosting for classification of imbalanced data. Pattern Recognition 40(12), 3358–3378 (2007)
33. Tax, D.M.J., Duin, R.P.W.: Data domain description using support vectors. In: ESANN, pp. 251–256 (1999)
34. Martinus, D., Tax, J.: One-class classification. PhD thesis, Delft University of Technology (2001)
35. Turney, P.D.: Cost-sensitive classification: Empirical evaluation of a hybrid genetic decision tree induction algorithm. J. Artif. Intell. Res (JAIR) 2, 369–409 (1995)
36. von Luxburg, U., Bousquet, O.: Distance-based classification with lipschitz functions. Journal of Machine Learning Research 5, 669–695 (2004)
37. Waters, R.: When will they ever stop bugging us? Financial Times, special report (2003)
38. Zadrozny, B., Elkan, C.: Learning and making decisions when costs and probabilities are both unknown. In: KDD, pp. 204–213 (2001)
39. Zhou, Z.-H., Liu, X.-Y.: On multi-class cost-sensitive learning. Computational Intelligence 26(3), 232–257 (2010)

One Shot Similarity Metric Learning for Action Recognition

Orit Kliper-Gross[1], Tal Hassner[2], and Lior Wolf[3]

[1] The Department of Mathematic and Computer Science,
The Weizmann Institute of Science, Rehovot, Israel
orit.kliper@weizmann.ac.il
[2] The Department of Mathematics and Computer Science,
The Open University, Raanana, Israel
hassner@openu.ac.il
[3] The Blavatnik School of Computer Science, Tel-Aviv University, Tel-Aviv, Israel
wolf@cs.tau.ac.il

Abstract. The One-Shot-Similarity (OSS) is a framework for classifier-based similarity functions. It is based on the use of background samples and was shown to excel in tasks ranging from face recognition to document analysis. However, we found that its performance depends on the ability to effectively learn the underlying classifiers, which in turn depends on the underlying metric.

In this work we present a metric learning technique that is geared toward improved OSS performance. We test the proposed technique using the recently presented ASLAN action similarity labeling benchmark. Enhanced, state of the art performance is obtained, and the method compares favorably to leading similarity learning techniques.

Keywords: Learned metrics, One-Shot-Similarity, Action Similarity.

1 Introduction

Analyzing videos of actions performed by humans is a subject of much research in Computer Vision and Pattern Recognition. The particular problem of action pair-matching is the task of determining if actors in two videos are performing the same action or not. This, when the two actors may be different people and when the viewing conditions may vary. Contrary to related image-similarity tasks such as pair-matching of face images [1], where class labels are well defined, this task is often ill-posed; actions are frequently not *atomic*, and so whether or not two videos present *same* or *not-same* actions is not well defined. In addition, when the videos are obtained "in the wild", with no control over viewing conditions and without the collaboration of the actors appearing in them, the task is even more challenging.

In this paper we focus on pair-matching (same/not-same classification) of action videos obtained in such unconstrained conditions. Performance in this task ultimately depends on the suitability of the similarity measure used to compare video pairs. Recent results on similar image-based challenges have shown

M. Pelillo and E.R. Hancock (Eds.): SIMBAD 2011, LNCS 7005, pp. 31–45, 2011.

that employing *background information* (sometimes called *side information*) can boost performance significantly. In our framework, the background information consists of a moderately large set of unlabeled examples, that are expected to be of different classes than the pair of samples we are comparing.

Specifically, the One-Shot-Similarity (OSS) measure [2] utilizes unlabeled non-class examples to obtain better estimates for the similarity of two face images [3]. OSS results consequently outperformed other methods on the LFW challenge [4]. OSS also compares favorably to other metric learning techniques in tasks related to ancient document analysis [5] and elsewhere [2].

Here, we report attempts to employ OSS on the recently introduced "Action Similarity Labeling" (ASLAN) data set [6], which includes thousands of videos from the web, in over 400 complex action classes. The ASLAN set was designed to capture the variability typical to unconstrained, "in the wild", action recognition problems and is currently the most comprehensive benchmark available for action similarity in videos (some example frames from the ASLAN set are presented in Figure 1).

Our tests on the ASLAN benchmark demonstrate that the performance gain obtained using OSS and background information for other tasks does not carry over to action similarity on the ASLAN set. While background-information might capture information vital for correctly measuring the similarity of two actions, benefiting from this information requires that the input space is suitable of this type of analysis. We therefore propose a novel scheme for supervised metric learning, the OSS-Metric Learning (OSSML). OSSML learns a projection matrix which improves the OSS relation between the example same and not-same training pairs in a reduced subspace of the original feature space. Our results demonstrate that OSSML significantly enhances action similarity performance on the ASLAN benchmark, compared to existing state-of-the-art techniques.

To summarize, this work makes the following contributions: (a) We have developed a new metric learning approach and applied it to the problem of action similarity (pair-matching) in videos. (b) We show how learned projections using background statistics enhance the performance over unsupervised metric learning (such as PCA). (c) We further show that applying two complementary weakly supervised criteria in an interleaving manner provides a substantial boost in performance, obtaining state-of-the-art results on the ASLAN benchmark.

The rest of this paper is structured as follows. Section 2 presents the OSSML and derives its formulation. Section 3 applies OSSML to action recognition on the ASLAN benchmark. Experimental results are presented in section 4. We conclude in section 5.

1.1 Related Work

Metric Learning. The choice of a suitable metric is crucial for the design of a successful pattern recognition system. The literature on the subject is therefore substantial. Some existing similarity measures are hand crafted (e.g., [7,8]). Alternatively, there is growing interest in methods which apply learning techniques to fit similarity measures and metrics to available training data (see [9]

Fig. 1. Examples of actions in the ASLAN set

for a comprehensive study). Most common to these techniques is the learning of a projection matrix from the data so that the Euclidean distance can perform better in the new subspace. Learning such a matrix is equivalent to learning a Mahalanobis distance in the original space.

The Relevant Component Analysis (RCA) method of Bar-Hillel et al. [10] is one such example. They learn a full rank Mahalanobis metric by using equivalence constraints on the training elements. Goldberger et al. [11] described the Neighborhood Component Analysis (NCA) approach for k-NN classification. NCA works by learning a Mahalanobis distance minimizing the leave-one-out cross-validation error of the k-NN classifier on a training set. Another method, designed for clustering by [12], also learns a Mahalanobis distance metric, here using semi-definite programming. Their method attempts to minimize the sum of squared distances between examples of the same label, while preventing the distances between differently labeled examples from falling below a lower bound.

In [13] a Large Margin Nearest Neighbor (LMNN) method was proposed, which employed semi-definite learning to obtain a Mahalanobis distance metric for which any collection of k-nearest neighbors always has the same class label. Additionally, elements with different labels were separated by large margins.

The Information Theoretic Metric Learning (ITML) approach of Davis et al. [14] solves a Bregman's optimization problem [15] to learn a Mahalanobis distance function. The result is a fast algorithm, capable of regularization by a known prior matrix, and is applicable under different types of constraints, including similarity, dissimilarity and pair-wise constraints. The Online Algorithm for Scalable Image Similarity (OASIS) [16] was proposed for online metric learning for sparse, high-dimensional elements.

Unlike the previously mentioned approaches, the recent method of Nguyen and Bai [17] attempts to learn a cosine similarity, rather than learning a metric for the Euclidean distance. This was shown to be particularly effective for pair-matching of face images on the Labeled Faces in the Wild (LFW) benchmark [1,18].

Similarities Employing Background Information. The first similarity measure in a recent line of work, designed to utilize background-information, is the One-Shot-Similarity (OSS) of [3,2]. Given two vectors I and J, their OSS score is computed by considering a training set of background sample vectors N. This set of vectors contains examples of items different from both I and J, but are otherwise unlabeled. We review the OSS score in detail in Sec. 2.1. This OSS has been shown to be key in amplifying performance on the LFW data set. Here, we extend the OSS approach by deriving a metric learning scheme for emphasizing the separation between same and not-same vectors when compared using the OSS.

2 One-Shot-Similarity Metric Learning (OSSML)

Given a set of training examples our goal is to learn a transformation matrix which improves OSS performance, as measured using cross-validation. We next derive this transformation for the case where the classifier underlying the OSS computation is a free-scale Fisher Linear Discriminant.

2.1 The Free-Scale LDA-Based, Symmetric OSS Score

Given two vectors I and J their One-Shot-Similarity (OSS) score is computed by considering a training set of background sample vectors N. This set contains examples of items not belonging to the same class as neither I nor J, but are otherwise unlabeled. A measure of the similarity of I and J is then obtained as follows: First, a discriminative model is learned with I as a single positive example, and N as a set of negative examples. This model is then used to classify the vector, J, and obtain a confidence score. A second such score is then obtained by repeating the same process with the roles of I and J switched. The particular nature of these scores depends on the classifier used. The final symmetric OSS score is the average of these two scores. Figure 2 summarizes these steps.

The OSS score can be fitted with almost any discriminative learning algorithm. In previous work, Fisher Linear Discriminant (FLD or LDA) [19,20] was mostly used as the underlying classifier. Similarities based on LDA can be efficiently computed by exploiting the fact that the background set N, which is the source of the negative samples, is used repeatedly, and that the positive class, which contains just one element, does not contribute to the within class covariance matrix.

The free-scale LDA-based One-Shot-Similarity is a simplified version in which the projection is done along the unnormalized vector. Although in general, the OSS score is not a positive definite kernel, it was shown in [2] that the free-scale LDA-based OSS version gives rise to a positive definite kernel and so is suitable for use in kernel machines, such as Support Vector Machines (SVM) [21]. The

```
One-Shot-Similarity(I, J,  N) =

     Model1 = train(I, N)
     Score1 = classify(J, Model1)

     Model2 = train(J, N)
     Score2 = classify(I, Model2)

     return ½(Score1+Score2)
```

Fig. 2. Computing the symmetric One-Shot-Similarity score for two vectors, **I** and **J**, given a set, **N**, of background examples

symmetric Free-Scale One-Shot-Similarity (FSOSS) between two vectors I and J given the negative set N, is expressed as:

$$FSOSS(I,J,N) = (I-\mu_N)^T S_w^+(J-\frac{I+\mu_N}{2})+(J-\mu_N)^T S_w^+(I-\frac{J+\mu_N}{2}) \quad (1)$$

Where,

μ_N is the mean of the negative set with $X_1,...X_r$ samples, and S_w^+ is the pseudo-inverse of $S_w = \frac{1}{r}\sum_{k=1}^{r}(X_k-\mu_N)(X_k-\mu_N)^T$. In practice, to allow for efficient computation, we apply PCA before the learning, and therefore there are more examples than dimensions, thus, S_w is invertible and S_w^+ is simply the inverse $(S_w)^{-1}$, which we will denote by, $(S_w)^{-1} = S^{-1}$.

2.2 Deriving the OSSML

Let $I_i, J_i \in R^n$ be the pairs of input vectors in the training set. Let $L_i \in \{0,1\}$ be the corresponding binary labels indicating if I_i and J_i belong to the same class or not. Our goal is to learn a linear transformation $A : R^n \longrightarrow R^m (m < n)$ which will be used to compute OSS in the transformed space. Specifically, we want to learn the linear transformation that will minimize the cross-validation error when similarities are computed by the OSSML score below. For each pair of vectors I, J, the OSS score in the transformed space (i.e. OSSML) is defined by:

$$\begin{aligned} &OSSML(I,J,N,A) = \\ &(AI-\mu_{AN})^T S_{AN}^+(AJ-\tfrac{AI+\mu_{AN}}{2}) + (AJ-\mu_{AN})^T S_{AN}^+(AI-\tfrac{AJ+\mu_{AN}}{2}) \end{aligned} \quad (2)$$

Here, N is the negative set, with r samples, A is the matrix to learn, AN is the negative set after applying A to each vector, μ_{AN} is the mean vector of the negative set after applying A, S_{AN}^+ is the pseudo-inverse of $S_{AN} = \frac{1}{r}\sum_{k=1}^{r}(AX_k-\mu_{AN})(AX_k-\mu_{AN})^T$, and $S_{AN} = AS_wA^T = ASA^T$ is invertible iff $S(=S_w)$ is invertible.

Replacing, S^{+}_{AN} by $S^{-1}_{AN} = (ASA^T)^{-1}$ We get,

$$\begin{aligned}
&OSSML(I, J, N, A) = \\
&\tfrac{1}{2}(AI - A\mu_N)^T(ASA^T)^{-1}(2AJ - AI - A\mu_N)+ \\
&\tfrac{1}{2}(AJ - A\mu_N)^T(ASA^T)^{-1}(2AI - AJ - A\mu_N) = \\
&\tfrac{1}{2}(I - \mu_N)^T A^T(ASA^T)^{-1}A(2J - I - \mu_N)+ \\
&\tfrac{1}{2}(J - \mu_N)^T A^T(ASA^T)^{-1}A(2I - J - \mu_N).
\end{aligned} \tag{3}$$

Using the following notations:

$$\begin{aligned}
a &= (I - \mu_N) \\
b &= (2J - I - \mu_N) \\
c &= (J - \mu_N) \\
d &= (2I - J - \mu_N)
\end{aligned}$$

We have,

$$OSSML(I, J, N, A) = \frac{1}{2}a^T A^T(ASA^T)^{-1}Ab + \frac{1}{2}c^T A^T(ASA^T)^{-1}Ad. \tag{4}$$

2.3 Objective Function

The objective function $f(A)$ is defined by:

$$f(A) = \sum_{i\in Pos} OSS(I_i, J_i, N, A) - \alpha \sum_{i\in Neg} OSS(I_i, J_i, N, A) - \beta||A - A_0||^2 \tag{5}$$

Where, Pos and Neg are the set of indices of the pairs belong to the same and not-same sets, respectively. Our goal is to maximize $f(A)$ with respect to A, given two parameters α and β, both non-negative. In practice we iterate on a range of β values, using cross-validation on part of the training data, as suggested by the CSML [17] algorithm. For A_0 we followed [17] and tried different $m \times n$ initial projections.

2.4 Free-Scale LDA-Based OSS Gradient

The objective function $f(A)$ is differentiable with respect to A. The gradient is given by:

$$\begin{aligned}
&\frac{\partial(f(A))}{\partial(A)} = \\
&\sum_{i\in Pos} \frac{\partial(OSS(I_i, J_i, N, A))}{\partial(A)} - \alpha \sum_{i\in Neg} \frac{\partial(OSS(I_i, J_i, N, A))}{\partial(A)} - 2\beta(A - A_0).
\end{aligned} \tag{6}$$

Using the notations in Equation 4, the free-scale LDA-based OSS derivative is given by,

$$\frac{\partial(OSS(I_i,J_i,N,A))}{\partial(A)} = \\ \frac{\partial(\frac{1}{2}{a_i}^T A^T(ASA^T)^{-1}Ab_i)}{\partial(A)} + \frac{\partial(\frac{1}{2}{c_i}^T A^T(ASA^T)^{-1}Ad_i)}{\partial(A)}. \tag{7}$$

This consists of two identical terms. Each can be written as:

$$\frac{1}{2}\frac{\partial(x^T A^T(ASA^T)^{-1}Ay)}{\partial(A)}$$

Denote by W the $(m \times n)$-dimensional matrix of the result obtained by deriving this term. Let $D = ASA^T$, where, A is an $(m \times n)$-dimensional matrix, S is an $(n \times n)$-dimensional matrix and thus, D is an $(m \times m)$-dimensional matrix.

We want to find the derivative of the function, $g(D,A) = x^T A^T D^{-1} Ay$, with respect to the matrix A.

D is a function of A, thus the chain rule can be written as:

$$[\frac{\partial g(D)}{\partial A}]_{ij} = \frac{\partial g(D)}{\partial A_{ij}} = \sum_{k=1}^{K}\sum_{l=1}^{L}\frac{\partial g(D)}{\partial D_{kl}}\frac{\partial D_{kl}}{\partial A_{ij}} = Tr[(\frac{\partial g(D)}{\partial D})^T\frac{\partial D}{\partial A_{ij}}]$$

Which is a matrix of the same dimensions as A (i.e. $m \times n$).

The total derivative W is therefore,

$$W_{ij} = [\frac{\partial(x^T A^T(ASA^T)^{-1}Ay)}{\partial A}]_{ij} = Tr[(\frac{\partial g(D)}{\partial D})^T\frac{\partial D}{\partial A_{ij}}] + [\frac{\partial g(D,A)}{\partial A}]_{ij} = \\ Tr[(\frac{\partial(x^T A^T D^{-1}Ay)}{\partial D})^T\frac{\partial D}{\partial A_{ij}}] + [\frac{\partial(x^T A^T D^{-1}Ay)}{\partial A}]_{ij} \tag{8}$$

where, $\frac{\partial g(D)}{\partial D}$ and $\frac{\partial D}{\partial A_{ij}}$ are $(m \times m)$-dimensional matrices. The last term, $\frac{\partial(x^T A^T D^{-1}Ay)}{\partial A}$, gives a matrix the same size as A and we take the ij entry.

1. From the following identity (see, for example, [22] for the various identities used throughout)

$$\frac{\partial(x^T X^{-1}y)}{\partial X} = -X^{-T}xy^T X^{-T},$$

we have

$$\frac{\partial(x^T A^T D^{-1}Ay)}{\partial D} = -D^{-1}Ax(Ay)^T D^{-1} = -(ASA^T)^{-1}Ax(Ay)^T(ASA^T)^{-1}$$

where, $X = D = ASA^T$ is an $(m \times m)$-dimensional symmetric matrix, and we use Ax and Ay instead of x and y.

2. Using the identity

$$\frac{\partial(X^T BX)}{\partial X_{ij}} = X^T BJ^{ij} + J^{ji}BX$$

we therefore have,

$$\frac{\partial D}{\partial A_{ij}} = \frac{\partial ASA^T}{\partial A^T_{ji}} = ASJ^{ji} + J^{ij}SA^T$$

Where, $X = A^T$, $B = S$, and J is a 4-dimensional tensor with $J^{il}_{jk} = \delta_{jl}\delta_{ki}$. J^{ji} is a matrix of the same dimensions as A^T which are, $(n \times m)$, with 1 at the ji entry, and 0 otherwise. We thus get a $(m \times m)$-dimensional matrix.

3. From the identity

$$\frac{\partial b^T X^T D X c}{\partial X} = D^T X b c^T + D X c b^T$$

we get,

$$\frac{\partial x^T A^T D^{-1} A y}{\partial A} = D^{-T} A x y^T + D^{-1} A y x^T = (ASA^T)^{-1} A x y^T + (ASA^T)^{-1} A y x^T$$

where, $X = A$, $D = D^{-1} = (ASA^T)^{-1}$, $b = x$ and $c = y$.

Finally, the total derivative in Equation 8 becomes:

$$\begin{aligned} &W_{ij} = [\tfrac{\partial(x^T A^T (ASA^T)^{-1} A y)}{\partial A}]_{ij} = \\ &Tr[(\tfrac{\partial(x^T A^T D^{-1} A y)}{\partial D})^T \tfrac{\partial(ASA^T)}{\partial A_{ij}}] + \tfrac{\partial(x^T A^T D^{-1} A y)}{\partial A} = \\ &Tr[(-(ASA^T)^{-1} A x (Ay)^T ((ASA^T)^{-1})^T (ASJ^{ji} + J^{ij} SA^T)] + \\ &((ASA^T)^{-1} A x y^T + (ASA^T)^{-1} A y x^T)_{ij} \end{aligned} \tag{9}$$

Which gives a scalar for each entry ij.

The general formula for W is given by,

$$\begin{aligned} &W(x, y)_{kl} = \\ &Tr[(-(ASA^T)^{-1} A x (Ay)^T ((ASA^T)^{-1})^T (ASJ^{lk} + J^{kl} SA^T)] + \\ &((ASA^T)^{-1} A x y^T + (ASA^T)^{-1} A y x^T)_{kl} \end{aligned} \tag{10}$$

for $k \in 1, ..., n$, $l \in 1, ...m$.

We have two such $(m \times n)$-dimensional W matrices for each (I_i, J_i) pair.

To summarize, Equation 6 becomes,

$$\begin{aligned} &\tfrac{\partial(f(A))}{\partial A} = \\ &\tfrac{1}{2} \sum_{i \in Pos} (W(a_i, b_i) + W(c_i, d_i)) - \\ &\tfrac{1}{2}\alpha \sum_{i \in Neg} (W(a_i, b_i) + W(c_i, d_i)) - \\ &2\beta(A - A_0) \end{aligned} \tag{11}$$

With W as above (Equation 10) for,

$$
\begin{aligned}
a_i &= (I_i - \mu_N) \\
b_i &= (2J_i - I_i - \mu_N) \\
c_i &= (J_i - \mu_N) \\
d_i &= (2I_i - J_i - \mu_N)
\end{aligned}
$$

3 Application to Action Recognition

In this section we apply OSSML to action similarity by measuring its performance on the ASLAN dataset.

3.1 ASLAN Data Set

The Action Similarity Labeling (ASLAN) collection is a new action recognition data set. This set includes thousands of videos collected from the web, in over 400 complex action classes. To standardize testing with this data, a "same/not-same" benchmark is provided, which addresses the action recognition problem as a non class-specific similarity problem instead of multi-class labeling. Specifically, the goal is to answer the following binary question – "does a pair of videos present the same action, or not?". This problem is sometimes referred to as the "unseen pair matching problem" (see for example [1]). Each video in the ASLAN collection is represented using each of the following state-of-the-art video descriptors: HOG, HOF and HNF [23]. Below, we use these descriptors, as made available by [6] without modification.

3.2 Same/Not-Same Benchmark

To report performance on the ASLAN database, the experimenter is asked to report aggregate performance of a classifier on ten separate experiments in a leave-one-out cross-validation scheme. Each experiment involves predicting the same/not-same labels for the video pairs in one of the ten "splits". Each such split includes 300 pairs of same actions and 300 pairs of not-same actions. In each experiment, nine of the splits are used for training, with the tenth split used for testing. The final parameters of the classifier under each experiment should be set using only the training data for that experiment, resulting in ten separate classifiers (one for each test set). The ASLAN benchmark has been designed such that these ten splits are mutually exclusive in the action labels they contain; if videos of a certain action appear in one split, no videos of that same action will appear in any other split. These tests therefore measure performance on general action similarity rather than the recognition of particular action classes.

3.3 Experimental Setup

We apply our experiments on each of the three descriptors available with the ASLAN data set. The dimension of each of the three descriptors is 5000. For each descriptor, we begin by applying PCA to get the vectors in a reduced n-dimensional space. We preform extensive tests with different PCA dimensions to choose a suitable subspace. We further reduce the dimension by applying OSSML as follows.

For each of the ten separate experiments we divide the nine training subsets such that one subset was used as a negative set, four subsets as validation samples and four subsets as training samples. We then use the training samples to find a matrix A that maximize $f(A)$ for a given α, β and initial matrix $A0$. Then, we use the validation samples to choose the next matrix A such that the accuracy on the validation sets is increased. We proceed iteratively until convergence.

For comparison we have implemented the Cosine Similarity Metric Learning (CSML) algorithm following the description in [17]. We have further used the CSML projection as an initial projection for our own OSSML algorithm.

Finally we have used a combination of similarity scores produced by different descriptors in the projected subspace to find optimal classifiers using linear SVM [21].

Results are reported by constructing an ROC curve and measuring both the area under curve (AUC) and the averaged accuracy $\pm$ standard errors for the ten splits.

4 Experimental Results

We first apply LDA-based OSS in the original 5000-dimensional descriptor space and compare it to the Cosine Similarity (CS). Table 1 reports the results of finding an optimal threshold on similarities calculated between vectors in the original descriptor space, as well as on the square root values of the descriptor entries (which makes sense for histograms [3]). Original vectors were L2 normalized before similarities were computed.

To allow for efficient computation, we next use PCA to reduce the dimension of the original space. PCA was preformed using different training sets for each experiment. We next choose an $n \times m$ initial projection matrix A_0 for the learning

Table 1. Original classification performance (no learning): Accuracy±Standard Error and (AUC), averaged over the 10-folds

		OSS	FSOSS	CS
HOG	original	$53.75 \pm .0.5(54.6)$	$51.90 \pm 0.4(51.5)$	$54.27 \pm 0.6(55.7)$
	sqrt	$53.20 \pm .0.7(53.7)$	$52.22 \pm .0.6(50.6)$	$53.47 \pm .0.6(54.2)$
HOF	original	$53.52 \pm .0.5(55.8)$	$52.63 \pm 0.4(53.3)$	$54.12 \pm 0.7(56.5)$
	sqrt	$54.80 \pm .0.6(56.0)$	$52.58 \pm 0.6(52.9)$	$53.83 \pm 0.7(56.0)$
HNF	original	$54.57 \pm 0.5(55.6)$	$52.60 \pm 0.4(52.4)$	$54.50 \pm 0.6(57.6)$
	sqrt	$54.27 \pm .0.6(54.9)$	$53.17 \pm 0.6(51.5)$	$53.93 \pm 0.73(55.8)$

algorithm (in our setting $n = 100$ and $m = 50$). We tried three different initial projections as suggested by [17]. We found that in our case best initial results were obtained by a simple $n \times m$ PCA projection. The initial PCA projection already improved the results over the original vector space. See the first block of Table 2.

We next perform three metric learning scenarios: CSML and OSSML with initial PCA projection, as well as OSSML with the matrix obtained by the CSML algorithm as the initial projection. We apply the projections obtained by each of these scenarios and calculated both CS and OSS scores in the projected subspace.

In the next three blocks of Table 2 we report the performances achieved by finding optimal thresholds for each of these scores. In the last column, we show the performances achieved by concatenating the scores of the three descriptors and finding an optimal classifier using linear SVM on a three-dimensional input vector. We further concatenate both scores from all three descriptors to form a six-dimensional vector given as an input to the linear SVM to get an optimal classifier. This is reported as CS+OSS on the third line of each algorithm.

Table 2. Classification performance on ASLAN: Accuracy±Standard Error and (AUC), averaged over the 10-folds. Please see text for more details.

		HOG	HOF	HNF	all descriptors
PCA init.	CS	$60.08 \pm 0.7(63.9)$	$57.07 \pm 0.7(60.1)$	$60.43 \pm 0.7(64.2)$	$61.10 \pm 0.7(65.2)$
	OSS	$59.83 \pm 0.7(63.1)$	$56.88 \pm 0.6(59.4)$	$59.80 \pm 0.7(63.0)$	$60.98 \pm 0.7(64.9)$
	CS+ OSS				$61.23 \pm 0.6(65.4)$
CSML	CS	$60.15 \pm 0.7(64.2)$	$58.62 \pm 1.0(61.8)$	$60.52 \pm 0.6(64.3)$	$62.90 \pm 0.8(67.4)$
	OSS	$60.00 \pm 0.9(63.8)$	$58.88 \pm 0.7(62.4)$	$59.98 \pm 0.7(63.3)$	$62.63 \pm 0.7(67.6)$
	CS+ OSS				$63.12 \pm 0.9(68.0)$
OSSML after PCA	CS	$60.22 \pm 0.7(64.1)$	$57.20 \pm 0.8(60.5)$	$60.10 \pm 0.7(64.3)$	$60.80 \pm 0.6(65.7)$
	OSS	$60.05 \pm 0.7(63.8)$	$58.05 \pm 0.8(60.7)$	$60.53 \pm 0.8(64.0)$	$62.32 \pm 0.8(66.7)$
	CS+ OSS				$62.52 \pm 0.8(66.6)$
OSSML after CSML	CS	$60.63 \pm 0.6(65.0)$	$59.53 \pm 0.9(63.6)$	$60.83 \pm 0.8(65.1)$	$63.17 \pm 0.8(68.0)$
	OSS	$60.00 \pm 0.8(64.3)$	$60.05 \pm 0.5(63.8)$	$60.75 \pm 0.8(64.1)$	$63.70 \pm 0.8(68.9)$
	CS+ OSS				$64.25 \pm 0.7(69.1)$

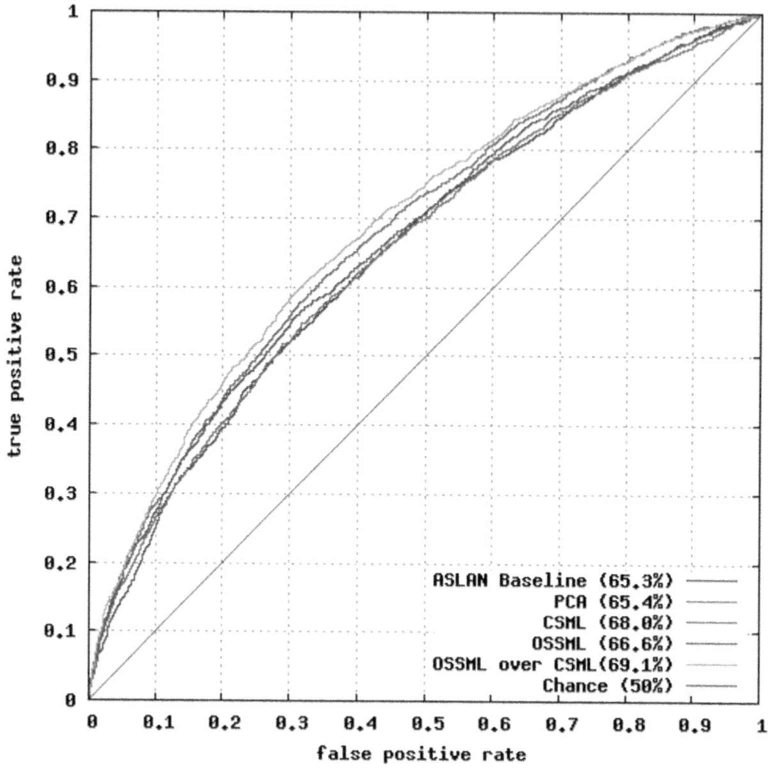

Fig. 3. ROC for the ASLAN benchmark

ROC curves of the results for View-2 of the ASLAN data set are presented in Figure 3. The results were obtained by repeating the classification process 10 times. Each time, we use nine sets for learning as specified in Section 3.3, and evaluate the results on the tenth set. ROC curve was constructed for all splits together (the outcome value for each pair is computed when this pair is a testing pair).

To gain further insight on our results, Figure 4 presents the most confident predictions made by our best scoring OSSML based method. The figure presents the most confident *correct* same and not-same predictions, and the most confident *incorrect* same and not-same predictions. Here, confidence was measured as the distance of the vector of similarities from the SVM hyperplane. These results emphasize the challenges of the ASLAN benchmark: as can be seen, many of the mistakes result from misleading context. Either "same" was predicted for two different actions because of similar background or camera motion, or "not-same" was predicted for the same action, based on very different backgrounds and motions.

Fig. 4. Most confident OSSML results. The Same/Not-Same labels are the ground truth labels, and the Correct/Incorrect labels indicate whether the method predicted correctly. For example, the top right quadrant displays same-action pairs that were most confidently labeled as not-same.

5 Conclusion

In this paper we have extended the usability of the recently proposed One-Shot-Similarity to cases in which the underlying metric is such that this similarity is ineffective. To learn a new metric, we construct a cost function that encourages either high or low similarity to pairs of samples depending on the associated same/not-same label.

Experiments on a recent and challenging action recognition benchmark reveal that the proposed metric learning scheme is effective and leads to the best reported results on this benchmark; However, not surprisingly, the degree of success depends on the specific initialization used. As an immediate but useful extension, we would like to apply similar methods to learn effective similarity scores between sets of vectors based on recent application of the One-Shot-Similarity to such problems [24].

References

1. Huang, G.B., Ramesh, M., Berg, T., Learned-Miller, E.: Labeled faces in the wild: A database for studying face recognition in unconstrained environments. Technical report, University of Massachusetts, Amherst, Technical Report 07-49 (2007)
2. Wolf, L., Hassner, T., Taigman, Y.: The one-shot similarity kernel. In: IEEE 12th International Conference on Computer Vision (ICCV), pp. 897–902 (2009)
3. Wolf, L., Hassner, T., Taigman, Y.: Descriptor based methods in the wild. In: Faces in Real-Life Images Workshop in European Conference on Computer Vision, ECCV (2008)
4. Wolf, L., Hassner, T., Taigman, Y.: Similarity scores based on background samples. In: Zha, H., Taniguchi, R.-i., Maybank, S. (eds.) ACCV 2009. LNCS, vol. 5995, pp. 88–97. Springer, Heidelberg (2010)
5. Wolf, L., Littman, R., Mayer, N., German, T., Dershowitz, N., Shweka, R., Choueka, Y.: Identifying join candidates in the Cairo Genizah. International Journal of Computer Vision, IJCV (2011)
6. Kliper-Gross, O., Hassner, T., Wolf, L.: The action similarity labeling challenge. IEEE Transactions of Pattern Analysis and Machine Intelligence (TPAMI) (2011), undergoing minor revisions
7. Belongie, S., Malik, J., Puzicha, J.: Shape context: A new descriptor for shape matching and object recognition. In: Advances in Neural Information Processing Systems (NIPS), vol. 13, pp. 831–837 (2001)
8. Zhang, H., Berg, A.C., Maire, M., Malik, J.: Svm-knn: Discriminative nearest neighbor classification for visual category recognition. In: IEEE Computer Society Conference on Computer Vision and Pattern Recognition (CVPR), vol. 2, pp. 2126–2136 (2006)
9. Yang, L., Jin, R.: Distance metric learning: A comprehensive survey, pp. 1–51. Michigan State Universiy, Ann Arbor
10. Bar-Hillel, A., Hertz, T., Shental, N., Weinshall, D.: Learning distance functions using equivalence relations. In: International Conference on Machine Learning (ICML), vol. 20, pp. 11–18 (2003)
11. Goldberger, J., Roweis, S., Hinton, G., Salakhutdinov, R.: Neighborhood components analysis. In: Advances in Neural Information Processing Systems (NIPS), vol. 17, pp. 513–520 (2005)
12. Xing, E.P., Ng, A.Y., Jordan, M.I., Russell, S.: Distance metric learning with application to clustering with side-information. In: Advances in Neural Information Processing Systems (NIPS), vol. 15, pp. 505–512 (2002)
13. Weinberger, K.Q., Blitzer, J., Saul, L.K.: Distance metric learning for large margin nearest neighbor classification. In: Advances in Neural Information Processing Systems (NIPS), vol. 18, pp. 1473–1480 (2006)
14. Davis, J.V., Kulis, B., Jain, P., Sra, S., Dhillon, I.S.: Information-theoretic metric learning. In: International Conference on Machine Learning (ICML), pp. 209–216 (2007)

15. Censor, Y., Zenios, S.A.: Parallel Optimization: Theory, Algorithms, and Applications. Oxford University Press, Oxford (1997)
16. Chechik, G., Sharma, V., Shalit, U., Bengio, S.: Large scale online learning of image similarity through ranking. The Journal of Machine Learning Research (JMLR) 11, 1109–1135 (2010)
17. Nguyen, H.V., Bai, L.: Cosine similarity metric learning for face verification. In: Kimmel, R., Klette, R., Sugimoto, A. (eds.) ACCV 2010, Part II. LNCS, vol. 6493, pp. 709–720. Springer, Heidelberg (2011)
18. (LFW results), vis-www.cs.umass.edu/lfw/results.html
19. Fisher, R.: The use of multiple measurements in taxonomic problems. Annals of Human Genetics 7, 179–188 (1936)
20. Hastie, T., Tibshirani, R., Friedman, J.H.: The elements of statistical learning. Springer, Heidelberg (2001)
21. Cortes, C., Vapnik, V.: Support-vector networks. Machine Learning 20, 273–297 (1995)
22. Petersen, K.B., Pedersen, M.S.: The matrix cookbook (2008), version 20081110
23. Laptev, I., Marszalek, M., Schmid, C., Rozenfeld, B.: Learning realistic human actions from movies. In: IEEE Conference on Computer Vision and Pattern Recognition (CVPR), pp. 1–8 (2008)
24. Wolf, L., Hassner, T., Maoz, I.: Face recognition in unconstrained videos with matched background similarity. In: IEEE Computer Society Conference on Computer Vision and Pattern Recognition, CVPR (2011)

On a Non-monotonicity Effect of Similarity Measures

Bernhard Moser[1], Gernot Stübl[1], and Jean-Luc Bouchot[2]

[1] Software Competence Center Hagenberg,
Softwarepark 21, A-4232 Hagenberg
{bernhard.moser,gernot.stuebl}@scch.at
[2] Department of Knowledge-Based Mathematical Systems,
Johannes Kepler University, Altenbergerstr. 69, A-4040 Linz
jean-luc.bouchot@jku.at

Abstract. The effect of non-monotonicity of similarity measures is addressed which can be observed when measuring the similarity between patterns with increasing displacement. This effect becomes the more apparent the less smooth the pattern is. It is proven that commonly used similarity measures like f-divergence measures or kernel functions show this non-monotonicity effect which results from neglecting any ordering in the underlying construction principles. As an alternative approach Weyl's discrepancy measure is examined by which this non-monotonicity effect can be avoided even for patterns with high-frequency or chaotic characteristics. The impact of the non-monotonicity effect to applications is discussed by means of examples from the field of stereo matching, texture analysis and tracking.

Keywords: Kernel functions, f-divergence, discrepancy measure, Lipschitz property, stereo matching, texture analysis, tracking.

1 Introduction

This paper is devoted to the question whether similarity measures behave monotonically when applied to patterns with increasing displacement. Misalignment of patterns is encountered in various fields of applied mathematics, particularly signal processing, time series analysis or computer vision. Particularly when dealing with patterns with high frequencies the comparison of the shifted pattern with its reference will show ups and downs with respect to the resulting similarity values induced by commonly used similarity measures. More precisely, let us think of a pattern M as a function $v : X \subseteq \mathbb{R}^n \rightarrow \mathbb{R}$. A translational shift by a vector $\mathbf{t}$ induces a displaced pattern $M_{\mathbf{t}}$ represented by $v_{\mathbf{t}}(.) = v(. - \mathbf{t})$. In this paper we study the monotonicity behavior of similarity measures S as function $\Delta_S[v, \mathbf{t}](\lambda) = S(v_{\mathbf{0}}, v_{\lambda\mathbf{t}})$ depending on the displacement factor $\lambda \geq 0$ along the vector $\mathbf{t}$. If $\Delta_S[v, \mathbf{t}](.)$ is monotonically increasing for a class $\mathcal{V}$ of patterns $v \in \mathcal{V}$ for any direction $\mathbf{t}$ we say that the similarity measure S satisfies the monotonicity condition (MC) with respect to the class $\mathcal{V}$. Unless mentioning $\mathcal{V}$ explicitly we restrict to the class of patterns with non-negative entries with bounded support.

M. Pelillo and E.R. Hancock (Eds.): SIMBAD 2011, LNCS 7005, pp. 46–60, 2011.

As main theoretical contribution of this paper a mathematical analysis in Section 2 and Section 3 show how this effect follows from construction principles which neglect any ordering between the elements of the patterns. While Section 2 refers to similarity and distance measures which rely on the aggregation of an element-wise operating function, Section 3 is devoted to the class of f-divergence measures which evaluate the frequencies of single values $v(x)$ of the pattern. For both classes of similarity measure examples are presented that demonstrate the non-monotonicity effect. In Section 4 an alternative construction principle based on the evaluation of partial sums is introduced and recalled from previous work, particularly [Mos09]. Theoretical results show that the non-monotonicity effect can be avoided. Finally, in Section 5 the impact of the non-monotonicity effect to applications in the field of stereo matching, tracking and texture analysis is discussed.

2 Construction Principles of Similarity Measures Induced by the Aggregation of Element-Wise Operating Functions

The analysis of formal construction principles of similarity measures based on the composition of an element-wise operating function and an aggregation operation leads to elucidating counter examples showing that commonly used similarity measures in general are not monotonic with respect to the extent of displacement.

Therefore we will have a look at similarity measures from a formal construction point of view. For example let us consider the elementary inner product $< .,. >$ of Euclidean geometry which is defined as

$$< \boldsymbol{x}, \boldsymbol{y} >= \sum_i x_i \cdot y_i. \tag{1}$$

Formular (1) is constructed by means of a composition of the algebraic product which acts coordinate-wise and the summation as aggregation function. Formally, (1) therefore follows the construction principle

$$\Delta_{[\mathcal{A},\mathcal{C}]}(f,g) := \mathcal{A}_x(\mathcal{C}(f(x),g(x))), \tag{2}$$

where $\mathcal{C}$ and $\mathcal{A}$ denote the coordinate-wise operating function and the aggregation, respectively. f, g refer to vectors, sequences or functions with x as index or argument and the expression $\mathcal{A}_x$ means the aggregation of all admissible x. The elements f, g denote the elements from some admissible space $\Psi \subset \{f : X \to \mathbb{R}\}$ for which the formal construction yields well defined real values. For example, in the case of (1) the n-dimensional Euclidean space $\mathbb{R}^n$ for $n \in \mathbb{N}$ or the Hilbert space of square-integrable sequences l^2 would be admissible.

In the following we draw conclusions about the monotonicity behavior of the induced function (2) by imposing certain algebraic and analytic properties on the coordinate-wise operating function $\mathcal{C}$ and the aggregation $\mathcal{A}$.

Theorem 1. *The construction*

$$\Delta_{[\mathcal{A},\mathcal{S},\mathcal{C}]}(f,g) := \mathcal{S}(\mathcal{A}_x(\mathcal{C}(f(x),g(x)))) \tag{3}$$

induces a function

$$\Delta_{[\mathcal{A},\mathcal{S},\mathcal{C}]} : \Psi \times \Psi \to \mathbb{R}$$

that does not satisfy the monotonicity condition (MC) under the assumption that Ψ is an admissible space of functions $f : \mathbb{Z} \subseteq \mathbb{R} \to \mathbb{R}$ that contains at least the set of pairwise differences of indicator functions of finite subsets of $\mathbb{Z}$, $\mathcal{C} : \mathbb{R}\times\mathbb{R} \to \mathbb{R}$ is a coordinate function that satisfies

(C1) *$\mathcal{C}$ is commutative,*
(C2) $\mathcal{C}(1,0) \neq \mathcal{C}(1,1)$,
(C3) $\mathcal{C}(0,0) = \min\{\mathcal{C}(1,0), \mathcal{C}(1,1)\}$,

the aggregation function $\mathcal{A} : \mathbb{R}^n \to \mathbb{R}$ is

(A1) *commutative and*
(A2) *strictly monotonically increasing or decreasing in each component, respectively,*

and the scaling function $\mathcal{S} : \mathbb{R} \to \mathbb{R}$ is strictly monotonically increasing or decreasing in each component, respectively.

Proof. Without loss of generality let us assume that the aggregation function is strictly monotonically increasing in each component.

We use the notation: $c_{01} := \mathcal{C}(0,1)$, $c_{11} := \mathcal{C}(1,1)$, $c_{00} := \mathcal{C}(0,0)$ and

$$h(.) := 1_{\{0\}}(.) + 1_{\{2\}}(.). \tag{4}$$

Consider

$$\begin{aligned}
\Delta_0 &= \Delta_{[\mathcal{A},\mathcal{S},\mathcal{C}]}(h(.), h(. - 0)) = \mathcal{S}(\mathcal{A}(c_{00}, \ldots, c_{00}, c_{11}, c_{00}, c_{11}, c_{00}, c_{00}, \ldots, c_{00})),\\
\Delta_1 &= \Delta_{[\mathcal{A},\mathcal{S},\mathcal{C}]}(h(.), h(. - 1)) = \mathcal{S}(\mathcal{A}(c_{00}, \ldots, c_{00}, c_{10}, c_{10}, c_{10}, c_{10}, c_{00}, \ldots, c_{00}))\\
\Delta_2 &= \Delta_{[\mathcal{A},\mathcal{S},\mathcal{C}]}(h(.), h(. - 2)) = \mathcal{S}(\mathcal{A}(c_{00}, \ldots, c_{00}, c_{10}, c_{00}, c_{11}, c_{00}, c_{10}, \ldots, c_{00})).
\end{aligned}$$

The case of $c_{10} < c_{11}$ implies $c_{00} = c_{01}$, hence a strictly increasing scaling function entails $\Delta_0 > \Delta_1 < \Delta_2$, and the case $c_{10} > c_{11}$, $c_{00} = c_{11}$ yields $\Delta_0 < \Delta_1 > \Delta_2$ which proves (4) to be a counter-example with respect to the monotonicity condition (MC). An analogous conclusion applies to a strictly decreasing scaling function. □

A direct consequence of Theorem 1 is that a binary operation $\odot : \mathbb{R}\times\mathbb{R} \to \mathbb{R}$ that preserves ordering in each argument, or reverses the ordering on both arguments, respectively, yields a further construction that cannot satisfy the monotonicity condition (MC) with respect to the class of patterns with non-negative entries with bounded support.

Corollary 1. *Let*

$$\Delta_1[\mathcal{A}_1, \mathcal{S}_1, \mathcal{C}_1](f,g) := \mathcal{S}_1(\mathcal{A}_{1x}(\mathcal{C}_1(f(x), g(x))))$$
$$\Delta_2[\mathcal{A}_2, \mathcal{S}_2, \mathcal{C}_2](f,g) := \mathcal{S}_2(\mathcal{A}_{2x}(\mathcal{C}_2(f(x), g(x))))$$

be functions following the construction principle (3) then

$$\Delta(f,g) = \Delta_1[\mathcal{A}_1, \mathcal{S}_1, \mathcal{C}_1](f,g) \odot \Delta_2[\mathcal{A}_2, \mathcal{S}_2, \mathcal{C}_2](f,g)$$

does not satisfy the monotonicity criterion (MC), where $\odot : \mathbb{R} \times \mathbb{R} \to \mathbb{R}$ *is an operation that is strictly monotonic of the same type in each component.*

Examples of similarity and distance measures following the construction principles of Theorem 1 or Corollary 1 are listed in Table 1.

Table 1. Examples of kernels and distance measures that follow the construction principles of Theorem 1 or Corollary 1 with summation as aggregation function

fomular	name	remark
$\\|f-g\\|_p$	Minkowski distance	$\mathcal{C}(a,b) = \|a-b\|^p$, $\mathcal{S}(x) = \sqrt[p]{x}$
$< f,g >= \sum_i f_i \cdot g_i$	inner product	$\mathcal{C}(a,b) = a \cdot b$
$e^{-\frac{1}{\sigma}\sum_i (f_i - g_i)^2}$	Gaussian kernel	$\mathcal{S}(x) = \exp(-x/\sigma)$
$-\sqrt{\\|f-g\\|^2 + c^2}$	multiquadratic	$\mathcal{S}(x) = -\sqrt{x+c^2}$
$\frac{1}{\sqrt{\\|f-g\\|^2+c^2}}$	inverse multiquadratic	$\mathcal{S}(x) = (\sqrt{x+c^2})^{-1}$
$\\|f-g\\|^{2n} \ln(\\|f-g\\|)$	thin plate spline	ln, x^n as scaling, $\odot(a,b) = a \cdot b$
$< f,g >^d, d \in \mathbb{N}$	polynomial kernel	(1) recursively applied, $\odot(a,b) = a \cdot b$
$(< f,g > +c)^d, d \in \mathbb{N}$	inh. polynomial kernel	(1) recursively applied, $\odot(a,b) = a \cdot b$
$\tanh(\kappa < x,y > +\theta)$	sigmoidal kernel	$\mathcal{S}(x) = \tanh(\kappa x + \theta)$

The following construction principle which does not require strictly monotonicity of the scaling function also leads to similarity measures that do not satisfy the monotonicity condition (MC).

Theorem 2. *The construction*

$$\Delta_{[\mathcal{A},\mathcal{S},\mathcal{C}]}(f,g) := \mathcal{S}(\mathcal{A}_x(\mathcal{C}(f(x), g(x)))) \tag{5}$$

induces a function

$$\Delta_{[\mathcal{A},\mathcal{S},\mathcal{C}]} : \Psi \times \Psi \to \mathbb{R}$$

that does not satisfy the monotonicity condition under the assumption that Ψ *is an admissible space of functions* $f : \mathbb{Z} \subseteq \mathbb{R} \to \mathbb{R}$ *that contains at least the set of pairwise differences of scaled indicator functions of finite subsets of* $\mathbb{Z}$, $\mathcal{C} : \mathbb{R} \times \mathbb{R} \to \mathbb{R}$ *is a continuous coordinate function that satisfies*

(C'1) *$\mathcal{C}$ is commutative,*
(C'2) *$\mathcal{C}(0,.)$ is strictly monotonic,*
(C'3) $\forall\alpha : \mathcal{C}(\alpha,\alpha) = 0$,

the aggregation function $\mathcal{A} : \mathbb{R}^n \to \mathbb{R}$ is continuous and satisfies (A1) and (A2) of Theorem 1 and the scaling function $\mathcal{S} : \mathbb{R} \to \mathbb{R}$ is

(S1) *continuous,*
(S2) *non-trivial in the sense that it is not constant on the range*

$$\mathcal{R} = \{\mathcal{A}(\mathcal{C}(\alpha,0),\mathcal{C}(\alpha,0),0,\ldots,0) \in \mathbb{R}_0^+ : \alpha \in \mathbb{R}\}.$$

Proof. Without loss of generality $0 = \mathcal{A}_x(0) = \mathcal{A}(0,\ldots,0)$. Set

$$h(.) := a \cdot 1_{\{0\}}(.) + b \cdot 1_{\{2\}}(.)$$

and, let us denote $\Theta_t(a,b) = \mathcal{A}_x(\mathcal{C}(f(x), f(x-t)))$.

Then, by applying (A1) we obtain

$$\begin{aligned}
\Theta_0(a,b) &= \mathcal{A}(0,\ldots,0,\mathcal{C}(0,0),\mathcal{C}(0,0),\mathcal{C}(0,0),\mathcal{C}(0,0),0,\ldots,0)\\
\Theta_1(a,b) &= \mathcal{A}(0,\ldots,0,\mathcal{C}(a,0),\mathcal{C}(a,0),\mathcal{C}(b,0),\mathcal{C}(b,0),0,\ldots,0)\\
\Theta_2(a,b) &= \mathcal{A}(0,\ldots,0,\mathcal{C}(a,0),\mathcal{C}(a,b),\mathcal{C}(b,0),\mathcal{C}(0,0),0,\ldots,0).
\end{aligned}$$

Let $\zeta \in \mathcal{R}$, $\zeta > 0$, and note that there is $a_0 > 0$ such that $\Theta_1(a_0, 0) = \zeta$. Observe that

$$\forall a \in [0, a_0]\, \exists\, b_a \in [0, a_0] : \Theta_1(a, b_a) = \zeta.$$

Let $\gamma_\zeta = \{(a, b_a) : \Theta_1(a, b_a) = \zeta\}$. Further, note that

$$\forall (a, b_a) \in \gamma_\zeta, a > 0 : \Theta_2(a, b_a) < \Theta_1(a, b_a) = \zeta$$

and

$$\underbrace{\lim_{a\to a_0^-} \Theta_2(a, b_a)}_{\Theta_2(a_0,0)} = \underbrace{\lim_{a\to a_0^-} \Theta_1(a, b_a)}_{\Theta_1(a_0,0)}.$$

Then $\forall \varepsilon > 0\, \exists \xi \in (\zeta - \varepsilon, \zeta)\, \exists (a_\xi, b_\xi) \in \gamma_\zeta$ we have

$$\xi = \Theta_2(a_\xi, b_\xi) < \Theta_1(a_\xi, b_\xi) = \zeta. \tag{6}$$

Let $s_0 = \mathcal{S}(0)$. Without loss of generality $s_0 > 0$. As $\mathcal{S}$ is not constant on $\mathcal{R}$, there is a $\zeta \in \mathcal{R}$ such that

$$s = \mathcal{S}(\zeta) \neq \mathcal{S}(0) = s_0.$$

Hence $\zeta > 0$. Without loss of generality $s < s_0$. Let $\xi = \inf\{\zeta > 0 : \mathcal{S}(\zeta) \leq s\}$. The continuity assumption of $\mathcal{S}$ implies $\xi > 0$. By (6) for all $n \in \mathbb{N}$ there is $\xi_n \in (\xi - \frac{1}{n}, \xi)$ for which there is $(a_n, b_n) \in \gamma_\xi$ with

$$\xi_n = \Theta_2(a_n, b_n) < \Theta_1(a_n, b_n) = \zeta.$$

Note that $\forall n \in \mathbb{N} : \mathcal{S}(\xi_n) > \mathcal{S}(\xi)$ and $\lim_n \mathcal{S}(\xi_n) = \mathcal{S}(\xi)$. Therefore, there is a n_0 with $\mathcal{S}(\xi_{n_0}) \in (s, s_0)$. For an illustration of the construction of ξ_{n_0} see Figure 2. By construction, for

$$h_0(.) := a_{n_0} \cdot 1_{\{0\}}(.) + b_{n_0} \cdot 1_{\{2\}}(.)$$

we obtain

$$0 = \Theta_0(a_{n_0}, b_{n_0}) < \Theta_2(a_{n_0}, b_{n_0}) < \Theta_1(a_{n_0}, b_{n_0})$$

which shows that the monotonicity condition (MC) cannot by satisfied, as

$$\mathcal{A}_x(\mathcal{C}(h_0(x), h_0(x-0))) < \mathcal{A}_x(\mathcal{C}(h_0(x), h_0(x-1))) > \mathcal{A}_x(\mathcal{C}(h_0(x), h_0(x-2)))$$

□

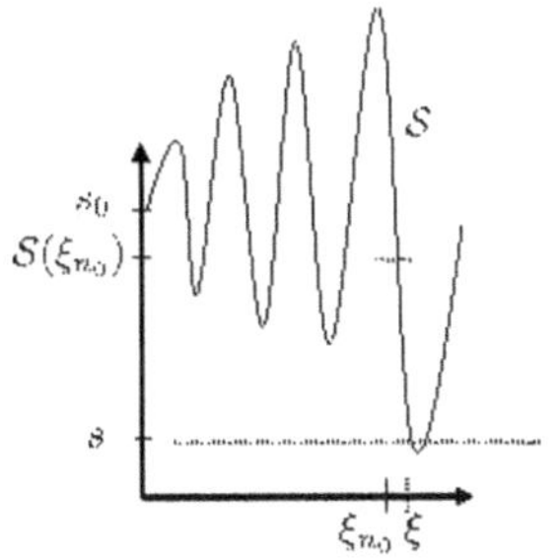

Fig. 1. Illustration of construction of ξ_{n_0}

Examples of similarity measures that meet the conditions of Theorem 5 are translational invariant kernels $\Phi(x, y) = \Phi(\|x - y\|)$ where $\phi : [0, \infty) \to \mathbb{R}$ is a continuous function that results from a Bessel transform of a finite non-negative Borel measure μ on $[0, \infty)$, i.e. $\phi(r) = \int_0^\infty \Omega_s(rt)d\mu(t)$ where $\Omega_1(r) = \cos r$ and $\Omega_s(r) = \Gamma(\frac{s}{2})\frac{s}{2}^{(s-2)/2} J_{(s-2)/2}(r)$, $s \geq 2$ and $J_{(s-2)/2}$ is the Bessel function of first kind of order $\frac{s-2}{2}$. For example there is the Dirichlet kernel $k(x, y) = \Phi_D(x)(\|x - y\|)$ provided by the continuous function $\Phi_D(x) = \sin\left((2n+1) \cdot \frac{x}{2}\right) / \sin\left(\frac{x}{2}\right)$ or the B_n-spline kernels $k(x, y) = B_{2p+1}(\|x - y\|)$ that result from multiple convolution of indicator functions, $B_n = \otimes_{i=1}^n 1_{[-\frac{1}{2}, \frac{1}{2}]}$, where the positive definite kernel property is only satisfied by odd orders.

For details on kernels and particularly translational invariant kernels see e.g. [SS01].

3 *f*-Divergence Measures

In this Section we concentrate on histogram based measures, see e.g. [TJ91]. The most prominent one is the *mutual information*, which for two discrete random variables X and Y can be defined as

$$I(X; Y) = \sum_{x,y} P_{XY}(x, y) \log\left(\frac{P_{XY}(x, y)}{P_X(x)P_Y(y)}\right) \tag{7}$$

where P_{XY} is the joint probability distribution of X and Y, and P_X and P_Y are the marginal probability distribution of X and Y respectively. This measure is commonly used in various fields of applications as for example in registering images, see e.g. [GGL08], [LZSC08]. Equation (7) is a special case of *Kullback-Leibler divergence*, [Kul59],

$$D_{\mathrm{KL}}(P\|Q) = \sum_z P(z) \log\left(\frac{P(z)}{Q(z)}\right) \tag{8}$$

which measures the deviation between the probability distributions P and Q. The mutual information is regained from (8) by setting $z = (x, y)$, $P(x, y) = P_{XY}(x, y)$ and $Q(x, y) = P_X(x)P_Y(y)$. A further generalization is provided by the class of f-divergence measures $D_{\mathrm{f}}(P\|Q)$, see e.g. [DD06, LV06], defined by

$$D_{\mathrm{f}}(P\|Q) = \sum_z Q(z)\mathrm{f}\left(\frac{P(z)}{Q(z)}\right) \tag{9}$$

where $f : [0, \infty] \to \mathbb{R} \cup \{+\infty\}$ is convex and continuous. These measures were introduced and studied independently by [Csi63], [Mor63] and [AS96]. The Kullback-Leibler divergence (8) results from (9) by means of $f(t) = t\log(t)$.

Theorem 3. *Let $f : [0, \infty] \to \mathbb{R} \cup \{+\infty\}$ be a strictly convex and continuous function. For two discrete sequences $A = (a_i)_{i=1}^n \in \mathcal{V}^n$ and $B = (b_i)_{i=1}^n \in \mathcal{V}^n$, $n \in \mathbb{N}$ let*

$$D_{\mathrm{f}}(A\|B) = \sum_{v,w\in\mathcal{V}} P_A(v)P_B(w) f\left(\frac{P_{A\,B}(v, w)}{P_A(v)P_B(w)}\right) \tag{10}$$

where $P_{A\,B}(v, w)$ denotes the joint frequency of occurrence of the pair of values (v, w), and $P_A(v)$, $P_B(w)$ denote the frequencies of v, w in the corresponding sequences A and B, respectively. Then there are sequences $h : \mathbb{Z} \to \mathcal{V}$ such that $\chi : \mathbb{N} \to [0, \infty]$ given by

$$\chi_t = D_f(A_0, A_t)$$

does not behave monotonically with respect to t, where $A_t(.) = 1_{1,\dots,n}(.) \cdot h(. - t)$.

Proof. Set $\mathcal{V} = \{0, 1\}$, and define $h(.) := \sum_{j=1}^m 1_{\{2\cdot j\}}(.)$ where $m \in \mathbb{N}$. Set $n = K \cdot m$ with $K \geq 3$. Then

$$P_{A_t}(0) = \tfrac{n-m}{n},\ P_{A_t}(1) = \tfrac{n-m}{n}$$

for $t \in \{0, 1, 2\}$, further

$$\begin{aligned}
&P_{A_0,A_0}(0,0) = \tfrac{n-m}{n},\ P_{A_0,A_0}(0,1) = 0,\ P_{A_0,A_0}(1,0) = 0,\ P_{A_0,A_0}(1,1) = \tfrac{m}{n},\\
&P_{A_0,A_1}(0,0) = \tfrac{n-2m}{n},\ P_{A_0,A_1}(0,1) = \tfrac{m}{n},\ P_{A_0,A_1}(1,0) = \tfrac{m}{n},\ P_{A_0,A_1}(1,1) = 0,\\
&P_{A_0,A_2}(0,0) = \tfrac{n-m}{n},\ P_{A_0,A_2}(0,1) = \tfrac{1}{n},\ P_{A_0,A_3}(1,0) = \tfrac{1}{n},\ P_{A_0,A_2}(1,1) = \tfrac{m-2}{n}.
\end{aligned}$$

By taking $n = K \cdot m$ into account we get

$$\frac{n^2}{m^2}\chi_0(K,m) = f\left(\frac{K}{K-1}\right)(K-1)^2 + 2f(0)(K-1) + f(K),$$

$$\frac{n^2}{m^2}\chi_1(K,m) = f\left(\frac{(K-2)K}{(K-1)^2}\right)(K-1)^2 + 2f\left(\frac{K}{K-1}\right)(K-1) + f(0),$$

$$\frac{n^2}{m^2}\chi_2(K,m) = f\left(\frac{K}{K-1}\right)(K-1)^2 + 2f\left(\frac{K}{K-1}\frac{1}{m}\right)(K-1) + f\left(K\frac{m-2}{m}\right).$$

Observe that because of the continuity of f for all $K \geq 2$ we obtain

$$\lim_{m\to\infty}(\chi_0(K,m) - \chi_2(K,m)) = 0. \tag{11}$$

As

$$\frac{(K-1)^2 - 2(K-1)}{(K-1)^2} + \frac{2(K-1)-1}{(K-1)^2} + \frac{1}{(K-1)^2} = 1$$

and

$$\frac{(K-2)K}{(K-2)^2}\frac{(K-1)^2 - 2(K-1)}{(K-1)^2} \cdot \frac{K}{K-1} + \frac{2(K-1)-1}{(K-1)^2} \cdot 0 + \frac{1}{(K-1)^2} \cdot K$$

the strict convexity of f implies

$$f\left(\frac{(K-2)K}{(K-2)^2}\right)$$

$$= \frac{(K-1)^2 - 2(K-1)}{(K-1)^2} \cdot f\left(\frac{K}{K-1}\right) + \frac{2(K-1)-1}{(K-1)^2} \cdot f(0) + \frac{1}{(K-1)^2} \cdot f(K)$$

and, therefore, for all $m > 2$ it follows that

$$\chi_0(K,m) - \chi_2(K,m) = \varepsilon_K > 0. \tag{12}$$

Together, formulae (11) and (12) imply that there are indices K_0 and m_0 such that $\chi_0(K_0,m_0) > \chi_1(K_0,m_0) < \chi_2(K_0,m_0)$ which proves the claim. □

Finally let us remark that an analogous proof shows that the claim of Theorem 3 is also true if the histograms P_X and P_Y are compared directly in the sense of definition (9).

4 The Monotonicity Property of the Discrepancy Measure

The concept of discrepancy measure was proposed by Hermann Weyl [Wey16] in the early 20-th century in order to measure deviations of distributions from uniformity. For details see, e.g. [BC09, Doe05, KN05]. Applications can be found in the field of numerical integration, especially for Monte Carlo methods in high dimensions, see e.g. [Nie92, Zar00, TVC07] or in computational geometry, see e.g. [ABC97, Cha00, KN99]. For applications to data storage problems on parallel disks see [CC04, DHW04] and half toning for images see [SCT02].

In the image processing context of registration and tracking, the discrepancy measure is applied in order to evaluate the auto-misalignment between a pattern P with its translated version P_T with lag or shift T. The interesting point about this is that based on Weyl's discrepancy concept distance measures can be constructed that guarantee the desirable registration properties: (R1) the measure vanishes if and only if the lag vanishes, (R2) the measure increases monotonically with an increasing lag, and (R3) the measure obeys a Lipschitz condition that guarantees smooth changes also for patterns with high frequencies. As the discrepancy measure as defined by (13)

$$\|\boldsymbol{f}\|_D := \sup\left\{\left|\sum_{i=m_1}^{m_2} f_i\right| : m_1, m_2 \in \mathbb{Z}\right\} \tag{13}$$

induces a norm on the space of vectors $\boldsymbol{f} = (f_1, \ldots, f_n) \in \mathbb{R}^n$ in the geometric sense we further on refer to it as discrepancy norm. As pointed out in [Mos09] Equation (13) is equivalent to

$$\|\boldsymbol{f}\|_D := \max(0, \max_{1\leq k\leq n} \sum_{i=0}^{k} f_i) - \min(0, \min_{1\leq k\leq n} \sum_{i=0}^{k} f_i) \tag{14}$$

which is advantageous in terms of computational complexity which amounts to $O(n)$ in comparison with $O(n^2)$ of the original definition (13). Note that the only arithmetical operations in the algorithm are summation, comparisons and inversion which on the one side are fast to compute and on the other side cheap in hardware design. In the context of this paper its dependency on the ordering of the elements is worth mentioning which is illustrated by the examples $\|(1, -1, 1)\|_D = 1$ and $\|(-1, 1, 1)\|_D = 2$. Note that alternating signals like $(-1, 1, -1, \ldots)$ lead to small discrepancy values, while reordering the signal e.g. in a monotonic way maximizes it.

As outlined in [Mos09] Equation (13) can be extended and generalized to arbitrary finite Euclidean spaces equipped with some measure μ in the following way:

$$\|f\|_{\mathcal{C}}^{(d)} = \sup_{c\in\mathcal{C}} \left|\int_c f d\mu\right| \tag{15}$$

where $\mathcal{C}$ refers to a set of Cartesian products of intervals. For example, let $\mathcal{B}^d$ denote the set of d-dimensional open boxes $I_1 \times I_2 \times \cdots \times I_d$ with open intervals I_i from the extended real line $[-\infty, \infty]$, and $\widetilde{\mathcal{B}}^d \subset \mathcal{B}^d$ the set of Cartesian products of intervals of the form $]-\infty, x[$, $]x, \infty[$. It can be shown that for all $d \in \mathbb{N}$ and non-negative $f \in \mathcal{L}(\mathbb{R}^d, \mu)$, $f \geq 0$, there holds

$$\|f - f \circ T_{\mathbf{t}}\|_{\mathcal{B}^d}^{(d)} = \|f - f \circ T_{\mathbf{t}}\|_{\widetilde{\mathcal{B}}^d}^{(d)} \tag{16}$$

where $T_{\mathbf{t}} = \mathbf{x} - \mathbf{t}$. Formulae 16 can be expressed by means of integral images and their higher dimensional variants which is crucial in terms of efficient computation. With this definitions the following result can be proven, for details and the proof see [Mos09].

Theorem 4. *Let $d \in \mathbb{N}$, let $f \in \mathcal{L}(\mathbb{R}^d, \mu)$, $f \geq 0$ and let $\Delta_{\mathcal{C}}[f](\mathbf{t}) = \|f - f \circ T_{\mathbf{t}}\|_{\mathcal{C}}$ denote the misalignment function $\mathbf{t} \in \mathbb{R}^d$. Further, let*

$$\delta_\mu[f](\mathbf{t}) = \sup_{C \in \mathcal{C}} \max\{\mu(C \backslash T_{\mathbf{t}}(C)), \mu(T_{\mathbf{t}}(C) \backslash C)\}.$$

Then for $\mathcal{C} = \mathcal{B}^d$ or $\mathcal{C} = \widetilde{\mathcal{B}}^d$ we have

1. *If f is non-trivial, i.e., $\int |f| d\mu > 0$ then $\Delta_{\mathcal{C}}[f](\mathbf{t}) = 0 \Longleftrightarrow \mathbf{t} = 0$*
2. *Lipschitz property: $\Delta_{\mathcal{C}}[f](\mathbf{t}) \leq \delta_\mu[f](\mathbf{t}) \|f\|_\infty$.*
3. *Monotonicity: $0 \leq \lambda_1 \leq \lambda_2 \Longrightarrow \Delta_{\mathcal{C}}[f](\lambda_1 \mathbf{t}) \leq \Delta_{\mathcal{C}}[f](\lambda_2 \mathbf{t})$ for arbitrary $\mathbf{t} \in \mathbb{R}^d$.*

Figure 2 illustrates the principle difference between the characteristics of the resulting misalignment functions induced by a measure, in this case normalized cross-correlation, that shows the non-monotonicity artefact on the one hand and the discrepancy norm on the other hand.

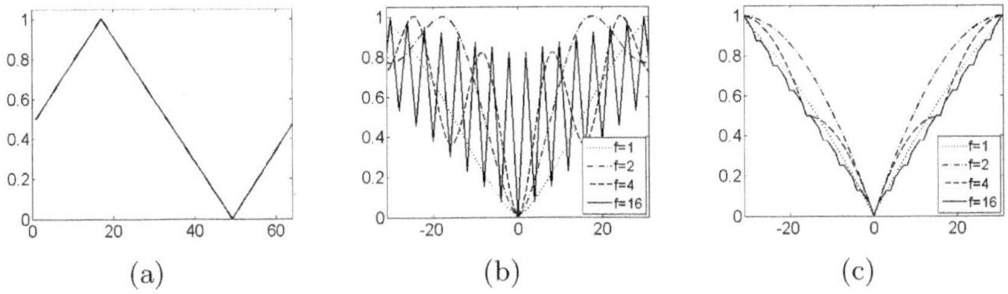

Fig. 2. Figure (a) shows a sawtooth function with frequency $\omega = 1$. In the other two figures misalignment functions for this sawtooth function and its variants with higher frequencies, $\omega = 2, 4, 16$ with respect to one minus the normalized cross-correlation, Figure (b), and the discrepancy norm, Figure (c), are shown. With increasing frequencies of the in Figure (b) the In contrast to Figure (b) the discrepancy norm induced misaligment functions in (c) show a monotonic behaviour with bounded slope due to the Lipschitz property.

5 Impact of the Non-monotonicity Effect on Applications

Misalignment is a phenomenon which can be observed in numerous situations in applied mathematics. In this paper we concentrate on examples from image processing in order to illustrate the relevance and impact of the monotonicity and Lipschitz property of the discrepancy measure in comparison to commonly used measures for which these properties cannot be guaranteed.

5.1 Image Tracking

Image tracking aims at identifying and localizing the movement of a pattern along a sequence of images. In this context a commonly used similarity measure is the so-called Bhattacharyya coefficient [Bha43] defined by

$$D_B(P_X, P_Y) = \sum_x \sqrt{P_X(x) P_Y(x)}. \tag{17}$$

See [CRM00] for details in the context of tracking. Note that $-D_B(P_X, P_Y)$ turns out to be a special f-divergence measure by means of $f(u) = -\sqrt{x}$.

Figure 3 depicts the cost functions of a person track on the CAVIAR (Context Aware Vision using Image-based Active Recognition) [1] database based on the discrepancy norm (second row) and the Bhattacharyya coefficient. It interesting to observe the robustness of the discrepancy norm at the presence of massive noise.

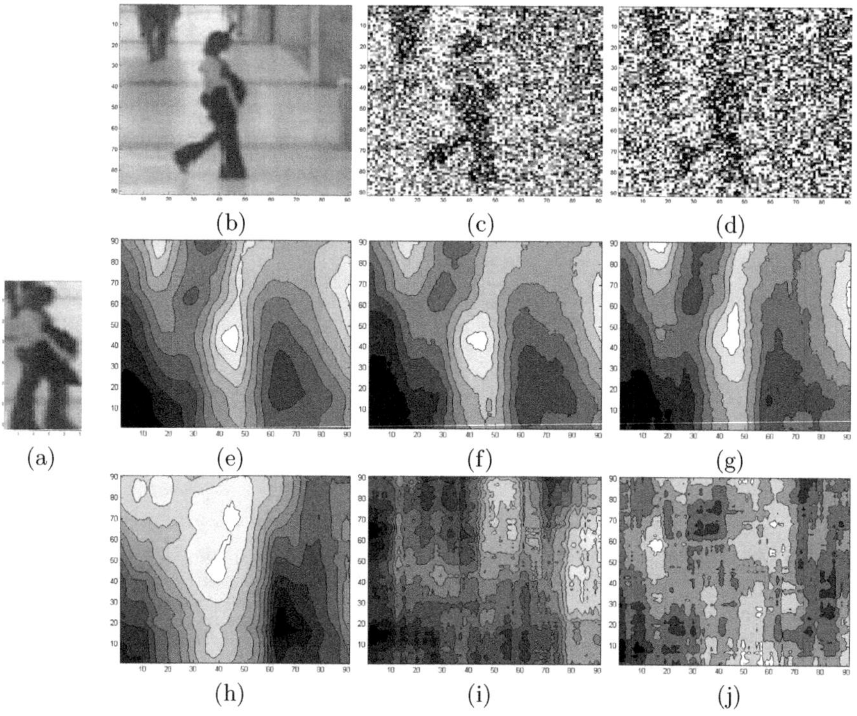

Fig. 3. Tracking of female from Figure 2(a) in a consecutive frame Figure (2b) and the same frame corrupted with additive gaussian noise with $SNR = 3$ in Figure 2(c) and $SNR = 1.5$ in Figure 2(d). Figures 2(e), (f) and (g) depict the corresponding cost function based on the discrepancy norm (DN) as similarity, whereas (h), (i) and (j) refer to the Bhattacharyya coefficient based similarity. The images are taken from frame 697 and frame 705 of the EC Funded CAVIAR project/IST 2001 37540 ("Shopping Center in Portugal", "OneLeaveShop2cor").

[1] http://homepages.inf.ed.ac.uk/rbf/CAVIAR/

5.2 Stereo Matching

Cost estimation in stereo matching is crucial for stereo vision, see [SS02]. Figure 4 illustrates the working principle of a typical stereo matching algorithm: the content of the white window in Figure 4(a) is compared with the windows along the white line in Figure 4(b). Figure 4(c) plots the comparison results with different matching cost functions. The x-value with the lowest dissimilarity is finally taken as disparity from which depth information can be derived.

Typically the sum of absolute distances (SAD), sum of squared distances (SSD) or cross correlation as well as their normalized and zero mean variants (NCC, ZSAD, etc.) are used as dissimilarity measures in this context. However these cost functions follow the construction principle of Equation (5) and suffer therefore from non-monotonic behaviour. Especially when adding white noise to the source images the number of local minima of these matching cost functions increase, whereas the discrepancy norm keeps mainly its monotonic behaviour, see Figure 4(c).

5.3 Defect Detection in Textured Surfaces

In the context of quality control typically reference image patches are compared to image patches which result from a sliding window procedure. For a discussion on similarity and a template matching based approach for detecting defects in regularly textured images see [BSM11]. Here an example is presented that

Fig. 4. Matching cost evaluation of sum of squared differences (SSD), normalized cross correlation (NCC) and discrepancy norm (DN) evaluated on the Middlebury Stereo 2003 Dataset [SS03], Teddy Example, at position x=192/y=300 with windowsize 10, depth 60. Figure 4(c) shows the evaluation of the white patch in Figures 4(a) along the white line in Figure 4(b). Whereas the results of Figures 4(d) and 4(e) with $SNR = 6.1$ are shown in Figure 4(f). DN is more robust regarding noise than the other costs.

demonstrates the behaviour of similarity measures showing the non-monotonicity effect versus the discrepancy norm. Fig. 5(b) depicts an example taken from the TILDA database [2]. As the presented texture shows a repetitive pattern it allows to apply a pattern matching approach and to compute the dissimilarity given some translational parameters. A defect-free pattern, depicted in Figure 5(a), is considered as a reference pattern and is then translated along the textured image. Each t_x and t_y displacement induces a dissimilarity value as illustrated in Figure 5(d) where the ordinate refers to the dissimilarity value. Observe the distinct local minumum of the discrepancy norm even in the presence of noise in Figures 5(e) and 5(f).

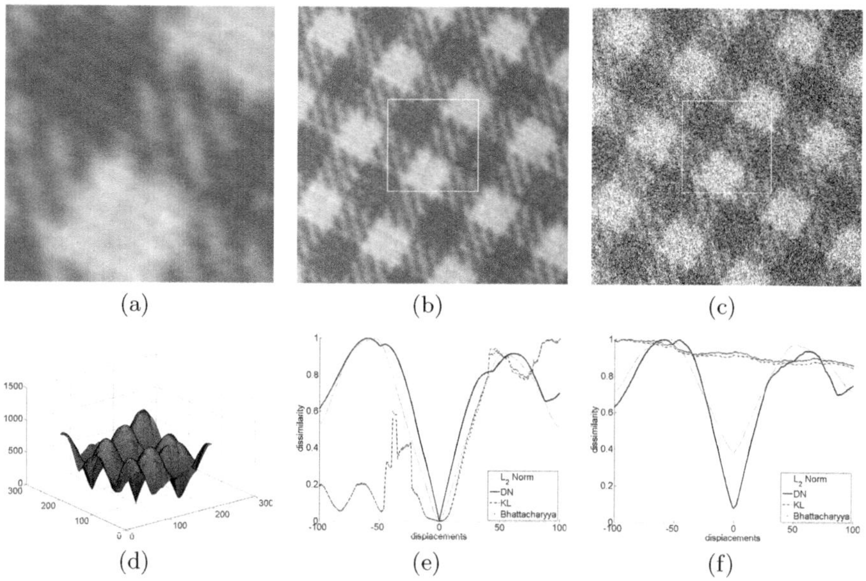

Fig. 5. Template matching example for regularly textured images. A defect-free reference template is shown in Figure (a) with corresponding patches (white square) in a noise free and a corrupted image by added white Gaussian noise, Figure (b) and Figure (c), respectively. Figure (d) plots a surface of dissimilarity values between the reference and the patches of Figure (b). Figures (e) (noise-free) and (f) (gaussian noise) show the behaviour of different cost functions along the x-axis: discrepancy norm (solid), L_2 norm (dotted), Bhattacharyya measure (square plotted) and mutual information (dashed-dotted).

6 Conclusion and Future Work

A non-monotonicity effect of commonly used similarity measures has been examined in the context of misaligned patterns. As it was shown this non-monotonicity

[2] Available from Universität Freiburg, Institut für Informatik, Lehrstuhl für Mustererkennung und Bildverarbeitung (LMB).

effect is caused by certain underlying construction principles. As the application section demonstrates this effect is worth thinking about for example in order to reduce local minima in resulting cost functions e.g. in the context of stereo matching. It remains future work to elaborate alternative similarity concepts as for instance based on Weyl's discrepancy measure to come up with cost functions that avoid the artefacts from the non-monotonicity effect.

Acknowledgement. This work was supported in part by the Austrian Science Fund (FWF) under grant no. P21496 N23 and the Austrian COMET program.

References

[ABC97] Alexander, J.R., Beck, J., Chen, W.W.L.: Geometric discrepancy theory and uniform distribution, pp. 185–207. CRC Press, Inc., Boca Raton (1997)

[AS96] Ali, S.M., Silvey, S.D.: A General Class of Coefficients of Divergence of One Distribution from Another. J. Roy. Statist. Soc. Ser. B 28, 131–142 (1996)

[BC09] Beck, J., Chen, W.W.L.: Irregularities of Distribution. Cambridge University Press, Cambridge (2009)

[Bha43] Bhattacharyya, A.: On a measure of divergence between two statistical populations defined by probability distributions. Bull. Calcutta Math. 35, 99–109 (1943)

[BSM11] Bouchot, J.-L., Stübl, G., Moser, B.: A template matching approach based on the discrepancy norm for defect detection on regularly textured surfaces. Accepted to Quality Control by Artificial Vision Conference, QCAV 2011 (June 2011)

[CC04] Chen, C.M., Cheng, C.T.: From discrepancy to declustering: Near-optimal multidimensional declustering strategies for range queries. J. ACM 51(1), 46–73 (2004)

[Cha00] Chazelle, B.: The Discrepancy Method: Randomness and Complexity. Cambridge University Press, Cambridge (2000)

[CRM00] Comaniciu, D., Ramesh, V., Meer, P.: Real-time tracking of non-rigid objects using mean shift, vol. 2, pp. 142–149 (2000)

[Csi63] Csiszár, I.: Eine informationstheoretische Ungleichung und ihre anwendung auf den Beweis der ergodizität von Markoffschen Ketten. Publ. Math. Inst. Hungar. Acad. 8, 95–108 (1963)

[DD06] Deza, M., Deza, E.: Dictionary of Distances. Elsevier, Amsterdam (2006)

[DHW04] Doerr, B., Hebbinghaus, N., Werth, S.: Improved bounds and schemes for the declustering problem. In: Fiala, J., Koubek, V., Kratochvíl, J. (eds.) MFCS 2004. LNCS, vol. 3153, pp. 760–771. Springer, Heidelberg (2004)

[Doe05] Doerr, B.: Integral approximations. Habilitation thesis, University of Kiel (2005)

[GGL08] Gao, Z., Gu, B., Lin, J.: Monomodal image registration using mutual information based methods. Image and Vision Computing 26(2), 164–173 (2008)

[KN99] Kuipers, L., Niederreiter, H.: Geometric Discrepancy: An Illustrated Guide. Algorithms and combinatorics, vol. 18. Springer, Berlin (1999)

[KN05] Kuipers, L., Niederreiter, H.: Uniform distribution of sequences. Dover Publications, New York (2005)

[Kul59] Kullback, S.: Information Theory and Statistics. Wiley, New York (1959)

[LV06] Liese, F., Vajda, I.: On Divergences and Informations in Statistics and Information Theory. IEEE Transactions on Information Theory 52(10), 4394–4412 (2006)

[LZSC08] Lu, X., Zhang, S., Su, H., Chen, Y.: Mutual information-based multimodal image registration using a novel joint histogram estimation. Computerized Medical Imaging and Graphics 32(3), 202–209 (2008)

[Mor63] Morimoto, T.: Markov processes and the h-theorem. Journal of the Physical Society of Japan 18(3), 328–331 (1963)

[Mos09] Moser, B.: Similarity measure for image and volumetric data based on Hermann Weyl's discrepancy measure. IEEE Transactions on Pattern Analysis and Machine Intelligence (2009), doi:10.1109/TPAMI.2009.50

[Nie92] Niederreiter, H.: Random Number Generation and Quasi-Monte Carlo Methods. Society for Industrial and Applied Mathematics, Philadelphia (1992)

[SCT02] Sadakane, K., Chebihi, N.T., Tokuyama, T.: Discrepancy-based digital halftoning: Automatic evaluation and optimization. In: WTRCV 2002, pp. 173–198 (2002)

[SS01] Schölkopf, B., Smola, A.J.: Learning with Kernels: Support Vector Machines, Regularization, Optimization, and Beyond, 1st edn. Adaptive Computation and Machine Learning. The MIT Press, Cambridge (2001)

[SS02] Scharstein, D., Szeliski, R.: A taxonomy and evaluation of dense two-frame stereo correspondence algorithms, Hingham, MA, USA, vol. 47, pp. 7–42. Kluwer Academic Publishers, Dordrecht (2002)

[SS03] Scharstein, D., Szeliski, R.: High-Accuracy Stereo Depth Maps Using Structured Light. In: IEEE Computer Society Conference on Computer Vision and Pattern Recognition, vol. 1, pp. 195–202 (June 2003)

[TJ91] Thomas, C.M., Joy, T.A.: Elements of Information Theory, 1st edn., p. 18. John Wiley & Sons, Inc., Chichester (1991)

[TVC07] Takhtamysheva, G., Vandewoestyneb, B., Coolsb, R.: Quasi-random integration in high dimensions. Image Vision Comput. 73(5), 309–319 (2007)

[Wey16] Weyl, H.: Über die Gleichverteilung von Zahlen mod. Eins. Math. Ann. 77, 313–352 (1916)

[Zar00] Zaremba, S.K.: The mathematical basis of Monte Carlo and Quasi-Monte Carlo methods. SIAM Review 10(3), 303–314 (1968)

Section-Wise Similarities for Clustering and Outlier Detection of Subjective Sequential Data

Oscar S. Siordia, Isaac Martín de Diego, Cristina Conde, and Enrique Cabello

Face Recognition and Artificial Vision Group, Universidad Rey Juan Carlos,
C. Tulipán, S/N, 28934, Móstoles, España
{oscar.siordia,isaac.martin,cristina.conde,enrique.cabello}@urjc.es

Abstract. In this paper, a novelty methodology for the representation and similarity measurement of sequential data is presented. First, a linear segmentation algorithm based on feature points is proposed. Then, two similarity measures are defined from the differences between the behavior and the mean level of the sequential data. These similarities are calculated for clustering and outlier detection of subjective sequential data generated through the evaluation of the driving risk obtained from a group of traffic safety experts. Finally, a novel dissimilarity measure for outlier detection of paired sequential data is proposed. The results of the experiments show that both similarities contain complementary and relevant information about the dataset. The methodology results useful to find patterns on subjective data related with the behavior and the level of the data.

Keywords: Subjective sequential data, Similarity, Clustering, Outlier.

1 Introduction

In the last few years, several representations of sequential data have been proposed, including Fourier Transforms [1], Wavelets [2], Symbolic Mappings [3] and, the most frequently used representation, Piecewise Linear Representation (see, for instance, [4,5,6,7]). Alternatively, the design of similarity measures for sequential data is addressed from a model-based perspective (see, for instance, [8,9]). In any case, the representation of the sequential data is the key to efficient and effective solutions. However, most of these representations imply sensitivity to noise, lack of intuitiveness, and the need to fine-tune many parameters [4]. In the present work, an alternative piecewise linear representation based on feature points is proposed. Similarity measures between sequential data is a common issue that has been treated in several ways. Usually, the statistical models fitted to the data are compared. Nevertheless, subjective sequential data are rarely considered. This kind of data corresponds to information collected from human opinions over a period of time. Although, it is not possible to successfully fit a unique model to all the data set since the changes on the level of the series usually respond to a great variety of factors, different model based approaches overcome this problem by employing one model per sequence [10].

M. Pelillo and E.R. Hancock (Eds.): SIMBAD 2011, LNCS 7005, pp. 61–76, 2011.

(a) Truck simulator (b) Driver top view (c) Road main view

Fig. 1. Truck simulator and sample frames of visual information acquired

The piecewise linear representation proposed in this work allows the definition of two similarity measures considering the behavior and the level of the sequential data, respectively. The proposed similarity measures were applied for clustering and outlier detection of a group of traffic safety experts' driving risk evaluations. Each expert provide two sequential risk evaluations of a simulated driving exercise. The data acquisition process was made as follows: a driving simulation exercise of ten minutes was recorded from a truck cabin simulator. Then, a group of 38 traffic safety experts were asked to evaluate the driving risk of the simulated exercise. One of the main objectives behind this project is to identify drivers' unsuitable behavior and lacks of attention.

The rest of the paper is organized as follows. Section 2 presents the process for the acquisition of the experts' evaluations. In Section 3, the piecewise linear representation algorithm for the linear segmentation of sequential data is developed. In Section 4, the section-wise similarities are defined. The evaluation of the performance of the proposed similarities on the experts' evaluations is presented in Section 5. Finally, Section 6 concludes.

2 CABINTEC Database

2.1 Data Acquisition

CABINTEC (âĂIJIntelligent cabin truck for road transportâĂİ) is an ongoing project focused on risk reduction for traffic safety [11]. The CABINTEC project is being developed in a highly realistic truck simulator (shown in Fig. 1(a)). The simulator was made using a real truck cockpit mounted over a stewart-platform to provide a natural driving sensation. Further, the driver's visual field is covered by a detailed simulated 3D scene. The data acquisition process consisted on the detailed monitoring of a simulated driving session of ten minutes in an interurban scenario that simulates a light traffic highway near San Sebastian (Spain). The driving exercise was carried out by professional drivers with more than 20 years of experience. The data acquired at the acquisition process consist of data registers of the vehicle dynamics and road characteristics, and visual information from two video sources: image sequences of driver's top view (Fig. 1(b)) and image sequences of the main view of the road (Fig. 1(c)). The data acquired in the truck simulator was used to make a detailed reproduction of the driving session to a

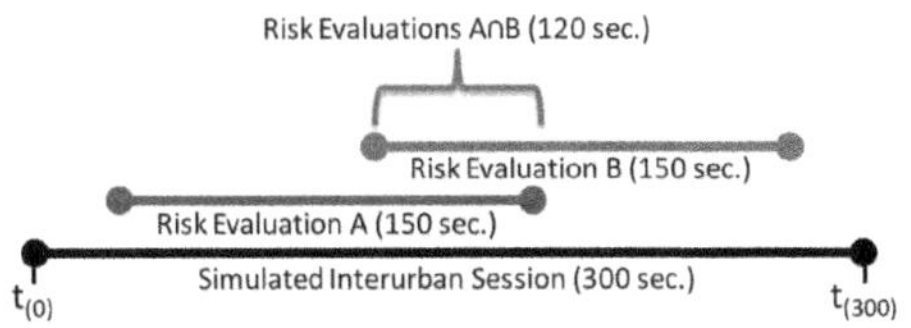

Fig. 2. Time line of the risk evaluations made by each traffic safety expert

group of traffic safety experts in a knowledge acquisition process. The knowledge acquisition process consisted on the risk evaluation, by a group of 38 traffic safety experts, of two partially overlapped sections of the simulated driving session (see Fig. 2). Each traffic safety expert was asked to evaluate the driving risk of the simulated session in the two different time periods in a randomly selected order. For that purpose, the simulation reproduction and knowledge acquisition tool called Virtual Co driver was used [12]. The Virtual Co driver system allows the evaluation of the driving risk through a Visual Analog Scale (VAS) in a range from 0 to 100, where 100 refers to the highest driving risk level. This method has been considered the best for subjective measurements (see, for instance, [13]). The main screen of the Virtual Co driver tool is shown in Fig. 3. The data considered for our CABINTEC database (shown in Fig. 4) consist on 76 risk evaluations (two for each traffic safety expert) obtained from the intersected time lapse between the two risk evaluations. Similar evaluations are expected for each expert. Hence, the capability of our acquisition methodology and the robustness of the subjective risk evaluations will be analyzed. In addition, wrong evaluations could be detected by comparing the two evaluations of the same expert. At first sight, given the high heterogeneity of the experts' VAS evaluations (see Fig. 4), it is hard to identify similar behavior between the curves. Further, given the subjectivity implied on the driving risk evaluation, small oscillations out of the main trend appear. These oscillations make it difficult to analyze subjective phenomena where a linear behavior along a temporary period of time is expected. To get a proper representation of sequential data, a piecewise representation is proposed in the next section.

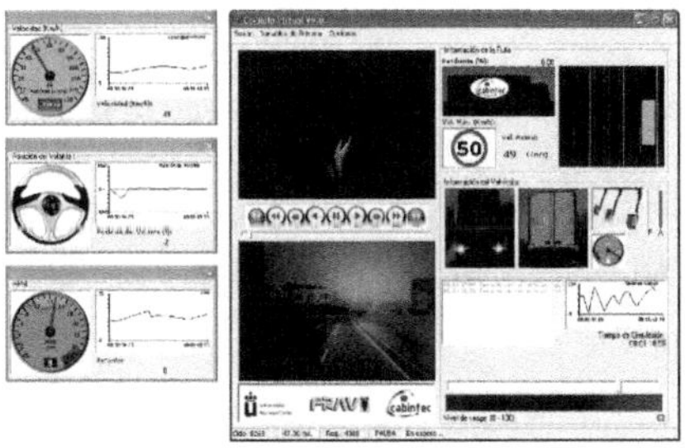

Fig. 3. Simulation reproduction and knowledge acquisition tool (Virtual Co driver)

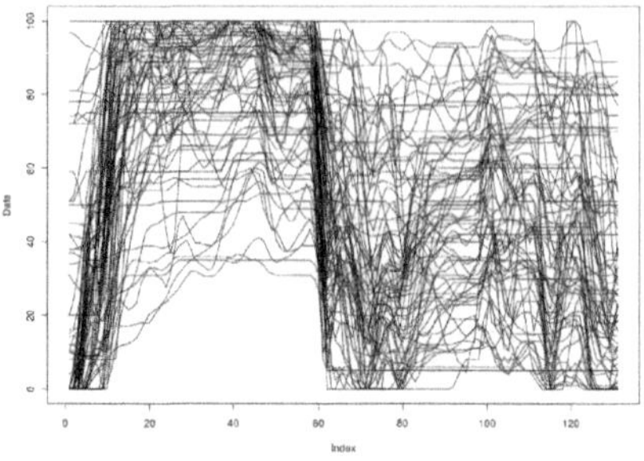

Fig. 4. Subjective sequential data acquired from the traffic safety experts

3 Trend Segmentation Algorithm

One of the main tasks of the present work is to define a proper similarity measure between subjective sequential data. Given the characteristics of sequential data (where sudden changes occur and where the key information is given by its trend), a piecewise representation of the data is appropriate. A variety of algorithms to obtain a proper linear representation of sequential data have been presented (see, for instance, [14], [15] and [16]). However, when working with subjective data, special considerations must be taken into account when selecting the cut points where a linear model will be fitted over the data. In this case, we propose a linear segmentation algorithm based on the time-honored idea of looking for feature points where extreme changes on the data trend occurs. We call this method Trend Segmentation Algorithm (TSA). On the first stage of the algorithm, the feature points of the VAS evaluation where the trend of the data presents a deviation from a straight course must be located. For that purpose the curvature of the data at each point needs to be calculated. Let $f(t)$ be a VAS evaluation at time $t = \{1, \ldots, T\}$. Following [17], the n-order tangent at time t is calculated as:

$$f^n(t) = wf(t) - \sum_{i=-n,\ i\neq 0}^{n} w_i f(t+i)\,, \tag{1}$$

where $w_i = 1/(2|i|)$, and w is the sum of all the weights w_i.

That is, we compute the tangent at t as a weighted average of the VAS evaluation in the n consecutive points surrounding t. The weight w_i is inversely proportional to the distance from the closest point to the point t. The curvature at each point t is computed as the absolute value of the difference between the tangent at that point and the tangent at point $t-1$:

$$C(t) = |f^n(t) - f^n(t-1)|\,. \tag{2}$$

A point t is a feature point if it satisfies one of the following conditions:

1. $t = 1$ or $t = T$ (initial and final point)
2. $C(t) > max(C(t+1), C(t-1))$ (local maximums)

Algorithm 1. Trend Segmentation Algorithm (TSA)

Input: VAS evaluation f, R^2_{min}
Output: $\{CP\}$ **(set of Cut Points)**
1. **Obtain the feature points of curve** $f \rightarrow \{FP\} = \{fp_1, fp_2, \ldots, fp_N\}$
2. **Repeat for each pair of consecutive feature points** fp_i, **and** fp_{i+1}
Fit a regression line $(\hat{Y})$ **in the current segment** $[fp_i \,, fp_{i+1}]$
if $(R^2(\hat{Y}) \geq R^2_{min})$ **then**
  Store the initial and final points of the current segment as cut points $(fp_i \in CP \,, fp_{i+1} \in CP)$
else
  Subdivide the segment to reduce the error and go to 2
end if
3. **Joint identical regression lines between the selected cut points.**

That is, the feature points are points with relevant changes in the curvature of the original VAS evaluation f. Notice that, since we work with a discretization of the curvature, there will be a smoothing effect depending of the n value. An example of the selection of feature points in a VAS evaluation using the 5-order curvature is shown in Fig. 5. In this example, a total of 38 points where the trend of the data suffered a relevant change were selected as feature points. Given a set of N feature points $\{FP\}$, the second stage of TSA consists on the selection of points where a piecewise linear model can be properly fitted (*Cut Points*=$\{CP\}$). As other segmentation algorithms, TSA needs some method to evaluate the quality of fit for a proposed segment. A measure commonly used in conjunction with linear regression is the coefficient of determination. Further, in order to ensure a linear fitting in each section, an Anderson-Darling Normality test is applied to the residuals of each fitted line (see, for instance, [18]). The pseudo code of the TSA is presented in (Algorithm 1). The input of the algorithm is the VAS evaluation f. The output of the algorithm will be a set of *Cut Points* among which a linear model can be fitted with an error lower or equal than the allowed

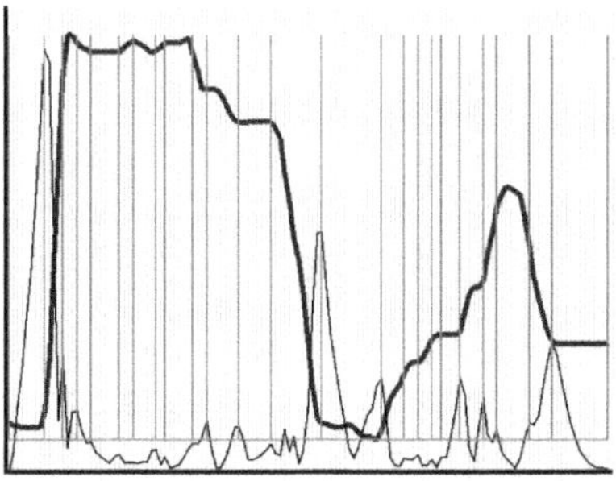

Fig. 5. Example of the selection of feature points (green marks) based on the curvature (black line) of a subjective sequential serie (blue line)

by the parameter R^2_{min}. Given a VAS evaluation f, all its feature points are obtained and stored in the set $\{FP\}$. Next, a linear model is tested in each segment defined by each pair of consecutive points in $\{FP\}$. If the regression error is low (R^2 is higher than R^2_{min}) then the feature points that define the segment are stored as *Cut Points*. Otherwise, the linear model is not proper for the observations in the segment and, as a consequence, the segment is divided. In this work we propose to store all the points in the segment as *Cut Points*. Finally, in order to reduce the number of generated sections, the consecutive segments with identical regression lines are joined together. Following the example shown in Fig. 5, the linear representation of the VAS evaluation after the application of TSA is shown in Fig. 6. In this example, 22 feature points were selected as *Cut Points*. That is, 21 linear sections were enough to represent the VAS evaluation with an R^2_{min} of 0.75. Notice that, the main advantage of the TSA algorithm is its special care when selecting *Cut Points* to fit a linear model. This righteousness becomes very important when working with subjective sequential data because the trend of the data is kept. In order to choose the optimal linear representation of a specific dataset, a trade-off between the global error and the complexity of the representation (number of generated segments) is considered by the minimization of:

$$C = \alpha(1 - R^2) + (1 - \alpha)\frac{\text{number of segments}}{T - 1}, \tag{3}$$

where the parameter α is set to 0.5 to grant similar relevance for both terms. In this case, R^2 is a global average over the R^2 of the linear models fitted in each of the segments obtained from TSA. In order to make comparable two linearized curves it is necessary to align the linear segments of each curve. To achieve this aim, an OR operation between the *Cut Points* selected from each curve is done. Figure 7 shows an example of the OR operation between the set of *Cut Points* selected from a two VAS evaluations. The outcome aligned segmentation for both VAS evaluations is shown in Fig. 7(c).

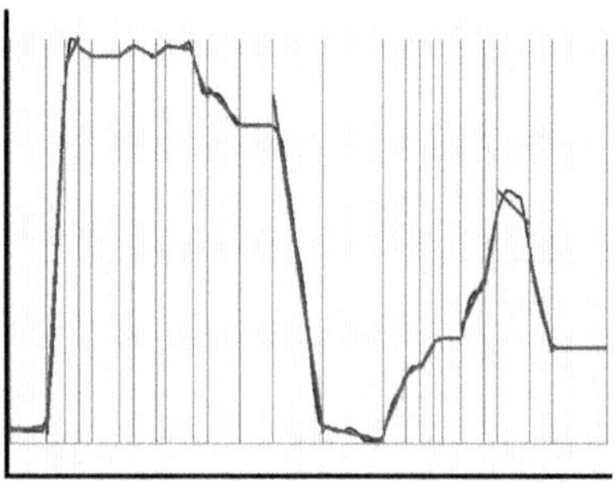

Fig. 6. Example of linear sections generated between the selected feature points

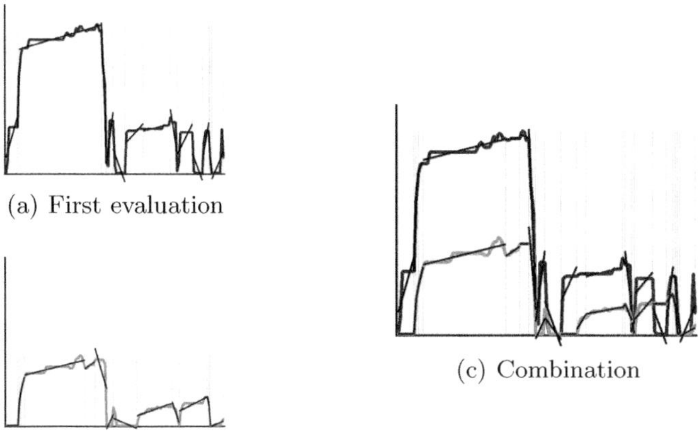

(a) First evaluation

(b) Second evaluation

(c) Combination

Fig. 7. Example of the TSA applied to two series acquired from the same traffic safety expert in different knowledge acquisition experiments

4 Similarity Definitions

One of the main tasks of the present work is to define a proper similarity measure between subjective sequential data. The similarity between two VAS evaluations can be measured in many ways. Given a pair of aligned linearized curves, it is possible to define a set of similarity measures taking advantage of the characteristics of the linear representation proposed in Section 3. In this work, we propose two similarity measures based on the difference of levels and the difference of angles between the linear regression lines obtained from the TSA representation of the curves.

4.1 Mean Level Based Similarity

Let $k = [t_{(1)}, t_{(2)}]$ be a common section defined for the curves f_i and f_j. Let $\hat{Y}_i = \beta_{0i} + x\beta_{1i}$ and $\hat{Y}_j = \beta_{0j} + x\beta_{1j}$ be the regression lines fitted in the section k of the curves f_i and f_j, respectively. The mean level similarity is based on the mean levels of the regression lines $\hat{Y}_i$ and $\hat{Y}_j$ over the section k (see Fig. 8(a)). The mean level similarity calculated in the section k, denoted by $s_0(k)$, is obtained as one minus the ratio between the Euclidean distance (d) of the mean levels of the regression lines $\dot{Y}_i$ and $\ddot{Y}_j$ and the worst possible distances between them:

$$s_0(k) = 1 - \frac{d}{\breve{d}}, \tag{4}$$

where $s_0(k)$ is in $[0, 1]$. The worst distance $\breve{d}$ is calculated from the maximum possible distance that the mean level of the curves could have in all the dataset. In this case, for a set of VAS evaluations ranging in $[0, 100]$, the maximum possible

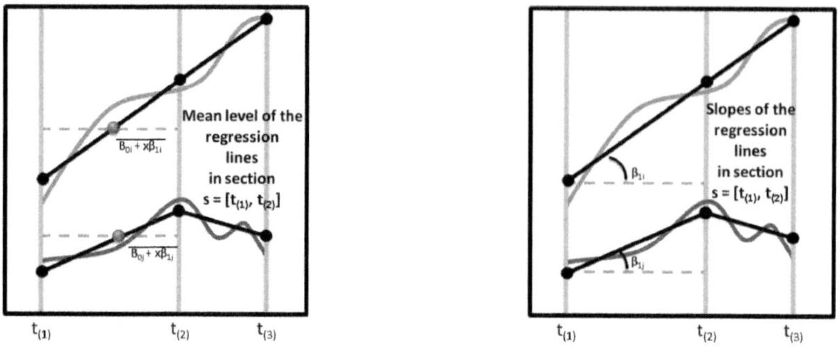

(a) Mean Level Similarity

(b) Angle Level Similarity

Fig. 8. Similarities between two sections of two segmented sequential series

distance $\breve{d}$ is 100. Finally, the overall mean level section-wise similarity for the curves f_i and f_j is calculated as the weighted sum of all the sectional similarities as follows:

$$S_0(f_i, f_j) = \frac{\sum_{k=1}^{K} w(k)\; s_0(k)}{\sum_{k=1}^{K} w(k)}, \tag{5}$$

where $w(k)$ is the width of the section $k = 1, \ldots, K$.

4.2 Angle Based Similarity

The angle based section-wise similarity considers the angle formed by the regression lines defined in the sections $k = 1, \ldots, K$. Let β_{1i} and β_{1j} be the slopes of the regression lines $\hat{Y}_i$ and $\hat{Y}_j$, respectively (see Figure 8(b)). The angle between the regression lines is calculated as:

$$\theta = atan(|\beta_{1i} - \beta_{1j}|). \tag{6}$$

The angle based similarity calculated in the section k, denoted by $s_1(k)$, is obtained as the relation between the angle θ and the worst possible angle $\breve{\theta}$ of the section k as follows:

$$s_1(k) = 1 - \frac{\theta}{\breve{\theta}_k}, \tag{7}$$

where $s_1(k)$ is in $[0, 1]$. The worst angle $\breve{\theta}$ is established as the maximum possible change in an analyzed section. The maximum possible angle between two regression lines at the section k can be calculated as:

$$\breve{\theta}_k = atan(|\frac{2\breve{d}}{w(k)}|), \tag{8}$$

where $w(k)$ is the width of the section $k = 1, \ldots, K$.

Finally, the overall angle based section-wise similarity for the curves f_i and f_j is calculated as the weighted sum of all the sectional similarities as follows:

$$S_1(f_i, f_j) = \frac{\sum_{k=1}^{K} w(k)\, s_1(k)}{\sum_{k=1}^{K} w(k)}, \tag{9}$$

where $w(k)$ is the width of the section $k = 1, \ldots, K$.

5 Experiments

Given the set of curves from the CABINTEC dataset, it is possible to generate similarity matrices with the definitions presented in the Section 4. For our purposes, an unique similarity matrix mas built:

$$S_{0,1} = \frac{S_0 + S_1}{2}. \tag{10}$$

In this case, as the proposed similarities matrices (S_0, and S_1) are obtained as the weighted mean of a set of similarities obtained from individual sections, a deviation from the Euclidianess may occur. Following [19], the deviation from Euclidianess of each similarity matrix of the CABINTEC dataset was calculated as the ratio of the smallest negative eigenvalue to the largest positive eigenvalue of the similarity matrices (r_{mm}). When the negative eigenvalues are relatively small in magnitude, those negative eigenvalues can be interpreted as a noise contribution. However, if the negative eigenvalues are relatively large, possibly important information could be rejected by neglecting them (see [20] for a complete description). The deviation of each matrix is presented in Table 1. Several techniques have been proposed to solve this problem ([20]). In this work, Multidimensional Scaling was applied to represent the data set in a Euclidean space. As mentioned before, the CABINTEC database consist of 76 VAS evaluations of a group of 38 traffic safety experts. That is, the same simulated driving session was evaluated twice for each expert. We will illustrate the performance of the similarity measures defined in Section 4 based on two kind of experiments on the CABINTEC dataset. The first one is a cluster experiment, whose main objective is to know if there are meaningful classes of experts that can be grouped together. In addition, it is possible to detect wrong evaluations when the two evaluations of the same experts are grouped in different clusters. The second experiment is based on a new measure for outlier detection. If there is a high difference between the two evaluations of the same expert, then the expert is considered an outlier and should be studied carefully.

Table 1. Euclidianess deviation of the similarity matrices of the dataset CABINTEC

Similarity	Lowest Eigenvalue	Highest Eigenvalue	Deviation from Euclidianess (r_{mm})
S_0	-0.1602	58.6125	0.0027
S_1	-0.0165	50.3231	0.0003

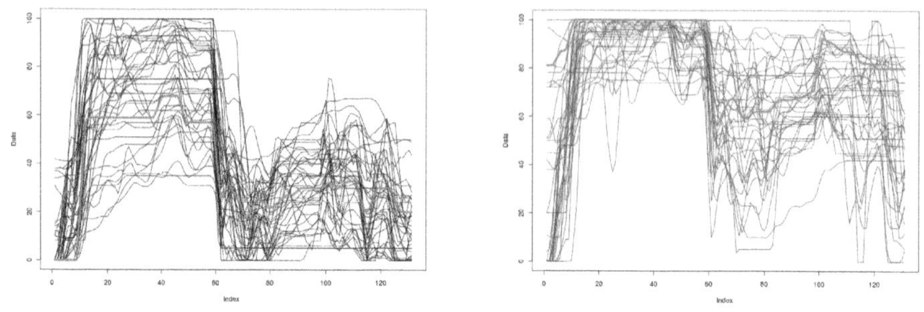

(a) Cluster 1 (b) Cluster 2

Fig. 9. Clusters of the CABINTEC database with the mean level and angle similarities

5.1 Clustering

Clustering is an initial and fundamental step in data analysis. It is an unsupervised technique whose goal is to reveal a natural partition of data into a number of meaningful subclasses or clusters. Accurate clustering requires a precise definition of the nearness between a pair of objects, in terms of either the pairwised similarity or distance. Clustering of sequential data differs from clustering of static feature data mainly in how to compute the similarity between two data objects. In general, depending upon the specific characteristics of the sequential data, different clustering studies provide different methods to compute this similarity. Once the similarity of sequential data is defined, many general-purpose clustering algorithms can be used to partition the data. In this work, we focus on clustering sequential data in which each sequential object is represented as a set of regression lines defined from a linearization algorithm. In our work, we test the capability of the similarity measure presented in (10) in order to achieve accurate clustering of the CABINTEC experts' evaluations. We will use this similarity to perform a partitioning clustering of the experts' evaluations into clusters around k representative objects or medoids among the sequential experts' evaluations of the dataset (see [21] for a complete description of the PAM algorithm). The clusters generated for the CABINTEC database are shown in Fig. 9. To apply PAM method, we will work with the dissimilarity defined as $1 - S_{0,1}$. For each cluster, the medoid (a representative VAS evaluation of the cluster) is remarked with a green line. In this case, two clearly identifiable patterns were found. In the simulated driving exercise, the driver received a phone call from second 5 to second 60. In the second cluster (Fig. 9(b)), the traffic safety experts considered the phone call as the maximum fault giving a 100 in their VAS evaluations. However, in the first cluster (Fig. 9(a)), the traffic safety experts did not consider to answer a phone call as the maximum risk in which a driver could fall. In this way, as the experts' evaluations bunched in cluster 2 were giving the maximum possible risk level during all the phone call, they were unable to penalize the action of driving with no hands on the steering wheel given from second 38 to second 50. On the other side, this action (no hands

Table 2. Clustering error of the CABINTEC database with several similarity measures

Method		Bad clustered experts	Error (%)
TSA	S_0	5	13.2
	S_1	12	31.6
	$\frac{S_0+S_1}{2}$	**1**	**2.6**
DTW		3	7.9
Euclidean distance		6	15.8
Hausdorff distance		12	31.6
Kendall correlation		16	42.1
Pearson correlation		17	44.7

on wheel) was detected and penalized by most of the experts bunched on the cluster 1. At the second half of the risk evaluation (from second 60) the experts of the first cluster punish in a moderated way a group of risky situations of the driver leaving a margin on their VAS range to punish riskier situations that could come. In the same way, the experts of the second cluster, detected most of the risky situations given at the second half of the evaluation. However, these experts continued with high VAS values until the end of the risk evaluation. The clusters generated with the similarities proposed in this work are very helpful to select the kind of data that will be considered in the future stages of the research. On the one hand, we have identified experts (cluster 2) whose major concern is the distraction of the driver while doing a secondary task (like a phone call). On the other hand, we have identified experts (cluster 1) that are more concerned about the driving efficiency regardless of the number of tasks of the driver. It is well known that is very difficult to conduct a systematic study comparing the impact of similarity metrics or distances on cluster quality, because objectively evaluating cluster quality is difficult in itself. In practice, manually assigned category labels are usually used as a baseline criteria for evaluating clusters. Nevertheless, in this case we know a relevant information: the expert that generated each evaluation. We estimate our clustering error as the number of experts such that the two evaluations of the same expert are grouped in different clusters. This error measure was used to compare the methodology proposed in this work with the clustering based on other well-known distance measures (DTW: Dynamic time warping, Euclidean and Hausdorff distance, and correlation of Kendall and Pearson). The results are shown in Table 2. The best result is achieved by the combination of the mean level and angle similarities. These results show the complementarity of both similarity measures achieving an error reduction from 13.2% and 31.6% to 2.6%.

Other Data. Additionally to the CABINTEC dataset, several well-known databases, out of the driving risk problem, were analyzed: the ECG200, Gun Point, Coffee, and Growth databases. A summary of these databases is shown in Table 3 (see [22] and [23] for a complete description). The Trend Segmentation Algorithm and the Similarity measure proposed in Section 4 were applied to all the series. Results are presented in Figure 10. For the ECG200 [22], two patterns were found among the 200 curves of the dataset. On the first one (see Fig. 10(b)), the main valley is generated faster with a steeper slope. After that, a decreasing behavior is observed until the end. On the second one (see Fig. 10(c)), the main valley is reached later with a moderated slope and an increasing behavior is observed until the end. In this case, it is clear that the angle and mean level similarities are useful to separate these patterns. In the same way, for the Gun Point database (see Fig. 10(e) and 10(f)) [22], the patterns found among the 200 curves are evidently dependent of the width of the main peak. For this clusters, the similarities presented in this paper shows relevance when separating the patterns. For the Coffee database (see Fig. 10(h) and 10(i)) [22], the two patterns found among the curves show a major relevance on the information given by the mean level similarity. In this case, the curves are mainly identified by its level since they have a similar angle behavior. Finally, for the Growth database (see Fig. 10(k) and 10(l)) [22], the patterns identified among the curves are clearly discovered by the behavior of their slope. In this case, each cluster is characterized by the tilt of each curves while they increase along their 31 registers.

5.2 Outlier Detection

One of the first tasks in any outlier detection method is to determine what an outlier is. This labor strongly depends on the problem under consideration. In this case, we are interested in the detection of experts that generated heterogeneous evaluations (or even random evaluations) during the acquisition process. An expert should be considered an outlier if a very high distance between the two risk evaluations of the experts is observed. Let f_i^1, and f_i^2 be the two evaluations obtained from expert i. Given the similarity measure presented in Section 4 two sets of evaluations are defined:

$$F(i)_{1,2} = \{f_j : S_{0,1}(f_i^1, f_j) > S_{0,1}(f_i^1, f_i^2)\}\,, \tag{11}$$

$$F(i)_{2,1} = \{f_j : S_{0,1}(f_i^2, f_j) > S_{0,1}(f_i^1, f_i^2)\}\,. \tag{12}$$

That is, $F(i)_{1,2}$ is the set of the experts' evaluations such that the similarities between them and the first evaluation of expert i are higher than the similarity between the two evaluations of expert i. Hence, the evaluations between evaluations 1 and 2 of expert i are considered.

$$\delta(i) = \#\{F(i)_{1,2} \cap F(i)_{2,1}\}\,. \tag{13}$$

Table 3. Summary of the databases considered in the clustering experiments

Database Name	Number of series	Time Series Length	Figure
ECG200	200	96	10(a)
Gun Point	200	150	10(d)
Coffee	56	286	10(g)
Growth	93	31	10(j)

ECG200 database

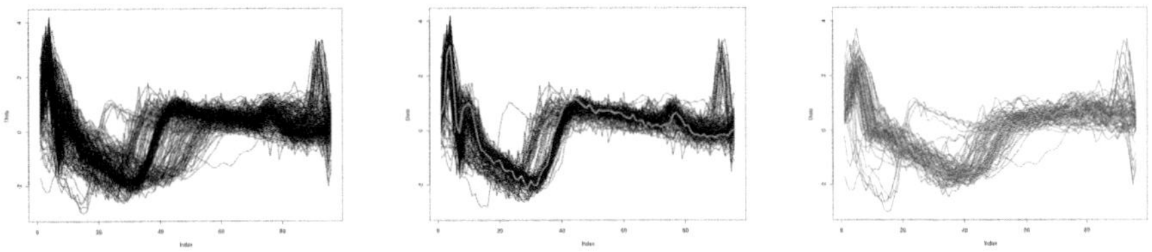

(a) Original data (b) Cluster 1 (c) Cluster 2

Gun Point database

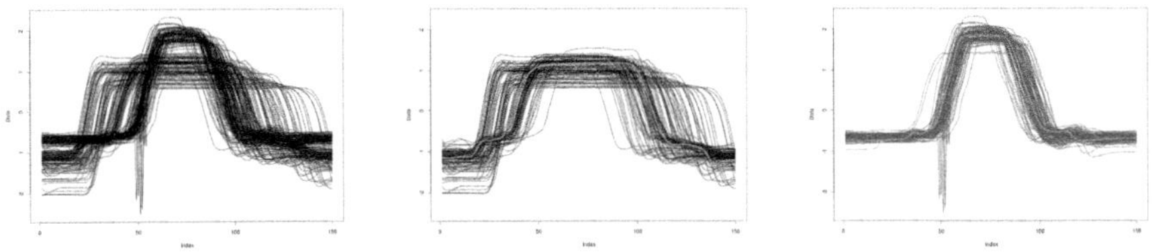

(d) Original data (e) Cluster 1 (f) Cluster 2

Coffee database

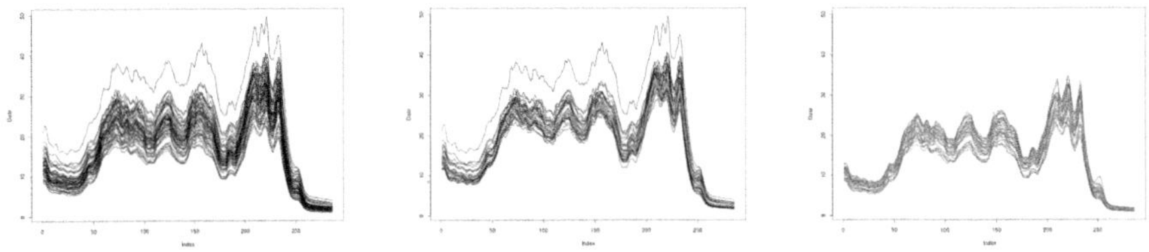

(g) Original data (h) Cluster 1 (i) Cluster 2

Growth database

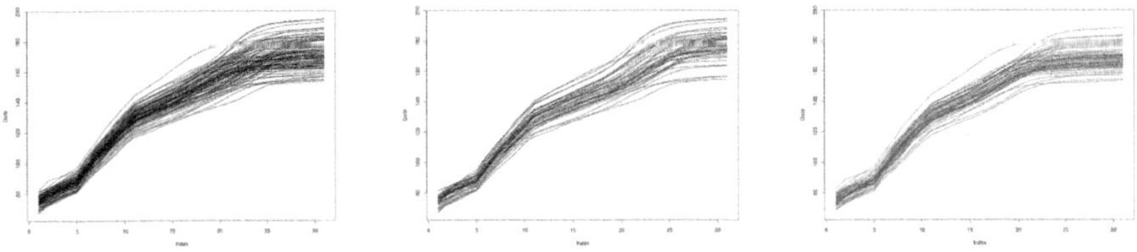

(j) Original data (k) Cluster 1 (l) Cluster 2

Fig. 10. Clustering of several databases with the mean level and angle similarities

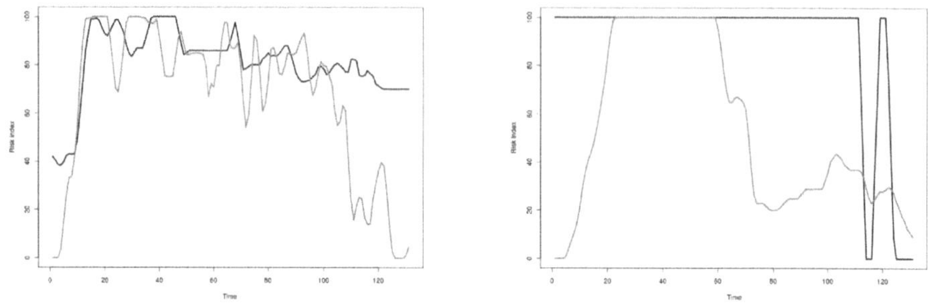

(a) Expert 22 (b) Expert 23

Fig. 11. Outliers of the CABINTEC database with the mean level and angle similarities

In the same way, $F(i)_{2,1}$ is the set of the experts' evaluations such that the similarities between them and the second evaluation of expert i are higher than the similarity between the two evaluations of expert i. Hence, the evaluations between evaluations 2 and 1 of expert i are considered. Given that, we deal with sequential data, in general $F(i)_{1,2} \neq F(i)_{2,1}$. To obtain the outliers evaluations in our experiments, we define the following dissimilarity measure: That is, given the similarity measure $S_{0,1}$, the dissimilarity measure evaluated on expert i equals the number of evaluations between his two evaluations. On the one hand, if the two evaluations of expert i are very similar, there will be very few elements in sets $F(i)_{1,2}$ and $F(i)_{2,1}$, and as a consequence, $\delta(i)$ will be very low. On the other hand, if the two evaluations of expert i are not similar, there will be very a lot of elements in sets $F(i)_{1,2}$ and $F(i)_{2,1}$, and as a consequence, $\delta(i)$ will be very high. Next, we calculate this dissimilarity measure in the CABINTEC database. Table 4 presents the values of the dissimilarity function (13) in the experts' VAS evaluations of the CABINTEC database.

Table 4. Dissimilarity measure for outliers detection in the CABINTEC database

δ value	**0**	**1**	**2**	**4**	**5**	**6**	**10**	**12**	**20**	**24**
Number of experts	24	5	2	1	1	1	1	1	1	1

Notice that in 24 out of 38 experts (63.2%) no other evaluations were found between the two expert's evaluations. That is, there are no neighbors in common between the first and the second evaluations of these experts. On the other hand, there were two experts with 20 and 24 neighbors in common between their two evaluations. That is, the two evaluations of the same expert are strongly different. Figure 11 shows the evaluations of these two experts that are considered as outliers. For the expert 22 (Fig. 11(a)), a group of contradictions could be observed between his two evaluations. In addition, from the second 100 , the first evaluation of the expert (green line), shows a decreasing risk value until the end of the evaluation and, on the other side, the second evaluation (blue line) shows a high level VAS evaluation the whole time. For the expert 23 (Fig. 11(b)), his second evaluation (blue line) shows a total disinterest on the experiment.

6 Conclusions

The main contribution of this paper, is a novelty methodology for the analysis of subjective sequential data. First, a linear segmentation algorithm for the proper representation of subjective data, based on the location of feature points, has been developed. This algorithm is useful to represent sequential data in a piecewise model emphasizing the trend of the data. Next, two similarity measures have been defined from the differences between the level and the angle of the lines of the piecewise representation. This similarities were defined in order to cover the two more relevant characteristics of the trend: behavior (angle) and scale (level). The methodology proposed in this work, focused on the representation and similarity measurement of subjective data, have been used for clustering several experts' risk evaluations of a simulated driving exercises. Further, a novel dissimilarity measure for outlier detection of paired sequential data have been proposed. The results of the cluster and outlier detection experiments show that both level and angle based similarities contain complementary and relevant information about the data trend. In the future, clustering of the individual segments of a linear segmentation representation of sequential data will be performed. In this way, potential high driving risk areas will be detected and studied for its prediction.

Acknowledgments. Supported by the Minister for Science and Innovation of Spain: CABINTEC (PSE-37010-2007-2) and VULCANO (TEC2009-10639-C04-04). Thanks to CONACYT and CONCYTEY from México for supporting the project through their scholarship programs.

References

1. Agrawal, R., Faloutsos, C., Swami, A.: Efficient similarity search in sequence databases. In: Lomet, D.B. (ed.) FODO 1993. LNCS, vol. 730. Springer, Heidelberg (1993)
2. Chan, K., Fu, W.: Efficient time series matching by wavelets. In: Proceedings of the 15th IEEE International Conference on Data Engineering (1999)
3. Perng, C., Wang, H., Zhang, S., Parker, S.: Landmarks: a new model for similarity-based pattern querying in time series databases. In: Proceedings of the 15th IEEE International Conference on Data Engineering (2000)
4. Keogh, E., Pazzani, M.: An enhanced representation of time series which allows fast and accurate classification, clustering and relevance feedback. In: KDD, pp. 239–243 (1998)
5. Lavrenko, V., Schmill, M., Lawrie, D., Ogilvie, P., Jensen, D., Allan, J.: Mining of concurrent text and time series. In: Proceedings of the 6th International Conference on Knowledge Discovery and Data Mining, pp. 37–44 (2000)

6. Park, S., Kim, S.W., Chu, W.W.: Segment-based approach for subsequence searches in sequence databases. In: Proceedings of the 16th ACM Symposium on Applied Computing (2001)
7. Wang, C., Wang, S.: Supporting content-based searches on time series via approximation. In: Proceedings of the 12th International Conference on Scientific and Statistical Database Management (2000)
8. Rabiner, L.: A tutorial on hidden markov models and selected applications in speech recognition. Proc. IEEE, 257–286 (1989)
9. García-García, D., Parrado-Hernandez, E., Díaz-de-Maria, F.: Anderson-darling: A goodness of fit test for small samples assumptions. P. Recognition 44, 1014–1022
10. Panuccio, A., Bicego, M., Murino, V.: A hidden markov model-based approach to sequential data clustering. In: Caelli, T.M., Amin, A., Duin, R.P.W., Kamel, M.S., de Ridder, D. (eds.) SPR 2002 and SSPR 2002. LNCS, vol. 2396, pp. 734–742. Springer, Heidelberg (2002)
11. Brazalez, A., et al.: CABINTEC: Cabina inteligente para el transporte por carretera. In: Proc. of the Congreso Español de Sistemas Inteligentes de Transporte (2008)
12. Siordia, O.S., Martín, I., Conde, C., Reyes, G., Cabello, E.: Driving risk classification based on experts evaluation. In: Proceedings of the 2010 IEEE Intelligent Vehicles Symposium (IV 2010), San Diego, CA, pp. 1098–1103 (2010)
13. Cork, R.C., Isaac, I., Elsharydah, A., Saleemi, S., Zavisca, F., Alexander, L.: A comparison of the verbal rating scale and the visual analog scale for pain assessment. Technical Report 1, Int. Journal of Anesthesiology (2004)
14. Keogh, E., Chu, S., Hart, D., Pazzani M.: Segmenting time series: A survey and novel approach. In: Data Mining in Time Series Databases, pp. 1–22 (1993)
15. Lachaud, J., Vialard, A., de Vieilleville, F.: Analysis and comparative evaluation of discrete tangent estimators. In: Andrès, É., Damiand, G., Lienhardt, P. (eds.) DGCI 2005. LNCS, vol. 3429, pp. 240–251. Springer, Heidelberg (2005)
16. Zhu, Y., Wu, D., Li, S.: A piecewise linear representation method of time series based on feature points. In: Apolloni, B., Howlett, R.J., Jain, L. (eds.) KES 2007, Part II. LNCS (LNAI), vol. 4693, pp. 1066–1072. Springer, Heidelberg (2007)
17. Basri, R., Costa, L., Geiger, D., Jacobs, D.: Determining the similarity of deformable shapes. Vision Research 38, 135–143 (1995)
18. Romeu, J.L.: Anderson-darling: A goodness of fit test for small samples assumptions. Selected Topics in Assurance Related Technologies 10(5), 1–6 (2003)
19. Pękalska, E., Duin, R.P.W., Günter, S., Bunke, H.: On not making dissimilarities euclidean. In: Fred, A., Caelli, T.M., Duin, R.P.W., Campilho, A.C., de Ridder, D. (eds.) SSPR&SPR 2004. LNCS, vol. 3138, pp. 1145–1154. Springer, Heidelberg (2004)
20. Pekalska, E., Paclík, P., Duin, R.P.W.: A generalized kernel approach to dissimilarity-based classification. Journal of Machine Learning Research, Special Issue on Kernel Methods 2(12), 175–211 (2001)
21. Kaufman, L., Rousseeuw, P.J.: Finding Groups in Data: An Introduction to Cluster Analysis. Wiley, New York (1990)
22. Keogh, E., Xi, X., Wei, L., Ratanamahatana, A.: The ucr time series classification/clustering (2006), `http://www.cs.ucr.edu/~eamonn/time_series_data/`
23. Ramsay, J., Silverman, B.: Functional Data Analysis, Secaucus, NJ, USA. Springer Series in Statistics (2005)

Hybrid Generative-Discriminative Nucleus Classification of Renal Cell Carcinoma

Aydın Ulaş[1,⋆], Peter J. Schüffler[2], Manuele Bicego[1], Umberto Castellani[1], and Vittorio Murino[1,3]

[1] University of Verona, Department of Computer Science, Verona, Italy
[2] ETH Zürich, Department of Computer Science, Zürich, Switzerland
[3] Istituto Italiano di Tecnologia, Genova, Italy

Abstract. In this paper, we propose to use advanced classification techniques with shape features for nuclei classification in tissue microarray images of renal cell carcinoma. Our aim is to improve the classification accuracy in distinguishing between healthy and cancerous cells. The approach is inspired by natural language processing: several features are extracted from the automatically segmented nuclei and quantized to visual words, and their co-occurrences are encoded as *visual topics*. To this end, a generative model, the probabilistic Latent Semantic Analysis (pLSA) is learned from quantized shape descriptors (visual words). Finally, we extract from the learned models a generative score, that is used as input for new classifiers, defining a hybrid generative-discriminative classification algorithm. We compare our results with the same classifiers on the feature set to assess the increase of accuracy when we apply pLSA. We demonstrate that the feature space created using pLSA achieves better accuracies than the original feature space.

Keywords: probabilistic Latent Semantic Analysis, renal cell carcinoma, SVM.

1 Introduction

The computer-based detection and analysis of cancer tissues represents a challenging yet unsolved task for researchers in both Medicine and Computer Science. The complexity of the data, as well as the intensive laboratory practice needed to obtain them, makes the development of such automatic tools very problematic. In this paper, we consider the problem of classifying cancer tissues starting from a tissue microarray (TMA), a technology which enables studies associating molecular changes with clinical endpoints [19]. With this technique, $0.6mm$ tissue cylinders are extracted from primary tumor blocks of hundreds of different patients, and are subsequently embedded into a recipient paraffin block. Such array blocks can then be used for simultaneous analysis of primary tumors on DNA, RNA, and protein level.

⋆ Corresponding author.

M. Pelillo and E.R. Hancock (Eds.): SIMBAD 2011, LNCS 7005, pp. 77–89, 2011.

Here we focus on the specific case of renal cell carcinoma (RCC). In order to analyse it, the tissue is transferred to an array and stained to make the morphology of cells and cell nuclei visible. Current image analysis software for TMAs requires extensive user interaction to properly identify cell populations on the TMA images, to select regions of interest for scoring, to optimize analysis parameters and to organize the resulting raw data. Because of these drawbacks, pathologists typically collect tissue microarray data by manually assigning a composite staining score for each spot. The manual rating and assessment of TMAs under the microscope by pathologists is quite inconsistent due to the high variability of cancerous tissue and the subjective experience of humans, as quoted in [15]. Manual scoring also introduces a significant bottleneck that limits the use of tissue microarrays in high-throughput analysis. Therefore, decisions for grading and/or cancer therapy might be inconsistent among pathologists. With this work, we want to contribute to a more generalized and reproducible system that automatically processes TMA images and thus helps pathologists in their daily work. One keypoint in the automatic TMA analysis for renal cell carcinoma

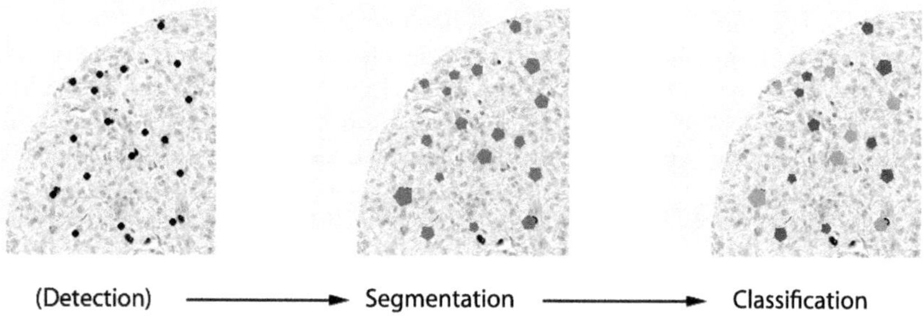

Fig. 1. The nuclei classification pipeline: detection, segmentation and classification into benign or cancerous

is the nucleus classification. In this context, the main goal is to automatically classify cell nuclei into cancerous or benign – this typically done by trained pathologists by eye. Clearly, prior to classification, the nucleus should be detected and segmented in the image.

In this paper, the problem of the classification of nuclei in renal cancer cells is investigated with the use of hybrid generative-discriminative schemes, representing a quite recent and promising trend of classification approaches [18,20]. The underlying idea is to take advantage of the best of the generative and the discriminative paradigms – the former based on probabilistic class models and *a priori* class probabilities, learnt from training data and combined via Bayes law to yield posterior probabilities, the latter aimed at learning class boundaries or posterior class probabilities directly from data, without relying on generative class models [21,24]. In the hybrid generative-discriminative scheme, the typical pipeline is to learn a generative model – suitable to properly describe the problem – from the data, and using it to project every object in a feature space (the so-called generative embedding space), where a discriminative classifier may be trained. This class of approaches have been successfully applied in many different scenarions, especially in the case of non-vectorial data (strings, trees, images) [28,8,22].

In particular, as for the generative model, we choose to employ the probabilistic Latent Semantic Analysis (pLSA) [17], a powerful methodology introduced in the text understanding community for unsupervised topic discovery in a corpus of documents, and subsequently largely applied in the computer vision community [12,8] as well as in the medical informatics domain [3,11,4]. Referring to the linguistic scenario, where these models have been initially introduced, the basic idea consists in characterizing a given document by the presence of one or more topics (e.g. sport, finance, politics), which may induce the presence of some particular words, and realizing that the topic distribution may be learned by looking at word co-occurrence in the whole corpus. In our case, similarly to [8,11], the documents are the cell nuclei images, whereas the words are visual features computed from the image – following the automated pipeline of TMA processing already proposed in [26]. Given a set of images, the visual features are quantized in order to define the so-called dictionary, and histograms of features describe the level of presence of the different visual words in every image. Then the pLSA model is learned to find local co-occurring patterns leading to the definition of the so-called *visual topics*. Finally, the topic distributions of each image represent the new space (the generative embedding space), where any discriminative classifier may be employed.

The proposed approach has been tested in a dataset composed by 474 cell nuclei images, employing different visual features as well as different classifiers in the generative embedding final space. The results were compared to those obtained working directly with the visual features, encouraging us in going ahead along this direction.

The paper is organized as follows. In Section 2, we introduce pLSA, and in Section 3, the data set and preprocessing used in this study is described. We explain the applied methods in Section 4, and illustrate our experiments in Section 5. Section 6 concludes the work.

2 Background: The Probabilistic Latent Semantic Analysis

The probabilistic Latent Semantic Analysis (pLSA) [17] is a probabilisitc generative model firstly introduced in the linguistic scenario, to describe and model documents. The basic idea underlying this model – and in general under the class of the so called topic models (another excellent example is the the Latent Dirichlet Allocation LDA [7]) – is that each document is characterized by the presence of one or more topics (e.g. sport, finance, politics), which may induce the presence of some particular words. From a probabilistic point of view, the document may be seen as a mixture of topics, each one providing a probability distribution over words. A topic model represents a generative model for documents, since a simple probabilistic procedure permits to specify how documents are generated. In particular, a new document may be generated in the following way: first choose a distribution over topics; then, for each word in that document, randomly select a topic according to its distribution, and draw a word from that topic. It is possible to invert the process, in order to infer the set of topics that were responsible for generating a collection of documents. The representation of documents and words with topic models has one clear advantage: each topic is individually interpretable, providing a probability distribution over words that picks out a coherent cluster of correlated terms. This may be really advantageous in the cancer detection context, since the final goal is to provide knowledge about complex systems, and provide possible hidden correlations.

A variety of probabilistic topic models have been used to analyze the content of documents and the meaning of words. These models all use the same fundamental idea – that a document is a mixture of topics – but make slightly different statistical assumptions; here we employed the probabilistic Latent Semantic Analysis, briefly presented in the following. Let us introduce the pLSA model from the original and most intuitive point of view, namely from the linguistic community perspective. As a starting point, the pLSA model takes as input a data set of N documents $\{d_i\}$, i=1,..., N, encoded by a set of words. Before applying pLSA, the data set is summarized by a co-occurrence matrix of size $M \times N$, where the entry $n(w_j, d_i)$ indicates the number of occurrences of the word w_j in the document d_i. The presence of a word w_j in the document d_i is mediated by a latent *topic* variable, $z \in T = \{z_1,..., z_Z\}$, also called *aspect* class, *i.e.*,

$$P(w_j, d_i) = \sum_{k=1}^{Z} P(w_j|z_k)P(z_k|d_i)P(d_i). \tag{1}$$

In practice, the topic z_k is a probabilistic co-occurrence of words encoded by the distribution $P(w|z_k)$, $w = \{w_1,..., w_M\}$, and each document d_i is compactly $(Z < M)$[1] modeled as a probability distribution over the topics, *i.e.*, $P(z|d_i)$, $z = \{z_1,..., z_Z\}$; $P(d_i)$ accounts for varying number of words. The hidden distributions of the model, $P(w|z)$ and $P(z|d)$, are learnt using Expectation-Maximization (EM), maximizing the model data-likelihood L:

$$L = \prod_{i=1}^{N} \prod_{j=1}^{M} P(w_j, d_i)^{n(w_j, d_i)} \tag{2}$$

The E-step computes the posterior over the topics, $P(z|w, d)$, and the M-step updates the parameters, $P(w|z)$ which identifies the model. Once the model has been learnt, the goal of inference is to estimate the topic distribution of a novel document. To do this, one can use the standard learning algorithm keeping fixed the parameters $P(w|z)$.

The typical classification scheme with pLSA is a standard generative approach, where one has to learn a model per-class and assign a new sample to

[1] Both Z and M are constants to be a-priori set.

the category whose model fits the point best, i.e., the model with highest likelihood (see Equation 2). Recently, other approaches successfully used meaningful distributions or other by-products coming from a generative model, as feature for a discriminative classifier. The intuition is that generative models like pLSA are built to understand how samples were generated, and they haven't any notion of discrimination; on the other hand, discriminative classifiers are built to separate the data and they are highly more effective if the data has been previously "explained" by a generative model. In this paper pLSA has been used in such a hybrid generative-discriminative context. LDA has an advantage over LSA in the sense that, even though you may overestimate the number of topics, it automatically finds the effective number of topics by discarding the unused topics. This can also be achieved using pLSA by applying information theoretic measures such as Bayesian Information Criterion (BIC). In this work, we do not report accuracies using LDA because the accuracies are similar as also been reported by [27,25,23]; and LSA is a simpler model.

3 The Tissue Microarray (TMA) Pipeline

In this section the tissue microarray pipeline is briefly summarized. For a full description please refer to [26]. In particular, first we describe how TMA are determined, followed by the image normalization and patching (how to segment nucleui). Finally, the image features we employed are described.

3.1 Tissue Micro Arrays

Small tissue spots of cancerous cell tissue are arranged on a glass array. They are stained with eosin which visualizes the morphological structure of the tissue. Further, immunohistochemical staining specifically stains MIB-1 expressing cell nuclei dark brown. Therefore, dark blue spots mark the cell nuclei (cancerous or benign), whereas dark brown spots show the MIB-1 positive nuclei.

The TMA slides were scanned with a magnification of 40x, resulting in three channel color images of size 3000x3000px per patient. Eight spots were exhaustively and independently labeled by two pathologists, marking the location and label of each cell nucleus (cancerous/benign) on the images [15].

The data set we employed in the evaluation comprises eight quarters of the images, which consist 100-200 cell nuclei, each (see Figure 2). Also, only those nuclei on which the two pathologists agreed on the label were retained.

3.2 Image Normalization and Patching

To minimize illumination variances among the scans the images were adjusted in contrast. Then, to get individual nuclei, we extracted patches of size 80x80 px, such that each patch has one nucleus in its center (see Figure 3). Both steps improved the following segmentation of cell nuclei.

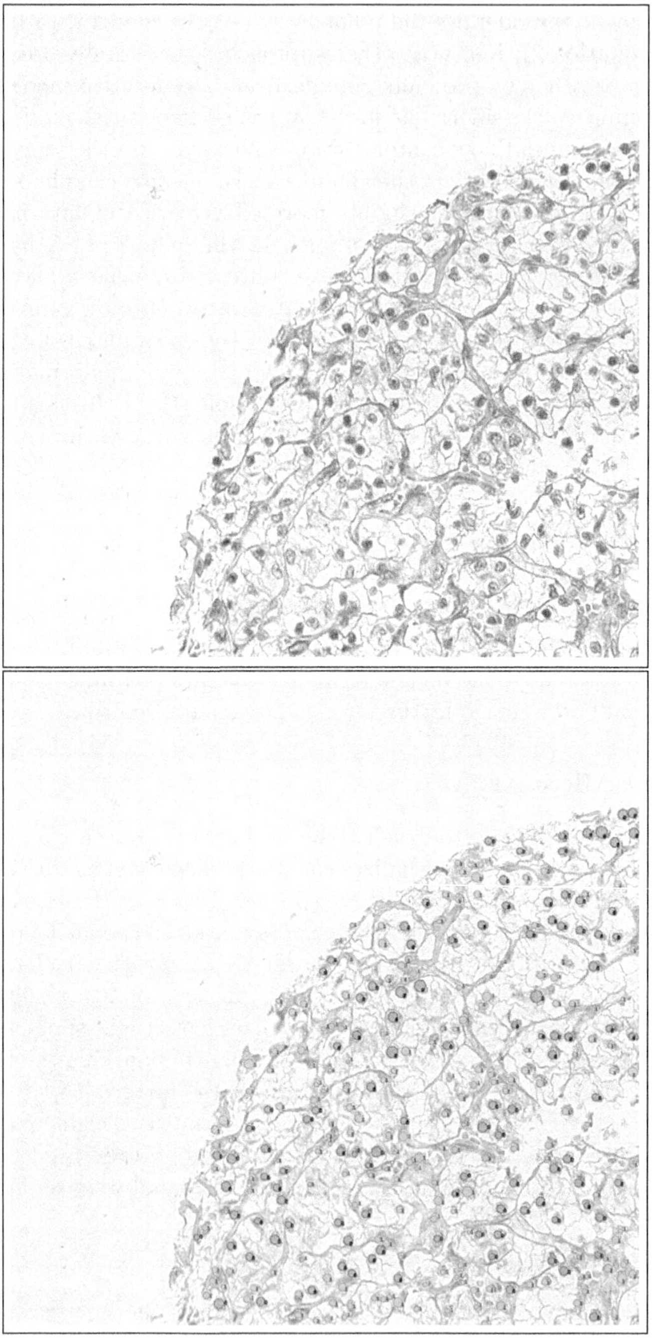

Fig. 2. Top: One 1500x1500px quadrant of a TMA spot from a RCC patient. **Bottom:** A pathologist exhaustively labeled all cell nuclei and classified them into malignant (black) and benign (red).

3.3 Segmentation

The segmentation of cell nuclei was performed with graphcut [10]. The gray intensities were used as unary potentials. The binary potentials were linearly weighted based on their distance to the center to prefer roundish objects lying in the center of the patch (see Figure 3). The contour of the segmented object was used to calculate several shape features as described in the following section.

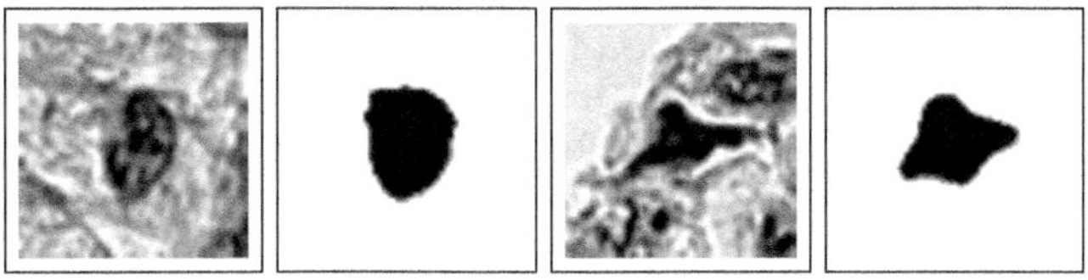

Fig. 3. Two examples of nucleus segmentation. The original 80x80 pixel patch are shown, each with the corresponding nucleus shape found with graphcut.

3.4 Feature Extraction

Features have been extracted from the patches, according to several intuitive guidelines used by pathologists to classify nuclei. They are based on pixel intensities as well as on shape descriptors. The features then have been summarized in histograms, representing the starting point of our algorithm. In [26], histograms have been directly used for classification: we will show in this paper that a significant benefit may be gained when an intermediate generative step is introduced before the final classification. The histograms are described in Table 1). The quantization of the features in histograms was reasonably chosen according to runtime and size of the underlying features. The loss of information due to this process was tried to be kept minimal. Other possible feature extraction methods such as curvature coefficients [5], wavelets [1], similarity based representations [14,6] have been left as future work.

4 Nuclei Classification

The hybrid generative discriminative approach employed to classify the nuclei can be summarized as follows:

1. **Nucleus Image Characterization via Feature Extraction and Summarization:** in this step each image is analysed following the pipeline described in the previous section, giving as output features, histograms.
2. **Generative Model Training:** given the training set, the pLSA generative model is trained. In particular, we straightforwardly assume that the visual features previously presented represent the words w_j, while the nuclei are the documents d. With such a point of view, the extracted histograms

Table 1. Features extracted from patch images for training and testing. All features are histograms.

Shortcut	Feature Description
ALL	**Patch Intensity**: A 16-bin histogram of gray scaled patch
FG	**Foreground Intensity**: A 16-bin histogram of nucleus
BG	**Background Intensity**: A 16-bin histogram of background
LBP	**Local Binary Patterns**: This local feature has been shown to bring considerable performance in face recognition tasks. It benefits from the fact that it is illumination invariant.
COL	**Color feature**: The only feature comprising color information. The colored patch (RGB) is rescaled to size 5x5. The 3x25 channel intensities are then concatenated to a feature vector of size 75.
FCC	**Freeman Chain Code**: The FCC describes the nucleus' boundary as a string of numbers from 1 to 8, representing the direction of the boundary line at that point ([16]). The boundary is discretized by subsampling with grid size 2. For rotational invariance, the first difference of the FCC with minimum magnitude is used. The FCC is represented in a 8-bin histogram.
SIG	**1D-signature**: Lines are considered from the object center to each boundary pixel. The angles between these lines form the signature of the shape ([16]). As feature, a 16-bin histogram of the signature is generated.
PHOG	**Pyramid histograms of oriented gradients**: PHOGs are calculated over a level 2 pyramid on the gray-scaled patches ([9]).

represent the counting vectors, able to describe how much a visual feature (namely a word) is present in a given image (namely a document). Given the histograms, pLSA is trained following the procedure described in Section 2. Only one model is trained for both classes, disregarding labels. Despite its simplicity – many other schemes may be used to fit the generative model in a classification task [2] – this option yielded promising results.

3. **Generative Embedding:** within this step, all the objects involved in the problem (namely training and testing patterns) are projected, through the learned model, to a vector space. In particular, for a given nucleus d, the representation $\phi(d)$ in the generative embedding space is defined as the estimated pLSA posteriors distribution (namely the mixture of topics characterizing the nuclei). In formulae we have that the

$$\phi(d) = [P(z|d)] = [P(z_1|d), \cdots P(z_Z|d)] \tag{3}$$

Our intuition is that the co-occurrence of visual features is different between healthy and cancerous cells. Since the co-occurrences are captured by the topic distribution $P(z|d)$, we are defining a meaningful score for discrimination. This representation with the topic posteriors has been already successfully used in computer vision tasks [12,8] as well as in the medical informatics domain [11,4].

4. **Discriminative Classification:** In the resulting generative embedding space any discriminative vector-based classifier may be employed. In this fashion, according to the generative/discriminative classification paradigm, we use the information coming from the generative process as discriminative features of a discriminative classifier.

5 Experiments

In this section the presented approach has been evaluated. In particular we give details about the experimental setup, together with the results and a discussion.

The classification experiments have been carried using a subset of the data presented in [26]. We selected a three patient subset preserving the cancerous/benign cell ratio. In particular, we employed three patients: from the labeled TMA images, we extracted 600 nuclei-patches of size 80x80 pixels. Each patch shows a cell nucleus in the center (see Figure 3). 474 (79 %) from the nuclei form our data set (as said before, we retain only those where the two pathologists agree on the label): 321 (67 %) benign and 153 (33 %) malignant nuclei.

The data of 474 nuclei samples is divided into ten folds (with stratification). We have eight representations (All, Bg, Col, Fcc, Fg, Lbp, Phog, and Sig); for each representation and each fold, we train pLSA on the training set and apply it to the test set. The number of topics has been chosen using leave-another-fold-out (of the nine training folds, we used 9-fold cross validation to estimate the best number of topics) cross validation procedure on the training set. In the obtained space, different classifiers have been tried. The obtained results have been compared with those obtained with the same classifier working on the original histograms (namely without the intermediate generative coding). In particular we employed the following classifiers (where not explicitly reported, all parameters have been tuned via cross validation on the training set)

- (svl): support vector machines with linear kernel (this represents the most widely employed solution with hybrid generative-discriminative approaches).
- (svp): support vector machines with polynomial kernel: after a preliminary evaluation, the degree p was set to 2.
- (svr): support vector machines with radial basis function kernel.
- (ldc): linear discriminant classifier
- (qdc): quadratic discriminant classifier
- (knn): k-nearest neighbor classifier
- (tree): decision tree

All results were computed by using PRTools [13] MATLAB toolbox. They are reported in tables 2 and 3, for the SVM family and for the other classifiers, respectively. The feature representations where the proposed approach overperforms the original space are marked with bold face (statistically significant difference with paired t-test, $p = 0.05$). In particular, results are averaged over ten runs. In all experiments the standard errors of the mean were inferior to 0.01 for support vector machines and 0.017 for other classifiers.

Table 2. Accuracies with SVM. ORIG is the original histogram based feature space, whereas PLSA stands for the proposed approach.

	svl		*svp*		*svr*	
	ORIG	PLSA	ORIG	PLSA	ORIG	PLSA
ALL	68.36	**74.26**	65.40	**75.06**	74.47	75.11
BG	72.88	70.82	66.79	**71.50**	**74.22**	71.92
COL	66.90	69.03	56.93	**70.32**	68.98	68.82
FCC	67.30	67.72	66.89	67.92	67.95	68.57
FG	70.68	71.97	64.12	**72.62**	70.49	71.09
LBP	68.61	69.43	42.36	**70.70**	68.79	70.47
PHOG	75.45	**79.67**	63.92	**79.22**	76.55	76.80
SIG	67.72	**68.34**	58.64	**67.69**	67.72	67.72

Table 3. Accuracies using different classifiers. ORIG is the original histogram based feature space, whereas PLSA stands for the proposed approach.

	ldc		*qdc*		*knn*		*tree*	
	ORIG	PLSA	ORIG	PLSA	ORIG	PLSA	ORIG	PLSA
ALL	71.71	70.21	69.55	69.01	72.35	**73.44**	*71.97	70.30
BG	**70.79**	68.31	68.48	67.52	**74.25**	71.29	62.25	**67.29**
COL	69.42	69.86	67.55	67.94	69.41	68.62	60.62	62.44
FCC	66.68	65.25	60.76	**65.19**	66.66	67.71		
FG	70.24	70.70	68.59	68.78	69.79	70.48	63.07	63.46
LBP	71.55	71.98	70.71	68.37	71.13	70.29	60.14	63.97
PHOG	75.29	*77.57	67.93	***74.62**	70.71	***74.69**	63.51	66.49
SIG	67.73	66.87	64.74	**68.95**	63.50	67.72	58.04	61.85

Observing the Table 2, we can see that the best accuracy using a SVM is 75.45% whereas the best accuracy on the pLSA space is 79.22 %. For most representations (except LBP, PHOG and COL), the accuracies of different kernels on the original space do not have large differences. We also observe that the data set is a difficult data set because there are some classifiers which have accuracy equal to the prior class distribution of the data set (67 per cent). We see that except the support vector machine with rbf kernel, the space constructed by pLSA always supercedes the original space (except BG on *svl*) in terms of average accuracy. The bold face in the table shows feature sets where pLSA space is more accurate than the original space using 10-fold CV paired t-test at $p = 0.05$.

By looking at the result with other classifiers (Table 3), we can again see that when we transform to the space with pLSA, we get higher accuracies with other classifiers but this time the difference is not strong as in support vector machines. The values with a "*" shows the best classification accuracy using that classifier and again bold face shows feature sets where pLSA space is more accurate than the original space. We can see that, although the number of feature sets where pLSA is better than the original space decreases, except for the decision tree, pLSA space gives the best results for all the classifiers.

5.1 Discussion

We have seen that by using the generative abilities of pLSA and applying the idea of natural language processing to shape features, we can project our data to another space where discriminative classifiers work better. We see that our algorithm automatically finds number of topics and on the space created by pLSA, we have the best results. We observe this behavior with support vector machine variants and also other classifiers.

In this preliminary work, we used a subset of all available subjects to test if the new space created by pLSA has advantages. We have seen that with the new space we have higher accuracy than applying on the original feature space. This promising result encourages us to use more data and apply other kernels to get better classification accuracies. In this work, we use the outputs of pLSA as features in a new space. Another approach would be to directly compute kernels after pLSA and use them for classification. We will explore this option as a future work.

6 Conclusion

In this paper, we propose the use of pLSA to transfer the given shape features into another space to get better classification accuracy for the classification of nuclei in TMA images of renal clear cell carcinoma. Our results show that the features computed by pLSA are more discriminative and achieves higher classification accuracies.

This study extends our previous works by using pLSA to project the data into another space which is more discriminative. We have used the outputs of pLSA as features in a new space but for future work, we plan to compute kernels from the outputs of pLSA and directly use them in kernel based classification. Since the outputs of pLSA are actually probability density functions, we believe that by computing the kernel directly and applying them in a kernel learning paradigm, we may achieve better classification accuracies.

In this work, we used image based feature sets for creating multiple features. In a further application of this scenario, the use of other modalities or other features (e.g. SIFT) extracted from these images, as well as the incorporation of complementary information of different modalities to achieve better classification accuracy is possible.

Acknowledgements. We thank Dr. Cheng Soon Ong very much for helpful discussions. Also, we acknowledge financial support from the FET programme within the EU FP7, under the SIMBAD project (contract 213250).

References

1. Bicego, M., Castellani, U., Murino, V.: Using hidden markov models and wavelets for face recognition. In: ICIAP, pp. 52–56 (2003)
2. Bicego, M., Cristani, M., Murino, V., Pękalska, E.z., Duin, R.P.W.: Clustering-based construction of hidden markov models for generative kernels. In: Cremers, D., Boykov, Y., Blake, A., Schmidt, F.R. (eds.) EMMCVPR 2009. LNCS, vol. 5681, pp. 466–479. Springer, Heidelberg (2009)
3. Bicego, M., Lovato, P., Ferrarini, A., Delledonne, M.: Biclustering of expression microarray data with topic models. In: Proceedings of the 2010 20th International Conference on Pattern Recognition, ICPR 2010, Washington, DC, USA, pp. 2728–2731 (2010)
4. Bicego, M., Lovato, P., Oliboni, B., Perina, A.: Expression microarray classification using topic models. In: Proceedings of the 2010 ACM Symposium on Applied Computing, SAC 2010, New York, NY, USA, pp. 1516–1520 (2010)
5. Bicego, M., Murino, V.: Investigating hidden markov models' capabilities in 2D shape classification. IEEE Transactions on Pattern Analysis and Machine Intelligence 26, 281–286 (2004)
6. Bicego, M., Murino, V., Figueiredo, M.A.: Similarity-based classification of sequences using hidden markov models. Pattern Recognition 37(12), 2281–2291 (2004)
7. Blei, D.M., Ng, A.Y., Jordan, M.I.: Latent dirichlet allocation. Journal of Machine Learning Research 3, 993–1022 (2003)
8. Bosch, A., Zisserman, A., Muñoz, X.: Scene classification via plsa. In: Leonardis, A., Bischof, H., Pinz, A. (eds.) ECCV 2006. LNCS, vol. 3954, pp. 517–530. Springer, Heidelberg (2006)
9. Bosch, A., Zisserman, A., Munoz, X.: Representing shape with a spatial pyramid kernel. In: CIVR 2007: Proceedings of the 6th ACM International Conference on Image and Video Retrieval, pp. 401–408. ACM, New York (2007)
10. Boykov, Y., Veksler, O., Zabih, R.: Efficient approximate energy minimization via graph cuts. IEEE Transactions on Pattern Analysis and Machine Intelligence 20(12), 1222–1239 (2001)
11. Castellani, U., Perina, A., Murino, V., Bellani, M., Rambaldelli, G., Tansella, M., Brambilla, P.: Brain morphometry by probabilistic latent semantic analysis. In: Jiang, T., Navab, N., Pluim, J.P.W., Viergever, M.A. (eds.) MICCAI 2010, Part II. LNCS, vol. 6362, pp. 177–184. Springer, Heidelberg (2010)
12. Cristani, M., Perina, A., Castellani, U., Murino, V.: Geo-located image analysis using latent representations. In: IEEE Conference on Computer Vision and Pattern Recognition, CVPR 2008, pp. 1–8 (2008)
13. Duin, R.P.W.: Prtools, a matlab toolbox for pattern recognition version 4.0.14 (2005), `http://www.prtools.org/`, `http://www.prtools.org/`
14. Elżbieta Pekalska, E., Duin, R.P.: The Dissimilarity Representation for Pattern Recognition. Foundations and Applications. World Scientific, Singapore (2005)
15. Fuchs, T.J., Wild, P.J., Moch, H., Buhmann, J.M.: Computational pathology analysis of tissue microarrays predicts survival of renal clear cell carcinoma patients. In: Metaxas, D., Axel, L., Fichtinger, G., Székely, G. (eds.) MICCAI 2008, Part II. LNCS, vol. 5242, pp. 1–8. Springer, Heidelberg (2008)
16. Gonzalez, R.C., Woods, R.E., Eddins, S.L.: Digital image processing using matlab (2003), 993475

17. Hofmann, T.: Unsupervised learning by probabilistic latent semantic analysis. Machine Learning 42(1-2), 177–196 (2001)
18. Jaakkola, T.S., Haussler, D.: Exploiting generative models in discriminative classifiers. In: Proceedings of the 1998 Conference on Advances in Neural Information Processing Systems, NIPS 1998, Cambridge, MA, USA, pp. 487–493 (1999)
19. Kononen, J., Bubendorf, L., et al.: Tissue microarrays for high-throughput molecular profiling of tumor specimens. Nat. Med. 4(7), 844–847 (1998)
20. Lasserre, J.A., Bishop, C.M., Minka, T.P.: Principled hybrids of generative and discriminative models. In: Proceedings of the IEEE Computer Society Conference on Computer Vision and Pattern Recognition, CVPR 2006, Washington, DC, USA, vol. 1, pp. 87–94 (2006)
21. Ng, A.Y., Jordan, M.I.: On discriminative vs generative classifiers: A comparison of logistic regression and naive Bayes. In: Advances in Neural Information Processing Systems, NIPS 2002, pp. 841–848 (2002)
22. Perina, A., Cristani, M., Castellani, U., Murino, V., Jojic, N.: A hybrid generative/discriminative classification framework based on free-energy terms. In: IEEE 12th International Conference on Computer Vision, ICCV 2009, October 2-29, pp. 2058–2065 (2009)
23. Perina, A., Cristani, M., Castellani, U., Murino, V., Jojic, N.: A hybrid generative/discriminative classification framework based on free-energy terms. In: Proceedings of the IEEE International Conference on Computer Vision, ICCV 2009, pp. 2058–2065 (2009)
24. Rubinstein, Y.D., Hastie, T.: Discriminative vs informative learning. In: Proceedings of International Conference on Knowledge Discovery and Data Mining, pp. 49–53. AAAI Press, Menlo Park (1997)
25. Russell, B.C., Freeman, W.T., Efros, A.A., Sivic, J., Zisserman, A.: Using multiple segmentations to discover objects and their extent in image collections. In: IEEE Computer Society Conference on Computer Vision and Pattern Recognition (CVPR 2006), vol. 2, pp. 1605–1614 (2006)
26. Schüffler, P.J., Fuchs, T.J., Ong, C.S., Roth, V., Buhmann, J.M.: Computational TMA analysis and cell nucleus classification of renal cell carcinoma. In: Goesele, M., Roth, S., Kuijper, A., Schiele, B., Schindler, K. (eds.) Pattern Recognition. LNCS, vol. 6376, pp. 202–211. Springer, Heidelberg (2010)
27. Sivic, J., Russell, B.C., Efros, A.A., Zisserman, A., Freeman, W.T.: Discovering objects and their localization in images. In: Proceedings of the IEEE International Conference on Computer Vision, ICCV 2005, vol. 1, pp. 370–377 (2005)
28. Tsuda, K., Kawanabe, M., Rätsch, G., Sonnenburg, S., Müller, K.R.: A new discriminative kernel from probabilistic models. Neural Computation 14, 2397–2414 (2002)

Multi-task Regularization of Generative Similarity Models

Luca Cazzanti[1], Sergey Feldman[2], Maya R. Gupta[2], and Michael Gabbay[1]

[1] Applied Physics Laboratory and
[2] Dept. Electrical Engineering
University of Washington
Seattle, USA

Abstract. We investigate a multi-task approach to similarity discriminant analysis, where we propose treating the estimation of the different class-conditional distributions of the pairwise similarities as multiple tasks. We show that regularizing these estimates together using a least-squares regularization weighted by a task-relatedness matrix can reduce the resulting maximum a posteriori classification errors. Results are given for benchmark data sets spanning a range of applications. In addition, we present a new application of similarity-based learning to analyzing the rhetoric of multiple insurgent groups in Iraq. We show how to produce the necessary task relatedness information from standard given training data, as well as how to derive task-relatedness information if given side information about the class relatedness.

Keywords: similarity, generative similarity-based classification, discriminant analysis, multi-task learning, regularization.

1 Introduction

Generative classifiers estimate class-conditional distributions from training samples, and then label a new sample as the class most likely to have generated it [21]. In standard metric-space learning problems, the class-conditional distributions' support is over the Euclidean space of feature vectors. For example, a standard metric-space generative classifier is quadratic discriminant analysis (QDA), which models each class as a multivariate Gaussian [16, 35]. More flexible generative models include Gaussian mixture models [21, 19] and locally Gaussian models [17].

In contrast, generative similarity-based classifiers build class-conditional probabilistic models of the similarities between training samples, and label any new sample as the class most likely to have generated its similarities to the training data. That is, in generative similarity-based classification, the class-conditional distributions' support is over a similarity space. Similarity discriminant analysis (SDA) models the class-conditional distributions of the similarities as exponential functions [7]. The local similarity discriminant classifier (local SDA) models as exponential functions the class-conditional distributions of the similarities of a test

M. Pelillo and E.R. Hancock (Eds.): SIMBAD 2011, LNCS 7005, pp. 90–103, 2011.

sample to the k-most similar samples from a training set [5]. Successful classification with local SDA, as with any generative similarity-based or feature-based classifier, depends on the ability to estimate numerically-stable model parameters. A standard approach to ensuring low variance parameter estimates is regularization.

This paper proposes a multi-task approach to regularizing the parameters of the class-conditional exponential models in the local SDA classifier. The motivating hypothesis of the multi-task approach is that learning multiple related tasks in parallel can reduce estimation variance when compared to learning the tasks individually. The successful application of the multi-task approach to many different problems empirically supports this hypothesis, as we briefly review in Sect. 4.

In this paper, the individual tasks consist of estimating the mean of the similarities between samples from pairs of classes. The standard single-task local SDA classifier estimates each of these class-conditional mean similarities independently. In the proposed multi-task approach, the mean estimates are regularized toward each other proportionally to their degree of relatedness, which is captured by a task relatedness matrix. The multi-task regularized mean estimates produce more robust local SDA exponential models which result in improved classification.

Our focus in this paper is on multi-task regularization for SDA. However, SDA is only one of many possible methods for similarity-based learning. Besides SDA, a different approach to generative classification based on pairwise similarities treats the vector of similarities between any sample and the training set as a feature vector and applies standard feature-space generative classifiers to the similarities-as-features. A drawback of this approach is that the model complexity grows linearly or exponentially with the size of the training set [29,28]. Other related research considers generative models for graphs [20], where a graph is modeled as being drawn from an exponential distribution.

Other similarity-based learning methods are not generative. Nearest-neighbor methods mirror standard metric space classifiers such as k-nearest neighbors (k-NN) and classify objects based on their most similar neighbors from a training set. Discriminative approaches to similarity-based classification also exist, owing to the popularity of kernel methods such as support vector machines (SVMs). One such approach treats the similarities as features, and mirrors the standard SVM trick of forming kernels by way of inner products (or exponential functions) operating on the vectors of similarities [18, 24].

Another approach treats the entire matrix of training pairwise similarities as the kernel. Since similarities are more general than inner products, the given similarity matrix may be indefinite and must be transformed into an admissible positive semi-definite kernel for use with an SVM [9, 37, 31, 10, 26, 8, 38]. SVM-KNN is a local SVM classifier that trains the SVM only on a test sample's k-most similar neighbors in similarity space [39]. For indefinite similarities, it was found to be advantageous to use local similarity-based classifiers such as SVM-KNN or kernel ridge interpolation weighted k-NN that approximate the local similarity matrix with a positive definite matrix, because lower-error matrix approximations are needed for local neighborhoods than for the entire matrix. For a recent, comprehensive review of similarity-based classifiers, see Chen et al. [9].

In Sect. 2 we briefly review the necessary background on local SDA and illustrate how the need for regularization arises. Section 3 introduces the proposed multi-task regularization for local SDA, shows that the regularized mean similarities have a closed-form solutions and discusses possible choices for the task relatedness matrix. Section 4 discusses other approaches to multi-task learning and contrasts them to the proposed approach. Section 5 reports experimental results on a set of benchmark similarity datasets spanning many different types of similarities, and Sect. 6 reports the results for a document classification problem where the documents are transcripts of statements made by Iraqi insurgent groups. Section 7 concludes with some open questions.

2 Background on Local Similarity Discriminant Analysis

Local SDA models the distribution of similarities as discrete exponentials, and takes its name from the discriminant curves that form the class boundaries in similarity space, in analogy to the standard feature-space classifier QDA, which forms discriminants in feature space. Also in analogy with feature-space generative classifiers, local SDA follows from the standard a posteriori Bayes classifier, which assigns a class label to a test sample x according to the rule

$$y = \arg\max_g P(x|Y = g)P(Y = g) ,$$

where $P(x|Y = g)$ is the probability of x having been generated from class g, and $P(Y = g)$ is the class g prior probability.

For similarity-based classification, assume that the test and training samples belong to an abstract space $\mathcal{B}$, such as the set of available Internet downloads, the set of amino acid sequences, or the set sonar echoes. Let $X \in \mathcal{B}$ be a random test sample with random class label $Y \in \{1, 2, \ldots, G\}$, and let $x \in \mathcal{B}$ denote the realization of X. Also assume that one can evaluate a relevant similarity function $s : \mathcal{B} \times \mathcal{B} \rightarrow \Omega$, where $\Omega \subset \mathbb{R}$ is assumed to be a finite discrete space without loss of generality, and $r = |\Omega|$. Alternatively, the pairwise similarity for all training and test samples considered could be given. Let $\mathcal{X} \subset \mathcal{B}$ be the set of n training samples, and $\mathcal{N}(x) \subset \mathcal{X}$ be the neighborhood of a test sample x, defined as its k-nearest (most similar) training samples. Also, let $\mathcal{N}_g(x) \subset \mathcal{N}(x)$ be the subset of x's neighbors that belong to class g.

The standard local SDA classifier makes the fundamental assumption that all the information about x's class label depends only on a set of local similarity statistics computed from $\mathcal{N}(x)$, $\mathcal{T}(x) = \bigcup_{h=1\ldots G} T_h(x)$, where $T_h(x)$ is the local similarity statistic computed from $\mathcal{N}_h(x)$. Given a test sample x, the local SDA classifier assigns x the label y according to the maximum a posteriori rule

$$y = \arg\max_g P(\mathcal{T}(x)|Y = g)P(Y = g) \tag{1}$$

$$= \arg\max_g \prod_{h=1}^{G} P_h(\mathcal{T}_h(x)|Y = g)P(Y = g), \tag{2}$$

where (2) is produced from (1) by assuming that the similarity statistics are independent such that the joint class-conditional probability is the product of the marginals.

Several choices are possible for the local similarity statistics $\mathcal{T}(x)$ [5, 7]. In practice, an effective choice are the sets of similarities between x and all its k most-similar neighbors from each class [32], so that $\mathcal{T}_h(x) = \{s(x,z)|z \in \mathcal{N}_h(x)\}$. With this choice, each class-conditional marginal pmf is modeled as the average of exponential functions of the similarities:

$$P_h(\mathcal{T}_h(x)|Y = g) \triangleq \frac{1}{k_h} \sum_{z \in \mathcal{N}_h(x)} \hat{P}(s(x,z)|Y = g)$$

$$= \frac{1}{k_h} \sum_{z \in \mathcal{N}_h(x)} \gamma_{gh} e^{\lambda_{gh} s(x,z)}, \tag{3}$$

where $k_h = |\mathcal{N}_h(x)|$.

Each of the parameters $\{\lambda_{gh}\}$ is determined by numerical minimization under the following method-of-moments constraint that the expected value of the similarity be equal to the average similarity computed from the neighborhood training samples:

$$E_{P_h(\mathcal{T}_h(x)|Y=g)}[s(X,z)] = \frac{\sum_{z_a \in \mathcal{N}_g(x)} \sum_{z_b \in \mathcal{N}_h(x)} s(z_a, z_b)}{k_g k_h}. \tag{4}$$

Each of the G^2 mean-constraints (4) is solved by one unique λ_{gh}, but there may be numerical difficulties. For example, when the neighborhood is small, when the discrete similarity domain consists of few distinct values, or when all of x's neighbors are equally maximally (or minimally) similar to each other, the local mean constraint could take on an extremal value:

$$E_{P(s(x,\mu_h)|Y=g)}[s(X, \mu_h)] = c,\ c \in \{\inf(\Omega), \sup(\Omega)\}. \tag{5}$$

There is no finite λ_{gh} solution to (5) – the solution to (5) is a Kronecker delta pmf, $\delta(s(x,z) - c)$. In practice, such degenerate pmfs can also arise when a finite λ_{gh} solution exists, but give rise to an exponential function so steep that it effectively acts like a Kronecker delta, which incorrectly concentrates all probability mass on an extremal similarity value c, causing classification errors.

The SDA formulation (3) mitigates, but does not eliminate, the deleterious effects of degenerate pmfs by modeling the class-conditional marginals as averages of exponentials, which smooth – or regularize – the effects of the components [32].

Other strategies considered in previous work included regularizing the exponential pmfs by convex combinations with averages of local exponential pmfs, and regularizing the model parameters (the exponents or the means) by convex combinations with baseline parameter values [6]. Yet another strategy considered a Bayesian estimation approach whereby the requirement that the pmfs be exponential was relaxed and the similarities were assumed multinomially distributed with Dirichlet priors on the parameters [32].

All previous strategies regularized each class-conditional pmf in isolation. In the following we present the main contribution of this paper: a multi-task strategy for regularizing the pmfs that exploits the relatedness between the classes.

3 Multi-task Regularization of Mean Similarity Estimates

Given a test sample x, we define as one task the problem of estimating the $(g\,,h)$ mean class-conditional pairwise similarity that appears on the right-hand-side of (4) to solve for the local exponential model. As discussed in the previous section, simply taking the empirical average can lead to numerical problems and non-finite estimates for λ_{gh}. Instead, we propose estimating all G^2 mean class-conditional pairwise similarities jointly as a multi-task problem. Then we use the $(g\,,h)$ multi-task estimate as the right-hand side of (4) to solve for a more stable exponential class-conditional model.

Denote the set of G^2 average similarities by $\{v_{gh}\}$, where v_{gh} is the average similarity between x's neighbors that belong to class g and x's neighbors that belong to class h. That is, $\{v_{gh}\}$ are the average similarities the on right side of (4). We find regularized estimates of the mean similarities

$$\{v^*_{gh}\}_{g,h=1}^{G} = \underset{\{\hat{v}_{gh}\}_{g,h=1}^{G}}{\arg\min} \sum_{g,h=1}^{G} \sum_{z_a \in \mathcal{N}_g(x)} \sum_{z_b \in \mathcal{N}_h(x)} (s(z_a, z_b) - \hat{v}_{gh})^2) + \eta \sum_{j,k=1}^{G} \sum_{l,m=1}^{G} A(v_{jk}, v_{lm})(\hat{v}_{jk} - \hat{v}_{lm})^2. \tag{6}$$

Substituting the solutions into the mean constraint equations (4) yields the regularized-mean constraints

$$E_{P_h(\mathcal{T}_h(x)|Y=g)}[s(X, z)] = v^*_{gh}\,, \tag{7}$$

whose numerical solutions produce the corresponding local SDA model parameters $\{\lambda^*_{gh}\}$.

The first term of (6) minimizes the empirical loss. If one solves (6) with no regularization ($\eta = 0$), the solutions are simply the empirical average similarities $\{v_{gh}\}$. The second term of (6) regularizes the average similarities proportionally to their degree of relatedness, which is captured by the $G^2 \times G^2$ matrix A. Each element $A(v_{jk}, v_{lm})$ quantifies the relatedness of the tasks. We base the task relatedness on the empirical average similarities v_{jk} and v_{lm}. We detail our choice for the relatedness A in Sect. 3.2.

The regularizing action of the second term of (6) shrinks the mean similarities toward each other, but weights the shrinkage by their relatedness. The effect in the degenerate case (5) is that the average similarity moves away from the extremal value c and shrinks toward the average similarity estimates for the other pmfs proportionally to their relatedness. Thus, the corresponding exponential class-conditional pmf estimate becomes feasible, that is the average similarity has been regularized.

Note that the regularization operates across classes: The average similarity of samples from class g to samples of class h, v_{gh}, is regularized toward the average similarity of the samples from class l to class m, v_{lm}. This is in contrast with other multi-task learning approaches, which associate a task with a sample; instead, the proposed approach associates each task to an exponential class-conditional marginal pmf, which is uniquely determined by the average local similarity parameter. Thus, matrix A captures the degree of relatedness between two exponential pmfs.

3.1 Closed-Form Solution

The minimization problem in (6) is convex and, if A is invertible, has the closed-form solution

$$v^* = (I - \tilde{A})^{-1}\tilde{v}\,, \tag{8}$$

where I is the diagonal unit matrix. The vector $\tilde{v} \in \mathbb{R}^{G^2}$ and the matrix $\tilde{A} \in \mathbb{R}^{G^2 \times G^2}$ have components:

$$\tilde{v}_{gh} = \frac{\sum_{z_a \in \mathcal{N}_g(x)} \sum_{z_b \in \mathcal{N}_h(x)} s(z_a, z_b)}{k_g k_h + \eta \sum_{l,m \neq g,h} A(v_{gh}, v_{lm})} \quad \text{and}$$

$$\tilde{A}(v_{gh}, v_{lm}) = \begin{cases} \frac{\eta A(v_{gh}, v_{lm})}{k_g k_h + \eta \sum_{g,h \neq l,m} A(v_{gh}, v_{lm})} & \text{for}\{g,h\} \neq \{j,k\} \\ 0 & \text{for}\{g,h\} = \{j,k\}. \end{cases}$$

These expressions result from setting to zero the partial derivatives of (6) with respect to $\hat{v}_{gh}$, assuming that the task relatedness A is symmetric, and simplifying.

3.2 Choice of Task Relatedness A

Ideally, the task relatedness matrix A conveys information about the strength of the connection between the tasks, but any symmetric invertible matrix can be used as the task relatedness matrix A. For the benchmark classification experiments in Sect. 5, we define A using a Gaussian kernel operating on the differences of the average similarities,

$$A(v_{jk}, v_{lm}) = e^{-(v_{jk} - v_{lm})^2/\sigma}\,. \tag{9}$$

The choice of the Gaussian kernel for A in (6) has an intuitive interpretation. When the average similarities v_{jk} and v_{lm} are close to each other (in the squared difference sense), the Gaussian kernel weights their contribution to the regularization more heavily. When the average similarities are far apart, their reciprocal regularizing influence is greatly diminished by the exponential decay of the Gaussian. The effect is to emphasize the reciprocal influence of closely related average similarities and to discount unrelated mean values, thus preventing unrelated tasks from introducing undue bias in the regularized estimates.

More generally, the task affinity may be mathematically-poorly-defined domain knowledge about how the classes in a particular problem relate to each other. For example, in the insurgent rhetoric classification problem of Sect. 6, we use side information to produce A based on a measure of relatedness between groups that is proportional to number of communiqués jointly released by insurgent groups. The proposed approach can flexibly incorporate such a priori side information about the tasks in the form of matrix A.

4 Related Work in Multi-Task Learning

Many new multi-task learning (MTL) methods have been proposed and shown to be useful for a variety of application domains [1, 2, 4, 14, 13, 23, 34, 40, 25]. Such methods comprise both discriminative and generative approaches that either learn the relatedness between tasks or, like this work, assume that a task-relatedness matrix is given.

Recently, multi-task learning research has focused on the problem of simultaneously learning multiple parametric models like multiple linear regression tasks and multiple Gaussian process regression [2, 4, 14]. Some of these multi-task methods jointly learn shared statistical structures, such as covariance, in a Bayesian framework [4]. Zhang and Yeung [40] assumed there exists a (hidden) covariance matrix for the task relatedness, and proposed a convex optimization approach to estimate the matrix and the task parameters in an alternating way. They develop their technique from a probabilistic model of the data and extend it to kernels by mapping the data to a reproducing kernel Hilbert space.

For SVMs, multi-task kernels have been defined [27]. Evgeniou et al. [13] proposed a MTL framework for kernels that casts the MTL problem as a single-task learning problem by constructing a special single kernel composed of the kernels from each task. The tasks are learned and regularized simultaneously.

Sheldon [33] builds on the work of Evgeniou et al. [13] and proposes a graphical multi-task learning framework where the tasks are nodes in a graph and the task relatedness information is captured by a kernel defined as the pseudoinverse of the weighted graph Laplacian. This task kernel penalizes distant tasks and shrinks more related tasks toward each other, but in practice must itself be regularized to avoid overfitting. The concept of a task network is also taken up by Kato et al. [23], who combine it with local constraints on the relatedness of pairs of tasks in a conic programming formulation to simultaneously solve for the tasks using kernel machines.

A recent approach integrates semisupervised learning with multi-task learning [25]. In that work both unlabeled and labeled data contribute to the simultaneous estimation of multiple tasks, and their contribution is weighted by their pairwise similarity,which is taken to be a radial basis kernel defined on the difference between feature vectors. We will not discuss in detail here related work in domain adaptation methods and transfer learning [11], which we differentiate as methods that compute some estimates for some tasks, and then regularize estimates for new tasks to the previous tasks' estimates.

The major difference between the existing and the proposed MTL approaches is that the existing approaches do not target similarity-based classifiers. The natural support for existing MTL methods is the Euclidean feature space, and adapting them to similarity-based learning remains an open question beyond the scope of this paper. In contrast, the proposed multi-task regularization naturally operates in similarity space and is ideally suited for generative similarity-based classifiers such as local SDA. Furthermore, as we discuss in Sect. 7, the proposed multi-task regularization approach can be extended to standard Euclidean-space classification and regression tasks.

5 Benchmark Classification Results

We compare the classification performance of the the multi-task regularized local SDA classifiers to the standard single-task local SDA classifier, where the chosen task affinity is the Gaussian kernel operating on the average similarities (9). For comparison, we also report classification results for the k-NN classifier in similarity space and for the SVM-KNN classifier, where the chosen SVM kernel is the inner product of vectors of similarities-as-features. We report classification results for six different benchmark similarity datasets from a variety of applications[1]. More classifier comparisons and details about these datasets can be found in Chen et al. [9].

The Amazon problem is to classify books as fiction or non-fiction, where the similarity between two books is the symmetrized percentage of customers who bought the first book after viewing the second book. There are 96 samples in this dataset, 36 from class *non-fiction*, and 60 from class *fiction*. This dataset is especially interesting because the similarity function strongly violates the triangle inequality and the minimality property of metrics (a sample should be maximally similar to itself), because customers often buy a different book if they first view a poorly-reviewed book.

The Aural Sonar problem is to distinguish 50 *target* sonar signals from 50 *clutter* sonar signals. Listeners perceptually evaluated the similarity between two sonar signals on a scale from 1 to 5. The pairwise similarities are the sum of the evaluations from two independent listeners, resulting in a perceptual similarity from 2 to 10 [30]. Perceptual similarities are often non-metric, in that they do not satisfy the triangle inequality.

The Patrol problem is to classify 241 people into one of 8 patrol units based on who people claimed was in their unit when asked to name five people in their unit [12]. The self-similarity is set to 1. Like the Amazon dataset, this is a sparse dataset and most of the similarities equal to zero.

[1] Datasets and software available at http://staff.washington.edu/lucagc

The Protein problem is to classify 213 proteins into one of four protein classes based on a sequence-alignment similarity [22].

The Voting problem is to classify 435 representatives into two political parties based on their votes [3]. The categorical feature vector of yes/no/abstain votes was converted into pairwise similarities using the value difference metric, which is a dissimilarity designed to be useful for classification [36]. The voting similarity is a pseudo-metric.

The Face Recognition problem consists of 945 sample faces of 139 people from the NIST Face Recognition Grand Challenge data set. There are 139 classes, one for each person. Similarities for pairs of the original three-dimensional face data were computed as the cosine similarity between integral invariant signatures based on surface curves of the face [15].

The six datasets are divided in 20 disjoint partitions of 80% training samples and 20% test samples. For each of the 20 partitions of each dataset we chose parameters using ten-fold cross-validation for each of the classifiers shown in the tables. Cross-validation parameter sets were based on recommendations in previously published papers and popular usage. The choice of neighborhood sizes was $\{2, 4, 8, 16, 32, 64, \min(n, 128)\}$. The regularizing parameter η and the kernel bandwidth σ were cross-validated independently of each other among the choices $\{10^{-3}, 10^{-2}, 0.1, 1, 10\}$.

Table 1 shows the mean error rates. Across five datasets multi-task local SDA outperforms single-task local SDA (one dataset is a tie) and for all six datasets it performs better than similarity k-NN. For Sonar and Voting, multi-task local SDA brings the performance closer to SVM-KNN.

Table 1. Percent test error averaged over 20 random test/train splits for the benchmark similarity datasets. Best results are in bold.

	Amazon 2 classes	Sonar 2 classes	Patrol 8 classes	Protein 4 classes	Voting 2 classes	FaceRec 139 classes
Multi-task Local SDA	**8.95**	14.50	**11.56**	**9.77**	5.52	**3.44**
Local SDA	11.32	15.25	**11.56**	10.00	6.15	4.23
Similarity k-NN	12.11	15.75	19.48	30.00	5.69	4.29[2]
SVM-KNN (sims-as-features)	13.68	**13.00**	14.58	29.65	**5.40**	4.23[2]

6 Iraqi Insurgent Rhetoric Analysis

We address the problem of classifying the rhetoric of insurgent groups in Iraq. The data consist of 1924 documents – translated jihadist websites or interviews with insurgent officials – provided by the United States government's Open Source Center. We consider the problem of classifying each document as having

[2] Results for k-NN and SVM-KNN were reported previously. The same train/test splits were used, but the cross-validation parameters were slightly different. See Chen et al. for details [9].

been released by one of eight insurgent groups operating in Iraq from 2003 to 2009.

Each document is represented by a 173-dimensional vector whose elements contain the frequency of occurrence of 173 keywords in the document. The dictionary of keywords was defined by one of the authors, who is an expert on insurgent rhetoric analysis. The chosen document similarity was the symmetrized relative entropy (symmetrized Kullback-Leibler divergence) of the normalized keyword frequency vectors.

For this problem, we compared two definitions of the task relatedness. One, we defined the task relatedness as proposed in Sect. 3. In addition, we derived a task relatedness from side information about the number of communiqués jointly released by two groups, shown in Table 2, where the j-th row and the k-th column denote the number of communiqués jointly released by the j-th and k-th insurgent groups. This side information was derived from a smaller, separate dataset. A higher number of joint statements indicates more cooperation among the leaders of the two groups and, typically, greater ideological affinity as well. Note that some groups work in isolation, while others selectively choose their collaborators.

Table 2. Number of Communiqués Jointly Released By Any Two Groups

	Group 1	Group 2	Group 3	Group 4	Group 5	Group 6	Group 7	Group 8
Group 1	0	0	0	0	7	8	6	2
Group 2	0	0	0	0	0	0	0	0
Group 3	0	0	0	0	0	0	0	0
Group 4	0	0	0	0	0	0	0	1
Group 5	7	0	0	0	0	6	5	1
Group 6	8	0	0	0	6	0	5	1
Group 7	6	0	0	0	5	5	0	1
Group 8	2	0	0	1	1	1	1	0

We conjecture that an appropriate multi-task regularization is to shrink the average document similarity estimates of more strongly connected groups toward each other. Recall that for local SDA there are G^2 mean-similarity constraints, where G is the number of classes. Each constraint is associated with its corresponding task of estimating the class-conditional marginal exponential pmf of the similarity between documents from group j and documents from group k, and consequently the task relatedness matrix A has dimensions $G^2 \times G^2$. In this problem there are $G = 8$ insurgent groups. Let the 8×8 matrix given in Table 2 be denoted by Q. We form the 64×64 task relatedness A from the joint communiqués Q as

$$A(v_{jk}, v_{lm}) = e^{-(Q_{jk}-Q_{lm})2/\sigma} . \tag{10}$$

This choice of task relatedness implies that the mean document similarities v_{jk} and v_{lm} should be strongly related if the number of joint communiqués released

Table 3. Percent leave-one-out cross-validation classification error for the insurgent rhetoric document classification problem. Best result is in bold.

Multi-task Local SDA (w/ joint statements task relatedness)	**52.34**
Multi-task Local SDA (w/ Gaussian kernel task relatedness)	52.75
Local SDA	54.52
Similarity k-NN	53.53
Guessing Using Class Priors	77.91

by groups (j, k) is the same as the number released by groups (l, m), and should be weakly related if the numbers differ greatly. Thus *the task relatedness measures the similarity between pairs of insurgent groups.* Furthermore, choosing a Gaussian kernel operating on all possible differences of the entries in matrix Q ensures that A is invertible.

Table 3 shows the leave-one-out cross-validation error rates for single-task, multi-task local SDA, and similarity k-NN. The neighborhood size and the parameters η and σ were cross validated from parameter choices identical to the benchmark datasets. In addition to the task relatedness derived from the side information Q, we tested the Gaussian kernel operating directly on the class-conditional document similarities in (9) without using any side information. For both choices of task relatedness, the performance of multi-task local SDA provides a small gain over the standard local SDA and similarity k-NN.

The communiqués-derived and the mean document similarity-derived task relatedness definitions represent two approaches to capturing the relationships between the insurgent groups. The former approach incorporates mathematically poorly-defined side information about the problem available from a separate data set, while the latter is purely data-driven from the document similarity data. The multi-task local SDA can flexibly accommodate both types of task knowledge. It is interesting that in this experiment both approaches lead to almost identical classification improvement over single-task local SDA.

Finally, many other definitions of document similarity are possible. While choosing the best similarity is an important practical problem, it is beyond the scope of this paper. In any case, the SDA classification framework, single- or multi-task, is independent of the chosen document similarity function, thus can accommodate any future choice of document similarity.

7 Discussion and Open Questions

In this paper, we have proposed treating the estimation of different class-conditional distributions in a generative model as multiple tasks, and shown that regularizing these estimates together with a simple least-squares similarity-based regularization can reduce classification errors.

It can be argued that regularizing the class-conditional distributions toward each other according to their relatedness implies that the class-conditional local SDA models are in fact correlated, which appears inconsistent with the assumptions that the class-conditional marginals in the SDA classifier (2) are independent. It might be possible to model the correlations directly in the SDA model without resorting to multi-task regularization, but this strategy must contend with the concomitant problem of having to estimate the task correlations in addition to the task-specific parameters, and makes the SDA classifier more complex. In constrast, the proposed multi-task regularization does not impose a particular structure on the task relatedness (i. e. correlation), which can be provided as domain-specific knowledge or computed directly – not estimated – from the task-specific parameters. We argue that this approach is more flexible, because it does not require modifying the original classifer, and more general, because it accommodates any problem-relevant task relatedness.

In the SDA model, the class-conditional pmf $P_j(T_j(x)|k)$ models the similarity of samples from class k to the samples of class j. Thus to tie the $P_j(T_j(x)|k)$ task to the $P_m(T_m(x)|l)$ task, we need the relatedness between the pair of classes $(j\,,k)$ to the pair of classes $(l\,,m)$. A simpler model would be to tie together tasks based only on one of the involved classes: Tie together the $P_j(T_j(x)|k)$ and $P_m(T_m(x)|l)$ tasks based only on the relatedness between the k-th and m-th classes or only on the relatedness between the j-th and l-th classes. Then the task-relatedness would simply be the class-relatedness.

Side information about class relatedness could be used, like the group relatedness given in the group rhetoric analysis in Sect. 6. In the absence of side information, class relatedness could be produced by first running a single-task classifier (like local SDA) and using the resulting class-confusion matrix as the task-relatedness matrix for the multi-task classifier. However, an advantage to the approach we took here of tying pairs of classes together is that we use the relatedness of both the (j,k) pair and the (l,m) pair, and by using a Gaussian RBF kernel to form A, an invertible A is always produced, ensuring a closed-form solution.

A more general nonparametric multi-task learning formulation would be

$$\{y_t^*\}_{t=1}^{U} = \underset{\{\hat{y}_t\}_{t=1}^{U}}{\arg\min} \sum_{t=1}^{U} \sum_{i=1}^{N_t} L(y_{ti}, \hat{y}_t) + \gamma J\left(\{\hat{y}_t\}_{t=1}^{T}\right), \tag{11}$$

where L is a loss function, J is a regularization function, U is the number of tasks, and N_t is the number of data points from task t. However, an advantage of the squared error formulation given in (6) is that is has a closed-form solution, as given in Sect. 3.1.

A number of theoretical questions can be asked about the proposed multi-task framework. Many MTL methods have a Bayesian interpretation, in that the task-specific random variables can be modeled as drawn from some shared prior, such that joint shrinkage towards the mean of that prior is optimal. Whether the proposed MTL can be derived from a Bayesian perspective is not clear. Also, ideally, the assumed multi-task similarities would perfectly represent the underlying statistical relatedness of the tasks. For what types of statistical relatedness is the proposed multi-task learning optimal, and what would the corresponding optimal task relatedness look like? Further, to what extent can one estimate an optimal task relatedness matrix of interest from the statistics of the tasks, with or without side information?

References

1. Agarwal, A., Daumé III, H., Gerber, S.: Learning multiple tasks using manifold regularization. In: Lafferty, J., Williams, C.K.I., Shawe-Taylor, J., Zemel, R., Culotta, A. (eds.) Advances in Neural Information Processing Systems, vol. 23, pp. 46–54 (2010)
2. Argyriou, A., Evgeniou, T., Pontil, M.: Convex multi-task feature learning. Machine Learning 73(3), 243–272 (2008)
3. Asuncion, A., Newman, D.J.: UCI machine learning repository (2007), `http://www.ics.uci.edu/~mlearn/MLRepository.html`
4. Bonilla, E.V., Chai, K.M.A., Williams, C.K.I.: Multi-task Gaussian process prediction. In: Platt, J., Koller, D., Singer, Y., Roweis, S. (eds.) Advances in Neural Information Processing Systems. MIT Press, Cambridge (2008)
5. Cazzanti, L., Gupta, M.R.: Local similarity discriminant analysis. In: Proc. Intl. Conf. Machine Learning (2007)
6. Cazzanti, L., Gupta, M.R.: Regularizing the local similarity discriminant analysis classifier. In: Proc. 8th Intl. Conf. Machine Learning and Applications (December 2009)
7. Cazzanti, L., Gupta, M.R., Koppal, A.J.: Generative models for similarity-based classification. Pattern Recognition 41(7), 2289–2297 (2008)
8. Chen, J., Ye, J.: Training svm with indefinite kernels. In: Proc. of the Intl. Conf. on Machine Learning (2008)
9. Chen, Y., Garcia, E.K., Gupta, M.R., Rahimi, A., Cazzanti, L.: Similarity-based classification: Concepts and algorithms. Journal of Machine Learning Research 10, 747–776 (2009)
10. Chen, Y., Gupta, M.R.: Learning kernels from indefinite similarities. In: Proc. of the Intl. Conf. on Machine Learning (2009)
11. Daumé III, H., Marcu, D.: Domain adaptation for statistical classifiers. Journal of Artificial Intelligence Research 26, 101–126 (2006)
12. Driskell, J.E., McDonald, T.: Identification of incomplete networks. Florida Maxima Corporation Technical Report (08-01) (2008)
13. Evgeniou, T., Micchelli, C., Pontil, M.: Learning multiple tasks with kernel methods. Journal of Machine Learning Research (6) (April 2005)
14. Evgeniou, T., Pontil, M.: Regularized multi–task learning. In: KDD 2004, pp. 109–117. ACM, New York (2004)
15. Feng, S., Krim, H., Kogan, I.A.: 3D face recognition using Euclidean integral invariants signature. In: IEEE/SP 14th Workshop on Statistical Signal Processing, SSP 2007 (2007)
16. Friedman, J.H.: Regularized discriminant analysis. Journal American Statistical Association 84(405), 165–175 (1989)
17. Garcia, E.K., Feldman, S., Gupta, M.R., Srivastava, S.: Completely lazy learning. IEEE Trans. Knowledge and Data Engineering 22(9), 1274–1285 (2010)
18. Graepel, T., Herbrich, R., Bollmann-Sdorra, P., Obermayer, K.: Classification on pairwise proximity data. In: Advances in Neural Information Processing Systems, vol. 11, pp. 438–444 (1998)

19. Gupta, M.R., Chen, Y.: Theory and use of the em method. Foundations and Trends in Signal Processing 4(3), 223–296 (2010)
20. Handcock, M., Hunter, D.R., Goodreau, S.: Goodness of fit of social network models. Journal American Statistical Association 103, 248–258 (2008)
21. Hastie, T., Tibshirani, R., Friedman, J.: The Elements of Statistical Learning. Springer, New York (2001)
22. Hofmann, T., Buhmann, J.: Pairwise data clustering by deterministic annealing. IEEE Trans. on Pattern Analysis and Machine Intelligence 19(1) (January 1997)
23. Kato, T., Kashima, H., Sugiyama, M., Asai, K.: Multi-task learning via conic programming. In: Platt, J., Koller, D., Singer, Y., Roweis, S. (eds.) Advances in Neural Information Processing Systems, vol. 20, pp. 737–744. MIT Press, Cambridge (2008)
24. Liao, L., Noble, W.S.: Combining pairwise sequence similarity and support vector machines for detecting remote protein evolutionary and structural relationships. Journal of Computational Biology 10(6), 857–868 (2003)
25. Liu, Q., Liao, X., Li, H., Stack, J.R., Carin, L.: Semisupervised multitask learning. IEEE Trans. Pattern Analysis and Machine Intelligence (6) (June 2009)
26. Luss, R., d'Aspremont, A.: Support vector machine classification with indefinite kernels. Mathematical Programming Computation 1(2), 97–118 (2009)
27. Micchelli, C.A., Pontil, M.: Kernels for multi–task learning. In: Advances in Neural Information Processing Systems (2004)
28. Pekalska, E., Duin, R.P.W.: Dissimilarity representations allow for building good classifiers. Pattern Recognition Letters 23(8), 943–956 (2002)
29. Pekalska, E., Paclíc, P., Duin, R.P.W.: A generalized kernel approach to dissimilarity-based classification. Journal of Machine Learning Research, 175–211 (2001)
30. Philips, S., Pitton, J., Atlas, L.: Perceptual feature identification for active sonar echoes. In: Proc. of the 2006 IEEE OCEANS Conf. (2006)
31. Roth, V., Laub, J., Kawanabe, M., Buhmann, J.M.: Optimal cluster preserving embedding of nonmetric proximity data. IEEE Trans. Pattern Anal. and Machine Intel. 25(12), 1540–1551 (2003)
32. Sadowski, P., Cazzanti, L., Gupta, M.R.: Bayesian and pairwise local similarity discriminant analysis. In: Proc. Intl. Workshop on Cognitive Information Processing (CIP), Isola d'Elba, Italy (June 2010)
33. Sheldon, D.: Graphical multi-task learning. In: Neural Information Processing Systems Workshops (2008), `http://web.engr.oregonstate.edu/~sheldon`,
34. Sheldon, D.: Graphical multi-task learning (2010) (unpublished manuscript), `http://web.engr.oregonstate.edu/~sheldon`
35. Srivastava, S., Gupta, M.R., Frigyik, B.: Bayesian quadratic discriminant analysis. Journal of Machine Learning Research 8, 1277–1305 (2007)
36. Stanfill, C., Waltz, D.: Toward memory-based reasoning. Communications of the ACM 29(12), 1213–1228 (1986)
37. Wu, G., Chang, E.Y., Zhang, Z.: An analysis of transformation on non-positive semidefinite similarity matrix for kernel machines. Tech. rep., University of California, Santa Barbara (March 2005)
38. Ying, Y., Campbell, C., Girolami, M.: Analysis of svm with indefinite kernels. In: Advances in Neural Information Processing Systems. MIT Press, Cambridge (2009)
39. Zhang, H., Berg, A.C., Maire, M., Malik, J.: SVM-KNN: discriminative nearest neighbor classification for visual category recognition. In: Proc. of the IEEE Conf. on Computer Vision and Pattern Recognition, pp. 2126–2136 (2006)
40. Zhang, Y., Yeung, D.Y.: A convex formulation for learning task relationships. In: Grünwald, P., Spirtes, P. (eds.) Proc. of the 26th Conference on Uncertainty in Artificial Intelligence, UAI 2010 (2010)

A Generative Dyadic Aspect Model for Evidence Accumulation Clustering

André Lourenço[1,3,2], Ana Fred[1,3], and Mário Figueiredo[1,3]

[1] Instituto de Telecomunicações
[2] Instituto Superior de Engenharia de Lisboa
[3] Instituto Superior Técnico, Lisboa, Portugal
alourenco@deetc.isel.ipl.pt,{afred,mario.figueiredo}@lx.it.pt

Abstract. Evidence accumulation clustering (EAC) is a clustering combination method in which a pair-wise similarity matrix (the so-called co-association matrix) is learnt from a clustering ensemble. This co-association matrix counts the co-occurrences (in the same cluster) of pairs of objects, thus avoiding the cluster correspondence problem faced by many other clustering combination approaches. Starting from the observation that co-occurrences are a special type of dyads, we propose to model co-association using a generative aspect model for dyadic data. Under the proposed model, the extraction of a consensus clustering corresponds to solving a maximum likelihood estimation problem, which we address using the expectation-maximization algorithm. We refer to the resulting method as *probabilistic ensemble clustering algorithm* (PEnCA). Moreover, the fact that the problem is placed in a probabilistic framework allows using model selection criteria to automatically choose the number of clusters. To compare our method with other combination techniques (also based on probabilistic modeling of the clustering ensemble problem), we performed experiments with synthetic and real benchmark data-sets, showing that the proposed approach leads to competitive results.

Keywords: Unsupervised learning, clustering, clustering Combination, generative models, model Selection.

1 Introduction

Although clustering is one of the oldest and most studied problems in statistical data analysis, pattern recognition, and machine learning, it is still far from being considered solved and continues to stimulate a considerable amount of research. Given a set of unlabeled objects, the classical goal of clustering is to obtain a partition of these objects into a set of K classes/groups/clusters (where K itself may be known or unknown). Numerous clustering algorithms having proposed in the past decades, but none can be considered of general applicability, mainly because each method is intimately attached to a particular answer to the key question that underlies clustering: "what is cluster?". For example, methods

M. Pelillo and E.R. Hancock (Eds.): SIMBAD 2011, LNCS 7005, pp. 104–116, 2011.

designed under the assumption that a cluster is a *compact* set of objects will fail to identify *connected* sets of objects [7].

Clustering combination techniques, which constitute a recent and promising research trend [1], [5], [8], [9], [17], [18], typically outperform stand-alone clustering algorithms and provide a higher degree of adaptability of the cluster structure to the data. The rationale behind clustering combination methods is that, in principle, a "better" and "more robust" partitioning of the data may be achieved by combining the information provided by an ensemble of clusterings than by using a single clustering (or clustering method).

Ensemble-based clustering techniques exploit the diversity of clustering solutions available in an ensemble of partitions, by proposing a consensus partition that leverages individual clustering results. One key aspect of this type of methods is that diversity can be created without any assumption about the data structure or underlying clustering algorithm(s). Moreover, ensemble methods are robust to incomplete information, since they may include partitions obtained from sub-sampled versions of the original dataset, from different data representations, from different clustering algorithms, and no assumptions need to be made about the number of clusters of each partition in the ensemble.

Evidence accumulation clustering. (EAC), proposed by Fred and Jain [8], [9], is an ensemble-based method that seeks to find consistent data partitions by considering pair-wise relationships. The method can be decomposed into three major steps:

(i) construction of the clustering ensemble;
(ii) accumulation of the "clustering evidence" provided by ensemble;
(iii) extraction of the final consensus partition from the accumulated evidence.

In the combination/accumulation step (ii), the clustering ensemble is transformed into matrix, termed the *co-occurrence matrix*, where each entry counts the number of clusterings in the ensemble in which each pair of objects were placed in the same cluster. A key feature of EAC is that obtaining the co-occurrence matrix does not involve any type of cluster correspondence, a non-trivial problem with which many other clustering ensemble methods have to deal.

The theory of dyadic data analysis, as defined by Hofmann et al. [13], fits perfectly with the EAC approach. In dyadic data, each elementary observation is a dyad (a pair of objects), possibly complemented with a scalar value expressing strength of association [13]. As explained in detail in Section 2, the co-association matrix obtained in the EAC approach can be interpreted as an aggregation of the information provided by an observed set of pairs of objects, thus can be seen as a dyadic dataset.

Hofmann et al. [13] proposed a systematic, domain independent framework for learning from dyadic data using generative mixture models. In this paper, we apply those ideas to the EAC formulation, yielding a generative model for the clustering ensemble. In the proposed approach, the consensus partition extraction step naturally consists in solving a *maximum likelihood estimation* (MLE) problem, which is addressed with the *expectation-maximization* (EM) algorithm [4]. We refer to the proposed method as *probabilistic ensemble clustering algorithm* (PEnCA).

One of the advantages of this MLE-based approach is the possibility of inclusion of a model selection criterion to estimate the number of cluster in the consensus partition. To that end, we can use a simple version of the *minimum description length* (MDL) criterion [15] or adaptation for mixtures [6] or even more recent and sophisticated methods [2].

This paper is organized as follows: in Section 2, we present the generative aspect model for the co-association matrix and a maximum likelihood estimation criterion for the consensus partition. Section 4 reviews some related work. Experimental results on both synthetic and real benchmark datasets are presented in Section 5. Finally, Section 6 concludes the paper by drawing some conclusions and giving pointers to future work.

2 Generative Model for Evidence Accumulation Clustering

2.1 Clustering Ensembles and Evidence Accumulation

The goal of evidence accumulation clustering (EAC) is to combine the results of an ensemble of clusterings into a single data partition, by viewing each clustering as an independent piece of evidence about the pairwise organization of the set of objects under study.

Consider a set of N objects $\mathcal{X} = \{1, \ldots, N\}$ to be clustered; without loss of generality[1], we simply index these objects with the integers from 1 to N. A *clustering ensemble* (CE), $\mathbb{P}$, is defined as a set of M different partitions of the set $\mathcal{X}$, that is, $\mathbb{P} = \{\mathcal{P}^1, \ldots, \mathcal{P}^M\}$, where each $\mathcal{P}^i$ is a partition with K_i clusters: $\mathcal{P}^i = \{C_1^i, \ldots, C_{K_i}^i\}$. This means that $C_k^i \subseteq \mathcal{X}$, for any $i = 1, ..., M$ and $k = 1, ..., K_i$, and that the following constraints are satisfied:

$$(k \neq j) \Rightarrow C_k^i \cap C_j^i = \emptyset, \quad \text{for } i = 1, ..., M \tag{1}$$

and

$$\bigcup_{k=1}^{K_i} C_k^i = \mathcal{X}, \quad \text{for } i = 1, ..., M. \tag{2}$$

Although higher-order information could be extracted from $\mathbb{P}$, the EAC approach focuses on the pair-wise information contained in $\mathbb{P}$, which is embodied in a sequence $\mathcal{S}$ of all the pairs of objects co-occurring in a common cluster of one of the partitions of the ensemble $\mathbb{P}$. Clearly, the number of pairs in $\mathcal{S}$ is

$$|\mathcal{S}| = \sum_{i=1}^{M} \sum_{k=1}^{K_i} |C_k^i| \left(|C_k^i| - 1\right), \tag{3}$$

[1] Any characteristics of the objects themselves (feature vectors, distances, ...) are only relevant for the individual clusterings of the ensemble and are thus encapsulated under the clustering ensemble obtained and irrelevant for the subsequent steps.

where $|\mathcal{C}_k^i|$ denotes the number of objects in the k-th cluster of partition $\mathcal{P}^i$. Each element of $\mathcal{S}$ is a pair $(y_m, z_m) \in \mathcal{X} \times \mathcal{X}$, for $m = 1, ..., |\mathcal{S}|$, such that there exists one cluster in one of the partitions, say $\mathcal{C}_k^i$, for which $y_m \neq z_m$, $y_m \in \mathcal{C}_k^i$ and $z_m \in \mathcal{C}_k^i$.

The $(N \times N)$ co-association matrix $\mathbf{C} = [C_{y,z}]$, which is the central element in the EAC approach, collects a statistical summary of $\mathcal{S}$ by counting the number of clusterings in which each pair of objects falls in the same cluster; formally, the element (y, z) of matrix $\mathbf{C}$ is defined as

$$C_{y,z} = \sum_{m=1}^{|\mathcal{S}|} \mathbb{I}\big((y_m, z_m) = (y, z)\big), \quad \text{for } y, z \in \mathcal{X} \tag{4}$$

where $\mathbb{I}$ is the indicator function (equal to one if its argument is a true propostion, and equal to zero if it is a false proposition). Naturally, matrix $\mathbf{C}$ is symmetrical because if some pair $(a, b) \in \mathcal{S}$, then also $(b, a) \in \mathcal{S}$. Because the set $\mathcal{S}$ does not contain pairs with repeated elements (of the form (z, z)), the diagonal elements are all zero.

2.2 Generative Model

Inspired by [11], [12], [13], we adopt a generative model for $\mathcal{S}$, by interpreting it as samples of $|\mathcal{S}|$ independent and identically distributed pairs of random variables $(Y_m, Z_m) \in \mathcal{X} \times \mathcal{X}$, for $m = 1, ..., |\mathcal{S}|$. Associated with each pair (Y_m, Z_m), there is a set of $|\mathcal{S}|$ multinomial latent class variable $R_m \in \{1, ..., L\}$, also independent and identically distributed, conditioned on which the variables Y_m and Z_m themselves are mutually independent and identically distributed, that is

$$P(Y_m = y, Z_m = z | R_m = r) = P(Y_m = y | R_m = r)\, P(Z_m = z | R_m = r) \tag{5}$$

and

$$P(Z_m = z | R_m = r) = P(Y_m = z | R_m = r), \tag{6}$$

for any $r \in \{1, ..., L\}$, and $z \in \{1, ..., N\}$. The rationale supporting the adoption of this model for clustering is that if there is an underlying cluster structure revealed by the observations in $\mathcal{S}$, then this structure may be captured by the the different conditional probabilities. For example, if $L = 2$ and there are two clearly separated clusters, $\{1, ..., T\}$ and $\{T+1, ..., N\}$, then $P(Y_m = z | R_m = 1)$ will have values close to zero, for $z \in \{T+1, ..., N\}$, and relatively larger values for $z \in \{T+1, ..., N\}$, whereas $P(Y_m = z | R_m = 2)$ will have the reverse behavior.

The modeling assumptions in (5) and (6) correspond to a mixture model for (Y_m, Z_m) of the form

$$P(Y_m = y, Z_m = z) = \sum_{r=1}^{L} P(Y_m = y | R_m = r)\, P(Y_m = z | R_m = r)\, P(R_m = r), \tag{7}$$

which induces a natural mechanism for generating a random sample from (Y_m, Z_m): start by obtaining a sample r of the random variable R_m (with probability $P(R_m = r)$); then, obtain two independent samples y and z, with probabilities $P(Y_m = y|R_m = r)$ and $P(Y_m = z|R_m = r)$.

The model is parameterized by the (common) probability distribution of the latent variables R_m, $(P(R_m = 1), ..., P(R_m = L))$, and by the L conditional probability distributions $(P(Y_m = 1|R_m = r), ..., P(Y_m = N|R_m = r))$, for $r = 1, ..., L$. We write these distributions compactly as an L-vector $\mathbf{p} = (p_1, ..., p_L)$, where $p_r = P(R_m = r)$ (for any $m = 1, ..., |\mathcal{S}|$) and an $L \times N$ matrix $\mathbf{B} = [B_{r,j}]$, where $B_{r,j} = P(Y_m = j|R_m = r) = P(Z_m = j|R_m = r)$ (for any $m = 1, ..., |\mathcal{S}|$). With this notation, we can write

$$P(Y = y, Z = z, R = r) = p_r\, B_{r,y}\, B_{r,z}, \tag{8}$$

and

$$P(Y = y, Z = z) = \sum_{r=1}^{L} p_r\, B_{r,y}\, B_{r,z}. \tag{9}$$

With the generative model in hand, we can now write the probability distribution for the observed set of pairs $\mathcal{S} = \{(y_m, z_m),\ m = 1, ..., |\mathcal{S}|\}$, assumed to be independent and identically distributed samples of (Y, Z):

$$P(\mathcal{S}|\mathbf{p}, \mathbf{B}) = \prod_{m=1}^{|\mathcal{S}|} \sum_{r=1}^{L} p_r\, B_{r,y_m}\, B_{r,z_m}. \tag{10}$$

Consider now the so-called complete data, which, in addition to $\mathcal{S}$ (the samples (y_m, z_m) of (Y_m, Z_m), for $m = 1, ..., |\mathcal{S}|$), also contains the corresponding (missing/latent) samples of the random variables R_m, $\mathcal{R} = \{r_m,\ m = 1, ..., |\mathcal{S}|\}$. The so-called complete likelihood is then

$$P(\mathcal{S}, \mathcal{R}|\mathbf{p}, \mathbf{B}) = \prod_{m=1}^{|\mathcal{S}|} p_{r_m} B_{r_m, y_m} B_{r_m, z_m} \tag{11}$$

$$= \prod_{m=1}^{|\mathcal{S}|} \prod_{r=1}^{L} \left(p_r\, B_{r,y_m}\, B_{r,z_m}\right)^{\mathbb{I}(r_m = r)}. \tag{12}$$

Although it would be computationally very easy, it is not possible to obtain maximum likelihood estimates of $\mathbf{p}$ and $\mathbf{B}$ from (12), because $\mathcal{R}$ is not observed. Alternatively, we will resort to the EM algorithm, which will provide maximum marginal likelihood estimates of $\mathbf{p}$ and $\mathbf{B}$, by maximizing $P(\mathcal{S}|\mathbf{p}, \mathbf{B})$ with respect to these parameters.

3 The Expectation Maximization Algorithm

According to the generative model described in the previous section, each possible value of $R_m \in \{1, ..., L\}$ corresponds to one of the L clusters and each probability $B_{r,j} = P(Y_m = j | R_m = r)$ is the probability that cluster r "owns" object j, which can be seen as a soft assignment. Consequently, estimating matrix $\mathbf{B}$ will reveal the underlying (consensus) cluster structure. We pursue that goal by using the EM algorithm [4], where $\mathcal{R}$ is the missing data.

3.1 The E-Step

The complete log-likelihood (the expectation of which is computed in the E-step) can be obtained from (12),

$$\log P(\mathcal{S}, \mathcal{R} | \mathbf{p}, \mathbf{B}) = \sum_{m=1}^{|\mathcal{S}|} \sum_{r=1}^{L} \mathbb{I}(r_m = r) \log\big(p_r\, B_{r,y_m}\, B_{r,z_m}\big). \tag{13}$$

The E-step consists in computing the conditional expectation of $\log P(\mathcal{S}, \mathcal{R} | \mathbf{p}, \mathbf{B})$ with respect to $\mathcal{R}$, conditioned on the current parameter estimates $\widehat{\mathbf{p}}$ and $\widehat{\mathbf{B}}$ and the observed $\mathcal{S}$, yielding the well-known Q-function. Since $\log P(\mathcal{S}, \mathcal{R} | \mathbf{p}, \mathbf{B})$ is a linear function of the (latent) binary indicator variables $\mathbb{I}(R_m = r)$,

$$Q(\mathbf{p}, \mathbf{B}; \widehat{\mathbf{p}}, \widehat{\mathbf{B}}) = \sum_{m=1}^{|\mathcal{S}|} \sum_{r=1}^{L} \mathbb{E}\left[\mathbb{I}(R_m = r) \,\middle|\, \mathcal{S}, \widehat{\mathbf{p}}, \widehat{\mathbf{B}}\right] \log\big(p_r\, B_{r,y_m}\, B_{r,z_m}\big) \tag{14}$$

$$= \sum_{m=1}^{|\mathcal{S}|} \sum_{r=1}^{L} \widehat{R}_{m,r} \log\big(p_r\, B_{r,y_m}\, B_{r,z_m}\big), \tag{15}$$

where

$$\widehat{R}_{m,r} \equiv \mathbb{E}\left[\mathbb{I}(R_m = r) \,\middle|\, \mathcal{S}, \widehat{\mathbf{p}}, \widehat{\mathbf{B}}\right] = P\left[R_m = r \,\middle|\, (y_m, z_m), \widehat{\mathbf{p}}, \widehat{\mathbf{B}}\right], \tag{16}$$

due to the independence assumption among the pairs and the fact that $\mathbb{I}(R_m = r)$ is a binary variable. The meaning of $\widehat{R}_{m,r}$ is clear: the conditional probability that the pair (y_m, z_m) was generated by cluster r. Finally, we can write

$$\widehat{R}_{m,r} = \frac{\widehat{p}_r\, \widehat{B}_{r,y_m}\, \widehat{B}_{r,z_m}}{\sum_{s=1}^{L} \widehat{p}_s\, \widehat{B}_{s,y_m}\, \widehat{B}_{s,z_m}}, \tag{17}$$

which is then plugged into (15).

3.2 The M-Step

The M-step consists in maximizing, with respect to $\mathbf{p}$ and $\mathbf{B}$, the Q-function, which we now write as

$$Q(\mathbf{p}, \mathbf{B}; \widehat{\mathbf{p}}, \widehat{\mathbf{B}}) = \sum_{m=1}^{|\mathcal{S}|} \sum_{r=1}^{L} \widehat{R}_{m,r} \log(p_r) + \sum_{m=1}^{|\mathcal{S}|} \sum_{r=1}^{L} \widehat{R}_{m,r} \log\big(B_{r,y_m}\, B_{r,z_m}\big), \tag{18}$$

showing that, as is common in EM for mixture models, the maximizations with respect to $\mathbf{p}$ and $\mathbf{B}$ can be carried out separately.

The maximization with respect to $\mathbf{p}$ (of course, under the constraints that $p_r \geq 0$, for $r = 1, ..., L$ and $\sum_{r=1}^{L} p_r = 1$) leads to the well-known

$$\widehat{p}_r^{\text{new}} = \frac{1}{|\mathcal{S}|} \sum_{m=1}^{|\mathcal{S}|} \widehat{R}_{m,r} \quad \text{for } r = 1, ..., L. \tag{19}$$

For the maximization with respect to $\mathbf{B}$, we begin by writing the relevant terms of (18) as

$$\sum_{m=1}^{|\mathcal{S}|} \sum_{r=1}^{L} \widehat{R}_{m,r} \log\big(B_{r,y_m} B_{r,z_m}\big) = \sum_{r=1}^{L} \sum_{y=1}^{N} \sum_{z=1}^{N} \widehat{C}^{\,r}_{y,z} \log\big(B_{r,y} B_{r,z}\big) \tag{20}$$

$$= \sum_{r=1}^{L} \sum_{y=1}^{N} \log\big(B_{r,y}\big) \sum_{z=1}^{N} \widehat{C}^{\,r}_{y,z} + \sum_{r=1}^{L} \sum_{z=1}^{N} \log\big(B_{r,z}\big) \sum_{y=1}^{N} \widehat{C}^{\,r}_{y,z} \tag{21}$$

$$= 2 \sum_{r=1}^{L} \sum_{y=1}^{N} \log\big(B_{r,y}\big) \sum_{z=1}^{N} \widehat{C}^{\,r}_{y,z} \tag{22}$$

where

$$\widehat{C}^{\,r}_{y,z} = \sum_{m=1}^{|\mathcal{S}|} \widehat{R}_{m,r}\, \mathbb{I}((y_m, z_m) = (y, z)), \tag{23}$$

for $r = 1, ..., L$ and $y, z \in \{1, ..., N\}$ and the equality in (22) is due to the symmetry relation $\widehat{C}^{\,r}_{y,z} = \widehat{C}^{\,r}_{z,y}$. Comparison of (23) with (4) shows that $\widehat{C}^{\,r}_{y,z}$ is a weighted version of the co-association matrix; instead of simply counting how many times the pair (y, z) appeared in a common cluster in the clustering ensemble, each of these appearances is weighted by the probability that that particular co-occurrence was generated by cluster r. We thus have L weighted co-association matrices, $\widehat{\mathbf{C}}^1$, ..., $\widehat{\mathbf{C}}^L$, whose elements are given by (23).

Finally, maximization of (22) with respect to $B_{r,y}$, under the constraints $B_{r,y} \geq 0$, for all $r = 1, ..., L$ and $y = 1, ..., N$, and $\sum_{y=1}^{N} B_{r,y} = 1$, for all $r = 1, ..., L$, leads to

$$\widehat{B}_{r,y}^{\text{new}} = \frac{\sum_{z=1}^{N} \widehat{C}^{\,r}_{y,z}}{\sum_{t=1}^{N} \sum_{z=1}^{N} \widehat{C}^{\,r}_{t,z}}. \tag{24}$$

3.3 Summary of the Algorithm and Interpretation of the Estimates

In summary, the proposed EM algorithm, termed PEnCA (probabilistic ensemble clustering algorithm) works as follows:

1. Given the set of objects, obtain an ensemble $\mathbb{P}$ of clusterings and, from this ensemble, build the set $\mathcal{S}$ of co-occurring pairs (see Section 2.1).
2. Choose a number of clusters, L, and initialize the parameter estimates $\widehat{\mathbf{p}}$ and $\widehat{\mathbf{B}}$.
3. Perform the E-step, by computing $\widehat{R}_{m,r}$, for $m = 1, ..., |\mathcal{S}|$ and $r = 1, ..., L$ according to (17).
4. Compute the weighted co-association matrices $\widehat{\mathbf{C}}^1, ..., \widehat{\mathbf{C}}^L$, according to (23).
5. Update the parameter estimates according to (19) and (24).
6. If some stopping criterion is satisfied, stop; otherwise go back to step 3.

The parameter estimates returned by the algorithm have clear interpretations: $\widehat{p}_1, ..., \widehat{p}_L$ are the probabilities of the L clusters; each distribution $\widehat{B}_{r,1}, ..., \widehat{B}_{r,N}$ can be seen as the sequence of degrees of ownership of the N objects by cluster r. This is in contrast with the original EAC work [8,9], where once a co-association matrix is obtained, a consensus clustering is sought by applying a some hard clustering algorithm. Notice that these soft ownerships are obtained even if all the clusterings in the ensemble are hard. It is also elementary to obtain an estimate of probability that object y belongs to cluster r (denoted as $\widehat{V}_{y,r}$), by applying Bayes law:

$$\widehat{V}_{y,r} = \hat{P}(R = r|Y = y) = \frac{\widehat{B}_{r,y}\,\widehat{p}_r}{\sum_{s=1}^{L} \widehat{B}_{s,y}\,\widehat{p}_s}. \tag{25}$$

4 Related Work

Topchy *et al.* introduced a combination method based on probabilistic model of the consensus partition, in the space of contributing clusters of the ensemble [18] [19]. As in present work, the consensus partition is found by solving a maximum likelihood estimation problem with respect to the parameters of a finite mixture distribution. Each mixture component is a multinomial distribution and corresponds to a cluster in the target consensus partition. As in this work, the maximum likelihood problem is solved using the EM algorithm. Our method differs from that of Topchy *et al.* in that it is based on co-association information.

Wang *et al.* extented the idea, with a model entitled *Bayesian cluster ensembles* (BCE) [20]. It is a mixed-membership model for learning cluster ensembles, assuming that they were generated by a graphical model. Although the posterior distribution cannot be calculated in closed, it is approximated using variational inference and Gibbs sampling. That work is very similar to the *latent Dirichlet allocation* (LDA) model [10], [16], but applied to a different input feature space.

Bulò *et al.* presented a method built upon the EAC framework where the co-association matrix was probabilisticly interpreted, and the extracted consensus solution consisted in a soft partition [3]. The method reduced the clustering problem to a polynomial optimization in the probability domain, solved using the Baum-Eagon inequality.

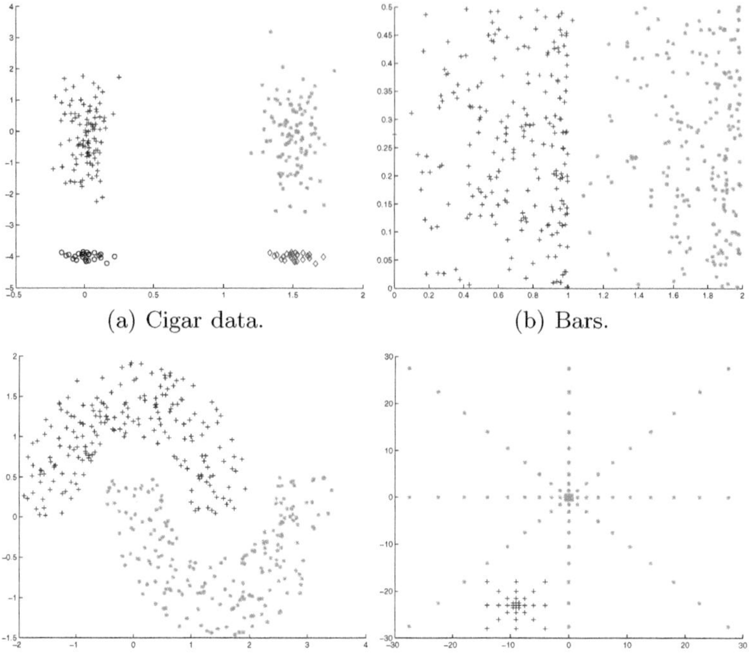

(a) Cigar data. (b) Bars.

(c) Half Rings. (d) Stars.

Fig. 1. Synthetic two-dimensional datasets

5 Experimental Results and Discussion

In this section, we present results for the evaluation of the proposed algorithm (which we refer to as PEnCA – *probabilistic ensemble clustering algorithm*) on several synthetic and real-world benchmark datasets from the well known UCI (University of California, Irvine) repository[2]. Figure 1 presents the four synthetic two-dimensional datasets used for this study.

To produce the clustering ensembles, we extend [14], where the classical K-means algorithm is used, and the several partitions in the ensembles are obtained by varying the numbers of clusters and the initialization. The minimum and the maximum number of clusters varied as a function of the number of samples, according to the following rule:

$\{K_{min}, K_{max}\} = \left\{\max\left(\lceil\sqrt{N}/2\rceil, \lceil N/50\rceil\right), K_{min} + 20\right\}$,

Figure 2 shows a co-association matrix obtained for the *Iris* dataset, using an ensemble produced with the proposed rule.

The color scheme of the representation ranges from white ($\mathcal{C}(y,z) = 0$) to black ($\mathcal{C}(y,z) = M$). Notice the evident block diagonal structure, and the clear separation the between the three clusters (Setosa, Versicolour, and Virginica).

[2] `http://www.ics.uci.edu/~mlearn/MLRepository.html`

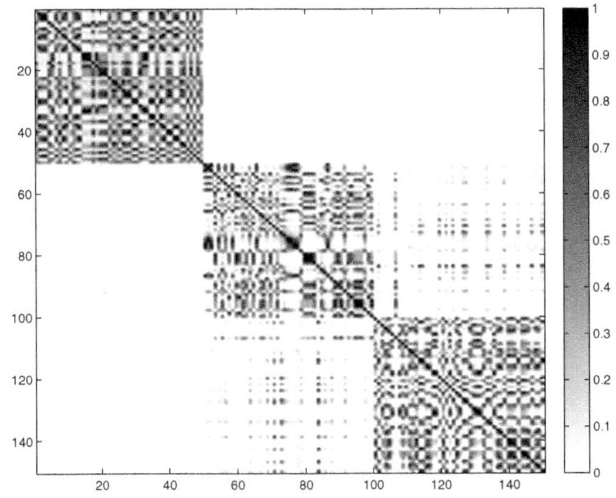

Fig. 2. Example of co-association matrix for the *Iris* dataset

Figure 3 presents the probabilistic assignment of each sample to each cluster, given by the posterior probabilities $\widehat{V}_{y,r}$ (see 25)) obtained after running the EM algorithm with $L = 3$. Notice that the assignments of the last fifty labels are noisier due to the not so clear separation of clusters 2 and 3, as can be seen in co-association matrix in Figure 2.

In a second set of experiments, we compared the results of PEnCA with those obtained with the approach from [18] (which we will refer to as MM – *mixture model*). The performance of the two methods was systematically assessed in terms of accuracy, by comparing the respective consensus partitions with ground truth clusterings. The accuracy is calculated using the *consistency index* (CI) [8]

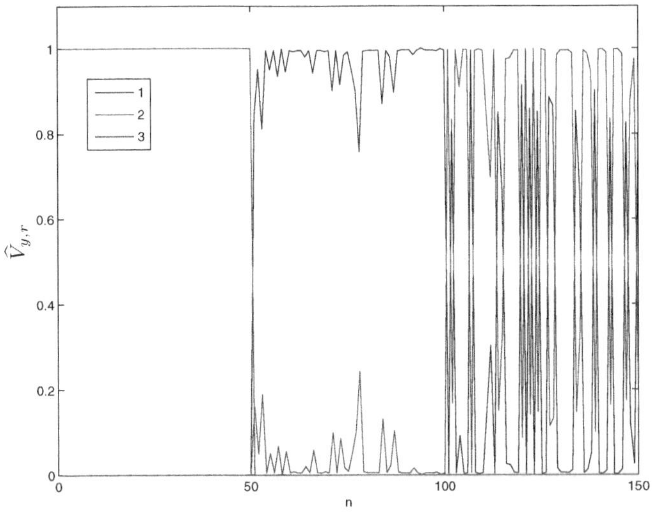

Fig. 3. Soft assignments obtained by PEnCA for the *Iris* dataset

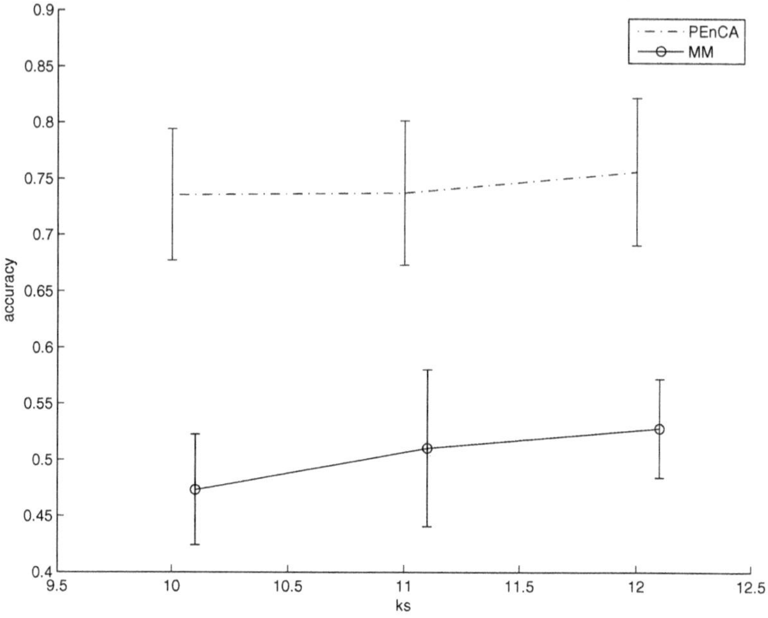

Fig. 4. Results on the *optdigits-r-tra-1000* dataset: accuracy (mean and standard deviation) over the several trials and for different number of aspects

which provides percentages of correct labels. For each ensemble, we have repeated the extraction of the consensus partition 10 times, in order to test the variability of the result and the dependence of the initialization.

Figure 4 shows the results for the *optdigits-r-tra-1000* dataset, the variability in the accuracy over the several trials, and for different numbers of clusters. The dashed and solid lines represent, respectively, the PEnCA and the MM results; blue and red represent results for ensemble (a) and (b). Notice that the

Table 1. Results obtained on the benchmark datasets (see text for details)

Data Set	N	K	PEnCA	MM
stars	114	2	**0.921**	0.737
cigar-data	250	4	0.712	**0.812**
bars	400	2	**0.985**	0.812
halfrings	400	2	**1.000**	0.797
iris-r	150	3	**0.920**	0.693
wine-normalized	178	3	**0.949**	0.590
house-votes-84-normalized	232	2	**0.905**	0.784
ionosphere	351	2	0.724	**0.829**
std-yeast-cellcycle	384	5	**0.729**	0.578
pima-normalized	768	2	**0.681**	0.615
Breast-cancers	683	2	**0.947**	0.764
optdigits-r-tra-1000	1000	10	**0.876**	0.581

variability in the accuracy on both models is of the same order of magnitude (in this example approximately 5% of the absolute value) and that PEnCA has always achieves higher accuracies than MM.

Finally, Table 1 reports the results obtained on several benchmark datasets (four synthetic and eight USI datasets).The best result for each dataset is shown in bold. These results show that PEnCA almost always achieves better accuracy than MM.

6 Conclusions and Future Work

In this paper, we have proposed a probabilistic generative model for consensus clustering, based on a dyadic aspect model for evidence accumulation clustering framework.

Given an ensemble of clusterings, the consensus partition is extracted by solving a maximum likelihood estimation problem via the expectation-maximization (EM).

The output of the method is a probabilistic assignment of each sample to each cluster, which is an advantage over previous works using the evidence accumulation framework.

Experimental assessment of the performance of the proposed method has shown that it outperforms another recent probabilistic approach to ensemble clustering.

One of the advantages of this framework is the possibility of inclusion of a model selection criterion. We hope to address this issue in future.

Ongoing work on different initialization schemes and strategies to escape from local solutions is being carried on.

Acknowledgements. This work was partially supported by Fundação para a Ciência e Tecnologia (FCT) under the grants SFRH/PROTEC/49512/2009 and PTDC/EIACCO/103230/2008 (Project EvaClue), and by the Future and Emerging Technologies Open Scheme (FET-Open) of the Seventh Framework Programme of the European Commission, under the SIMBAD project (contract 213250).

References

1. Ayad, H.G., Kamel, M.S.: Cumulative voting consensus method for partitions with variable number of clusters. IEEE Trans. Pattern Anal. Mach. Intell. 30(1), 160–173 (2008)
2. Buhmann, J.: Information theoretic model validation for clustering. In: IEEE International Symposium on Information Theory (2010)
3. Bulò, S.R., Lourenço, A., Fred, A., Pelillo, M.: Pairwise probabilistic clustering using evidence accumulation. In: Hancock, E.R., Wilson, R.C., Windeatt, T., Ulusoy, I., Escolano, F. (eds.) SSPR&SPR 2010. LNCS, vol. 6218, pp. 395–404. Springer, Heidelberg (2010)

4. Demspter, A., Laird, N., Rubin, D.: Maximum likelihood from incomplete data via the EM algorithm. Journal of the Royal Statistical Society (B) 39, 1–38 (1977)
5. Fern, X.Z., Brodley, C.E.: Solving cluster ensemble problems by bipartite graph partitioning. In: Proc. ICML 2004 (2004)
6. Figueiredo, M., Jain, A.K.: Unsupervised learning of finite mixture models. IEEE Trans. Pattern Anal. Mach. Intell. 24(3), 381–396 (2002)
7. Fischer, B., Roth, V., Buhmann, J.: Clustering with the connectivity kernel. In: Thrun, S., Saul, L., Schölkopf, B. (eds.) Neural Information Processing Systems – NIPS, vol. 16 (2004)
8. Fred, A.: Finding consistent clusters in data partitions. In: Kittler, J., Roli, F. (eds.) MCS 2001. LNCS, vol. 2096, pp. 309–318. Springer, Heidelberg (2001)
9. Fred, A., Jain, A.: Combining multiple clustering using evidence accumulation. IEEE Trans. Pattern Analysis and Machine Intelligence 27(6), 835–850 (2005)
10. Griffiths, T.L., Steyvers, M.: Finding scientific topics. Proc. Natl. Acad. Sci. USA 101 suppl. 1, 5228–5235 (2004)
11. Hofmann, T.: Unsupervised learning from dyadic data, pp. 466–472. MIT Press, Cambridge (1998)
12. Hofmann, T., Puzicha, J.: Statistical models for co-occurrence data. Technical report, Cambridge, MA, USA (1998)
13. Hofmann, T., Puzicha, J., Jordan, M.I.: Learning from dyadic data. In: Advances in Neural Information Processing Systems (NIPS), vol. 11. MIT Press, Cambridge (1999)
14. Lourenço, A., Fred, A., Jain, A.K.: On the scalability of evidence accumulation clustering. In: ICPR, Istanbul, Turkey (August 23-26, 2010)
15. Rissanen, J.: Stochastic COmplexity in Statistical Inquiry. World Scientific, Singapore (1989)
16. Steyvers, M., Griffiths, T.: Latent Semantic Analysis: A Road to Meaning. In: Probabilistic Topic Models. Lawrence Erlbaum, Mahwah (2007)
17. Strehl, A., Ghosh, J.: Cluster ensembles - a knowledge reuse framework for combining multiple partitions. J. of Machine Learning Research 3 (2002)
18. Topchy, A., Jain, A., Punch, W.: A mixture model of clustering ensembles. In: Proc. of the SIAM Conf. on Data Mining (April 2004)
19. Topchy, A., Jain, A.K., Punch, W.: Clustering ensembles: Models of consensus and weak partitions. IEEE Trans. Pattern Anal. Mach. Intell. 27(12), 1866–1881 (2005)
20. Wang, H., Shan, H., Banerjee, A.: Bayesian cluster ensembles. In: 9th SIAM International Conference on Data Mining. SIAM, Philadelphia (2009)

Supervised Learning of Graph Structure

Andrea Torsello and Luca Rossi

Dipartimento di Scienze Ambientali, Informatica e Statistica,
Università Ca' Foscari Venezia, Italy
{torsello,lurossi}@dsi.unive.it

Abstract. Graph-based representations have been used with considerable success in computer vision in the abstraction and recognition of object shape and scene structure. Despite this, the methodology available for learning structural representations from sets of training examples is relatively limited. In this paper we take a simple yet effective Bayesian approach to attributed graph learning. We present a naïve node-observation model, where we make the important assumption that the observation of each node and each edge is independent of the others, then we propose an EM-like approach to learn a mixture of these models and a Minimum Message Length criterion for components selection. Moreover, in order to avoid the bias that could arise with a single estimation of the node correspondences, we decide to estimate the sampling probability over all the possible matches. Finally we show the utility of the proposed approach on popular computer vision tasks such as 2D and 3D shape recognition.

1 Introduction

Graph-based representations have been used with considerable success in computer vision in the abstraction and recognition of object shape and scene structure, as they can concisely capture the relational arrangement of object primitives, in a manner which can be invariant to changes in object viewpoint. Despite their many advantages and attractive features, the methodology available for learning structural representations from sets of training examples is relatively limited, and the process of capturing the modes of structural variation for sets of graphs has proved to be elusive.

Recently, there has been considerable interest in learning structural representations from samples of training data, in particular in the context of Bayesian networks, or general relational models [6]. The idea is to associate random variables with the nodes of the structure and to use a structural learning process to infer the stochastic dependency between these variables. However, these approaches rely on the availability of correspondence information for the nodes of the different structures used in learning. In many cases the identity of the nodes and their correspondences across samples of training data are not known, rather, the correspondences must be recovered from structure.

In the last few years, there has been some effort aimed at learning structural archetypes and clustering data abstracted in terms of graphs. In this context

M. Pelillo and E.R. Hancock (Eds.): SIMBAD 2011, LNCS 7005, pp. 117–132, 2011.

spectral approaches have provided simple and effective procedures. For example Luo and Hancock [8] use graph spectral features to embed graphs in a low dimensional space where standard vectorial analysis can be applied. While embedding approaches like this one preserve the structural information present, they do not provide a means of characterizing the modes of structural variation encountered and are limited by the stability of the graph's spectrum under structural perturbation. Bonev et al. [3], and Bunke et al. [4] summarize the data by creating super-graph representation from the available samples, while White and Wilson [18] use a probabilistic model over the spectral decomposition of the graphs to produce a generative model of their structure. While these techniques provide a structural model of the samples, the way in which the supergraph is learned or estimated is largely heuristic in nature and is not rooted in a statistical learning framework. Torsello and Hancock [14] define a superstructure called tree-union that captures the relations and observation probabilities of all nodes of all the trees in the training set. The structure is obtained by merging the corresponding nodes and is critically dependent on the order in which trees are merged. Further, the model structure and model parameter are tightly coupled, which forces the learning process to be approximated through a series of merges, and all the observed nodes must be explicitly represented in the model, which then must specify in the same way proper structural variations and random noise. The latter characteristic limits the generalization capabilities of the model. Torsello [15] recently proposed a generalization for graphs which allowed to decouple structure and model parameters and used a stochastic process to marginalize the set of correspondences, however the approach does not deal with attributes and all the observed nodes still need be explicitly represented in the model. Further, the issue of model order selection was not addressed. Torsello and Dowe [16] addressed the generalization capabilities of the approach by adding to the generative model the ability to add nodes, thus not requiring to model explicitly isotropic random noise, however correspondence estimation in this approach was cumbersome and while it used a minimum message length principle for selecting model-complexity, that could be only used to choose from different learned structures since it had no way to change the complexity while learning the model.

2 Generative Graph Model

Consider the set of undirected graphs $S = (g_1, \ldots, g_l)$, our goal is to learn a generative graph model $\mathcal{G}$ that can be used to describe the distribution of structural data and characterize the structural variations present the set. To develop this probabilistic model, we make an important simplifying assumption: We assume that the model is a mixture of naïve models where observation of each node and each edge is independent of the others, thus imposing a conditional independence assumption similar to naïve Bayes classifier, but allowing correlation to pop up by mixing the models.

The naïve graph model $\mathcal{G}$ is composed by a structural part, i.e., a graph $G = (V, E)$, and a stochastic part. The structural part encodes the structure, here

V are all the nodes that can be generated directly by the graph, and $E \subseteq V \times V$ is the set of possible edges. The stochastic part, on the other hand, encodes the variability in the observed graph. To this end we have a series of binary random variables θ_i associated with each node and τ_{ij} associated with each edge, which give us respectively the probability that the corresponding node is generated by the model, and the probability that the corresponding edge is generated, conditioned on the generation of both endpoints. Further, to handle node- and edge-attributes, we assume the existence of generative models W_i^n and $W_{i,j}^e$ that model the observable node and edge attribute respectively, and that are parametrized by the (possibly vectorial) quantities ω_i^n and $\omega_{i,j}^e$. Note that θ_i and W_i^n need not be independent, nor do τ_{ij} and $W_{i,j}^e$. With this formalism, the generation of a graph from a naïve model is as follows: First we sample from the node binary indicator variables θ_i determining which nodes are observed, then we sample the variables $\tau_{i,j}$ indicating which edges between the observed nodes are generated, and finally we sample the attributes W_i^n and $W_{i,j}^e$ for all observed nodes and edges, thus obtaining the full attributed graph.

Clearly, this approach can generate only graphs with fewer or equal nodes than V. This constraint limits the generalization capability of the model and forces one to model explicitly even the observed random isotropic noise. To correct this we add the ability to generate nodes and edges not explicitly modeled by the core model. This is obtained by enhancing the stochastic model with an external node observation model that samples a number of random *external nodes*, i.e., nodes not explicitly modeled in the generative model. The number of external nodes generated is assumed to follow a geometric distribution of parameter $1 - \bar{\theta}$, while the probability of observing edges that have external nodes as one of the endpoints is assumed to be the result of a Bernoulli trial with a common observation probability $\bar{\tau}$. Further, we assume common attribute models $\bar{W}^n$ and $\bar{W}^e$ for external nodes and edges, parametrized by the quantities $\bar{\omega}^n$ and $\bar{\omega}^e$. This way external nodes allow us to model random isotropic noise in a compact way.

After the graph has been sampled from the generative model, we lose track of the correspondences between the sample's nodes and the nodes of the model that generated them. We can model this by saying that an unknown random permutation is applied to the nodes of the sample. For this reason, the observation probability of a sample graph depends on the unknown correspondences between sample and model nodes.

Figure 1 shows a graph model and the graphs that can be generated from it with the corresponding probabilities. Here model is unattributed with null probability of generating external nodes. The numbers next to the nodes and edges of the model represent the values of θ_i and $\tau_{i,j}$ respectively. Note that, when the correspondence information (letters in the Figure) is dropped, we cannot distinguish between the second and third graph anymore, yielding the final distribution.

Given the node independence assumptions at the basis of the naïve graph model, if we knew the correspondences σ_g mapping the nodes of graph g to the

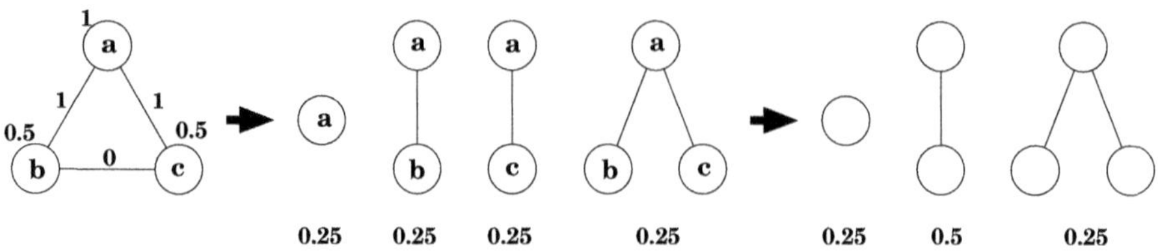

Fig. 1. A structural model and the generated graphs. When the correspondence information is lost, the second and third graph become indistinguishable.

nodes of the model $\mathcal{G}$, we could very easily compute the probability of observing graph g from model $\mathcal{G}$:

$$P(g|\mathcal{G},\sigma_g) = (1-\bar{\theta}) \prod_{i \in V} P(g_{\sigma_g^{-1}(i)}|\theta_i, \omega_i^n) \cdot \prod_{(i,j)\in E} P(g_{\sigma_g^{-1}(i),\sigma_g^{-1}(j)}|\tau_{i,j}, \omega_{i,j}^e) \cdot$$
$$\cdot \prod_{i \notin V} P(g_{\sigma_g^{-1}(i)}|\bar{\theta}, \bar{\omega^n}) \cdot \prod_{(i,j)\notin E} P(g_{\sigma_g^{-1}(i),\sigma_g^{-1}(j)}|\bar{\tau}, \bar{\omega^e}),$$

where the indexes $i \in V$ and $(i,j) \in E$ indicate product over the internal nodes and edges, while, with an abuse of the formalism, we write $i \notin V$ and $(i,j) \notin E$ to refer to external nodes and edges. With the ability to compute the probability of generating any graph from the model, we can compute the complete data likelihood and do maximum likelihood estimation of the model $\mathcal{G}$, however, here we are interested in the situation where the correspondences are not known and must be inferred from the data as well.

Almost invariably, the approaches in the literature have used some graph matching technique to estimate the correspondences and use them in learning the model parameters. This is equivalent to defining the sampling probability for node g as $P(g|\mathcal{G}) = \max_{\sigma \in \Sigma_n} P(g|\mathcal{G},\sigma)$. However, as shown in [15], assuming the maximum likelihood estimation, or simply a single estimation, for the correspondences yields a bias in the estimation as shown in Figure 2. Here, the graph distribution obtained from the model in Figure 1 is used to infer a model, however, since each node of the second sample graphs is always mapped to the same model node, the resulting inferred model is different from the original one and it does not generate the same sample distribution.

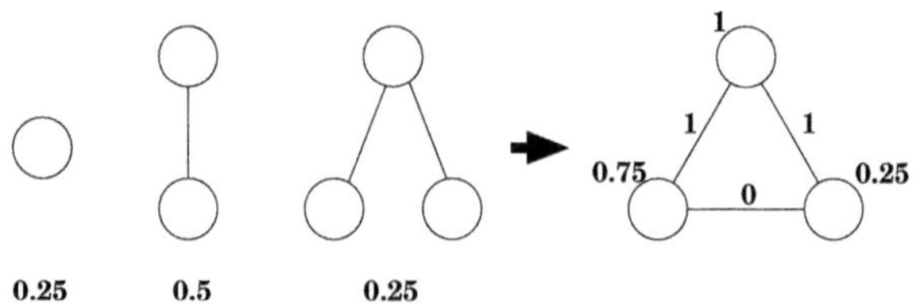

Fig. 2. Model estimation bias. If a single node correspondence is taken into account the estimated model will exhibit a bias towards one of multiple possible correspondences.

To solve this bias Torsello [15] proposed to marginalize the sampling probability over all possible correspondences, which, once extended to deal with external nodes, results in the probability

$$P(\hat{g}|\mathcal{G}) = \sum_{\sigma \in \Sigma_n^m} P(g|\mathcal{G}, \sigma)P(\sigma) = \frac{1}{|\Sigma_g|} \sum_{\sigma \in \Sigma_n^m} P(g|\mathcal{G}, \sigma), \tag{1}$$

where $\hat{g}$ is is the quotient of g modulo permutation of its nodes, i.e., the representation of g where the actual order of the nodes is ignored, Σ_n^m is the set of all possible partial correspondences between the m nodes of graph g and the n nodes of model $\mathcal{G}$, and Σ_g is the set of symmetries of g, i.e., the set of graph isomorphisms from g onto itself.

Clearly, averaging over all possible correspondences is not possible due to the super-exponential growth of the size of Σ_n^m; hence, we have to resort to an estimation approach. In [15] was proposed an importance sampling approach to compute a fast-converging estimate of $P(g|\mathcal{G})$. Note that similar importance sampling approaches marginalizing over the space of correspondences have been used in [2] and [11]. In particular, in the latter work the authors show that the estimation has expected polynomial behavior.

2.1 Correspondence Sampler

In order to estimate $P(g|\mathcal{G})$, and to learn the graph model, we need to sample correspondences with probability close to the posterior $P(\sigma|g, \mathcal{G})$. Here we generalize the approach in [15] for models with external nodes, also eliminating the need to pad the observed graphs with dummy nodes to make them of the same size of the graph model.

Assume that we know the node-correspondence matrix $M = (m_{ih})$, which gives us the marginal probability that model node i corresponds to graph node h. Note that, since model nodes can be deleted (not observed) and graph nodes can come from the external node model, we have that $\forall h, \sum_i m_{ih} \leq 1$ and $\forall i, \sum_h m_{ih} \leq 1$. We turn the inequalities into equalities by extending the matrix M into a $(n+1) \times (m+1)$ matrix $\bar{M}$ adding $n+m$ slack variables, where the first n elements of the last column are linked with the probabilities that a model node is not observed, the first m elements of the last row are linked with the probability that an observed node is external and element at index $n+1, m+1$ is unused. $\bar{M}$ is a partial doubly-stochastic matrix, i.e., its first n rows and its first m columns add up to one.

With this marginal node-correspondence matrix to hand, we can sample a correspondence as follows: First we can sample the correspondence for model node 1 picking a node h_1 with probability m_{1,h_1}. Then, we to condition the node-correspondence matrix to the current match by taking into account the structural information between the sampled node and all the others. We do this by multiplying $\bar{m}_{j,k}$ by $P(g_{h_1,k}|\mathcal{G}_{1,j})$, i.e., the probability that the edges/non-edges between k and h_1 map to the model edge $(1, j)$. The multiplied matrix is then projected to a double-stochastic matrix $\bar{M}_1^{h_1}$ using a Sinkhorn projection [13] adapted to partial doubly-stochastic matrix, where the alternate row and column normalization is performed only on the first n rows and m columns. We can then sample a correspondence for model node 2 according to the distribution of the second row of $\bar{M}_1^{h_1}$ and compute the conditional matching probability $\bar{M}_{1,2}^{h_1,h_2}$ in much the same way we computed $\bar{M}_1^{h_1}$. and iterate until we have sampled a complete set of correspondences, obtaining a fully deterministic conditional matching probability $\bar{M}_{1,\dots,n}^{h_1,\dots,h_n}$, corresponding to a correspondence σ, that has been sampled with probability $P(\sigma) = (\bar{M})_{1,h_1} \cdot (\bar{M}_1^{h_1})_{2,h_2} \cdot \dots \cdot (\bar{M}_{1,\dots,n-1}^{h_1,\dots,h_{n-1}})_{n,h_n}$.

2.2 Estimating the Model

With the correspondence samples to hand, we can easily perform a maximum likelihood estimation of each model parameter by observing that, by construction of the model, conditioned on the correspondences the node and edge observation are independent to one another. Thus, we need only to maximize the node and edge models independently, ignoring what is going on in the rest of the graph. Thus, we define the sampled node and edge likelihood functions as

$$\mathcal{L}_i(S, \mathcal{G}) = \prod_{g \in S} \sum_{\sigma} \frac{P(g_{\sigma(i)} | \theta_i, \omega_i^n)}{P(\sigma)}$$

$$\mathcal{L}_{i,j}(S, \mathcal{G}) = \prod_{g \in S} \sum_{\sigma} \frac{P(g_{\sigma(i),\sigma(j)} | \tau_{i,j}, \omega_{i,j}^e)}{P(\sigma)}$$

from which we can easily obtain maximum likelihood estimates of the parameters θ_i, ω_i^n, $\tau_{i,j}$, and $\omega_{i,j}^e$.

Further, we can use th samples to update the initial node-correspondence matrix in the following way

$$\bar{M}' = \frac{1}{\sum_\sigma \frac{P(\sigma|g,\mathcal{G})}{P(\sigma)}} \sum_\sigma \frac{P(\sigma|g,\mathcal{G})}{P(\sigma)} M_\sigma$$

where M_σ is the deterministic correspondence matrix associated with σ. Thus in our learning approach we start with a initial guess for the node-correspondence matrix and improve on it as we go along. In all our experiments we initialize the matrix based only on local node information, i.e. $m_{i,h}$ is equal the probability that model node i generates the attributes of graph model h.

The only thing left to estimate is the value of $|\Sigma_g|$, but that can be easily obtained using our sampling approach observing that it is proportional to the probability of sampling an isomorphism between g and a deterministic model obtained from g by setting the values of $\tau_{i,j}$ to 1 or 0 according the existence of edge (i,j) in g, and setting $\bar{\theta} = 0$. It interesting to note that in this corner case, our sampling approach turns out to be exactly the same sampling approach used in [1] to show that the graph isomorphism problem can be solved in polynomial time. Hence, our sampling approach is expected polynomial for deterministic model. and we can arguably be confident that it will perform similarly well for low entropy models.

2.3 Model Selection

Given this sampling machinery to perform maximum likelihood estimation of the model parameters for the naïve models, we adopt a standard EM approach to learn mixtures of naïve models.

This, however, leaves us with a model selection problem, since model likelihood decreases with the number of mixture components as well as with the size of the naïve models. To solve this problem we follow [16] in adopting a minimum message length approach to model selection, but we deviate from it in that we use the message length to prune an initially oversized model.

Thus we seek to minimize the combined cost of a two part message resulting in the penalty function

$$I_1 = \frac{D}{2}\log\left(\frac{|S|}{2\pi}\right) + \frac{1}{2}\log(\pi D) - 1 - \sum_{g\in S}\log\left(P(g|\mathcal{G},\sigma_g)\right), \qquad (2)$$

where $|S|$ is the number of samples and D the number of parameters for the structural model.

The learning process is initiated with a graph model that has several mixture components, each with more nodes that have been observed in any graph in the training set. We iteratively perform the EM learning procedure on the oversized model and, with the observation probabilities to hand, we decide whether to prune a node from a mixture component or a whole mixture component and after the model reduction we reiterate the EM parameter estimation and the pruning until no model simplification reduces the message length.

The pruning strategy adopted is a greedy one, selecting the operation that guarantees the largest reduction in message length given the current model parameters. Note that this greedy procedure does not guarantee optimality since the estimate is clearly a lower bound, as the optimum after the pruning can be in a very different point in the model-parameter space, but it does still give a good initialization for leaving the reduced parameter set.

In order to compute the reduction in message length incurred by removing a node, while sampling the correspondences we compute the matching probability not only of the current model, but also of the models obtained from the current one with any singe node removal. Note, however, that this does not increase the time complexity of the sampling approach and incurs only in a small penalty.

3 Experimental Evaluation

In order to asses the performance of the proposed approach, we run several experiments on graphs arising from different classification problems arising from 2D and 3D object recognition tasks, as well as one synthetic graph-classification testbed. The generative model is compared against standard nearest neighbor and nearest prototype classifiers based on the distances obtained using several graph matching techniques at the state of the art. In all cases the prototype is selected by taking the set-median of the training set. The performance of the generative model is assessed in terms of the classification performance for the classification task to hand. For this reason, for all the experiments we plot the precision and recall values:

$$\text{precision} = \frac{tp}{tp + fp} \qquad \text{recall} = \frac{tp}{tp + fn}$$

where tp indicates the true positives, tn the true negatives and fn the false negatives.

With the exception to the last set of experiments, all the graphs used have a single numerical attribute associated to each node and no attributes linked with the edges. The last set of experiments, on the other hand, is based on edge-weighted graphs with no node attribute.

For the node-attributed graphs, we adopted the rectified Gaussian model used in [14]. To this end, we define a single stochastic node observation model X_i for each node i. We assume X_i is normally distributed with mean μ_i and standard deviation σ_i. When sampling node i from the graph model, a sample x_i is drawn from X_i. If $x_i \geq 0$ then the node is observed with weight $w_i = x_i$, otherwise the node will not be present in the sampled graph. Hence the node observation probability is $\theta_i = 1 - \text{erfc}(\mu_i / \sigma_i)$ where erfc is the complementary error function

$$\text{erfc} = \int_x^\infty \frac{1}{\sqrt{2\pi}} \exp\left(-\frac{1}{2}s^2\right) ds \,.$$

The edge observation model, on the other hand is a simple Bernoulli process.

3.1 Shock Graphs

We experimented on learning models for shock graphs, a skeletal based representation of shape. We extracted graphs from a database composed of 150 shapes divided into 10 classes of 15 shapes each. Each graph had a node attribute that reflected the size of the boundary feature generating the corresponding skeletal segment. Our aim was to compare the classification results obtained learning a generative model to what can be obtained using standard graph matching techniques and a nearest neighbor classifier. Figure 3 shows the shape database, the matrix of extracted edit distances between the shock graphs, and a multidimensional scaling representation of the distances; here numbers correspond to classes. As we can see, recognition based on this representation is a hard problem, as the class structure is not very clear in these distances and there is considerable class overlap.

In Figure 4 we compare the classification performance obtained with the nearest neighbor and nearest prototype rules with the one obtained by learning the generative models and using Bayes decision rule for classification, i.e., assigning each graph to the class of the model with largest probability of generating it. Note that the graphs are never classified with a model that had the same graph in the training set, thus in the case of the 15 training samples, the correct class had only 14 samples, resulting in a leave-one-out scheme. Figure 4 shows a clear

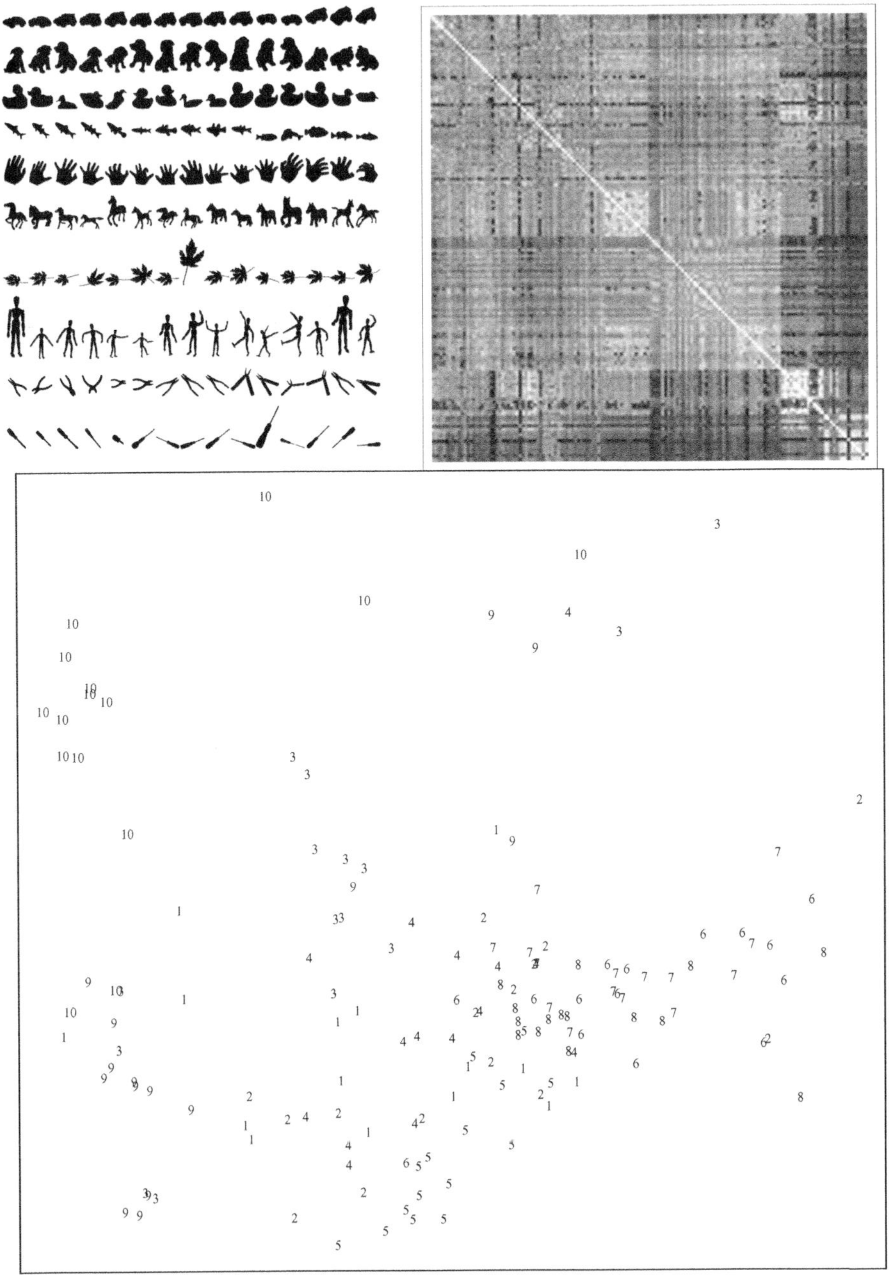

Fig. 3. Top row: Left, shape database; right, edit distance matrix. Bottom row: Multidimensional Scaling of the edit distances.

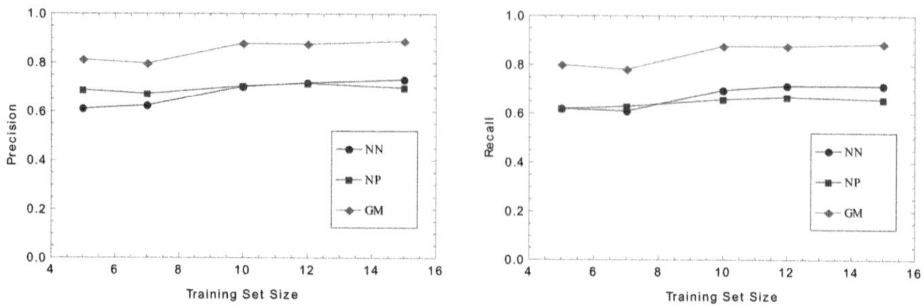

Fig. 4. Precision and Recall on the shock graph dataset as the number of training samples increases

improvement of about 15% on both precision and recall values regardless the number of samples in the training set, thus proving that learning the modes of structural variation present in a class rather than assuming an isotropic behavior with distance, as has been done for 40 years in structural pattern recognition, gives a clear advantage.

3.2 3D Shapes

The second test set is based on a 3D shape recognition task. We collected a number of shapes from the McGill 3D Shape Benchmark [12] and we extracted their medial surfaces. The final dataset was obtained by transforming these skeletal representations into an attributed graph. Figure 5 shows the shapes, their graph distance matrix and a Multidimensional Scaling representaion of the distances. The distances between the graphs were computed using the normalized metric described in [17], which in turn relies on finding a maximal isomorphism between the graphs, for which we adopted the association graph-based approach presented in [10]. Both the distance matrix and the Multidimensional Scaling show that the classes are well separated, resulting in a relatively easy classification task.

Once again we tested the generative model performance against the nearest neighbor and the nearest prototype classifier. Figure 6 confirms our intuition that this was indeed an easy task, since both the nearest neighbor and the nearest prototype classifiers achieve the maximum performance. Yet, the generative model performs extremely well, even when the training set contains just a very few samples. As for the performance gap between the nearest neighbor and the generative model, it is probably due to the very naïve way of estimating the initial node correspondences, and could be probably reduced using a more sophisticated initialization.

3.3 Synthetic Data

To further assess the effectiveness of the proposed approach we tested it on synthetically generated data, where the data generation process is compatible

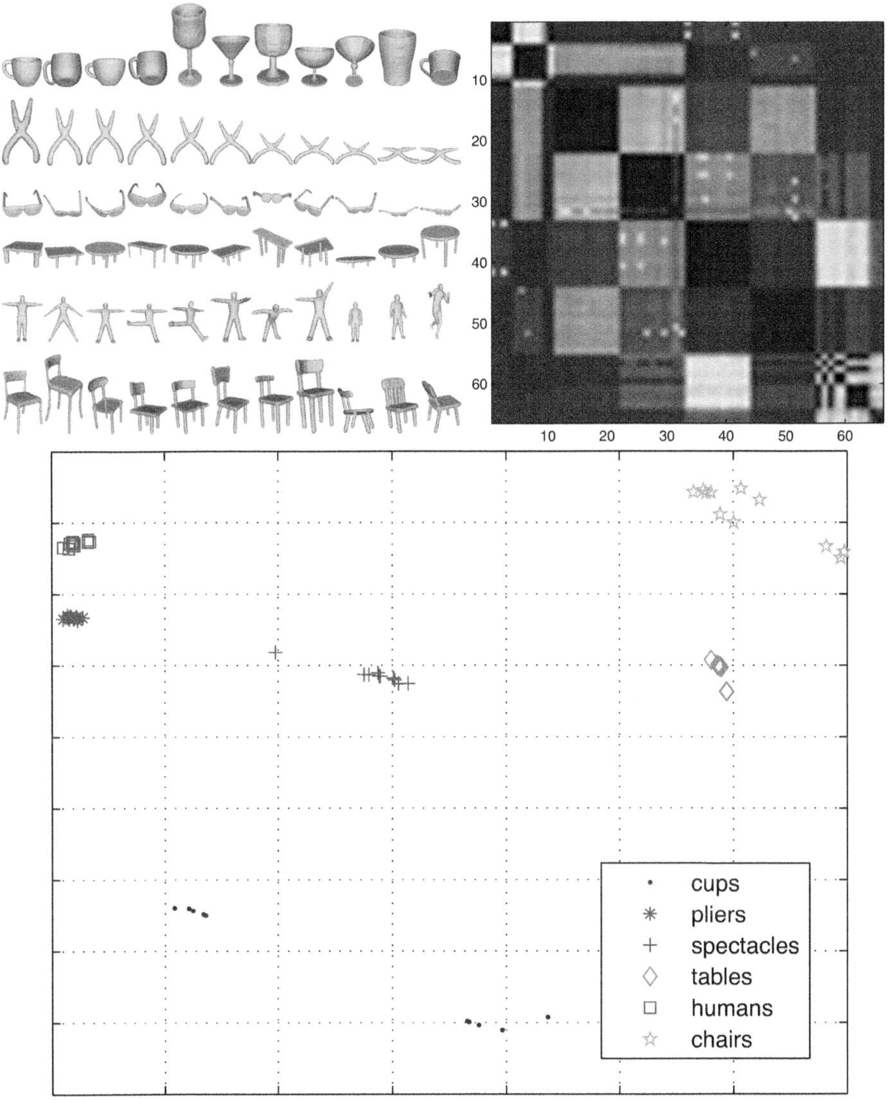

Fig. 5. Top row: Left, shape database; right, distance matrix. Bottom row: Multidimensional Scaling of the graph distances.

with the naïve model adopted in the proposed learning approach. To this end, we have randomly generated 6 different weighted graph prototypes, with size ranging from 3 to 8 nodes. For each prototype we started with an empty graph and then we iteratively added the required number of nodes each labeled with a random mean and variance. Then we added the edges and their associated observation probabilities up to a given edge density. Given the prototypes, we sampled 15 observations from each class being careful to discard graphs that

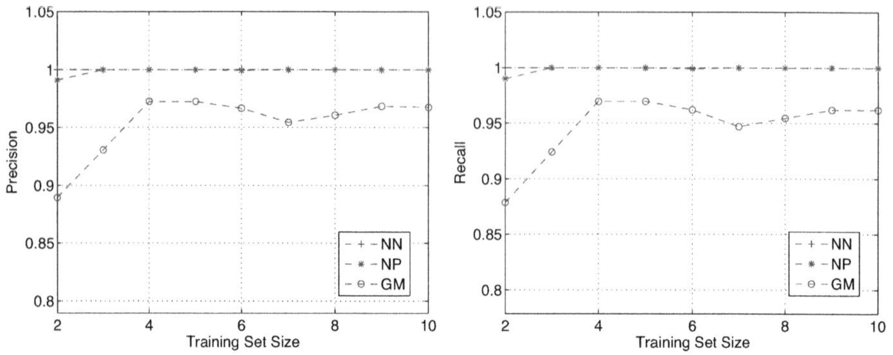

Fig. 6. Precision and Recall on the 3D shapes dataset

were disconnected. Then we proceeded as in the previous set of experiments computing the dissimilarities between the graphs and learning the graph models.

Generating the data with the same model used for learning might seem to give an unfair advantage to our generative model, but the goal of this set of experiments is asses the ability of the learning procedure to obtain a good model even in the presence of very large model-overlap. A positive result can also provide evidence for the validity of the optimization heuristics.

Figure 7 shows the distance matrix of the synthetic data and the corresponding Multidimensional Scaling representation. There is a considerable overlap between different classes, which renders the task particularly challenging for the nearest neighbor and nearest prototype classifiers. Yet, our generative model was able to learn and describe this large intra class variability, thus coping with the class overlap. Figure 8 plots the precision and recall curves for this set of experiments. Even with a relatively small training set, our approach achieves nearly 90% precision and recall, and as the number of observed samples increases, it yields perfect classification. On the other hand, the nearest neighbor classifier is not able to increase its precision and recall above the 84% limit, while the nearest prototype approach exhibits even lower performance.

3.4 Edge-Weighted Graphs

In the finals set of experiments, we applied the approach to an object recognition task. To this end we used a subset of the COIL-20 dataset [9]. For each image we extracted the most salient points using a Matlab implementation of the corner detector described in [7], the salient points where connected according to a Delaunay triangulation, thus resulting in an edge-weighted graph, were the edge-weights correspond to the distance between the salient points.

With this representation we used different node and edge observation models. Since nodes are not attributed, we used simple Bernoulli models for them. For the edges, on the other hand, we used a combined Bernoulli and Gaussian model: a Bernoulli process establishes whether the edge is observed, and if it is the weight is drawn according to an independent Gaussian variable. The reason for

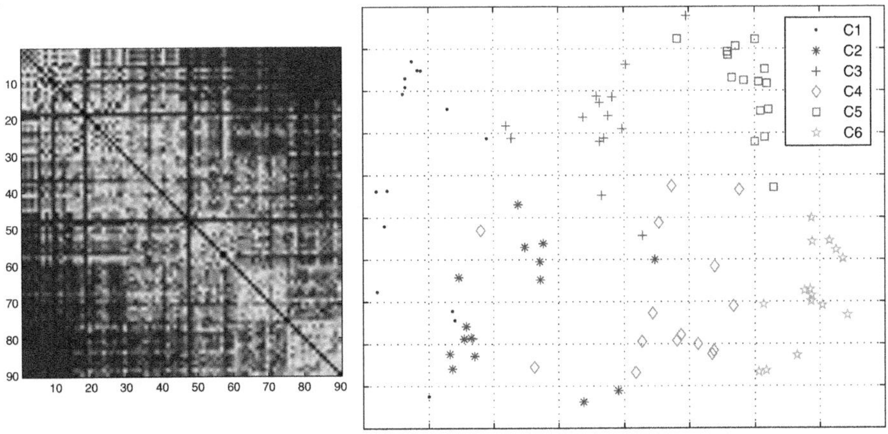

Fig. 7. Distance matrix and MDS of distances for the Synthetic Dataset

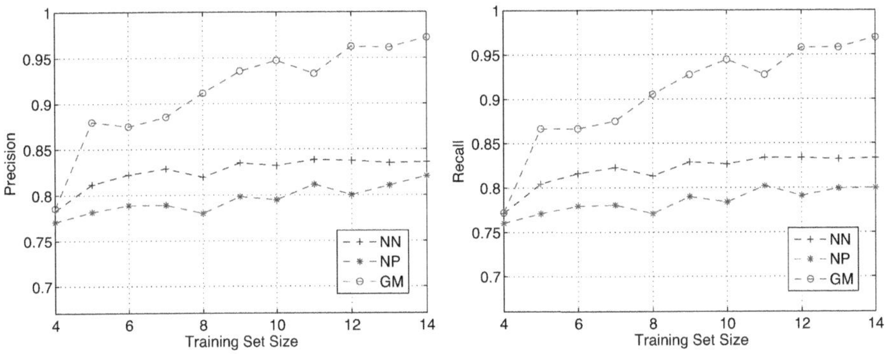

Fig. 8. Precision and Recall on the synthetic dataset

this different weight model resides in the fact that the correlation between the weight and the observation probability that characterized the rectified Gaussian model did not fit the characteristics of this representation.

To compute the distances for the nearest neighbor and nearest prototype rule, we used the graph matching algorithm described in [5], which is capable of dealing with edge-weighted graphs. Once the correspondences where computed, we adopted the same metric as before. As Figure 9 shows, the generated dataset is even more complex than the synthetic one. This is mainly due to the instability of the corner detector, which provided several spurious nodes resulting in very large intra-class structural variability.

Figure 10 shows that even on this difficult dataset, we significantly outperform both the nearest neighbor and nearest prototype classifiers, emphasizing once again the advantages of our structural learning approach.

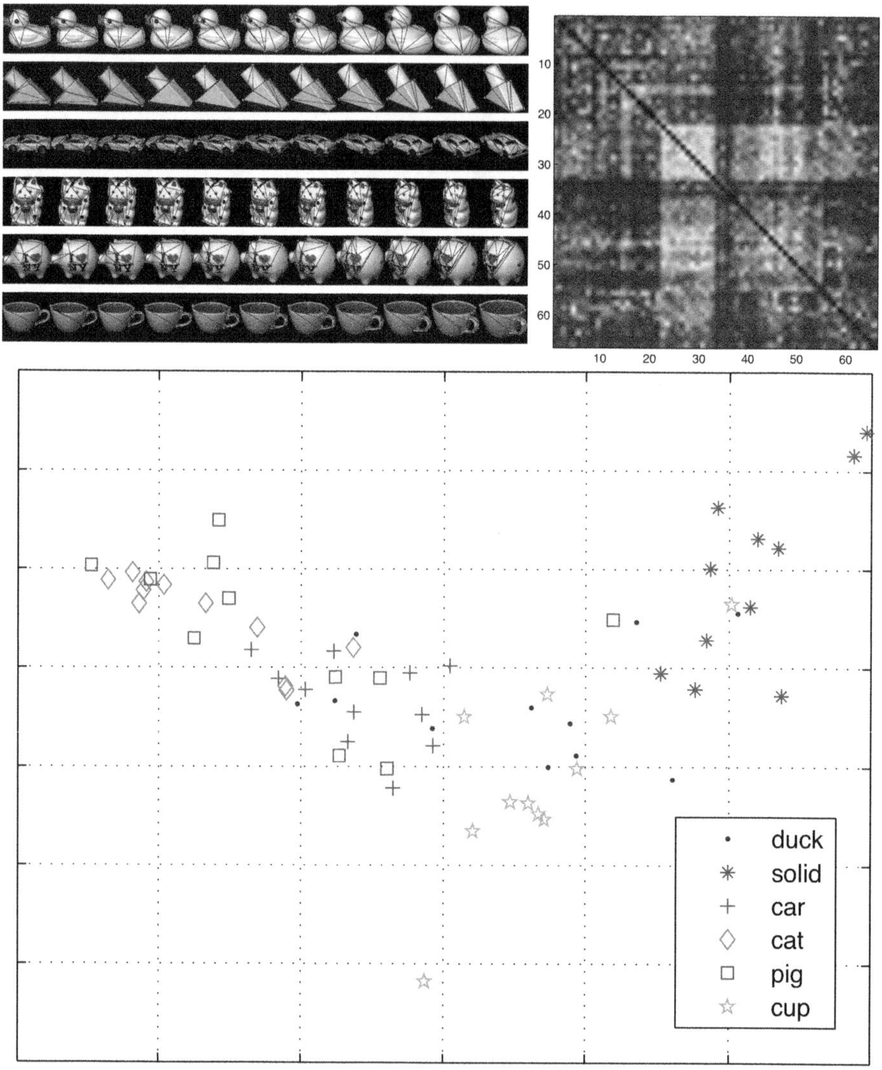

Fig. 9. Top row: Left, shape database; right, distance matrix. Bottom row: Multidimensional Scaling of the graph distances.

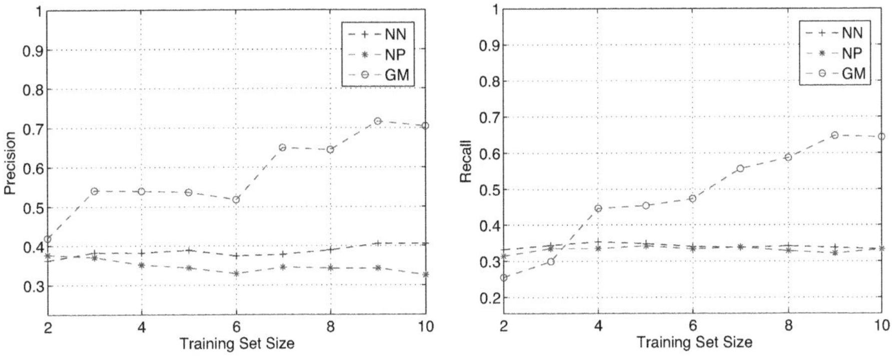

Fig. 10. Precision and Recall on the COIL-20 dataset

4 Conclusions

In this paper we have addressed to problem of learning a generative model for graphs from samples. The model is based on a naïve node independence assumptions, but mixes such simple models in order to capture node correlation. The correspondences are estimated using a fast sampling approach, the node and edge parameters are then learned using maximum likelihood estimates, while model selection adopts a minimum descriptor length principle.

Experiments performed on a wide range of real world object recognition tasks as well as on synthetic data show that learning the graph structure gives a clear advantage over the isotropic behavior assumed by the vast majority of the approaches in the structural pattern recognition literature. In particular, the approach very clearly outperforms both the nearest neighbor and the nearest prototype rules regardless of the matching algorithm and the distance metric adopted.

References

1. Babai, L., Erdös, P., Selkow, S.M.: Random Graph Isomorphism. SIAM J. Comput. 9(3), 635–638 (1980)
2. Beichl, I., Sullivan, F.: Approximating the permanent via importance sampling with application to the dimer covering problem. J. Comput. Phys. 149(1), 128–147 (1999)
3. Bonev, B., et al.: Constellations and the Unsupervised Learning of Graphs. In: Escolano, F., Vento, M. (eds.) GbRPR. LNCS, vol. 4538, pp. 340–350. Springer, Heidelberg (2007)
4. Bunke, H., et al.: Graph Clustering Using the Weighted Minimum Common Supergraph. In: Hancock, E.R., Vento, M. (eds.) GbRPR 2003. LNCS, vol. 2726, pp. 235–246. Springer, Heidelberg (2003)
5. Cour, T., Srinivasan, P., Shi, J.: Balanced graph matching. In: Advances in NIPS (2006)

6. Friedman, N., Koller, D.: Being Bayesian about Network Structure. Machine Learning 50(1-2), 95–125 (2003)
7. He, X.C., Yung, N.H.C.: Curvature scale space corner detector with adaptive threshold and dynamic region of support. In: Proceedings of the Pattern Recognition, 17th International Conference on (ICPR 2004), vol. 2, pp. 791–794. IEEE Computer Society, Washington, DC, USA (2004)
8. Luo, B., Hancock, E.R.: A spectral approach to learning structural variations in graphs. Pattern Recognition 39, 1188–1198 (2006)
9. Nene, S.A., Nayar, S.K., Murase, H.: Columbia Object Image Library (COIL-20). Technical report (February 1996)
10. Pelillo, M.: Replicator equations, maximal cliques, and graph isomorphism. em Neural Computation 11(8), 1933–1955 (1999)
11. Rabbat, M.G., Figueiredo, M.A.T., Nowak, R.D.: Network Inference From Co-Occurrences. IEEE Trans. Information Theory 54(9), 4053–4068 (2008)
12. Siddiqi, K., et al.: Retrieving Articulated 3D Models Using Medial Surfaces. Machine Vision and Applications 19(4), 261–274 (2008)
13. Sinkhorn, R.: A relationship between arbitrary positive matrices and double stochastic matrices. Ann. Math. Stat. 35, 876–879 (1964)
14. Torsello, A., Hancock, E.R.: Learning Shape-Classes Using a Mixture of Tree-Unions. IEEE Trans. Pattern Anal. Machine Intell. 28(6), 954–967 (2006)
15. Torsello, A.: An Importance Sampling Approach to Learning Structural Representations of Shape. In: IEEE CVPR (2008)
16. Torsello, A., Dowe, D.: Learning a generative model for structural representations. In: Wobcke, W., Zhang, M. (eds.) AI 2008. LNCS (LNAI), vol. 5360, pp. 573–583. Springer, Heidelberg (2008)
17. Torsello, A., Hidovic-Rowe, D., Pelillo, M.: Polynomial-time metrics for attributed trees. IEEE Trans. Pattern Anal. Mach. Intell. 27, 1087–1099 (2005)
18. White, D., Wilson, R.C.: Spectral Generative Models for Graphs. In: Int. Conf. Image Analysis and Processing, pp. 35–42. IEEE Computer Society, Los Alamitos (2007)

An Information Theoretic Approach to Learning Generative Graph Prototypes

Lin Han, Edwin R. Hancock, and Richard C. Wilson

Department of Computer Science, University of York

Abstract. We present a method for constructing a generative model for sets of graphs by adopting a minimum description length approach. The method is posed in terms of learning a generative supergraph model from which the new samples can be obtained by an appropriate sampling mechanism. We commence by constructing a probability distribution for the occurrence of nodes and edges over the supergraph. We encode the complexity of the supergraph using the von-Neumann entropy. A variant of EM algorithm is developed to minimize the description length criterion in which the node correspondences between the sample graphs and the supergraph are treated as missing data.The maximization step involves updating both the node correspondence information and the structure of supergraph using graduated assignment. In the experimental part, we demonstrate the practical utility of our proposed algorithm and show that our generative model gives good graph classification results. Besides, we show how to perform graph clustering with Jensen-Shannon kernel and generate new sample graphs.

1 Introduction

Relational graphs provide a convenient means of representing structural patterns. Examples include the arrangement of shape primitives or feature points in images, molecules and social networks. Whereas most of traditional pattern recognition and machine learning is concerned with pattern vectors, the issue of how to capture variability in graph, tree or string representations has received relatively little attention in the literature. The main reason for the lack of progress is the difficulty in developing representations that can capture variations in graph-structure. This variability can be attributed to a) variations in either node or edge attributes, b) variations in node or edge composition and c) variations in edge-connectivity.

This trichotomy provides a natural framework for analyzing the state-of-the-art in the literature. Most of the work on Bayes nets in the graphical models literature can be viewed as modeling variations in node or edge attributes [1]. Examples also include the work of Christmas et al.[2] and Bagdanov et al. [3] who both use Gaussian models to capture variations in edge attributes. The problems of modeling variations in node and edge composition are more challenging since they focus on modeling the structure of the graph rather than its attributes.

M. Pelillo and E.R. Hancock (Eds.): SIMBAD 2011, LNCS 7005, pp. 133–148, 2011.

The problem of learning edge structure is probably the most challenging of those listed above. Broadly speaking there are two approaches to characterizing variations in edge structure for graphs. The first of these is graph spectral, while the second is probabilistic. In the case of graph spectra, many of the ideas developed in the generative modeling of shape using principal components analysis can be translated relatively directly to graphs using simple vectorization procedures based on the correspondences conveyed by the ordering of Laplacian eigenvectors [5,4]. Although these methods are simple and effective, they are limited by the stability of the Laplacian spectrum under perturbations in graph-structure. The probabilistic approach is potentially more robust, but requires accurate correspondence information to be inferred from the available graph structure. If this is to hand, then a representation of edge structure can be learned. To date the most effective algorithm falling into this category exploits a part-based representation [8].

In this paper, we focus on the third problem and aim to learn a generative model that can be used to describe the distribution of structural variations present in a set of sample graphs, and in particular to characterize the variations of the edge structure present in the set. We follow Torsello and Hancock [6] and pose the problem as that of learning a generative supergraph representation from which we can sample. However, their work is based on trees, and since the trees are rooted the learning process can be effected by performing tree merging operations in polynomial time. This greedy strategy does not translate tractably to graphs where the complexity becomes exponential, and we require different strategies for learning and sampling. Torsello and Hancock realize both using edit operations, here on the other hand we use a soft-assign method for optimization and then generate new instances by Gibbs sampling.

Han, Wilson and Hancock propose a method of learning a supergraph model in [23] where they don't take into account the complexity of the supergraph model. Here, we take an information theoretic approach to estimating the supergraph structure by using a minimum description length criterion. By taking into account the overall code-length in the model, MDL allows us to select a supergraph representation that trades-off goodness-of-fit with the observed sample graphs against the complexity of the model. We adopt the probabilistic model in [7] to furnish the required learning framework and encode the complexity of the supergraph using its von-Neumann entropy[11] (i.e. the entropy of its Normalized Laplacian eigenvalues). Finally, a variant of EM algorithm is developed to minimize the total code-length criterion, in which the correspondences between the nodes of the sample graphs and those of the supergraph are treated as missing data. In the maximization step, we update both the node correspondence information and the structure of supergraph using graduated assignment. This novel technique is applied to a large database of object views, and used to learn class prototypes that can be used for the purposes of object recognition.

The remainder of this paper is organized as follows. Section 2 outlines the probabilistic framework which describes the distribution of the graph data. Section 3 explains how we encode our model so as to formulate the problem in hand in a minimum description length setting. In Section 4, we present the EM algorithm for minimizing the code-length. Section 5 provides experimental results that support our approach. Finally, section 6 offers some conclusions.

2 Probabilistic Framework

We are concerned with learning a structural model represented in terms of a so-called supergraph that can capture the variations present in a sample of graphs. In Torsello and Hancock's work [6] this structure is found by merging the set of sample trees, and so each sample tree can be obtained from it by edit operations. Here, on the other hand, we aim to estimate an adjacency matrix that captures the frequently occurring edges in the training set. To commence our development we require the *a posteriori* probabilities of the sample graphs given the structure of the supergraph and the node correspondences between each sample graph and the supergraph. To compute these probabilities we use the method outlined in [7].

Let the set of sample of graphs be $\mathcal{G} = \{G_1, ...G_i, ...G_N\}$, where the graph indexed i is $G_i = (V_i, E_i)$ with V_i the node-set and E_i the edge-set. Similarly, the supergraph which we aim to learn from this data is denoted by $\Gamma = (V_\Gamma, E_\Gamma)$, with node-set V_Γ and edge-set E_Γ. Further, we represent the structure of the two graphs using a $|V_i| \times |V_i|$ adjacency matrix D^i for the sample graph G_i and a $|V_\Gamma| \times |V_\Gamma|$ adjacency matrix M for the supergraph model Γ. The elements of the adjacency matrix for the sample graph and those for the supergraph are respectively defined to be

$$D_{ab} = \begin{cases} 1 & \text{if } (a,b) \in E_D \\ 0 & \text{otherwise} \end{cases} , \quad M_{\alpha\beta} = \begin{cases} 1 & \text{if } (\alpha,\beta) \in E_\Gamma \\ 0 & \text{otherwise} \end{cases} . \tag{1}$$

We represent the correspondence matches between the nodes of the sample graph and the nodes of the supergraph using a $|V_i| \times |V_\Gamma|$ assignment matrix S^i which has elements

$$s^i_{a\alpha} = \begin{cases} 1 \text{ if } a \rightarrow \alpha \\ 0 \text{ otherwise} \end{cases} . \tag{2}$$

where $a \rightarrow \alpha$ implies that node $a \in V_i$ is matched to node $\alpha \in V_\Gamma$.

With these ingredients, according to Luo and Hancock [7] the *a posteriori* probability of the graphs G_i given the supergraph Γ and the correspondence indicators is

$$P(G_i|\Gamma, S^i) = \prod_{a \in V_i} \sum_{\alpha \in V_\Gamma} K^i_a \exp[\mu \sum_{b \in V_i} \sum_{\beta \in V_\Gamma} D^i_{ab} M_{\alpha\beta} s^i_{b\beta}] . \tag{3}$$

where

$$\mu = \ln \tfrac{1-P_e}{P_e} , \quad K^i_a = P_e^{|V_i| \times |V_\Gamma|} B^i_a . \tag{4}$$

In the above, P_e is the error rate for node correspondence and B^i_a is the probability of observing node a in graph G_i , the value of which depends only on the identity of the node a . $|V_i|$ and $|V_\Gamma|$ are the number of the nodes in graph G_i and supergraph Γ.

3 Model Coding Using MDL

Underpinning minimum description length is the principle that learning, or finding a hypothesis that explains some observed data and makes predictions about data yet unseen, can be viewed as finding a shorter code for the observed data [10,13,9]. To formalize this idea, we encode and transmit the observed data and the hypothesis, which in our case are respectively the sample graphs $\mathcal{G}$ and the supergraph structure Γ. This leads to a two-part message whose total length is given by

$$\mathcal{L}(\mathcal{G}, \Gamma) = LL(\mathcal{G}|\Gamma) + LL(\Gamma) . \tag{5}$$

3.1 Encoding Sample Graphs

We first compute the code-length of the graph data. For the sample graph-set $\mathcal{G} = \{ G_1, ...G_i, ...G_N \}$ and the supergraph Γ, the set of assignment matrices is $\mathcal{S} = \{S^1, ...S^i, ...S^N\}$ and these represent the correspondences between the nodes of the sample graphs and those of the supergraph. Under the assumption that the graphs in $\mathcal{G}$ are independent samples from the distribution, using the *a posteriori* probabilities from Section 2 the likelihood of the set of sample graphs is

$$P(\mathcal{G}|\Gamma, \mathcal{S}) = \prod_{G_i \in \mathcal{G}} \prod_{a \in V_i} \sum_{\alpha \in V_\Gamma} K_a^i \exp[\mu \sum_{b \in V_i} \sum_{\beta \in V_\Gamma} D_{ab}^i M_{\alpha\beta} s_{b\beta}^i] . \tag{6}$$

Instead of using the *Shannon-Fano code* [12], which is equivalent to the negative logarithm of the above likelihood function, we measure the code-length of the graph data using its average. Our reason is that if we adopt the former measure, then there is a bias to learning a complete supergraph that is fully connected. The reason will become clear later-on when we outline the maximization algorithm in Section 4, and we defer our justification until later. Thus, the graph code-length is $LL(\mathcal{G}|\Gamma) = -\frac{1}{|\mathcal{G}|} \sum_{G_i \in \mathcal{G}} \log P(G_i|\Gamma, S^i)$ which is the average over the set of sample graphs $\mathcal{G}$.

3.2 Encoding the Supergraph Model

Next, we require to compute a code-length to measure the complexity of the supergraph. For two-part codes the MDL principle does not give any guideline as to how to encode the hypotheses. Hence every code for encoding the supergraph structure is allowed, so long as it does not change with the sample size N. Here the code-length for describing supergraph complexity is chosen to be measured using the von-Neumann entropy [11]

$$H = \frac{-\sum_k \frac{\lambda_k}{2} \ln \frac{\lambda_k}{2}}{|V_\Gamma|} . \tag{7}$$

where $|V_\Gamma|$ is the number of nodes in the supergraph and λ_k are the eigenvalues of the normalized Laplacian matrix of the supergraph $\hat{L}$ whose elements are

$$\hat{L}_{\alpha\beta} = \begin{cases} 1 & \text{if } \alpha = \beta \\ -\frac{1}{\sqrt{T_\alpha T_\beta}} & \text{if } (\alpha, \beta) \in E_\Gamma \\ 0 & \text{otherwise} \end{cases} . \tag{8}$$

where $T_\alpha = \sum_{\xi \in V_\Gamma} M_{\alpha\xi}$ and $T_\beta = \sum_{\xi \in V_\Gamma} M_{\beta\xi}$. The normalized Laplacian matrix is commonly used as a graph representation and graph cuts [18,19] and its eigenvalues are in the range $0 \leq \lambda_k \leq 2$ [17]. Divided by 2, the value of $\frac{\lambda_k}{2}$ is constrained between 0 and 1, and the von-Neumann entropy derived thereby is an intrinsic property of graphs that reflects the complexity of their structures better than other measures. We approximate the entropy $-\frac{\lambda_k}{2} \ln \frac{\lambda_k}{2}$ by the quadratic entropy $\frac{\lambda_k}{2}(1 - \frac{\lambda_k}{2})$, to obtain

$$H = \frac{-\sum_k \frac{\lambda_k}{2} \ln \frac{\lambda_k}{2}}{|V_\Gamma|} \simeq \frac{\sum_k \frac{\lambda_k}{2}(1 - \frac{\lambda_k}{2})}{|V_\Gamma|} = \frac{\sum_k \lambda_k}{2|V_\Gamma|} - \frac{\sum_k \lambda_k^2}{4|V_\Gamma|} . \tag{9}$$

Using the fact that $Tr[\hat{L}^n] = \sum_k \lambda_k^n$, the quadratic entropy can be rewritten as

$$H = \frac{Tr[\hat{L}]}{2|V_\Gamma|} - \frac{Tr[\hat{L}^2]}{4|V_\Gamma|} . \tag{10}$$

Since the normalized Laplacian matrix $\hat{L}$ is symmetric and it has unit diagonal elements, then according to equation(8) for the trace of the normalized Laplacian matrix we have

$$Tr[\hat{L}] = |V_\Gamma| . \tag{11}$$

Similarly, for the trace of the square of the normalized Laplacian, we have

$$\begin{aligned} Tr[\hat{L}^2] &= \sum_{\alpha \in V_\Gamma} \sum_{\beta \in V_\Gamma} \hat{L}_{\alpha\beta} \hat{L}_{\beta\alpha} = \sum_{\alpha \in V_\Gamma} \sum_{\beta \in V_\Gamma} (\hat{L}_{\alpha\beta})^2 \\ &= \sum_{\substack{\alpha,\beta \in V_\Gamma \\ \alpha = \beta}} (\hat{L}_{\alpha\beta})^2 + \sum_{\substack{\alpha,\beta \in V_\Gamma \\ \alpha \neq \beta}} (\hat{L}_{\alpha\beta})^2 \\ &= |V_\Gamma| + \sum_{(\alpha,\beta) \in E_\Gamma} \frac{1}{T_\alpha T_\beta} . \end{aligned} \tag{12}$$

Substituting Equation(11) and (12) into Equation (10), the entropy becomes

$$H = \frac{|V_\Gamma|}{2|V_\Gamma|} - \frac{|V_\Gamma|}{4|V_\Gamma|} - \sum_{(\alpha,\beta) \in E_\Gamma} \frac{1}{4|V_\Gamma| \, T_\alpha T_\beta} = \frac{1}{4} - \sum_{(\alpha,\beta) \in E_\Gamma} \frac{1}{4|V_\Gamma| \, T_\alpha T_\beta} . \tag{13}$$

As a result, the approximated complexity of the supergraph depends on two factors. The first is the order of supergraph, i.e. the number of nodes of the supergraph. The second is the degree of the nodes of the supergraph.

Finally, by adding together the two contributions to the code-length, the overall code-length is

$$\mathcal{L}(\mathcal{G},\Gamma) = LL(\mathcal{G}|\Gamma) + LL(\Gamma) = \tag{14}$$
$$-\frac{1}{|\mathcal{G}|}\sum_{G_i\in\mathcal{G}}\sum_{a\in V_i}\log\{\sum_{\alpha\in V_\Gamma} K_a^i \exp[\mu\sum_{b\in V_i}\sum_{\beta\in V_\Gamma} D_{ab}^i M_{ab} s_{b\beta}^i]\} + \frac{1}{4} - \sum_{(\alpha,\beta)\in E_\Gamma}\frac{1}{4|V_\Gamma|\, T_\alpha T_\beta}\,.$$

Unfortunately, due to the mixture structure, the direct estimation of the supergraph structure M from the above code-length criterion is not tractable in closed-form. For this reason, we resort to using the expectation maximization algorithm.

4 Expectation-Maximization

Having developed our computational model which poses the problem of learning the supergraph as that of minimizing the code-length, in this section, we provide a concrete algorithm to locate the supergraph structure using our code-length criterion. The minimization of the code-length is equivalent to the maximization of its negative, and we develop an EM algorithm to realize the maximization. We view the node correspondence information between the sample graphs and supergraph as missing data, and regard the structure of the supergraph as the set of parameters to be estimated. In the two interleaved steps of the EM algorithm, the expectation step involves recomputing the *a posteriori* probability of node correspondence while the maximization step involves updating both the structure of the supergraph and the node correspondence information.

4.1 Weighted Code-Length Function

We follow Figueiredo and Jain's MDL setting of the EM algorithm [16] and make use of Luo and Hancock's log-likelihood function for correspondence matching. According to Luo and Hancock [7], treating the assignment matrix as missing data, the weighted log-likelihood function for observing a sample graph G_i, i.e. for it to have been generated by the supergraph Γ is

$$\bar{\Lambda}^{(n+1)}(G_i|\Gamma, S^{i,(n+1)}) = \sum_{a\in V_i}\sum_{\alpha\in V_\Gamma} Q_{a\alpha}^{i,(n)}\{\ln K_a^i + \mu\sum_{b\in V_i}\sum_{\beta\in V_\Gamma} D_{ab}^i M_{\alpha\beta}^{(n)} s_{b\beta}^{i,(n+1)}\}\,. \tag{15}$$

where the superscript n indicates that quantity is taken at iteration n of the EM algorithm and $Q^{i,(n)}$ is a matrix with elements $Q_{a\alpha}^{i,(n)}$ that are set equal to the *a posteriori* probability of node a in G_i being matched to node α in Γ at iteration n of the EM algorithm.

With the above likelihood function and the code-length developed in the previous section, Figueiredo and Jain's formulation of EM involves maximizing

$$\Lambda^{(n+1)}(\mathcal{G}|\Gamma,\mathcal{S}^{(n+1)}) = \frac{1}{|\mathcal{G}|}\sum_{G_i\in\mathcal{G}}\sum_{a\in V_i}\sum_{\alpha\in V_\Gamma} Q_{a\alpha}^{i,(n)}\{\ln K_a^i + \mu\sum_{b\in V_i}\sum_{\beta\in V_\Gamma} D_{ab}^i M_{\alpha\beta}^{(n)} s_{b\beta}^{i,(n+1)}\}$$
$$-\frac{1}{4} + \sum_{(\alpha,\beta)\in E_\Gamma}\frac{1}{4|V_\Gamma|\,T_\alpha^{(n)}T_\beta^{(n)}} \ . \qquad (16)$$

The expression above can be simplified since the first term under the curly braces contributes a constant amount

$$\sum_{G_i\in\mathcal{G}}\sum_{a\in V_i}\sum_{\alpha\in V_\Gamma} Q_{a\alpha}^{i,(n)}\ln K_a^i = \sum_{G_i\in\mathcal{G}}\sum_{a\in V_i}\ln K_a^i \ . \qquad (17)$$

Based on this observation, the critical quantity in determining the update direction is

$$\hat{\Lambda}^{(n+1)} = \qquad (18)$$
$$\frac{1}{|\mathcal{G}|}\sum_{G_i\in\mathcal{G}}\sum_{a\in V_i}\sum_{\alpha\in V_\Gamma}\sum_{b\in V_i}\sum_{\beta\in V_\Gamma} Q_{a\alpha}^{i,(n)} D_{ab}^i M_{\alpha\beta}^{(n)} s_{b\beta}^{i,(n+1)} - \frac{1}{4} + \sum_{(\alpha,\beta)\in E_\Gamma}\frac{1}{4|V_\Gamma|T_\alpha^{(n)}T_\beta^{(n)}} \ .$$

4.2 Maximization

In order to optimize our weighted code-length criterion, we use graduated assignment [15] to update both the assignment matrices $\mathcal{S}$ and the structure of the supergraph, i.e. the supergraph adjacency matrix M. The updating process is realized by computing the derivatives of $\hat{\Lambda}^{(n+1)}$, and re-formulating the underlying discrete assignment problem as a continuous one using softmax[14].

In the maximization step, we have two parallel iterative update equations. The first update mode involves softening the assignment variables, while the second aims to modify the edge structure in the supergraph. Supergraph edges that are unmatchable become disjoint by virtue of having weak connection weights and cease to play any significant role in the update process. Experiments show that the algorithm appears to be numerically stable and appears to converge uniformly.

Updating Assignment Matrices: To update the assignment matrices, we commence by computing the partial derivative of the weighted code-length function in Equation (18) with respect to the elements of the assignment matrices, which gives

$$\frac{\partial\hat{\Lambda}^{(n+1)}}{\partial s_{b\beta}^{i,(n+1)}} = \frac{1}{|\mathcal{G}|}\sum_{a\in V_i}\sum_{\alpha\in V_\Gamma} Q_{a\alpha}^{i,(n)} D_{ab}^i M_{\alpha\beta}^{(n)} \ . \qquad (19)$$

To ensure that the assignment variables remain constrained to lie within the rage [0,1], we adopt the soft-max update rule

$$s_{a\alpha}^{i,(n+1)} \longleftarrow \frac{\exp[\frac{1}{T}\frac{\partial \hat{\Lambda}^{(n+1)}}{\partial s_{a\alpha}^{i,(n+1)}}]}{\sum_{\alpha' \in V_\Gamma} \exp[\frac{1}{T}\frac{\partial \hat{\Lambda}^{(n+1)}}{\partial s_{a\alpha'}^{i,(n+1)}}]} \ . \tag{20}$$

The value of the temperature T in the update process has been controlled using a slow exponential annealing schedule of the form suggested by Gold and Rangarajan[15]. Initializing T^{-1} with a small positive value and allowing it to gradually increase, the assignment variable $s_{a\alpha}^{i,(n+1)}$ corresponding to the maximum $\frac{\partial \hat{\Lambda}^{(n+1)}}{\partial s_{a\alpha}^{i,(n+1)}}$ approaches 1 while the remainder approach 0.

Updating Supergraph Structure: The partial derivative of the weighted code-length function in Equation (18) with respect to the elements of the supergraph adjacency matrix is equal to

$$\frac{\partial \hat{\Lambda}^{(n+1)}}{\partial M_{\alpha\beta}^{(n)}} = \frac{1}{|\mathcal{G}|} \sum_{G_i \in \mathcal{G}} \sum_{a \in V_i} \sum_{b \in V_i} Q_{a\alpha}^{i,(n)} D_{ab}^{i} s_{b\beta}^{i,(n+1)} - \frac{1}{4|V_\Gamma|(T_\alpha^{(n)})^2} \sum_{(\alpha,\beta') \in E_\Gamma} \frac{1}{T_{\beta'}^{(n)}} \ . \tag{21}$$

The soft-assign update equation for the elements of the supergraph adjacency matrix is

$$M_{\alpha\beta}^{(n+1)} \longleftarrow \frac{\exp[\frac{1}{T}\frac{\partial \hat{\Lambda}^{(n+1)}}{\partial M_{\alpha\beta}^{(n)}}]}{\sum_{(\alpha',\beta') \in E_\Gamma} \exp[\frac{1}{T}\frac{\partial \hat{\Lambda}^{(n+1)}}{\partial M_{\alpha'\beta'}^{(n)}}]} \ . \tag{22}$$

In the case of the updating of the assignment matrix elements, in each row and each column of the recovered assignment matrix no more than one element can take on unit value. By contrast, in the case of the recovered supergraph adjacency matrix there may exist multiple elements in each row or column with a unit value. To deal with this problem, in practice we set a threshold, and then recover the adjacency matrix by setting all elements larger than the threshold to unity and set the remaining elements to zero. This is repeated each time we decrease the temperature T in the annealing schedule.

From Equation (21), it is interesting to note that the derivatives of $\hat{\Lambda}^{(n+1)}$ with respect to the elements of supergraph adjacency matrix are dependent on the frequency of sample-set edges that are in correspondence with the same supergraph edge. To illustrate this point, if we approximate the matrix Q using S, then the first term in Equation (21) becomes the expectation value of the permutated adjacency matrices for the sample graphs. As a result, the elements of the supergraph adjacency matrix reflect the frequency of corresponding edges in the sample-set. The thresholding process selects frequent edges and removes unfrequent ones.

Recall that in Section 3 we discussed the encoding of the sample graphs, and chose to use the average of *Shannon-Fano code*. We can now elucidate that the reason for this choice is that as the number of the sample graphs increases, for instance in the limit as the size of the graph sample-set $\mathcal{G}$ increases, i.e. $N \to \infty$, the sum of permuted adjacency matrices of the sample graphs might dominate the magnitude of the second term in Equation (21). Thus the update algorithm might induce a complete supergraph that is fully connected. Hence, we choose to use its average rather than its sum.

4.3 Expectation

In the expectation step of the EM algorithm, we compute the *a posteriori* correspondence probabilities for the nodes of the sample graphs to the nodes of the supergraph. Applying Bayes rule, the *a posteriori* correspondence probability for the nodes of the sample graph G_i at iteration $n+1$ are given by

$$Q_{a\alpha}^{i,(n+1)} = \frac{\exp[\sum_{b\in V_i}\sum_{\beta\in V_\Gamma} D_{ab}^i M_{\alpha\beta}^{(n)} s_{b\beta}^{i,(n)}]\pi_\alpha^{i,(n)}}{\sum_{\alpha'\in V_\Gamma}\exp[\sum_{b\in V_i}\sum_{\beta\in V_\Gamma} D_{ab}^i M_{\alpha'\beta}^{(n)} s_{b\beta}^{i,(n)}]\pi_{\alpha'}^{i,(n)}} . \tag{23}$$

In the above equation, $\pi_{\alpha'}^{i,(n)} = \langle Q_{a\alpha'}^{i,(n)}\rangle_a$, where $\langle\ \rangle_a$ means average over a.

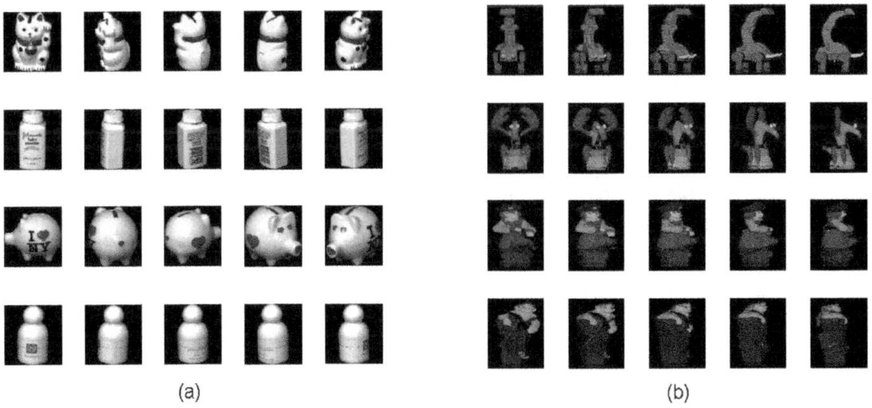

Fig. 1. (a)Example images in the COIL dataset. (b)Example images in the toys dataset.

5 Experiments

In this section, we report experimental results aimed at demonstrating the utility of our proposed generative model on real-world data. We use images from two datasets for experiments. The first dataset is the COIL [20] which consists of images of 4 objects, with 72 views of each object from equally spaced directions over 360°. We extract corner features from each image and use the detected feature points as nodes to construct sample graphs by Delaunay triangulation. The second dataset is a dataset consisting of views of toys, and contains images of 4 objects with 20 different views of each object. For this second dataset, the feature keypoints used to construct Delaunay graphs are extracted using the SIFT [21] detector. Some example images of the objects from these two datasets are given in Figure 1.

The first part of our experimental investigation aims to validate our supergraph learning method. We test our proposed algorithm on both of the two datasets and in order to better analyze our method, we initialize the supergraph in our EM algorithm with different structures. For the COIL dataset, we initialize the supergraph structure with the median graph, i.e. the sample graph with the largest *a posteriori* probability from the supergraph. On the other hand, to initialize the structure of the supergraph in the toys dataset, we match pairs of graphs from a same object using the discrete relaxation algorithm [22]. Then we concatenate(merge) the common structures over for the sample graphs from a same object to form an initial supergraph. The initial supergraph constructed in this way preserves more of the structural variations present in the set of sample graphs. The median graph, on the other hand, captures more of the common salient information. We match the sample graphs from the two datasets against their supergraphs both using graduated assignment[15] and initialize the assignment matrices in our algorithm with the resulting assignment matrices. Using these settings, we iterate the two steps of the EM algorithm 30 times, and observe how the complexity of the supergraph, the average log-likelihood of the sample graphs and the overall code-length vary with iteration number. Figures 2 and 3 respectively shows the results for the COIL and toys datasets illustrated in Figure 1.

From Figure 2(a) it is clear that the von-Neumann entropy of the supergraph increases as the iteration number increases. This indicates that the supergraph structure becomes more complex with an increasing number of iterations. Figure 2(b) shows that the average of the log-likelihood of the sample graphs increases during the iterations. Figure 2(c) shows that the overall-code length decreases and gradually converges as the number of iterations increases. For the toys dataset, the von-Neumann entropy in Figure 3(a) shows an opposite trend and decreases as the number of iterations increases. The reason for this is that the initial supergraph we used for this dataset, i.e. the concatenated supergraph, accommodates too much structural variation from the sample graphs. The reduction of the von-Neumann entropy implies some trivial edges are eliminated or relocated. As a result the supergraph structure both condenses and simplifies with increasing iteration number. Although the complexity of the graphs behaves differently, the average of the likelihood of the graphs in Figure 3(b) and the overall-code length in Figure 3(c) exhibit a similar behaviour to those for the COIL dataset. In other words, our algorithm behaves in a stable manner both increasing the likelihood of sample graphs and decreasing the overall code-length on both datasets.

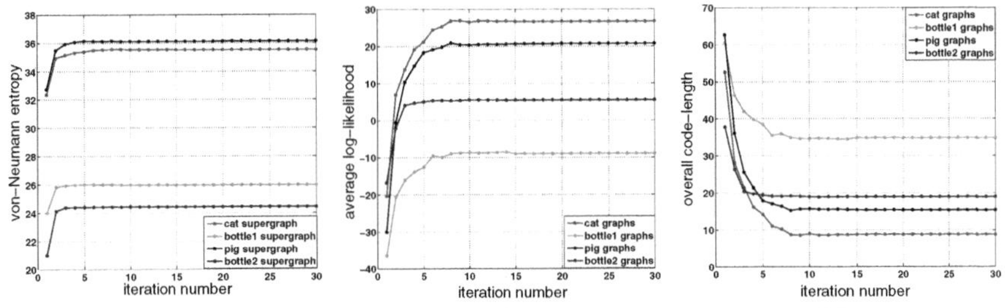

(a) (b) (c)

Fig. 2. COIL dataset: (a)variation of the complexity of the supergraph, encoded as von-Neumann entropy, during iterations, (b) variation of average log-likelihood of the sample graphs during iterations and (c) variation of the overall code-length during iterations

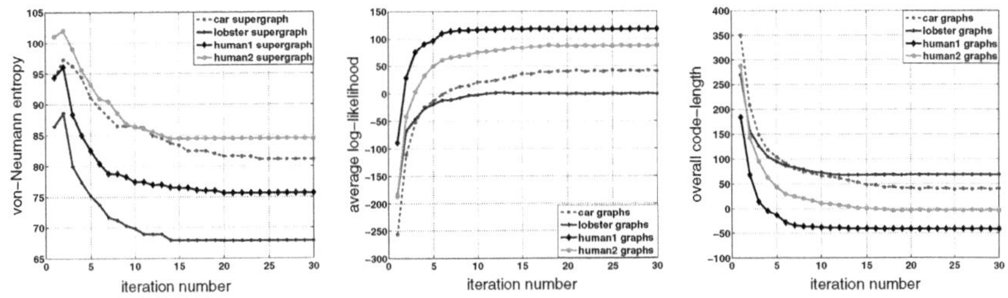

(a) (b) (c)

Fig. 3. Toy dataset: (a)variation of the complexity of the supergraph, encoded as von-Neumann entropy, during iterations, (b) variation of the average log-likelihood of the sample graphs during iterations and (c) variation of the overall code-length during iterations

Our second experimental goal is to evaluate the effectiveness of our learned generative model for classifying out-of-sample graphs. From the COIL dataset, we aim 1) to distinguish images of cats from pigs on the basis of their graph representations and 2) distinguish between images of different types of bottle. For the toys dataset, on the other hand, we aim to distinguish between images of the four objects. To perform these classification tasks, we learn a supergraph for each object class from a set of samples and use Equation (3) to compute the *a posteriori* probabilities for each graph from a separate (out-of-sample) test-set. The class-label of the test graph is determined by the class of the supergraph which gives the maximum *a posteriori* probability. The classification rate is the fraction of correctly identified objects computed using 10-fold cross validation. To perform the 10-fold cross validation for the COIL dataset, we index the 72 graphs from a same object according to their image view direction from 0° to 360°, and in each fold we select 7 or 8 graphs that are equally spaced over the angular interval as test-set, and the remainder are used as as sample-set for training. The similar applies for the toys dataset. For comparison, we have also investigated the results obtained using two alternative constructions of the supergraph. The first of these is the median graph or concatenated graph used to initialize our algorithm. The second is the supergraph learned without taking its complexity into account, which means, this supergraph is learned by maximizing the likelihood function of the sample graphs given in equation (6). Table 1 shows the classification results obtained with the three different supergraph constructions. From the three constructions, it is the supergraphs learned using the MDL principle that achieve the highest classification rates on all the three classification tasks.

Table 1. Comparison of the classification results. The bold values are the average classification rates from 10-fold cross validation, followed by their standard error.

Classification Rate	cat & pig	bottle1 & bottle2	four objects (Toys)
learned supergraph(by MDL)	**0.824** ± 0.033	**0.780** ± 0.023	**0.763** ± 0.026
median graph/concatenated graph	**0.669** ± 0.052	**0.651** ± 0.023	**0.575**± 0.020
learned supergraph	**0.807** ± 0.056	**0.699** ± 0.029	**0.725** ± 0.022

We have also compared our method with a feature-based classifier. Here we apply a K-nearest neighbor classifier to the Laplacian spectrum of the graph. We perform experiments that are reported on the classification task from the COIL dataset involving images of the cat and pig. To do this, we compute the eigenvalues of the Laplacian matrix of each sample graph, and encode the spectrum as a set of eigenvalues of decreasing magnitude. Using these Laplacian spectra, we find that 10-fold cross-validation with a 3NN classifier gives an average correct classification rate of 0.625. To investigate how our learned supergraph improves the classification result. We visualize the classifications results delivered by the two methods in Figure 4. The bottom shows the classification result obtained using our generative model. Here the test images are arranged into series according to their a posterior classification probabilities. The vertical line is the Bayes decision boundary between the two objects (cat to the left and pig to the right). Each images is labeled with its index and actual identity. In the top row we show the images that are classified in error using the 3-NN classifier. Object images 56cat, 26cat, 66cat, 36cat and 26pig that are misclassified using the 3NN, are correctly classified using our learned supergraph.

Next, we investigate how to embed graphs from different objects into pattern space so as to cluster the graphs according to object identity. Here we combine the Jensen-Shannon divergence with the von-Neumann entropy to measure the

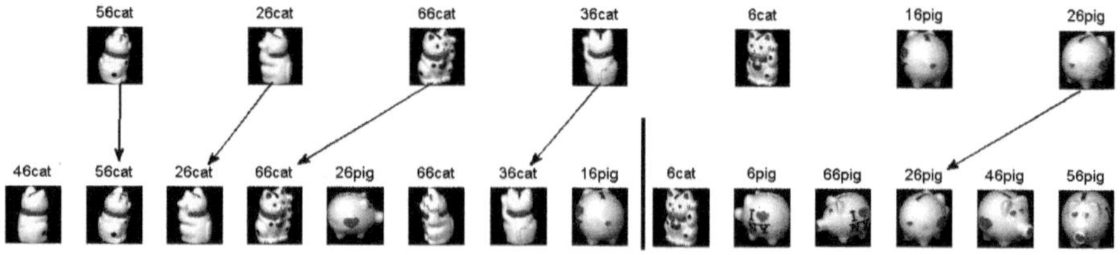

Fig. 4. Improvement of our classification result

pairwise dissimilarity between graphs. We then apply kernel PCA to the Jensen-Shannon kernel to effect the embedding. We construct a supergraph for each pair of graphs and measure their dissimilarity using the Jensen-Shannon divergence computed from the von-Neumann entropy,

$$JSD(G_i, G_j) = H(G_i \otimes G_j) - \frac{H(G_i) + H(G_j)}{2} \quad . \tag{24}$$

In the above equation, $G_i \otimes G_j$ represents the supergraph for graphs G_i, G_j, and $H(\cdot)$ denotes the von-Neumann entropy of the corresponding graph. From the Jensen-Shannon divergence we construct a kernel $K(G_i, G_j) = JSD(G_i, G_j)$ and with the kernel matrix we embed the graphs into pattern space by kernel PCA. In order to assess the quality of the method, we compare our embedding result with that obtained by using edit distance to measure graph dissimilarity. In Figure 5, we illustrate the Jensen-Shannon embedding onto a 2D space for two object clustering tasks. The first row shows the embeddings of graphs from images of cat (red) and pig (blue). The second row shows the embedding of the graphs from two types of bottle images (bottle1 as black scatter points and bottle2 as green scatter points). The left column displays the clustering results by edit distance and the right column gives the result by Jensen-Shannon divergence. It is clear from Figure 5 that the Jensen-Shannon kernel embedding gives better clustering results than the edit distance embedding. This is especially the case for the cat and pig objects, where the cat graphs and pig graphs are heavily overlapped in the edit-distance embedding.

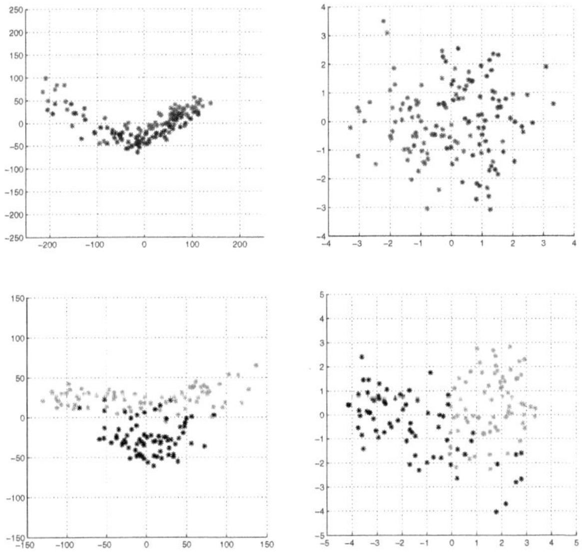

Fig. 5. Comparison of graph clusterings obtained from Jensen-Shannon kernel and edit distance. Row 1: cat (red) and pig (blue). Row 2: bottle1(black) and bottle2 (green). Column 1: edit distance and Column 2: Jensen-Shannon kernel.

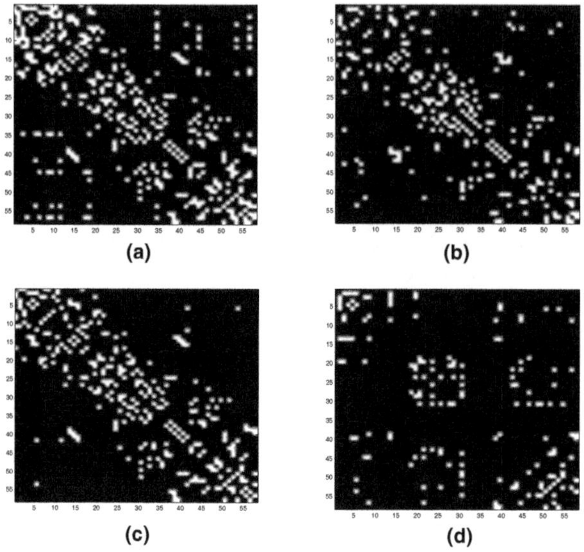

Fig. 6. The adjacency matrices of four graphs. (a) the learned supergraph, (b) a generated sample graph that has high likelihood, (c) the median graph, (d) a generated sample graph with low likelihood.

Finally, we explore whether our generative model can be used to generate new sample graphs. Given a supergraph structure, we use Gibbs sampling to generate some new samples. From the newly generated graphs, we select a graph that has high generating likelihood together with a graph that has low likelihood, and compare their structure with that of the median graph and the supergraph. We use black and white squares to indicate zero and unit entries respectively to represent the elements of the adjacency matrices. The adjacency matrices for the four graphs are shown in Figure 6. The example supergraph here is learned using Delaunay graphs from the 72 pig images. From Figure 6, it is clear that the supergraph, median graph and high likelihood sample graph have very similar structure. On the other hand, the low likelihood sample graph shows a very different structure. It is also important to note that the structure of the supergraph is more complex than that of the median graph, which supports our observation that the von-Neumann entropy in Figure 2(a) increases with iteration number.

6 Conclusion

In this paper, we have presented an information theoretic framework for learning a generative model of the variations in sets of graphs. The problem is posed as that of learning a supergraph. We provide a variant of EM algorithm to demonstrate how the node correspondence recover and supergraph structure estimation can be couched in terms of minimizing a description length criterion. Empirical results on real-world dataset support our proposed method by a) validating our learning algorithm and b) showing that our learned supergraph outperforms two alternative supergraph constructions. We also have illustrated how to embed graphs using supergraphs with Jensen-Shannon divergence and investigated the performance of our generative model on generating new sample graphs. Our future work will aim to fit a mixture of supergraph to data sampled from multiple classes to perform graph clustering.

References

1. Friedman, N., Koller, D.: Being Bayesian about network structure.A Bayesian approach to structure discovery in Bayesian networks. Machine Learning, 95–125 (2003)
2. Christmas, W.J., Kittler, J., Petrou, M.: Probabilistic feature labeling schemes: modeling compatibility coefficient distribution. Image and Vision Computing 14, 617–625 (1996)
3. Bagdanov, A.D., Worring, M.: First order Gaussian graphs for efficient structure classification. Pattern Recognition 36, 1311–1324 (2003)
4. Cootes, T.F., Edwards, G.J., Taylor, C.J.: Active Appearance Models. IEEE PAMI 23, 681–685 (2001)
5. Luo, B., Hancock, E.R.: A spectral approach to learning structural variations in graphs. Pattern Recognition 39, 1188–1198 (2006)
6. Torsello, A., Hancock, E.R.: Learning shape-classes using a mixture of tree-unions. IEEE PAMI 28, 954–967 (2006)
7. Luo, B., Hancock, E.R.: Structural graph matching using the EM alogrithm and singular value decomposition. IEEE PAMI 23, 1120–1136 (2001)
8. White, D., Wilson, R.C.: Parts based generative models for graphs. In: ICPR, pp. 1–4 (2008)
9. Rissanen, J.: Modelling by Shortest Data Description. Automatica, 465–471 (1978)
10. Rissanen., J.: Stochastic complexity in statistical inquiry. World Scientific, Singapore (1989)
11. Passerini, F., Severini, S.: The von neumann entropy of networks, arXiv:0812.2597 (2008)
12. Cover, T., Thomas, J.: Elements of Information Theory. John Wiley&Sons, New York (1991)
13. Grunwald, P.: Minimum Description Length Tutorial. In: Advances in Minimum Description Length: Theory and Applications (2005)
14. Bridle, J.S.: Training stochastic model recognition algorithms as networks can lead to maximum mutual information estimation of parameters. In: Advances in Neural Information Processing Systems, vol. 2, pp. 211–217 (1990)
15. Gold, S., Rangarajan, A.: A Graduated Assignment Algorithm for Graph Matching. IEEE PAMI 18, 377–388 (1996)
16. Figueiredo, M.A.T., Jain, A.K.: Unsupervised learning of finite mixture models. IEEE PAMI 24, 381–396 (2002)
17. Wilson, R.C., Zhu, P.: A study of graph spectra for comparing graphs and trees. Pattern Recognition 41, 2833–2841 (2008)
18. Shi, J., Malik, J.: Normalized cuts and image segmentation. In: CVPR, pp. 731–737 (1997)

19. Robles-Kelly, A., Hancock, E.R.: A riemannian approach to graph embedding. Pattern Recognition 40, 1042–1056 (2007)
20. Nene, S.A., Nayar, S.K., Murase, H.: Columbiaobjectimagelibrary (COIL100). Technical Report CUCS-006-96. Department of Computer Science, Columbia University (1996)
21. Lowe, D.G.: Distinctive image features from scale invariant keypoints. IJCV 99, 91–110 (2004)
22. Wilson, R.C., Hancock, E.R.: Structural matching by discrete relaxation. IEEE PAMI 19, 634–648 (1997)
23. Han, L., Wilson, R.C., Hancock, E.R.: A Supergraph-based Generative Model. In: ICPR, pp. 1566–1569 (2010)

Graph Characterization via Backtrackless Paths

Furqan Aziz, Richard C. Wilson, and Edwin R. Hancock

Department of Computer Science,
The University of York, YO10 5GH, UK
{furqan,wilson,erh}@cs.york.ac.uk

Abstract. Random walks on graphs have been extensively used for graph characterization. Positive kernels between labeled graphs have been proposed recently. In this paper we use *backtrackless* paths for gauging the similarity between graphs. We introduce *efficient* algorithms for characterizing both labeled and unlabeled graphs. First we show how to define efficient kernels based on backtrackless paths for labeled graphs. Second we show how the pattern vectors composed of backtrackless paths of different lengths can be use to characterize unlabeled graphs. The proposed methods are then applied to both labeled and unlabeled graphs.

Keywords: Backtrackless paths, Graph kernels, Graph Clustering.

1 Introduction

Many real world data such as texts, molecules, or shapes can be represented using graphs. It is for this reason that graph based methods are widely used in many applications including network analysis[17], world wide webs[18], and problems in machine learning[19]. To compare such objects, the problem then reduces to the problem of comparing graphs. However, subgraph isomorphism is known to be NP-complete, and so computing the exact solution can be computationally intractable. For this reason inexact and decomposition methods have been used instead. Inexact methods include the use of approximate methods to compute graph edit-distance [15,16]. Decomposition Methods include the idea of decomposing graphs into substructures such as paths, cycles, and trees. Similarity between graphs can be measured using frequencies of matching substructures.

For labeled graphs, kernel methods are becoming increasingly popular because of their high performance[10]. A number of kernels, defined on substructures such as paths, trees and cycles, have been proposed [4,3,1]. One of the most popular polynomial time algorithms for labeled graph is the random walk kernel[1]. The idea behind the random walk kernel is to measure the similarity between graphs based on the matching of random walks of different lengths. One of the problem with the random walk kernel is "tottering" which means that it can move in one direction and return to the same vertex instantly[8]. Mahá et al[8] have proposed a method for reducing tottering by transforming the graph into an equivalent directed graph that does not allow cycles of length 2 and then define a kernel on the transformed graph. The size of the transformed graph, however, is $|\mathcal{V}| + 2|\mathcal{E}|$, and in most cases computing such a kernel is not practical.

M. Pelillo and E.R. Hancock (Eds.): SIMBAD 2011, LNCS 7005, pp. 149–162, 2011.

Unlabeled graphs can be classified using feature vectors that can be constructed from the number of walks, cycles, or trees on a graph. Recently Peng et al[11,12,13] have proposed the use of the coefficients of the reciprocal of Ihara zeta function to characterize and measure the similarities between graphs. These coefficients are related to the number of prime cycles in a graph and can be computed from the eigenvalues of the adjacency matrix of the oriented line graph. The method, however, cannot successfully classify graphs which have branches, for example graphs of chemical compounds. Moreover, computing such pattern vector can also be computationally expensive as the size of oriented line graph can be $O(\mathcal{V}^2)$ in the worst case.

These disadvantages in existing graph clustering methods are due to competing requirements in their design[4]. Not only should a kernel give good measure of similarity between graphs, it should also both have the polynomial time complexity and applied to a large class of graphs of different structures. The problem with the random walk kernel is its expressiveness which can be improved by both avoiding cycles of length 2 and by label enrichment[8]. However such an extension can badly increase the execution time of the kernel, making it impractical to apply it to dense graphs. In this paper our goal is to efficiently classify graphs with higher accuracy based on backtrackless walks on graphs. We use backtrackless kernels for labeled graphs, whose worst case time complexity is the same as that of the random walk kernel. For unlabeled graph, we use a feature vector composed of backtrackless walks of different length. To evaluate the performance of the backtrackless paths, we apply the proposed methods on both synthetic and real world data and compare its accuracy with existing methods. Finally we give a comparison of the run time of our approach with that of alternative approaches.

2 Backtrackless Walks on Graphs

A graph G consists of a finite set of vertices (or nodes) $\mathcal{V}$ and a finite set of edges $\mathcal{E} \subset \mathcal{V} \times \mathcal{V}$. In this paper n denotes the size of the graph, i.e., the number of vertices in the graph, and m denotes the number of edges in the graph. For a labeled graph there is additionally a set of labels $\mathcal{L}$ along with a function $l : \mathcal{V} \cup \mathcal{E} \rightarrow \mathcal{L}$ which assigns a label to each edge and/or vertex of the graph. A labeled graph can be vertex-labeled which assigns labels to the vertices only, edge-labeled which assigns labels to the edges only, or fully labeled which assigns labels to both edges and vertices. Any edge-labeled(or vertex-labeled) graph can be considered fully labeled if we consider that all of the edges(or vertices) of the graph are assigned the same label. Similarly an unlabeled graph can be considered as a labeled graph, that assigns the same label to each vertex and edge. In this paper we will consider the case of both labeled and unlabeled graphs.

A random walk w in a graph is a sequence of vertices $v_1, v_2, ...v_k$ where $v_i \in \mathcal{V}$ such that $(v_i, v_{i+1}) \in \mathcal{E}$. A walk has backtracking if $v_{i-1} = v_{i+1}$, for some i, $2 \leq i \leq k-1$, where k is the length of the walk. A walk is backtrackless if it has no backtracking. Gärtner et al[1] and Kashima et al[6] have defined graph kernels based on matching random walks in graphs. In this paper our focus is to efficiently classify graphs based on backtrackless paths of the graph. The motivation here is that the random walk totters and can add noise to the representation of the graph. Figure 2 shows an example of the difference between the number of backtrackless walks and random walks of length 3 in the graph of Figure 1. The i, jth entry in Figure 2(a) shows the number of random walks of length 3 from vertex i to vertex j. Similarly, the i, jth entry of Figure 2(b) shows the number of backtrackless walks of length 3 from vertex i to vertex j. These matrices show that there are a total of 74 random walks of length 3 in the graph of Figure 1(a), while there are only 26 backtrackless walks of same length in the graph of Figure 1(a). In particular there are 6 random walks of length 3 from vertex 1 to vertex 4, which are $(1, 2, 1, 4), (1, 5, 1, 4), (1, 4, 1, 4), (1, 2, 3, 4), (1, 4, 3, 4), (1, 4, 5, 4)$. Out of these random walks only $(1, 2, 3, 4)$ is a backtrackless walk, and therefore there is only one backtrackless walk of length 3 from node 1 to node 4. Now suppose that the vertices 1, 2, 3, 4, 5 of the graph are assigned the labels x, y, x, y, w respectively. Then the sequence x-y-x-y might correspond to path (1,4,1,4) or (1,2,3,4). By preventing tottering, the first option can be eliminated.

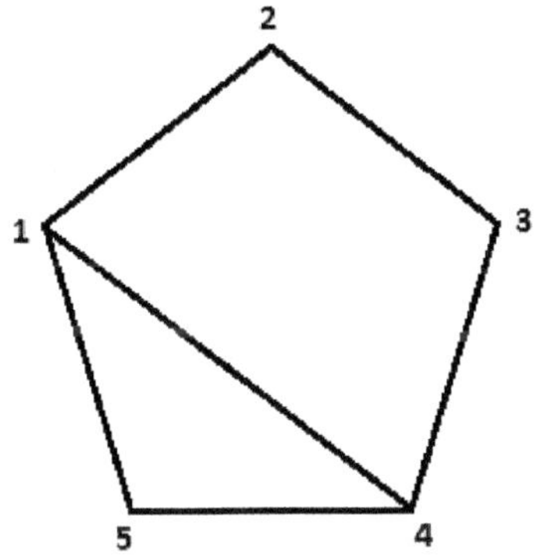

$$\begin{bmatrix} 0 & 1 & 0 & 1 & 1 \\ 1 & 0 & 1 & 0 & 0 \\ 0 & 1 & 0 & 1 & 0 \\ 1 & 0 & 1 & 0 & 1 \\ 1 & 0 & 0 & 1 & 0 \end{bmatrix}$$

(a) Graph (b) Adjacency Matrix

Fig. 1. Graph and its adjacency matrix

One way of locating backtrackless walks of different lengths, is to transform the graph to a form that enforces a backtrackless structure. One such transformation is the Perron-Frobenius operator which converts a graph into a oriented line graph. The oriented line graph is of size $2m$. The i, jth entry of kth power of the adjacency matrix of a oriented line graph gives the number of backtrackless paths of length k from vertex i to vertex j if $i \neq j$, while it gives the number of prime cycles of length k starting at vertex i if $i = j$. A prime cycle is a cycle with no backtrackless paths and no tails. A cycle has a tail if any of its cyclic permutation has backtracking.

To construct the oriented line graph $OLG(\mathcal{V}_L, \mathcal{E}_L)$ of the original graph $G(\mathcal{V}, \mathcal{E})$, we first convert the graph into its equivalent digraph, $DG(\mathcal{V}_D, \mathcal{E}_D)$, by replacing each edge by a pair of directed arcs. The oriented line graph is the directed graph whose vertex set $\mathcal{V}_L$ and edge set $\mathcal{E}_L$ are defined as follows

$$\begin{bmatrix} 2 & 5 & 1 & 6 & 4 \\ 5 & 0 & 4 & 1 & 2 \\ 1 & 4 & 0 & 5 & 2 \\ 6 & 1 & 5 & 2 & 4 \\ 4 & 2 & 2 & 4 & 2 \end{bmatrix} \quad \begin{bmatrix} 2 & 1 & 1 & 1 & 0 \\ 1 & 0 & 1 & 1 & 2 \\ 1 & 1 & 0 & 1 & 2 \\ 1 & 1 & 1 & 2 & 0 \\ 0 & 2 & 2 & 0 & 2 \end{bmatrix}$$

(a) Random Walks (b) Backtrackless Walks

Fig. 2. Random Walks vs Backtrackless walks of length 3

$\mathcal{V}_L = \mathcal{E}_D,$
$\mathcal{E}_L = \{((u,v),(v,w)) \in \mathcal{E}_D \times \mathcal{E}_D : u,v,w \in \mathcal{V}, u \neq w\}$

Figure 3(a) shows an example of a graph, Figure 3(b) shows its equivalent digraph, and Figure 3(c) shows the oriented line graph of the original graph. A path between any two different vertices in the oriented line graph corresponds to a backtrackless path in the original graph, while a path between the same vertices corresponds to a prime cycle in the original graph.

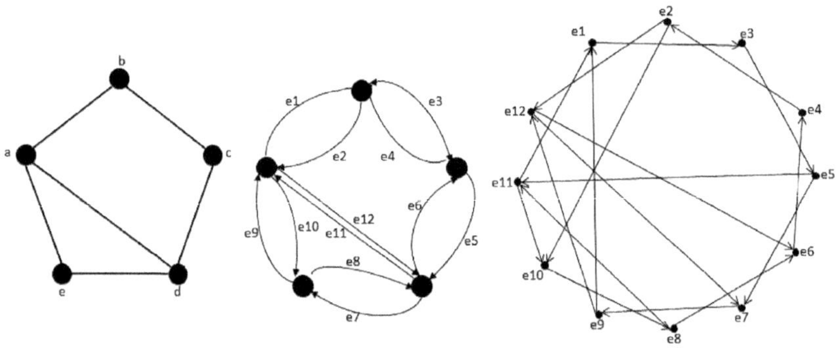

(a) Graph (b) Diagraph (c) Oriented line graph

Fig. 3. Graph and its oriented line graph

Our objective in this paper is to use backtrackless paths for classifying graphs. Mahé et al have proposed a graph kernel based on backtrackless path for labeled graphs. However the cost of computing their kernel is very high and so in most cases it cannot be applied to practical problems. In this paper, we propose efficient methods for classifying both labeled and unlabeled graphs. We propose a kernel for labeled graphs based on backtrackless paths whose time complexity is the same as that of the random walk kernel. For unlabeled graphs we use pattern vectors constructed from backtrackless paths of different lengths.

3 Kernels for Labeled Graphs

In this section we review the literature on existing kernels for labeled graphs and their extensions. A graph kernel is a positive definite kernel on the set of graphs $\mathcal{G}$. For such kernel $\kappa : \mathcal{G} \times \mathcal{G} \to \mathbb{R}$ it is known that a map $\Phi : \mathcal{G} \to \mathcal{H}$ into a Hilbert space $\mathcal{H}$ exists, such that $\kappa(G, G') = \langle \Phi(G), \Phi(G') \rangle$ for all $G, G' \in \mathcal{G}$ [10]. Graph kernels can be defined on random walks [1], shortest paths [4], cyclic patterns [3], and trees [2] in the graph. In this paper we propose an efficient method for computing graph kernels based on backtrackless paths of the graph.

Gärtner et al [1] have defined graph kernel using random walks, which is based on the idea of counting the number of matching walks in two input graphs. Their kernel for the two input graphs $G_1 = (V_1, E_1)$ and $G_2 = (V_2, E_2)$ is given by the direct product graph $G_\times$:

$$\kappa(G_1, G_2) = \sum_{i,j=1}^{|V_\times|} \sum_{k=0}^{\infty} \epsilon_k \left[A_\times^k\right]_{i,j} \tag{1}$$

where $A_\times$ is the adjacency matrix of $G_\times = (V_\times, E_\times)$, which is defined as

$$\begin{gathered} V_\times(G_1 \times G_2) = \{(v_1, v_2) \in V_1 \times V_2 : label(v_1) = label(v_2)\} \\ E_\times(G_1 \times G_2) = \{((u_1, u_2), (v_1, v_2)) \in V_\times^2(G_1 \times G_2) : \\ (u_1, v_1) \in E_1 \wedge (u_2, v_2) \in E_2 \wedge label(u_1, v_1) = label(u_2, v_2)\} \end{gathered}$$

and $(\epsilon_1, \epsilon_2, \epsilon_3, ...)$ is a sequence of constants, chosen such that (1) converges.

As pointed out in [8,4], one of the problem with the random walk graph kernel is that of tottering. A tottering walk can move to one direction and then instantly return to the starting position. This results in many redundant paths in the graphs, which may decrease the discriminative powers of the kernels. To reduce tottering, Mahé et al[8] have defined a kernel based on backtrackless walks instead of random walks. They first transform the graph into a directed graph of size $n + 2m$ that captures the backtrackless structure of the original graph. They then define the kernel on the transformed graphs. Since the oriented line graph is also related to the backtrackless structure of the graph with a size of only $2m$, the same kernel can be defined on an oriented line graph. Let T_1 and T_2 be the adjacency matrices of the oriented line graphs of the graphs G_1 and G_2 respectively. The kernel can be defined as

$$\kappa(G_1, G_2) = \sum_{i,j=1}^{|\mathcal{V}_\times|} \sum_{k=0}^{\infty} \epsilon_k \left[T_\times^k\right]_{i,j} \tag{2}$$

where $T_\times$ is the adjacency matrix of the direct product graph of T_1 and T_2.

The use of backtrackless kernels in practice is, however, limited because of the computational cost of such kernels. The problem is the size of the transformed graph which is $O(m_1 m_2)$. In the worst case when $m = O(n^2)$, the size of the product graph can be $O(n_1^2 n_2^2)$. In such cases the computational cost of computing the kernel can be very high and computing such kernels in most cases may not be feasible.

To overcome this problem, in this paper we use a method that efficiently computes kernels on backtrackless walks using the adjacency matrix of the original graph instead of the transformed graph. To commence, we introduce an $n \times n$ matrix A_k whose (i,j)th entry is given by

$$(A_k)_{i,j} = \begin{cases} \text{number of paths in G of length k with no backtracking} \\ \text{starting at i and ending at j.} \end{cases} \tag{3}$$

Here i, j run over the vertices of G. Since there is no backtracking in paths of unit length, we define $A_1 = A$. To locate the paths of length $k \geq 2$, we use the following theorem [21]

Theorem 1. *(Recursions for the matrices A_k). Let A be the adjacency matrix of a simple graph G and Q be a $n \times n$ diagonal matrix whose ith diagonal entry is the degree of the ith node minus 1. Then*

$$A_k = \begin{cases} A & \text{if } k = 1 \\ A^2 - (Q + I) & \text{if } k = 2 \\ A_{k-1}A - A_{k-2}Q & \text{if } k \geq 3 \end{cases} \tag{4}$$

The proof of the above theorem can be found in [21]. We now define a kernel on A_m as

$$\kappa\left(G_1, G_2\right) = \sum_{i,j=1}^{|V_\times|} \sum_{k=0}^{\infty} \epsilon_k \left[(A_\times)_k\right]_{i,j} \tag{5}$$

where $A_\times$ is the product graph and the (i,j)th entry of $(A_\times)_k$ is the number of backtrackless paths of length k in G, starting from vertex i and ending at vertex j. Since kernel defined here is same as one defined in 2, therefore it is valid positive definite kernel if we choose a sequence of positive coefficients ϵ_i such that (5) converges[5]. Here we propose to choose $\epsilon_i = \epsilon^i$ for $i \geq 1$ and $0 < \epsilon < 1$. The value of ϵ depends on the particular dataset that we are using. In practice, we select a smaller value for dense graphs and a larger value for sparse graphs. This is because for dense graphs, the paths with larger length add more noise to the structural representation of the graph.

The graph kernel introduced here can be computed efficiently. This is because the size of the product graph in this case is $O(n_1 n_2)$ which is much smaller than the size of the product graph for the oriented line graph or the transformed graph used by Mahé[8]. By using dynamic programming, in which we first compute A_1 and A_2, and then iteratively compute A_k, for $k \geq 3$, we can speed up the running time of our kernel.

4 Pattern Vectors for Unlabeled Graphs

In this section we review methods for measuring the similarity between unlabeled graphs. Although kernels on random walks and other substructures can be efficiently applied to labeled graphs, where the number of unique labels assigned to nodes and edges are sufficiently large, such kernels can be very inefficient in the case of unlabeled graphs. For unlabeled graphs, the size of the product graph is $n_1 \times n_2$. Computing the higher powers of such matrices can be computationally very expensive.

One way to overcome this problem is to first define a vector representation for a graph based on the frequency with which a particular substructure appears in the graph, and then take the dot product of these vectors for different graphs to gauge the similarity between unlabeled graphs[7,20]. Recently Peng et al[11,12,13] have used pattern vectors constructed from the coefficients of the reciprocal of Ihara zeta function. The Ihara zeta function associated to a finite connected graph G is defined to be a function of $u \in \mathbb{C}$ [23]

$$\zeta_G(u) = \prod_{c \in [C]} \left(1 - u^{l(c)}\right)^{-1} \tag{6}$$

The product is over equivalence classes of primitive closed backtrackless, tail-less cycles. Here $l(c)$ is the length of the cycle c. The Ihara zeta function can also be written in the form of a determinant expression [22]

$$\zeta_G(u) = \frac{1}{\det(I - uT)} \tag{7}$$

where T is the Perron-Frobenius operator. So the reciprocal of the Ihara zeta function can be written in terms of the determinant of the matrix T, and hence in the form of a polynomial of degree 2m:

$$\zeta_G(u)^{-1} = \det(I - uT) = c_0 + c_1 u + c_2 u^2 + c_3 u^3 + ... + c_{2m} u^{2m} \tag{8}$$

Peng et al [11] have used these coefficients to cluster unlabeled graphs. Since these coefficients are related to the prime cycles, such a feature vector reduces tottering.

There are two problems with pattern vectors composed of Ihara coefficients. The first problem is the computational cost of computing such vectors. The Ihara coefficients can be computed from the eigenvalues of the oriented line graph[14]. The worst case complexity for finding such vectors of fixed length can be $O(n^6)$. The second problem is that the pattern vectors constructed from the Ihara coefficients may fail to convey meaning in case where the graph has branches. The reason is that the Ihara zeta function is defined on the number of prime cycles of the graph and ignores the branches in the graph. To avoid the second problem here we use pattern vector based on the frequencies of backtrackless paths of different lengths in the graph. We propose to use the pattern vector $\boldsymbol{v_G} = [\epsilon_1 l_1, \epsilon_2 l_2, ..., \epsilon_k l_k]$, where l_i is the number of backtrackless paths of length i and $(\epsilon_1, \epsilon_2, ..., \epsilon_k)$ is a sequence of weights. Since paths with larger length may give some redundant information, we assign these weights in such a way that the number of paths with smaller length get higher weights. Here we propose $\epsilon_i = \epsilon^i$ for $i \geq 1$ and $0 < \epsilon < 1$. The value of l_1 can be computed from the adjacency matrix of the graph. To compute l_k for $i \geq 2$, we can use the adjacency matrix of the oriented line graph. So the coefficients l_k for $k \geq 2$ can be computed as

$$l_k = \sum_{i,j=1}^{|\mathcal{V}|} \left[T^{k-1}\right]_{i,j} \tag{9}$$

Since we are computing our feature vector using the adjacency matrix of oriented line graph which captures the backtrackless structure of the graph, the pattern vector introduced here can be applied to a larger class of graphs. The worst case computational cost of computing the feature vector is, however, $O(n^6)$. To reduce the computational cost, we use A_k defined in (3) instead of T. So we compute each l_k, for $k \geq 1$, as

$$l_k = \sum_{i,j=1}^{|\mathcal{V}|} [A_k]_{i,j} \tag{10}$$

Using (10), the cost of computing the proposed pattern vector of some constant length is $O(n^3)$, which is smaller then the cost of computing pattern vectors from coefficients of Ihara zeta function.

5 Experiments

In this section we apply our proposed method to both real and synthetic datasets. The purpose of the experiments on synthetic dataset is to evaluate whether the backtrackless walks to distinguish between different graphs under controlled structural errors. For the real-world data we have selected two different datasets. i.e., MUTAG[9] and COIL.

5.1 Synthetic Data

We commence by investigating the relationship between graph edit distance and the Euclidean distance between pattern vectors composed of Ihara coefficients. The edit distance between two graphs G_1 and G_2 is the minimum edit cost taken over all sequences of edit operations that transform G_1 to G_2. In our experiment we choose a seed graph and construct a new graph by randomly deleting certain number of edges from the seed graph. The edit cost between seed graph and the newly generated graph is then equal to the number of edges deleted.

To start with, we generate 100 random points in Euclidean space and construct a Delaunay triangulation over the point positions. We use the resulting graph with 100 nodes and 288 edges as our seed graph. We next generate 1000 graphs by randomly deleting up to 30 edges of the seed graph. For each graph we compute backtrackless paths of length up to 10 using (10) and construct a pattern vector in the form $\boldsymbol{v_G} = [\epsilon_1 l_1, \epsilon_2 l_2, ..., \epsilon_{10} l_{10}]$. Here we choose $\epsilon = 0.1$. We compute the feature distance between the pattern vectors $\boldsymbol{v_i}$ and $\boldsymbol{v_j}$ as $d_{ij} = \sqrt{(\boldsymbol{v_i} - \boldsymbol{v_j})^T (\boldsymbol{v_i} - \boldsymbol{v_j})}$. The experimental results are shown in Figure 4, which shows the feature distance between pattern vectors composed of backtrackless walks of seed graph and edited graph as a function of edit distance. i.e., number of edges deleted. Similarly Figure 4(b) shows the feature distance between pattern vectors composed of random walks of the seed graph and the edited graph as a function of the edit distance. Small variance in figure 4(a) compared to figure 4(b) shows that backtrackless paths offer more stability to noise.

To compare the stability of the feature vector composed of backtrackless walks with the feature vector composed of random walks and the feature vector composed of Ihara coefficients we have shown the relative standard deviation as a function of edit distance for all the three methods in Figure 4(c). It is clear from Figure 4(c) that backtrackless walks provide a more stable representation of the graph when compared to either random walks or the Ihara coefficients.

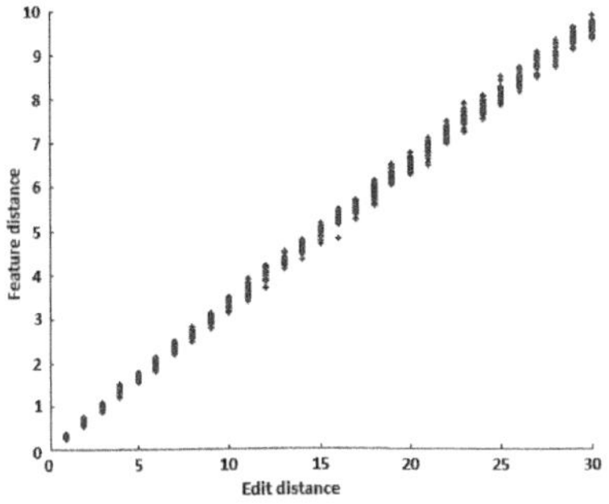

(a) Backtrackless walk

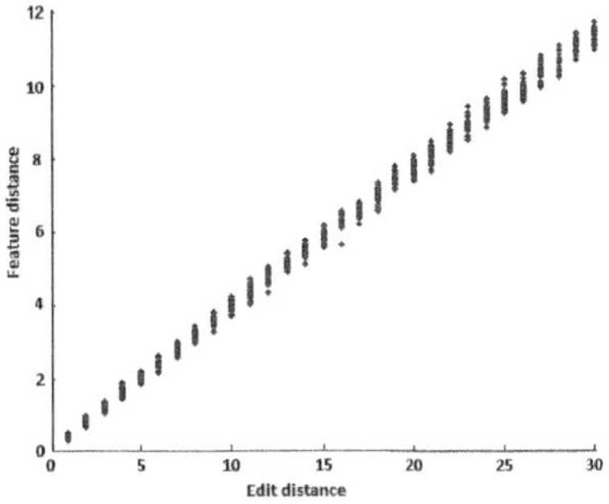

(b) Random walk

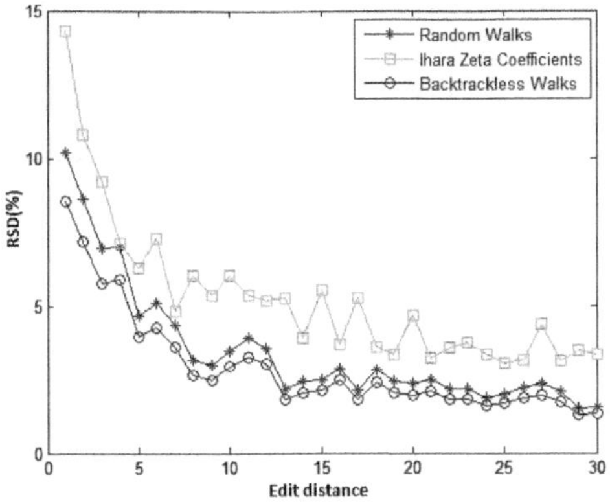

(c) Percent relative standard deviation

Fig. 4. Effect of Edit distance

5.2 Real-World Dataset

In this section we compare our method with alternative methods on real-world data. We choose two real-world datasets namely Mutag[9] and COIL. We then compare our method to existing methods. We use KNN classifier to measure the classification accuracy of data.

Mutag Dataset: Mutag is a collection of 188 chemical compounds. The task, in this dataset, is to predict whether each of 188 compounds has mutagenicity or not. The maximum number of vertices is 40 and the minimum number of vertices is 14, while the average number of vertices is 26.03. The vertices and edges of each compound are labeled with real numbers between 0 and 1.

COIL Dataset: The second dataset consists of graphs extracted from the images in the COIL dataset. Here the task is to classify thirty images of each of three objects, into three different object classes. To establish a graph on the images of objects, we first extract feature points from the image. For this purpose, we use the Harris corner detector[25]. We then construct a Delaunay graph using the selected feature points as vertices. Figure 5(a) shows some of the object views (images) used for our experiments and Figure 5(b) shows the corresponding Delaunay triangulations.

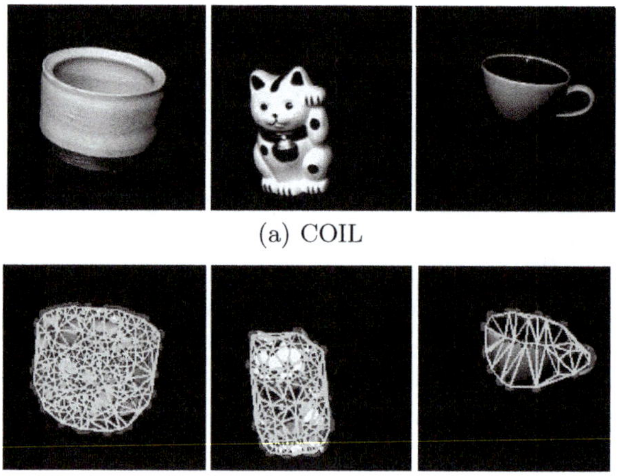

(a) COIL

(b) Delaunay triangulation

Fig. 5. COIL objects and their Delaunay triangulations

Experiments and Results: To evaluate the performance of our kernel on labeled graphs we use the Mutag dataset. We have compared our method with the random walk kernel[1]. The classification accuracies are estimated using 10-fold cross-validation and are shown in Table 1. The classification accuracy of our method is 91.1%, while that of random walk kernel is 90.0%. Results show that by reducing tottering, we can improve classification accuracy.

To evaluate the performance of the pattern vector extracted from backtrackless walks on a graph, we first apply our method to the COIL dataset. We compute backtrackless paths of length up to 10 using Equation (10) and construct a pattern vector of the form $\boldsymbol{v_G} = [\epsilon_1 l_1, \epsilon_2 l_2, ..., \epsilon_{10} l_{10}]$. In this case we choose $\epsilon = 0.1$. Finally we perform PCA on the feature vectors to embed them into a 3-dimensional space. Figure 6 shows the embedding. We have compared our method to both pattern vectors constructed from random walks on a graph and pattern vectors constructed from the coefficients of Ihara zeta function for the graph. Table 1 shows

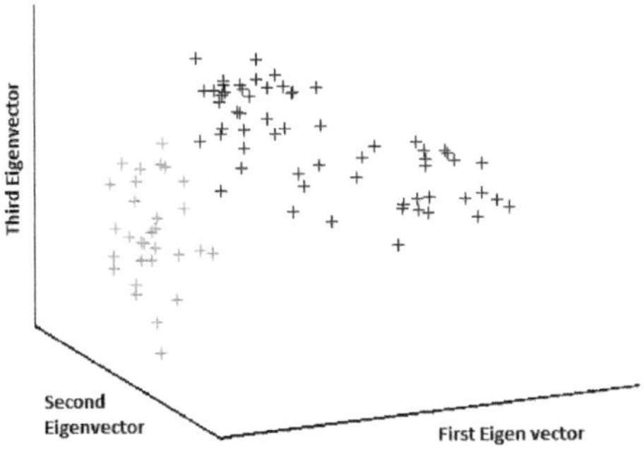

Fig. 6. Performance of clustering

the accuracies of these methods on the COIL dataset. The accuracy of the feature vector constructed from backtrackless walks is 95.5%, while the accuracy for both feature vectors from random walk and feature vectors from the Ihara coefficients is 94.4% . This shows that even on md2 graphs (graphs with degree of each vertex at least 2), the feature vector constructed from backtrackless paths outperforms that constructed from the coefficients of the reciprocal of the Ihara zeta function. We have also applied the shortest path kernel[4] to the same dataset and its accuracy was only 86.7%. In other words our results show that the kernel based on backtrackless path outperforms alternative kernels.

Finally, we evaluate the performance of our feature vector on unlabeled graphs from the Mutag dataset. Table 1 shows the accuracies of each of the three feature vectors. The results show that, in the case of graphs having branches, the coefficients of the reciprocal of the Ihara zeta function are not very effective in distinguishing such graphs.

Table 1. Experimental Results

Method	Dataset	Accuracy
Random walk kernel	Mutag(labeled)	90.0%
Backtrackless walk kernel	Mutag(labeled)	91.1%
Feature vector from Random walk	COIL(unlabeled)	94.4%
Feature vector from backtrackless random walk	COIL(unlabeled)	95.5%
Feature vector from Ihara coefficients	COIL(unlabeled)	94.4%
Shortest Path Kernel	COIL(unlabeled)	86.7%
Feature vector from Random walk	Mutag(unlabeled)	89.4%
Feature vector from backtrackless random walk	Mutag(unlabeled)	90.5%
Feature vector from Ihara coefficients	Mutag(unlabeled)	80.5%

6 Timing Analysis

Our kernel avoids tottering, however it remains an important question that how it compares to known kernels in terms of computational complexity. In this section our goal is to compare the time complexity and the execution time of different methods.

Suppose we are dealing with two graphs with n_1 and n_2 nodes respectively, where both n_1 and n_2 are bounded by n. To compute the random walk kernel we first have to determine the direct product graph. The size of the adjacency matrix of the direct product graph can be $O(n^2)$ in worst case. We then have to compute the product of adjacency matrix of the direct product graph. So the worst case time of computing the random walk kernel is $O(n^6)$. In practice, the run time can be improved[1]. However, the worst case run time remains the same. To compute the kernel on the transformed graph, we first have to transform the graph in a representation that captures its backtrackless structure. The number of vertices in each transformed graph can be $O(n^2)$, and so the size of the adjacency matrix of their direct product graph can be $O(n^4)$. The worst case time complexity of computing the kernel in such cases can be $O(n^{12})$. The worst case running time for our method still remains $O(n^6)$, since we are computing the kernel using the adjacency matrix of that of the graph without transforming it.

In practice the execution time of our method is close to that of random walk kernel. To show this, we use the synthetic data used in Section 5.1. For each graph, we compute random walks of length 10, backtrackless walks of length 10 using our method, and backtrackless walks of length 10 by transforming the graph to an oriented line graph. The execution time for each method on 1000 graphs is shown in Table 2. It is clear that even on sparse graphs our method performs very well compared to that based on the transformed graph.

Table 2. Execution time comparison

Method	Execution Time (Seconds)
Random walk	9.98
Backtrackless random walk using our method	12.30
Backtrackless random walk using transformed graph	313.14

7 Strengths and Weaknesses

We conclude by discussing the advantages and disadvantages of using backtrackless paths in graphs as a measure of similarity. The disadvantages of most of the kernel methods are their expressiveness and running time. The shortest path kernel[4] avoids the problem of tottering, however it uses only the shortest paths between the nodes. The kernel based on cyclic patterns[2] uses all possible cyclic pattern, but is not polynomial. The major advantage of using backtrackless walks instead of random walks is that such kernels not only reduce tottering, but they also retain the expressivity of the random walks and can be computed in polynomial time.

There are however some limitations of the methods based on backtrackless walks. Although such methods reduce tottering, they cannot completely avoid the problem. This happens when a graph contains a triangle. For such a case, a path of length 6 may corresponds to a path that traverses six different edges or a path that traverses the same triangle twice. Another problem with backtrackless paths is that although the theoretical time for both methods is the same, in practice the random walk kernel performs better. This is due to the fact that the power series for adjacency matrix of the product graph can be efficiently computed[1].

8 Conclusion

In this paper we have presented methods for measuring the similarity between graphs based on frequencies of backtrackless paths of different lengths. We have proposed efficient methods for both labeled graphs and unlabeled graphs and applied on both synthetic and real world data. The proposed scheme for labeled graphs gives better results than those for the random walk kernel. For unlabeled graphs our scheme is superior to one that uses feature vector from the coefficient of the reciprocal of the Ihara zeta function both in terms of time and accuracy.

Acknowledgements. We acknolwedge support form the EU FET project SIMBAD. ERH is supported by a Royal Society Wolfson Research Merit Award.

References

1. Gärtner, T., Flach, P., Wrobel, S.: On graph kernels: Hardness results and efficient alternatives. In: Schölkopf, B., Warmuth, M.K. (eds.) COLT/Kernel 2003. LNCS (LNAI), vol. 2777, pp. 129–143. Springer, Heidelberg (2003)
2. Qiangrong, J., Hualan, L., Yuan, G.: Cycle kernel based on spanning tree. In: Proc. of International Conference on Electrical and Control Engineering 2010, pp. 656–659 (2010)
3. Horváth, T., Gärtner, T., Wrobel, S.: Cyclic pattern kernels for predictive graph mining. In: Proceedings of the Tenth ACM SIGKDD International Conference on Knowledge Discovery, pp. 158–167 (2004)
4. Borgwardt, K.M., Kriegel, H.: Shortest-path kernels on graphs. In: Proceedings of 5th IEEE Internationl Conference on Data Mining (ICDM 2005), pp. 74–81 (2005)
5. Vishwanathan, S.V.N., Schraudolph, N.N., Kondor, R., Borgwardt, K.M.: Graph Kernels. Journal of Machine Learning Research, 1201–1242 (2010)
6. Kashima, H., Tsuda, K., Inokuchi, A.: Marginalized kernels between labeled graphs. In: Proceedings of the Twentieth International Conference on Machine Learning, pp. 321–328. AAAI Press, Menlo Park (2003)
7. Kashima, H., Inokuchi, A.: Kernels for Graph Classification. In: ICDM Workshop on Active Mining (2002)
8. Mahé, P., Ueda, N., Akutsu, T., Perret, J., Vert, J.: Extensions of Marginalized Graph Kernels. In: Proceedings of the 21st International Conference on Machine Learning (2004)
9. Srinivasan, A., Muggleton, S.H., Sternberg, M.J.E., King, R.D.: Theories for mutagenicity: a study in first-order and feature-based induction. Artificial Intelligence 85, 277–299 (1996)
10. Schölkopf, B., Smola, A.J.: Learning with kernels. MIT Press, Cambridge
11. Ren, P., Wilson, R.C., Hancock, E.R.: Pattern vectors from the Ihara zeta function. In: 19th International Conference on Pattern Recognition, pp. 1–4 (2008)

12. Ren, P., Wilson, R.C., Hancock, E.R.: Graph Characteristics from the Ihara Zeta Function. In: da Vitoria Lobo, N., Kasparis, T., Roli, F., Kwok, J.T., Georgiopoulos, M., Anagnostopoulos, G.C., Loog, M. (eds.) S+SSPR 2008. LNCS, vol. 5342, pp. 257–266. Springer, Heidelberg (2008)
13. Ren, P., Wilson, R.C., Hancock, E.R.: Hypergraphs, Characteristic Polynomials and the Ihara Zeta Function. In: Jiang, X., Petkov, N. (eds.) CAIP 2009. LNCS, vol. 5702, pp. 369–376. Springer, Heidelberg (2009)
14. Ren, P., Aleksic, T., Emms, D., Wilson, R.C., Hancock, E.R.: Quantum walks, Ihara zeta functions and cospectrality in regular graphs. Quantum Information Processing (in press)
15. Bunke, H.: On a relation between graph edit distance and maximum common subgraph. Pattern Recognition Lett. 18(8), 689–694 (1997)
16. Riesen, K., Bunke, H.: Approximate graph edit distance computation by means of bipartite graph matching. Image Vision Comput., 950–959 (2009)
17. Wasserman, S., Faust, K.: Social Network Analysis: Methods and Applications. Cambridge University Press, Cambridge (1994)
18. Broder, A., Kumar, R., Maghoul, F., Raghavan, P., Rajagopalan, S., Stata, R., Tomkins, A., Wiener, J.: Graph structure in the web. Computer Networks 33, 309–320 (2000)
19. Chapelle, O., Schölkopf, B., Zien, A.: Semi-Supervised Learning. MIT Press, Cambridge (2006)
20. Kramer, S., Raedt, L.D.: Feature construction with version spaces for Biochemical Applications. In: Proceedings of th 18th ICML (2001)
21. Stark, H.M., Terras, A.A.: Zeta Functions of Finite Graphs and Coverings. Adv. in Math. 121, 124–165 (1996)
22. Kotani, M., Sunada, T.: Zeta function of finite graphs. Journal of Mathematics 7(1), 7–25 (2000)
23. Bass. H.: The IharaSelberg zeta function of a tree lattice. Internat. J. Math., 717–797 (1992)
24. Scott, G., Storm, C.K.: The coefficients of the Ihara Zeta Function. Involve - a Journal of Mathematics 1(2), 217–233 (2008)
25. Harris, C., Stephens, M.: A combined corner and edge detector. In: Fourth Alvey Vision Conference, Manchester, UK, pp. 147–151 (1988)

Impact of the Initialization in Tree-Based Fast Similarity Search Techniques

Aureo Serrano, Luisa Micó, and Jose Oncina

Departamento de Lenguajes y Sistemas Informáticos,
Universidad de Alicante,
P.O. box 99, E-03080 Alicante, Spain
{aserrano,mico,oncina}@dlsi.ua.es
http://www.dlsi.ua.es

Abstract. Many fast similarity search techniques relies on the use of pivots (specially selected points in the data set). Using these points, specific structures (indexes) are built speeding up the search when queering. Usually, pivot selection techniques are incremental, being the first one randomly chosen.

This article explores several techniques to choose the first pivot in a tree-based fast similarity search technique. We provide experimental results showing that an adequate choice of this pivot leads to significant reductions in distance computations and time complexity.

Moreover, most pivot tree-based indexes emphasizes in building balanced trees. We provide experimentally and theoretical support that very unbalanced trees can be a better choice than balanced ones.

1 Introduction

Similarity search has become a fundamental task in many application areas, including data mining, pattern recognition, computer vision, multimedia information retrieval, biomedical databases, data compression or statistical data analysis. The simplest, yet most popular method for this task is the well-known k-Nearest Neighbor (kNN) classifier. However, one of the main constraints of using this technique to classify large datasets is its complexity: finding the k-Nearest Neighbors for a given query is linear on the database size. A classical method to speed up the search is to rely in some property of the dissimilarity measure to build up a data structure (index) in preprocess time. Once the index has been built, similarity queries can be answered with a significant reduction in the number of distance computations.

In this work we are going to focus our attention in dissimilarity functions that fulfills the conditions of being a distance and then define a metric space (A review of such techniques can be found in [3][7][18].) According to Navarro and Reyes [12], algorithms to search in metric spaces can be divided in pivot-based and clustering algorithms:

- *Pivot-based* algorithms use a set of distinguished objects (pivots) of the datasets. Usually, the distances between pivots and some (or all) the objects in the database are stored in the index. This information, along with

M. Pelillo and E.R. Hancock (Eds.): SIMBAD 2011, LNCS 7005, pp. 163–176, 2011.

the properties of the distance function, is used in query time to avoid some distance computations.
- *Clustering* algorithms divide the spaces in zones as compact as possible, storing a representative point for each zone and extra information that permit to discard a zone at query time.

According to Hjaltason and Samet [7] and Zezula et al.[18], the algorithms can be divided in:

- *Ball partitioning* algorithms, that requires only one pivot to divide a set S into two subsets using a spherical cut.
- *Generalized hyperplane partitioning* algorithms, where the division is done using two pivots.
- *Distance matrix* algorithms, where precomputed distances between the objects in the datasets are stored to be used in query time.

For example, the Vantage Point Tree (vp-tree) algorithm [17] is a *pivot-based* algorithm that uses *ball partitioning* metric trees. The simplest method selects randomly the vantage points. However, the author argues that a more careful selection procedure can yield better search performance.

One of the first works about the selection of pivots was done by Shapiro in 1977 [14]. He found that if the data set belongs to a uniform distribution on a hypercube in the Euclidean space, it is better to pick (vantage) points near corners of the hypercube as pivots to improve search performance. Taking into account these results, Yianilos argues that choosing the points near corners as pivots can be shown to minimize the boundary of the ball that is inside the hypercube, increasing search efficiency.

Other well-known example of *pivot-based* method was proposed by Ullmann in 1991 [15]. Ullmann defines a metric tree (gh-tree) using *generalized hyperplane partitioning*. Instead of picking just one object for partitioning the space as in the vp-tree, this method picks two pivots, usually, the samples farthest from each other, dividing the set of remaining samples based on the closest pivot. Similar strategies were applied in Faloutsos and Lin [5] or Merkwirth et al. [10].

Despite the taxonomy proposed by Navarro and Reyes, some clustering algorithms also use pivots to build indexes. GNAT (Geometric Near-neighbor Access Tree) [2] is a *clustering* algorithm, that is a generalization of a gh-tree, and then, where more than two pivots should be chosen to divide the data set at each node. The method for choosing the pivot samples is based on a philosophy similar to that of Yianilos for the vp-tree (and also suggested by others [1][14]). The method first randomly selects a set of candidate pivot samples from the dataset. Next, the first pivot is selected randomly from the candidates, and the remaining pivots are selected iteratively as the farthest away from the previously selected.

A bisector tree, proposed by Kalantari and McDonald [8], is a gh-tree augmented with the maximum distance to a sample in its subtree. Moreover, if in this structure one of the two pivots in each non leaf node is inherited from its parent node, the monotonous bisector tree (mb-tree) is obtained [13]. Since this strategy leads to fewer pivot objects, its use reduces the number of distance computations during search (provided the distances of pivot objects are propagated downward during search), at the lower cost of a worse partitioning and a deeper tree. It should be clear that many different configurations are possible for obtaining a mb-tree, since there are many options to choose the second pivot at each step for the next decomposition. For example, one strategy is to select as the second pivot the one that tries to associate the same number of objects with each node (then, obtaining a balanced tree).

In the last few years we worked with MDF-trees. This indexes can be viewed as a particularization of the mb-tree. In order to build an MDF-tree, first a pivot is chosen from the database (usually randomly). The algorithm proceeds by dividing the database in two sets each time a node of the tree is split. To split a node, two pivots are chosen, the corresponding to the new left node is the pivot of the node to be split and the right pivot is the farthest element of the left pivot. Then, the objects of the original node are distributed according to its nearest pivot. This structure stores some additional information (i.e. the distance from the node pivot to the farthest object of the node) [4].

However, the selection of the first pivot (root of the tree) has not received special attention. Note that in mb-trees, the selection of the first pivot is affecting all levels of the tree because the decomposition of the space is done in a top-down manner.

In this paper we are interested in the initialization of MDF-trees, this index is used as the basis for building other more complex indexes ([11][4]). In this case the initialization involves only the selection of the representative of the root.

In this paper an experimental survey of several initializations for the MDF-tree has been done. Although these initializations involves only the selection of the representative of the tree root, significant variations on the properties of the trees and efficiency of the search can be observed.

Moreover, we show that, in this type of trees, it is not a good idea to force the tree to be balanced. The main reason is that forcing the nodes to be of equal size leads to big overlapping regions. We show that it is better to force to have wide unbalanced trees in order to reduce the overlapping regions.

In the next section, a quick review of the construction of the MDF-tree is presented. In section 3 different initialization proposals are detailed. In section 4 experiments have been carried out on several artificial and real datasets. Finally, some concluding remarks are depicted in Section 6.

2 The MDF-Tree

The MDF tree is a binary indexing structure based on a *hyperplane partitioning* approach [11][4]. The main difference with mb-trees is related to the selection of the representatives (pivots) each time a node is split.

2.1 Building an MDT-Tree

In order to build an MDF-tree, firstly a pivot is randomly selected as the root of the tree (first level). Secondly, the farthest object to the root is chosen as the second pivot, then the rest of objects are distributed according to the closest pivot. This procedure is recursively repeated until each leaf node has only one object (see Figure 3). It is interesting to observe that the root of the tree is propagated recursively through all the levels of the tree as the left node.

Algorithm 1 describes how an MDF-tree is built. The function `build_tree` `(`ℓ`,`S`)` takes as arguments the future representative of the root node (ℓ) and the set of objects to be included in the tree (excluding ℓ) and returns the MDF-tree that contains $S \cup \{\ell\}$. The first time that `build_tree(`ℓ`,`S`)` is called, ℓ is selected *randomly* among the data set. In the algorithm, M_T is the pivot corresponding to T, r_T is the covering radius, and T_L (T_R) is the left (right) subtree of T.

Algorithm 1. build_tree(ℓ, S)

Data:
  $S \cup \{\ell\} = D$: set of points to include in T;
  ℓ: future left representative of T
create MDF-tree T
if S *is empty* **then**
  $M_T = \ell$
  $r_T = 0$
else
  $r = \text{argmax}_{x \in S}\, d(\ell, x)$
  $r_T = d(\ell, r)$
  $S_\ell = \{x \in S | d(\ell, x) < d(r, x)\}$
  $S_r = \{x \in S | d(\ell, x) \geq d(r, x)\} - \{r\}$
  T_L = `build_tree(`ℓ`,`S_ℓ`)`
  T_R = `build_tree(`r`,`S_r`)`
end
return T

2.2 The Search Algorithm

Given a query point, the search algorithm proceeds in a top down procedure.

At each step, the search algorithm computes the distance to the representatives of each child node and updates the current nearest neighbor candidate if necessary. Next, using the distance from the sample to the representatives and the radius of the node, it tries to discard each of the nodes. At last, the search continues with each of the undiscarded nodes.

Note that since in MDF-trees the representative of the left node is the same as the representative of its father, the distance computation of the query point to the left representative can be avoided. Then, only one distance is computed each time a node is explored (see alg. 2.)

As pruning rule, here we are going to consider the simplest one. Given a query point x and the current NN candidate nn, no object in the tree T can be nearest to x than the current NN candidate if (see fig. 1)

$$d(x, nn) \leq d(rep(T), x) - r_T$$

Algorithm 2. search_tree(T, x)

```
Data:
   T: tree node;
   x: sample
if not exists T_L then return
if not exists T_R then
 |  if not pruned T_L then search(T_L, x)
 |  return
end
d_r = d(rep(T_R), x); update nearest neighbour
if d_ℓ < d_r then
 |  if not pruned T_L then search (T_L, x)
 |  if not pruned T_R then search (T_R, x)
end
else
 |  if not pruned T_R then search (T_R, x)
 |  if not pruned T_L then search (T_L, x)
end
```

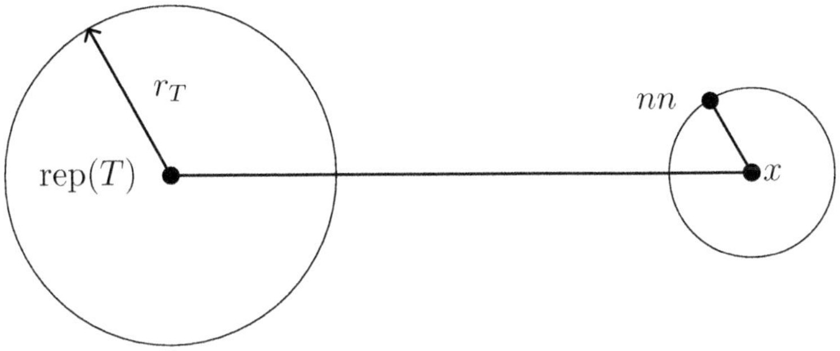

Fig. 1. Pruning rule

Note that as a consequence of this rule if the representatives of the children of a node are too near or their radius are too large, an overlapping region will appear where none of the children can be pruned (see fig. 2). This (usually unavoidable) situation provokes the algorithm to explore both subtrees.

The MDF-tree building procedure tries to weaken this effect by choosing, as representative for the right child, the farthest object of the left representative. Unfortunately, this usually leads to large radius.

3 Initialization Methods

As stated in the previous section, it is necessary to choose a pivot that will act as the root of the tree for construction purposes. To our knowledge, no work has been done before to study alternative initialization choices. In this work, we present experimental results (both for tree construction and for search performance) when performing different root initializations.

Let we enumerate the methods used for this purpose.

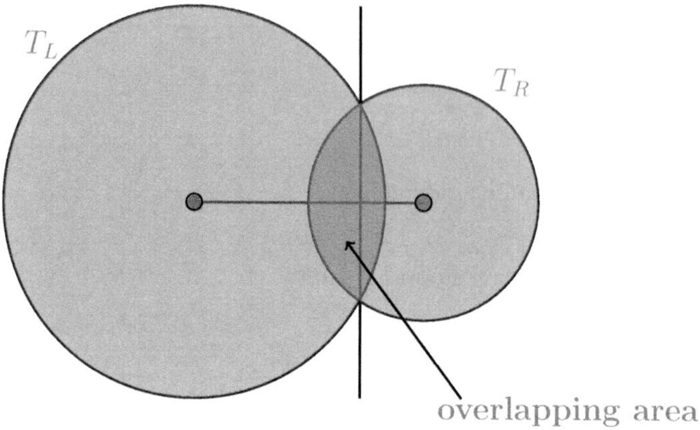

Fig. 2. Overlapping region

3.1 *Random* Method

This initialization is the usual method applied in the MDF-tree [11][4]. It consists on selecting randomly a sample from the database.

3.2 *Outlier* Method

The aim of this method is to choose an outlier as initialization. In this method, we first choose randomly one sample from the database, and then the most distant sample from it is selected as root of the tree.

The hypothesis is that by choosing two, probably, very distant points at the first level, and recursively dividing the space, the resulting subspaces will have similar size, producing a very balanced tree.

Given a dataset D, and given $p \in D$ randomly chosen, we select r as the root of the tree, where

$$r = \text{argmax}_{t \in D}\, d(p, t)$$

Figure 3 is and example of the partition an the MDF-tree produced by a set of points in a two dimensional space. As expected, the tree is reasonably balanced.

3.3 *Median* Method

The aim now is to choose a "centered" point as initialization. In this case, we choose the point that minimizes the sum of the distance to all the others, i.e. the set median of the training set.

Given a dataset D, we select the root of the tree r, where

$$r = \text{argmin}_{p \in D} \sum_{t \in D} d(p, t)$$

An example, using the same data set than in fig. 3, can be seen in fig. 4. Note that now the tree is very unbalanced.

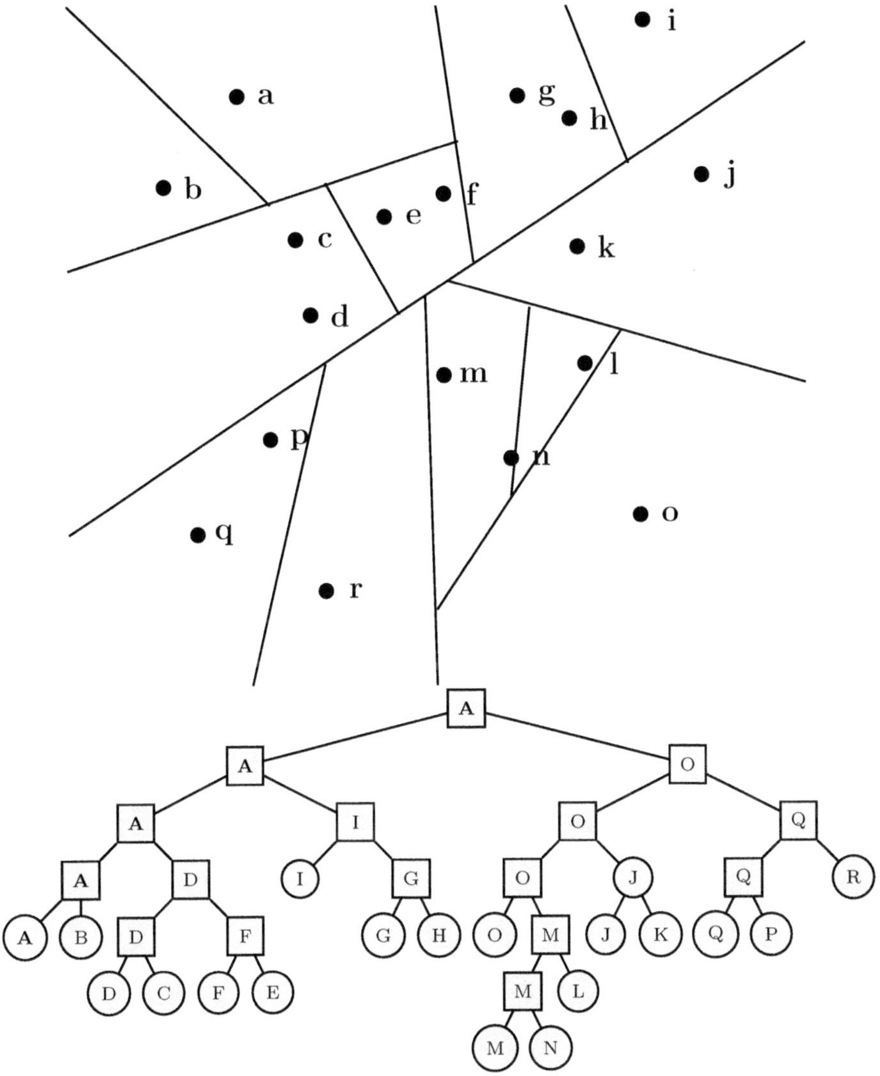

Fig. 3. Example of a space partitioning produced by a MDF-tree in a two-dimensional space (top). Given a random object, "L", in this example the root is the most distant object to "L" (label "A"), and then is propagated through all the levels of the three through the left child. The same criterion is used recursively for the propagation of the rest of pivots. The decomposition continues until there are only one object in each leaf node (down).

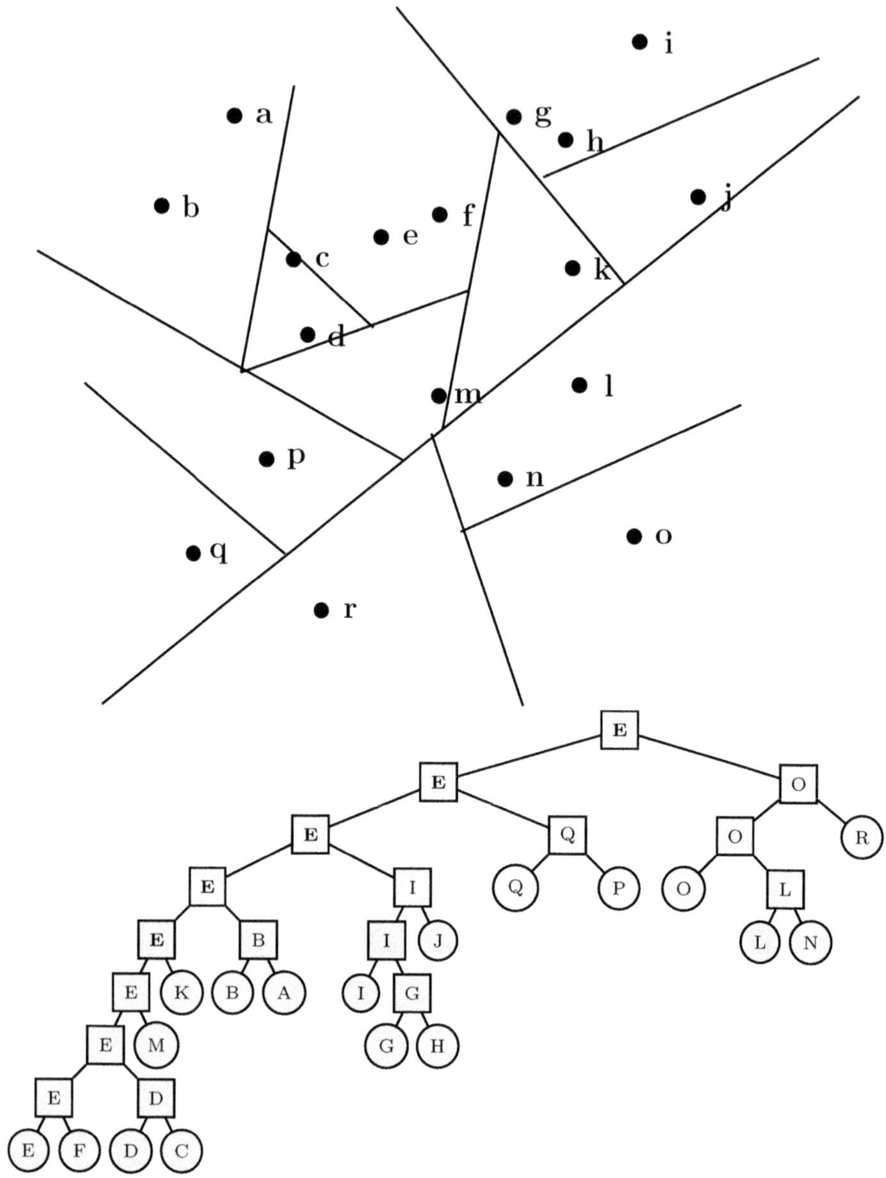

Fig. 4. Example of a space partitioning produced by a MDF-tree in a two-dimensional space (top). In this example the root is the set median of the set. The decomposition continues until there are only one object in each leaf node (down).

4 Experiments

We have carried out a series of experiments using synthetic and real data to study the influence of the different methods for the first pivot selection in the MDF-tree.

Two sets of databases were used in our experiments:

1. Synthetic prototype sets, generated from uniform distributions in the unit hypercube, from dimension 2 to 20. Each point in the plot shows the result of a experiment using 50 000 samples as training set, an 10 000 samples as test. The Euclidean distance was used as dissimilarity measure.
2. Two string databases:
   - A database of 69 069 words of an English dictionary was used. A training set of 50 000 samples with 10 000 test samples were used for the experiments. The words for the samples are randomly chosen from the entire dictionary. In order to obtain reliable results, several experiments were carried out, changing the value of the random seed to obtain different set of words in each case.
   - A database of 61 293 strings representing contour chains [6] of the handwritten digits in NIST database. A training set of 10 000 samples with 1 000 test samples were used for the experiments. Several experiments with a distinct random seed were carried out.

   In both cases, the edit distance [9][16] was used as dissimilarity measure. Edit distance between two strings is the minimum cost sequence of character insertions, deletions and substitutions to make equal the two strings. In our experiments the cost of apply any of the three operations are the same.

Figure 5 shows the depths of the trees using Random, Outlier and Median initializations, for a dataset with 50 000 samples uniformly distributed points in the unit hypercube for dimensions varying form 2 to 20. Unlike the other initializations, the depth of the tree for the Median initialization grows quickly with the dimension of the space. This is due to the fact that, in general, the space around the median is usually more populated than in the other choices.

To analyze the behavior of the trees during the search, several experiments were done. Figure 6 (left) shows the average number of distance computations in a nearest neighbor search for the three initialization. The same datasets as in the previous experiments were used. Figure 6 (ref) shows the time spent, in microseconds, by each search. The time was measured on a cpu running at 2660 MHz under a Linux system.

It can be observed that, unexpectedly, in high dimensional spaces the Median initialization (the method that obtained deepest trees) reduces significantly the number of distance computations with respect to the classical approaches (Random and Outlier).

Similar results have been obtained using the English dictionary and the NIST Database. Results can be seen in tables 1, 2 and 3.

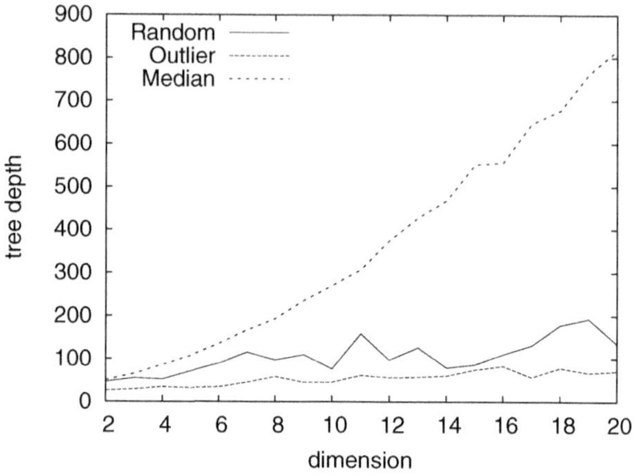

Fig. 5. Tree depths using Random, Outlier and Median initialization in the Euclidean Space

Table 1. Tree depths using Random, Outlier and Median initializations

	Random	Outlier	Median
English dic.	184.7	97.2	361.8
NIST	137.1	119.8	203.3

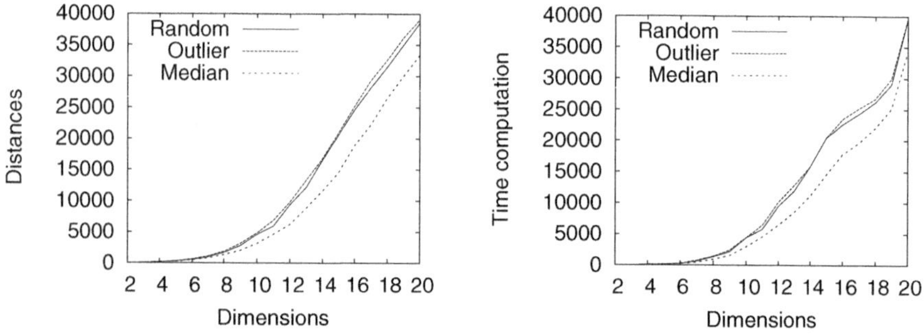

Fig. 6. Average number of distance computations (on the left) and time (in seconds) using Random, Outlier and Median initialization in the Euclidean Space

Table 2. Average number of distance computations using Random, Outlier and Median initializations

	Random	Outlier	Median
English dic.	4402.6	5324.6	3241.9
NIST	1713.8	1845.9	1501.2

Table 3. Time (in microseconds) using Random, Outlier and Median initializations

	Random	**Outlier**	**Median**
English dic.	16446.6	19906,4	12268.6
NIST	87769.9	95037.9	78800.6

5 Non Balanced Trees

In order to find an explanation to this result the MDF-tree was studied deeply.

Let suppose we have a very big database were a good candidate to NN is found quickly and its distance to the query object is negligible with respect to the radius of the nodes.

In a node we can distinguish four regions depending on two criteria:

- if we are in the left (right) node region.
- if we are in the overlapping region or not.

Let we call r the probability that a random point in the node goes to the left child. Let we call s the probability that a point falls in the overlapping region. We are going to assume now that this probabilities depends only on the size of the node.

In order to check if this is assumable, for each node of some MDF-tree, we have counted the number of points in the node and the number of points in the left child. The trees were obtained from a database of 20 000 points uniformly distributed in 5, 10 and 15 dimensional unit hypercube. The euclidean distance was used as dissimilarity function. The experiments were repeated using the Outlier and the Median initialization techniques. The results of this experiment is shown in fig. 7. Similarly, the number of points in the node versus the number of points in the overlapping region was represented in fig. 8. It can be seen that the ratios are quite linear (perhaps with the exception of the last point). Then the slope gives us the parameter r and s respectivelly. Table 4 shows their values.

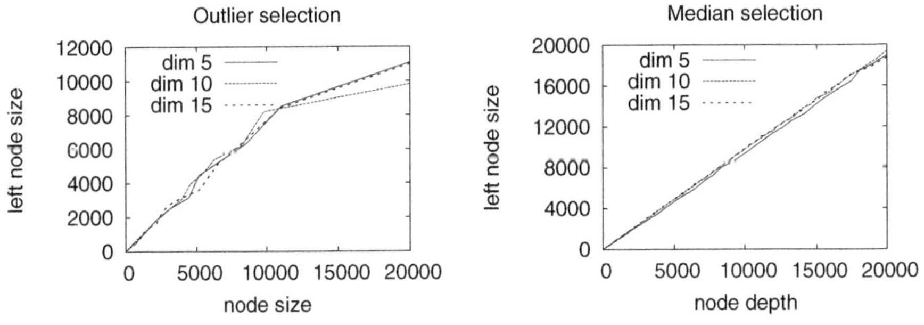

Fig. 7. Left node size versus parent node size in MDF-tree with Outlier and Median initializations for uniformly dirtributed points in the 5, 10 and 15 dimensional unit hypercube

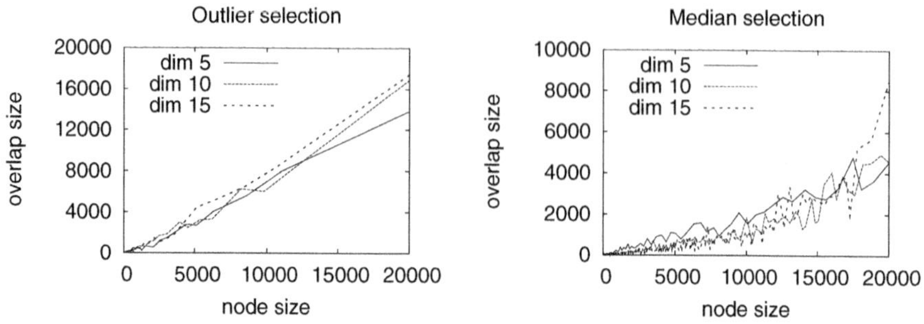

Fig. 8. Orevlapping node size versus parent node size in MDF-tree with Outlier and Median initializations for uniformly distributed points in the 5, 10 and 15 dimensional unit hypercube

Table 4. Values of the parameters r and s

dim.	param. r		param. s	
	Outlier	Median	Outlier	Median
5	0.65	0.94	0.67	0.20
10	0.63	0.97	0.75	0.15
15	0.65	0.97	0.81	0.15

Note that parameter r is smaller for the Outlier than for the Median initialization. That means that the trees are more balanced for the Outlier than for the Median initialization. In fact, for the Median initialization, the trees are very unbalanced.

Note also that parameter s is smaller for the Median than for the Outlier initialization. Assuming the distance to the NN is negligible, if a query point falls in the overlapping region, the algorithm should search in both children, otherwise it search only in one of them.

In this situation, the Median initialization is displacing the frontier of the two children towards the right one and reducing the overlapping region at the expenses of increasing the depth of the tree.

To get an idea of how efficient the effect can be, we can estimate the expected number of distance computations.

In order to do that we need to know the following probabilities:

- Probability of being in left node but not in the overlapping region: $r(1-s)$
- Probability of being in the left node and in the overlapping region: rs.
- Probability of being in the right node and in the overlapping region: $(1-r)s$.
- Probability of being in the right node but not in the overlapping region: $(1-r)(1-s)$.

The the expected number of distance computations in a tree with n objects ($c(n)$) can be expressed as:

$$\begin{aligned} c(n) &= r(1-s)\,c(rn) + s\,[c(rn) + c((1-r)n)] + (1-r)(1-s)\,c((1-r)n) + 1 \\ &= (r(1-s)+s)\,c(rn) + (s + (1-r)(1-s))\,c((1-r)n) + 1 \end{aligned}$$

and obviously, $c(n) = 1$ if $n \leq 1$.

Table 5 shows the expected number of distance computations corresponding to the parameters in table 4.

Table 5. Expected number of distance computations

dim.	Outlier	Median
5	5502	879
10	10235	2103
15	16291	2374

6 Conclusions

In this work we show that an appropriate initialization technique can lead to significant distance computations reductions in MDF-trees based search algorithms.

Surprisingly, and far from what intuitively was expected, the method that produces a more degenerate tree is the one that computes the least number of distances. Moreover, the reduction is more important as the dimensionality of the data increases.

The lesson learnt from this work is that balanced trees can not be taken as a guide to increase the performance of the algorithm. We have developed a simple theory to explain why very unbalanced trees can lead to significant distance computation reductions.

Many questions remains open:

- Can we devise an expression to link the reduction factor r (which is related with the balance degree of the tree) with the overlapping factor s? This expression will guide us to find which is the optimal relative volume of the chidren nodes.
- In our case, we are manipulating the relative value of the children nodes just by choosing an initial pivot. Can we propagate this idea to the selection of pivots in all the nodes?
- Can we extrapolate this results to other tree based indexes?

Acknowledgements. The authors thank the Spanish CICyT for partial support of this work through projects TIN2009-14205-C04-C1, the IST Programme of the European Community, under the PASCAL Network of Excellence, (IST–2006-216886), and the program CONSOLIDER INGENIO 2010 (CSD2007-00018).

References

1. Bozkaya, T., Özsoyoglu, Z.M.: Indexing large metric spaces for similarity search queries. ACM Trans. Database Syst. 24(3), 361–404 (1999)
2. Brin, S.: Near neighbor search in large metric spaces. In: Proceedings of the 21st International Conference on Very Large Data Bases, pp. 574–584 (1995)
3. Chávez, E., Navarro, G., Baeza-Yates, R., Marroquin, J.L.: Searching in metric spaces. ACM Computing Surveys 33(3), 273–321 (2001)
4. Gómez-Ballester, E., Micó, L., Oncina, J.: Some approaches to improve tree-based nearest neighbour search algorithms. Pattern Recognition 39(2), 171–179 (2006)
5. Faloutsos, C., Lin, K.: Fastmap: a fast algorithm for indexing, data-mining and visualization of traditional and multimedia datasets. In: Proceedings of the 1995 ACM SIGMOD International Conference on Management of Data, SIGMOD 1995, pp. 163–174. ACM, New York (1995)
6. Freeman, H.: Boundary encoding and processing. Picture Processing and Psychopictorics, 241–266 (1970)
7. Hjaltason, G.R., Samet, H.: Index-driven similarity search in metric spaces. ACM Trans. Database Syst. 28(4), 517–580 (2003)
8. Kalantari, I., McDonald, G.: A data structure and an algorithm for the nearest point problem. IEEE Trans. Software Engineering 9, 631–634 (1983)
9. Levenshtein, V.I.: Binary codes capable of correcting deletions, insertions, and reversals. Doklady Akademii Nauk 163(4), 845–848 (1965)
10. Merkwirth, C., Parlitz, U., Lauterborn, W.: Fast nearest-neighbor searching for nonlinear signal processing. Physical Review 62, 2089–2097 (2000)
11. Micó, L., Oncina, J., Carrasco, R.C.: A fast branch and bound nearest neighbor classifier in metric spaces. Pattern Recognition Letters 17, 731–773 (1996)
12. Navarro, G., Reyes, N.: Dynamic spatial approximation trees. J. Exp. Algorithmics 12, 1–68 (2008)
13. Noltemeier, H., Verbarg, K., Zirkelbach, C.: Monotonous bisector* trees – a tool for efficient partitioning of complex scenes of geometric objects. In: Monien, B., Ottmann, T. (eds.) Data Structures and Efficient Algorithms. LNCS, vol. 594, pp. 186–203. Springer, Heidelberg (1992)
14. Shapiro, M.: The choice of reference points in best-match file searching. Commun. ACM 20, 339–343 (1977)
15. Uhlmann, J.K.: Satisfying general proximity/similarity queries with metric trees. Inf. Process. Lett. 40(4), 175–179 (1991)
16. Wagner, R.A., Fischer, M.J.: The string-to-string correction problem. Journal of the ACM 21(1), 168–173 (1974)
17. Yianilos, P.N.: Data structures and algorithms for nearest neighbor search in general metric spaces. In: Proceedings of the ACM-SIAM Symposium on Discrete Algorithms, pp. 311–321 (1993)
18. Zezula, P., Amato, G., Dohnal, V., Batko, M.: Similarity Search: The Metric Space Approach. Springer, Heidelberg (2006)

Multiple-Instance Learning with Instance Selection via Dominant Sets

Aykut Erdem and Erkut Erdem

Hacettepe University, 06800 Beytepe, Ankara, Turkey
aykut.erdem@hacettepe.edu.tr, erkut@cs.hacettepe.edu.tr

Abstract. Multiple-instance learning (MIL) deals with learning under ambiguity, in which patterns to be classified are described by bags of instances. There has been a growing interest in the design and use of MIL algorithms as it provides a natural framework to solve a wide variety of pattern recognition problems. In this paper, we address MIL from a view that transforms the problem into a standard supervised learning problem via instance selection. The novelty of the proposed approach comes from its selection strategy to identify the most representative examples in the positive and negative training bags, which is based on an effective pairwise clustering algorithm referred to as dominant sets. Experimental results on both standard benchmark data sets and on multi-class image classification problems show that the proposed approach is not only highly competitive with state-of-the-art MIL algorithms but also very robust to outliers and noise.

1 Introduction

In recent years, multiple-instance learning (MIL) [7] has emerged as a major machine learning paradigm, which aims at classifying bags of instances with class label information available for the bags but not necessarily for the instances. In a typical MIL setting, a *negative bag* is composed of only negative instances, whereas a bag is considered *positive* if it contains at least one positive instance, leading to a learning problem with ambiguously labeled data. MIL paradigm provides a natural framework to handle many challenging problems in various domains, including drug-activity prediction [7], document classification [1], content-based image retrieval [25], object detection [21], image categorization [5,4], and visual tracking [2,10].

In general, MIL methods can be grouped into two main categories. The first class of approaches, including the APR [7], DD [16], EM-DD [24] methods, uses *generative* models to represent the target concept by a region in the instance feature space which covers all the true positive instances while remaining far from every instance in the negative bags. Alternatively, the second class of works employs *discriminative* learning paradigm to address the MIL problems. The methods in this group are mainly the generalizations of the standard single-instance learning (SIL) methods to the MIL setting, *e.g.* mi-SVM and MI-SVM [1], MI-Kernel [9], MIO [12], Citation KNN [22] and MILBoost-NOR [21].

Recently, a new group of SVM-based methods has been proposed for MIL, namely the DD-SVM [5], MILES [4], MILD_B [13] and MILIS [8] methods, which tackles multi-instance problems by transforming them into standard SIL problems. The basic

M. Pelillo and E.R. Hancock (Eds.): SIMBAD 2011, LNCS 7005, pp. 177–191, 2011.

idea is to embed each bag into a feature space based on a representative set of instances selected from the training bags and to learn a classifier in this feature space. The major difference between these methods is how they select instance prototypes, which will be detailed in the next section. However, it should be noted here that a good set of prototypes is vital to the success of any method.

In this paper, a new instance selection mechanism is proposed for multiple-instance learning. The novelty comes from utilizing *dominant sets* [18], an effective pairwise clustering framework, to model the distributions of negative instances and accordingly to select a set of instance prototypes from the positive and negative training bags. Therefore, the proposed approach is named MILDS, Multiple-Instance Learning with instance selection via Dominant Sets. The main contributions are as follows: (i) The constructed feature space is usually of a lower dimension compared to those of other instance-selection based MIL approaches [5,4,8]. This is mainly due to the use of clustering performed on the instances from the negative training bags. (ii) The presented approach is highly insensitive to noise in the bag labels as the dominant sets framework is proven to be very robust against outliers that might exist in the data. (iii) The proposed binary MIL formulation can be easily generalized to solve multi-class problems in a natural way due to the proposed cluster-based representation of data. (iv) The experimental results demonstrate that the suggested approach is highly competitive with the state-of-the-art MIL approaches.

The remainder of the paper is organized as follows: Section 2 summarizes the previous work on instance-selection based MIL and provides background information on the dominant sets framework. Section 3 presents the proposed MILDS algorithm. Section 4 reports experimental results on some benchmark data sets and on multi-class image classification problems. Finally, Section 5 concludes the paper with a summary and possible directions for future work.

2 Background

2.1 Instance-Selection Based MIL

As mentioned in the introduction, the existing instance-selection based MIL methods, namely DD-SVM [5], MILES [4], MILD_B [13] and MILIS [8], can be differentiated mainly by the procedures they follow in identifying the set of instance prototypes used to map bags into a feature space. Below, we review these differences in detail.

In DD-SVM, a diverse density (DD) function [16] is used in identifying the instance prototypes. Within each training bag, the instance having the largest DD value is chosen as a prototype for the class of the bag. Then, a standard SVM in combination with radial basis function (RBF) is trained on the corresponding embedding space. The performance of DD-SVM is highly affected by the labeling noise since a negative bag close to a positive instance drastically reduces the DD value of the instance, thus its chance to be selected as a prototype.

In MILES, there is no explicit selection of instance prototypes. All the instances in the training bags are employed to build a very high-dimensional feature space, and then the instance selection is implicitly performed via learning a 1-norm SVM classifier.

As expected, the main drawback of MILES stems from its way of constructing the embedding space. Its computational load grows exponentially as the volume of the training data increases.

In [13], an instance-selection mechanism based on a conditional probability model is developed to identify the true positive instance in a positive bag. For each instance in a positive bag, a decision function is formulated whose accuracy on predicting the labels of the training bags is used to measure true positiveness of the corresponding instance. The authors of [13] use this instance selection mechanism to devise two MIL methods, MILD_I and MILD_B, for *instance-level* and for *bag-level* classification problems, respectively. Here, MILD_B is of our interest, which defines the instance-based feature space by the most positive instances chosen accordingly from each positive bag, and like DD-SVM, trains a standard SVM with the RBF kernel in that feature space.

In MILIS, instances in the negative bags are modeled as a probability distribution function based on kernel density estimation. Initially, the most positive (*i.e.* the least negative) instance and the most negative instance are selected respectively in each positive bag and each negative bag based on the distribution estimate. These instance prototypes form the feature space for the bag-level embedding in which a linear SVM is trained. To increase the robustness, once a classifier is learnt, MILIS employs an alternating optimization scheme for instance selection and classifier training to update the selected prototypes and the weights of the support vectors. As a final step, it includes an additional feature pruning step which removes all features with small weights.

2.2 Clustering with Dominant Sets

Our instance selection strategy makes use of a pairwise clustering approach known as *dominant sets* [18]. In a nut shell, the concept of a dominant set can be considered as a generalization of a maximal clique to edge-weighted graphs. Suppose the data to be clustered is represented in terms of their similarities by an undirected edge-weighted graph with no self-loops $G = (V, E, w)$, where V is the set of nodes, $E \subseteq V \times V$ is the set of edges, and $w : E \rightarrow \mathbb{R}_+$ is the positive weight (similarity) function. Further, let $A = [a_{ij}]$ denote the $n \times n$ adjacency matrix of G where $a_{ij} = w(i,j)$ if $(i,j) \in E$ and is 0 otherwise. A dominant set is formulated based on a recursive characterization of the weight $\mathrm{w}_S(i)$ of element i w.r.t. to a set of elements S (A curious reader may refer to [18] for more details), as:

Definition 1. *A nonempty subset of vertices $S \subseteq V$ such that $\sum_{i \in T} \mathrm{w}_T(i) > 0$ for any nonempty $T \subseteq S$, is said to be* dominant *if:*

1. $\mathrm{w}_S(i) > 0,$ *for all* $i \in S,$
2. $\mathrm{w}_{S \cup \{i\}}(i) < 0,$ *for all* $i \notin S.$

The above definition of a dominant set also formalizes the notion of a *cluster* by expressing two basic properties: (i) elements within a cluster should be very similar (*high internal homogeneity*), (ii) elements from different clusters should be highly dissimilar (*high external inhomogeneity*).

Consider the following generalization of the Motzkin-Straus program [17] to an undirected edge-weighted graph $G{=}(V, E, w)$:

$$\begin{array}{ll} \text{maximize} & f(\mathbf{x}) = \mathbf{x}^T A\mathbf{x} \\ \text{subject to} & \mathbf{x} \in \Delta \end{array} \tag{1}$$

where A is the weighted adjacency matrix of graph G, $\Delta{=}\{\mathbf{x} \in \mathbb{R}^n \mid \mathbf{x}{\geq}\mathbf{0} \text{ and } \mathbf{e}^T\mathbf{x}{=}1\}$ is the standard simplex in $\mathbb{R}^n$ with $\mathbf{e}$ being a vector of ones of appropriate dimension. The support of $\mathbf{x}$ is defined as the set of indices corresponding to its positive components, *i.e.* $\sigma(\mathbf{x}) = \{i{\in}V \mid x_i > 0\}$. The following theorem (from [18]) provides a one-to-one relation between dominant sets and strict local maximizers of (1).

Theorem 1. *If S is a dominant subset of vertices, then its weighted characteristic vector $\mathbf{x} \in \Delta$ defined as:*

$$x_i = \begin{cases} \frac{\mathrm{w}_S(i)}{\sum_{j\in S} \mathrm{w}_S(j)} & \text{if } i \in S \\ 0 & \text{otherwise} \end{cases} \tag{2}$$

is a strict local solution of (1). Conversely, if $\mathbf{x}$ is a strict local solution of (1), then its support $S = \sigma(\mathbf{x})$ is a dominant set, provided that $\mathrm{w}_{S\cup\{i\}}(i) \neq 0$ for all $i \notin S$.

The cohesiveness of a dominant set (cluster) S can be measured by the value of the objective function $\mathbf{x}^T A\mathbf{x}$. Moreover, the similarity of an element j to S can be directly computed by $(A\mathbf{x})_j$ where

$$(A\mathbf{x})_j \begin{cases} = \mathbf{x}^T A\mathbf{x} \text{ if } j{\in}\sigma(\mathbf{x}) \\ \leq \mathbf{x}^T A\mathbf{x} \text{ if } j{\notin}\sigma(\mathbf{x}) \,. \end{cases} \tag{3}$$

As a final remark, it should be noted that the spectral methods in [20,11] maximize the same quadratic function in Eq. (1). However, they differ from dominant sets in their choice of the feasible region. The solutions obtained with these methods are constrained to lie in the sphere defined by $\mathbf{x}^T\mathbf{x} = 1$ instead of the standard simplex Δ used in the dominant sets framework. This subtle difference is crucial for our practical purposes. First, the components of the weighted characteristic vector give us a measure of the participation of the corresponding data points in the cluster. Second, this constraint provides robustness against noise and outliers [18,15].

3 Proposed Method

In this section, we present a novel multiple-instance learning framework called MILDS, which transforms a MIL problem into a SIL problem via instance selecting. Unlike the similar approaches in [5,4,13,8], it makes use of the *dominant sets* clustering framework [18] for instance selection to build a more effective embedding space. We first restrict ourselves to the *two-class* case. However, as will be described later in Section 3.4, extension to *multi-class* MIL problems is quite straightforward.

3.1 Notations

Let $B_i = \{B_{i1}, \ldots, B_{ij}, \ldots, B_{in_i}\}$ denote a bag of instances where B_{ij} denotes the jth instance in the bag, and $y_i \in \{+1, -1\}$ denote the label of bag i. For the sake of simplicity, we will denote a positive bag as B_i^+ and a negative bag as B_i^-. Further, let $\mathcal{B} = \{B_1^+, \ldots, B_{m^+}^+, B_1^-, \ldots, B_{m^-}^-\}$ denote the set of m^+ positive and m^- negative training bags. Note that each bag may contain different number of instances, and each instance may have a label which is not directly observable.

3.2 Instance Selection with Dominant Sets

Recall the two assumptions of the classical MIL formulation that a bag is positive if it contains at least one positive instance, and all negative bags contains only negative instances [7]. This means that positive bags may contain some instances from the negative class but there is no such ambiguity in the negative bags (provided that there is no labeling noise). Just like in [13,8], our instance selection strategy is heavily based on this observation. However, unlike those approaches, to select the representative set of instances we do not explicitly estimate either a probability density function or a conditional probability. Instead, we try to model the negative data by clustering the instances in the negative bags, and then making decisions according to the distances to the extracted clusters. As will be clear throughout the paper, the dominant sets framework provides a natural scheme to carry out these tasks in an efficient way.

Denote $\mathcal{N} = \{I_i \mid i = 1, \ldots, M\}$ as the collection of negative instances from all of the negative training bags, *i.e.* the set defined by $\{B_{ij}^- \in B_i^- \mid i = 1, \ldots, m^-\}$. Construct the matrix $A = [a_{ij}]$ composed of the similarities between the negative instances as:

$$a_{ij} = \begin{cases} exp\left(-\frac{d(I_i, I_j)^2}{2\sigma^2}\right) & \text{if } i \neq j \\ 0 & \text{otherwise} \end{cases} \tag{4}$$

where $d(\cdot, \cdot)$ is a distance measure that depends on the application and σ is a scale parameter. In the experiments, the Euclidean distance was used.

To extract the clusters in $\mathcal{N}$, the iterative *peeling-off strategy* suggested in [18] is employed. In specific, at each iteration, a dominant set (a cluster) is found by solving the quadratic program in (1). Then, the instances in the cluster are removed from the similarity graph, and this process is reiterated on the remaining instances. In theory, the clustering process stops when all the instances are covered, but in dealing with large and noisy data sets, this is not very practical. Hence, in our experiments, an upper bound on the number of extracted clusters was introduced that at most m^- (*i.e.* the number of negative bags) most coherent dominant sets were selected according to internal coherency values measured by the corresponding values of the objective function. Notice that, in this way, *instance pruning* is carried our in an early stage. This is another fundamental point which distinguishes our work from the approaches in [4,8] as these two methods perform instance pruning implicitly in the SVM training step. Moreover, this provides robustness to noise and outliers.

Suppose $\mathcal{C} = \{C_1, \ldots, C_k\}$ denotes the set of clusters extracted from the collection of negative training instances $\mathcal{N}$. A representative set for $\mathcal{N}$ is found by selecting one prototype from each cluster $C_i \in \mathcal{C}$. Recall that each cluster C_i is associated with a characteristic vector $\mathbf{x}^{C_i}$ whose components give us a measure of the participation of the corresponding instances in the cluster [18]. Hence, the instance prototype z_i^- representing the cluster C_i is identified based on the corresponding characteristic vector $\mathbf{x}^{C_i}$ as:

$$z_i^- = I_{j^*} \text{ with } j^* = \underset{j \in \sigma(\mathbf{x}^{C_i})}{\arg\max}\, x_j^{C_i} \quad . \tag{5}$$

In selecting the representative instances for the positive class, however, the suggested clustering-based selection strategy makes no sense on the collection of positive bags because the bags may contain some negative instances which may collectively form one or more clusters, thus if applied, the procedure may result in some instance prototypes belonging to the negative class. Hence, for selecting prototypes for the positive class, a different strategy is employed. In particular, the most positive instance in each positive bag is identified according to its relationship to the negative training data.

For a positive bag $B_i^+ = \left\{B_{i1}^+, \ldots, B_{in_i^+}^+\right\}$, let $A^\dagger$ be an $n_i^+ \times |\mathcal{N}|$ matrix composed of the similarities between the instances in B_i^+ and the negative training instances in $\mathcal{N}$, computed like in (4). The *true positive* (*i.e.* the *least negative*) instance in B_i^+, denoted with z_i^+, is picked as the instance which is the most distant from the extracted negative clusters in $\mathcal{C}$ as follows:

$$z_i^+ = B_{ij^*}^+ \text{ with } j^* = \underset{j=1,\ldots,n_i^+}{\arg\min} \frac{\sum_{\ell=1,\ldots,k} (A^\dagger \mathbf{x}^{C_\ell})_j \times |C_\ell|}{\sum_{\ell=1,\ldots,k} |C_\ell|} \tag{6}$$

where the term $(A^\dagger \mathbf{x}^{C_\ell})_j$ is the weighted similarity of the instance B_{ij}^+ to the cluster C_ℓ, and $|\cdot|$ denotes the cardinality of the set[1]. Intuitively, in (6), larger clusters have more significance in the final decision than the smaller ones.

To illustrate the proposed selection process, consider the two-dimensional synthetic data given in Fig. 1(a). It contains 8 positive bags and 8 negative bags, each having at least 8 and at most 10 instances. Each instance is randomly drawn from one of the five normal distributions: $\mathcal{N}([4,8]^T, I)$, $\mathcal{N}([0,4]^T, I)$, $\mathcal{N}([-1,12]^T, I)$, $\mathcal{N}([-4,-2]^T, I)$ and $\mathcal{N}([6,2]^T, I)$ with I denoting the identity matrix. A bag is labeled positive if it contains at least one instance from the first two distributions. In Fig. 1(a), positive and negative instances are respectively represented by crosses and circles, and drawn with colors showing the labels of the bags they belong: blue for positive and red for negative bags. The result of the proposed instance selection method is given in Fig. 1(b). The extracted negative clusters are shown in different colors, and the selected instance prototypes are indicated by squares. Notice that the dominant sets framework correctly captured the multi-modality of the negative class, and the prototypes selected from the extracted clusters are all close to the centers of the given negative distributions. Moreover, the true positive instances in the positive bags were successfully identified.

[1] Note that since the zero-components of $\mathbf{x}^{C_\ell}$ have no effect on estimating z_i^+s, in practice highly reduced versions of $A^\dagger$s are utilized in the computations.

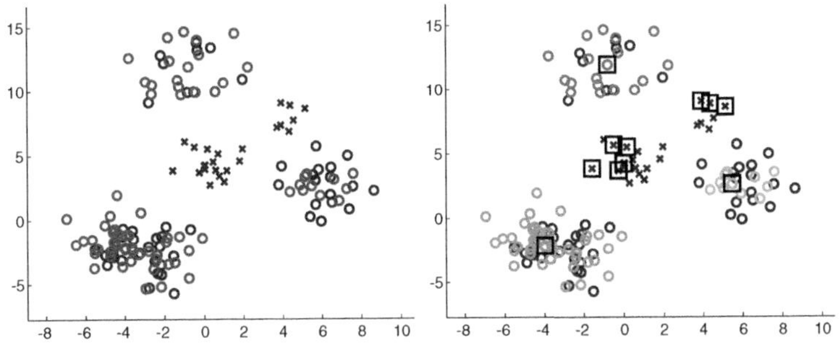

(a) (b)

Fig. 1. Synthetic data set (best viewed in color). (a) Raw data. (b) The instance selection process. See text for details.

3.3 Classification

We can now describe our classification scheme. Suppose $\mathcal{Z}=\{z_1^-, \ldots, z_k^-, z_1^+, \ldots, z_{m^+}^+\}$ denote the set of selected instance prototypes, where k is the number of extracted negative clusters, m^+ is the number of positive training bags[2]. A similarity measure $s(z, B_i)$ between a bag B_i and an instance prototype z is defined by

$$s(z, B_i) = \max_{B_{ij} \in B_i} exp\left(-\frac{d(z, B_{ij})^2}{2\sigma^2}\right) \tag{7}$$

which calculates the similarity between z and its nearest neighbor in B_i. Then, we define an embedding function φ which maps a bag B to a $(k+m^+)$-dimensional vector space by considering the similarities to the instance prototypes:

$$\varphi(B)= \left[s(z_1^-, B), \ldots, s(z_k^-, B), s(z_1^+, B), \ldots, s(z_{m^+}^+, B)\right]^T \tag{8}$$

For classification, the embedding in (8) can be used to convert the MIL problem into a SIL problem. In solving the SIL counterpart, we choose to train a standard linear SVM which has a single regularization parameter C needed to be tuned. In the end, we come up with a linear classifier to classify a test bag B as:

$$f(B; \mathbf{w}) = \mathbf{w}^T \varphi(B) + b \tag{9}$$

where $\mathbf{w} \in \mathbb{R}^{|\mathcal{Z}|}$ is the weight vector, b is the bias term. The label of a test bag B is simply estimated by:

$$y(B) = sign(f(B; \mathbf{w})) \tag{10}$$

The outline of the proposed MIL framework is summarized in Algorithm 1.

[2] Note that one can always select more than one instance from each cluster or each positive bag. A detailed analysis of this issue on the performance will be reported in a longer version.

Algorithm 1. Summary of the proposed MILDS framework.

Input : Training bags $\{B_1^+, \ldots, B_{m^+}^+, B_1^-, \ldots, B_{m^-}^-\}$

1 Apply dominant sets to cluster all the instances in the negative training bags
2 Select k ($\leq m^-$) instance prototypes from the extracted k negative clusters via Eq. (5)
3 Select m^+ instance prototypes from the positive bags via Eq. (6)
4 Form the instance-based embedding in Eq. (8) using the selected prototypes
5 Train a linear SVM classifier based on the constructed feature space

Output: The set of selected instance prototypes $\mathcal{Z}$ and the SVM classifier $f(B; \mathbf{w})$ with weight $\mathbf{w}$

3.4 Extension to Multi-class MIL

The proposed approach can be straightforwardly extended to solve multi-class MIL problems by employing a *one-vs-rest* strategy. In particular, one can train c binary classifiers, one for each class against all other classes. Then, a test bag can be classified according to the classifier with the highest decision value. Note that an implementation of this idea forms a different instance-based embedding for each binary subproblem. Here, we propose a second type of embedding which results from using a set of representative instances common for all classes, as:

$$\begin{aligned}\phi(B) = [&s(z_1^1, B), s(z_2^1, B), \ldots, s(z_{m_1}^1, B),\\ &s(z_1^2, B), s(z_2^2, B), \ldots, s(z_{m_2}^2, B),\\ &\vdots\\ &s(z_1^c, B), s(z_2^c, B), \ldots, s(z_{m_c}^c, B)\,]\end{aligned} \tag{11}$$

where z_i^k is the ith instance prototype selected from class k (note that the number of prototypes may differ from class to class). In this case, training data is kept the same for all binary subproblems, only the labels differ, and this makes the training phase much more efficient. This second approach is denoted with milDS to distinguish it with the naive multi-class extension of MILDS.

In milDS, instance selection is performed as follows. Let $\mathcal{I}^k = \{I_i^k \mid i = 1, \ldots, M_k\}$ denote the collection of instances in bags belonging to class k, *i.e.* the set defined by $\{B_{ij} \in B_i \mid \text{for all } B_i \in \mathcal{B} \text{ with } y(B_i) = k\}$. First, for each class k, the pairwise similarity matrix A_k of instances $\mathcal{I}^k$ is formed, and accordingly a set of clusters $\mathcal{C}^k = \{C_1^k, \ldots, C_{m_k}^k\}$ is extracted via dominant sets framework[3]. Then, an instance prototype from each cluster C_i^k is identified according to:

$$z_i^k = I_{j^*}^k \text{ with } j^* = \underset{j \in \sigma(\mathbf{x}^{C_i^k})}{\arg\max} \; x_j^{C_i^k} / \beta_{ik}(j) \tag{12}$$

where the function $\beta_{ik}(j)$ measures the similarity of jth instance in C_i^k to all the remaining classes. The basic idea is to select the most representative element in C_i^k which is also quite dissimilar to the remaining training data from other classes. However, here we make a simplification and estimate $\beta_{ik}(j)$ by considering only the most closest class:

[3] In the experiments, for each class k, we extract at most m_k clusters that is equal to the number of training bags belonging to class k.

$$\beta_{ik}(j) = \max_{\substack{m=1,\dots,c \\ m \neq k}} \frac{\sum_{C_\ell^m \in \mathcal{C}^m} (A_{km} \mathbf{x}^{C_\ell^m})_j \times |C_\ell^m|}{\sum_{C_\ell^m \in \mathcal{C}^m} |C_\ell^m|} \tag{13}$$

with A_{km} denoting the $M^k \times M^m$ matrix of similarities between the instances in $\mathcal{I}^k$ and the instances in $\mathcal{I}^m$.

The embedding procedure described above gives rise to a feature space whose dimensionality is at most $\sum_k m_k$, *i.e.* the sum of the total number of clusters extracted for each class.

3.5 Computational Complexity

From a computational point of view, the most time consuming step of the proposed MILDS method and its multi-class extensions is the calculation of pairwise distances, which is also the case for [4,13,8]. In addition, there is the cost of clustering negative data with dominant sets. In this matter, a dominant set can be computed in quadratic time using the approach in [19]. An important point here is that the size of the input graphs becomes smaller and smaller at each iteration of the employed peeling off strategy, and this further introduces an increase in the efficiency of the clustering step.

4 Experimental Results

In this section, we present two groups of experiments to evaluate the proposed MILDS algorithm. First, we carry out a thorough analysis on some standard MIL benchmark data sets. Following that, we investigate image classification by casting it as a multi-class MIL problem. In the experiments, LIBSVM [3] package was used for training linear SVMs. In addition to the SVM regularization parameter C, our algorithm has only a single scale parameter σ that needs to be tuned. The best values for C and σ are selected by using n-fold cross validation from the sets $\{2^{-10}, 2^{-9}, \dots, 2^{10}\}$ and $linspace(0.05\mu, \mu, 20)$, respectively, with μ being the mean distance between pair of instances in the training data and $linspace(a, b, n)$ denoting the set n linearly spaced numbers between and including a and b.

4.1 Benchmark Data Sets

We evaluate our MILDS method on five popular MIL benchmark data sets used in many multiple-instance learning studies, namely *Musk1*, *Musk2*, *Elephant*, *Fox* and *Tiger*. In *Musk1* and *Musk2*, the task is to predict drug activity from structural information. Each drug molecule is considered as a bag in which the instances represents different structural configurations of the molecule. In *Elephant*, *Fox* and *Tiger*, the goal is to differentiate images containing elephants, tigers and foxes from those that do not, respectively. Each image is considered as a bag, and each region of interest within the image as an instance. The details of the data sets are given in Table 1.

For experimental evaluation, we use the most common setting, 10 times 10-fold cross validation (CV). That is, we report the classification accuracies averaged over 10 runs

Table 1. Information about the MIL benchmark data sets

data set	bags pos./neg.	avg. inst./bag	dim
Musk1	47/45	5.17	166
Musk2	39/63	64.69	166
Elephant	100/100	6.96	230
Fox	100/100	6.60	230
Tiger	100/100	6.10	230

where the parameter selection is carried our by using 10-fold cross validation. Our results are shown in Table 2 together with those of 12 other MIL algorithms in the literature [13,8,4,5,10,12,14,1,24]. All reported results are also based on 10-fold CV averaged over 10 runs[4], with the exception of MIForest, which is over 5 runs, and MILIS and MIO, which are over 15 runs. The results demonstrate that our proposed approach is competitive with and often better than the state-of-the-art MIL methods. In three out of five MIL benchmark data sets, it outperforms several MIL approaches. However, it is more important to note that it gives the best performance among the instance-selection based MIL approaches.

Table 2. Classification accuracies of various MIL algorithms on standard benchmark data sets. The best performances are indicated in bold typeface.

Algorithm	*Musk1*	*Musk2*	*Elephant*	*Fox*	*Tiger*
MILDS	**90.9**	86.1	**84.8**	**64.3**	81.5
MILD_B [13]	88.3	86.8	82.9	55.0	75.8
MILIS [8]	88.6	91.1	*n/a*	*n/a*	*n/a*
MILES [4]	83.3	**91.6**	84.1	63.0	80.7
DD-SVM [5]	85.8	91.3	83.5	56.6	77.2
MILD_I [13]	89.9	88.7	83.2	49.1	73.4
MIForest [10]	85.0	82.0	84.0	64.0	82.0
MIO [12]	88.3	87.7	*n/a*	*n/a*	*n/a*
Ins-KI-SVM [14]	84.0	84.4	83.5	63.4	82.9
Bag-KI-SVM [14]	88.0	82.0	84.5	60.5	**85.0**
mi-SVM [1]	87.4	83.6	82.2	58.2	78.9
MI-SVM [1]	77.9	84.3	81.4	59.4	84.0
EM-DD [24]	84.8	84.9	78.3	56.1	72.1

In Table 3, for each instance-selection based MIL approach, we report the average dimensions of the corresponding embedding spaces. MILES has the highest dimension since it utilizes all the training instances in the mapping. On *Musk2* and *Fox*, our MILDS approach does not offer any advantage in terms of dimension reduction, but for the other data sets, it decreases the dimension $\sim 6-23\%$, as compared to MILIS and DD-SVM. Among all, MILD_B has the lowest dimension as it only uses positive instance

[4] Note that the results of MILD_B and MILD_I on *Musk1* and *Musk2* are different than reported in [13]. This is because, for a complete comparison, we downloaded the source codes of MILD_B and MILD_I available at the authors' webpage and repeated the experiments on all the five data sets with our setting of 10 times 10-fold CV.

Table 3. The dimensions of the embedding spaces averaged over 10 runs of 10-fold CV

Algorithm	*Musk1*	*Musk2*	*Elephant*	*Fox*	*Tiger*
MILDS	75.0	92.0	169.4	180.0	139.2
MILD_B	42.4	35.2	90.0	90.0	90.0
MILIS	83.0	92.0	180.0	180.0	180.0
MILES	429.4	5943.8	1251.9	1188.0	1098.0
DD-SVM	83.0	92.0	180.0	180.0	180.0

prototypes in its embedding scheme. However, as can be seen in Table 2, neglecting the negative prototypes results in a poor performance compared to the other approaches.

4.2 Image Classification

The multi-class extensions of our approach have been investigated on image classification problems. In specific, we used the COREL data set which contains 2000 natural images from 20 diverse categories, each having 100 examples. Each image is considered as a bag of instances with instances corresponding to regions of interest obtained via segmentation. Each region is represented by a 9-dimensional feature vector describing shape and local image characteristics (refer to [5,4] for details). Some example images from the data set are given in Fig. 2.

In our evaluation, we used the same experimental setup described in [4], and performed two groups of experiments, which are referred to as *1000-Image* and *2000-Image*, respectively. In *1000-Image*, only the first ten categories are considered whereas in *2000-Image*, all the twenty categories in the data set are employed. On both experiments, five times two-fold CV is performed. The average categorization accuracies are presented in Table 4. As can be seen from the results, the performance of *MILDS* and *milDS* are competitive with the state-of-the-art MIL approaches. Especially for the larger *2000-Image* data set, our milDS method gives the best result.

Fig. 2. Example images randomly drawn from the COREL data set. For each category, the average number of regions per image is given inside the parentheses.

Table 4. Classification accuracies of various MIL algorithms on COREL *1000-Image* and *2000-Image* data sets. The best performances are indicated in bold typeface.

Algorithm	*1000-Image*	*2000-Image*
milDS	82.2	**70.6**
MILDS	83.0	69.4
MILD_B [13]	79.6	67.7
MILIS [8]	**83.8**	70.1
MILES [4]	82.6	68.7
DD-SVM [5]	81.5	67.5
MIForest [10]	59.0	66.0
MissSVM [26]	78.0	65.2
mi-SVM [1]	76.4	53.7
MI-SVM [1]	74.7	54.6

Recall that in MILDS, each classifier trained for distinguishing a specific category from the rest is built upon a different embedding space, or in other words, the set of selected prototypes varies in every subproblem. For each subproblem in *1000-Image*, Fig. 3 shows the instance prototype identified in one of the training images from the target class. Notice that the prototypes are selected from the discriminative regions for that class. On the other hand, in milDS, the set of selected instance prototypes is the same for all the subproblems. This second selection strategy provides a rich way to include contextual relationships in representing visual categories. In some respects, it resembles the vocabulary generation step of the *bag-of-words* approach [6]. The subtle difference is that a similarity-based mapping is employed here instead of a frequency-based one. Fig. 4 shows five prototypes among the full set of representative instances selected for the *Horse* and *Battle ships* categories. Observe that for the *Horse* category, selected prototypes include not just horses but also the regions corresponding to grass regions. Likewise, for the *Battle ships* category, there are additional prototypes representing sky and sea regions.

4.3 Sensitivity to Labeling Noise

Lastly, we analyzed the sensitivity to labeling noise. For that purpose, we repeated the experiment in [4] which involves distinguishing *Historical buildings* from *Horses* in COREL data set. In this experiment, we compared our method with MILES, MILIS, MILD_B with varying degrees of noise levels where the results are based on five times 2-fold CV. For each noise level, $d\%$ of positive and $d\%$ of negative images are randomly selected from the training set, and then their labels are changed to form the noisy labels. Fig. 5 shows the average classification accuracies. When the level of labeling noise is low ($d \leq 5\%$), there is no considerable difference in the performances. As the noise level increases, the performance of MILIS degrades. MILES gives comparable results to MILDS and MILD_B for the noise levels up to $d \leq 25\%$, but gives relatively poor outcomes afterwards. Overall, MILDS is the most robust MIL algorithm to labeling noise among all the tested MIL algorithms. Its performance remains almost the same over all levels of the labeling noise. This is expected, since dominant sets is known to be quite robust to outliers [18,15].

Fig. 3. Sample instance prototypes selected by the *MILDS* algorithm. For each image category, the first row shows a sample training image from that category, and the bottom row illustrates the selected prototype region (shown in white) on the corresponding segmentation map.

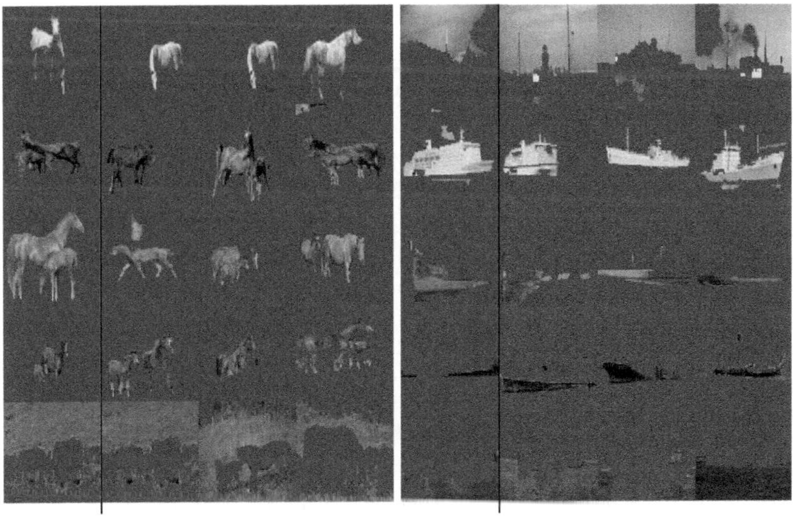

Fig. 4. Sample instance prototypes selected by the *milDS* algorithm for the *Horse* and the *Battle ships* categories. The leftmost columns are the prototypes. The rightmost three columns show other sample regions from the corresponding extracted clusters. The regions in each cluster share similar visual characteristics.

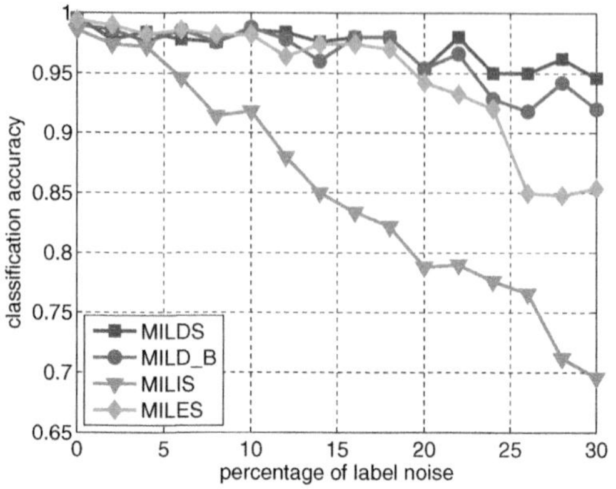

Fig. 5. Sensitivity of various MIL algorithms to labeling noise. MILDS produces the most robust results.

5 Summary and Future Work

In this paper, we proposed an effective MIL scheme, MILDS, which offers a new solution to select a set of instance prototypes, for transforming a given MIL problem into a standard SIL problem. This instance selection approach enables us to successfully identify the most representative examples in the positive and negative training bags. Its success lies in the use of dominant sets pairwise clustering framework. Our empirical results show that the proposed algorithm is competitive with state-of-the-art MIL methods and also robust to labeling noise. As a future work, we plan to extend our approach to multi-instance multi-label learning setting [27,23].

References

1. Andrews, S., Tsochantaridis, I., Hofmann, T.: Support vector machines for multiple-instance learning. In: NIPS, pp. 1073–1080 (2003)
2. Babenko, B., Yang, M.H., Belongie, S.: Visual tracking with online multiple instance learning. In: CVPR, pp. 983–990 (2009)
3. Chang, C.C., Lin, C.J.: LIBSVM: A library for support vector machines (2001), software `http://www.csie.ntu.edu.tw/~cjlin/libsvm`
4. Chen, Y., Bi, J., Wang, J.Z.: MILES: Multiple-instance learning via embedded instance selection. IEEE Trans. Pattern Anal. Mach. Intell. 28(12), 1931–1947 (2006)
5. Chen, Y., Wang, J.Z.: Image categorization by learning and reasoning with regions. J. Mach. Learn. Res. 5, 913–939 (2004)
6. Csurka, G., Dance, C.R., Fan, L., Willamowski, J., Bray, C.: Visual categorization with bags of keypoints. In: ECCV Int. Workshop Stat. Learning in Comp. Vis. (2004)
7. Dietterich, T.G., Lathrop, R.H., Lozano-Pérez, T.: Solving the multiple instance problem with axis-parallel rectangles. Artif. Intell. 89(1-2), 31–71 (1997)
8. Fu, Z., Robles-Kelly, A., Zhou, J.: MILIS: Multiple instance learning with instance selection. IEEE Trans. Pattern Anal. Mach. Intell. 33(5), 958–977 (2011)

9. Gärtner, T., Flach, P.A., Kowalczyk, A., Smola, A.J.: Multi-instance kernels. In: ICML, pp. 179–186 (2002)
10. Leistner, C., Saffari, A., Bischof, H.: MIForests: Multiple-instance learning with randomized trees. In: Daniilidis, K., Maragos, P., Paragios, N. (eds.) ECCV 2010, Part VI. LNCS, vol. 6316, pp. 29–42. Springer, Heidelberg (2010)
11. Leordeanu, M., Hebert, M.: A spectral technique for correspondence problems using pairwise constraints. In: ICCV, vol. 2, pp. 1482–1489 (2005)
12. Li, M., Kwok, J., Lu, B.L.: Online multiple instance learning with no regret. In: CVPR, pp. 1395–1401 (2010)
13. Li, W.J., Yeung, D.Y.: MILD: Multiple-instance learning via disambiguation. IEEE Trans. on Knowl. and Data Eng. 22, 76–89 (2010)
14. Li, Y.F., Kwok, J.T., Tsang, I.W., Zhou, Z.H.: A convex method for locating regions of interest with multi-instance learning. In: Buntine, W., Grobelnik, M., Mladenić, D., Shawe-Taylor, J. (eds.) ECML PKDD 2009, Part II. LNCS, vol. 5782, pp. 15–30. Springer, Heidelberg (2009)
15. Liu, H., Yan, S.: Common visual pattern discovery via spatially coherent correspondences. In: CVPR, pp. 1609–1616 (2010)
16. Maron, O., Lozano-Pérez, T.: A framework for multiple instance learning. In: NIPS, pp. 570–576 (1998)
17. Motzkin, T.S., Straus, E.G.: Maxima for graphs and a new proof of a theorem of Turán. Canad. J. Math. 17, 533–540 (1965)
18. Pavan, M., Pelillo, M.: Dominant sets and pairwise clustering. IEEE Trans. on Pattern Anal. and Mach. Intell. 29(1), 167–172 (2007)
19. Rota Bulò, S., Bomze, I., Pelillo, M.: Fast population game dynamics for dominant sets and other quadratic optimization problems. In: Hancock, E.R., Wilson, R.C., Windeatt, T., Ulusoy, I., Escolano, F. (eds.) SSPR&SPR 2010. LNCS, vol. 6218, pp. 275–285. Springer, Heidelberg (2010)
20. Sarkar, S., Boyer, K.L.: Quantitative measures of change based on feature organization: Eigenvalues and eigenvectors. Comput. Vis. Image Understand. 71(1), 110–136 (1998)
21. Viola, P., Platt, J.C., Zhang, C.: Multiple instance boosting for object detection. In: NIPS, pp. 1419–1426 (2006)
22. Wang, J., Zucker, J.-D.: Solving multiple-instance problem: A lazy learning approach. In: ICML (2000)
23. Zha, Z.J., Hua, X.S., Mei, T., Wang, J., Qi, G.J., Wang, Z.: Joint multi-label multi-instance learning for image classification. In: CVPR (2008)
24. Zhang, Q., Goldman, S.A.: EM-DD: An improved multi-instance learning technique. In: NIPS, pp. 561–568 (2002)
25. Zhang, Q., Goldman, S.A., Yu, W., Fritts, J.: Content-based image retrieval using multiple-instance learning. In: ICML, pp. 682–689 (2002)
26. Zhou, Z.H., Xu, J.M.: On the relation between multi-instance learning and semi-supervised learning. In: ICML, pp. 1167–1174 (2007)
27. Zhou, Z.H., Zhang, M.L.: Multi-instance multi-label learning with applications to scene classification. In: NIPS, pp. 1609–1616 (2006)

Min-sum Clustering of Protein Sequences with Limited Distance Information

Konstantin Voevodski[1], Maria-Florina Balcan[2], Heiko Röglin[3], Shang-Hua Teng[4], and Yu Xia[5]

[1] Department of Computer Science, Boston University, Boston, MA 02215, USA
[2] College of Computing, Georgia Institute of Technology, Atlanta, GA 30332, USA
[3] Department of Computer Science, University of Bonn, Bonn, Germany
[4] Computer Science Department, University of Southern California, Los Angeles, CA 90089, USA
[5] Bioinformatics Program and Department of Chemistry, Boston University, Boston, MA 02215, USA

Abstract. We study the problem of efficiently clustering protein sequences in a limited information setting. We assume that we do not know the distances between the sequences in advance, and must query them during the execution of the algorithm. Our goal is to find an accurate clustering using few queries. We model the problem as a point set S with an unknown metric d on S, and assume that we have access to *one versus all* distance queries that given a point $s \in S$ return the distances between s and all other points. Our one versus all query represents an efficient sequence database search program such as BLAST, which compares an input sequence to an entire data set. Given a natural assumption about the approximation stability of the *min-sum* objective function for clustering, we design a provably accurate clustering algorithm that uses few one versus all queries. In our empirical study we show that our method compares favorably to well-established clustering algorithms when we compare computationally derived clusterings to gold-standard manual classifications.

1 Introduction

Biology is an information-driven science, and the size of available data continues to expand at a remarkable rate. The growth of biological sequence databases has been particularly impressive. For example, the size of GenBank, a biological sequence repository, has doubled every 18 months from 1982 to 2007. It has become important to develop computational techniques that can handle such large amounts of data. Clustering is very useful for exploring relationships between protein sequences. However, most clustering algorithms require distances between all pairs of points as input, which is infeasible to obtain for very large protein sequence data sets. Even with a *one versus all* distance query such as BLAST (Basic Local Alignment Search Tool) [AGM+90], which efficiently compares a sequence to an entire database of sequences, it may not be possible to use it n times to construct the entire

M. Pelillo and E.R. Hancock (Eds.): SIMBAD 2011, LNCS 7005, pp. 192–206, 2011.

pairwise distance matrix, where n is the size of the data set. In this work we present a clustering algorithm that gives an accurate clustering using only $O(k \log k)$ queries, where k is the number of clusters.

We analyze the correctness of our algorithm under a natural assumption about the data, namely the (c, ϵ) approximation stability property of [BBG09]. Balcan et al. assume that there is some relevant "target" clustering C_T, and optimizing a particular objective function for clustering (such as min-sum) gives clusterings that are structurally close to C_T. More precisely, they assume that any c-approximation of the objective is ϵ-close to C_T, where the distance between two clusterings is the fraction of misclassified points under the optimum matching between the two sets of clusters. Our contribution is designing an algorithm that given the (c, ϵ)-property for the *min-sum* objective produces an accurate clustering using only $O(k \log k)$ *one versus all* distance queries, and has a runtime of $O(k \log(k) n \log(n))$. We conduct an empirical study that compares computationally derived clusterings to those given by gold-standard classifications of protein evolutionary relatedness. We show that our method compares favorably to well-established clustering algorithms in terms of accuracy. Moreover, our algorithm easily scales to massive data sets that cannot be handled by traditional algorithms.

The algorithm presented here is related to the one presented in [VBR+10]. The *Landmark-Clustering* algorithm presented there gives an accurate clustering if the instance satisfies the (c, ϵ)-property for the k-median objective. However, if the property is satisfied for the *min-sum* objective the structure of the clustering instance is quite different, and the algorithm given in [VBR+10] fails to find an accurate clustering in such cases. Indeed, the analysis presented here is also quite different. The min-sum objective is also considerably harder to approximate. For k-median the best approximation guarantee is $(3 + \epsilon)$ given by [AGK+04]. For the min-sum objective when the number of clusters is arbitrary there is an $O(\delta^{-1} \log^{1+\delta} n)$-approximation algorithm with running time $n^{O(1/\delta)}$ for any $\delta > 0$ due to [BCR01]. In addition, min-sum clustering satisfies the *consistency* property of Kleinberg [Kle03, ZBD09], while k-median does not [Kle03]. The min-sum objective is also more flexible because the optimum clustering is not always a Voronoi decomposition (unlike the optimum k-median clustering).

There are also several other clustering algorithms that are applicable in our limited information setting [AV07, AJM09, MOP01, CS07]. However, because all of these methods seek to approximate an objective function they will not necessarily produce an accurate clustering in our model if the (c, ϵ)-property holds for values of c for which finding a c-approximation is NP-hard. Other than [VBR+10] we are not aware of any results providing both provably accurate algorithms and strong query complexity guarantees in such a model.

2 Preliminaries

Given a metric space $M = (X, d)$ with point set X, an unknown distance function d satisfying the triangle inequality, and a set of points $S \subseteq X$, we would like to find a k-clustering C that partitions the points in S into k sets $C_1, \ldots, C_k$ by using *one versus all* distance queries.

The *min-sum* objective function for clustering is to minimize $\Phi(C) = \sum_{i=1}^{k} \sum_{x,y \in C_i} d(x, y)$. We reduce the min-sum clustering problem to the related *balanced k-median* problem. The balanced k-median objective function seeks to minimize $\Psi(C) = \sum_{i=1}^{k} |C_i| \sum_{x \in C_i} d(x, c_i)$, where c_i is the median of cluster C_i, which is the point $y \in C_i$ that minimizes $\sum_{x \in C_i} d(x, y)$. As pointed out in [BCR01], in metric spaces the two objective functions are related to within a factor of 2: $\Psi(C)/2 \leq \Phi(C) \leq \Psi(C)$. For any objective function Ω we use OPT_Ω to denote its optimum value.

In our analysis we assume that S satisfies the (c, ϵ)-property of [BBG09] for the min-sum and balanced k-median objective functions. To formalize the (c, ϵ)-property we need to define a notion of distance between two k-clusterings $C = \{C_1, \ldots, C_k\}$ and $C' = \{C'_1, \ldots, C'_k\}$. As in [BBG09], we define the distance between C and C' as the fraction of points on which they disagree under the optimal matching of clusters in C to clusters in C':

$$\mathrm{dist}(C, C') = \min_{\sigma \in S_k} \frac{1}{n} \sum_{i=1}^{k} |C_i - C'_{\sigma(i)}|,$$

where S_k is the set of bijections $\sigma\colon \{1, \ldots, k\} \to \{1, \ldots, k\}$. Two clusterings C and C' are said to be ϵ-*close* if $\mathrm{dist}(C, C') < \epsilon$.

We assume that there exists some unknown relevant "target" clustering C_T and given a proposed clustering C we define the error of C with respect to C_T as $\mathrm{dist}(C, C_T)$. Our goal is to find a clustering of low error. The (c, ϵ) approximation stability property is defined as follows.

Definition 1. *We say that the instance (S, d) satisfies the (c, ϵ)-property for objective function Ω with respect to the target clustering C_T if any clustering of S that approximates OPT_Ω within a factor of c is ϵ-close to C_T, that is, $\Omega(C) \leq c \cdot \mathrm{OPT}_\Omega \Rightarrow \mathrm{dist}(C, C_T) < \epsilon$.*

We note that because any $(1 + \alpha)$-approximation of the balanced k-median objective is a $2(1+\alpha)$-approximation of the min-sum objective, it follows that if the clustering instance satisfies the $(2(1 + \alpha), \epsilon)$-property for the min-sum objective, then it satisfies the $(1 + \alpha, \epsilon)$-property for balanced k-median.

3 Algorithm Overview

In this section we present a clustering algorithm that given the $(1+\alpha, \epsilon)$-property for the balanced k-median objective finds an accurate clustering using few distance queries. Our algorithm is outlined in Algorithm 1 (with some implementation details omitted). We start by uniformly at random choosing n' points that we call *landmarks*, where n' is an appropriate number. For each landmark that we choose we use a *one versus all* query to get the distances between this landmark and all other points. These are the only distances used by our procedure.

Our algorithm then expands a ball B_l around each landmark l one point at a time. In each iteration we check whether some ball B_{l^*} passes the test in line 7. Our test considers the size of the ball and its radius, and checks whether their product is greater than the threshold T. If this is the case, we consider all balls that overlap B_{l^*} on any points, and compute a cluster that contains all the points in these balls. Points and landmarks in the cluster are then removed from further consideration.

Algorithm 1. Landmark-Clustering-Min-Sum(S, d, k, n', T)

1: choose a set of landmarks L of size n' uniformly at random from S;
2: $i = 1$, $r = 0$;
3: **while** $i \leq k$ **do**
4:    **for** each $l \in L$ **do**
5:       $B_l = \{s \in S \mid d(s, l) \leq r\}$;
6:    **end for**
7:    **if** $\exists l^* \in L : |B_{l^*}| \cdot r > T$ **then**
8:       $L' = \{l \in L : B_l \cap B_{l^*} \neq \emptyset\}$;
9:       $C_i = \{s \in S : s \in B_l \text{ and } l \in L'\}$;
10:       remove points in C_i from consideration;
11:       $i = i + 1$;
12:    **end if**
13:    increment r to the next relevant distance;
14: **end while**
15: **return** $C = \{C_1, \ldots C_k\}$;

A complete description of this algorithm can be found in the next section. We now present our theoretical guarantee for Algorithm 1.

Theorem 1. *Given a metric space $M = (X, d)$, where d is unknown, and a set of points S, if the instance (S, d) satisfies the $(1 + \alpha, \epsilon)$-property for the balanced-k-median objective function, we are given the optimum objective value* OPT, *and each cluster in the target clustering C_T has size at least $(6+240/\alpha)\epsilon n$, then* Landmark-Clustering-Min-Sum$(S, d, k, n', \frac{\alpha \mathrm{OPT}}{40\epsilon n})$ *outputs a clustering that is $O(\epsilon/\alpha)$-close to C_T with probability at least $1 - \delta$. The algorithm uses $n' = \frac{1}{(3+120/\alpha)\epsilon} \ln \frac{k}{\delta}$* one versus all distance queries, *and has a runtime of $O(n'n \log n)$.*

We note that $n' = O(k \ln \frac{k}{\delta})$ if the sizes of the target clusters are balanced. In addition, if we do not know the value of OPT, we can still find an accurate clustering by running Algorithm 1 from line 2 with increasing estimates of T until enough points are clustered. Theorem 2 states that we need to run the algorithm $n'n^2$ times to find a provably accurate clustering in this setting, but in practice much fewer iterations are sufficient if we use larger increments of T. It is not necessary to recompute the landmarks, so the number of distance queries that are required remains the same. We next give some high-level intuition for how our procedures work.

Given our approximation stability assumption, the target clustering must have the structure shown in Figure 1. Each target cluster C_i has a "core" of well-separated points, where any two points in the cluster core are closer than a

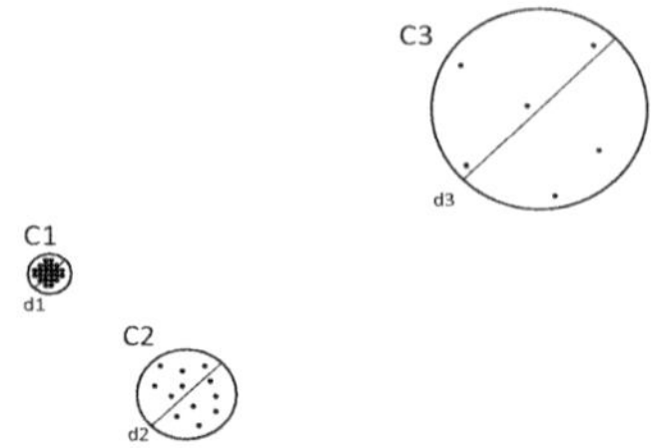

Fig. 1. Cluster cores C_1, C_2 and C_3 are shown with diameters d_1, d_2 and d_3, respectively. The diameters of the cluster cores are inversely proportional to their sizes.

certain distance d_i to each other, and any point in a different core is farther than cd_i, for some constant c. Moreover, the diameters of the cluster cores are inversely proportional to the cluster sizes: there is some constant θ such that $|C_i| \cdot d_i = \theta$ for each cluster C_i. Given this structure, it is possible to classify the points in the cluster cores correctly if we extract the smaller diameter clusters first. In the example in Figure 1, we can extract C_1, followed by C_2 and C_3 if we choose the threshold T correctly and we have selected a landmark from each cluster core. However, if we wait until some ball contains all of C_3, C_1 and C_2 may be merged.

4 Algorithm Analysis

In this section we give a complete description of our algorithm and present its formal analysis. We describe the structure of the clustering instance that is implied by our approximation stability assumption, and give the proof of Theorem 1. We also state and prove Theorem 2, which concerns what happens when we do not know the optimum objective value OPT and must estimate one of the parameters of our algorithm.

4.1 Algorithm Description

A detailed description of our algorithm is given in Algorithm 2. In order to efficiently expand a ball around each landmark, we first sort all landmark-point pairs (l, s) by $d(l, s)$ (not shown). We then consider these pairs in order of increasing distance (line 7), skipping pairs where l or s have already been clustered; the clustered points are maintained in the set $\bar{S}$.

In each iteration we check whether some ball B_{l^*} passes the test in line 19. Our actual test, which is slightly different than the one presented earlier, considers the size of the ball and the *next largest* landmark-point distance (denoted by r_2), and checks whether their product is greater than the threshold T. If this is the case, we consider all balls that overlap B_{l^*} on any points, and compute a cluster that contains all the points in these balls. Points and landmarks in the cluster are then removed from further consideration by adding the clustered points to $\bar{S}$, and removing the clustered points from any ball.

Our procedure terminates once we find k clusters. If we reach the final landmark-point pair, we stop and report the remaining unclustered points as part of the same cluster (line 12). If the algorithm terminates without partitioning all the points, we assign each remaining point to the cluster containing the closest clustered landmark (not shown). In our analysis we show that if the clustering instance satisfies the $(1+\alpha, \epsilon)$-property for the balanced k-median objective function, our procedure will output exactly k clusters.

The most time-consuming part of our algorithm is sorting all landmark-points pairs, which takes $O(|L|n \log n)$, where n is the size of the data set and L is the set of landmarks. With a simple implementation that uses a hashed set to store the points in each ball, the total cost of computing the clusters and removing clustered points from active balls is at most $O(|L|n)$ each. All other operations take asymptotically less time, so the overall runtime of our procedure is $O(|L|n \log n)$.

Algorithm 2. Landmark-Clustering-Min-Sum(S, d, k, n', T)

1: choose a set of landmarks L of size n' uniformly at random from S;
2: **for** each $l \in L$ **do**
3: $B_l = \emptyset$;
4: **end for**
5: $i = 1$, $\bar{S} = \emptyset$;
6: **while** $i \leq k$ **do**
7: $(l, s) =$ GetNextActivePair();
8: $r_1 = d(l, s)$;
9: **if** $((l', s') =$ PeekNextActivePair()$) != $ null **then**
10: $r_2 = d(l', s')$;
11: **else**
12: $C_i = S - \bar{S}$;
13: break;
14: **end if**
15: $B_l = B_l + \{s\}$;
16: **if** $r_1 == r_2$ **then**
17: continue;
18: **end if**
19: **while** $\exists l \in L - \bar{S} : |B_l| > T/r_2$ and $i \leq k$ **do**
20: $l^* = \text{argmax}_{l \in L - \bar{S}} |B_l|$;
21: $L' = \{l \in L - \bar{S} : B_l \cap B_{l^*} \neq \emptyset\}$;
22: $C_i = \{s \in S : s \in B_l \text{ and } l \in L'\}$;
23: **for** each $s \in C_i$ **do**
24: $\bar{S} = \bar{S} + \{s\}$;
25: **for** each $l \in L$ **do**
26: $B_l = B_l - \{s\}$;
27: **end for**
28: **end for**
29: $i = i + 1$;
30: **end while**
31: **end while**
32: **return** $C = \{C_1, \ldots C_k\}$;

4.2 Structure of the Clustering Instance

We next describe the structure of the clustering instance that is implied by our approximation stability assumption. We denote by $C^* = \{C_1^*, \ldots, C_k^*\}$ the optimal balanced-k-median clustering with objective value OPT=$\Psi(C^*)$. For each cluster C_i^*, let c_i^* be the median point in the cluster. For $x \in C_i^*$, define $w(x) = |C_i^*|d(x, c_i^*)$ and let $w = \text{avg}_x w(x) = \frac{\text{OPT}}{n}$. Define $w_2(x) = \min_{j \neq i}|C_j^*|d(x, c_j^*)$.

It is proved in [BBG09] that if the instance satisfies the $(1+\alpha, \epsilon)$-property for the balanced k-median objective function and each cluster in C^* has size at least $\max(6, 6/\alpha) \cdot \epsilon n$, then at most 2ϵ-fraction of points $x \in S$ have $w_2(x) < \frac{\alpha w}{4\epsilon}$. In addition, by definition of the average weight w at most $120\epsilon/\alpha$-fraction of points $x \in S$ have $w(x) > \frac{\alpha w}{120\epsilon}$.

We call point x *good* if both $w(x) \leq \frac{\alpha w}{120\epsilon}$ and $w_2(x) \geq \frac{\alpha w}{4\epsilon}$, else x is called bad. Let X_i be the *good* points in the optimal cluster C_i^*, and let $B = S \setminus \cup X_i$ be the bad points. Lemma 1, which is similar to Lemma 14 of [BBG09], proves that the optimum balanced k-median clustering must have the following structure:

1. For all x, y in the same X_i, we have $d(x, y) \leq \frac{\alpha w}{60\epsilon|C_i^*|}$.
2. For $x \in X_i$ and $y \in X_{j \neq i}$, $d(x, y) > \frac{\alpha w}{5\epsilon} / \min(|C_i^*|, |C_j^*|)$.
3. The number of bad points is at most $b = (2 + 120/\alpha)\epsilon n$.

4.3 Proof of Theorem 1 and Additional Analysis

We next present the proof of Theorem 1. We give an outline of our arguments, which is followed by the complete proof. We also state and prove Theorem 2.

Proof Outline. We first give an outline of our proof of Theorem 1. Our algorithm expands a ball around each landmark, one point at a time, until some ball is large enough. We use r_1 to refer to the current radius of the balls, and r_2 to refer to the next relevant radius (next largest landmark-point distance). To pass the test in line 19, a ball must satisfy $|B_l| > T/r_2$. We choose T such that by the time a ball satisfies the conditional, it must overlap some good set X_i. Moreover, at this time the radius must be large enough for X_i to be entirely contained in some ball; X_i will therefore be part of the cluster computed in line 22. However, the radius is too small for a single ball to overlap different good sets and for two balls overlapping different good sets to share any points. Therefore the computed cluster cannot contain points from any other good set. Points and landmarks in the cluster are then removed from further consideration. The same argument can then be applied again to show that each cluster output by the algorithm entirely contains a single good set. Thus the clustering output by the algorithm agrees with C^* on all the good points, so it must be closer than $b + \epsilon = O(\epsilon/\alpha)$ to C_T.

Complete Proof. We next give a detailed proof of Theorem 1.

Proof. Since each cluster in the target clustering has more than $(6+240/\alpha)\epsilon n$ points, and the optimal balanced-k-median clustering C^* can differ from the target clustering by fewer than ϵn points, each cluster in C^* must have more than $(5+240/\alpha)\epsilon n$ points. Moreover, by Lemma 1 we may have at most $(2+120/\alpha)\epsilon n$ bad points, and hence each $|X_i| = |C_i^* \setminus B| > (3+120/\alpha)\epsilon n \geq (2+120/\alpha)\epsilon n + 2 = b+2$. We will use $s_{\min}$ to refer to the $(3+120/\alpha)\epsilon n$ quantity.

Our argument assumes that we have chosen at least one landmark from each good set X_i. Lemma 2 argues that after selecting $n' = \frac{n}{s_{\min}} \ln \frac{k}{\delta} = \frac{1}{(3+120/\alpha)\epsilon} \ln \frac{k}{\delta}$ landmarks the probability of this happening is at least $1-\delta$. Moreover, if the target clusters are balanced in size: $\max_{C \in C_T} |C| / \min_{C \in C_T} |C| < c$ for some constant c, because the size of each good set is at least half the size of the corresponding target cluster, it must be the case that $2 s_{\min} c \cdot k \geq n$, so $n/s_{\min} = O(k)$.

Suppose that we order the clusters of C^* such that $|C_1^*| \geq |C_2^*| \geq \ldots |C_k^*|$, and let $n_i = |C_i^*|$. Define $d_i = \frac{\alpha w}{60 \epsilon |C_i^*|}$ and recall that $\max_{x,y \in X_i} d(x,y) \leq d_i$. Note that because there is a landmark in each good set X_i, for radius $r \geq d_i$ there exists some ball containing all of X_i. We use $B_l(r)$ to denote a ball of radius r around landmark l: $B_l(r) : \{s \in S \mid d(s,l) \leq r\}$.

Applying Lemma 3 with all the clusters in C^*, we can see that as long as $r \leq 3d_1$, a ball cannot contain points from more than one good set and balls overlapping different good sets cannot share any points. Also, when $r \leq 3d_1$ and $r < d_i$, a ball $B_l(r)$ containing points from X_i does not satisfy $|B_l(r)| \geq T/r$. To see this, consider that for $r \leq 3d_1$ any ball containing points from X_i has size at most $|C_i^*| + b < \frac{3n_i}{2}$; for $r < d_i$ the size bound $T/r > T/d_i = \frac{\alpha w}{40\epsilon} / \frac{\alpha w}{60 \epsilon |C_i^*|} = \frac{3n_i}{2}$. Finally, when $r = 3d_1$ some ball $B_l(r)$ containing all of X_1 does satisfy $|B_l(r)| \geq T/r$. For $r = 3d_1$ there is some ball containing all of X_1, which must have size at least $|C_1^*| - b \geq n_1/2$. For $r = 3d_1$ the size bound $T/r = n_1/2$, so this ball is large enough to satisfy this conditional. Moreover, for $r \leq 3d_1$ the size bound $T/r \geq n_1/2$. Therefore a ball containing only bad points cannot pass our test for $r \leq 3d_1$ because the number of bad points is at most $b < n_1/2$.

Consider the smallest radius r^* for which some ball $B_{l^*}(r^*)$ satisfies $|B_{l^*}(r^*)| \geq T/r^*$. It must be the case that $r^* \leq 3d_1$, and B_{l^*} overlaps with some good set X_i because we cannot have a ball containing only bad points for $r^* \leq 3d_1$. Moreover, by our previous argument because B_{l^*} contains points from X_i, it must be the case that $r^* \geq d_i$, and therefore some ball contains all the points in X_i. Consider a cluster $\hat{C}$ of all the points in balls that overlap B_{l^*}: $\hat{C} = \{s \in S \mid s \in B_l \text{ and } B_l \cap B_{l^*} \neq \emptyset\}$, which must include all the points in X_i. In addition, B_{l^*} cannot share any points with balls that overlap other good sets because $r^* \leq 3d_1$, therefore $\hat{C}$ does not contain points from any other good set. Therefore the cluster $\hat{C}$ entirely contains some good set and no points from any other good set.

These facts suggest the following conceptual algorithm for finding a clustering that classifies all the good points correctly: increment r until some ball satisfies $|B_l(r)| \geq T/r$, compute the cluster containing all points in balls that overlap $B_l(r)$, remove these points, and repeat until we find k clusters. We can argue that each cluster output by the algorithm entirely contains some good set and no points from any other good set. Each time we consider the clusters $C \subseteq C^*$ whose good sets have not yet been output, order them by size, and consider the diameters d_i of their good sets. We apply Lemma 3 with C to argue that while $r \leq 3d_1$ the radius is too small for the computed cluster to overlap any of the remaining good sets. As before, we argue that by the time we reach $3d_1$ we must output some cluster. In addition, when $r \leq 3d_1$ we cannot output a cluster of only bad points and whenever we output a cluster overlapping some good set X_i, it must be the case that $r \geq d_i$. Therefore each computed cluster must entirely contain some good set and no points from any other good set. If there are any unclustered points upon the completion of the algorithm, we can assign the remaining points to any cluster. Still, we are able to classify all the good points correctly, so the reported clustering must be closer than $b + \text{dist}(C^*, C_T) < b + \epsilon = O(\epsilon/\alpha)$ to C_T.

It suffices to show that even though our algorithm only considers discrete values of r corresponding to landmark-point distances, the output of our procedure exactly matches the output of the conceptual algorithm described above. Consider the smallest (continuous) radius r^* for which some ball $B_{l_1}(r^*)$ satisfies $|B_{l_1}(r^*)| \geq T/r^*$. We use d_{real} to refer to the largest landmark-point distance that is at most r^*. Clearly, by the time our algorithm reaches $r_1 = d_{real}$ it must be the case that B_{l_1} passes the test on line 19: $|B_{l_1}| > T/r_2$, and this test is not passed by any ball at any prior time. Moreover, B_{l_1} must be the largest ball passing our test at this point because if there is another ball B_{l_2} that also satisfies our test when $r_1 = d_{real}$ it must be the case that $|B_{l_1}| > |B_{l_2}|$ because B_{l_1} satisfies $|B_{l_1}(r)| \geq T/r$ for a smaller r. Finally because there are no landmark-point pairs (l, s) with $r_1 < d(l, s) < r_2$, $B_l(r_1) = B_l(r^*)$ for each landmark $l \in L$. Therefore the cluster that we compute on line 22 for $B_{l_1}(r_1)$ is equivalent to the cluster the conceptual algorithm computes for $B_{l_1}(r^*)$. We can repeat this argument for each cluster output by the conceptual algorithm, showing that Algorithm 2 finds exactly the same clustering.

We note that when there is only one good set left the test in line 19 may not be satisfied anymore if $3d_1 \geq \max_{x,y \in S} d(x, y)$, where d_1 is the diameter of the remaining good set. However, in this case if we exhaust all landmark-points pairs we report the remaining points as part of a single cluster (line 12), which must contain the remaining good set, and possibly some additional bad points that we consider misclassified anyway.

Using a hashed set to keep track of the points in each ball, our procedure can be implemented in time $O(|L|n \log n)$, which is the time necessary to sort all landmark-point pairs by distance. All other operations take asymptotically less time. In particular, over the entire run of the algorithm, the cost of computing the clusters in lines 21-22 is at most $O(n|L|)$, and the cost of removing clustered points from active balls in lines 23-28 is also at most $O(n|L|)$. □

Theorem 2. *If we are not given the optimum objective value* OPT, *then we can still find a clustering that is $O(\epsilon/\alpha)$-close to C_T with probability at least $1 - \delta$ by running Landmark-Clustering-Min-Sum at most $n'n^2$ times with the same set of landmarks, where the number of landmarks $n' = \frac{1}{(3+120/\alpha)\epsilon} \ln \frac{k}{\delta}$ as before.*

Proof. If we are not given the value of OPT then we have to estimate the threshold parameter T for deciding when a cluster develops. Let us use T^* to refer to its correct value ($T^* = \frac{\alpha \mathrm{OPT}}{40\epsilon n}$). We first note that there are at most $n \cdot n|L|$ relevant values of T to try, where L is the set of landmarks. Our test in line 19 checks whether the product of a ball size and a ball radius is larger than T, and there are only n possible ball sizes and $|L|n$ possible values of a ball radius.

Suppose that we choose a set of landmarks L, $|L| = n'$, as before. We then compute all $n'n^2$ relevant values of T and order them in ascending order: $T_i \leq T_{i+1}$ for $1 \leq i < n'n^2$. Then we repeatedly execute Algorithm 2 starting on line 2 with increasing estimates of T. Note that this is equivalent to trying all continuous values of T in ascending order because the execution of the algorithm does not change for any T' such that $T_i \leq T' < T_{i+1}$. In other words, when $T_i \leq T' < T_{i+1}$, the algorithm will give the same exact answer for T_i as it would for T'.

Our procedure stops the first time we cluster at least $n - b$ points, where b is the maximum number of bad points. We give an argument that this gives an accurate clustering with an additional error of b.

As before, we assume that we have selected at least one landmark from each good set, which happens with probability at least $1 - \delta$. Clearly, if we choose the right threshold T^* the algorithm must cluster at least $n - b$ points because the clustering will contain all the good points. Therefore the first time the algorithm clusters at least $n - b$ points for some estimated threshold T, it must be the case that $T \leq T^*$. Lemma 4 argues that if $T \leq T^*$ and the number of clustered points is at least $n - b$, then the reported partition must be a k-clustering that contains a distinct good set in each cluster. This clustering may exclude up to b points, all of which may be good points. Still, if we arbitrarily assign the remaining points we will get a clustering that is closer than $2b + \epsilon = O(\epsilon/\alpha)$ to C_T. □

Lemma 1. *If the balanced k-median instance satisfies the $(1 + \alpha, \epsilon)$-property and each cluster in C^* has size at least* $\max(6, 6/\alpha) \cdot \epsilon n$ *we have:*

1. *For all x, y in the same X_i, we have $d(x, y) \leq \frac{\alpha w}{60\epsilon|C_i^*|}$.*
2. *For $x \in X_i$ and $y \in X_{j \neq i}$, $d(x, y) > \frac{\alpha w}{5\epsilon} / \min(|C_i^*|, |C_j^*|)$.*
3. *The number of bad points is at most $b = (2 + 120/\alpha)\epsilon n$.*

Proof. For part 1, since $x, y \in X_i \subseteq C_i^*$ are both good, they are at distance of at most $\frac{\alpha w}{120\epsilon|C_i^*|}$ to c_i^*, and hence at distance of at most $\frac{\alpha w}{60\epsilon|C_i^*|}$ to each other.

For part 2 assume without loss of generality that $|C_i^*| \geq |C_j^*|$. Both $x \in C_i^*$ and $y \in C_j^*$ are good; it follows that $d(y, c_j^*) \leq \frac{\alpha w}{120\epsilon|C_j^*|}$, and $d(x, c_j^*) > \frac{\alpha w}{4\epsilon|C_j^*|}$ because $|C_j^*| d(x, c_j^*) \geq w_2(x) > \frac{\alpha w}{4\epsilon}$. By the triangle inequality it follows that

$$d(x, y) \geq d(x, c_j^*) - d(y, c_j^*) \geq \frac{\alpha w}{\epsilon|C_j^*|}\left(\frac{1}{4} - \frac{1}{120}\right) > \frac{\alpha w}{5\epsilon} / \min(|C_i^*|, |C_j^*|),$$

where we use that $|C_j^*| = \min(|C_i^*|, |C_j^*|)$.

Part 3 follows from the maximum number of points that may not satisfy each of the properties of the good points and the union bound. □

Lemma 2. *After selecting $\frac{n}{s}\ln\frac{k}{\delta}$ points uniformly at random, where s is the size of the smallest good set, the probability that we did not choose a point from every good set is smaller than $1-\delta$.*

Proof. We denote by s_i the cardinality of X_i. Observe that the probability of not selecting a point from some good set X_i after $\frac{nc}{s}$ samples is $(1-\frac{s_i}{n})^{\frac{nc}{s}} \leq (1-\frac{s_i}{n})^{\frac{nc}{s_i}} \leq (e^{-\frac{s_i}{n}})^{\frac{nc}{s_i}} = e^{-c}$. By the union bound the probability of not selecting a point from every good set after $\frac{nc}{s}$ samples is at most ke^{-c}, which is equal to δ for $c = \ln\frac{k}{\delta}$. □

Lemma 3. *Given a subset of clusters $C \subseteq C^*$, and the set of the corresponding good sets X, let $s_{\max} = \max_{C_i \in C} |C_i|$ be the size of the largest cluster in C, and $d_{\min} = \frac{\alpha w}{60\epsilon s_{\max}}$. Then for $r \leq 3d_{\min}$, a ball cannot overlap a good set $X_i \in X$ and any other good set, and a ball containing points from a good set $X_i \in X$ cannot share any points with a ball containing points from any other good set.*

Proof. By part 2 of Lemma 1, for $x \in X_i$ and $y \in X_{j\neq i}$ we have

$$d(x,y) > \frac{\alpha w}{5\epsilon} / \min(|C_i^*|, |C_j^*|).$$

It follows that for $x \in X_i \in X$ and $y \in X_{j\neq i}$ we must have $d(x,y) > \frac{\alpha w}{5\epsilon} / \min(|C_i^*|, |C_j^*|) \geq \frac{\alpha w}{5\epsilon}/|C_i^*| > \frac{\alpha w}{5\epsilon}/s_{\max} = 12d_{\min}$, where we use the fact that $|C_i| \leq s_{\max}$. So a point in a good set in X and a point in any other good set must be farther than $12d_{\min}$.

To prove the first part, consider a ball B_l of radius $r \leq 3d_{\min}$ around landmark l. In other words, $B_l = \{s \in S \mid d(s,l) \leq r\}$. If B_l overlaps a good set in $X_i \in X$ and any other good set, then it must contain a point $x \in X_i$ and a point $y \in X_{j\neq i}$. It follows that $d(x,y) \leq d(x,l) + d(l,y) \leq 2r \leq 6d_{\min}$, giving a contradiction.

To prove the second part, consider two balls B_{l_1} and B_{l_2} of radius $r \leq 3d_{\min}$ around landmarks l_1 and l_2. Suppose B_{l_1} and B_{l_2} share at least one point: $B_{l_1} \cap B_{l_2} \neq \emptyset$, and use s^* to refer to this point. It follows that the distance between any point $x \in B_{l_1}$ and $y \in B_{l_2}$ satisfies $d(x,y) \leq d(x,s^*) + d(s^*,y) \leq [d(x,l_1) + d(l_1,s^*)] + [d(s^*,l_2) + d(l_2,y)] \leq 4r \leq 12d_{\min}$.

If B_{l_1} overlaps with $X_i \in X$ and B_{l_2} overlaps with $X_{j\neq i}$, and the two balls share at least one point, there must be a pair of points $x \in X_i$ and $y \in X_{j\neq i}$ such that $d(x,y) \leq 12d_{\min}$, giving a contradiction. Therefore if B_{l_1} overlaps with some good set $X_i \in X$ and B_{l_2} overlaps with any other good set, $B_{l_1} \cap B_{l_2} = \emptyset$. □

Lemma 4. *If $T \leq T^* = \frac{\alpha w}{40\epsilon}$ and the number of clustered points is at least $n-b$, then the clustering output by Landmark-Clustering-Min-Sum using the threshold T must be a k-clustering that contains a distinct good set in each cluster.*

Proof. Our argument considers the points that are in each cluster that is output by the algorithm. Let us call a good set *covered* if any of the clusters $C_1, \ldots, C_{i-1}$ found so far contain points from it. We will use $\bar{C}^*$ to refer to the clusters in C^* whose good sets are not *covered*. It is critical to observe that if $T \leq T^*$ then if C_i contains points from an *uncovered* good set, C_i cannot overlap with any other good set.

To see this, let us order the clusters in $\bar{C}^*$ by decreasing size: $|C_1^*| \geq |C_2^*| \geq \ldots |C_j^*|$, and let $n_i = |C_i^*|$. As before, define $d_i = \frac{\alpha w}{60\epsilon|C_i^*|}$. Applying Lemma 3 with $\bar{C}^*$ we can see that for $r \leq 3d_1$, a ball of radius r cannot overlap a good set in $\bar{C}^*$ and any other good set, and a ball containing points from a good set in $\bar{C}^*$ cannot share any points with a ball containing points from any other good set. Because $T \leq T^*$ we can also argue that by the time we reach $r = 3d_1$ we must output some cluster.

Given this observation, it is clear that the algorithm can cover at most one new good set in each cluster that it outputs. In addition, if a new good set is covered this cluster may not contain points from any other good set. If the algorithm is able to cluster at least $n - b$ points, it must cover every good set because the size of each good set is larger than b. So it must report k clusters where each cluster contains points from a distinct good set. □

5 Experimental Results

We present some preliminary results of testing our *Landmark-Clustering-Min-Sum* algorithm on protein sequence data. Instead of requiring all pairwise similarities between the sequences as input, our algorithm is able to find accurate clusterings by using only a few BLAST calls. For each data set we first build a BLAST database containing all the sequences, and then compare only some of the sequences to the entire database. To compute the distance between two sequences, we invert the bit score corresponding to their alignment, and set the distance to infinity if no significant alignment is found. In practice we find that this distance is almost always a metric, which is consistent with our theoretical assumptions.

In our computational experiments we use data sets created from the Pfam [FMT+10] (version 24.0, October 2009) and SCOP [MBHC95] (version 1.75, June 2009) classification databases. Both of these sources classify proteins by their evolutionary relatedness, therefore we can use their classifications as a ground truth to evaluate the clusterings produced by our algorithm and other methods. These are the same data sets that were used in the [VBR+10] study, therefore we also show the results of the original *Landmark-Clustering* algorithm on these data, and use the same amount of distance information for both algorithms: $30k$ queries for each data set, where k is the number of clusters. In order to run *Landmark-Clustering-Min-Sum* we need to set the parameter T. Because in practice we do not know its correct value, we use increasing estimates of T until we cluster enough of the points in the data set; this procedure is similar to the algorithm for the case when we don't know the optimum objective value OPT and hence don't know T. We set the k parameter using the number of clusters in the ground truth clustering. In order to compare a computationally derived clustering to the one given by the gold-standard classification, we use the distance measure from the theoretical part of our work.

Because our Pfam data sets are so large, we cannot compute the full distance matrix, so we can only compare with methods that use a limited amount of distance information. A natural choice is the following algorithm: uniformly at random choose a set of landmarks L, $|L| = d$; embed each point in a d-dimensional space using distances to L; use k-means clustering in this space (with distances given by the Euclidian norm). This procedure uses exactly d one versus all distance queries, so we can set d equal to the number of queries used by the other algorithms. For SCOP data sets we are able to compute the full distance matrix, so we can compare with a spectral clustering algorithm that has been shown to work very well on these data [PCS06].

From Figure 2 we can see that *Landmark-Clustering-Min-Sum* outperforms k-means in the embedded space on all the Pfam data sets. However, it does not perform better than the original *Landmark-Clustering* algorithm on most of these data sets. When we investigate the structure of the ground truth clusters in these data sets, we see that the diameters of the clusters are roughly the same. When this is the case the original algorithm will find accurate clusterings as well [VBR+10]. Still, *Landmark-Clustering-Min-Sum* tends to give better results when the original algorithm does not work well (data sets 7 and 9).

Figure 3 shows the results of our computational experiments on the SCOP data sets. We can see that the three algorithms are comparable in performance here. These results are encouraging because the spectral clustering algorithm significantly outperforms other clustering algorithms on these data [PCS06].

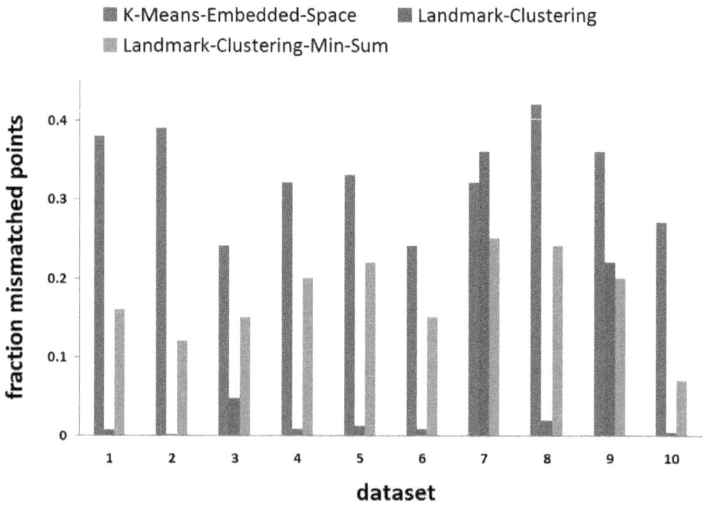

Fig. 2. Comparing the performance of k-means in the embedded space (blue), *Landmark-Clustering* (red), and *Landmark-Clustering-Min-Sum* (green) on 10 data sets from Pfam. Datasets **1-10** are created by uniformly at random choosing 8 families from Pfam of size s, $1000 \leq s \leq 10000$.

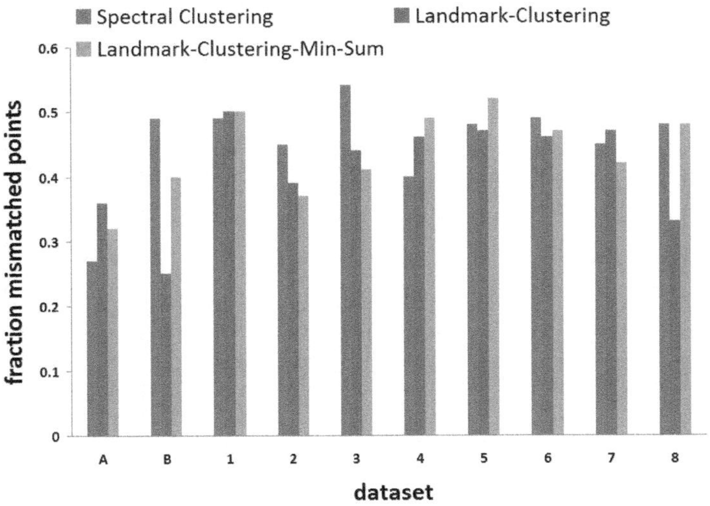

Fig. 3. Comparing the performance of spectral clustering (blue), *Landmark-Clustering* (red), and *Landmark-Clustering-Min-Sum* (green) on 10 data sets from SCOP. Data sets **A** and **B** are the two main examples from [PCS06], the other data sets (**1-8**) are created by uniformly at random choosing 8 superfamilies from SCOP of size s, $20 \leq s \leq 200$.

Moreover, the spectral algorithm needs the full distance matrix as input and takes much longer to run. When we examine the structure of the SCOP data sets, we find that the diameters of the ground truth clusters vary considerably, which resembles the structure implied by our approximation stability assumption, assuming that the target clusters vary in size. Still, most of the time the product of the cluster sizes and their diameters varies, so it does not quite look like what we assume in the theoretical part of this work.

We plan to conduct further studies to find data where clusters have different scale and there is an inverse relationship between cluster sizes and their diameters. This may be the case for data that have many outliers, and the correct clustering groups sets of outliers together rather than assigns them to arbitrary clusters. The algorithm presented here will consider these sets to be large diameter, small cardinality clusters. More generally, the algorithm presented here is more robust because it will give an answer no matter what the structure of the data is like, whereas the original *Landmark-Clustering* algorithm often fails to find a clustering if there are no well-defined clusters in the data. The *Landmark-Clustering-Min-Sum* algorithm presented here also has fewer hyperparameters and is easier to use in practice when we do not know much about the data.

6 Conclusion

We present a new algorithm that clusters protein sequences in a limited information setting. Instead of requiring all pairwise distances between the sequences as input, we can find an accurate clustering using few BLAST calls. We show that our algorithm produces accurate clusterings when compared to gold-standard classifications, and we expect it to work even better on data who structure more closely resembles our theoretical assumptions.

Acknowledgments. This work was supported in part by NSF grant CCF-0953192 and a Microsoft Research Faculty Fellowship.

References

[AGK+04] Arya, V., Garg, N., Khandekar, R., Meyerson, A., Munagala, K., Pandit, V.: Local search heuristics for k-median and facility location problems. SIAM J. Comput. 33(3) (2004)

[AGM+90] Altschul, S.F., Gish, W., Miller, W., Myers, E.W., Lipman, D.J.: Basic local alignment search tool. J. Mol. Biol. 215(3), 403–410 (1990)

[AJM09] Ailon, N., Jaiswal, R., Monteleoni, C.: Streaming k-means approximation. In: Proc. of 23rd Conference on Neural Information Processing Systems, NIPS (2009)

[AV07] Arthur, D., Vassilvitskii, S.: k-means++: the advantages of careful seeding. In: Proc. of 18th ACM-SIAM Symp. on Discrete Algorithms, SODA (2007)

[BBG09] Balcan, M.F., Blum, A., Gupta, A.: Approximate clustering without the approximation. In: Proc. of 20th ACM-SIAM Symp. on Discrete Algorithms, SODA (2009)

[BCR01] Bartal, Y., Charikar, M., Raz, D.: Approximating min-sum k-clustering in metric spaces. In: Proc. of 33rd ACM Symp. on Theory of Computing, STOC (2001)

[CS07] Czumaj, A., Sohler, C.: Sublinear-time approximation algorithms for clustering via random sampling. Random Struct. Algorithms 30(1-2), 226–256 (2007)

[FMT+10] Finn, R.D., Mistry, J., Tate, J., Coggill, P., Heger, A., Pollington, J.E., Gavin, O.L., Gunesekaran, P., Ceric, G., Forslund, K., Holm, L., Sonnhammer, E.L., Eddy, S.R., Bateman, A.: The pfam protein families database. Nucleic Acids Res. 38, D211–D222 (2010)

[Kle03] Kleinberg, J.: An impossibility theorem for clustering. In: Proc. of 17th Conference on Neural Information Processing Systems, NIPS (2003)

[MBHC95] Murzin, A.G., Brenner, S.E., Hubbard, T., Chothia, C.: Scop: a structural classification of proteins database for the investigation of sequences and structures. J. Mol. Biol. 247, 536–540 (1995)

[MOP01] Mishra, N., Oblinger, D., Pitt, L.: Sublinear time approximate clustering. In: Proc. of 12th ACM-SIAM Symp. on Discrete Algorithms, SODA (2001)

[PCS06] Paccanaro, A., Casbon, J.A., Saqi, M.A.S.: Spectral clustering of protein sequences. Nucleic Acids Res. 34(5), 1571–1580 (2006)

[VBR+10] Voevodski, K., Balcan, M.F., Röglin, H., Teng, S., Xia, Y.: Efficient clustering with limited distance information. In: Proc. of 26th Conference on Uncertainty in Artifcial Intelligence, UAI (2010)

[ZBD09] Zadeh, R.B., Ben-David, S.: A uniqueness theorem for clustering. In: Proc. of 25th Conference on Uncertainty in Artifcial Intelligence, UAI (2009)

Model-Based Clustering of Inhomogeneous Paired Comparison Data

Ludwig M. Busse and Joachim M. Buhmann

Department of Computer Science, ETH Zurich,
8092 Zurich, Switzerland
{ludwig.busse,jbuhmann}@inf.ethz.ch

Abstract. This paper demonstrates the derivation of a clustering model for paired comparison data. Similarities for non-Euclidean, ordinal data are handled in the model such that it is capable of performing an integrated analysis on real-world data with different patterns of missings.

Rank-based pairwise comparison matrices with missing entries can be described and compared by means of a probabilistic mixture model defined on the symmetric group. Our EM-method offers two advantages compared to models for pairwise comparison rank data available in the literature: (i) it identifies groups in the pairwise choices based on similarity (ii) it provides the ability to analyze a data set of heterogeneous character w.r.t. to the structural properties of individal data samples.

Furthermore, we devise an active learning strategy for selecting paired comparisons that are highly informative to extract the underlying ranking of the objects. The model can be employed to predict pairwise choice probabilities for individuals and, therefore, it can be used for preference modeling.

1 Introduction

Objects $o_a, o_b, \ldots$ of a given set of objects $\mathcal{O}$ can be characterized in the most elementary form by a preference relation. Such pairwise comparisons, that yield so-called paired comparison data, encode the preferences of objects in many different contexts. Comparing two objects o_a and o_b with an operator $<$, i.e. measuring whether object o_a is bigger, higher, more preferred, ... than object o_b endows an otherwise unstructured pair of objects with a very elementary piece of information (1-bit). Neither the actual difference between the two objects is important nor are there any compulsary restrictions placed on the operator (e.g. transitivity). The data type is a comparison matrix, where objects $o_a, o_b, \ldots, o_m$ are compared pairwise to each other:

$$\mathbf{X} = (x_{ab}) \in \mathbb{B}^{m \times m} = \{0,1\}^{m \times m}$$

The comparison operator can be specified dependent on the application at hand. Here, we focus in particular on preference data.

A data set consists of $i = 1, \ldots, n$ samples:

$$\mathcal{X} = \left\{\mathbf{X}^{(i)}\right\} = \left\{(x_{ab})^{(i)}\right\}$$

M. Pelillo and E.R. Hancock (Eds.): SIMBAD 2011, LNCS 7005, pp. 207–221, 2011.

In this work, we aim at finding structure in pairwise comparison rank data. A famous simple model for pairwise comparisons is the Babington Smith model (a thorough overview is provided in [19]).

Many data arise as pairwise comparisons (rather than as points in an Euclidean vector space $\mathbb{R}^n$). Suppose we have a number of objects o_a, o_b, ... which are to be considered according to some common quality. If the quality is measurable in some objective way, the objects yield variate values, and the problem is amenable to treatment by standard machine learning methods. However, it may happen for either theoretical or for practical reasons that the quality is not measurable or cannot be measured robustly. We then have to rely for a discussion of the variation of the quality based on a comparison of the objects among themselves. The method of pairwise comparisons provides reliable and informative data about the relative quality[1].

A widely used methods of comparison ranks the object according to a suitable application criterion. The objects are arranged in the order in which they possess the quality under consideration (*total order*). The ranking method is not appropriate [14] when the quality considered is not known to be representable by a linear variable. It is not necessarily unreasonable that object $o_a < o_b$, $o_b < o_c$ and $o_c < o_a$, if the objects deal for example with tastes in music, eatables or film stars; and in practice this in not uncommon [14]. Such "inconsistent" information can never appear in a ranking for if o_a is preferred to o_b and o_b to o_c, then o_a must automatically be shown as preferred to o_c. The use of rankings thus destroys what may be valuable information.

When preference relations are evaluated under a single criterion, there is one dominant total order (ranking assumption). However, noise can result in probabilistically intransitive data. In this paper, we consider a probabilistic model for pairwise comparison data, establishing a probability distribution over rankings. The model allows for intransitivities and places equal probability mass on all rankings that are equally consistent with the given pairwise comparisons. Noisy real-world data can be handled in a meaningful way.

[1] Data derived from paired comparison experiments: Many situations naturally produce pairwise comparisons such as sporting events which involve two teams (e.g. football, basketball). The records of wins and losses for the teams constitute the data. In other situations, such as food tasting, pairwise comparisons are helpful because of the difficulty of distinguishing preferences when more than two objects are considered simultaneously. Though direct *rankings* are popular to elicit *preferences* e.g. in music, movies, and food, giving a ranking for more than, say, 5 objects is quite a difficult and time-consuming task for an interviewee to complete. Deciding between just 2 objects at a time is easier than infering complete rankings and thus, pairwise comparison generates data of superior quality. An alternative to asking someone to rank the m objects is to have the ranker choose which of each pair of objects is preferred. With many objects being up for consideration (e.g. products), we must expect the stated pairwise preference data to have missings. Pairwise comparison matrices might be incomplete because respondents do not express all preferences or are indifferent.

We derive a mixture model for cluster analysis and provide an EM algorithm for parameter estimation (unsupervised inference). The model and parameter estimator can tolerate missings in the data, incase not all paired comparisons are made or available to the data analyst.

We also devise a strategy for automatically selecting paired comparisons that are "significant" to extract a ranking.

The model framework introduced above is instantiated for the application of *preference modeling*. Cluster analysis of paired comparison data attempts to find groups of preference choices. Preference data of surveys often suffer from missing values since respondents might answer to only a few paired comparisons, possibly a different set of paired comparisons for each respondent causing heterogeneity in the data. We present a mixture approach for similarity-based pattern analysis of such discrete, non-Euclidean, and inhomogeneous preference data by a single probabilistic model. The usefulness of the method is demonstrated by that predictions (=recommendations) for individuals can be made based on the cluster solution.

This paper is organized as follows: A model for heterogeneous paired comparison data comprising different clusters and missings is presented in Sec. 3, and its algorithmic estimation from data in Sec. 4. Sec. 5 proposes a strategy for selecting pairwise comparisons. In Sec. 6, we point out that the method is helpful for predicting preferences. Experimental results are reported in Sec. 7.

2 Relevant Work

Learning to rank and *ordinal regression* are presently popular research topics. In [7], the problem of learning how to order instances, given feedback in the form of preference judgments, is tackled. Another *supervised* approach to learning a preference function is [10]. Here, the training information consists of samples with partial and possibly inconsistent information about their associated rankings. From these, a ranking function is induced. Learning a preference function, defined over pairs, for producing a ranking is also presented in [2]. An approach to ensemble learning is introduced in [15], which takes ranking rather than classification as fundamental. Multiple input rankings are combined according to the degree of expertise that each ranker has. A supervised pairwise/listwise approach to ranking is developed in [6], and in [21], the problem of consensus finding for a group of rankers is considered.

Unsupervised learning on rank and pairwise data is mostly considered in the context of Collaborative Filtering (see [23] for a survey of techniques). A model for the cluster analysis of rank-type data is developed in [4], which is now relaxed to accomodate for paired comparison data. Learning Mallows models with pairwise preferences was very recently developed in [17].

3 Modeling Paired Comparison Data

When modeling paired comparison data there are two options: i) To model the pairwise comparison process (physical/mechanical/behavioral/neurological processes). ii) To model the population of n pairwise comparison givers (comparators). Here, we focus in this second, data-analytic approach.

Suppose there are m *objects*, also called *items*. By permuting the objects one can form all $m!$ possible rankings. Considering the simplex $P_{m!}$, we wish to define a probability model, i.e. a family of probability distributions, i.e. a subset of $P_{m!}$, parametrized by θ in a space Θ: $\{P(\theta)|\theta \in \Theta\} \subset P_{m!}$, where $P(\theta)$ is a function from Θ to $P_{m!}$. The set of possible rankings of m objects has a group structure and is referred to as the symmetric group of order m, denoted $\mathbb{S}_m$. The distribution on $\mathbb{S}_m$ will be given through its density $P_\pi(\theta) = P[\Pi = \pi; \theta]$, $\pi \in \mathbb{S}_m, \theta \in \Theta$.

Please note that a *ranking* $\pi \in \mathbb{S}_m$ is a permutation of the object indices, i.e. indicating the ranks. Inverting a ranking gives the corresponding *ordering* $\varpi \in T_m$. An ordering lists the objects according to their order.

In *sufficient statistic models*, the parameter θ "touches the data π" only through functions $s(\pi)$. Section 9E of [8] motivate the *exponential family distributions*: if $s = (s_1, s_2, \ldots, s_p)$, then:

$$P_\theta(\pi^{(1)}, \ldots, \pi^{(n)}) = \exp(\sum_{j=1}^{p} \theta_j s_j - n\psi(\theta)).$$

We now look at an exponential family model using the pairwise comparisons $\mathrm{I}[\pi_a < \pi_b]$ implied by a ranking π as sufficient statistics. $\mathrm{I}[\pi_a < \pi_b]$ is the 0/1 indicator variable indicating whether the rank of object o_a is smaller than the rank of object o_b in the ranking π (meaning that object o_a is bigger/higher/more preferred/...). The model assumes that the structure resides in the pairwise comparisons. The general model is based on the $\binom{m}{2} \times 1$ parameter p whose indices ab, $a < b$ are ordered. The p_{ab} is interpreted as the probability object o_a would be preferred to object o_b if only that comparison were to be made. Note that $p_{ba} = 1 - p_{ab}$.

A ranking is obtained by making independently all the pairwise comparisons using those probabilities. The probability that the pairwise comparisons are consistent with an ordering $\varpi \in T_m$ is

$$Z(p) = \sum_{\varpi \in T_m} \prod_{a<b} p_{\varpi_a \varpi_b}$$

The probability of an ordering ϖ given that the pairwise comparisons are consistent is the probability that the comparisons yield ϖ divided by the probability they are consistent. The Babington Smith model [19] thus has the density

$$P_p(\varpi) = \frac{1}{Z(p)} \prod_{a<b} p_{\varpi_b \varpi_b}.$$

Remark: A Babington Smith model has weak stochastic transitivity, if for a, b,

$$p_{ab} \geq \frac{1}{2} \text{ and } p_{bc} \geq \frac{1}{2} \Rightarrow p_{ac} \geq \frac{1}{2}$$

and has strong stochastic transitivity if

$$p_{ab} \geq \frac{1}{2} \text{ and } p_{bc} \geq \frac{1}{2} \Rightarrow p_{ac} = \max\{p_{ab}, p_{bc}\}$$

We now write down the exponential model defined over the space of rankings, where the sufficient statistics consist of the $\bar{m} = \binom{m}{2}$ pairwise comparisons x_{ab} for $a < b$. The model is

$$\mathbf{M}(\pi|\theta) = \exp(\theta'\mathbf{X}(\pi) - \psi(\theta)), \quad \pi \in \mathbb{S}_m \tag{1}$$

where $\theta = (\theta_{12}, \theta_{13}, \ldots, \theta_{m-1,m})$,
$\mathbf{X}(\pi) = \mathbf{X}^{\pi}$ with $\mathbf{X} = (x_{12}, x_{13}, \ldots, x_{m-1,m})$,
$x_{ab}^{\pi} = I[\pi_a < \pi_b]$ (the pairwise comparisons implied by the ranking π),
$1 \leq a < b \leq m$;
ψ is the normalizing constant.

Note that the symmetric group (of rankings) is the model space, whereas the data space consists of all pairwise comparisons (matrices). The model enforces transitivities by comparing the measured, possibly intransitive choices with rank induced pairwise choices. Objects are ranked by determining the maximum likelihood ranking. Rankings with equal maximal likelihood are averaged.

The choice parameters p are related to the θ's through

$$p_{ab} = \frac{\exp(-\theta_{ab})}{1 + \exp(-\theta_{ab})}, \quad a, b \in \mathcal{O}. \tag{2}$$

The quantity $\mathbf{X}(\pi)$ plays the role of a dissimilarity measure. The model exemplifies the derivation of a suitable similarity information for non-Euclidean data that can be used in order to perform learning.

Given a sample of size n, the maximum likelihood estimator exists if and only if $0 < \hat{x}_{ab} < 1$ for all $a < b$. If $\hat{x}_{ab} = 0\ (= 1)$, then set $\hat{\theta}_{ab} = +\infty\ (-\infty)$. Let $H = \{(a, b)|a < b, 0 < \hat{x}_{ab} < 1\}$ be the set of pairs remaining, and $\mathbb{S}_m^*$ be the subset of rankings that conform to the sample, i.e.
$\mathbb{S}_m^* = \{\pi \in \mathbb{S}_m | \pi_a < (>)\ \pi_b \text{ if } \hat{x}_{ab} = 0\ (= 1)\}$.

The loglikelihood is

$$l^*(\theta, \hat{\mathbf{X}}) = \sum_{\substack{a<b \\ (a,b) \in H}} n\theta_{ab}\hat{x}_{ab} - n\psi^*(\theta) \tag{3}$$

with

$$\exp(\psi^*(\theta)) = \frac{1}{m!} \sum_{\pi \in \mathbb{S}_m^*} \exp\Big(\sum_{\substack{a<b \\ (a,b) \in H}} \theta_{ab} I[\pi_a < \pi_b]\Big) \tag{4}$$

3.1 Model-Based Clustering

For cluster analysis, the observed paired comparison data is assumed to consist of K groups. Each group is modeled by a Babington Smith distribution (cf. equation 1):

$$\mathbf{M}^{(k)}(\pi|\theta^{(k)}) = \exp(\theta^{(k)'}\mathbf{X}(\pi) - \psi(\theta^{(k)})), \quad \pi \in \mathbb{S}_m$$

The component distributions are joined in a mixture model,

$$\mathbf{M}(\pi) = \sum_{k=1}^{K} c^{(k)}\mathbf{M}^{(k)}(\pi|\theta^{(k)}), \tag{5}$$

with the mixture weights $(c^{(1)}, \ldots, c^{(K)})$ forming a partition of 1. Model parameters can be estimated with an expectation-maximization (EM) algorithm [20], or more sophisticated latent variable estimation algorithms such as Deterministic Annealing [11].

3.2 Missings

When measuring paired comparison data (e.g. elicit pairwise preferences in a survey), we have to expect that the pairwise comparison matrices may contain missings. That is, at position (a, b) in a matrix we do not have the information 0 or 1 but rather a $*$ indicating that this paired comparison is missing.

To further complicate the problem, in both cases below the pattern of missings might vary between the n pairwise comparison matrices constituting the samples.

Missings may occur for different reasons. The number of pairwise comparisons between m objects is $\frac{m(m-1)}{2}$. Instead of insisting on having all paired comparisons, the analyst might only measure/ask for a subset of the paired comparisons in order to make the experiment more cheap or comfortable. For example, he might query each pair with a probability p_q so that the number of necessary paired comparisons is only a fraction of all pairs.

A further reason for missings in a paired comparison dataset is that – though all paired comparisons are queried – some are not available. Some measurements might be unavailable, whether occuring by chance or built into the design of the experiment (e.g. to save costs or in an industrial experiment some results are missing because of mechanical breakdowns unrelated to the experimental process). Respondents in a survey might not answer all questions because they are indifferent w.r.t. to a paired comparison (i.e. object o_a and o_b are seen equally preferred; in an opinion survey some interviewees may be unable to express a preference for one object over another) or respondents get tired and are not willing to answer all the questions posed.

Sometimes it is natural to treat the values that are not observed as missing, in the sense that there are true underlying values that would have been observed if the industrial equipment had been better maintained or survey techniques had been better. Sometimes, however, it is less clear that a well-defined preference has been masked by the nonresponse. Instead, the lack of a response is essentially an additional point in the sample space.

Excluding units that have missing values is generally inappropriate, since the investigator is usually interested in making inferences about the entire target population and since the removal of a subsample of common characteristic might cause a systematic bias.

In the following, an option for handling heterogeneous (i.e.: different patterns of missings within the samples) data in a probabilistic model is given. The performance of any missing-data method depends heavily on the mechanisms that lead to missing values. Data *missing completely at random* (MCAR) means that the missingness is not related to the data under study. Data can be missing at random (MAR, missingness is related to the observed data but not to the missing data) and there are also nonignorable missing-data mechanisms. For a thorough review of statistical analysis with missing data see the book of [16].

Notation:
$\text{Mis}^{(i)} = \{(a,b)|$ paired comparison between (a,b) missing in sample $i\}$
is the set of missings in sample i.

MODEL-BASED COMPLETION

Assuming that there are "true" values underlying at the missing matrix positions which are just masked (i.e. for each sample there is an unobservable complete pairwise comparison matrix), we can try to estimate these unobserved true values. We can explicitly estimate a maximum likelihood completion to a partial pairwise comparison matrix by treating the missing pairwise comparisons as latent information, and assuming complete pairwise comparison matrices to be distributed according to the model, e.g. the Babington-Smith model. An estimate of the full pairwise comparison matrix is obtained with an EM-type algorithm (latent variable estimation algorithm), which alternatingly reestimates the model parameters from current completion estimates, and then reestimates completions based on the current model (estimate the true frequencies of the full pairwise comparison matrices in the sample, then maximize the resulting likelihood).

In the E-step, the current parameter estimates are used to estimate the expected value of the sufficient statistics for the complete data. In the M-step, the estimated sufficient statistics are used to obtain maximum likelihood estimates of the model parameters.

This iterative EM procedure naturally suits into the clustering EM algorithm announced in section 3.1 and detailed in section 4. Having missings in the data adds more latent variables besides the unknown cluster assignments. The method can be used as basis for partial paired comparison data clustering, by performing completions based on the data currently assigned to a cluster during the clustering E-step, and performing maximum likelihood estimation for the mixture components given the current completion estimates during the M-step. Model-based completions can be performed based on the current cluster solution.

4 Model Inference

Heterogeneous, partial paired comparison data drawn from K distinct groups can now be described by a mixture model. The generative model for the data is

$$\mathbf{M}(\pi|c,\theta) = \sum_{k=1}^{K} c^{(k)} \frac{1}{m!} \exp(\theta^{(k)'}\mathbf{X}(\pi) - \psi^*(\theta^{(k)}, \mathrm{Mis}^{(\pi)})), \quad \pi \in \mathbb{S}_m \tag{6}$$

with the normalizing constant ψ depending on the cluster-specific $\theta^{(k)}$ and the sample-specific pattern of missings $\mathrm{Mis}^{(\pi)}$ by

$$\exp(\psi^*(\theta^{(k)}, \mathrm{Mis}^{(\pi)})) = \frac{1}{m!} \sum_{\rho \in \mathbb{S}^*_m} \exp(\sum_{\substack{a<b \\ (a,b)\in H}} \sum_{(a,b)\notin \mathrm{Mis}^{(\pi)}} \theta^{(k)}_{ab} I[\rho_a < \rho_b]).$$

For inference based on maximum likelihood (ML) estimation, for the mixture model described above, the overall ML estimator of the model parameters is approximated with an expectation-maximization (EM) algorithm [20]. In this section, we derive estimation equations for the heterogeneous data model, and discuss the implementation of an efficient EM algorithm for paired comparison data.

For data $\mathbf{X}^{(i)}$, $i = 1, \ldots, n$ and K clusters, define cluster assignments $q^{(i)} = (q^{(i)(1)}, \ldots, q^{(i)(K)})$. If $\mathbf{X}^{(i)}$ is assigned to cluster k, then $q^{(i)(k)} = 1$ and all other entries are 0. These assignment probabilities $q^{(i)(k)}$ ($q^{(i)(k)} \in [0,1]$, $\sum_k q^{(i)(k)} = 1$) are hidden variables of the EM estimation problem.

The E-step of the algorithm computes estimates of the assignment probabilities conditional on the current parameter configuration of the model. For samples that are only partially available, we want to make the cluster assignments maximally non-committal w.r.t. missings (i.e. paired comparisons not given). This involves establishing a uniform probability distribution over the missing values (maximum entropy argument), i.e. the restricted model assigns equal probabilities to all paired comparison matrices consistent with the given values regardless of what actual values the missings might have (uniform distribution over the missings). The maximum entropy approach avoids hidden assumptions about missing pairwise comparison entries. To summarize, for computing cluster assignments, the lack of knowledge about some paired comparisons is handled by substituting with the set of pairwise comparison matrices consistent with the given pairwise comparisons. The parameters θ are comparable for paired comparison matrices with different pattern of missings. Formally, this holds because the model is a distribution on the consistent completions (all possible matrices that are consistent with the given pairwise comparisons form an equivalence class).

Given estimates of the component parameter $\theta^{(k)}$ and the mixture weight $c^{(k)}$ for each cluster k, assignment probabilities are estimated as

$$q^{(i)(k)} = \frac{c^{(k)}\mathbf{M}(\pi^{(i)}|\theta^{(k)})}{\sum_{k'=1}^{K} c^{(k')}\mathbf{M}(\pi^{(i)}|\theta^{(k')})}.$$

In the M-step, assignment probabilities are assumed to be given. For each cluster, the parameters to be estimated are $c^{(k)}$ and $\theta^{(k)}$. As for any mixture model

EM algorithm, the mixture weights are straightforwardly computed as $c^{(k)} = \frac{1}{n}\sum_{i=1}^{n} q^{(i)(k)}$.

For ML estimation of the component parameters $\theta^{(k)}$, consider the Newton-Raphson method. To find the estimates of the $\theta_{ab}^{(k)}$ for each mode, the Newton-Raphson method can be applied to the negative log-likelihood:

$$-l^{*}(\theta^{(k)}, \hat{\mathbf{X}}) = \sum_{\substack{a<b \\ (a,b)\in H}} \sum_{i=1}^{n} q^{(i)(k)} \theta_{ab}^{(k)} \hat{x}_{ab}^{(i)} - \sum_{i=1}^{n} q^{(i)(k)} \psi^{*}(\theta^{(k)}) \tag{7}$$

In practice, the normalizing constants $\psi^{*}(\theta^{(k)}, \mathrm{Mis}^{(\pi)})$ can be expensive to compute if m is large. We therefore derived a MCMC sampler to approximate $l^{*}(\theta^{(k)})$ and $\psi^{*}(\theta^{(k)}, \mathrm{Mis}^{(\pi)})$.

Suppose that θ_0 is close to the ML estimate. A sample of rankings $\pi_{s_1}, \pi_{s_2}, \ldots, \pi_{s_s} \sim \mathbf{M}(\pi|\theta_0)$ is a random sample of rankings from the distribution defined by the paired comparison model with parameter θ_0. Make use of the law of large numbers to estimate an expectation (ML estimate in exponential families is the value $\hat{\theta}_0$ for which the expected value of the statistics is equal to the observed value) by a sample mean $\approx \frac{1}{s}\sum_{r=1}^{s} \exp((\theta - \theta_0)'\mathbf{X}(\pi_{s_r}))$ (further details of derivation omitted).

E-step: At the current parameter value $\theta^{(k)}$, a Monte Carlo simulation of the Markov ranking is made; this simulation is used to estimate cumulants (or moments) of the distribution. The approximated log-likelihood for cluster k is:

$$l^{*}(\theta^{(k)}, \hat{\mathbf{X}}) \approx \sum_{i=1}^{n} q^{(i)(k)} \Big\{ -\ln\{\frac{1}{s}\sum_{r=1}^{s} \exp((\theta^{(k)} - \theta_0^{(k)})'(\mathbf{X}(\pi_{s_r}^{(k)}) - \mathbf{X}(\pi^{(i)})))\}\Big\} \tag{8}$$

For sampling, simulate a discrete-time Markov chain whose stationary distribution is the distribution we want to sample from. Change (or not) the current ranking, according to some rule dependent on θ_0. Begining with an initial ranking, the elements of this ranking are stochastically updated, the updating mechanism circles through the ranking again and again, this defining a stochastic process which is a Markov chain. Approximate random draws e.g. by Gibbs sampling or Metropolis-Hastings.

Details for a Metropolis-Hastings type of sampler: As an elementary change, we define a transposition in the ranking, i.e. two random ranks are exchanged. π_{τ} denotes the ranking with transposition. The change takes effect with probability $\sim \min(1, p_{\tau})$, with $p_{\tau} = \exp(\theta_0)'(\mathbf{X}(\pi_{\tau}) - \mathbf{X}(\pi))$, otherwise the change is discarded.

5 Selection of Comparisons

As pointed out in section 3.2, we should not rely on having all paired comparisons available, since the number of pairwise comparisons grows quadratically with the number m of objects. Sometimes we have no control on *which* pairwise comparisons we can measure or get a response to. In other settings, however, we are able to *select* pairwise comparisons that data is aquired for. In a survey, for example, instead of asking for all pairwise comparisons, the interviewer can choose a subset of questions. It is thus reasonable to think of a strategy for the selection of comparisons.

We here again assume that there is a ranking underlying the paired comparisons (otherwise we see no argument why some paired comparisons are more "informative" than others). Under this transitivity assumption, the task reduces to the problem of *sorting* a partially ordered set (poset; the partial order induced by the paired comparisons). That is, like with any comparison-based sorting algorithm, one constructs a linear order (ranking) by queries "<" on pairs of objects. The two differences to standard sorting are: (i.) the query operation ("<") might be expensive (e.g. time-consuming measurement, limited attention of respondents in surveys); (ii.) the query operation ("<") might be noisy (e.g. flipped with a probability p_{Error}). We now give a method for selecting paired comparisons ensuring that the first paired comparisons queried are the most informative to construct the ranking. The method might not be robust to errors in the paired comparisons, in particular if errors occur between distant objects. For an error bound analysis for QuickSort with noisy comparison operation (resp. intransitivities) we refer to [1]. Probabilistic QuickSort always needs $O(n \log n)$ calls to the comparison oracle and, moreover, it is not clear whether the first queries yield the most valuable information about the ranking.

Let us try to make sure that the gain of information (for the ranking) is monotonically decreasing in the sequence of paired comparisons that are queried. The motivation is that only a limited number of comparisons can be queried due to cost or time constraints; for example, in a survey the interviewer does not even know when the interviewee will stop answering the questions. Technically, the problem rephrases as: Each additional comparison that is queried should reduce most the cardinality of the set of rankings (total orders) consistent with the partial order, since finally we would like to identify the single one underlying ranking. The method below is thus based on the theory of linear extensions [13].

Let P denote a poset (here: paired comparisons acquired so far) and $|E(P)|$ is the set of its linear extensions (here: all rankings consistent with the paired comparisons given). Suppose that we can choose any pair $o_a, o_b \in \{o_1, \ldots, o_m\}$ and ask an oracle to compare them. Having gotten the answer, say o_a precedes o_b, we add the relation $a < b$ and all its transitive consequences to P and obtain a new partial order $P^1 = P\&[a < b]$. We call the oracle again and ask it to compare a new pair of objects as long as $|E(P^q)| > 1$. In a finite number q of queries we sort the original poset P, i.e. obtain a total linear order $P^q = \pi \in E(P)$. Clearly, one has the information theory worst-case lower bound $q \geq \log_2 |E(P)|$ on the number of queries. For any poset P with $|E(P)| > 1$ linear extensions there exists a pair of objects $a, b \in \{1, \ldots, m\}$ such that:

$$\max\{\frac{|E(P\&[a < b])|}{|E(P)|}, \frac{|E(P\&[b < a])|}{|E(P)|}\} \leq \beta \tag{9}$$

The inequality (9) says that in any poset P there exists a comparison a, b which decreases the number of linear extensions by at least β. β is conjectured to be 2/3 and it is known [12] that inequality (9) holds with $\beta = 8/11$. The latter result implies that using 8/11-balanced test comparison one can sort an arbitrary poset P in at most $q \leq 2.2 \log_2 |E(P)|$ queries. [12] also show that computing the "balancing constants" $\beta_{ab} = |E(P\&[a < b])|/|E(P)| = \text{Prob}\{a < b \text{ in } E(P)\}$ is #P-hard. However, one can compute approximations to the balancing constants in time $O(T)$, where T is the complexity of nearly uniform generation of linear extensions of P. Therefore, a well-balanced comparison in a given poset can also be found with high probability in time $O(T)$. Now, the following fact [12]: Let $r_a = \frac{1}{|E(P)|} \sum_{\pi \in E} \pi(a)$ be the average rank of $a \in \{1, \dots, m\}$ over the set of linear extensions of P, then an arbitrary pair a, b of objects such that $|r_a - r_b| < 1$ is an 8/11-balanced comparison in K. The strategy is to minimize $|\hat{r}_a - \hat{r}_b|$ over $a, b \in \{1, \dots, m\}$. Intuitively, this approach favors comparing objects that are close to each other. This is particularly helpful to refine the underlying ranking, while it is – for exactly the same reason – of disadvantage for estimating a pairwise model, since comparisons between objects that are far apart (high absolute value of θ_{ab}) are more discriminative.

For averaging the ranks $\hat{r}_a$ of objects we need a nearly uniform generator of linear extensions of the poset (Markov chain with uniform stationary distribution for combinatorial object "linear extension"). For algorithm and details, please consult [13].

6 Application: Preference Prediction

Finally, we like to stress the usefulness of the probabilistic paired comparison model for preference modeling. A powerful approach to preference elicitation is the use of rankings, where the members of a population order items, values, or products according to their degree of preference or importance. The task of ranking, however, can be tedious. Deciding between just two items at a time is easier, and such pairwise preference data often naturally or implicitly arises (e.g. a dog is presented with two feeding dishes. The one that the dog eats first is the more preferred one).

Identifying Groups of Choices: The mixture model defined above expresses the separation of the comparators observed in the data into different groups or types, each of which exhibits a "typical" preference behavior. The interpretation of the θ_{ab}'s for each group is that a positive value codes a preference of object o_a over o_b by the group (when $\theta_{ab} \to \infty$: o_a is always preferred to o_b). A value of 0 means indifference or neutrality w.r.t. to the two objects at hand, whereas a negative value of θ_{ab} indicates that object o_a is seen as less preferable than o_b. The soft preference probabilities p_{ab} between objects can be used to construct the utility weights (as described in [22], for example) that a society and its groups assign to the different objects/options o_a, o_b.

Recommendations: The method is helpful to estimate preference relations on the set of objects, i.e. to predict the choice probabilities between two objects for

Table 1. Estimation errors on synthetic data with $K = 2$ and $K = 3$ clusters. The distances between the cluster centers and the cluster overlaps are varied.

Setting			Results
K	τ_d	λ / p	error$_{L2}$ $\hat{\theta}$
2	6	1.0 / 0.73	0.43 ± 0.10
	3	1.0 / 0.73	0.55 ± 0.12
		0.5 / 0.62	0.52 ± 0.17
			l-approximation: 0.94 ± 0.60
3	4-5	1.5 / 0.82	1.14 ± 0.42
	2-4	1.5 / 0.82	0.84 ± 0.27
		0.5 / 0.62	0.74 ± 0.13

an individual. The prediction of the preference between objects o_a and o_b for individual i based on the cluster solution is given by the posterior:

$$p_{ab}^{(i)} = \sum_{k=1}^{K} q^{(i)(k)} \frac{\exp(-\theta_{ab}^{(k)})}{1 + \exp(-\theta_{ab}^{(k)})} \tag{10}$$

7 Experimental Results

The experiments include synthetic and real-world paired comparison data derived from rankings. The mixture analysis with artificial data drawn from a density with known parameters is conducted to check the method's capability of recovering parameters from paired comparison data. Additional experiments are conducted on a data set from a study on change in mass politics described in [3], where Germans expressed their preference regarding political goals. All experiments are performed with the EM algorithm described in section 4.

7.1 Synthetic Data

Synthetic pairwise comparison data observations were derived from rankings drawn at random from a mixture of Mallows models [18]. Sample experiments for $m = 4$ objects and $K = 2$ and 3 clusters are shown in Tab 1. τ_d are the mutual Kendall distances between the cluster centers; λ is an inverse spread (a lower value resulting in an higher overlap between the clusters) and $1 - p$ is the inverse flip probability of a pairwise comparison. In the setting of 2 equally sized clusters $n = 150$ samples were used, for the 3 clusters, including a small one, $n = 300$ samples were used. The quality of parameter estimates is reported as the L2 error to the true θ. The Bayesian Information Criterion (BIC) [20] estimate of the number of clusters was correct except for very near cluster centers and/or broad cluster overlaps.

With the distance between the cluster centers decreasing, the estimation errors increase. The estimation errors become smaller when the cluster have a higher spread (small λ). Approximating the likelihood by sampling generally increases the estimation error.

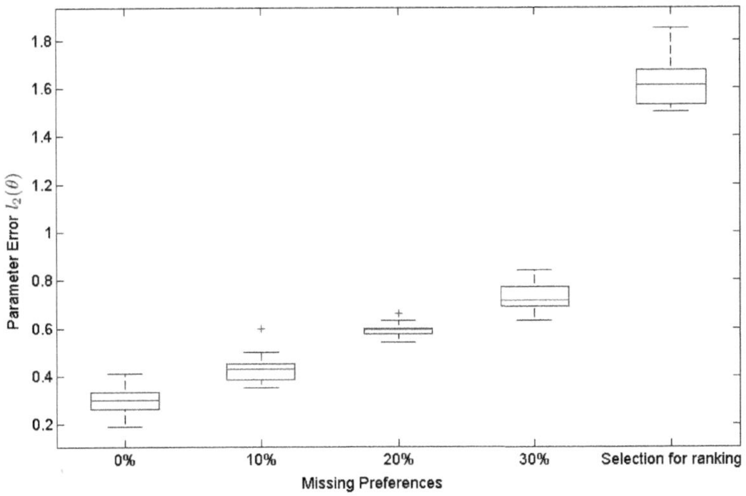

Fig. 1. Missings in the data set: Estimation error of θ versus different sorts of incomplete data

We also measured the parameter recovery error depending on different types of missings in the data, i.e. with the paired comparison matrices only partially available in the sample (here: $n = 500$). The value of the method being capable of handling missings is illustrated in Fig. 1, where from left to right the number of missings increases (Remark: thereby, the effective sample size is reduced, may possibly reduce e.g. the costs of measuring or time of surveying!). First, the algorithm sees all pairwise comparisons (the full information is available). In the second scenario, in each pairwise comparison matrix, each entry is available with probability 0.9. It is a genuine advantage of the proposed model that it can handle samples containing different patterns of missing at the same time. Previously, when the data analyst was confronted with such heterogenous data it was often common practice that he had to delete incomplete samples or to analyse them separately. Next, random 80% and 70% of the pairwise comparisons got accessible to the inference procedure. Finally, we used the method described in section 5 to automatically determine the subset of paired comparisons for ranking construction. As expected, the error is significantly higher compared to random selection for the reason given at the end of section 5: comparisons between near objects are helpful to refine the underlying ranking, while for discriminating between clusters distant objects are more helpful.

7.2 Political Goals German Data

The political goals data set of real-world rankings from a study on change in mass politics: A sample of 2262 Germans expressed their preference on four political goals based on their perceived personal importance: *Order*, *Say*, *Prices*, *Freedom*. We analyzed the paired comparisons by EM estimation of the above mixture

Table 2. Political Goals: Preference probabilities for the two clusters found: "Materialism" and "Post-materialism"

Pair $(o_a, o_b) \rightarrow$	(O,S)	(O,P)	(O,F)	(S,P)	(S,F)	(P,F)
$\hat{p}_{ab}^{(Mat.)}$	77%	48%	86%	29%	53%	76%
$\hat{p}_{ab}^{(Post-mat.)}$	43%	37%	29%	58%	57%	49%

model and found two clusters in agreement with the original classification by [3] of the goals into *Materialist* and *Post-materialist* (see Tab. 2). The analysis in [19] by a simple Babington Smith model "lefts a significant proportion of the data unexplained". We measured the prediction quality of our method by deleting 10% random subsamples of the paired comparisons. The trained model was able to predict the capped paired choice probabilities with a prediction error of 8.65% $\pm$ 0.78%. To the best of our knowledge, there does not exist an alternative method for comparison that is able to make predictions on this granularity of individual paired choices.

8 Conclusion

A probabilistic mixture model for the analysis of inhomogeneous paired comparison data was introduced. Our modeling approach permits the integration of data with different patterns of missings by estimating a model-based distribution on the subset of matrices consistent with the information given and thus can combine estimate contributions in a meaningful way.

The assumption throughout this line of work is that there is a ranking underlying the order relation. A ranking (or total order) orders objects according to some criterion, neglecting any "distance" between the objects. In practice, paired comparisons (or partial orders) are sometimes easier to acquire. In fact, when rankings are distributed according to the well-known Mallows model with modal ranking σ and inverse spread λ, the flip probabilities of the induced paired comparisons directly relate to the spread of the rank model. An advantage of models based on ranks is that parameters can be tied in order to reduce the number of free parameters (see [9,4]).

The underlying ranking assumption is valid as long as there is a single criterion under which the objects are evaluated, or the objects map to a linear scale. What can be done in case of intransitivities ($o_a < o_b$, $o_b < o_c$, and $o_c < o_a$) that arise systematically due to conflicting multiple criteria? Intransitivities can be consistently resolved and used to estimate utility weights for multicriteria decision making ([5]).

References

1. Ailon, N., Mohri, M.: An Efficient Reduction of Ranking to Classification, Technical Report, TR2007-903 (2007)
2. Ailon, N., Mohri, M.: Preference-Based Learning to Rank. Machine Learning 80, 189–211 (2010)

3. Barnes, S.H., Kaase, M.: Political Action: Mass Participation in Five Western Countries. Sage, Beverly Hills (1979)
4. Busse, L.M., Orbanz, P., Buhmann, J.M.: Cluster Analysis of Heterogeneous Rank Data. In: International Conference on Machine Learning (2007)
5. Busse, L.M., Buhmann, J.M.: Multicriteria Scaling for Utilities under Intransitivities (to appear, 2011)
6. Cao, Z., Qin, T., Liu, T.-Y., Tsai, M.-F., Li, H.: Learning to Rank: From Pairwise Approach to Listwise Approach, Microsoft Tech. Report (2007)
7. Cohen, W.W., Schapire, R.E., Singer, Y.: Learning to Order Things. In: Advances in Neural Information Processing Systems, vol. 10 (1998)
8. Diaconis, P.: Group Representations in Probability and Statistics, Institute of Mathematical Statistics (1988)
9. Fligner, M.A., Verducci, J.S.: Distance based rank models. Journal of the Royal Statistical Society B 48(3), 359–369 (1986)
10. Fürnkranz, J., Hüllermeier, E.: Pairwise Preference Learning and Ranking. In: Lavrač, N., Gamberger, D., Todorovski, L., Blockeel, H. (eds.) ECML 2003. LNCS (LNAI), vol. 2837, pp. 145–156. Springer, Heidelberg (2003)
11. Hofmann, T., Buhmann, J.: Pairwise Data Clustering by Deterministic Annealing. IEEE Transactions on Pattern Analysis and Machine Intelligence 19(1), 1–14 (1997)
12. Kahn, J., Saks, M.: Every poset has a good comparison. In: Proc. 16-th Symposium on Theory of Computing, pp. 299–301 (1984)
13. Karzanov, A., Khachiyan, L.: On the Conductance of Order Markov Chains. Order 8, 7–15 (1991)
14. Kendall, M.G., Babington Smith, B.: On the Method of Paired Comparisons. Biometrika 31, 324–345 (1940)
15. Lebanon, G., Lafferty, J.D.: Cranking: Combining Rankings Using Conditional Probability Models on Permutations. In: International Conference on Machine Learning (2002)
16. Little, R.J.A., Rubin, D.B.: Statistical analysis with missing data. Wiley series in probability and mathematical statistics. Applied probability and statistics, NJ (2002)
17. Lu, T., Boutilier, C.: Learning Mallows Models with Pairwise Preferences. In: International Conference on Machine Learning (2011)
18. Mallows, C.L.: Non-null ranking models I. Biometrika 44, 114–130 (1957)
19. Marden, J.I.: Analyzing and Modeling Rank Data. Chapman & Hall, Boca Raton (1995)
20. McLachlan, G.J., Krishnan, T.: The EM Algorithm and Extensions. John Wiley & Sons, Chichester (1997)
21. Meila, M., Phadnis, K., Patterson, A., Bilmes, J.: Consensus ranking under the exponential model. In: Conference on Uncertainty in Artificial Intelligence, UAI (2007)
22. Saaty, T.L.: A scaling method for priorities in hierarchical structures. Journal of Mathematical Psychology 15, 234–281 (1977)
23. Su, X., Khoshgoftaar, T.M.: A Survey of Collaborative Filtering Techniques. In: Advances in Artificial Intelligence (2009)

Bag Dissimilarities for Multiple Instance Learning

David M.J. Tax, Marco Loog, Robert P.W. Duin,
Veronika Cheplygina, and Wan-Jui Lee

Pattern Recognition Laboratory, Delft University of Technology,
Mekelweg 4, 2628 CD Delft, The Netherlands
D.M.J.Tax@tudelft.nl

Abstract. When objects cannot be represented well by single feature vectors, a collection of feature vectors can be used. This is what is done in Multiple Instance learning, where it is called a bag of instances. By using a bag of instances, an object gains more internal structure than when a single feature vector is used. This improves the expressiveness of the representation, but also adds complexity to the classification of the object. This paper shows that for the situation that not a single instance determines the class label of a bag, simple bag dissimilarity measures can significantly outperform standard multiple instance classifiers. In particular a measure that computes just the average minimum distance between instances, or a measure that uses the Earth Mover's distance, perform very well.

Keywords: pattern recognition, multiple instance learning, dissimilarity representation.

1 Introduction

Standard pattern recognition assumes that objects are represented by a feature vector, containing measurements on the objects that are informative for the class separability [7]. Unfortunately, for complex real world objects this is often insufficient. By using a single feature vector, much of the internal structure of the object is lost. Take for instance an image, that can contain several regions with very different characteristics: a person, a face, a tree in the background, a blue sky. It is a priori not clear how important each region is for the classification problem at hand. Only when a very clear classification task is requested, suitable features may be selected and extracted. Otherwise, the representation should be flexible enough to encode all information in the image, and let the classifier optimize its model to get a good performance.

When the representation requires more flexibility, the single feature representation may be replaced by a collection of feature vectors. For instance in the case of image classification or image retrieval, it is customary to segment the image in more-or-less homogeneous subparts, and to represent the full image by a collection of feature vectors. This is what is called Multiple Instance Learning (MIL)[5]. Objects are represented by a set (called *bag*) of feature vectors

M. Pelillo and E.R. Hancock (Eds.): SIMBAD 2011, LNCS 7005, pp. 222–234, 2011.

(called *instances*), and each object can belong to the positive or negative class. Typically, it is assumed that objects from the positive class contain at least one instance from a so-called *concept*. The task of a classifier is then to identify if one of the instances belong to the concept, and label the object then to the positive class. Many MIL algorithms therefore contain an optimization strategy to search for the most informative instance per bag, and create a model of the concept [20,13,22,1].

For the situation that no clear concept can be defined, or the situation that most instances in a bag actually contribute to the class discrimination, a more global approach in comparing bags can be defined. Instead of focusing on the single most informative instance in a bag, a similarity measure between sets of feature vectors is defined [9,15,2,12]. In most cases the goal is to define a Mercer kernel between the bags, such that a standard support vector classifier can be trained. By this one tries to implicitly reduce the complexity of a bag of instances back to a simple vector representation. The advantage is that the well understood procedures of pattern recognition can be applied, but the drawback is that a part of the representational power is lost.

When the demand for Mercer kernels is relaxed, more powerful dissimilarity measures can be defined. Actually, any (dis)similarity can be constructed, as long it may be informative for the class separability [17]. This is at the expense that it cannot be directly plugged into the support vector classifier. The alternative is then to apply a classifier that can operate on distances, like the k-nearest neighbor classifier or a nearest mean classifier, or to use a dissimilarity space approach [8,14]. In a dissimilarity space approach the dissimilarities are treated as new features, such that *any* classifier can be trained on these features. The distance character of the dissimilarities is then not used, but as features they can still contribute to a good class separation.

In this paper we propose a few simple dissimilarity measures between bags, based on pairwise dissimilarities between instances. These dissimilarities capture a more global differences between instance distributions of bags. This is done in section 2. We show in section 4 that for quite some multiple instance problems, the more global dissimilarity measures are very informative in that the classifiers trained on top of them give very good classification performance. In section 5 we conclude and have a bit more discussion on the results.

2 Bag Dissimilarities

Assume an object i is represented by a bag $B_i = \{\mathbf{x}_{ik}, k = 1, ..., n_i\}$ containing n_i instances, where each instance is represented by a vector $\mathbf{x} \in \mathbb{R}^d$. In the training set $\{(B_i, y_i), i = 1, ..., N\}$ each bag is labeled positive $y_i = +1$ or negative $y_i = -1$. Given the bag of instances, a classifier has to predict its class label $\hat{y}_i = f(B_i)$. First define the pairwise dissimilarities of instances in the bags B_i and B_j:

$$D_{ij} = D(B_i, B_j) = \begin{pmatrix} D(\mathbf{x}_{i1}, \mathbf{x}_{j1}) & \dots & D(\mathbf{x}_{i1}, \mathbf{x}_{jn_j}) \\ D(\mathbf{x}_{i2}, \mathbf{x}_{j1}) & \dots & D(\mathbf{x}_{i2}, \mathbf{x}_{jn_j}) \\ \vdots & & \vdots \\ D(\mathbf{x}_{in_i}, \mathbf{x}_{j1}) & \dots & D(\mathbf{x}_{in_i}, \mathbf{x}_{jn_j}) \end{pmatrix}, \tag{1}$$

where $D(\mathbf{x}_{ik}, \mathbf{x}_{jl})$ defines the distance between instance k from bag B_i and instance l from bag B_j. In principle, any distance $D(\mathbf{x}_i, \mathbf{x}_j)$ can be used, but in this paper the squared Euclidean distance is used.

The classic approach for the classification of a bag B is to first identify a concept $C \in \mathbb{R}^d$, and to check for each instance if it is member of this concept.

$$f(B_i) = \begin{cases} +1, & \text{if} \quad \exists \mathbf{x}_{ik} \in C \\ -1, & \text{otherwise} \end{cases} \tag{2}$$

In section 3 a few approaches using concepts are explained in more depth.

Instead of focussing on the single most informative instance from a bag, a bag can be described by its full distribution of its instances. This assumes that all instances in a bag are informative about the bag label and not a single instance can determine the class label. It is then possible to define a dissimilarity matrix $d_{ij} = d(B_i, B_j)$ between bags, that is measuring the difference between (or overlap in) the distributions of B_i and B_j.

A drawback may be that the distances obtained in such manner may not be euclidean, or even metric. Therefore only methods that directly operate on distances can be applied, for instance a k-nearest neighbor (k-nearest bag) classifier would be suitable. The alternative approach is to interpret the distances to the other bags as new features, and to train classifiers on this new dissimilarity space [14]:

$$f(B_i) = f((d_{i1}, d_{i2}, ..., d_{iR})) \tag{3}$$

Typically, the distances to all training bags can be used so $R = N$, but reductions in complexity and computational requirements can be obtained when a smaller representation set is chosen $R << N$.

We did not specify the dissimilarity d_{ij} between bags yet. In this paper we consider two approaches, the first using bag distribution dissimilarities (section 2.1) and the second using the pairwise instance dissimilarities (section 2.2).

2.1 Bag Distribution Dissimilarities

To characterize bag differences in terms of differences between distributions of the instances would mean that for each bag a probability density has to be estimated, and next the difference between the distributions of two bags. It is not only very hard to estimate a high dimensional probability density function in a high dimensional feature space, it is also very computational demanding to estimate the difference, or overlap, of two distributions. Therefore approximations are made, and the following approximate distribution comparisons are considered:

Mahalanobis Distance. The distribution of each bag is approximated by a single Gaussian distribution with mean μ and covariance matrix Σ. The difference between two Gaussian distributions is computed using the Mahalanobis distance:

$$d_{ij} = (\mu_i - \mu_j)^T \left(\frac{1}{2}\Sigma_i + \frac{1}{2}\Sigma_j\right)^{-1} (\mu_i - \mu_j) \tag{4}$$

Note that the *averaged* covariance matrix is used of the covariance matrices Σ_i and Σ_j of the two bags. That means that when the number of instances per bag is low, and the feature dimensionality is high, it can become hard (or, in fact, impossible) to invert the averaged covariance matrix.

Earth Mover's Distance. The Earth Mover's distance measures the dissimilarity between two distributions p_i and p_j by measuring the effort to turn one distibution p_i, one 'pile of earth', into another one p_j. [16] In case of a discrete probability mass, the probability has to be moved over distances $D_{ij}(k,l)$ as defined in (1). For the MIL bag similarity that we consider, we assume that each instance in bag B_i contains $1/n_i$ of the total probability mass. The Earth Mover's distance is defined by the minimum amount of work that is needed to transform distribution p_i into p_j:

$$d_{ij} = \min_{f_{kl}} \sum_{k,l} f_{kl} D_{ij}(k,l) \tag{5}$$

where f_{kl} defines the flow between instance k and instance l, and with the additional constraints that $f_{kl} \geq 0$, $\forall k,l$, $\sum_l f_{kl} \leq 1/n_i$, $\sum_k f_{kl} \leq 1/n_j$ and $\sum_{kl} f_{kl} = 1$.

2.2 Pairwise Instance Dissimilarities

Instead of modeling full probability densities, the empirical distances between instances can be used.

To get a single dissimilarity measure between bags B_i and B_j, the matrix in (1) has to be reduced to a single scalar. A collection of operations O_1, .., O_5 is defined that first reduce the rows and columns of the matrix to (two) vectors, and then reduces the vectors to a scalar. In figure 1 a graphical representation of the general family of operations on the dissimilarity D_ij is shown. The first two operations perform a row and column wise reduction:

$$\tilde{\mathbf{d}}_i = O_1(D(\mathbf{x}_{i1}, \mathbf{x}_{j1}), ..., D(\mathbf{x}_{in_i}, \mathbf{x}_{j1})) \tag{6}$$

$$\tilde{\mathbf{d}}_j = O_2(D(\mathbf{x}_{i1}, \mathbf{x}_{j1}), ..., D(\mathbf{x}_{i1}, \mathbf{x}_{jn_j})) \tag{7}$$

where the individual operators reduce a vector to a scalar: $O_i : \mathbb{R}^n \to \mathbb{R}$. On these reduced vectors, the final bag dissimilarity is defined:

$$d_{ij} = O_5(O_3(\tilde{\mathbf{d}}_i), O_4(\tilde{\mathbf{d}}_j)). \tag{8}$$

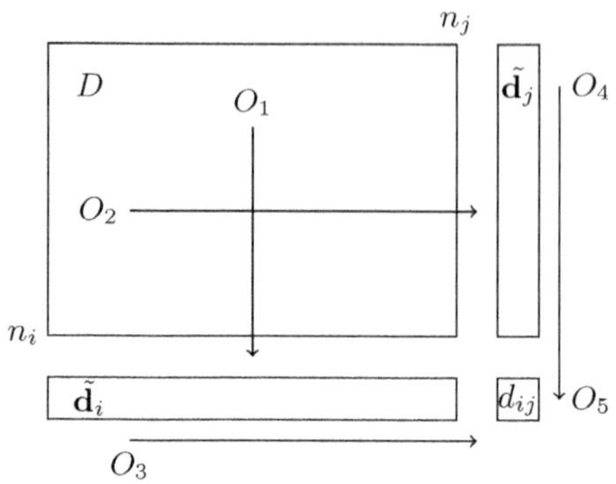

Fig. 1. The operations that can be performed on a general dissimilarity matrix D between bags B_i and B_j

(Note that d_{ij} contains a single scalar dissimilarity, while D_{ij} contains the full instance dissimilarity matrix.) Often a symmetric dissimilarity matrix is preferred, $d_{ij} = d_{ji}$, and therefore the operations are defined in a symmetric way: $O_1 = O_2$ and $O_3 = O_4$.

This reduction of the full dissimilarity matrix using these operations generalizes many approaches, depending on the choices for O_i. This results in well-known and new bag similarity measures:

Overall Minimum. $O_1 = O_2 = \min$, $O_3 = O_4 = \min$, $O_5 = \min$: Use the overall minimum pairwise distance between instances. This is expected to be quite noisy because a single instance determines the final distance between bags. When the number of instances per bag is low, and there is a very dense concept C, i.e. it is covering a small area in the feature space, this measure may actually work.

Mean Minimum Distance. $O_1 = O_2 = \min$, $O_3 = O_4 = \text{mean}$, $O_5 = \text{mean}$ The mean minimum distance between bags, where for each instance the closest instance in the other bag is found, and where the minimum distances are averaged over all the instances. This is certainly not as noise sensitive as the overall minimum, and captures more of the general similarity between the distributions of the two bags. This does not work if there is a single instance that determines the class label.

Standard Haussdorf Distance. $O_1 = O_2 = \min$, $O_3 = O_4 = \max$, $O_5 = \max$: The standard Haussdorf distance between bags, where for each instance the closest instance in the other bag is found, and from all the closest matches, the lastest distance is used to define the bag distance. The advantage is that the Haussdorf distance defines a metric, but it is sensitive to a single outlier instance, that can dominate the full bag distance.

Modified Haussdorf. $O_1 = O_2 = \min$, $O_3 = O_4 = \max$, $O_5 = \min$: The modified Haussdorf distance between bags [6] that is less sensitive to single outliers.

2.3 Linear Assignment Dissimilarity

The operations that are defined in (8) matches instances independently of each other; each element in (6) or (7) are computed individually. By performing a linear assignment [11], instances in bag B_i are matched to bag B_j. When one bag is larger than the other, instances of the largest bag are not matched, and will not contribute to the distance between the two bags. Define $I_{kl} = 1$ when instances k and l are matched, and $I_{kl} = 0$ otherwise, then the bag dissimilarity is defined as:

$$d_{ij} = \sum_{k,l} I_{kl} D_{ij}(k, l). \quad (9)$$

3 Standard MIL Classifiers

The original model proposed by [5] was an axis-parallel rectangle that was grown and shrunk to best cover the area of the concept. Several parameters determine the optimization of the rectangle, and one of them (τ) defines a slight extrapolation around to box to become a bit resistant against noise. It is applied to a drug discovery problem where molecules have to be distinguished based on their shape into active and inactive molecules. It appears that this rectangular model fits well with the molecule shape classification, but it is less successful in other applications.

A probabilistic description of the MIL problem was given by [13]. The concept is modeled by a general probabilistic model, where typically an axis-parallel Gaussian is used. Unfortunately, the optimization of the parameters requires a computationally expensive maximization of an likelihood that is adapted to include the constraint that at least one of the instances in a positive bag has a high concept probability. Because the error landscape is very wild, several random initialisations are tried, and the solution with the highest likelihood is used.

Newer methods often avoid the modeling of the concept by a density model, and try to separate concept instances from background instances using a discriminative approach. Two of them include the MISVM [1] and the MiBoost [19]. The first uses a support vector classifier, in which one instance from each positive bag is selected as being the 'witness', i.e. each bag is reduced to its most positive member. The second is a variant of boosting, where in each boosting step a weight per instance is updated. The weight indicates how informative this instance seems to be in the prediction of the class label of the bag.

The above mentioned methods assume the presence of a concept. Other methods avoid this assumption, and try to apply standard pattern recognition techniques directly to the MIL problem. The first approach is to extract features from the bag of instances, like the average instance, or the minimum and maximum feature values that appear in the bag, and train a standard classifier on this feature vector [9]. A second approach is to ignore the MIL problem and to label all instances according to their bag label. [21] Then a standard classifier can be fitted to the fully labeled instance dataset. To classify a new bag of instances, first all instances are classified, and then a simple combining rule like taking the maximum, or majority voting is applied. Finally, an idea similar to the bag of words in the natural language processing can be applied. In particular, in MILES [4] all instances in the training set are considered words (or potential concepts), and new bags are represented by their similarity to each of the words. On these long similarity vectors a sparse classifier is fitted to select the most informative words.

4 Experiments

To show the benefits and limitations of the bag similarities, classification experiments are performed on some standard real world MIL datasets. The datasets often deal with image classification, where with different procedures segments are extracted, different features per segment are computed and different classes are defined. [3,1,4]. Two non-image problems are the classical drug discovery problems Musk1 and Musk2, in which molecules are described by 166 shape features [5], and the webpage classification, in which webpages are described by a collection of pages that have links to the original page. In table 1 some characteristics are shown of the datasets that are considered in this paper. The datasets are chosen to show some variability in the number of features, the number of bags, and the average number of instances per bag.

Table 1. Some characteristics of the standard MIL datasets used in this paper

dataset	nr.inst.	dim.	pos. bags	neg. bags	min. inst/bag	median inst/bag	max. inst/bag
MUSK 1 [5]	476	166	47	45	2	4	40
MUSK 2 [5]	6598	166	39	63	1	12	1044
Corel African [4]	7947	9	100	1900	2	3	13
Corel Historical [4]	7947	9	100	1900	2	3	13
SIVAL AjaxOrange [10]	47414	30	60	1440	31	32	32
Web atheism [23]	5443	200	50	50	22	58	76
Web motorcycles [23]	4730	200	50	50	22	49	73
Web mideast [23]	3373	200	50	50	15	34	55
Corel Fox [1]	1320	230	100	100	2	6	13
Corel Tiger [1]	1220	230	100	100	1	6	13
Corel Elephant [1]	1391	230	100	100	2	7	13

In tables 2, 3 and 4 the results of the classifiers mentioned in Section 2 are shown. Three different types of classifiers are used: the standard MIL classifiers in the top block, the k-nearest neighbor that is directly operating on the distances defined in Section 2 given in the middle block, and finally classifiers that use the distances as features in the last block.

For the Axis-parallel Rectangle classifier (APR) the τ parameter is varied, because that appears to have the most significant influence on the performance. The other parameters are fixed. For the Diverse Density 100 random restarts of the optimization is chosen. In the miBoost the number of boosting runs was set to $M = 100$. For the MI-SVM and MILES the kernel was chosen to be an RBF kernel, where the width parameter σ was roughly optimized (using 5 candidates). For the MI-SVM the linear kernel was also applied for comparison.

The more simple MIL classifiers includes first the Linear Discriminant Analysis (LDA) trained on all instances, with a maximum combination rule to get from instance to bag labels. The next two classifiers represent a bag of instances by the mean instance (where the feature values are averaged) or the minimum and maximum feature value, respectively. On this new feature vector a LDA is trained. The last simple MIL classifier applies a bag of words approach, where first k cluster centers are obtained by applying k-means clustering on all instances, next the bags are represented by the number of instances that are assigned to each cluster, and finally a (linear) support vector classifier is trained on the histograms.

The standard MIL classifier are compared to the classifiers that work with the bag dissimilarities. Five different dissimilarities are considered here, the 'Overall Minimum' (minmin.) dissimilarity, the 'Mean Minimum' (mindist) distance, the 'Hausdorff' (haussd.) distance, the Mahalanobis (mahal.) distance, the Earth Mover's distance (emd) and, finally, the linear assignment (lin.ass.) distance. The classifier that is used for classifying distance data is the k-nearest neighbor. The k is optimized on the training set using leave-one-out crossvalidation.

Furthermore, all classifiers are implemented, trained and evaluated using a Matlab toolbox [18]. In quite some cases the performance as mentioned in the literature could not be reproduced. This might be caused by the fact that the optimization of the free parameters in the methods was not so extensive as in the original papers. In this paper a reasonable range of parameters was chosen and an internal crossvalidation was used to find the final optimal value. In some cases (in particular the Diverse Density) the optimization was so slow, that just a fixed parameter setting was chosen. Furthermore, all features have been rescaled to zero mean and unit variance on the training set. The reported performance is the area under the ROC curve ($\times 100$). A performance of 50.0 means that the two classes are not separated at all, a performance of 100.0 is perfect.

From the results in Tables 2, 3 and 4 several things can be concluded:

Datasets that contain a clear concept often do not gain much by the use of bag similarities. That is visible in datasets Musk 1, Musk 2, AjaxOrange, Corel Tiger and Corel Elephant. For datasets in which many instances contain some information about the class label, like in the webpage classification, but also a bit in Corel African, Corel Historical and Corel Fox, the bag dissimilarity measures are informative.

It is not always the case that using a nearest neighbor classifier on the distances gives the highest performance. In particular on the webpage classification problems significant improvements can be made by using a k-nearest neighbor classifier (or a Parzen classifier) in the dissimilarity space. On the other hand, on the Corel African and Corel Historical datasets, training a classifier in the dissimilarity space slightly deteriorates the results. This is probably caused by the fact that the dissimilarity space is quite large here because the number of training bags is high: 90% of 2000 = 1800D.

Table 2. AUC performances (100×) of the classifiers on datasets Musk1, Musk2, Corel African and Corel Historical. Results are obtained using five times 10-fold stratified crossvalidation. Results [(1)] cannot be obtained because some bags in Musk2 are too large to compute the Earth Mover's distance between bags.

classifier	Musk 1	Musk 2	Corel African	Corel Historical
Standard MIL classifiers				
APR $\tau = 0.999$	81.8 (1.3)	82.5 (1.2)	50.5 (0.0)	50.5 (0.1)
APR $\tau = 0.995$	78.9 (1.7)	80.8 (2.3)	57.4 (0.8)	61.4 (0.4)
Diverse Density (100 restarts)	89.4 (1.3)	**93.2 (0.0)**	85.6 (0.1)	83.4 (0.7)
MiBoost ($M = 100$ rounds)	80.3 (3.1)	49.3 (3.7)	68.0 (0.0)	80.4 (1.6)
MI-SVM (linear kernel)	70.3 (3.0)	81.5 (2.1)	63.4 (2.0)	78.9 (0.6)
MI-SVM (RBG kernel)	**92.9 (1.3)**	NaN (0.0)	NaN (0.0)	**90.8 (1.0)**
MILES (RBF kernel)	**92.8 (1.4)**	**95.3 (1.5)**	58.9 (9.2)	60.8 (12.8)
Simple MIL with LDA, max-comb.	72.9 (3.4)	76.7 (3.4)	68.8 (0.2)	74.4 (0.2)
LDA on mean-inst	85.7 (1.4)	87.6 (2.8)	77.2 (0.3)	86.2 (0.1)
LDA on extremes	**92.4 (1.9)**	88.9 (4.0)	88.5 (0.1)	85.3 (0.2)
BagOfWords (k=10)+linear SVM	72.7 (4.7)	63.7 (6.1)	75.1 (3.2)	78.4 (3.9)
BagOfWords (k=100)+linear SVM	78.7 (5.5)	71.2 (3.1)	83.4 (1.8)	85.6 (2.6)
Distance-based classifiers on bag dissimilarities				
minmin+k-NND	90.1 (1.4)	84.0 (1.9)	86.6 (0.4)	84.1 (1.2)
mindist+k-NND	86.3 (2.0)	83.2 (1.6)	**92.7 (0.7)**	**90.7 (1.1)**
haussd.+k-NND	89.0 (1.6)	84.2 (0.8)	86.7 (0.9)	88.5 (1.0)
mahal.+k-NND	61.8 (2.8)	65.7 (5.7)	67.3 (0.7)	63.2 (1.2)
emd+k-NND	90.1 (2.7)	(1)	**92.0 (0.7)**	88.8 (1.7)
lin.ass.+kNND	84.7 (1.6)	76.5 (2.7)	69.9 (0.6)	87.8 (0.4)
Standard classifiers on bag dissimilarity space				
minmin.+Parzen Classifier	**94.7 (3.0)**	92.3 (2.7)	90.4 (0.6)	84.0 (0.6)
mindist.+Parzen Classifier	61.2 (6.0)	50.0 (0.0)	83.4 (0.9)	86.0 (0.5)
haussd.+Parzen Classifier	86.9 (0.7)	92.1 (2.5)	79.1 (0.6)	84.3 (0.5)
mahal.+Parzen Classifier	52.1 (0.9)	65.8 (2.4)	46.3 (2.4)	52.4 (1.3)
emd+Parzen Classifier	87.4 (3.4)	(1)	89.4 (0.4)	85.4 (0.7)
lin.ass.+Parzen Classifier	83.3 (2.7)	72.2 (2.9)	83.5 (0.7)	86.2 (0.5)
minmin.+k-NN	**93.3 (1.5)**	90.7 (3.9)	88.7 (0.8)	83.5 (1.3)
mindist.+k-NN	88.8 (3.0)	83.8 (1.4)	81.7 (1.1)	85.5 (1.0)
haussd.+k-NN	89.2 (2.7)	91.6 (1.0)	77.0 (0.7)	80.0 (1.3)
mahal.+k-NN	72.0 (3.1)	61.6 (2.7)	53.3 (1.6)	57.0 (0.8)
emd+k-NN	**92.4 (1.4)**	(1)	86.9 (1.1)	79.6 (1.5)
lin.ass.+k-NN	88.6 (2.1)	72.6 (3.7)	81.5 (1.4)	84.7 (1.4)

Table 3. AUC performances (100×) of the classifiers on datasets SIVAL AjaxOrange, webpage Atheism, webpage Motorcycles and webpage Mideast. Results are obtained using five times 10-fold stratified crossvalidation. Results [(2)] cannot be obtained because the linear programming optimizer required more than 128GB of memory, which was not available.

classifier	AjaxOrange	alt.atheism	rec.motorcycles	politics.mideast
Standard MIL classifiers				
APR $\tau = 0.995$	48.4 (0.8)	50.0 (0.0)	50.0 (0.0)	49.8 (0.4)
Diverse Density (100 restarts)	55.5 (2.9)	52.2 (2.4)	46.4 (2.9)	40.2 (2.5)
MiBoost ($M = 100$ rounds)	56.5 (2.4)	50.0 (0.0)	NaN (0.0)	50.3 (1.5)
MI-SVM (linear kernel)	**93.6 (2.6)**	69.8 (2.8)	76.4 (4.0)	79.8 (2.3)
MI-SVM (RBG kernel)	NaN (0.0)	45.5 (7.1)	49.7 (5.4)	46.1 (2.4)
MILES (RBF kernel)	[(2)]	47.1 (4.5)	44.7 (4.8)	54.1 (1.8)
Simple MIL with LDA, max-comb.	89.3 (0.3)	81.6 (1.2)	80.4 (2.1)	75.0 (3.1)
LDA on mean-inst	82.3 (0.9)	83.7 (2.1)	84.4 (1.8)	78.1 (1.7)
LDA on extremes	90.3 (0.3)	50.0 (0.0)	51.2 (0.4)	65.0 (1.8)
BagOfWords (k=100)+linear SVM	81.2 (2.5)	54.0 (0.0)	65.2 (9.3)	58.6 (6.8)
Distance-based classifiers on bag dissimilarities				
minmin+k-NND	53.6 (1.2)	50.0 (0.0)	50.0 (0.0)	52.8 (2.2)
mindist+k-NND	62.9 (1.3)	59.2 (1.9)	58.4 (0.5)	53.4 (1.1)
haussd.+k-NND	72.4 (1.3)	72.8 (3.0)	68.7 (3.2)	67.1 (1.8)
mahal.+k-NND	64.0 (1.6)	47.7 (4.4)	45.0 (3.4)	58.5 (6.0)
emd+k-NND	77.6 (2.6)	56.0 (1.2)	60.8 (0.4)	57.2 (1.3)
lin.ass.+kNND	71.6 (1.4)	69.2 (1.7)	53.7 (2.9)	58.5 (3.2)
Standard classifiers on bag dissimilarity space				
minmin.+Parzen Classifier	55.7 (1.6)	49.8 (0.4)	50.0 (0.0)	50.4 (2.3)
mindist.+Parzen Classifier	78.0 (1.3)	78.9 (2.8)	78.4 (0.5)	75.2 (1.9)
haussd.+Parzen Classifier	71.8 (0.9)	73.8 (2.0)	82.0 (2.2)	73.8 (0.9)
mahal.+Parzen Classifier	75.3 (0.9)	54.2 (3.3)	43.7 (3.5)	61.9 (1.8)
emd+Parzen Classifier	78.7 (1.1)	**89.7 (1.3)**	77.6 (1.5)	**87.8 (1.1)**
lin.ass.+Parzen Classifier	78.9 (0.6)	80.1 (2.4)	84.2 (2.8)	84.3 (3.1)
minmin.+k-NN	56.0 (1.6)	50.0 (0.0)	50.0 (0.0)	47.8 (2.7)
mindist.+k-NN	70.6 (2.6)	84.9 (1.6)	**86.6 (2.0)**	82.2 (1.5)
haussd.+k-NN	68.9 (1.9)	85.6 (2.1)	**89.2 (3.5)**	77.2 (3.2)
mahal.+k-NN	70.8 (1.5)	51.2 (3.6)	56.3 (3.8)	55.8 (4.6)
emd+k-NN	72.0 (2.4)	**90.0 (1.4)**	**80.7 (0.7)**	82.6 (1.7)
lin.ass.+k-NN	70.1 (0.8)	82.1 (2.3)	82.9 (2.4)	80.8 (3.8)

Table 4. AUC performances (100×) of the classifiers on datasets Corel Fox, Corel Tiger, and Corel Elephant. Results are obtained using five times 10-fold stratified crossvalidation.

classifier	Corel Fox	Corel Tiger	Corel Elephant
Standard MIL classifiers			
APR $\tau = 0.995$	55.2 (1.2)	57.9 (1.6)	74.6 (3.2)
Diverse Density (100 restarts)	66.5 (1.6)	79.3 (0.2)	90.8 (0.0)
MiBoost (M = 100 rounds)	53.5 (1.4)	74.2 (1.3)	88.9 (1.3)
MI-SVM (linear kernel)	54.4 (1.5)	80.1 (1.1)	84.1 (1.3)
MI-SVM (RBF kernel)	69.6 (1.4)	**86.5 (1.4)**	91.1 (1.2)
MILES (RBF kernel)	69.8 (1.7)	**87.2 (1.7)**	88.3 (1.1)
Simple MIL with LDA, max-comb.	57.9 (1.4)	83.4 (1.3)	**90.8 (1.6)**
LDA on mean-inst	58.5 (2.8)	**86.5 (1.2)**	89.7 (1.3)
LDA on extremes	62.9 (3.0)	84.8 (1.0)	**91.3 (1.3)**
BagOfWords (k=10)+linear SVM	51.8 (4.6)	71.2 (4.0)	73.0 (1.9)
Distance-based classifiers on bag dissimilarities			
minmin+k-NND	65.7 (1.3)	83.4 (1.2)	83.4 (1.1)
mindist+k-NND	63.9 (1.5)	76.4 (1.3)	87.9 (1.7)
haussd.+k-NND	63.5 (3.0)	80.9 (1.2)	80.9 (2.2)
mahal.+k-NND	58.8 (2.9)	58.8 (2.9)	66.3 (4.1)
emd+k-NND	61.3 (2.1)	85.5 (0.9)	86.8 (2.3)
lin.ass.k+NND	57.5 (4.1)	78.9 (2.4)	72.8 (2.5)
Standard classifiers on bag dissimilarity space			
minmin.+Parzen Classifier	61.2 (4.0)	74.3 (2.8)	86.7 (0.7)
mindist.+Parzen Classifier	62.3 (1.9)	70.7 (1.2)	74.9 (4.2)
haussd.+Parzen Classifier	59.8 (1.7)	66.9 (2.2)	73.2 (1.1)
mahal.+Parzen Classifier	68.9 (3.4)	68.9 (3.4)	64.9 (1.7)
emd+Parzen Classifier	54.3 (2.1)	67.8 (1.5)	76.5 (2.2)
lin.ass.+Parzen Classifier	64.4 (1.9)	64.6 (1.4)	69.6 (2.1)
minmin.+k-NN	67.0 (1.4)	78.6 (1.4)	87.8 (1.1)
mindist.+k-NN	59.6 (3.1)	73.7 (1.3)	76.0 (1.8)
haussd.+k-NN	56.7 (3.8)	70.6 (1.9)	77.8 (0.9)
mahal.+k-NN	**75.0 (3.8)**	75.0 (3.8)	65.6 (1.1)
emd+k-NN	61.4 (0.9)	76.5 (0.6)	76.3 (1.0)
lin.ass.+k-NN	65.0 (3.1)	68.7 (2.9)	71.8 (2.3)

5 Conclusions

In some MIL problems not a single instance may be decisive, but the full distribution of all the instances in a bag. For these situations bag dissimilarities are defined that characterize the difference in distribution between bags. For the webpage classification problem this resulted in very good performances, while for other problems, where a single concept can be expected, the bag dissimilarity is far less successful. It seems that most webpages that link to another webpage, contain information about the linked-to webpage, and therefore selecting just one single most informative webpage is not optimal. For other problems, like the image classification problem, the different segments appear to be more independent, in that detecting the single most informative segment is often best. This effect is also enhanced by the fact that in the image classification problems images often do not have many segments (around 3-6), so it is hard to treat these few instances as a distribution.

When the given the bag dissimilarities are interpreted as new features to represent the bag, a classifier can be trained on these distance features. In this paper only the k-nearest neighbor and the Parzen classifier are considered. Although the choice of the classifier has some influence on the final performance, the choice of the bag dissimilarity is more important. One well-performing dissimilarity is using the Earth Mover's Distance.

Acknowledgments. We acknowledge the financial support from the FET programme within the EU FP7, under the project "Similarity-based Pattern Analysis and Recognition - SIMBAD" (contract 213250).

References

1. Andrews, S., Hofmann, T., Tsochantaridis, I.: Multiple instance learning with generalized support vector machines. In: Proceedings of the AAAI National Conference on Artificial Intelligence (2002)
2. Blaschko, M.B., Hofmann, T.: Conformal multi-instance kernels. In: NIPS 2006 Workshop on Learning to Compare Examples, pp. 1–6 (2006)
3. Carson, C., Thomas, M., Belongie, S., Hellerstein, J.M., Malik, J.: Blobworld: A system for region-based image indexing and retrieval. In: Huijsmans, D.P., Smeulders, A.W.M. (eds.) VISUAL 1999. LNCS, vol. 1614, pp. 509–517. Springer, Heidelberg (1999)
4. Chen, Y., Bi, J., Wang, J.: MILES: Multiple-instance learning via embedded instance selection. IEEE Transactions on Pattern Analysis and Machine Intelligence 28(12), 1931–1947 (2006)
5. Dietterich, T., Lathrop, R., Lozano-Perez, T.: Solving the multiple instance problem with axis-parallel rectangles. Artificial Intelligence 89(1-2), 31–71 (1997)
6. Dubuisson, M., Jain, A.: Modified Hausdorff distance for object matching. In: 12th Internat. Conference on Pattern Recognition, vol. 1, pp. 566–568 (1994)
7. Duda, R., Hart, P., Stork, D.: Pattern Classification, 2nd edn. John Wiley & Sons, Chichester (2001)

8. Duin, R.P., Pekalska, E.: The dissimilarity space: bridging structural and statistical pattern recognition. Pattern Recognition Letters (in press, accepted manuscript 2011)
9. Gärtner, T., Flach, P., Kowwalczyk, A., Smola, A.: Multi-instance kernels. In: Sammut, C., Hoffmann, A. (eds.) Proceedings of the 19th International Conference on Machine Learning, pp. 179–186. Morgan Kaufmann, San Francisco (2002)
10. Goldman, S.: SIVAL (spatially independent, variable area, and lighting) benchmark (1998), `http://www.cs.wustl.edu/~sg/accio/SIVAL.html`
11. Kuhn, H.: The hungarian method for the assignment problem. Naval Research Logistics Quarterly 2, 83–97 (1955)
12. Kwok, J.T., Cheung, P.M.: Marginalized multi-instance kernels. In: Proceedings of International Joint Conference on Artificial Intelligence, pp. 901–906 (2007)
13. Maron, O., Lozano-Pérez, T.: A framework for multiple-instance learning. In: Advances in Neural Information Processing Systems, vol. 10, pp. 570–576. MIT Press, Cambridge (1998)
14. Pekalska, E.: The Dissimilarity representations in pattern recognition. Concepts, theory and applications. Ph.D. thesis, Delft University of Technology (January 2005)
15. Ray, S., Craven, M.: Supervised versus multiple instance learning: an empirical comparison. In: ICML 2005: Proceedings of the 22nd International Conference on Machine Learning, pp. 697–704. ACM, New York (2005)
16. Rubner, Y., Tomasi, C., Guibas, L.: A metric for distributions with applications to image databases. In: Proceedings of the IEEE International Conference on Computer Vision, pp. 59–66 (1998)
17. Sörensen, L., Loog, M., Tax, D.M.J., Lee, W.J., de Bruijne, M., Duin, R.P.W.: Dissimilarity-based multiple instance learning. In: Hancock, E.R., Wilson, R.C., Windeatt, T., Ulusoy, I., Escolano, F. (eds.) SSPR&SPR 2010. LNCS, vol. 6218, pp. 129–138. Springer, Heidelberg (2010)
18. Tax, D.: MIL, a Matlab toolbox for multiple instance learning, version 0.7.9 (May 2011), `http://prlab.tudelft.nl/david-tax/mil.html`
19. Viola, P., Platt, J., Zhang, C.: Multiple instance boosting for object dection. In: Advances in Neural Inf. Proc. Systems (NIPS 2005), pp. 1419–1426 (2005)
20. Weidmann, N., Frank, E., Pfahringer, B.: A two-level learning method for generalized multi-instance problems. In: Lavrač, N., Gamberger, D., Todorovski, L., Blockeel, H. (eds.) ECML 2003. LNCS (LNAI), vol. 2837, pp. 468–479. Springer, Heidelberg (2003)
21. Xu, X., Frank, E.: Logistic regression and boosting for labeled bags of instances. In: Dai, H., Srikant, R., Zhang, C. (eds.) PAKDD 2004. LNCS (LNAI), vol. 3056, pp. 272–281. Springer, Heidelberg (2004)
22. Zhang, Q., Goldman, S.: EM-DD: An improved multiple-instance learning technique. In: Advances in Neural Information Processing Systems, vol. 14, MIT Press, Cambridge (2002)
23. Zhou, Z.H., Jiang, K., Li, M.: Multi-instance learning based web mining. Applied Intelligence 22(2), 135–147 (2005)

Mutual Information Criteria for Feature Selection

Zhihong Zhang and Edwin R. Hancock

Department of Computer Science, University of York, UK

Abstract. In many data analysis tasks, one is often confronted with very high dimensional data. The feature selection problem is essentially a combinatorial optimization problem which is computationally expensive. To overcome this problem it is frequently assumed either that features independently influence the class variable or do so only involving pairwise feature interaction. In prior work [18], we have explained the use of a new measure called multidimensional interaction information (MII) for feature selection. The advantage of MII is that it can consider third or higher order feature interaction. Using dominant set clustering, we can extract most of the informative features in the leading dominant sets in advance, limiting the search space for higher order interactions. In this paper, we provide a comparison of different similarity measures based on mutual information. Experimental results demonstrate the effectiveness of our feature selection method on a number of standard data-sets.

1 Introduction

High-dimensional data pose a significant challenge for pattern recognition. The most popular methods for reducing dimensionality are variance based subspace methods such as PCA. However, the extracted PCA feature vectors only capture sets of features with a significant combined variance, and this renders them relatively ineffective for classification tasks. Hence it is crucial to identify a smaller subset of features that are informative for classification and clustering. The idea underpinning feature selection is to a) reduce the dimensionality of the feature space, b) speed up and reduce the cost of a learning algorithm, c) obtain the feature subset which is most relevant to classification. Mutual information provides a principled way of measuring the mutual dependence of two variables, and has been used by a number of researchers to develop information theoretic feature selection criteria. For example, Batti [1] has developed the Mutual Information Based Feature Selection (MIFS) criterion, where the features are selected in a greedy manner. Given a set of existing selected features S, at each step it locates the feature x_i that maximize the relevance to the class $I(x_i; C)$. The selection is regulated by a proportional term $\beta I(x_i; S)$ that measures the overlap information between the candidate feature and existing features. The parameter β may significantly affect the features selected, and its control remains an open problem. Peng et al [11] on the other hand, use the so-called Maximum-Relevance Minimum-Redundancy criterion (MRMR), which is equivalent to MIFS with

M. Pelillo and E.R. Hancock (Eds.): SIMBAD 2011, LNCS 7005, pp. 235–249, 2011.

$\beta = \frac{1}{n-1}$. Yang and Moody's [15] Joint Mutual Information (JMI) criterion is based on conditional MI and selects features by checking whether they bring additional information to an existing feature set. This method effectively rejects redundant features. Kwak and Choi [8] improve MIFS by developing MIFS-U under the assumption of a uniform distribution of information for input features. It calculates the MI based on a Parzen window, which is less computationally demanding and also provides better estimates.

However, there are two limitations for the above MI feature selection methods. Firstly, they assume that each individual relevant feature should be dependent with the target class. This means that if a single feature is considered to be relevant it should be correlated with the target class, otherwise the feature is irrelevant [3]. So only a small set of relevant features is selected, and larger feature combinations are not considered. The second weakness is that most of the methods simply consider pairwise feature dependencies, and do not check for third or higher order dependencies between the candidate features and the existing features. To overcome the above problem, Zhang and Hancock [18] introduce the so called multidimensional interaction information (MII) $I(F;C) = I(f_1, \ldots, f_m; C)$ to select the optimal subset of features. The main reason for using $I(F;C)$ as feature selection criterion is that: because $I(F;C)$ is a measure of the reduction of uncertainty in class C due to the knowledge of feature vector $F = \{f_1, \ldots, f_m\}$, selecting features that maximize $I(F;C)$, from an information theoretic perspective, translates into selecting those features that contain the maximum information about class C.

In prior work[18], we have proposed a graph-based method to feature selection. In this feature selection scheme, the original features are clustered into different clusters based on dominant-set clustering and each cluster just includes a small set of features. As dominant set clustering can group most of the informative features into the leading dominant set based on suitable similarity measure, this allows us to limit the search space for further feature selection. The similarity measure used for clustering is based on mutual information. We compare the similaity measure with other two well known alternative measures of similarity, namely Pearson's correlation coefficient (ρ) which based on distance and the Least square regression error (e) is made. Using the Parzen window for probability distribution estimation, we then apply a greedy strategy to incrementally select the features that maximizes the multidimensional mutual information between the already selected features and the output class set.

2 Dominant-Set Clustering Algorithm

There are several different methods for clustering features, well-known examples are: k-means algorithm [9] is built for all sample, but requires a user to supply the number of clusters in advance. In addition, it can not detect clusters of arbitrary shapes. The Self Organizing Map(SOM) [14] is a type of artificial neural network which can produce a low-dimensional space for the input data objects using a neighborhood function to cluster nodes. As same with k-means algorithm, it does not explicitly optimize any measure of the total dissimilarity to locate clusters. Again, it requires the number of clusters as user input. In this paper, we use dominant set clustering which is suitable for both subspace and high dimensional data clustering. In addition, it does not require the user to provide the number of clusters and can also handle outliers efficiently. Most importantly, it can group most of the informative features into cluster based on a suitable similarity measure.

2.1 Concept of Dominant Set

The dominant set[10], is a combinational concept in graph theory that generalizes the notion of a maximal complete subgraph from simple graphs to edge-weighted graphs. In fact, dominant sets turn out to be equivalent to maximal cliques. The definition of the dominant set simultaneously emphasizes internal homogeneity and together with external inhomogeneity. Thus it is can be used as a general definition of a "cluster". To provide an example, assume there are N training samples, each having 5 feature vectors. In order to capture the dominant features from these 5 features (represented as $F_1, \ldots, F_5$), we construct a graph $G = (V, E)$ with node-set V, edge-set $E \subseteq V \times V$ and edge weight matrix W whose elements are in the interval $[0, 1]$. Each vertex represents a feature and the edge between two features represents their pairwise relationship. The weight on the edge reflects the degree of relevance between two features. Therefore, we represent the graph G with the corresponding edge-weight or weighted relevance matrix. In our example, in Fig. 1, features $\{F_1, F_2, F_3\}$ form the dominant set, since the edge weights "internal" to that set (0.6, 0.7 and 0.9) are larger than the sum of those between the internal and external features (which is between 0.05 and 0.25).

For the graph $G = (V, E)$ above, we can locate the dominant set by finding the solutions of a quadratic program that maximizes the functional

$$f(\mathbf{x}) = \frac{1}{2}\mathbf{x}^T \mathbf{W} \mathbf{x} \ . \tag{1}$$

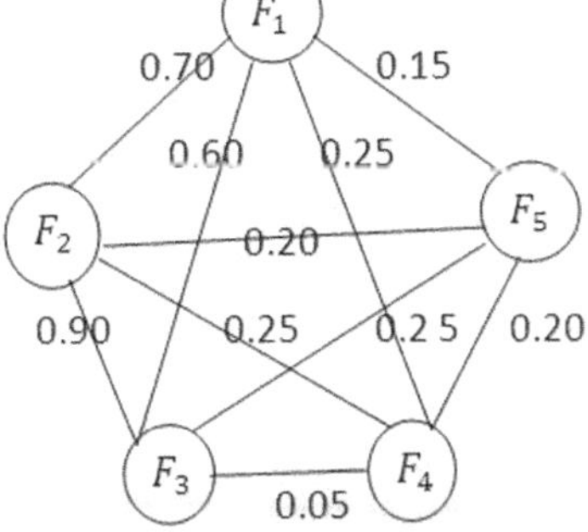

Fig. 1. The subset of features $\{F_1, F_2, F_3\}$ is dominant

subject to $\mathbf{x} \in \triangle$, where $\triangle = \{\mathbf{x} \in \mathbb{R}^n : \mathbf{x} \geq 0 and \sum_{i=1}^{n} x_i = 1\}$ and $\mathbf{W}$ is the relevance weight matrix between features. The dominant set corresponds in the strict sense with solutions of the quadratic program. Let u denote a strict local solution of the above program. It has been proved by [10] that $\sigma(u) = \{i|u_i > 0\}$ is equivalent to a dominant set of the graph represented by the edge-weight matrix $\mathbf{W}$. In addition, the local maximum of $f(u)$ indicates the "cohesiveness" of the corresponding cluster. The replicator equation can be used to solve the program using the iterative update equation:

$$x_i(t+1) = x_i(t)\frac{(\mathbf{W}\mathbf{x}(t))_i}{\mathbf{x}(t)^T\mathbf{W}\mathbf{x}(t)} . \tag{2}$$

where $x_i(t)$ corresponded to the $i-th$ feature vector at iteration t of the update process.

2.2 Dominant-Set Clustering Algorithm

Pavan et al have demonstrated that the concept of a dominant set provides an effective framework for iterative pairwise clustering. Consider a set of features represented by an undirected edge-weighted graph with no self-loops. Let the graph be denoted by $G = (V, E, \omega)$ where $V = 1, \ldots, n$ is the vertex set, $E \subseteq V \times V$ is the edge set, and ω is the weight function. Each vertex represents a feature and the weight residing on the edge between two nodes represents the pairwise affinity of the corresponding features. To cluster the features into coherent groups, a dominant set of the weighted graph is iteratively located, and then removed from the graph. This process is repeated until the node-set of the graph is empty. The main property of a dominant set is that the overall similarity among the internal features is greater than that between the external features and the internal features.

3 Feature Similarity Measure

There are different similarity measure methods that can be used for clustering and different methods may lead to different cluster results. As a result, we need to carefully select the most suitable measure to use. In general, the Euclidean distance is widely used as the distance or similarity measure for clustering [7]. However, Euclidean distance only accounts for a data which follows a particular distribution [16], it is not effective to reflect functional similarity such as positive and negative correlation and interdependency. Rao [12] introduced two approaches to measure the linear dependency between variables, namely, a)Pearson's correlation coefficient (ρ), b) Least square regression error (e).

Pearson's Correlation Coefficient (ρ): The Correlation coefficient (ρ) between two random variables x and y is defined as:

$$\rho(x, y) = \frac{cov(x, y)}{\sqrt{var(x)var(y)}} . \tag{3}$$

where $var()$ denotes the variance of a variable and $cov(x, y)$ is the covariance between two random variables. From the above definition, we can see that Pearson's correlation coefficient quantifies the linear dependency between two variables x and y. When the $\rho(x, y)$ is large (i.e. 1 or -1), this implies that variable x and variable y are closely related, otherwise, when $\rho(x, y)$ is equal to 0, this means that two variables are totally unrelated. As a result, the method can be used to detect positive and negative correlation. However, there are two limitations which unsuit the utility of Pearson coefficient to used for dominant set clustering. First, it is not robust to outliers and as a result it may assign a high similarity score to a pair of dissimilar features. Second, as it is sensitive to rotation and invariant to scaling, the two pairs of variables having different variances may give the same value of the similarity measure.

Least Square Regression Error (e)**:** The dependency of two variables x and y can be modeled by the linear model, $y = a + bx$. As a result, the degree of dependency between them can be measure by the error in predicting y from the linear model. The parameters of the model a and b can be learned by minimizing the mean square error as follows:

$$e(x, y)^2 = \frac{1}{n} \sum (e(x, y)_i)^2 . \tag{4}$$

where $e(x, y)_i = y_i - a - bx_i$, $a = \bar{y}$, $b = \frac{cov}{(x,y)var(x)}$ and $e(x, y) = var(y)(1 - \rho(x, y)^2)$. From this definition, we can see that the least square regression error (e) quantifies the amount of variance of y unexplained by the linear model. As with Pearson's correlation coefficient (ρ), it is sensitive to rotation and scaling.

4 Feature Selection Using Dominant-Set Clustering

In this paper we aim to utilize the dominant-set clustering algorithm for feature selection. Using a graph representation of the features, there are three steps to the algorithm, namely a) computing the relevance matrix $\mathbf{W} = (\mathbf{w}_{ij})_{n \times n}$ based on the mutual information between feature vectors, b) dominant-set clustering to cluster the feature vectors and c) selecting the optimal feature set from leading dominant set using the multidimensional interaction information (MII) criterion. In the remainder of this paper we describe these elements of our feature selection algorithm in more detail.

4.1 Computing the Similarity Matrix

Instead of using the Euclidean distance, Pearson's correlation coefficient (ρ) or the least square regression error (e), our similarity measure employs an mutual information measure to evaluate the interdependence of features. The use of this mutual information measure allows dominant set clustering to discover the informative features and group them into cluster. In accordance with Shannon's information theory [13], the uncertainty of a random variable Y can be measured by the entropy $H(Y)$. For two variables X and Y, the conditional entropy

$H(Y|X)$ measures the remaining uncertainty about Y when X is known. The mutual information (MI) represented by $I(X;Y)$ quantifies the information gain about Y provided by variable X. The relationship between $H(Y)$, $H(Y|X)$ and $I(X;Y)$ is $I(X;Y) = H(Y) - H(Y|X)$.

As defined by Shannon, the initial uncertainty for the random variable Y is expressed as:

$$H(Y) = -\sum_{y \in Y} P(y) \log P(y) . \tag{5}$$

where $P(y)$ is the prior probability density function over Y. The remaining uncertainty in the variable Y if the variable X is known is defined by the conditional entropy $H(Y|X)$

$$H(Y|X) = -\int_x p(x)\{\sum_{y \in Y} p(y|x) \log p(y|x)\}dx . \tag{6}$$

where $p(y|x)$ denotes the posterior probability for variable Y given another random variable X. After observing the variable vector x, the amount of additional information gain is given by the mutual information (MI)

$$I(X;Y) = H(Y) - H(Y|X) = \sum_{y \in Y} \int_x p(y,x) log \frac{p(y,x)}{p(y)p(x)} dx . \tag{7}$$

From the above definition, we can see that mutual information quantifies the information which is shared by two variables X and Y. When the $I(X;Y)$ is large, this implies that variable X and variable Y are closely related, otherwise, when $I(X;Y)$ is equal to 0, this means that two variables are totally unrelated. Therefore, in our feature selection scheme, the relevance of pairs of feature vectors is computed using mutual information. Suppose there are N training samples, each having K feature vectors. The kth feature vector for the lth training sample is f_k^l, so we can represent the kth feature vector for the N training samples as the long vector $F_k = \{f_k^1, f_k^2, \ldots, f_k^N\}$. The entropy of the feature vector F_k where $(k = 1, 2, \ldots, K)$ can be computed using Equation (3). For two feature vectors F_{k1} and F_{k2}, their mutual information $I(F_{k1}, F_{k2})$ can be computed by Equation (5). The relevance degree between two feature vectors F_{k1} and F_{k2} can be defined as [17]:

$$\mathbf{W}(F_{k1}, F_{k2}) = \frac{2I(F_{k1}, F_{k2})}{H(F_{k1}) + H(F_{k2})} . \tag{8}$$

where $k1, k2 \in K$ and the higher the value of $\mathbf{W}(F_{k1}, F_{k2})$ the more relevant are the features F_{k1} and F_{k2}. Otherwise, if $\mathbf{W}(F_{k1}, F_{k2}) = 0$, the two features are totally unrelated. In addition, for the above computation, we use the Parzen-Rosenblatt window method to estimate the probability density function of random variables F_{k1} and F_{k2} [11]. The Parzen probability density estimation formula is given by: $p(x) = \frac{1}{N}\phi(\frac{x-x_i}{h})$, where $\phi(\frac{x-x_i}{h})$ is the window function and h is the window width. Here, we use a Gaussian as the window function, so $\phi(\frac{x-x_i}{h}) = \frac{1}{(2\pi)^{\frac{d}{2}} h^d |\Sigma|^{\frac{1}{2}}} \exp(\frac{(x-x_i^T)\Sigma^{-1}(x-x_i)}{-2h^2})$, where Σ is the covariance of $(x - x_i)$, d is the length of vector x. When $d = 1$, $p(x)$ estimates the marginal density and when $d = 2$, $p(x)$ estimates the joint density of variables such as F_{k1} and F_{k2}.

4.2 Dominant-Set Clustering

The dominant-set clustering algorithm commences from the relevance matrix and iteratively bi-partitions the features into a dominant set and a non-dominant set. It therefore produces the dominant-set progressively and hierarchically. The clustering process stops when all the features are grouped into one of the dominant-sets. We can formulate the dominant-set clustering algorithm in the following: a) Initialize $\mathbf{W}^t$ by the similarity matrix $\mathbf{W}$, where $t = 1$. b) Calculate the local solution of Equation(1) by Equation(2): u^t and $f(u^t)$. c) Get the dominant set: $DS^t = \sigma(u^t)$. d) Split out DS^t from $\mathbf{W^t}$ and get a new similarity matrix $\mathbf{W^{t+1}}$. e) If $\mathbf{W^{t+1}}$ is not empty, $\mathbf{W^t} = \mathbf{W^{t+1}}$ and $t = t + 1$, then go to step b; else exit

4.3 Selecting Key Features

In accordance with Shannon's information theory [13], the uncertainty of a random variable Y can be measured by the entropy $H(Y)$. For two variables X and Y, the conditional entropy $H(Y|X)$ measures the remaining uncertainty about Y when X is known. The mutual information (MI) represented by $I(X;Y)$ quantifies the information gain about Y provided by variable X. The relationship between $H(Y)$, $H(Y|X)$ and $I(X;Y)$ is $I(X;Y) = H(Y) - H(Y|X)$.

As defined by Shannon, the initial uncertainty for the random variable Y is expressed as:

$$H(Y) = -\sum_{y \in Y} P(y) \log P(y) \ . \tag{9}$$

where $P(y)$ is the prior probability density function over Y. The remaining uncertainty in the variable Y if the variable X is known is defined by the conditional entropy $H(Y|X)$

$$H(Y|X) = -\int_x p(x)\{\sum_{y \in Y} p(y|x) \log p(y|x)\} dx \ . \tag{10}$$

where $p(y|x)$ denotes the posterior probability for variable Y given another random variable X. After observing the variable vector x, the amount of additional information gain is given by the mutual information (MI)

$$I(X;Y) = H(Y) - H(Y|X) = \sum_{y \in Y} \int_x p(y,x) log \frac{p(y,x)}{p(y)p(x)} dx \ . \tag{11}$$

In addition, for the above computation, we use Parzen-Rosenblatt window method to estimate the probability density function of random variables F_{k1} and F_{k2} [11].

The Parzen probability density estimation formula is given by: $p(x) = \frac{1}{N}\phi(\frac{x-x_i}{h})$, where $\phi(\frac{x-x_i}{h})$ is the window function and h is the window width. Here, we use a Gaussian as the window function, so $\phi(\frac{x-x_i}{h}) = \frac{1}{(2\pi)^{\frac{d}{2}} h^d |\Sigma|^{\frac{1}{2}}} \exp(\frac{(x-x_i^T)\Sigma^{-1}(x-x_i)}{-2h^2})$, where Σ is the covariance of $(x - x_i)$, d is the length of vector x. When $d = 1$, $p(x)$ estimates the marginal density and when $d = 2$, $p(x)$ estimates the joint density of variables such as F_{k1} and F_{k2}.

The multidimensional interaction information between feature vector $F = \{f_1, \ldots, f_m\}$ and class variable C is:

$$I(F;C) = I(f_1, \ldots, f_m; C) = \sum_{f_1,\ldots,f_m} \sum_{c \in C} P(f_1, \ldots, f_m; c) \times \log \frac{P(f_1, \ldots, f_m; c)}{P(f_1, \ldots, f_m)P(c)} . \tag{12}$$

The main reason for using $I(F;C)$ as a feature selection criterion is that: because $I(F;C)$ is a measure of the reduction of uncertainty in class C due to knowledge of the feature vector $F = \{f_1, \ldots, f_m\}$, from an information theoretic perspective selecting features that maximize $I(F;C)$ translates into selecting those features that contain the maximum information about class C. In practice and as noted in the introduction, locating a feature subset that maximizes $I(F;C)$ presents two problems: 1) it requires an exhaustive "combinatorial" search over the feature space, and 2) it demands large training sample sizes to estimate the higher order joint probability distribution in $I(F;C)$ with a high dimensional kernel [8]. Bearing these obstacles in mind, most of the existing related papers approximate $I(F;C)$ based on the assumption of lower-order dependencies between features. For example, the first-order class dependence assumption includes only first-order interactions. That is it assumes that each feature independently influences the class variable, so as to select the mth feature, f_m, $P(f_m|f_1, \ldots, f_{m-1}, C) = P(f_m|C)$. A second-order feature dependence assumption is proposed by Guo and Nixon [5] to approximate $I(F;C)$, and this is arguably the most simple yet effective evaluation criterion for selecting features. The approximation is given as

$$I(F;C) \approx \widehat{I}(F;C) = \sum_i I(f_i;C) - \sum_i \sum_{j>i} I(f_i;f_j) + \sum_i \sum_{j>i} I(f_i;f_j|C) . \tag{13}$$

By using $\widehat{I}(F;C)$ instead of $I(F;C)$, it is possible to locate a subset of informative features by implementing a greedy "pick-one-feature-at-a-time" selection procedure. Given K features, out of which m are to be selected ($m < K$), this involves two steps: 1) select the first feature f'_{max} that maximizes $I(f';C)$, and 2) select $m-1$ subsequent features that maximize the criterion in Equation (8), i.e., select the second feature f''_{max} that maximizes $I(f'';C) - I(f'';f'_{max}) + I(f'';f'_{max}|C)$, select the third feature f'''_{max} that maximizes $I(f''';C) - I(f''';f'_{max}) - I(f''';f''_{max}) + I(f''';f'_{max}|C) + I(f''';f''_{max}|C)$ and so on.

Although an MII based on the second-order feature dependence assumption can select features that maximize class-separability and simultaneously minimize dependencies between feature pairs, there is no reason to assume that the final optimal feature subset is formed by pairwise interactions between features. In fact, it neglects the fact that third or higher order dependencies can be lead to an optimal feature subset.

The primary reason for using the approximation $\widehat{I}(F;C)$ for feature selection instead of directly using multidimensional interaction information $I(F;C)$ is that $I(F;C)$ requires estimation of the joint probability distribution of features using a large training sample. Consider the joint distribution $P(F) = P(f_1, \ldots, f_m)$, by the chain rule of probability

$$P(f_i, \ldots, f_m) = P(f_1)P(f_2|f_1) \times P(f_3|f_2, f_1) \cdots P(f_m|f_1, f_2 \cdots f_{m-1}) \ , \quad (14)$$

$$P(F;C) = P(f_1, \ldots f_m;C) = P(C)p(f_1|C)P(f_2|f_1,C)P(f_3|f_1,f_2,C)$$
$$\times P(f_4|f_1,f_2,f_3,C) \cdots P(f_i|f_1,\ldots,f_m,C) \ . \quad (15)$$

In our feature selection scheme, the original features are clustered into different dominant-sets based on dominant-set clustering and each dominant-set just includes a small set of features. Therefore, for each dominant set, we do not need to use the approximation $\widehat{I}(F;C)$. Instead, we can directly use the multidimensional interaction information $I(F;C)$ criterion for feature selection. Using Parzen windows for probability distribution estimation, we then apply the greedy strategy to select the feature that maximizes the multidimensional mutual information between the features and the output class set. As a result the first feature $f^{'}_{max}$ maximizes $I(f^{'}, C)$, the second selected feature $f^{''}_{max}$ maximizes $I(f^{''}, f^{'}, C)$, the third feature $f^{'''}_{max}$ maximizes $I(f^{'''}, f^{''}, f^{'}, C)$, and so on. For each dominant set, we repeat this procedure until $|S| = k$.

5 Classification

After finding the discriminating features, we apply the variational EM (VBEM) algorithm [2] to fit a mixture of Gaussians model to the selected feature subset. After learning the mixture model, we use the a posteriori probability, see Equation(16), to classify sample. Given a sample, we first compute its selected feature vector b through feature selection. Then we compute its a posteriori probabilities r_c, the mean vectors $\hat{b}_c$, and the precision matrices Λ_c, where $c \in c_1, \ldots, c_l$ and l is the number of class for the data. For example, in binary class, if $r_{c_1} > r_{c_2}$ then the sample is classified as class c_1. Otherwise, the sample is classified as c_2. The posterior probabilities are given by

$$r_{nk} \propto \pi_k |\Lambda_k|^{\frac{-1}{2}} \exp\{\frac{1}{2}(x_n - \mu_k)^T \Lambda_k (x_n - \mu_k)\} \ . \quad (16)$$

where $k = 1, \ldots, K$ is the mixture component, $n = 1, \ldots, N$ denotes the data index. Model parameters π_k, μ_k and Λ_k are respectively a priori probability, the mean of selected feature vectors and precision matrices of the kth component. In the variational Bayesian EM (VBEM) algorithm, all of these model parameters are characterized by hyper-parameters, which take into account the uncertainty in the parameter estimation. The parameters r_{nk} are called posteriori probability because they represent the responsibility the kth component takes in explaining the nth observation. The posteriori probability can be arranged into a matrix $R = (r_{nk})$ and will have to satisfy the following conditions:

$$0 \leq r_{nk} \leq 1 \,. \tag{17}$$

6 Experiments and Comparisons

The data sets used to test the performance of our proposed algorithm are the benchmark data sets from the NIPS 2003 feature selection challenge and the UCI Machine Learning Repository. Table. 1 summarizes the properties of these data-sets. Our proposed feature selection method (referred to as the DS*plus*MII method) (which utilizes the multidimensional interaction information (MII) criterion and dominant-set clustering for feature selection) involves grouping a set of informative features into cluster from the original feature set by dominant-set clustering and then applying MII criterion into the cluster for feature selection. In order to examine the performance of our proposed method DS*plus*MII, we need to know how meaningful the cluster obtained based on mutual information is and what more useful information they contain. In view of this, we should first examine how discriminative the features in the leading dominant set. Next, we could use the extracted features for classification to check the performance. Our proposed scheme for evaluation and comparison can be outlined as follows: a) the study of the cluster performance obtained by different similarity measure methods(i.e., the Pearson's correlation coefficient (ρ) and Least square regression error (e)). b) the study of classification results based on the selected feature subset captured by MII in the dominant sets and compared with other MI-based criterion methods(i.e., the MRMR algorithm [11] and the MIFS algorithm [1]).

6.1 Cluster Performance Evaluation Using Different Similarity Measures

As we mentioned before, our proposed algorithm is capable of grouping informative features in the leading dominant set by dominant set clustering based on a suitable similarity measure. Different similarity measures will lead to different clustering results, which means that an unsuitable similarity measure may group less informative features into a cluster. Therefore, we should carefully select which similarity measure to use. Here, we study the clustering results obtained by using three different similarity measures for dominant-set clustering(DS). In order to examine the discriminability of the features grouped in the

Table 1. Summary of UCI and NIPS benchmark data sets

Data-set	Examples	Features	Classes
Madelon	2000	500	2
Breast cancer	699	10	2
Pima	768	8	2
Australian	690	14	2

Table 2. J value comparisons of dominant set using different feature similarity measure

Data-set	Similarity Measure:MI	Similarity Measure: (ρ)	Similarity Measure: (e)
Madelon	1.1082	1.0024	1.0094
Breast cancer	5.1513	5.1513	5.1513
Pima	1.3716	1.3716	1.0177
Australian	2.2546	2.2006	1.2090

leading dominant set, we will use the multidimensional interaction information (MII) criterion. Then, a criterion function is used to measure the discrimination of the selected key features. This is a well known measure of class separability introduced by Devijiver and Kittler [4], and given by

$$J(Y) = \frac{|S_w + S_b|}{|S_w|} = \prod_{k=1}^{d}(1+\lambda_k) \ . \tag{18}$$

where Y denotes the feature set, λ_k, $k = 1 \ldots d$, are the eigenvalues of matrix $S_w^{-1}S_b$, and S_w and S_b are the between and within class scatter matrices. Table. 2 shows the comparative cluster results of our mutual information based similarity measure with other two similarity measures in terms of the measured J value. The subset obtained by our mutual information based similarity measure is more discriminative, giving the highest J value.

6.2 Classification Results Using Selected Feature Subset

After obtaining the discriminating features, we apply a variational Bayesian EM(VBEM) algorithm to learn a Gaussian mixture model on the selected feature subset for the purpose of classification. We compare classification results from our proposed feature selection method (referred to as the DS*plus*MII method) (which utilizes the multidimensional interaction information (MII) criterion and dominant-sets for feature selection) with those obtained using k-means algorithm [9] and alternative existing MI-based criterion methods, namely a) Maximum-Relevance Minimum-Redundancy (MRMR), b) Mutual Information Based Feature Selection (MIFS).

Based on the feature subsets selected by our proposed DS*plus*MII method, We first examine the classification performance using different sized feature subsets by selecting the top k features ranked by their incremental gain. In the classification performance evaluation process, we employ a posteriori probability, see

Equation(16), to perform classification, we got the classification accuracy by the percentage of the data, which are predicted correctly. For the purpose of comparison, we repeated the feature selection process using the k-means algorithm, MRMR algorithm and MIFS algorithm.

The Madelon data set is a 2 classes problem originally proposed in the NIPS'2003 feature selection challenge [6]. The data points grouped into 32 clusters placed on the vertices of a five dimensional hypercubes. As a result, there are only 5 informative features, but 15 redundant features and 480 probes. In Fig. 2, we present the top 14 features ranked by the incremental gain calculated by MII. The classification accuracies obtained on different feature subsets are shown in the right hand side of Fig. 2. From the figure, it is clear that using the leading 6 features (476, 339, 379, 154, 443, 456), we achieve 90% classification accuracy. Because of the unsupervised nature of the VBEM algorithm and the gaussian mixture model, the classification accuracy of 90% demonstrates the adequate separability provided by the selected feature subset. For comparison, we also visualize the classification results of using the feature subset obtained by MRMR;

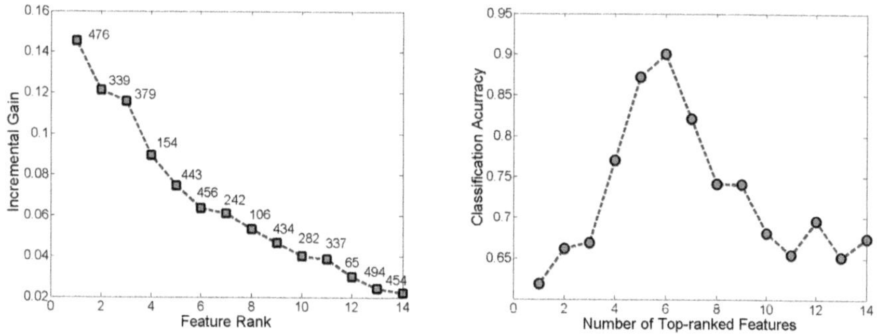

(a) Top-ranked Features by Incremental Gain

(b) Classification result

Fig. 2. The result on Madelon data set for our algorithm. The values of the Incremental gain for the top 14 features are presented in the left part along with the feature indices, while the classification accuracies are plotted in the right part.

In Fig. 3, the top-ranked features ranked by MRMR are presented in the left hand part, and the classification accuracies using the top-ranked features incrementally are presented in the right hand part. The best result is about 63.1% using 9 features, which is much worse than the result of our algorithm as shown in Fig. 2. The poor classification performance may be explained by our observation that most of the selected top features are not in the 1st dominant set and ranked very low by DS*plus*MII. On the other hand, we find that for MRMR there is a tendency to overestimate the redundancy between features, since they neglect the conditional redundancy term $I(x_i, S|C)$. As a result some important features can be discarded, which in turn leads to information loss.

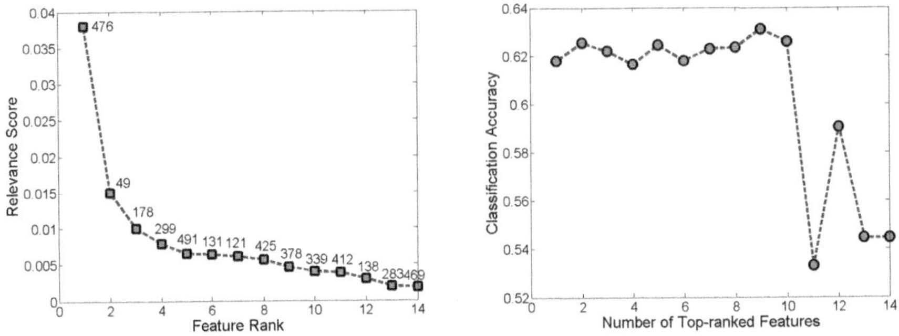

(a) Top-ranked Features by Relevance Score

(b) Classification result

Fig. 3. The result on Madelon data set using MRMR for feature ranking. The values of the relevance score for the top 14 features are presented in the left part along with the feature indices, while the classification accuracies are plotted in the right part.

Table 3. The classification accuracy on the top features selected by different methods in the Breast Cancer data set

No.of Features Selected	DS*plus*MII	MRMR	MIFS
2	88.84%	88.84%	88.84%
3	96.3%	87.98%	84.4%
4	96.3%	87.55%	82.51%

The experimental results in Table. 3, 4 and 5 show that DS*plus*MII is, by and large, superior to the other feature clustering and feature selection methods by selecting a smaller set of discriminative features than the others as reflected by the classification results. As shown by the results, DS*plus*MII outperforms MIFS and MRMR algorithms in all cases except in the Pima dataset, in which all the four methods yield a comparable classification rate. It is interesting to note that the performance achieves a 96.3% when using the 3 features selected by DS*plus*MII and maintain at the same accuracy even when more features are selected(see Table. 3). Similaly, 83.77% is achieved when 3 features are selected by DS*plus*MII and its performance remains at this level even when more features are selected(see Table. 5). This implies that the discriminative information exists in a small set of features which can be used to fit the mixture Gaussian models to the data. In addition, in breast cancer, we find out that the leading 4 selected features are all from the first dominant set found by dominant set clustering. This again supports the fact that the first dominant set captures the greatest number of informative features. From Table. 4, it is clear that using the leading three features, then all the four methods achieve 75.91% classification accuracy, which is higher than that obtained using other sized feature subsets. Using fewer or more features both deteriorate the accuracy. This implies that classification of samples is based on a very few of the most important features.

Table 4. The classification accuracy on the top features selected by different methods in the Pima data set

No.of Features Selected	DS*plus*MII	MRMR	MIFS
2	74.09%	74.09%	74.09%
3	75.91%	75.91%	75.91%
4	72.79%	70.31%	70.31%

Table 5. The classification accuracy on the top features selected by different methods in the Australian data set

No.of Features Selected	DS*plus*MII	MRMR	MIFS
3	83.77%	68.84%	64.35%
4	83.77%	69.13%	64.35%
5	83.77%	69.28%	83.62%

7 Conclusions

This paper has presented a new graph theoretic approach to feature selection. The proposed feature selection method offers two major advantages. First, dominant-set clustering can capture the most informative features based on MI-based similarity measure. Second, the MII criteria takes into account high-order feature interactions, overcoming the problem of overestimated redundancy. As a result the features associated with the greatest amount of joint information can be preserved.

References

1. Battiti, R.: Using Mutual Information for Selecting Features in Supervised Neural Net Learning. IEEE Transactions on Neural Networks 5(4), 537–550 (2002)
2. Bishop, C.: Pattern Recognition and Machine Learning, vol. 4. Springer, New York (2006)
3. Cheng, H., Qin, Z., Qian, W., Liu, W.: Conditional Mutual Information Based Feature Selection. In: IEEE International Symposium on Knowledge Acquisition and Modeling, pp. 103–107 (2008)
4. Devijver, P.A., Kittler, J.: Pattern Recognition: A Statistical Approach, vol. 761. Prentice-Hall, London (1982)
5. Guo, B., Nixon, M.: Gait Feature Subset Selection by Mutual Information. IEEE Transactions on Systems, Man and Cybernetics, Part A: Systems and Humans 39(1), 36–46 (2008)
6. Guyon, I., Gunn, S., Nikravesh, M., Zadeh, L.: Feature extraction, foundations and applications (2006)
7. Jiang, D., Tang, C., Zhang, A.: Cluster analysis for gene expression data: a survey. IEEE Transactions on Knowledge and Data Engineering 16(11), 1370–1386 (2004)
8. Kwak, N., Choi, C.: Input Feature Selection by Mutual Information Based on Parzen Window. IEEE TPAMI 24(12), 1667–1671 (2002)

9. MacQueen, J., et al.: Some Methods for Classification and Analysis of Multivariate Observations. In: Proceedings of the Fifth Berkeley Symposium on Mathematical Statistics and Probability, California, USA, vol. 1, pp. 281–297 (1967)
10. Pavan, M., Pelillo, M.: A New Graph-Theoretic Approach to Clustering and Segmentation. In: IEEE Computer Society Conference on Computer Vision and Pattern Recognition, vol. 1 (2003)
11. Peng, H., Long, F., Ding, C.: Feature Selection Based on Mutual Information: Criteria of Max-Dependency, Max-Relevance, and Min-Redundancy. IEEE Transactions on Pattern Analysis and Machine Intelligence, 1226–1238 (2005)
12. Rao, C.: Linear statistical Inference and Its Applications (1965)
13. Shannon, C.: A Mathematical Theory of Communication. ACM SIGMOBILE Mobile Computing and Communications Review 5(1), 3–55 (2001)
14. Tamayo, P., Slonim, D., Mesirov, J., Zhu, Q., Kitareewan, S., Dmitrovsky, E., Lander, E., Golub, T.: Interpreting patterns of gene expression with self-organizing maps: Methods and application to hematopoietic differentiation. Proceedings of the National Academy of Sciences of the United States of America 96(6), 2907 (1999)
15. Yang, H., Moody, J.: Feature Selection Based on Joint Mutual Information. In: Proceedings of International ICSC Symposium on Advances in Intelligent Data Analysis, pp. 22–25 (1999)
16. Yu, J., Tian, Q., Amores, J., Sebe, N.: Toward robust distance metric analysis for similarity estimation. In: IEEE Computer Society Conference on Computer Vision and Pattern Recognition, vol. 1, pp. 316–322. IEEE, Los Alamitos (2006)
17. Zhang, F., Zhao, Y., Fen, J.: Unsupervised Feature Selection based on Feature Relevance. In: International Conference on Machine Learning and Cybernetics, vol. 1, pp. 487–492 (2009)
18. Zhang, Z., Hancock, E.: A graph-based approach to feature selection. In: Jiang, X., Ferrer, M., Torsello, A. (eds.) GbRPR 2011. LNCS, vol. 6658, pp. 205–214. Springer, Heidelberg (2011)

Combining Data Sources Nonlinearly for Cell Nucleus Classification of Renal Cell Carcinoma

Mehmet Gönen[1], Aydın Ulaş[2,⋆], Peter Schüffler[3], Umberto Castellani[2], and Vittorio Murino[2,4]

[1] Aalto University School of Science, Department of Information and Computer Science, Helsinki Institute for Information Technology (HIIT), Espoo, Finland
[2] University of Verona, Department of Computer Science, Verona, Italy
[3] ETH Zürich, Department of Computer Science, Zürich, Switzerland
[4] Istituto Italiano di Tecnologia (IIT), Genova, Italy

Abstract. In kernel-based machine learning algorithms, we can learn a combination of different kernel functions in order to obtain a similarity measure that better matches the underlying problem instead of using a single fixed kernel function. This approach is called *multiple kernel learning* (MKL). In this paper, we formulate a nonlinear MKL variant and apply it for nuclei classification in tissue microarray images of *renal cell carcinoma* (RCC). The proposed variant is tested on several feature representations extracted from the automatically segmented nuclei. We compare our results with single-kernel support vector machines trained on each feature representation separately and three linear MKL algorithms from the literature. We demonstrate that our variant obtains more accurate classifiers than competing algorithms for RCC detection by combining information from different feature representations nonlinearly.

Keywords: multiple kernel learning, renal cell carcinoma, support vector machines.

1 Introduction

Empirical success of kernel-based machine learning algorithms such as *support vector machines* (SVMs) is very much dependent on the kernel function used. Kernel selection is generally handled by choosing the best-performing kernel function among a set of kernel functions on a separate validation set. Instead of using a single fixed kernel function, *multiple kernel learning* (MKL) algorithms learn a combination of different kernel functions in order to obtain a similarity measure that better matches the underlying problem [8].

Most of the MKL algorithms proposed in the literature combine the kernels linearly (i.e., linear sum, convex sum, and conic sum) [1,12,14]. Similar to nonlinear classifier combination rules, we can also combine kernels nonlinearly to

⋆ Corresponding author.

M. Pelillo and E.R. Hancock (Eds.): SIMBAD 2011, LNCS 7005, pp. 250–260, 2011.

obtain better kernels [5,7,13]. We formulate a nonlinear MKL variant derived from [5] and test it on cell nucleus classification of *renal cell carcinoma* (RCC) using *tissue microarray* (TMA) images by comparing it with single-kernel SVMs and linear MKL algorithms. Our experiments demonstrate that although it is more costly to use the proposed nonlinear MKL approach, the increase in accuracy is worth its computational complexity.

The paper is organized as follows: Section 2 introduces the data set used in this study. We explain the methods applied in Section 3 and give our experimental results in Section 4. We conclude the paper in Section 5.

2 Data Set

Cancer tissue analysis consists of several consecutive estimation and classification steps which require intensive laboratory practice. The TMA technology enables studies associating molecular changes with clinical endpoints [11]. In this technique, 0.6 mm tissue cylinders are extracted from primary tumor blocks of hundreds of different patients, and are subsequently embedded into a recipient paraffin block. Such array blocks can then be used for simultaneous analysis of primary tumors on DNA, RNA, and protein level.

In this work, we consider the computer based classification of tissue from RCC after such a workflow has been applied. The tissue has been transferred to an array and stained to make the morphology of cells and cell nuclei visible. Current image analysis software for TMAs requires extensive user interaction to properly identify cell populations on the TMA images, to select regions of interest for scoring, to optimize analysis parameters and to organize the resulting raw data. Because of these drawbacks, pathologists typically collect the TMA data by manually assigning a composite staining score for each spot. Such manual scoring can result in serious inconsistencies between data collected during different microscopy sessions. Manual scoring also introduces a significant bottleneck that limits the use of TMAs in high-throughput analysis.

The manual rating and assessment of TMAs under the microscope by pathologists is quite inconsistent due to the high variability of cancerous tissue and the subjective experience of humans, as shown in [6]. Therefore, decisions for grading and/or cancer therapy might be inconsistent among pathologists. With this work, we want to contribute to a more generalized and reproducible system that automatically processes the TMA images and thus helps pathologists in their daily work.

In a previous study, an automated pipeline of TMA processing was already proposed, concentrating on the investigation of various image features and associated kernels on the performance of an SVM classifier for cancerous cells [15]. In this work, we follow this workflow (see Fig. 1) and extend the nucleus classification using different MKL strategies to combine information from multiple sources (in our case different representations). By considering different types of features, in Section 4, we show that nonlinear MKL reaches significantly better accuracies than linear MKL algorithms and single-kernel SVMs.

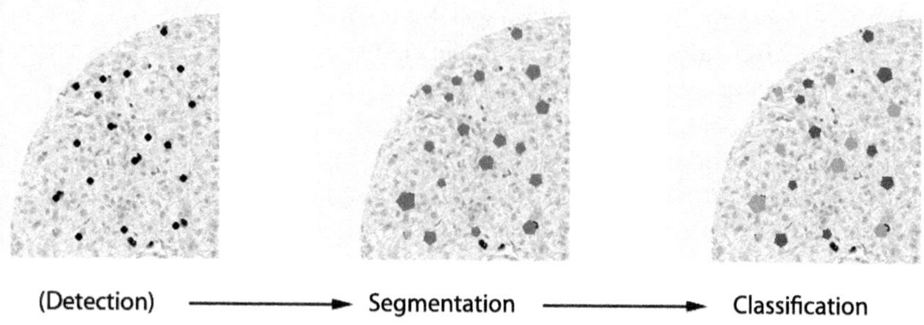

Fig. 1. One key point in the automatic TMA analysis for RCC is the nucleus classification. Nuclei are eosin stained and visible in the TMA image as dark blue spots. We want to do the classification of cell nuclei into cancerous or benign, which is recently done by trained pathologists with their eyes. The automatic approach comprises nucleus detection on the image, the segmentation of the nuclei and the classification, all based on training data labeled by two human experts.

2.1 Tissue Micro Arrays

Tissue Micro Arrays comprise several hundreds of roundish 1mm spots on one carrier plate. Each spot is a small piece of tissue, consisting of several hundreds cancerous and healthy cells. The morphological structure of the cells is made visible under light microscope by eosin staining. Further, proliferating cell nuclei expressing the protein MIB-1 (Ki-67 antigen) are immunohistochemically made visible by brown staining.

The TMA spots are scanned and stored for processing. The images are three channel color images of size 3000 px $\times$ 3000 px. The labeled dataset comprises eight tissue spots from eight patients, each showing 100–200 cells (see Fig. 2).

The TMA images are independently labeled by two pathologists [6]. Therefore, locations and disease states (cancer/non cancer) of each cell in the TMA image are known. From eight labeled TMA images, we extracted 1633 nuclei-patches of size 80 px $\times$ 80 px. Each patch shows a cell nucleus in the center (see Fig. 3). 1273 (78 per cent) from the nuclei form our data set, where the two pathologists agree on the label: 891 (70 per cent) benign and 382 (30 per cent) malignant nuclei.

2.2 Image Normalization and Patching

To minimize illumination variances among the scans, the TMA images were adjusted in contrast. For classification of the individual nuclei, we extracted patches from the whole image such that each 80 px $\times$ 80 px patch has one nucleus in the center (see Fig. 3).

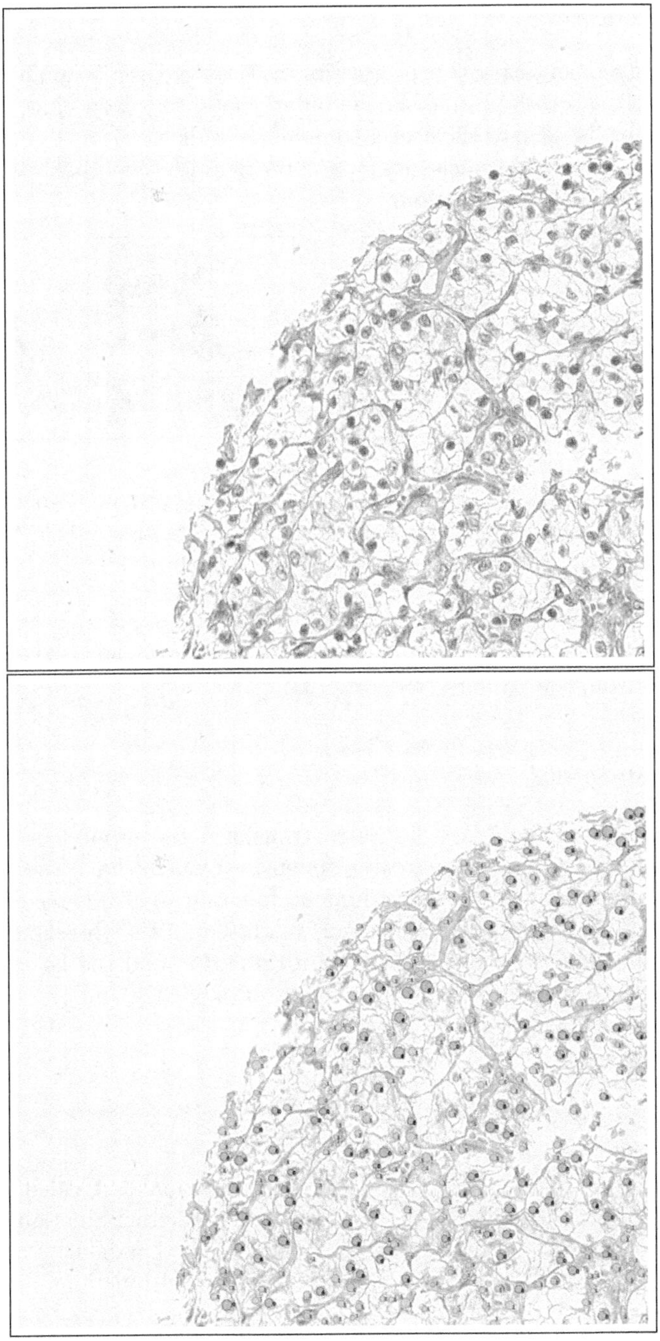

Fig. 2. Top: One 1500 px × 1500 px quadrant of a TMA spot from a RCC patient. **Bottom:** A pathologist exhaustively labeled all cell nuclei and classified them into malignant (black) and benign (red).

2.3 Segmentation

For graphcut segmentation [3], the gray intensities were used as unary potentials. As cell nuclei tend to be roundish, the binary potentials were linearly weighted based on their distance to the center to prefer roundish objects (see Fig. 3). The border of the segmented nuclei was used to calculate several shape features as described in the following section.

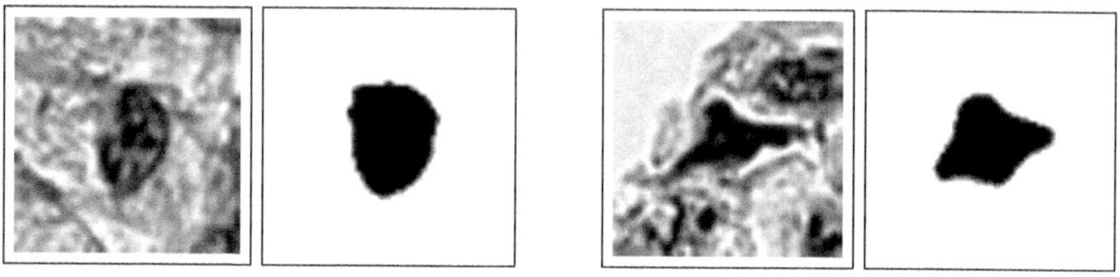

Fig. 3. Two examples of nucleus segmentation. The original 80 px × 80 px patches are shown, each with the corresponding nucleus shape found with graphcut.

2.4 Feature Extraction

For training and testing the various classifiers, we extracted several histogram-like features from the patches (see Table 1).

3 Methodology

The main idea behind SVMs [16] is to transform the input feature space to another space (possibly with a greater dimension) where the classes are linearly separable. After training, the discriminant function of SVM becomes $f(\boldsymbol{x}) = \langle \boldsymbol{w}, \Phi(\boldsymbol{x}) \rangle + b$, where $\boldsymbol{w}$ is the vector of weights, b is the threshold, and $\Phi(\cdot)$ is the mapping function. Using the dual formulation and the kernel trick, one does not have to define this mapping function explicitly and the discriminant function can be written as

$$f(\boldsymbol{x}) = \sum_{i=1}^{N} \alpha_i y_i k(\boldsymbol{x}_i, \boldsymbol{x}) + b$$

where $k(\boldsymbol{x}_i, \boldsymbol{x}_j) = \langle \Phi(\boldsymbol{x}_i), \Phi(\boldsymbol{x}_j) \rangle$ is the kernel function that calculates a similarity measure between data instances. Selecting the kernel function is the most important issue in the training phase; it is generally handled by choosing the best-performing kernel function among a set of kernel functions on a separate validation set.

In recent years, MKL methods have been proposed [8], for learning a combination k_η of multiple kernels instead of selecting only one:

$$k_\eta(\boldsymbol{x}_i, \boldsymbol{x}_j; \boldsymbol{\eta}) = f_\eta(\{k_m(\boldsymbol{x}_i^m, \boldsymbol{x}_j^m)_{m=1}^P\}; \boldsymbol{\eta}) \quad (1)$$

Table 1. Features extracted from patch images for training and testing. All features are histograms.

Name	Feature Description
ALL	**Patch Intensity**: A 16-bin histogram of gray scaled patch.
FG	**Foreground Intensity**: A 16-bin histogram of nucleus.
BG	**Background Intensity**: A 16-bin histogram of background.
LBP	**Local Binary Patterns**: This local feature has been shown to bring considerable performance in face recognition tasks. It benefits from the fact that it is illumination invariant.
COL	**Color Feature**: The only feature comprising color information. The colored patch (RGB) is rescaled to size 5×5. The 3×25 channel intensities are then concatenated to a feature vector of size 75.
FCC	**Freeman Chain Code**: The FCC describes the nucleus' boundary as a string of numbers from 1 to 8, representing the direction of the boundary line at that point [9]. The boundary is discretized by subsampling with grid size 2. For rotational invariance, the first difference of the FCC with minimum magnitude is used. The FCC is represented in a 8-bin histogram.
SIG	**1D-Signature**: Lines are considered from the object center to each boundary pixel. The angles between these lines form the signature of the shape [9]. As feature, a 16-bin histogram of the signature is generated.
PHOG	**Pyramid Histograms of Oriented Gradients**: PHOGs are calculated over a level 2 pyramid on the gray-scaled patches [2].

where the combination function f_η forms a single kernel from P base kernels using the parameters η. Different kernels correspond to different notions of similarity and instead of searching which works best, the MKL method does the picking for us, or may use a combination of kernels. MKL also allows us to combine different representations possibly coming from different sources or modalities.

3.1 Linear Multiple Kernel Learning

There is significant work on the theory and application of MKL and most of the proposed algorithms use a linear combination function such as convex sum or conic sum. Fixed rules use the combination function in (1) as a fixed function of the kernels, without any training. Once we calculate the combined kernel, we train a single kernel machine using this kernel. For example, we can obtain a valid kernel by taking the mean of the combined kernels.

Instead of using a fixed combination function, we can also have a function parameterized by a set of parameters and then we have a learning procedure to optimize these parameters as well. The simplest case is to parameterize the sum rule as a weighted sum:

$$k_\eta(\boldsymbol{x}_i, \boldsymbol{x}_j; \boldsymbol{\eta}) = \sum_{m=1}^{P} \eta_m k_m(\boldsymbol{x}_i^m, \boldsymbol{x}_j^m)$$

with $\eta_m \in \mathbb{R}$. Different versions of this approach differ in the way they put restrictions on the kernel weights: [1,12,14]. For example, we can use arbitrary weights (i.e., linear combination), nonnegative kernel weights (i.e., conic combination), or weights on a simplex (i.e., convex combination).

3.2 Nonlinear Multiple Kernel Learning

A linear combination may be restrictive and nonlinear combinations are also possible [5,7,13]. [5] developed a nonlinear kernel combination method based on kernel ridge regression (KRR) and polynomial combination of kernels. The nonlinear combination can be formulated as

$$k_\eta(\boldsymbol{x}_i, \boldsymbol{x}_j) = \sum_{\boldsymbol{q} \in \mathcal{Q}} \eta_{q_1 q_2 \ldots q_P} k_1(\boldsymbol{x}_i^1, \boldsymbol{x}_j^1)^{q_1} k_2(\boldsymbol{x}_i^2, \boldsymbol{x}_j^2)^{q_2} \ldots k_P(\boldsymbol{x}_i^P, \boldsymbol{x}_j^P)^{q_P}$$

where $\mathcal{Q} = \{\boldsymbol{q} \colon \boldsymbol{q} \in \mathbb{Z}_+^P, \ \sum_{m=1}^P q_m \leq d\}$ and $\eta_{q_1 q_2 \ldots q_P} \geq 0$. The number of parameters to be learned is too large and the combined kernel is simplified in order to reduce the learning complexity:

$$k_\eta(\boldsymbol{x}_i, \boldsymbol{x}_j) = \sum_{\boldsymbol{q} \in \mathcal{R}} \eta_1^{q_1} \eta_2^{q_2} \ldots \eta_P^{q_P} k_1(\boldsymbol{x}_i^1, \boldsymbol{x}_j^1)^{q_1} k_2(\boldsymbol{x}_i^2, \boldsymbol{x}_j^2)^{q_2} \ldots k_P(\boldsymbol{x}_i^P, \boldsymbol{x}_j^P)^{q_P}$$

where $\mathcal{R} = \{\boldsymbol{q} \colon \boldsymbol{q} \in \mathbb{Z}_+^P, \ \sum_{m=1}^P q_m = d\}$ and $\boldsymbol{\eta} \in \mathbb{R}^P$. For example, when $d = 2$, the combined kernel function becomes

$$k_\eta(\boldsymbol{x}_i, \boldsymbol{x}_j) = \sum_{m=1}^{P} \sum_{h=1}^{P} \eta_m \eta_h k_m(\boldsymbol{x}_i^m, \boldsymbol{x}_j^m) k_h(\boldsymbol{x}_i^h, \boldsymbol{x}_j^h). \tag{2}$$

The combination weights are optimized by solving the following min-max optimization problem:

$$\underset{\boldsymbol{\eta} \in \mathcal{M}}{\text{mininimize}} \ \underset{\boldsymbol{\alpha} \in \mathbb{R}^N}{\text{maximize}} \ \boldsymbol{y}^\top \boldsymbol{\alpha} - \frac{1}{2} \boldsymbol{\alpha}^\top (\mathbf{K}_\eta + \lambda \mathbf{I}) \boldsymbol{\alpha}$$

where $\mathcal{M}$ is a positive, bounded, and convex set. Two possible choices for the set $\mathcal{M}$ are the ℓ_1-norm and ℓ_2-norm bounded sets defined as

$$\begin{aligned} \mathcal{M}_1 &= \{\boldsymbol{\eta} \colon \boldsymbol{\eta} \in \mathbb{R}_+^P, \ \|\boldsymbol{\eta} - \boldsymbol{\eta}_0\|_1 \leq \Lambda\} \\ \mathcal{M}_2 &= \{\boldsymbol{\eta} \colon \boldsymbol{\eta} \in \mathbb{R}_+^P, \ \|\boldsymbol{\eta} - \boldsymbol{\eta}_0\|_2 \leq \Lambda\} \end{aligned} \tag{3}$$

where $\boldsymbol{\eta}_0$ and Λ are two model parameters. A projection-based gradient-descent algorithm can be utilized to solve this min-max optimization problem. At each iteration, $\boldsymbol{\alpha}$ is obtained by solving a KRR problem with the current kernel matrix and $\boldsymbol{\eta}$ is updated with the gradients calculated using $\boldsymbol{\alpha}$ while considering the bound constraints on $\boldsymbol{\eta}$ due to $\mathcal{M}_1$ or $\mathcal{M}_2$.

We formulate a variant of this method by replacing KRR with SVM as the base learner. In that case, the optimization problem becomes

$$\underset{\boldsymbol{\eta} \in \mathcal{M}}{\text{mininimize}} \ J_{\eta} = \underset{\boldsymbol{\alpha} \in \mathcal{A}}{\text{maximize}} \ \mathbf{1}^\top \boldsymbol{\alpha} - \frac{1}{2} \boldsymbol{\alpha}^\top ((\boldsymbol{y}\boldsymbol{y}^\top) \odot \mathbf{K}_{\eta}) \boldsymbol{\alpha}$$

where $\odot$ denotes the element-wise product between matrices and $\mathcal{A}$ is defined as

$$\mathcal{A} = \{\boldsymbol{\alpha} \colon \boldsymbol{\alpha} \in \mathbb{R}_+^P, \ \ \boldsymbol{y}^\top \boldsymbol{\alpha} = 0, \ \ \boldsymbol{\alpha} \leq C\}.$$

Note that the simultaneous optimization of $\boldsymbol{\eta}$ and $\boldsymbol{\alpha}$ is not possible. Hence, we use a two-step optimization strategy to optimize them alternatively even though it is prone to sticking at local optima. We solve this optimization problem again using a projection-based gradient-descent algorithm. When updating the kernel parameters at each iteration, the gradients of J_{η} with respect to $\boldsymbol{\eta}$ are used. These gradients can be written as

$$\frac{\partial J_{\eta}}{\partial \eta_m} = -\frac{1}{2} \sum_{h=1}^{P} \eta_h \boldsymbol{\alpha}^\top ((\boldsymbol{y}\boldsymbol{y}^\top) \odot \mathbf{K}_h \odot \mathbf{K}_m) \boldsymbol{\alpha}.$$

4 Experiments

4.1 Experimental Methodology

1273 nuclei samples were divided into ten folds with stratification. We then trained single-kernel SVMs with different kernels for each feature representation and combined the feature representations using four different MKL algorithms on these folds. In our experiments, we used three different kernel functions: the linear kernel (`LIN`), the second-degree polynomial kernel (`POL`), and the Gaussian kernel (`GAU`). Using a rule of thumb, the width parameter of the Gaussian kernel was chosen as $\sqrt{D}$ where D is the dimensionality of the corresponding feature representation.

We implemented single-kernel SVM and four MKL algorithms in MATLAB and solved the canonical SVM optimization problems with the LIBSVM software [4]. `SVM` denotes the single-kernel SVMs trained on each feature representation separately. `RBMKL` denotes the rule-based MKL algorithm that trains an SVM with the mean of the combined kernels. `SimpleMKL` is the iterative algorithm of [14] that uses projected gradient updates and trains single-kernel SVMs at each iteration. `GLMKL` denotes the group Lasso-based MKL algorithms proposed by [10,17]. In our implementation, we used ℓ_1-norm on the kernel weights and learned a convex combination of the kernels. `NLMKL` denotes the nonlinear MKL variant derived from [5], which uses the quadratic kernel given in (2) and selects the kernel weights from the set $\mathcal{M}_1$ in (3). In our implementation, $\boldsymbol{\eta}_0$ is taken as $\mathbf{0}$ and Λ is assigned to 1 arbitrarily.

As a summary, we have eight representations (ALL, FG, BG, LBP, COL, FCC, SIG, and PHOG), three kernels (LIN, POL, and GAU), and five algorithms (SVM, RBMKL, SimpleMKL, GLMKL, and NLMKL).

4.2 Results

Table 2 reports the single-kernel SVM accuracies for all feature representation and kernel function pairs. We see that the best performance was obtained as 76.9 per cent using (PHOG, GAU) pair. Independent of the kernel function used, feature representations BG and PHOG gave consistently higher accuracies than other representations.

Table 2. Single-kernel SVM accuracies

	LIN	POL	GAU
ALL	70.0±0.2	71.9±2.9	68.7±2.9
FG	70.0±0.2	71.2±3.7	65.9±4.3
BG	70.2±0.6	72.7±3.8	69.6±3.1
LBP	70.0±0.2	63.6±2.7	68.4±6.3
COL	70.2±3.0	62.9±3.5	67.2±3.4
FCC	70.0±0.2	69.8±0.7	62.9±5.5
SIG	70.0±0.2	69.6±3.4	66.0±3.0
PHOG	76.0±3.4	70.5±3.3	**76.9±2.7**

Next, using four different MKL algorithms, we combined eight kernels calculated on the feature representations with the same kernel function. Table 3 lists the results of best single-kernel SVMs and four MKL algorithms trained. We can achieve an accuracy of 83.3 per cent by combining eight GAU kernels with NLMKL. This result is better than all other MKL settings and single-kernel SVMs. In the last column of Table 3, the results of combining all possible feature representation and kernel function pairs (i.e., 24 kernels) in a single learner are shown. NLMKL is still the best MKL algorithm even though the average accuracy decreases to 83.1 per cent.

To give a feel of complexity, we also measured the time required to run each method. Table 4 gives the running times in seconds. We can see that NLMKL takes more time because of the second order dependency to the number of kernels in

Table 3. MKL accuracies

	LIN	POL	GAU	LIN+POL+GAU
SVM	76.0±3.4	72.7±3.8	76.9±2.7	NA
RBMKL	77.3±4.0	77.2±2.4	82.7±3.6	81.8±3.8
SimpleMKL	77.1±3.3	77.3±2.3	81.8±3.8	81.6±3.9
GLMKL	77.1±3.5	76.5±3.2	81.8±4.3	81.8±3.8
NLMKL	77.9±3.9	79.2±3.8	**83.3±3.6**	83.1±3.5

Table 4. Time required for each method (in seconds). Single kernel time measurements are summed over all representations.

	LIN	POL	GAU	LIN+POL+GAU
SVM	4.45	5.81	3.52	NA
RBMKL	1.56	0.87	1.35	2.57
SimpleMKL	35.55	11.07	11.71	32.81
GLMKL	11.11	4.61	5.20	14.27
NLMKL	45.25	39.21	44.28	323.83

the gradient computations. This difference becomes more apparent when we increase the number of combined kernels. The running time can be reduced by caching the element-wise products between the kernel matrices.

4.3 Discussion

In this paper, we formulated a nonlinear MKL algorithm derived from [5] and we have seen that proposed algorithm performs better than single-kernel SVMs and three linear MKL algorithms. When we were combining linear kernels on the feature representations, we observed that linear MKL algorithms achieved to outperform single-kernel SVMs, whereas the nonlinear MKL algorithm improved the average accuracy most thanks to the nonlinearity in kernel combination. Even though the kernels were nonlinear when we were combining polynomial and Gaussian kernels, the nonlinear MKL algorithm got better accuracies than single-kernel SVMs and linear MKL algorithms. We have seen that when we use the nonlinear MKL algorithm, we achieved 6.4 per cent improvement in accuracy compared to single-kernel SVMs.

5 Conclusion

In this paper, we formulate a nonlinear MKL algorithm variant and use it for the classification of nuclei in TMA images of RCC. We used SVMs extensively through different feature sets in our previous work [15]. This study extends our previous work using several feature sets in a nonlinear MKL setting and compares the results with single-kernel SVMs and several linear MKL algorithms.

We have seen that the nonlinear MKL algorithm performs better than single kernel SVMs and linear MKL algorithms in all of the experiments. The proposed nonlinear MKL variant learns a better similarity measure than linear MKL algorithms by combining the input kernels nonlinearly. In this work, we used image-based feature sets for creating multiple feature representations. In a further application of this scenario, the use of other modalities or other features (e.g., SIFT) extracted from these images as well as the incorporation of complementary information of different modalities to achieve better classification accuracy is possible.

Acknowledgements. We acknowledge financial support from the FET programme within the EU FP7, under the SIMBAD project (contract 213250).

References

1. Bach, F.R., Lanckriet, G.R.G., Jordan, M.I.: Multiple kernel learning, conic duality, and the SMO algorithm. In: Proceedings of the 21st International Conference on Machine Learning (2004)
2. Bosch, A., Zisserman, A., Munoz, X.: Representing shape with a spatial pyramid kernel. In: Proceedings of the 6th ACM International Conference on Image and Video Retrieval (2007)
3. Boykov, Y., Veksler, O., Zabih, R.: Efficient approximate energy minimization via graph cuts. IEEE Transactions on Pattern Analysis and Machine Intelligence 20, 1222–1239 (2001)
4. Chang, C.C., Lin, C.J.: LIBSVM: A Library for Support Vector Machines (2001)
5. Cortes, C., Mohri, M., Rostamizadeh, A.: Learning non-linear combinations of kernels. In: Advances in Neural Information Processing Systems, vol. 22 (2009)
6. Fuchs, T.J., Wild, P.J., Moch, H., Buhmann, J.M.: Computational pathology analysis of tissue microarrays predicts survival of renal clear cell carcinoma patients. In: Metaxas, D., Axel, L., Fichtinger, G., Székely, G. (eds.) MICCAI 2008, Part II. LNCS, vol. 5242, pp. 1–8. Springer, Heidelberg (2008)
7. Gönen, M., Alpaydın, E.: Localized multiple kernel learning. In: Proceedings of the 25th International Conference on Machine Learning (2008)
8. Gönen, M., Alpaydın, E.: Multiple kernel learning algorithms. Journal of Machine Learning Research 12, 2211–2268 (2011)
9. Gonzalez, R.C., Woods, R.E., Eddins, S.L.: Digital Image Processing Using MATLAB. Prentice-Hall, Inc., Englewood Cliffs (2003)
10. Kloft, M., Brefeld, U., Sonnenburg, S., Zien, A.: ℓ_p-norm multiple kernel learning. Journal of Machine Learning Research 12, 953–997 (2011)
11. Kononen, J., Bubendorf, L., Kallioniemi, A., Barlund, M., Schraml, P., Leighton, S., Torhorst, J., Mihatsch, M.J., Sauter, G., Kallioniemi, O.P.: Tissue microarrays for high-throughput molecular profiling of tumor specimens. Nature Medicine 4, 844–847 (1998)
12. Lanckriet, G.R.G., Cristianini, N., Bartlett, P., Ghaoui, L.E., Jordan, M.I.: Learning the kernel matrix with semidefinite programming. Journal of Machine Learning Research 5, 27–72 (2004)
13. Lewis, D.P., Jebara, T., Noble, W.S.: Nonstationary kernel combination. In: Proceedings of the 23rd International Conference on Machine Learning (2006)
14. Rakotomamonjy, A., Bach, F.R., Canu, S., Grandvalet, Y.: SimpleMKL. Journal of Machine Learning Research 9, 2491–2521 (2008)
15. Schüffler, P.J., Fuchs, T.J., Ong, C.S., Roth, V., Buhmann, J.M.: Computational TMA analysis and cell nucleus classification of renal cell carcinoma. In: Goesele, M., Roth, S., Kuijper, A., Schiele, B., Schindler, K. (eds.) Pattern Recognition. LNCS, vol. 6376, pp. 202–211. Springer, Heidelberg (2010)
16. Vapnik, V.N.: Statistical Learning Theory. John Wiley and Sons, Chichester (1998)
17. Xu, Z., Jin, R., Yang, H., King, I., Lyu, M.R.: Simple and efficient multiple kernel learning by group Lasso. In: Proceedings of the 27th International Conference on Machine Learning (2010)

Supervised Segmentation of Fiber Tracts

Emanuele Olivetti[1,2] and Paolo Avesani[1,2]

[1] NeuroInformatics Laboratory (NILab), Fondazione Bruno Kessler, Trento, Italy
[2] Centro Interdipartimentale Mente e Cervello (CIMeC) Università degli Studi di Trento, Italy

Abstract. In this work we study the problem of supervised tract segmentation from tractography data, a vectorial representation of the brain connectivity extracted from diffusion magnetic resonance images. We report a case study based on a dataset where for each tractography of three subjects the segmentation of eight major anatomical tracts was manually operated by expert neuroanatomists. Domain specific distances that encodes the dissimilarity of tracts do not allow to define a positive semi-definite kernel function. We show that a dissimilarity representation based on such distances enables the successful design of a classifier. This approach provides a robust encoding which proves to be effective using a linear classifier. Our empirical analysis shows that we obtain better tract segmentation than previously proposed methods.

1 Introduction

Brain connectivity analysis involves the investigation of the connections between different brain areas. *Anatomical* connectivity refers to the structural links between different areas that develops in the white matter of the brain. *Functional* connectivity investigates the correlation between the brain activity of anatomically remote areas. *Effective* connectivity is concerned with finding a causal link between different brain structures. In this work we are interested in anatomical connectivity.

Diffusion MRI (dMRI) is a magnetic resonance imaging technique [3,24] that allows to reconstruct white matter fiber tracts as a set of *streamlines* by means of deterministic tractography algorithms [13]. A streamline is a vectorial representation of thousands of neuronal axons expressing structural connectivity. The whole set of streamlines of a brain is called *tractography* (see Figure 1) and given that the resolution of modern MRI scanners is in the order of $1mm^3$, a full brain tractography consists of $\approx 3 \times 10^5$ streamlines.

The segmentation of the network of neuronal links into known anatomically structures is a task of interest in neurological studies, for example for the study of Alzheimer disease [6]. Neuroanatomy and neuroscience research study brain tracts through both invasive brain dissection and non-invasive MRI techniques. Segmenting a given tract from a tractography is a difficult task because of the variability of the brain anatomy among different subjects. The segmentation process is slow and requires an expert neuroanatomist.

M. Pelillo and E.R. Hancock (Eds.): SIMBAD 2011, LNCS 7005, pp. 261–274, 2011.

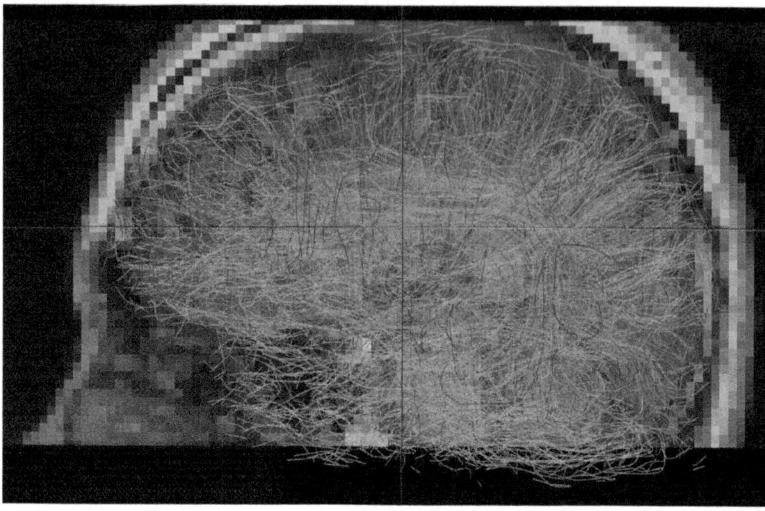

Fig. 1. A tractography (whole set of polylines) made of $\approx 3\times 10^5$ streamlines (polylines) describes the pathways of neural axons within the brain. Only 3% of the streamlines are shown to improve readability. Colors represents the main direction of each streamline.

From the point of view of algorithmic approaches, this segmentation task has traditionally been addressed with unsupervised techniques over only diffusion data [26]. Such techniques often rely on expert-crafted streamline-streamline distance functions encoding informative relationships for the segmentation task, then followed by a clustering algorithm (agglomerative, k-means, Gaussian mixture model, etc. see [25] for a recent brief review).

Supervised tract segmentation instead aims at learning how to segment the tractography from expert-made examples provided as input. Supervised tract segmentation has received little attention so far in the literature. To the best of our knowledge only a few different approaches have been proposed. The first is based on a B-spline representation of the streamlines followed by classification via the nearest-neighbor algorithm with respect to an atlas (see [12]). The second is based on spectral clustering [15] and the most recent on hierarchical Dirichlet processes [25]. A related work to this problem is [17] where both structural and functional connectivity are studied jointly in a pairwise approach with the goal of assessing the contributions of structural information and functional information when segmenting the tracts.

Similarly to [12], in this work we propose to address the supervised segmentation problem as a classification problem. A novel contribution of this work is to leverage the expert-crafted streamline-streamline distance functions available from the literature and to use them in a dissimilarity based [20] representation of the problem. Moreover we note that the widely adopted kernel-based classification algorithms cannot directly embed such distance functions into a kernel because the kernel would violate the necessary assumption of being positive semi-definite [20,7,23].

This paper is structured as follows. In Section 2 we formally introduce the problem of supervised tract segmentation, we illustrate the most common streamline-streamline distance functions. We briefly discuss the issue with embedding such distance functions into kernels. We then introduce the dissimilarity based representation and describe how we use it for the tract segmentation problem. In Section 3 we present an application of the proposed dissimilarity-based approach on a real dataset of dMRI-based tractographies from three subjects. We illustrate both the single subject and the across-subject segmentation results on multiple tracts and compare the result with a nearest neighbor approach proposed in [12]. In Section 4 we discuss the results supporting the claim that the dissimilarity-based approach is straightforward and effective for the tract segmentation task.

2 Methods

Segmenting a given tractography is the task of partitioning it into subsets of streamlines. *Supervised* segmentation is the task of partitioning according to provided examples. An example is an expert-made assignment of streamlines to categories of interest, like neuroanatomic fiber tracts. Supervised segmentation uses examples to guide the segmentation of further tractography data. In this work we restrict the segmentation task to segmenting a single specific fiber tract of interest at a time and we assume to have available examples. In this setting each streamline can be class-labeled as being member of the fiber tract of interest or not. For this reason the supervised segmentation problem becomes a binary classification problem.

The proposed method comprises two steps, namely an alignment/registration step, that is meant to bring tractography data from different subjects to a common space, and the actual segmentation step. Once a segmentation of the fiber tract of a given subject is made available, the task is to segment the same fiber tract in the tractography of a new subject. While the registration step aims to reduce the variance of the tractography between two subjects, the segmentation step aims to generalize the pattern of a specific neuroanatomic fiber tract.

2.1 Basic Definitions and Notation

Let the polyline $s = \{\boldsymbol{x}_1, \ldots, \boldsymbol{x}_{n_s}\}$, where $\boldsymbol{x} \in \mathbb{R}^3$, be a *streamline* reconstructed from dMRI data by means of deterministic tractography algorithms [13]. Let $T = \{s_1, \ldots, s_M\}$ be the *tractography* defined as a set of streamlines. We assume that T is sampled according to a probability distribution $\mathfrak{T}$ which incorporates the variance of data related to the dMRI measurement process and the variability of subjects. Current dMRI techniques operated on adult humans generate tractographies of size in the order of 3×10^5 streamlines. Let τ be an anatomical fiber tract of interest, e.g. the arcuate fasciculus (see Figure 3), and let $t \subset T$ be its corresponding streamline-based approximation within given the tractography. A neuroanatomist segmenting a tract t from the tractography T corresponds to a mapping $f : T \mapsto \{0, 1\}$ where

$$f(s) = \begin{cases} 1 \text{ if } s \text{ in } t \\ 0 \text{ otherwise} \end{cases} \quad (1)$$

In the machine learning terminology the function f is called *classifier* and each pair $(s, f(s))$ is a class-labeled *example*. In practice f is not available and the problem is then to infer an approximation g from data. We may have many samples of t for the same fiber tract τ, e.g. the arcuate fasciculus, when the annotation is operated by different neuroanatomists. The labeling is prone to error and has to be considered an approximation of the true fiber tract.

A classifier g is learned from examples by training a classification algorithm which optimize a loss function L. Common classification algorithms are the k-nearest neighbor (kNN) [8] and the Support Vector Machines (SVMs) [5]. A usual loss function is the $0-1$ loss $L(s, g(s) = I(s, g(s))$ where I is the indicator function.

2.2 Evaluation Criteria

Claiming that a segmentation algorithm is effective requires evidence of the goodness of its results. An evaluation criterion is necessary to assess its effectiveness. A traditional measure of the quality of predictions of a classifier is its *generalization error* which is its expected loss

$$\epsilon = E_{P_{XY}}[L(g(x), y)]. \quad (2)$$

Note that classification algorithms do not minimize ϵ directly because P_{XY} is not available in practice. The goal is then to control it indirectly by minimization of accessible quantities, like the *empirical error*

$$\epsilon_{emp} = \frac{1}{n} \sum_{i=1 \ldots n} L(g(x_i), y_i) \quad (3)$$

where $\{(x_i, y_i)\}_{i=1 \ldots n}$ is the train set. The empirical error on an *independent* test set is a popular and unbiased point estimate of ϵ.

Many other general evaluation criteria can be adopted [22] but for the specific application of tractography segmentation the following score was proposed by the board of an international brain connectivity competition (PBCC) held in 2009 [1]

$$r = \frac{TP - FP}{TP + FP} \quad (4)$$

where TP is the number of *true positive* streamlines, i.e. the correctly predicted streamlines which expert defined as being part of the given tract of interest. Conversely FP is the number of *false positive* streamlines which are predicted as being part of the tract of interest but actually do not. This score can be rewritten as the difference between two known scores, i.e. precision and false positive rate (FPR)

[1] `http://pbc.lrdc.pitt.edu/?q=2009a-staff`

$$r = \frac{TP}{TP+FP} - \frac{FP}{TP+FP} = \text{precision} - \text{FPR}. \tag{5}$$

The actual definition of the PBCC2009 score takes into account a small amount of *uncertain* streamlines, about which different experts might disagree and that lie at the border between t and its neighboring streamlines. For simplicity we refer in the following only to the streamlines labeled with high degree of confidence by the experts.

2.3 Distances

The main body of the literature about tract segmentation (see Section 1) refers to distances between pair of streamlines as a leading way to incorporate domain specific information when clustering streamlines. See [26] for a recent survey about these distances. A popular group of distances is the modified Hausdorff distances [9] and among the most popular [26] are

- $\boldsymbol{d}_1(s_A, s_B) = \frac{1}{n_{s_A}} \sum_{i=1}^{n_{s_A}} d(\boldsymbol{x}_i^A, s_B)$
- $\boldsymbol{d}_2(s_A, s_B) = \min_{i=1,\dots,n_{s_A}} d(\boldsymbol{x}_i^A, s_B)$
- $\boldsymbol{d}_3(s_A, s_B) = max_{i=1,\dots,n_{s_A}} d(\boldsymbol{x}_i^A, s_B)$

where (see Figure 2)

$$d(\boldsymbol{x}_i^A, s_B) = \min_{j=1,\dots,n_{s_B}} ||\boldsymbol{x}_i^A - \boldsymbol{x}_j^B||_2 \tag{6}$$

which can be combined in order to get the symmetric versions:

- $\boldsymbol{h}_a(\boldsymbol{d}, s_A, s_B) = \frac{\boldsymbol{d}(s_A, s_B) + \boldsymbol{d}(s_B, s_A)}{2}$
- $\boldsymbol{h}_b(\boldsymbol{d}, s_A, s_B) = \min(\boldsymbol{d}(s_A, s_B), \boldsymbol{d}(s_B, s_A))$
- $\boldsymbol{h}_c(\boldsymbol{d}, s_A, s_B) = \max(\boldsymbol{d}(s_A, s_B), \boldsymbol{d}(s_B, s_A))$

Note that all distances defined above are not metric [9] because $\boldsymbol{d}(s_A, s_B) = 0$ does not imply that $s_A = s_B$. This fact has consequences when trying to incorporate these domain-specific distances in classification algorithms as explained in the following sections.

2.4 Classification Algorithms and Feature Space

Among the many classification algorithms available in the literature [4] we are interested in those that can exploit the distances introduced in Section 2.3. Two leading class of algorithms are the nearest neighbor (NN) and the kernel-based classification algorithms, like support vector machines (SVMs).

The k-nearest neighbor (k-NN) algorithm is among the simplest and most studied distance-based classification algorithm [11]. Given a dataset D_{train} of class-labeled streamlines and a distance function d, the k-NN is instantiated as a classifier and predicts the class-label c of new streamline s from majority vote

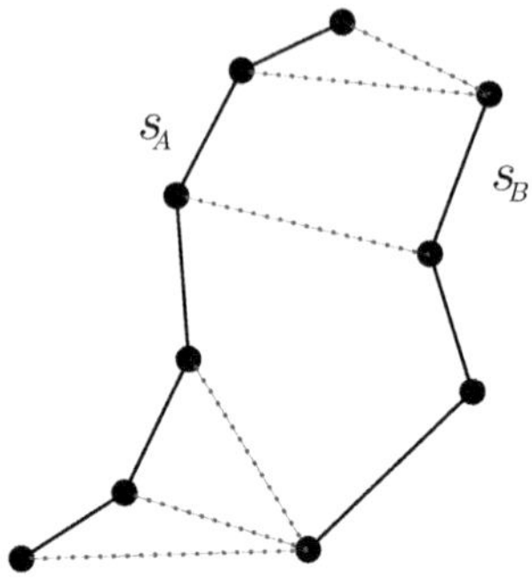

Fig. 2. Many distances between two streamlines, s_A and s_B (solid line), that are proposed in the literature are based on the set of minimum distances between each point of s_A to s_B. The set of minimal distances is represented here as dotted lines.

among k nearest neighbors [2] streamlines of s in D_{train}. The optimal value of the structural parameter k can be defined from prior knowledge or it can be estimated from data as explained for example in [16]. For metric distances k-NN is asymptotically optimal in the Bayes sense [8]. k-NN is known to suffer limitations due to the impact of noisy examples [19].

Kernel-based classification algorithms define an extremely popular class of algorithms which is characterized by a mapping ϕ of the data from the original space into a new, possibly infinite-dimensional, Euclidean feature space, $x \to \phi(x)$, $x \in \mathcal{X}$. The mapping is meant to enhance the linear separability of the data among the classes. The *kernel function* $k : \mathcal{X} \times \mathcal{X} \mapsto \mathbb{R}$ corresponds to the inner product of elements in this new feature space, $k(x, x') = \langle \phi(x), \phi(x') \rangle$ where $x, x' \in \mathcal{X}$.

Kernels can be interpreted as similarity functions between objects. Not every similarity function is a kernel because the similarity might lack the inner product representation. The availability of the mapping ϕ for a kernel is equivalent to being a positive semi-definite (psd) function [23]. It is common practice to derive kernels from problem-specific distance function [23]. In this case a necessary condition for a *valid* kernel is that the underlying distance function is a *metric*, i.e. it has the reflectivity, positivity, symmetry and triangle inequality properties. Violating this requirement leads to an *indefinite* kernel.

Indefinite kernels present several issue for *empirical risk minimization*-based (ERM) classification algorithms like SVM. The first is non-convexity of the optimization problem, which suffers the problem of local minima. Even adopting ad-hoc optimization algorithms (e.g., *sequential minimal optimization* (SMO) [21]) the amount of computation could be greatly increased and lead to saddle points which does not guarantee the usual generalization properties. See [7].

In the application of tractography segmentation discussed in this paper the domain-specific distances described in Section 2.3 are not metrics. This means that it is not straightforward to derive a valid kernel from them.

---

[2] Ties are broken at random.

Numerous solutions have been proposed to learn from indefinite kernels by operating directly on the kernel matrix. Unfortunately each solution is usually based on strong assumptions which are difficult to ascertain in practical cases. See [7] for a detailed discussion and references.

2.5 Dissimilarity Space

A generalization of the traditional kernel approach is the use of dissimilarity-based representation spaces [20,2]. This representation requires only a generic similarity or dissimilarity function $d : \mathcal{X} \times \mathcal{X} \rightarrow \mathbb{R}$ and a representation set $R = \{x_1, \dots, x_n\}$, where $x_i \in \mathcal{X}$, $i = 1, \dots, n$ are called *prototypes* or *landmarks*. A mapping $\psi_R : \mathcal{X} \rightarrow \mathbb{R}^n$ is defined such that $v = \psi_R(x) = [d(x, x_1), \dots, d(x, x_n)]^T \in \mathbb{R}^n$. Given a dataset $D = \{x_1, \dots, x_m\}$ where $x_i \in \mathcal{X}$, $i = 1, \dots, m$, its dissimilarity representation is $\mathsf{D} = \{\psi_R(x_1), \dots, \psi_R(x_m)\} = \{v_1, \dots, v_m\}$ and $v_i \in \mathbb{R}^n$, $i = 1, \dots, m$. In [2] ψ_R is called *empirical similarity map* and $R \subseteq D$.

The dataset in the new representation can be processed by the vast majority of the classification algorithm in the literature. Successful attempts were reported when using k-NN, Fisher Linear Discriminant, Support Vector Classification with linear kernel, Linear Programming machines and the linear and quadratic normal density classifiers [20,19].

An open problem of the dissimilarity based representation is the definition of the set of prototypes. Even though many heuristics were proposed [19], the random selection among the available data has been proved effective, robust and simple. Moreover theoretical results about the goodness of selecting random prototypes was presented in [2].

In this work we adopt the dissimilarity space approach for the tractography segmentation problem. The dissimilarity function is defined as the symmetric version of $\boldsymbol{d}_1$ introduced in Section 2.3. We define the dissimilarity function δ as

$$\delta(s_A, s_B) = d_1(s_A, s_B) + d_1(s_B, s_A). \tag{7}$$

Moreover we select prototypes at random from the set of streamlines available in the dataset. Further details are presented in Section 3. After mapping the dataset to $\mathbb{R}^n$ by means of the dissimilarity representation we train a classifier to perform the segmentation task as described in Section 3.

2.6 Fiber Tract Segmentation

We propose a two steps method to segment a given fiber tract within a the tractography of a new/unseen subject. The first step is registration, the second is segmentation.

The registration step comprises the projection of the tractography in a common reference space takes place by two subsequent registrations, *global* one and *local* one. The tractography is first warped in MNI space [10]. MNI is a reference brain representation built by a process of averaging more than 300 MRI scans. We call this step *global* registration across subject. The second step is to compute a *local* registration specific of the tract of interest. Target tractography is transformed by an affine transformation in order to match the source tract.

After the registration we assume that all available streamlines belong to the same distribution in order to match the definitions in Section 2.1. Segmenting the tract of interest τ on the new subject is then reduced to bringing all tractographies to a common space and then training a classifier from the streamlines segmented by the expert and predicting the class label of unlabeled ones.

The segmentation of tract τ suffers scalability issues. The first obvious reason is the size of the tractography $|T| \approx 3 \times 10^5$. A preliminary improvement to reduce this issue is to focus the segmentation of the fiber tract τ to a subset of T which is a superset of t. We denote this superset as S. This initial reduction of the problem can be performed in several ways. A first solution is to let the neuroanatomist manually select the superset from the tractography. Another approach is to automatically select the superset by collecting all streamlines within a certain distance from few landmarks defined by prior knowledge. As it will be illustrated in detail in Section 3.1 the results that we present are based on expert-made supersets whose size lie in the range of $|S| \approx 3000 - 8000$ streamlines.

3 Experiments and Results

This Section is organized as follows: a first part is devoted to introduce the dataset; in the second part we illustrate the experimental setup and the results for the classification of streamlines on a single subject; the last part reports the results for the segmentation of the tracts across subjects.

3.1 Dataset: PBCC2009 Spring Edition

The dataset used in our study was released by the University of Pittsburgh as materials for the Pittsburgh Brain Connectivity Competition 2009[3]. In Spring 2009 the scientific board of the competition proposed an open public contest to the scientific community about mapping the human connectome. The idea was to encourage researchers coming from different areas of expertise to work on a common task and be evaluated on the same data.

The contest was organized around four different challenges. Our focus here is restricted to challenge 2: supervised fiber tract segmentation. The data distributed as competition materials included MRI images such as structural, diffusion (dMRI) and functional (fMRI) together with expert annotations. Those data were acquired on three different subjects. The deterministic tractography was reconstructed in DSI space [14], using the Diffusion Toolkit TrackVis [4].

All the data mentioned above were accessible to a committee of experts that manually annotated a collection of fiber tracts for each of the subjects involved in the experiments. The manual annotation concerned 8 different fiber tracts: arcuate fasciculus, cingulum, corticospinal tract, forceps, fornix, inferior optical frontal fasciculus (ioff), subcallosal fasciculus, uncinate fasciculus. Some of them

[3] `http://www.braincompetition.org`
[4] `http://www.trackvis.org`

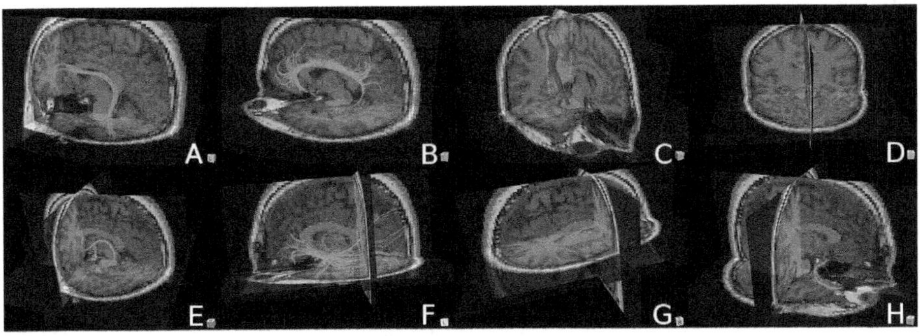

Fig. 3. The tracts of PBCC 2009 dataset, spring edition: arcuate fasciculus (A), cingulum (B), corticospinal tract (C), forceps major (D), fornix (E), inferior optical frontal fasciculus (ioff) (F), subcallosal fasciculus (G), uncinate fasciculus (H)

were annotated on the same hemisphere for all subjects (fornix, ioff, forceps and uncinate) while others were annotated on different hemisphere in different subjects (arcuate, cingulum, corticospinal and subcallosal) Figure 3 illustrates the patterns of the different tracts, while Table 1 reports the quantitative aspects.

Table 1. PBCC2009 Spring Edition Dataset: the size of the annotated tracts for each subject together with to which hemisphere, either left or right, they belonged to

	tract	Subj 0		Subj 1		Subj 2	
A	Arcuate	96	L	406	R	228	R
B	Cingulum	539	L	185	R	194	L
C	Corticospinal	175	R	331	L	243	L
D	Forceps	366	-	385	-	263	-
E	Fornix	54	L	109	L	47	L
F	Ioff	433	L	266	L	282	L
G	Subcallosal	27	R	18	R	34	L
H	Uncinate	82	R	80	R	122	R

For each tract and of each subject two sets of streamlines were annotated. The first set is made of the streamlines that actually comprise the tract; the second set is a sample of streamlines, called *superset*, which includes a large neighborhood of the tract. These supersets contain on average 3000-8000 streamlines while the tracts comprise only tens to hundreds of streamlines.

3.2 Single Subject Segmentation

A first experiment was designed to investigate the supervised segmentation task of each given fiber tract on a single subject. In this experiment we assumed to have part of the tractography already partitioned by an expert neuroanatomist and the task is to segment the remaining part. Even though this task is of minor neuroscientific interest it aimed to assess the goodness of the dissimilarity representation for the supervised tract segmentation without the bias introduced by the coregistration.

In Table 2 we present the PBCC2009 score averaged over 4 datasets created by drawing $n = 100$ prototypes at random without replacement. The classifier used on these dataset was SVM with linear kernel. The score estimation process was 10-fold CV.

Table 2. PBCC 2009 Spring Edtion: PBCC2009 score for single subject segmentation (std-mean ≈ 0.02) using the dissimilarity-based representation and linear SVM

tract	Subj1	Subj2	Subj3
arcuate	0.94	0.96	0.93
cingulum	0.85	0.89	0.92
corticosp.	0.94	0.95	0.92
forceps	0.98	0.94	0.92
fornix	0.81	0.86	0.72
ioff	0.70	0.72	0.90
subcall.	0.92	0.83	0.87
uncinate	0.84	0.75	0.63

3.3 Predictions Cross-Subjects

A second experiment was designed to evaluate the proposed approach when segmenting a tract on the tractography of an unseen subject after training a classifier on the same tract annotated on a different subject. We restricted our analysis to learning from only one annotated tract.

We followed the pipeline explained in Section 2.6 for each tract and for each pair of subjects. We first coregistered the tractographies of each subjects in the pair, then we encoded the training dataset with the dissimilarity representation. The dataset for the training step was designed considering all the streamlines belonging to the given tract and an equal number of streamlines in the neighborhood of the tract. For both sets of streamlines the corresponding representation in the dissimilarity space was computed. Two learning process were performed by training the 1-NN classifier in the euclidean space and the linear SVM in the dissimilarity space. After the training stage, the test was performed on the superset of the tract from the tractography of the target subject. Finally the PBCC2009 score was computed according to the definition in Section 2.2.

We report the results for the following tracts: arcuate, corticospinal, forceps major and inferior occipito-frontal cortex. We discarded all the other tracts from this second experiment because the expert-made segmentations varied excessively across subjects both from the point of view of the size (see Table 1) and the shape. This issue is due to the anatomical variability across subjects that cannot be significantly reduced by the current coregistration procedure. Another possible explanation is that the variability across segmentations is due to unclear guidelines for the manual annotation.

Table 3. Cross-Subject Segmentation of the *arcuate fasciculus*. For each pair of subjects the PBCC2009 score is computed both for 1-NN (baseline) and the proposed method based on the dissimilarity representation and linear SVM.

train $\mapsto$ test	1-NN	dis.+LinSVM
$1_L \mapsto 2_R$	0.224	**0.328**
$1_L \mapsto 3_R$	0.338	**0.711**
$2_R \mapsto 1_L$	−0.021	**0.333**
$2_R \mapsto 3_R$	0.697	**0.860**
$3_R \mapsto 1_L$	0.260	**0.792**
$3_R \mapsto 2_R$	**0.229**	0.187

Table 4. Cross-Subject Segmentation of the *corticospinal tract*. For each pair of subjects the PBCC2009 score is computed both for 1-NN (baseline) and the proposed method based on the dissimilarity representation and linear SVM.

train $\mapsto$ test	1-NN	dis.+LinSVM
$1_R \mapsto 2_L$	0.402	**0.767**
$1_R \mapsto 3_L$	0.091	**0.387**
$2_L \mapsto 1_R$	0.446	**0.749**
$2_L \mapsto 3_L$	**0.852**	0.588
$3_L \mapsto 1_R$	0.417	**0.869**
$3_L \mapsto 2_L$	0.459	**0.698**

4 Discussion

The results illustrated in Section 3 provide empirical evidence that the dissimilarity space representation is effective for the supervised fiber tract segmentation. The proposed approach allows to exploit the domain knowledge by encoding of the appropriate distance measures defined by the domain experts. Results in Table 2 shows that accurate classification is attained on single subject experiments where the anatomical variability across subject is not present as a confound.

For the most challenging task of supervised fiber tract segmentation across subject, we focus the analysis on the comparison between a dissimilarity based and a distance based approaches. The empirical results in Table 3, 4, 5 and 6 show that the dissimilarity-based representation provides a more robust encoding of the problem since a linear classifier, i.e. linear SVM, performs even better than the non-linear classifier 1-NN (proposed in [12]) in 20 over 24 cases.

In some cases the poor score results could be related to a large variance of the tract annotated on different brains. As discussed in Section 3.3 the major sources of variance are the anatomical variability among subjects and the process of annotation among different experts. Currently the training process relies on a single tract segmentation even though encoded as several streamlines. In order to capture the more general pattern of a tract across the population of subjects it is then necessary to rely on annotations from more subjects.

Table 5. Cross-Subject Segmentation of the *forceps major*. For each pair of subjects the PBCC2009 score is computed both for 1-NN (baseline) and the proposed method based on the dissimilarity representation and linear SVM.

train $\mapsto$ test	1-NN	dis.+LinSVM
$1 \mapsto 2$	**0.732**	0.506
$1 \mapsto 3$	**0.323**	0.194
$2 \mapsto 1$	0.158	**0.544**
$2 \mapsto 3$	0.658	**0.726**
$3 \mapsto 1$	0.014	**0.347**
$3 \mapsto 2$	0.366	**0.743**

Table 6. Cross-Subject Segmentation of the *inferior occipito-frontal fasciculus* (ioff). For each pair of subjects the PBCC2009 score is computed both for 1-NN (baseline) and the proposed method based on the dissimilarity representation and linear SVM.

train $\mapsto$ test	1-NN	dis.+LinSVM
$1_L \mapsto 2_L$	−0.853	**0.323**
$1_L \mapsto 3_L$	−1.170	**0.567**
$2_L \mapsto 1_L$	−0.095	**0.189**
$2_L \mapsto 3_L$	−0.025	**0.415**
$3_L \mapsto 1_L$	0.090	**0.229**
$3_L \mapsto 2_L$	−0.049	**0.203**

The results of this work support the efficacy of the dissimilarity-based representation with respect to other approaches. Nevertheless the tract segmentation problem across subjects still presents major issues related to the high variability of the tracts across subjects. In order to obtain an accurate cross-subject segmentation of the fiber tracts the step of coregistration between tractographies must be improved. A possible improvement along this direction is the use of non-affine transformations such as voxel-based morphometry [1]. It is an advance techniques for the coregistration of MRI brain images. From the pattern recognition side the adaptation of the classifier to a test set with a slightly different underlying distribution is addressed by the literature on transfer learning and domain adaptation [18].

Acknowledgment. The authors would like to thank Prof. Walter Schneider of the Learning Research Development Center of the University of Pittsburgh for sharing the complete dataset of the PBCC2009 Spring Edition contest. The release of the annotation of the tracts of all subjects allowed this investigation.

References

1. Ashburner, J., Friston, K.J.: Voxel-Based Morphometry The Methods. NeuroImage 11(6), 805–821 (2000)
2. Balcan, M.-F., Blum, A., Srebro, N.: A theory of learning with similarity functions. Machine Learning 72(1), 89–112 (2008)

3. Basser, P.J., Mattiello, J., LeBihan, D.: MR diffusion tensor spectroscopy and imaging. Biophysical Journal 66(1), 259–267 (1994)
4. Bishop, C.M.: Pattern Recognition and Machine Learning, 1st edn. Information Science and Statistics. Springer, Heidelberg (2006); corr. 2nd printing edn. (October 2007)
5. Boser, B.E., Guyon, I., Vapnik, V.: A Training Algorithm for Optimal Margin Classifiers. In: Computational Learing Theory, pp. 144–152 (1992)
6. Bozzali, M., Falini, A., Franceschi, M., Cercignani, M., Zuffi, M., Scotti, G., Comi, G., Filippi, M.: White matter damage in Alzheimer's disease assessed in vivo using diffusion tensor magnetic resonance imaging. Journal of Neurology, Neurosurgery & Psychiatry 72(6), 742–746 (2002)
7. Chen, Y., Garcia, E.K., Gupta, M.R., Rahimi, A., Cazzanti, L.: Similarity-based Classification: Concepts and Algorithms. J. Mach. Learn. Res. 10, 747–776 (2009)
8. Devroye, L., Györfi, L., Lugosi, G.: A Probabilistic Theory of Pattern Recognition. Stochastic Modelling and Applied Probability, corrected edn. Springer, Heidelberg (1996)
9. Dubuisson, M.P., Jain, A.K.: A modified Hausdorff distance for object matching. In: Proceedings of 12th International Conference on Pattern Recognition, vol. 1, pp. 566–568. IEEE Comput. Soc. Press, Los Alamitos (1994)
10. Evans, A.C., Collins, D.L., Millst, S.R., Brown, E.D., Kelly, R.L., Peters, T.M.: 3D statistical neuroanatomical models from 305 MRI volumes. In: Nuclear Science Symposium and Medical Imaging Conference, pp. 1813–1817 (1993)
11. Hastie, T., Tibshirani, R., Friedman, J.: The Elements of Statistical Learning: Data Mining, Inference, and Prediction, 2nd edn. Springer Series in Statistics, corr. 3rd printing 5th printing. edn. Springer, Heidelberg (2009)
12. Maddah, M., Mewes, A.U.J., Haker, S., Grimson, W.E.L., Warfield, S.K.: Automated Atlas-Based Clustering of White Matter Fiber Tracts from DTMRI. In: Duncan, J.S., Gerig, G. (eds.) MICCAI 2005. LNCS, vol. 3749, pp. 188–195. Springer, Heidelberg (2005)
13. Mori, S., van Zijl, P.C.M.: Fiber tracking: principles and strategies a technical review. NMR Biomed. 15(7-8), 468–480 (2002)
14. Nezamzadeh, M., Van Wedeen, J., Wang, R., Zhang, Y., Zhan, W., Young, K., Meyerhoff, D.J., Weiner, M.W., Schuff, N.: In-vivo investigation of the human cingulum bundle using the optimization of MR diffusion spectrum imaging. European Journal of Radiology 75(1) (July 2010)
15. O'Donnell, L.J., Westin, C.-F.F.: Automatic tractography segmentation using a high-dimensional white matter atlas. IEEE Transactions on Medical Imaging 26(11), 1562–1575 (2007)
16. Olivetti, E., Mognon, A., Greiner, S., Avesani, P.: Brain Decoding: Biases in Error Estimation. In: First Workshop on Brain Decoding: Pattern Recognition Challenges in NeuroImaging (WBD) (August 2010)
17. Olivetti, E., Veeramachaneni, S., Greiner, S., Avesani, P.: Brain connectivity analysis by reduction to pair classification. In: 2nd International Workshop on Cognitive Information Processing (CIP), pp. 275–280 (June 2010)
18. Pan, S.J., Yang, Q.: A Survey on Transfer Learning. IEEE Transactions on Knowledge and Data Engineering 22(10), 1345–1359 (2010)
19. Pekalska, E., Duin, R., Paclik, P.: Prototype selection for dissimilarity-based classifiers. Pattern Recognition 39(2), 189–208 (2006)
20. Pekalska, E., Paclik, P., Duin, R.P.W.: A generalized kernel approach to dissimilarity-based classification. J. Mach. Learn. Res. 2, 175–211 (2002)

21. Platt, J.C.: Fast training of support vector machines using sequential minimal optimization, pp. 185–208. MIT Press, Cambridge (1999)
22. Schiavo, R.A., Hand, D.J.: Ten More Years of Error Rate Research. International Statistical Review 68(3), 295–310 (2000)
23. Schölkopf, B., Smola, A.J.: Learning with Kernels: Support Vector Machines, Regularization, Optimization, and Beyond, 1st edn. Adaptive Computation and Machine Learning. The MIT Press, Cambridge (2001)
24. Tuch, D.S., Reese, T.G., Wiegell, M.R., Makris, N., Belliveau, J.W., Van Wedeen, J.: High angular resolution diffusion imaging reveals intravoxel white matter fiber heterogeneity. Magn. Reson. Med. 48(4), 577–582 (2002)
25. Wang, X., Grimson, Westin, C.-F.: Tractography segmentation using a hierarchical Dirichlet processes mixture model. NeuroImage 54(1), 290–302 (2011)
26. Zhang, S., Correia, S., Laidlaw, D.H.: Identifying White-Matter Fiber Bundles in DTI Data Using an Automated Proximity-Based Fiber-Clustering Method. IEEE Transactions on Visualization and Computer Graphics 14(5), 1044–1053 (2008)

Exploiting Dissimilarity Representations for Person Re-identification

Riccardo Satta, Giorgio Fumera, and Fabio Roli

Dept. of Electrical and Electronic Engineering,
University of Cagliari,
Piazza d'Armi, 09123 Cagliari, Italy
{riccardo.satta,fumera,roli}@diee.unica.it

Abstract. Person re-identification is the task of recognizing an individual that has already been observed over a network of video-surveillance cameras. Methods proposed in literature so far addressed this issue as a classical *matching* problem: a descriptor is built directly from the view of the person, and a similarity measure between descriptors is defined accordingly. In this work, we propose a general dissimilarity framework for person re-identification, aimed at transposing a generic method for person re-identification based to the commonly adopted multiple instance representation, into a dissimilarity form. Individuals are thus represented by means of dissimilarity values, in respect to common prototypes. Dissimilarity representations carry appealing advantages, in particular the compactness of the resulting descriptor, and the extremely low time required to match two descriptors. Moreover, a dissimilarity representation enables various new applications, some of which are depicted in the paper. An experimental evaluation of the proposed framework applied to an existing method is provided, which clearly shows the advantages of dissimilarity representations in the context of person re-identification.

Keywords: person re-identification, dissimilarity representation, multiple instance.

1 Introduction

In video-surveillance, it is often desirable to recognize a person who has already been observed over a network of camera sensors. Such task, commonly referred to as "person re-identification", is useful for a number of practical security applications, both online (i.e. tracking a person over different, non-overlapping cameras) and offline (i.e. retrieval of all the video sequences which contain an individual of interest given as query).

Typically, the low resolution of the frames taken by the sensors of the network, and the variety of possible poses, makes face recognition techniques ineffective (see Fig. 1). A common approach is thus to look at the global appearance of the individual, building a descriptor that represents the whole body.

Person re-identification has been modeled so far as a classical *matching* problem: a descriptor is built directly from the blob containing the person, and some

M. Pelillo and E.R. Hancock (Eds.): SIMBAD 2011, LNCS 7005, pp. 275–289, 2011.

Fig. 1. Example of image pairs representing the same individual taken from two different non-overlapping views, extracted from the ViPER benchmark dataset [7]

distance measure between descriptors is defined accordingly. The problem of how to build a suitable descriptor has been addressed in various ways. In fact, there is not an agreement on what features provide the best discriminant capabilities. Many of the existing methods, however, are based on the common idea of representing the human body as a *bag of instances*, defined as a set of randomly taken image patches or strips, or a set of interest points [14].

Regardless of the chosen features, often the descriptors of different people share a lot of redundant information. Their images can indeed contain similar instances, tipically associated to similar characteristics of their clothes (see Fig. 2). Our intuition is based on the above premise; instead of creating the descriptor of a person directly from its image, we propose to represent an individual by means of a vector of dissimilarity values between the bag of instances drawn from its image, and a number of pre-defined bags of instances named *visual prototypes*, each corresponding to some specific "visual" characteristics obtained from a given set of template users.

Dissimilarity-based representations for pattern recognition is a recently introduced and very promising research field [11]. In the context of person re-identification, a dissimilarity representation carries appealing advantages. In particular, in terms of the compactness of the descriptor, and of the computational requirements of the matching phase, which can be implemented as a comparison between vectors. We point out that, to the best of our knowledge, this work is the first attempt to exploit a dissimilarity representation in a *matching* task, in which only one (or a few) example per class is given, that is the case of person re-identification. The adopted representation is somewhat similar to that used in the so-called "visual words" methods, largely used in scene categorization (see for instance [17]). In visual words methods, a visual codebook is built offline, and then every sample is described in terms of the frequency (count of the occurrences) of every visual word. However, differently from visual words approaches, in the dissimilarity paradigm the *whole* sample is compared with every prototype, while in visual words approaches one looks for all the occurrences of every visual word *inside* the sample. Moreover, in a visual words method, for each visual concept the occurrences are simply counted, without considering the *degree* of presence, represented instead by a dissimilarity value. Note that a similar way to consider prototypes has been exploited in [3] for the specific task of image classification.

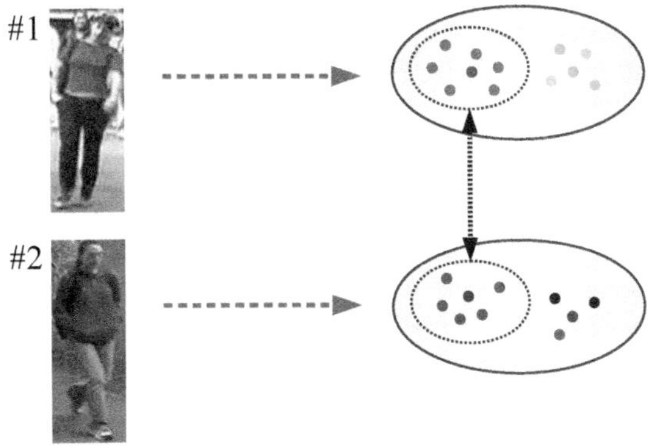

Fig. 2. An example of two pedestrians sharing clothing characteristics. Some of the instances of pedestrian #1 are similar to some of the instances extracted from pedestrian #2. Instances are represented by coloured dots. Here, only the upper body part is considered.

A dissimilarity representation also enables several new applications. An interesting one is *people grouping*, i.e. clustering individuals in the dissimilarity space so that each cluster contains only people of similar appearance, or that share the same visual characteristics. People grouping can be useful to reduce the number of candidates to be matched against a specific query, thus greatly lowering computational requirements when the number of individuals is huge, and to automatically group people in a scene, whose "role" can be inferred from their appearance (i.e. policemen, members of a sport team).

Moreover, representing individuals with vectors allows one to easily switch from a matching to a *learning* paradigm, where a classifier can be learned from a set of vectors of the same individual, for example representing different view points and poses, or of a group of individuals which share some common characteristic. A classifier is potentially able to generalize an appearance model of the individual (or group), and may represent an effective way to accumulate views taken by different frames, instead of keeping in memory all the feature vectors representing the same individual and matching every query against all of them.

The aim of this work is to provide a general dissimilarity framework for person re-identification, which we named "Multiple Component Dissimilarity" (MCD). This framework builds upon a recently proposed framework for person re-identification methods, the Multiple Component Matching (MCM) framework [14], which embeds the concept of multiple instances representation. MCM is able to frame, partially or completely, the great part of the existing methods. We will show how a generic method that can be framed in MCM can be turned into a dissimilarity-based form. We will also apply our MCD framework to an existing person re-identification method, and provide a preliminary experimental evaluation.

The paper is organized as follows. In Sect. 2 we briefly survey previous works on person re-identification, and provide details on the Multiple Component Matching framework. Then, in Sect. 3 the proposed dissimilarity framework is presented. We apply the proposed framework to an existing person re-identification method in Sect. 4 and provide an experimental evaluation. Finally, in Sect. 5 we sum up the proposed work and provide future research directions.

2 Background

In this Section, first an overview of the approaches to person re-identification available in literature is provided, then we describe the Multiple Component Matching framework for person re-identification.

2.1 Previous Works on Person Re-identification

As mentioned in Sect. 1, person re-identification has been considered in literature as a matching problem, where the task consists in associating an individual from a probe gallery to the corresponding identity in a template gallery.

In [5], the human body is subdivided with respect to its symmetry properties: anti-symmetry separates torso and legs, while symmetry is divides left and right parts. The descriptor is made up of three local features: colour histograms, *maximally stable colour regions* (MSCR) and *recurrent high-structured patches* (RHSP), all extracted from torso and legs separately. To obtain MSCR and RHSP, several patches are sampled at random, mainly near symmetry axes; then, clustering algorithms are used to find the most significant ones. The matching distance is a combination of the distances computed on the individual features.

In [2], an human body parts detector is used to find in the body of each individual fifteen non-overlapping square cells, that have proven to be "stable regions" of the silhouette. For each cell a covariance descriptor based on colour gradients is computed. Descriptor generation and matching is performed through a pyramid matching kernel.

In [1] two methods were proposed. In the first, Haar-like features are extracted from the whole body, while in the second the body is divided into upper and lower part, each described by the MPEG7 Dominant Colour descriptor.

An approach based on harvesting SIFT-like interest points from different frames of a video sequence is described in [9]. Different frames are used also in [6], where two methods are proposed. The first one is based on interest points. The second one exploits a part subdivision of the human body based on decomposable triangulated graphs and dynamic programming to find the optimal deformation of this model for the different individuals.

In [8] the problem of defining the best descriptor for person re-identification is addressed. Different features are extracted, and their weights are computed by a boosting algorithm. Features are computed from randomly taken strips.

The approach proposed in [15] is based of global color descriptors (histograms, spatiograms, color/path-length) computed from the whole blob containing the person. A graph-based method is then used to reduce the dimensionality of the descriptors.

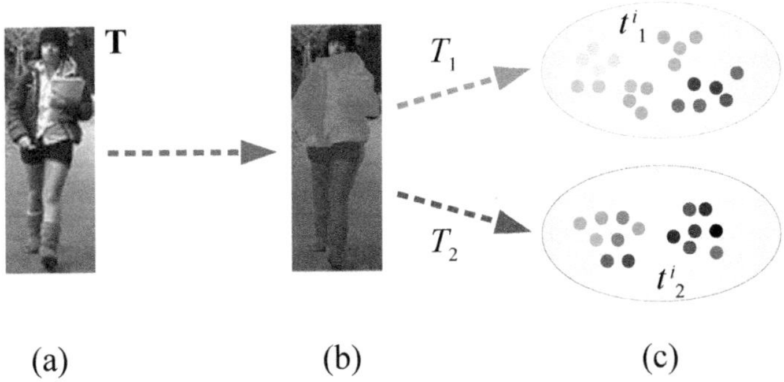

Fig. 3. An example of the MCM representation. Considering the individual in (a), a toy subdivision in two parts, upper-body (in green) and lower-body (in red), is applied (b). Every part is composed by several instances, or components (c), here represented by coloured dots.

In [13] person re-identification is considered as a relative ranking problem, exploiting a discriminative subspace built by means of an Ensemble RankSVM. Colour and texture-based features are extracted from six fixed horizontal regions.

Despite the methods summarised above exhibit many differences, it can be noted that many of them are based on a *multiple instance* representation, by taking several patches, strips, interest points. In addition, most works exploit some *part-based* model of the body, which is divided accordingly into regions/parts. These two concepts, multiple instance representation and part subdivision, provide the foundation for the Multiple Component Matching Framework [14], which is depicted in the following subsection.

In [14] the authors also proposed a direct implementation of their framework, where a two-part subdivision is adopted (torso-legs) and each part is described by a set of random and partly overlapping patches. Each patch is represented by its colour histogram.

2.2 The Multiple Component Matching Framework

In this section we describe the Multiple Component Matching (MCM) framework for person re-identification. This framework has been presented in [14], and aims to provide a common foundation for existing and future methods for person re-identification. It is able to provide an unique view for the great part of the methods proposed so far in literature. Therefore, we have chosen to adopt MCM as the underlying paradigm for our proposed dissimilarity framework.

MCM is based on concepts that have found to underly most previous works, namely multiple instance representation, and part subdivision. The individual is represented by means of bags of instances, or "set of components" in MCM terminology. Such components can be any kind of local features: patches, strips, interest points. To take into account the peculiarities of the human body, MCM also embeds the concept of part subdivision. For each part, a different set of components is considered.

Formally, let $\mathcal{T} = \{\mathbf{T}_1, \ldots, \mathbf{T}_N\}$ be the *template gallery*, each corresponding to an individual. Every template $\mathbf{T}_i$ is represented as an ordered sequence of a predefined number of M sets, corresponding to the M parts into which an image is subdivided:

$$\mathbf{T}_i = \{T_{i,1}, \ldots, T_{i,M}\} \tag{1}$$

Following a multiple-instance representation, every part $T_{i,j}$ is a set of an arbitrary number $n_{i,j}$ of components (a simple example is depicted in Fig. 3), and is described by the corresponding feature vectors $\mathbf{t}_{i,j}^k$:

$$T_{i,j} = \{\mathbf{t}_{i,j}^1, \ldots, \mathbf{t}_{i,j}^{n_{i,j}}\}, \mathbf{t}_{i,j}^k \in \mathbb{X}, \tag{2}$$

where $\mathbb{X}$ denotes the feature space (assumed the same for all sets, for the sake of simplicity, and without losing generality). Given a probe $\mathbf{Q}$, which is represented as a sequence of parts as described above, the task of MCM is to find the most similar template $\mathbf{T}^* \in \mathcal{T}$, with respect to a similarity measure $D(\cdot, \cdot)$:

$$\mathbf{T}^* = \arg\min_{\mathbf{T}_i} D(\mathbf{T}_i, \mathbf{Q}). \tag{3}$$

The similarity measure D between sequences is defined as a combination of similarity measures $d(\cdot, \cdot)$ between sets:

$$D(\mathbf{T}_i, \mathbf{Q}) = f\Big(d(T_{i,1}, Q_1), \ldots, d(T_{i,M}, Q_M)\Big). \tag{4}$$

D can be any combination of the set distances, like a weighted average in which the coefficients reflect the relevance of the corresponding regions. Concerning the similarity measure d, it can be any distance measure betwen sets. A possible measure is the *k-th Hausdorff Distance* proposed by Wang and Zucker [16], which has been used in [14]. It is defined as the k-th ranked distance of the minimum distances between each element of one set and each element of the other. Comparing two sets $X = \{x_i\}$ and $Y = \{y_i\}$, we have

$$d_H(X, Y) = \max\big(h_k(X, Y), h_k(Y, X)\big) \tag{5}$$

where

$$h_k(X, Y) = \underset{x \in X}{k\text{-th}} \min_{y \in Y}(\|x - y\|) \tag{6}$$

Note that another metric has to be defined, namely the distance measure $\|x - y\|$ between the components of the sets.

Conveniently choosing the parameters of the MCM framework (part subdivision adopted, components extracted and corresponding representation, and the distance measures d and D), different specific implementations can be obtained. In particular, many of the existing methods for person re-identification can be described, fully or partially, by means of this framework.

3 The Multiple Component Dissimilarity Framework for Person Re-identification

Here we illustrate the proposed Multiple Component Dissimilarity (MCD) framework for person re-identification. This framework builds upon the MCM framework described above, and aims at defining a dissimilarity-based version of a generic method for person re-identification which can be framed into MCM.

Consider a generic target MCM method which adopts a multiple instances representation and (possibly, but not necessary) a part subdivision, and assume that a template gallery $\mathcal{T} = \{\mathbf{T}_1, \ldots, \mathbf{T}_N\}$ is given. A probe individual $\mathbf{Q}$, which can be any element of the probe gallery, is given as well. As in MCM, the task is to find the most similar template to $\mathbf{Q}$. The proposed MCD framework requires four steps:

1. define a set of prototypes for each body part;
2. represent each element of $\mathcal{T}$ via dissimilarity vectors, one for each part;
3. represent $\mathbf{Q}$ via dissimilarity vectors, one for each part;
4. find the element of $\mathcal{T}$ which is most similar to $\mathbf{Q}$ in the dissimilarity space.

The first three steps are aimed at transposing the original problem into a dissimilarity space, while the fourth step corresponds to Eq. 3 in MCM, where this time we compare dissimilarity vectors.

Step one is to define a distinct set of *visual prototypes* for each body part. These prototypes will be used to build a dissimilarity vector for each part of each element of $\mathcal{T}$, and of $\mathbf{Q}$. The prototypes are extracted from the template gallery $\mathcal{T}$.

In MCM, each individual is represented as a set of components for each of its parts. We chose to represent each visual prototype as a set of components as well. Accordingly, the dissimilarity between a visual prototype and an individual can be computed by means of the same distance measure d between sets of components adopted by the target method (Eq. 4). This allows one to easily and directly define a dissimilarity version of any method framed in MCM, without the need of defining a new dissimilarity measure between descriptors and prototypes.

Considering the m-th body part, the procedure for defining the corresponding prototypes is the following. First, all the components belonging to the m-th part of every element of $\mathcal{T}$ are put together forming a single set of components. Then, a clustering algorithm is applied to this set; prototypes will be defined as the clusters found.

Any clustering method can be adopted, for example the well known K-Means algorithm. To reduce computational and memory requirements, it may be preferable to have prototypes made up by a reduced number of components. Thus, one can also define a two-stage clustering procedure: first, the components belonging to each individual are separately clustered; then, a second clustering is carried out on the centroids obtained at the first-stage. Note that many other algorithms to find out prototypes have been proposed in literature (see for example [12]).

This procedure ends up with a prototype gallery $\mathcal{P}$, made by M sets of prototypes, one set for each body part:

$$\mathcal{P} = \{\mathbf{P}_1, \dots, \mathbf{P}_M\} \tag{7}$$

with the m-th set of prototypes having a cardinality $N_{P,m}$

$$\mathbf{P_m} = \{P_{m,1}, \dots, P_{m,N_{P,m}}\} \tag{8}$$

It turns out that the parameters of the clustering algorithm, which govern the number of prototypes $N_{P,m}$ for each part, are important, but not crucial: as will be shown in Sect. 4, performance does not vary drastically in respect to $N_{P,m}$.

Fig. 4 sums up the process of prototypes generation in a case where the number of parts is two.

Once prototypes have been defined, we can build a dissimilarity representation of each element of $\mathcal{T}$, and of $\mathbf{Q}$. Such dissimilarity representation is made up of a different dissimilarity vector for each part. More formally, given an individual $\mathbf{I}$ composed by m parts $I_1, \dots, I_m$, the dissimilarity representation is the following:

$$\mathbf{I^{Dis}} = \{I_1^{Dis}, \dots, I_m^{Dis}\} \tag{9}$$

where each I_i^{Dis} is a vector of dissimilarity measures corresponding to the i-th part:

$$I_i^{Dis} = \left[d(I_i, P_{i,1}) \dots d(I_i, P_{i,N_{P,i}})\right] \tag{10}$$

By means of Eq. 9 and Eq. 10, all the elements $\mathbf{T}_i$ of the template gallery $\mathcal{T}$ can be described via their dissimilarity representation $\mathbf{T^{Dis}}_i$.

Once the data has been transposed into a dissimilarity space, the problem of finding the best match in the template gallery given a query $\mathbf{Q}$ can be addressed similarly to Eq. 3 of MCM:

$$\mathbf{T^{Dis}}^* = \arg\min_{\mathbf{T^{Dis}}_i} D(\mathbf{T^{Dis}}_i, \mathbf{Q}), \tag{11}$$

where the superscript **Dis** indicates a dissimilarity representation. D can be the same fusion rule of Eq. 4, this time applied to distance measures d_{Dis} between dissimilarity vectors. Considering a generic dissimilarity template $\mathbf{T^{Dis}}$ and a probe $\mathbf{Q^{Dis}}$, we have therefore:

$$D(\mathbf{T^{Dis}}, \mathbf{Q^{Dis}}) = f\Big(d_{Dis}(T_1^{Dis}, Q_1), \dots, d_{Dis}(T_M^{Dis}, Q_M)\Big). \tag{12}$$

The distance measure d_{Dis}, can be defined as any distance measure between vectors, for example the euclidean distance.

The proposed dissimilarity representation exhibits clear advantages. First, in place of a complex descriptor, for each individual we have a set of a limited number of dissimilarity vectors, one for each part of the body, thus saving a great amount of memory for descriptors storage. Note that also the prototypes need to be stored, however the number of their elements can be conveniently reduced, for example

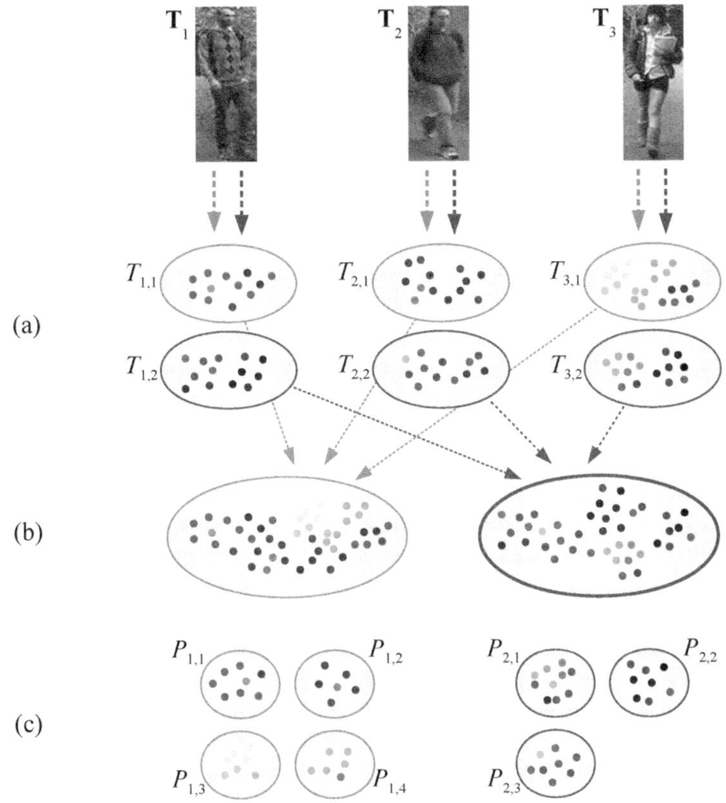

Fig. 4. Generation of the prototype gallery in MCD. Considering a template gallery of three individuals, represented as a set of components for each part according to MCM (a), all the components corresponding of each part are put together (b), then a clustering operator is applied and a number of prototypes is generated for each part (c). In this example, two parts are considered, upper (in green) and lower (in red) body.

by adopting a two-stage clustering scheme as explained previously. Furthermore, the matching becomes as simple as computing a distance between vectors, which is almost an immediate operation with modern CPUs. Such extremely fast matching can lead to several useful applications, like finding the identity of an individual among a huge number of candidates, almost in real-time.

The MCD framework we proposed can be used to define a dissimilarity version of any method which can be framed in MCM. In particular, in the following Section we apply MCD to the implementation of MCM proposed in [14].

4 Application of MCD

In this section, we provide a preliminary analysis of the application of MCD to an existing person re-identification method. We have chosen MCMimpl, a direct implementation of MCM proposed in [14] which has shown to attain state-of-the-art performance.

In MCMimpl, first the mask which separates the individual from the background is obtained by a STEL generative model [10]. The body is then divided into two parts, torso and legs, exploiting the anti-symmetry properties of the human silhouette. From each part, random and partly overlapping patches are extracted and described via a colour histogram in the HSV colour space. The distance between two sets corresponding to the same part is evaluated by the k-th Hausdorff Distance (which has been introduced in Sect. 2.2), while the final matching distance is the average of the distances of the parts.

To apply MCD, first a proper clustering algorithm to find the prototypes must be chosen. We adopted a two-stage clustering scheme, where at first patches belonging to every template are clustered with the Mean-Shift clustering algorithm [4], which does not make any assumption on the shape of the distribution nor the number of clusters. The only parameter of Mean-Shift is the bandwidth BW, which governs how spread is each cluster. The resulting centroids (actually, the real patch nearest to each centroid) are put together and clustered again, this time via the classical K-Means method. Here, the only parameter is the number of clusters K. We have chosen to adopt K-Means for the second clustering stage, since applying Mean-Shift resulted in too unbalanced clusters (many of which composed by only 1 or 2 elements). Instead, Mean-Shift has proven to be more effective in clustering the patches of a single individual.

Fig. 5 shows the result of applying this clustering algorithm to patches extracted accordingly to $MCMimpl$. A set of 10 individuals is considered, taken from the ViPER dataset [7]. Note that some prototypes look quite similar; however, all the different visual characteristics are reasonably well captured in distinct prototypes.

Concerning the d_{Dis} distance measure (Eq. 12) between dissimilarity vectors, we adopt the euclidean distance. Finally, the overall matching distance (D in Eq. 12) is the average of the distances of the single parts.

Preliminary Evaluation

A preliminary experimental evaluation of the dissimilarity version of the target method, $MCMimpl$, is provided in the following. The dissimilarity version is denoted as $MCMimpl^{Dis}$.

We changed the parameters of $MCMimpl$ originally used in [14], reducing the size of the patches and increasing their number, thus obtaining an higher granularity, that we have found to be more effective in capturing the visual characteristics. We extracted 300 random rectangular patches from each part, whose width and height are in the range $[8\%, 12\%]$ of the width and the height of the part.

The bandwidth parameter of Mean-Shift clustering was set to $BW = 0.3$ for all the experiments.

Table 1. Short comparison between $MCMimpl$ and its dissimilarity version $MCMimpl^{Dis}$. The size of the descriptor is computed considering 32 bit floats values, and for $MCMimpl^{Dis}$ is referred to a number of prototypes of 80 for both torso and legs. Matching time is evaluated on a 2.4 GHz CPU, and refers for both methods to a non-optimized C++ implementation.

	$MCMimpl$	$MCMimpl^{Dis}$
Size of the descriptor	$96KB$	$640B$
Average matching time	$28.6ms$	$< 0.01ms$

In Table 1, a short comparison between the original method and its dissimilarity version is provided. In particular, we reported the size of the descriptor and the average time required for matching.

As can be seen, the size of the descriptor for $MCMimpl^{Dis}$ is reduced by two orders of magnitude: the original descriptor, in fact, is made up of 300 different local patches for each part (torso and legs), every patch being represented by a vector of 40 features (see [14] for further details). The dissimilarity descriptor, instead, is composed by a vector of N_P elements for each part, N_P being the number of prototypes (assumed the same for all the parts).

The matching time has been evaluated as the average of 6300 single comparisons, and, as can be seen, it is also greatly reduced, being almost immediate, and leads to a matching rate of over 10^5 candidates *per second.*

We evaluated also the matching performance of $MCMimpl^{Dis}$. Given a template gallery and a probe gallery, a common way to assess the performance of a person re-identification method is the Cumulative Matching Characteristics curve, that is, the average probability of finding the correct match of the elements of the probe gallery, in the template gallery. Here, we build both the template and the probe gallery from a sub-set of the ViPER benchmark dataset [7], made up of the first 126 pedestrian. In this dataset, for every person two non-overlapping views are available. The template gallery is made up of the first view of each pedestrian, while the probe gallery is built by each second view.

In Fig. 6 we report the average CMC curve over 10 different folds of 63 pedestrians. The CMC curve of the original method $MCMimpl$ is also plotted in blue, as reference.

Performance vary in respect to the number of prototypes N_P, which in these experiments is the same for all the body parts. In Fig. 7 the performance versus N_P is evaluated by means of the area of the first 20% of the CMC curve (denoted as $AUC_{20\%}$). We chose to consider the first part of the curve only, since in real application scenarios the interest is usually on the first ranks. The plot of Fig. 6 corresponds to a $N_P = 80$.

The proposed framework is aimed at taking advantages related to the compactness of the dissimilarity representation, rather than incrementing the pure matching performance. We point out that such advantages do not depend to the specific target method considered. However, note that performance attained by the dissimilarity version are comparable to that of the original method. Furthermore, the dissimilarity version slightly outperforms the original method in the first part of the curve, which as stated previously is usually the most interesting.

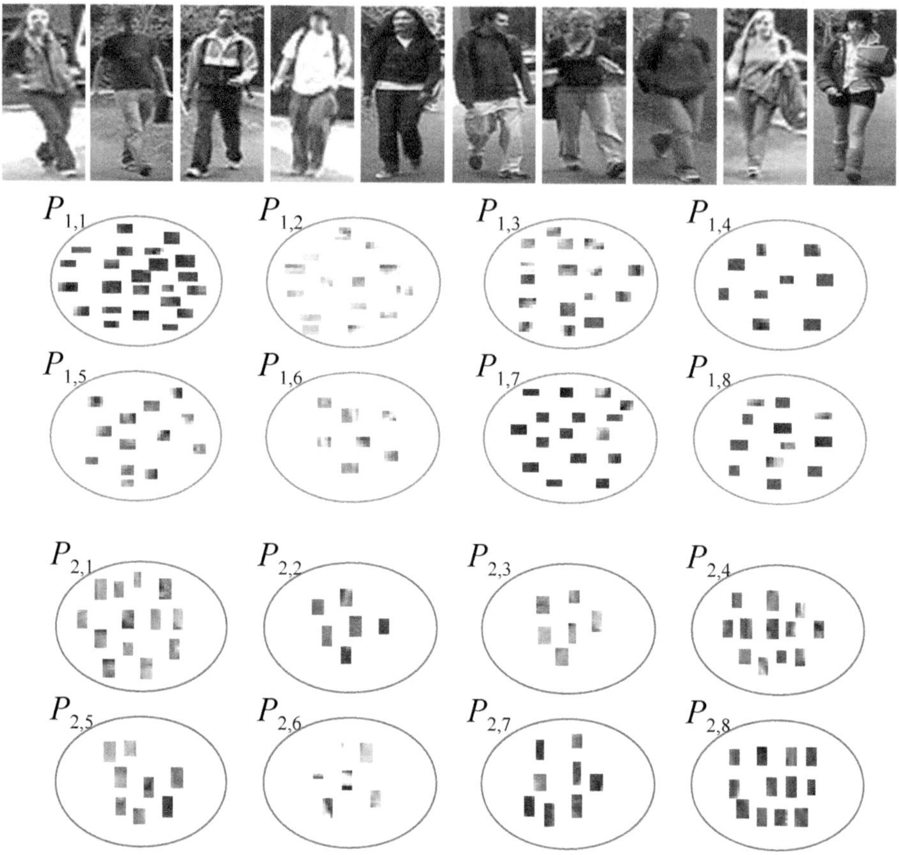

Fig. 5. Patch clustering results, for a set of 10 individuals. In green, prototypes related to the *torso* body part; in red, prototypes related to the *legs* body part. The number of prototypes is set to 8 for both the parts.

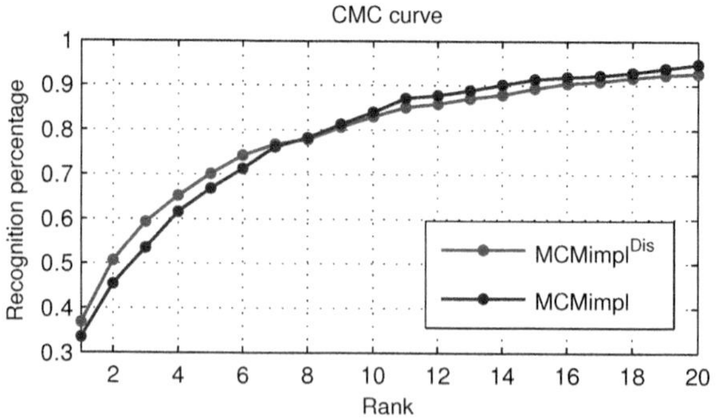

Fig. 6. Average Cumulative Matching Characteristics curve over 10 runs on a sub-set of the ViPER dataset. In blue, performance attained by the reference method $MCMimpl$; in red, performance attained by its dissimilarity version $MCMimpl^{Dis}$.

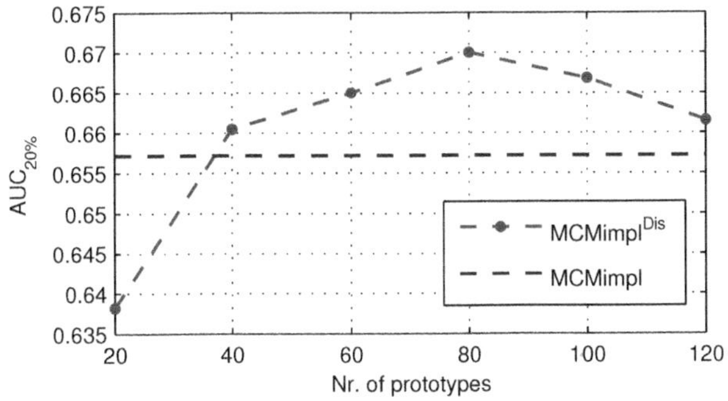

Fig. 7. $AUC_{20\%}$ attained by $MCMimpl^{Dis}$ in respect to the number of prototypes (in red). The blue line depicted as reference is the $AUC_{20\%}$ of $MCMimpl$.

5 Conclusions and Future Work

In this paper, we proposed a framework, named "Multiple Component Dissimilarity" (MCD), aimed at transposing a generic method for person re-identification to a dissimilarity-based form. MCD is completely general, and does not impose constraints on the specific features used by the target method considered. It only requires that the target method exploits a multiple instances representation.

Dissimilarity representations carry interesting benefits to the problem of person re-identification. The first one is the compactness of the resulting dissimilarity descriptors; regardless of the complexity of the local features adopted by the target method, the dissimilarity descriptor will be as compact as a vector of dissimilarities. The second advantage is then obvious, as once samples are described in such form, a comparison between descriptors is almost immediate, being the computation of differences between vectors extremely cheap in terms of computational requirements.

The proposed MCD framework has been applied to an existing person re-identification method, and an experimental evaluation in respect to this method has been provided. Future studies shall include a more comprehensive analysis which consider different person re-identification approaches. Methods depicted in [5,9,6] are good candidates to apply MCD.

A dissimilarity representation can be exploited to enable several interesting applications. Here, we briefly describe some of them.

The first possible application is *people grouping*. Once we have a set of individuals described by dissimilarity vectors, we can cluster them in the dissimilarity space, so that we obtain clusters of people sharing a similar appearance. Since it is reasonable that every individual shares different characteristics with different groups of people, a "fuzzy" of "soft" clustering should be adopted, which does not hardly assign every individual to a single cluster.

People grouping can be useful in a number of tasks. For example, it can be used as a preprocessing phase to reduce the number the candidates prior to perform matching: we can first find clusters that the query is more likely to belong to, then perform matching only against templates belonging to these clusters. This can lead to a great reduction of computational requirements when the cardinality of the template gallery is huge. Note that only the first phase (grouping) exploits dissimilarity representations, while the second phase (matching inside a single group) can be run using any person re-identification method. We can also use people grouping to perform tasks that are not strictly related to the classic person re-identification problem. For example, we can exploit it to find people that share similar appearance in a scene. Individuals whose role can be assigned in respect to their appearance (for instance, policemen, vigilantes, firemen) can be therefore grouped automatically.

Another application that a dissimilarity representation can enable, is *appearance learning*, i.e. learn the appearance of an individual from a series of dissimilarity vectors. A great practical problem in person re-identification is how to accumulate different frames of the same person in a single descriptor. Most of the techniques proposed so far deal with only one template image per person, while the few methods that consider different images adopt approaches that vary from harvesting all the information obtained from all the frames, to clustering techniques aimed at reducing the number of local features that build the final descriptor. A classifier could be a great way to build a descriptor of an individual starting from a series of frames. In fact, each frame can be described as a dissimilarity vector, and these vectors can form a training set. Then, we can train a one-class or an one-versus-all classifier to learn the appearance of the individual.

The appearance of people that show similar visual characteristics (for example policemen, firemen, sport teams) can also be learned. Furthermore, appearance learning could be applied in scenarios not related to security and surveillance, for example to recognize different traditional dressings in cultural heritage applications.

References

1. Bak, S., Corvee, E., Bremond, F., Thonnat, M.: Person re-identification using haar-based and dcd-based signature. In: AVSS, pp. 1–8 (2010)
2. Bak, S., Corvee, E., Bremond, F., Thonnat, M.: Person re-identification using spatial covariance regions of human body parts. In: AVSS (2010)
3. Carli, A., Castellani, U., Bicego, M., Murino, V.: Dissimilarity-based representation for local parts. In: Proceedings of the 2nd IEEE International Workshop on Cognitive Information Processing (CIP) (2010)
4. Comaniciu, D., Meer, P.: Mean shift: A robust approach toward feature space analysis. IEEE Trans. Pattern Anal. Mach. Intell. 24, 603–619 (2002)
5. Farenzena, M., Bazzani, L., Perina, A., Murino, V., Cristani, M.: Person re-identification by symmetry-driven accumulation of local features. In: CVPR (2010)
6. Gheissari, N., Sebastian, T.B., Hartley, R.: Person reidentification using spatiotemporal appearance. In: CVPR (2006)
7. Gray, D., Brennan, S., Tao, H.: Evaluating appearance models for recognition, reacquisition, and tracking. In: PETS (2007)
8. Gray, D., Tao, H.: Viewpoint invariant pedestrian recognition with an ensemble of localized features. In: Forsyth, D., Torr, P., Zisserman, A. (eds.) ECCV 2008, Part I. LNCS, vol. 5302, pp. 262–275. Springer, Heidelberg (2008)

9. Hamdoun, O., Moutarde, F., Stanciulescu, B., Steux, B.: Interest points harvesting in video sequences for efficient person identification. In: VS (2008)
10. Jojic, N., Perina, A., Cristani, M., Murino, V., Frey, B.: Stel component analysis: Modeling spatial correlations in image class structure. In: CVPR, pp. 2044–2051 (2009)
11. Pekalska, E., Duin, R.P.W.: The Dissimilarity Representation for Pattern Recognition: Foundations And Applications (Machine Perception and Artificial Intelligence). World Scientific Publishing Co., Inc., River Edge (2005)
12. Pekalska, E., Duin, R.P.W., Paclik, P.: Prototype selection for dissimilarity-based classifiers. Pattern Recognition 39 (February 2006)
13. Prosser, B., Zheng, W., Gong, S., Xiang, T.: Person re-identification by support vector ranking. In: BMVA, pp. 21.1–21.11 (2010)
14. Satta, R., Fumera, G., Roli, F., Cristani, M., Murino, V.: A multiple component matching framework for person re-identification. In: ICIAP (in press, 2011), arXiv:1105.2491 `http://arxiv.org/abs/1105.2491`
15. Truong Cong, D.N., Achard, C., Khoudour, L., Douadi, L.: Video sequences association for people re-identification across multiple non-overlapping cameras. In: Foggia, P., Sansone, C., Vento, M. (eds.) ICIAP 2009. LNCS, vol. 5716, pp. 179–189. Springer, Heidelberg (2009)
16. Wang, J., Zucker, J.D.: Solving the multiple-instance problem: A lazy learning approach. In: ICML (2000)
17. Yang, J., Jiang, Y.G., Hauptmann, A.G., Ngo, C.W.: Evaluating bag-of-visual-words representations in scene classification. In: Proceedings of the International Workshop on Multimedia Information Retrieval, pp. 197–206 (2007)

A Study of Embedding Methods under the Evidence Accumulation Framework

Helena Aidos and Ana Fred

Instituto de Telecomunicações, Instituto Superior Técnico, Lisbon, Portugal
{haidos,afred}@lx.it.pt

Abstract. In this paper we address a voting mechanism to combine clustering ensembles leading to the so-called co-association matrix, under the Evidence Accumulation Clustering framework. Different clustering techniques can be applied to this matrix to obtain the combined data partition, and different clustering strategies may yield too different combination results. We propose to apply embedding methods over this matrix, in an attempt to reduce the sensitivity of the final partition to the clustering method, and still obtain competitive and consistent results. We present a study of several embedding methods over this matrix, interpreting it in two ways: (i) as a feature space and (ii) as a similarity space. In the first case we reduce the dimensionality of the feature space; in the second case we obtain a representation constrained to the similarity matrix. When applying several clustering techniques over these new representations, we evaluate the impact of these transformations in terms of performance and coherence of the obtained data partition. Experimental results, on synthetic and real benchmark datasets, show that extracting the relevant features through dimensionality reduction yields more consistent results than applying the clustering algorithms directly to the co-association matrix.

Keywords: clustering ensembles, co-association matrix, evidence accumulation clustering, embedding methods.

1 Introduction

Clustering is one of the central problems in Pattern Recognition and Machine Learning. Given a set of unlabeled data, its typical goal is to group objects into clusters, such that objects within a cluster are similar, and objects in distinct clusters are dissimilar. Assuming that clusters are disjoint, the clustering process leads to a data partition. Hundreds of clustering algorithms exist, handling differently issues such as cluster shape, density, noise. k-means is one of the most studied and used algorithms [9,18].

Recently, taking advantage of the diversity of clustering solutions produced by clustering algorithms over the same dataset, an approach known as *Clustering Ensemble methods*, has been proposed and gained an increasing interest [4,16,10,1]. Given a set of data partitions - a clustering ensemble (CE) - these methods propose a consensus partition based on a combination strategy, having in general a leveraging effect over the single data partitions in the CE.

We can generate clustering ensembles following two approaches: choice of data representation or choice of clustering algorithms or algorithmic parameters. In the first

M. Pelillo and E.R. Hancock (Eds.): SIMBAD 2011, LNCS 7005, pp. 290–305, 2011.

case, we can get different representations of objects by applying different preprocessing mechanisms or feature extraction techniques, or just by sampling the data a number of times. We can also have clustering ensembles if we use several clustering algorithms or just the same algorithm with different parameter values.

Fred and Jain [5] proposed a clustering ensemble approach based on the combination of information provided by a set of different partitions of a given dataset, through the Evidence Accumulation method. To combine all the different partitions, Fred and Jain [5] proposed a voting scheme, which leads to a pairwise relationships matrix, called "co-association matrix". The final data partition is obtained by applying a clustering algorithm over the co-association matrix. One main advantage of this voting scheme is that it can deal with partitions having different number of clusters and different data representations.

The application of different clustering techniques to this matrix may yield different solutions. We propose to use embedding methods (also called dimensionality reduction (DR) methods) over this matrix, in an attempt to reduce the sensitivity of the combined data partition to the clustering method, and obtain better and more consensual results. We present a study of the performance and coherence of the solutions when different clustering techniques are applied to the resulting data representations. To obtain those representations we will follow two approaches: interpret the co-association matrix as a feature space, and as a similarity space.

The first approach is similar to the one proposed by Kuncheva *et al.* [11]: we will view the co-association matrix as a feature space, but instead of using the full feature space, we will reduce its dimension using several dimensionality reduction (DR) methods. These DR techniques aim to take a set of data points in a high-dimensional space and output a new set of data points in a lower-dimensional space, in a way that preserves the topology of the high-dimensional data. This new data representation is commonly called an *embedding* of the original dataset. We will empirically show that the use of DR methods to remove redundant features improves the quality and consistency of the final partition for different clustering techniques.

In the other approach we view the co-association matrix as a similarity space, as in [5]. However, instead of applying directly the clustering techniques to this matrix, we will first apply DR methods to it. Many DR methods take as input some distance measure between points (usually in a distance matrix whose (i, j) entry contains the distance between data points i and j). Therefore, if one converts the similarity measures in the co-association matrix into distance (or dissimilarity) measures, one can input this dissimilarity matrix into the DR methods directly. The resulting low-dimensional data points are then clustered with several clustering techniques. Again, we intend to study if there exists consistency and an improvement in the quality of the solutions.

The dimensionality reduction methods used have different characteristics such as: linear vs. nonlinear; preserving local structure vs. preserving global structure; preserve spatial distances vs. preserving graph distances. This means that different embedding strategies may influence differently the solutions; we intend to study if there exists a class of embedding methods suitable for certain types of datasets (well separate clusters, touching clusters).

This paper is organized as follows: Section 2 gives a brief explanation of the embedding algorithms used in the study. Section 3 explains the evidence accumulation approach, including the construction of the co-association matrix. Section 4 explains the new methodology proposed in this paper and the two interpretations we give to this matrix. Section 5 describes the datasets used in this study and the experimental results for the two interpretations of the co-association matrix: feature space (section 5.2) and similarity space (section 5.3). We summarize and discuss the main findings in Section 6. Conclusions are drawn in Section 7.

2 Embedding Methods

To perform embeddings we will use several unsupervised DR methods: Locality Preserving Projections (LPP) [7]. Neighborhood Preserving Projections (NPE) [6], Sammon's mapping [15], Curvilinear Component Analysis (CCA) [3], Isomap [17], Curvilinear Distance Analysis (CDA) [13], Locally Linear Embedding (LLE) [14] and Laplacian Eigenmap (LE) [2]. We now briefly introduce each of these algorithms.

2.1 Nonlinear Methods

The *Locally Linear Embedding* (LLE) [14] assumes that the data manifold is smooth and sampled densely enough such that each data point lies close to a locally linear subspace on the manifold. In other words, the manifold smoothness and sampling should be enough to locally approximate the manifold by a hyperplane. LLE makes a locally linear approximation of the whole data manifold; it first estimates a local coordinate system for each data point from its k-nearest neighbors. To produce the embedding, LLE finds low-dimensional coordinates that preserve the previously estimated local coordinate systems as well as possible. Technically, LLE first minimizes the reconstruction error $E(\mathbf{W}) = \sum_i \|\mathbf{x}_i - \sum_j W_{i,j}\mathbf{x}_j\|^2$ with respect to the coefficients $W_{i,j}$, under the constraints that $W_{i,j} = 0$ if i and j are not neighbors, and $\sum_j W_{i,j} = 1$. After finding these weights, the low-dimensional configuration of points is next found by minimizing $E(\mathbf{Y}) = \sum_i \|\mathbf{y}_i - \sum_j W_{i,j}\mathbf{y}_j\|^2$ with respect to the low-dimensional representation $\mathbf{y}_i$ of each data point.

The *Laplacian Eigenmap* (LE) [2] uses a graph embedding approach. An undirected k-nearest neighbor graph is formed, where each data point is a vertex. Points i and j are connected by an edge with weight $W_{i,j} = 1$ if j is among the k nearest neighbors of i, otherwise the edge weight is set to zero; this simple weighting method has been found to work well in practice [2]. To find a low-dimensional embedding of the graph, the algorithm tries to put points that are connected in the graph as close to each other as possible and does not care what happens to the other points. Technically, it minimizes $\frac{1}{2}\sum_{i,j} \|\mathbf{y}_i - \mathbf{y}_j\|^2 W_{i,j} = \mathbf{y}^T\mathbf{L}\mathbf{y}$ with respect to the low-dimensional point locations $\mathbf{y}_i$, where $\mathbf{L} = \mathbf{D} - \mathbf{W}$ is the graph Laplacian and $\mathbf{D}$ is a diagonal matrix with elements $\mathrm{D}_{ii} = \sum_j W_{i,j}$. This cost function has an undesirable trivial solution: having all points in the same position would have a cost of zero, which would be a global minimum of the cost function. In practice, the low-dimensional configuration is found by solving the generalized eigenvalue problem $\mathbf{Ly} = \lambda\mathbf{Dy}$ [2]. The smallest eigenvalue corresponds to the trivial solution, but the eigenvectors corresponding to the next smallest eigenvalues yield the desired LE solution.

Isomap [17] is a variant of Multidimensional Scaling (MDS) [12], which finds a configuration of output coordinates matching a given distance matrix. Isomap does not compute pairwise input-space distances as simple Euclidean distances but as *geodesic distances* along the manifold of the data (technically, along a graph formed by connecting all k-nearest neighbors). Given these geodesic distances the output coordinates are found by standard linear MDS. When output coordinates are found for such input distances, the manifold structure in the original data becomes unfolded; it has been shown that this algorithm is asymptotically able to recover certain types of manifolds.

Curvilinear component analysis (CCA) [3] is a variant of MDS [12] that tries to preserve only distances between points that are near each other in the embedding. This is achieved by weighting each term in the MDS cost function by a coefficient that depends on the corresponding pairwise distance in the embedding. In our case, this coefficient is simply 1 if the distance is below a predetermined threshold and 0 if it is larger. This approach is similar to Isomap but the determination of whether two points are neighbors is done in the output space in CCA, rather than in the input space as in Isomap.

Curvilinear distance analysis Curvilinear Distance Analysis (CDA) [13] is an extension of CCA. The idea is to replace in MDS the Euclidean distances in the original space with geodesic distances in the same manner as in the Isomap algorithm. Otherwise the algorithm is similar to CCA.

2.2 Linear Methods

Locality Preserving Projections (LPP) [7] is a linear dimensionality reduction method that preserves local neighborhood information. It shares many properties of nonlinear techniques such as Laplacian Eigenmaps or Locally Linear Embedding, since it is a linear approximation of the nonlinear Laplacian Eigenmaps.

Neighborhood Preserving Projections (NPE) [6] is a linear dimensionality reduction method that preserves the local structure of the data. It has similar properties to LPP, but it is a linear approximation of Locally Linear Embedding (LLE), which means that it has properties similar to that method.

3 Evidence Accumulation: The Co-association Matrix

Let $X = \{x_1, x_2, \ldots, x_n\}$ be a set of n objects or samples represented in a feature space or some other data representation. A clustering algorithm takes X as input and groups the n patterns into k clusters, forming a partition P. A *clustering ensemble*, $\mathbb{P}$, is a set of N different partitions of the data X:

$$\mathbb{P} = \{P^1, P^2, \ldots, P^N\} \tag{1}$$

$$P^1 = \{C_1^1, C_2^1, \ldots, C_{k_1}^1\}$$

$$\vdots$$

$$P^N = \{C_1^N, C_2^N, \ldots, C_{k_N}^N\},$$

where C_j^i is the jth cluster in data partition P^i, which has k_i clusters and n_j^i is the cardinality of C_j^i, with $\sum_{j=1}^{k_i} n_j^i = n, i = 1, \ldots, N$.

The *evidence accumulation* approach, proposed by Fred and Jain [5], is a three-step cluster ensemble method: 1- build the clustering ensemble (CE); 2- combine evidence in the CE, mapping it into a co-association matrix; 3- extract the consensus partition by applying a clustering algorithm over the co-association matrix. The basic idea is that patterns belonging to a "natural" cluster are very likely to be assigned to the same cluster in different data partitions. Taking the co-occurrences of pairs of patterns in the same cluster as votes for their association, the N data partitions of n patterns yield a $n \times n$ co-association matrix:

$$\mathcal{C}(i,j) = \frac{n_{ij}}{N}, \tag{2}$$

where n_{ij} is the number of times the pattern pair (i, j) is assigned to the same cluster among the N partitions.

In its normalized form, as per expression (2), matrix $\mathcal{C}$ can be given different interpretations, either probabilistic or simply as pairwise similarity. Another issue is how to address and use this matrix for clustering purposes. In the following we propose a novel methodology by applying DR techniques.

4 Dimensionality Reduction in Evidence Accumulation Clustering

We propose a new methodology called Dimensionality Reduction in Evidence Accumulation Clustering (DR-EAC), which is based on the Evidence Accumulation Clustering (EAC) method described above. As said before, the evidence accumulation approach is a three-step cluster ensemble method; we now propose a four-step method. We build the clustering ensemble (step 1) and the co-association matrix (step 2) similarly to the evidence accumulation approach. However, instead of applying a clustering algorithm directly to the co-association matrix, we apply a DR technique to it (which is now step 3). As detailed below, we propose two ways to do this, depending on how one interprets the co-association matrix. This DR technique outputs a low-dimensional dataset, which is then fed into a clustering algorithm (which is now step 4). We now discuss each of these four steps in more detail.

1) Build the Clustering Ensemble. As referred before, there are several ways to produce a clustering ensemble. In this study we build a clustering ensemble by running the k-means algorithm to produce a total of $N = 200$ data partitions, each one with k clusters, k being an integer randomly drawn between $k_{min} = \max\{\sqrt{n}/2, n/50\}$ and $k_{max} = k_{min} + 20$, where n is the number of samples of the dataset.

2) Obtain the co-association matrix. We begin by computing the co-association matrix according to equation (2). Then, we interpret this matrix in one of two possible ways:

- *Co-associations viewed as Features:* One way to look at matrix $\mathcal{C}$ is to say that its i-th row represents a new set of features for the i-th data point, an idea originally proposed by Kuncheva *et al.* [11]. Thus, each pattern is now represented by how many times it was grouped together with all other patterns.

- *Co-association viewed as Similarities:* We can transform the co-association matrix $\mathcal{C}$, which is a similarity matrix, into a dissimilarity matrix (or distance matrix). Since many DR methods can take as input a matrix of pairwise distances (or dissimilarities), if we transform this matrix of similarities into a matrix of dissimilarities we can exploit this property. Since the elements of $\mathcal{C}$ lie between 0 and 1, we use a very simple transformation: the new dissimilarity matrix has the element (i, j) given by $1 - \mathcal{C}(i, j)$.

3) Apply Dimensionality Reduction techniques. We apply DR techniques to obtain a new representation of the data, preserving the topology of the original data. For the DR methods we need to choose a target dimension to reduce the data to and, in some cases, we also have to choose a parameter of the method (usually the number of nearest neighbors to consider). In all cases we let each algorithm choose the most suitable parameter and dimension by an intrinsic criterion. This intrinsic criterion can be the value of the cost function that each algorithm has to minimize, or the reconstruction error. For example, in Isomap we chose the parameter (which is the number of nearest neighbors used to construct a graph) which minimizes the residual variance [17]. It is beyond the scope of this paper to detail how these parameters should be chosen; the relevant information can be found in the references cited in Section 2.

4) Extract the consensus partition. After we get the embedded data, we apply eight well-known clustering algorithms: k-means, single-link, complete-link, average-link, Ward-link, centroid-link, median-link and weighted-link [9].

4.1 Quality Measures

We use two quality measures to assess the results: consistency index (CI) and normalized mutual information (NMI).

The CI simply measures the fraction of patterns correctly grouped together compared to the ground-truth labeling. It takes values between 0 and 1, and it is a measure of the accuracy of the clustering.

The NMI [16] is a symmetric measure of the information shared between two partitions. Consider the partition P^a, which describes a labeling of the n patterns in the dataset X into k_a clusters. If one takes frequency counts as approximations for probabilities, the entropy of the data partition P^a is given by $H(P^a) = -\sum_{i=1}^{k_a} \frac{n_i^a}{n} \log\left(\frac{n_i^a}{n}\right)$, where n_i^a represents the number of patterns in cluster $C_i^a \in P^a$. The agreement between two partitions P^a and P^b is given by their mutual information:

$$I(P^a, P^b) = \sum_{i=1}^{k_a} \sum_{j=1}^{k_b} \frac{n_{ij}^{ab}}{n} \log\left(\frac{\frac{n_{ij}^{ab}}{n}}{\frac{n_i^a}{n} \cdot \frac{n_j^b}{n}}\right),$$

whith n_{ij}^{ab} the number of shared patterns between clusters $C_i^a \in P^a$ and $C_j^b \in P^b$.

The NMI is then defined by

$$NMI(P^a, P^b) = \frac{I(P^a, P^b)}{\sqrt{H(P^a)H(P^b)}}.$$

It is similar to the widely used mutual information, but normalized to be in the interval $[0, 1]$. For each DR method, we compute the NMI between all 28 pairs of clustering algorithms[1]. We then take the average of these 28 NMI values to obtain the average NMI for that DR method. This average NMI will measure how consistent the partitions are among the 8 clustering algorithms after applying that DR method.

5 Experimental Results

We will apply the new methodology described in section 4 to several datasets, in an attempt to improve the quality and robustness of the solutions, compared to the evidence accumulation approach. We will apply the clustering algorithms mentioned in section 4 to the co-association matrix directly (in both interpretations), an approach we will denote by EAC_F (Evidence Accumulation Clustering in the feature space) and EAC (Evidence Accumulation Clustering in the sense presented by [5]). The idea is to verify empirically whether the use of embedding methods and subsequent clustering algorithms is advantageous relative to the application of clustering algorithms on the co-association matrix directly. Also, we will try to find some correspondence between pairs of embedding and clustering methods suitable for some types of data. In that sense, we will study synthetic data and real data, with the synthetic data divided in two broad meta-sets: datasets with separate clusters and datasets with touching clusters.

5.1 Data

We used 18 datasets: 10 synthetic datasets (5 well-separated and 5 with touching clusters), and 8 real datasets from the UCI Machine Learning Repository[2]. The synthetic datasets were chosen to take into account a wide variety of situations: well-separated and touching clusters; gaussian and non-gaussian clusters; arbitrary shapes; and diverse cluster densities. These synthetic datasets are shown in figure 1. The *Iris* dataset consists of three species of Iris plants (Setosa, Versicolor and Virginica). This dataset is characterized by four features and 50 samples in each cluster. *Std Yeast* is composed of 384 samples (genes) over two cell cycles of yeast cell data. This dataset is characterized by 17 features and consisting of five clusters corresponding to the five phases of the cell cycle. The *Pima* dataset is composed of 768 samples (genes) from National Institute of Diabetes and Digestive and Kidney Diseases, it has 8 features and two clusters. *Wine* consists of the results of a chemical analysis of wines grown in the same region in Italy divided into three clusters with 59, 71 and 48 patterns described by 13 features. *Optdigits* is a subset of Handwritten Digits dataset containing only the first 100 patterns of each digit, from a total of 1000 data samples characterized by 64 attributes. The *Wisconsin Breast-Cancer* dataset consists of 683 patterns represented by nine features and has two clusters. The *House Votes* dataset consists of votes for each of the U.S. House of Representatives Congressmen on the 16 key votes identified by the Congressional Quarterly Almanac. It is composed by two clusters and only the patterns without missing values

[1] 28 is the number of off-diagonal elements in the upper triangular part of the matrix containing the NMI between pairs of clustering algorithms, which is an 8-by-8 matrix.

[2] `http://archive.ics.uci.edu/ml`

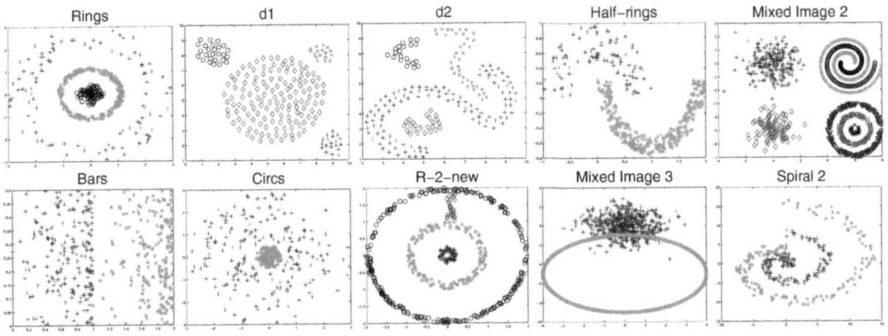

Fig. 1. Synthetic datasets

were considered, for a total of 232 samples (125 democrats and 107 republicans). The *Crabs* dataset consists of 200 patterns represented by 5 features and has two classes. Pima, House Votes, Crabs and Wine were normalized to have unit variance.

5.2 Experiment 1: Feature Space

In this section we interpret the co-association matrix as a new feature space, as described in Section 4. The application of clustering algorithms directly to the co-association matrix viewed as a feature space, is here denoted by EAC_F.

Analyzing the average NMI in figure 2 over all clustering algorithms used to obtain the final partition, we notice that LE and LPP are the ones that produce more coherent solutions for the synthetic datasets with separate clusters (figure 2 top), which indicates that they are robust to the extraction algorithm. CCA and CDA are the algorithms with the most dispersion in the solutions for all datasets. Unlike for separate clusters, the NMI for datasets with touching clusters (figure 2 middle) shows that no DR algorithm is robust to the choice of the clustering algorithm. In the real datasets, LE is the most consistent DR algorithm in half of the datasets (Wine, Std Yeast, Optdigits and Iris).

Even if the NMI is high, it is not necessarily true that we have a high CI (i.e. that the results of the clustering algorithms are good), it only means that the clustering algorithms obtained similar final partitions. However, the use of that measure is a good indicator that the embedded space yields good clustering results regardless of the clustering algorithm. This is an advantage, since we do not know *a priori* which is the most suitable clustering algorithm for a certain kind of data.

Table 1 contains the best CI values (first row of each dataset) and the corresponding clustering algorithm used for that solution; it also presents the average CI over all the clustering algorithms (second row of each dataset). Based on figure 2 we have claimed that LE and LPP are the ones that produce the most coherent solutions for the synthetic datasets with separate clusters; Table 1 corroborates these findings, since LE and LPP usually yield maximum CI for several clustering algorithms.

In synthetic datasets with separate clusters, LE and LPP, which are local algorithms, combine well with multiple hierarchical clustering algorithms. Isomap and Sammon, which are global and nonlinear, combine well with single-link, which is also the best clustering algorithm for EAC_F.

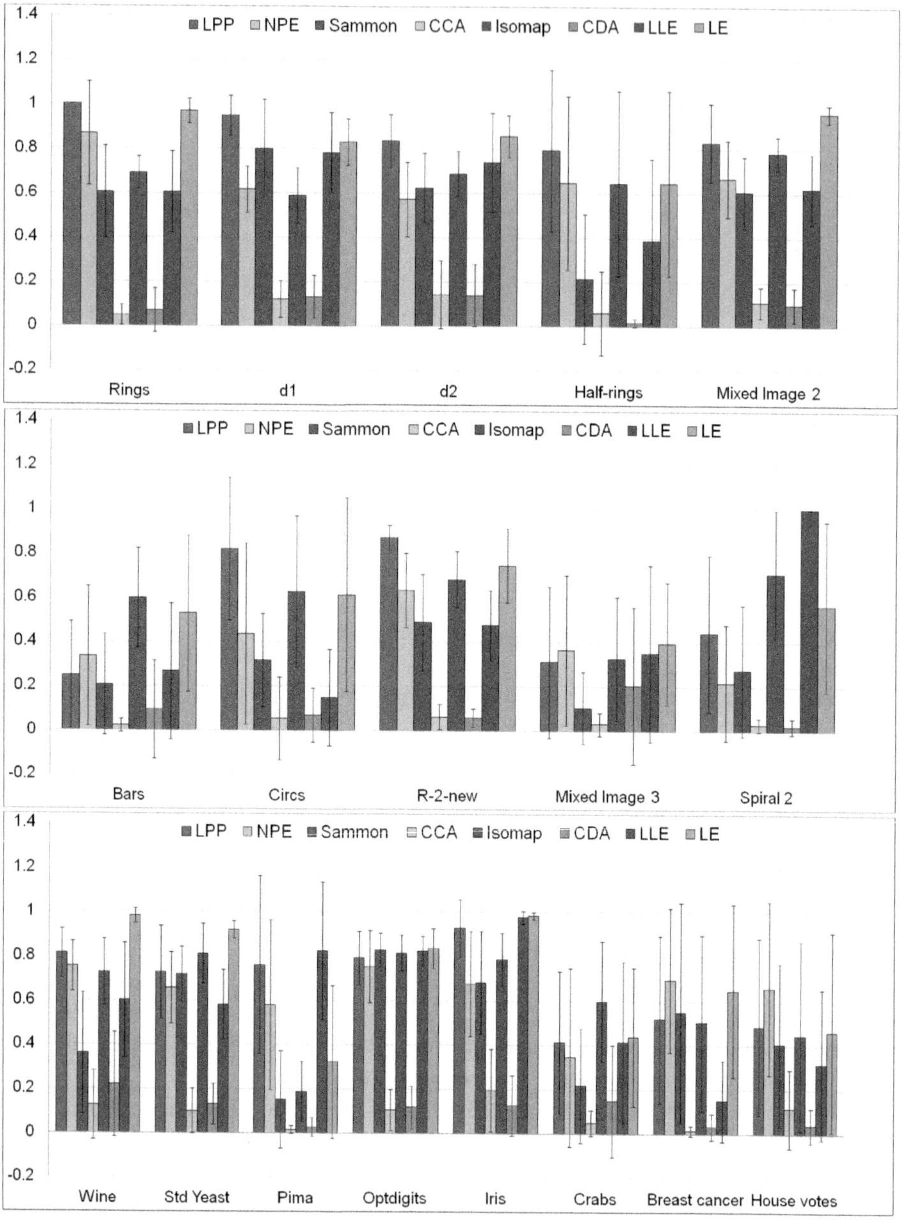

Fig. 2. Mean and standard deviation of Normalized Mutual Information over the clustering algorithms for each dataset and each embedding method. The co-association matrix was interpreted as features. *Top:* Synthetic datasets with separate clusters. *Middle:* Synthetic datasets with touching clusters. *Bottom:* Real datasets.

The analysis of the CI values for the synthetic datasets with touching clusters, shown in Table 1, shows that LPP, Isomap and LE are, on average values, better than EAC_F. In terms of maximum values, EAC_F outperforms the DR-based methods only in one dataset (R-2-new), and still by a very small margin; while it is outperformed in all remaining datasets.

The best DR-clustering algorithm pairs, for synthetic datasets with touching clusters, are LPP with k-means, Sammon with Ward-link and CDA with k-means. The overall best DR is Isomap, which is in first place in maximum CI for 4 out of 5 datasets.

The analysis of CI values for real datasets (see Table 1), shows that all DR methods do relatively well when compared to EAC_F, except for CCA and CDA. Isomap and Sammon are the two best DR algorithms when compared to the remaining DR techniques, especially in the Optdigits dataset. CCA and CDA are the worst overall methods, especially in the Std Yeast and Optdigits datasets.

These results show the advantage of performing DR over using EAC_F. In fact, from Table 1, using DR gives in general the best CI in all datasets, both in terms of maximum CI and of average CI.

Overall, for both synthetic and real datasets, there is no DR algorithm which is always robust in terms of NMI. However, LE and LPP (which is a linear version of LE), seem to have this property, especially in synthetic datasets with separate clusters. For the real datasets, LPP and LE present the best results, except in the Optdigits dataset, which yields better results with a global DR method (like Isomap and Sammon), instead of a local method.

5.3 Experiment 2: Similarity Space

In this section we interpret the entries of the co-association matrix as similarity values. We transform these into dissimilarity values, as described in Section 4. We plug-in this dissimilarity matrix into the embedding methods and will add "EA-" (from "Evidence Accumulation") before the acronyms of the DR methods to emphasize the dependency of this matrix.

The analysis of NMI values for the synthetic datasets with separate clusters, shown in Figure 3, shows that EA-LE and EA-LLE yield the most coherent clustering results, except for the Half-rings dataset. For the Mixed Image 2 dataset, local algorithms (EA-LPP, EA-NPE, EA-LLE and EA-LE) and global algorithms that preserve "geodesic" distances (EA-Isomap, EA-CDA) have very coherent results. However, the analysis of the CI values (Table 2) immediately shows that results are not good for that dataset. This suggest that the co-association matrix might not be the best clustering ensemble approach for this dataset.

Similar to the feature space, the analysis of NMI values for synthetic datasets with touching clusters (figure 3 middle) suggests that no DR algorithm is robust to the choice of clustering algorithm; except the EA-Sammon in the Mixed Image 3. For the real datasets (figure 3 bottom) EA-LE is the DR algorithm with the most consistent results, except for the Pima, Crabs and Breast cancer datasets.

The best overall DR methods, for the synthetic datasets with separate clusters, are EA-LE and EA-LLE. EA-Isomap, EA-CCA, EA-CDA and EA-LE yield the best results

Table 1. Consistency index (%) for co-association matrix interpreted as features. *(First row)* Best CI and clustering algorithm(s) which yield that CI value. Legend: (1) k-means, (2) single-link, (3) complete-link, (4) average-link, (5) Ward-link, (6) centroid-link, (7) median-link, (8) weighted-link. *(Second row)* Average CI (%) over all clustering methods. The gray cells correspond to the best NMI presented in figure 2 and the best average CI are shown in bold.

		EAC_F	LPP	NPE	Sammon	CCA	Isomap	CDA	LLE	LE
Synthetic data with separate clusters	Rings	100	100	61.25	100	50.00	100	52.00	85.50	100
		(2)	(1-8)	(1)	(2)	(2)	(2)	(4)	(5)	(2-8)
		65.28	**100**	55.13	64.78	43.00	73.56	45.75	66.06	99.47
	d1	100	100	82.00	100	70.00	100	70.50	72.50	100
		(2-8)	(2-8)	(6)	(2,4-8)	(2,6)	(2)	(2)	(2)	(2,8)
		98.44	**98.19**	65.25	91.75	54.75	65.31	50.13	69.69	85.88
	d2	100	93.50	51.00	100	59.00	69.00	60.50	50.50	67.00
		(2)	(7)	(7)	(2)	(6)	(2)	(4)	(2)	(3,4,6)
		76.31	**73.87**	42.56	73.00	49.87	59.56	49.25	44.88	61.69
	Half-rings	100	100	69.75	100	81.75	100	74.75	100	100
		(2)	(1,2,4-8)	(2,4-8)	(2)	(5)	(1,2)	(2,6,7)	(2)	(2,4-8)
		72.19	**93.31**	65.81	72.09	66.19	59.87	63.56	88.28	86.63
	Mixed Image 2	65.70	71.80	36.60	71.60	22.90	71.40	23.70	47.00	71.60
		(2)	(2)	(5)	(2)	(6)	(2)	(1)	(5)	(3)
		54.44	63.69	32.50	51.90	21.10	57.45	22.61	38.52	**70.66**
Synthetic data with touching clusters	Bars	99.25	99.25	79.25	99.25	59.50	99.25	73.75	76.00	96.00
		(5)	(4,5)	(1)	(5)	(1)	(2,3)	(1)	(7)	(1)
		68.19	75.25	64.78	68.19	53.09	**90.16**	58.78	62.84	76.84
	Circs	99.50	100	58.75	99.50	63.00	100	84.50	59.00	99.50
		(2,5,8)	(1-6,8)	(1)	(2,8)	(5)	(1,8)	(1)	(8)	(5)
		80.00	**96.16**	54.94	80.56	55.62	91.37	62.31	55.31	66.91
	R-2-new	90.20	77.40	44.40	89.20	50.40	82.80	51.20	57.20	78.60
		(4)	(1)	(2)	(4,5)	(6)	(4)	(7)	(5)	(1)
		66.60	**73.95**	40.55	70.52	39.52	71.22	42.57	51.67	71.52
	Mixed Image 3	84.90	71.90	66.80	74.60	54.80	89.50	74.80	55.30	83.80
		(5)	(1)	(3)	(5)	(8)	(3)	(1)	(3,5)	(4)
		61.52	67.10	58.16	61.59	52.15	73.42	55.59	53.17	**74.92**
	Spiral 2	77.67	77.67	64.33	77.67	58.67	85.00	51.67	85.00	85.00
		(2)	(2)	(8)	(2)	(1)	(2)	(1)	(1-8)	(2,5,7,8)
		63.50	70.96	56.54	61.12	52.50	82.54	50.75	**85.00**	81.33
Real data	Wine	96.07	98.31	90.45	96.07	72.47	96.63	84.27	61.24	96.63
		(8)	(3)	(3)	(5)	(1)	(5,6)	(1)	(5)	(1)
		75.91	94.03	77.18	71.07	46.49	88.48	58.43	47.68	**94.66**
	Std Yeast	60.94	63.80	58.07	61.20	37.24	61.20	35.94	60.16	71.35
		(4)	(1)	(7)	(8)	(4)	(3)	(6)	(5)	(3,5,7)
		54.88	58.36	50.10	54.10	33.33	57.19	32.49	51.14	**66.83**
	Pima	64.71	64.71	65.36	66.02	65.10	64.71	65.23	64.71	64.58
		(2,7)	(1,2,4,6-8)	(2)	(7)	(4)	(2)	(2,7)	(5)	(2)
		56.95	64.34	63.95	57.86	60.90	60.12	60.16	**64.49**	57.03
	Optdigits	87.90	49.60	52.00	85.40	22.50	84.10	17.60	46.30	55.90
		(8)	(5)	(5)	(1)	(5)	(3)	(1)	(3)	(5)
		69.75	31.06	39.34	**74.42**	17.46	71.18	14.53	43.91	38.61
	Iris	84.00	90.67	70.67	90.67	58.67	94.00	49.33	53.33	90.67
		(5,8)	(3)	(3)	(2,8)	(1)	(1)	(1)	(2,4-8)	(1-3,7,8)
		63.17	84.83	62.08	68.42	45.17	86.58	39.75	53.00	**90.42**
	Crabs	65.00	56.00	58.00	65.00	57.00	70.50	54.00	67.00	70.50
		(2)	(3)	(1,5)	(2)	(5)	(2)	(3)	(7)	(4,6)
		59.94	53.12	53.31	57.37	52.50	55.87	51.56	58.00	**62.81**
	Breast Cancer	62.96	68.81	58.13	64.86	64.86	94.58	74.23	75.55	68.67
		(2)	(5)	(2,3,7,8)	(2-4,6-8)	(2,6,7)	(4-8)	(1)	(8)	(1)
		56.81	61.11	56.44	61.68	60.65	**86.09**	64.81	67.84	60.45
	House Votes	89.22	88.36	81.90	87.93	81.47	87.07	61.21	64.66	74.14
		(1)	(1)	(5)	(1)	(1)	(3)	(5)	(1)	(1)
		74.52	71.28	63.31	**73.81**	59.37	69.34	54.69	57.81	62.88

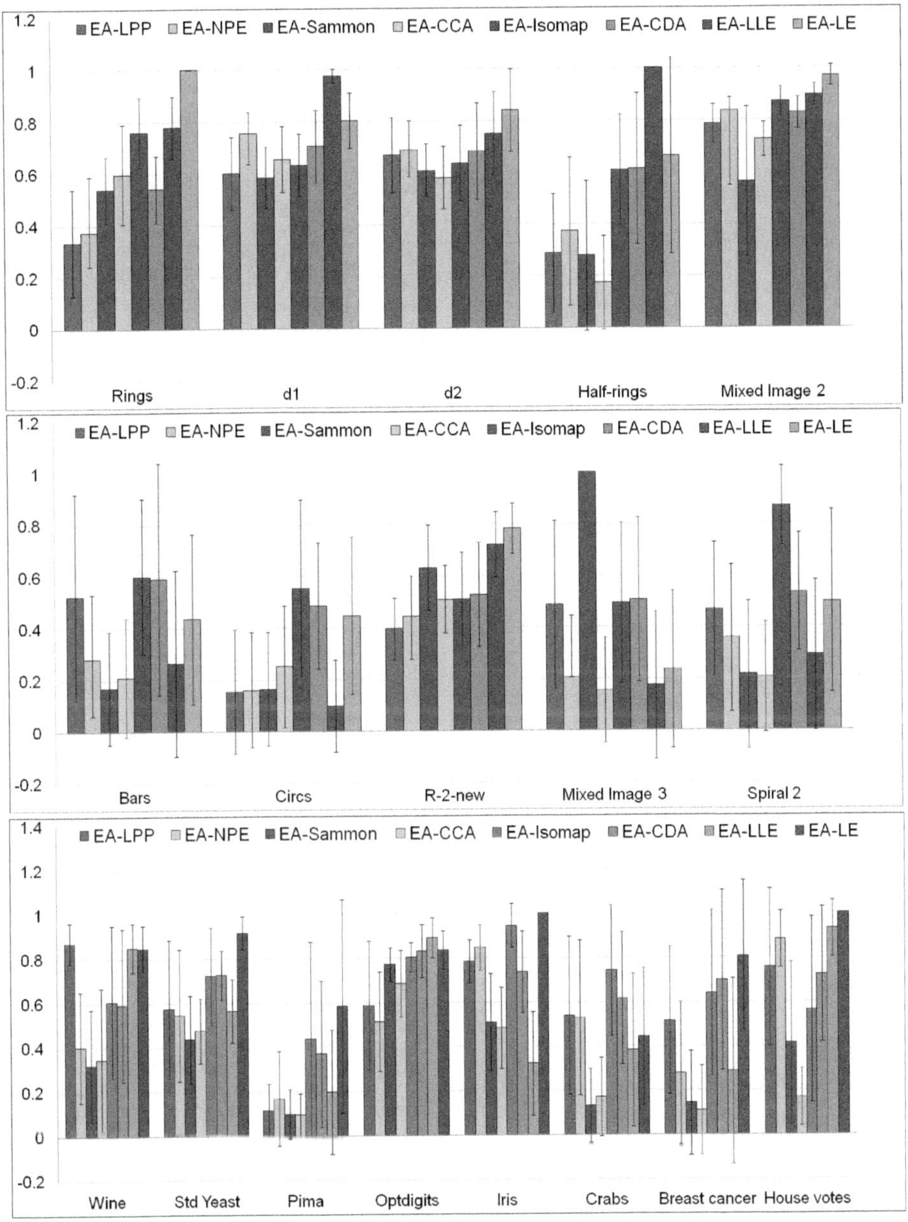

Fig. 3. Mean and standard deviation of Normalized Mutual Information over the clustering algorithms for each dataset and each embedding method. The co-association matrix was interpreted as similarities. *Top:* Synthetic datasets with separate clusters. *Middle:* Synthetic datasets with touching clusters. *Bottom:* Real datasets.

Table 2. Consistency index (%) for co-association matrix interpreted as similarities. *(First row)* Best CI and clustering algorithm(s) which yield that CI value. Legend: (1) k-means, (2) single-link, (3) complete-link, (4) average-link, (5) Ward-link, (6) centroid-link, (7) median-link, (8) weighted-link. *(Second row)* Average CI (%) over all clustering methods. The gray cells correspond to the best NMI presented in figure 3 and the best average CI are shown in bold.

		EAC	EA-LPP	EA-NPE	EA-Sammon	EA-CCA	EA-Isomap	EA-CDA	EA-LLE	EA-LE
Synthetic data with separate clusters	Rings	100	74.00	74.00	77.50	77.50	63.25	79.00	81.00	100
		(2,4,8)	(2)	(2)	(1)	(2)	(7,8)	(1)	(7,8)	(1-8)
		74.79	58.69	56.59	70.41	68.44	61.47	72.53	73.50	**100**
	d1	100	100	90.50	100	100	100	100	90.00	100
		(2,4-8)	(2,4)	(2)	(2)	(2)	(2)	(2,7)	(2)	(2)
		94.07	74.31	69.06	59.62	61.31	67.62	77.06	**87.81**	71.75
	d2	100	100	61.50	66.50	100	88.50	100	100	79.00
		(2)	(2)	(2)	(4)	(2)	(2)	(2)	(2)	(2)
		70.21	59.87	48.56	59.31	60.75	60.06	59.94	56.50	**64.50**
	Half-rings	100	94.75	88.00	81.75	93.25	100	100	100	100
		(2,4,8)	(4)	(8)	(2)	(6)	(2)	(2)	(1-8)	(2,4-8)
		82.86	81.06	80.12	64.59	68.69	79.62	72.41	**100**	90.84
	Mixed Image 2	72.40	67.50	67.70	60.00	70.80	71.00	70.80	66.90	68.10
		(8)	(6)	(2)	(1)	(2)	(2)	(2)	(2)	(2-4,6-8)
		53.34	60.10	61.46	50.72	60.31	63.45	62.81	64.09	**67.05**
Synthetic data with touching clusters	Bars	99.25	100	75.25	69.75	99.50	99.50	74.00	99.00	99.25
		(4)	(5,8)	(1)	(4,6)	(6)	(3,5)	(1)	(4)	(5)
		74.25	88.69	65.53	61.00	77.53	**90.28**	61.84	77.66	69.84
	Circs	99.50	81.00	78.75	82.25	71.00	99.50	99.50	78.75	99.50
		(2,4,5)	(3)	(5)	(1)	(3)	(1,4-6)	(2)	(5)	(2,5)
		76.54	63.50	62.47	66.22	61.37	**88.97**	73.78	63.37	76.47
	R-2-new	89.20	58.80	58.80	65.80	60.60	63.20	79.80	59.80	80.60
		(5)	(2)	(2)	(2)	(2)	(2)	(2)	(2)	(8)
		65.77	44.32	47.55	60.32	45.62	45.12	44.92	53.77	**67.80**
	Mixed Image 3	88.70	92.40	75.00	50.10	85.10	89.60	91.90	82.60	76.10
		(5)	(5)	(5)	(1-8)	(5)	(4)	(3)	(1)	(5)
		67.14	**82.00**	66.34	50.10	68.42	79.95	**82.00**	60.31	68.12
	Spiral 2	85.00	56.33	55.67	65.33	77.67	84.00	91.33	60.33	85.00
		(2)	(4,5,7)	(5,8)	(1)	(2)	(1,5)	(7,8)	(7)	(2,5,7,8)
		63.43	54.29	53.67	58.54	61.00	79.25	**81.92**	54.75	78.79
Real data	Wine	93.82	98.31	73.03	97.75	97.19	94.94	94.94	91.01	91.57
		(8)	(3)	(5)	(1)	(1)	(5)	(4,6)	(2)	(3-6)
		72.12	**92.84**	61.45	70.86	68.40	82.80	82.94	85.74	86.24
	Std Yeast	67.71	72.14	72.14	72.92	72.40	67.45	72.40	51.04	63.28
		(4)	(8)	(5)	(4)	(4)	(7)	(3)	(5)	(4-6,8)
		51.79	**63.38**	59.89	50.13	52.11	60.03	60.87	41.89	61.36
	Pima	65.10	71.35	65.63	64.71	68.49	64.71	64.71	65.76	64.71
		(6,7)	(7)	(6)	(2,4)	(4)	(2,3,6-8)	(2)	(7)	(2-4,6-8)
		62.91	**65.74**	61.95	60.81	60.03	62.04	58.41	64.13	63.49
	Optdigits	80.70	56.60	23.60	81.90	82.70	82.60	80.90	47.10	72.00
		(5)	(5)	(1)	(5)	(5)	(5)	(5)	(5)	(5)
		55.41	43.86	20.92	70.91	64.61	70.74	**72.30**	36.24	60.35
	Iris	90.67	90.00	95.33	89.33	90.67	94.67	90.67	79.33	90.67
		(2,4,5,8)	(4,6)	(1,3,8)	(5)	(2)	(1)	(2)	(1)	(1-8)
		75,62	83.92	88.75	70.75	67.75	**91.17**	71.83	57.25	90.67
	Crabs	71.00	54.00	88.00	70.50	71.00	71.00	71.00	66.00	74.50
		(2)	(1)	(1,4-6)	(5)	(2)	(2)	(2)	(3)	(5)
		57.56	52.06	**78.31**	56.13	56.87	56.87	56.44	62.12	63.44
	Breast Cancer	69.84	95.75	81.41	94.29	85.65	97.07	97.22	88.43	96.05
		(3)	(1,4)	(1)	(1)	(4)	(1)	(1)	(5)	(1)
		62.12	88.54	71.34	75.35	65.96	92.22	**92.90**	72.29	64.79
	House Votes	88.36	90.09	90.09	89.22	94.40	88.36	89.22	59.91	66.81
		(4)	(1)	(4-6)	(3,4)	(4)	(3)	(1)	(3)	(1-8)
		68.53	84.80	**88.79**	72.90	70.53	81.14	85.67	59.54	66.81

with single-link. For the synthetic datasets with touching clusters, the best DR methods are EA-Isomap and EA-LE, when used with the appropriate clustering algorithm.

For the Std Yeast dataset the worst results correspond to nonlinear local DR methods (EA-LLE and EA-LE). For the Optdigits dataset, the worst results correspond to local methods (EA-LPP, EA-NPE, EA-LLE and EA-LE), while nonlinear global methods perform very well. In the House votes dataset, the best DR algorithms in average CI are linear methods (EA-LPP and EA-NPE) and nonlinear global methods that preserves "geodesic" distances (EA-Isomap and EA-CDA). These last two algorithms also have very good results for the Breast cancer dataset.

From Table 2, we notice that there exists at least one DR method that outperforms or equals EAC for each dataset, showing that there is an advantage in performing DR.

Like in the feature space, single-link is the best extraction method, except for real datasets. In real datasets, k-means and Ward link work better.

Overall, nonlinear methods are more suitable for this space, with local methods working better in synthetic data with separate clusters.

6 Discussion

There are some interesting findings to draw from all the above data. First, there is an advantage in using DR techniques on the co-association matrix to improve clustering results. However, care must be taken in choosing the right DR technique for each dataset.

Second, the use of DR techniques usually improves the average consistency index (CI) values over the co-association matrix. This suggests that using DR makes the clustering results less dependent on the choice of the specific clustering algorithm.

Although no DR algorithm consistently outperforms all the others, some algorithms do well in specific circumstances. Good results are obtained from datasets with separate clusters using LPP and LE (local DR methods). For datasets with touching clusters, Isomap and LE (nonlinear DR methods) yield the overall best results. Importantly, in real datasets no DR algorithm stood out from the others, and considerable variability was detected from dataset to dataset, again stressing out that the choice of the appropriate DR technique is crucial.

To further investigate this aspect, we have computed the measures N1[3] and silhouette for the real datasets studied in this paper. Those values are presented in table 3. Datasets Std Yeast and Pima stand out for having high values of N1, and in those datasets local DR methods yield the best clustering results in terms of average CI. On the other hand, datasets Optdigits and Breast Cancer stand out for having low values of N1 and the best results in those datasets come from global DR methods. Also, Crabs and Std Yeast have low values of the silhouette index and local DR methods perform well with these datasets. Given the relatively small number of datasets and DR methods used in this paper, we present these associations not as proven rules, but rather as temporary guidelines. We will actively research these types of associations using more datasets and more DR methods in the future.

[3] As explained in [8] "This method constructs a class-blind minimum spanning tree over the entire dataset, and counts the number of points incident to an edge going across the two classes. The fraction of such points over all points in the dataset is used as the N1 measure."

Table 3. N1 and Silhouette measures for the real datasets studied in this paper, and type of DR method that yields the best average CI for both types of spaces (feature and similarity spaces). The question mark (?) indicates datasets where the best DR type is different in the two spaces.

Real Datasets	N1	Silhouette	Best DR type
Wine	0.118	0.4368	local
Std Yeast	0.388	0.2274	local
Pima	0.438	0.1524	local
Optdigits	0.059	0.2892	global
Iris	0.100	0.6565	?
Crabs	0.160	0.0442	local
Breast Cancer	0.057	0.7178	global
House Votes	0.159	0.4471	?

There are some differences between using the co-association matrix as features or as similarities. For example, CCA and CDA perform poorly in the former case but considerably better in the latter. On the other hand, Sammon performs better in the feature space relative to the similarity space.

It is interesting to note that the DR algorithms which have the highest NMI values for each dataset are very often the ones which have also the highest average CI values. In other words, it seems that the DR algorithms which yield the most consistent partitions also yield the best partitions. Furthermore, for each dataset, the highest NMI between the feature space and the similarity space very often corresponds to the highest average CI as well. This suggests that NMI (a measure which does not need to know the true partition) can help predict the CI (which does use the true partition).

7 Conclusions

This study shows that the use of dimensionality reduction (DR) techniques in clustering ensembles presents interesting advantages in accuracy and robustness. Future work is needed to study the influence of different strategies to construct the clustering ensemble, and the influence of parameter choice for the DR and clustering algorithms.

We also reported some interesting associations between types of datasets and appropriate DR methods; however, further work is needed to draw conclusive information.

Acknowledgments. We acknowledge financial support from the FET programme within the EU FP7, under the SIMBAD project (contract 213250). This work was partially supported by the Portuguese Foundation for Science and Technology (FCT), scholarship number SFRH/BD/39642/2007, and grant PTDC/EIA-CCO/103230/2008.

References

1. Ayad, H.G., Kamel, M.S.: Cluster-based cumulative ensembles. In: Oza, N.C., Polikar, R., Kittler, J., Roli, F. (eds.) MCS 2005. LNCS, vol. 3541, pp. 236–245. Springer, Heidelberg (2005)

2. Belkin, M., Niyogi, P.: Laplacian eigenmaps and spectral techniques for embedding and clustering. In: Advances in Neural Information Processing Systems (NIPS 2001), vol. 14, pp. 585–591 (2002)
3. Demartines, P., Hérault, J.: Curvilinear component analysis: a self-organizing neural network for nonlinear mapping of data sets. IEEE Trans. on Neural Networks 8(1), 148–154 (1997)
4. Fred, A.: Finding consistent clusters in data partitions. In: Kittler, J., Roli, F. (eds.) MCS 2001. LNCS, vol. 2096, pp. 309–318. Springer, Heidelberg (2001)
5. Fred, A., Jain, A.: Combining multiple clusterings using evidence accumulation. IEEE Trans. on Pattern Analysis and Machine Intelligence 27(6), 835–850 (2005)
6. He, X., Cai, D., Yan, S., Zhang, H.J.: Neighborhood preserving embedding. In: Proc. of the 10th Int. Conf. on Computer Vision (ICCV 2005), vol. 2, pp. 1208–1213 (2005)
7. He, X., Niyogi, P.: Locality preserving projections. In: Advances in Neural Information Processing Systems (NIPS 2003), vol. 16 (2004)
8. Ho, T.K., Basu, M., Law, M.H.C.: Measures of Geometrical Complexity in Classification Problems. In: Data Complexity in Pattern Recognition, Advanced Information and Knowledge Processing, 1st edn., vol. 16, pp. 3–23. Springer, Heidelberg (2006)
9. Jain, A.K., Murty, M.N., Flynn, P.J.: Data clustering: a review. ACM Computing Surveys 31(3), 264–323 (1999)
10. Kuncheva, L.I., Hadjitodorov, S.T.: Using diversity in cluster ensembles. In: Proc. of the Int. Conf. on Systems, Man and Cybernetics, vol. 2, pp. 1214–1219 (2004)
11. Kuncheva, L.I., Hadjitodorov, S.T., Todorova, L.P.: Experimental comparison of cluster ensemble methods. In: Proc. of the 9th Int. Conf. on Information Fusion, FUSION 2006 (2006)
12. Lee, J.A., Verleysen, M.: Nonlinear Dimensionality Reduction. Information Science and Statistics. Springer, Heidelberg (2007)
13. Lee, J.A., Lendasse, A., Verleysen, M.: Nonlinear projection with curvilinear distances: Isomap versus curvilinear distance analysis. Neurocomputing 57, 49–76 (2004)
14. Roweis, S.T., Saul, L.K.: Nonlinear dimensionality reduction by locally linear embedding. Science 290, 2323–2326 (2000)
15. Sammon, J.W.: A nonlinear mapping for data structure analysis. IEEE Trans. on Computers 18(5), 401–409 (1969)
16. Strehl, A., Ghosh, J.: Cluster ensembles - a knowledge reuse framework for combining multiple partitions. Journal of Machine Learning Research 3, 583–617 (2002)
17. Tenenbaum, J.B., de Silva, V., Langford, J.C.: A global geometric framework for nonlinear dimensionality reduction. Science 290, 2319–2323 (2000)
18. Theodoridis, S., Koutroumbas, K.: Pattern Recognition. Elsevier Academic Press (2003)

A Study on the Influence of Shape in Classifying Small Spectral Data Sets

Diana Porro-Muñoz[1,2], Robert P.W. Duin[2], Isneri Talavera[1], and Mauricio Orozco-Alzate[3]

[1] Advanced Technologies Application Center (CENATAV), Cuba
[2] Pattern Recognition Lab, TU Delft, The Netherlands
[3] Universidad Nacional de Colombia Sede Manizales, Colombia
{dporro,italavera}@cenatav.co.cu,r.duin@ieee.org, morozcoa@bt.unal.edu.co

Abstract. Classification of spectral data has raised a growing interest in may research areas. However, this type of data usually suffers from the curse of dimensionality. This causes most statistical methods and/or classifiers to not perform well. A recently proposed alternative which can help avoiding this problem is the Dissimilarity Representation, in which objects are represented by their dissimilarities to representative objects of each class. However, this approach depends on the selection of a suitable dissimilarity measure. For spectra, the incorporation of information on their shape, can be significant for a good discrimination. In this paper, we make a study on the benefit of using a measure which takes shape of spectra into account. We show that the shape-based measure not only leads to better classification results, but that a certain number of objects is enough to achieve it. The experiments are conducted on three one-dimensional data sets and a two-dimensional one.

Keywords: Object representation, classification,small sample size, dissimilarity representation, spectral data.

1 Introduction

Classification of unknown objects is one of the main problems in many research areas. Object representation plays an important role in this task. In practical classification problems, the number of training samples is usually very small, represented by a very large number of features which are not always the best to describe them. Many studies have been done on this issue; when only a certain number of objects is available, a peaking phenomenon occurs in the classification accuracy as the number of features is increased. This is known as the curse of dimensionality [1, 2, 3]. Hence, the ideal situation in order to obtain a good classifier would be to have at least as many samples as features. It appears to be difficult to achieve this in a number of real-world problems.

A type of data which has raised a growing interest in advanced approaches to its automatic analysis is the spectral data. It is due to the increasing possibilities

M. Pelillo and E.R. Hancock (Eds.): SIMBAD 2011, LNCS 7005, pp. 306–320, 2011.

of the different research fields e.g. chemometrics and signal processing, to obtain it, and the usefulness of the spectral information to describe and differentiate samples of different classes. This is the type of application where data sets are small because the cost to obtain them is very high, and they are usually much smaller than the dimensionality of the space. The traditional way of representing spectra is by sampling, as a sequence of individual observations made on the objects. The higher the sampling resolution, the more accurate the spectrum is described, which implies a representation in a high-dimensional space. However, this way of representation is not good for traditional procedures. It makes them suffer the curse of dimensionality. Furthermore, discriminative knowledge about spectra e.g. the continuity between the measured values, shape, is not taken into account in the traditional high-dimensional feature-based representation. Thus, it does not help avoiding the problem.

Recent works have studied alternative object representations instead of features, demonstrating that the curse of dimensionality can be avoided [3]. A recently developed alternative in the field of pattern recognition is the Dissimilarity Representation (DR) [4]. It is based on the important role that pairwise dissimilarities between objects play. Classifiers may be built in the dissimilarity space generated by a representation set. In this way, the geometry and the structure of a class are determined by a user defined dissimilarity measure, in which application background information may be expressed. It is important to remark that, any traditional classifier that is defined on feature spaces can also be used in the dissimilarity space.

With the DR, the problem of building classifiers in high-dimensional spaces can be tackled, as the dimensionality will depend now on the size of the representation set (usually smaller or equal to the size of the training set). However, the main issue in this approach is the selection of a suitable measure for the problem at hand. The more discriminative information we take into account when designing the dissimilarity measure, the more compact the classes are. The centroid of the data should remain approximately the same and the average distance to this mean should decrease or be constant [3], requiring less samples for its description and a good classification accuracy.

Due to benefits that the DR has shown, it has been explored in several applications like the discrimination of spectral data [4, 5, 6, 7]. In this paper, we will make an exhaustive experimental study on the DR for spectral data. We will focus on the usefulness of taking the shape of the curve into account in the dissimilarity measure. It will be shown that this can help achieving good classification results in small sample size problems. Recently, the use of the DR was also extended to 2D spectral data i.e. objects represented by matrices, where two types of spectral features are described [8]. Thus, the study will be generalized to this type of data. We will use three one-dimensional spectral data set and a 2D spectral one. In the experiments we compare the classification accuracy in measures which do not take shape into account with a measure which does. This analysis is done for several training set sizes and representation set sizes, to see how the measures influence the results. Moreover, for the measure which takes shape into account, we study the sensitivity of the results to the optimization of the parameters (Gaussian filter parameter). The paper is structured as follows. In Section 2, a brief introduction to the DR will be done. Also, the 1D and 2D measures to be used in the experiments are referenced. Following, the data sets and experiments will be described in Section 3. Finally, a discussion and the drawn conclusions will be presented in Section 4.

2 Introduction to Dissimilarity Representation Approach

The Dissimilarity Representation (DR) [4] was proposed as a more flexible representation of the objects than the feature representation, with the purpose of having more information about the structure of the objects. It is seen as a link between the statistical and structural approaches, as both types of patterns can be described by the (dis)similarity measure. The DR is also based on the role that (dis)similarities play in a class composition. Objects from the same class should be similar and objects from different classes should be different (compactness property). Hence, it should be easier for the classifiers to discriminate between them.

Using the DR, classifiers are trained in the space of the proximities between objects, instead of the traditional feature space. Thus, in place of the feature matrix $\mathbf{X} \in \mathbb{R}^{n \times q}$, where **n** runs over the objects and **q** over the variables, the set of objects is represented by the matrix $\mathbf{D}(\mathbf{X}, \mathbf{R})$. This matrix contains the dissimilarity values $d(x_i, r_j)$ between each object x_i of $\mathbf{X}$ and the objects r_j of the representation set $\mathbf{R}(r_1, ..., r_h)$. We build from this matrix a dissimilarity space. Objects are represented in this space by the column vectors of the dissimilarity matrix. Each dimension corresponds to the dissimilarities with one of the representation objects.

When an object is represented by a matrix $\mathbf{Y} \in \mathbb{R}^{m \times l}$, the theory of the DR is the same [8]. In fact, one of the advantages of the DR is that it can be generated from any representation of the objects e.g. vectors of numbers, graphs, as long as we have a proper dissimilarity measure. Hence, to obtain the dissimilarity space, a mapping $\phi(\cdot, R) : \mathbb{R}^{m \times l} \to \mathbb{R}^h$ is defined, such that for every object $\mathbf{Y}$, $\phi(\mathbf{Y}, R) = [d(\mathbf{Y}, r_1), d(\mathbf{Y}, r_2), ..., d(\mathbf{Y}, r_h)]$. Classifiers are then built in this space, as in any feature space.

The elements of $\mathbf{R}$ are called prototypes, and have preferably to be selected by a prototype selection method [4]. These prototypes are usually the most representative objects of each class, $\mathbf{R} \subseteq \mathbf{X}$ or $\mathbf{X}$ itself, resulting in a square dissimilarity $\mathbf{D}(\mathbf{X}, \mathbf{X})$. $\mathbf{R}$ and $\mathbf{X}$ can also be chosen as different sets. As dissimilarities are computed to $\mathbf{R}$, a dimensionality reduction is reached if a good, small set can be found, resulting in less computationally expensive classifiers.

2.1 1D and 2D Dissimilarity Measures for Spectral Data

A general dissimilarity measure for all types of data does not exist. Thus, the selection of the suitable measure for the problem at hand is the key issue in the DR approach. In recent studies, some 1D [6, 9] and 2D [8] measures have been studied and proposed for spectral data. Such is the case of the very well known Manhattan (L1-norm) and Euclidean distances. However, although the previous dissimilarities are of the most used measures in the comparisons of chemical spectral data, the connectivity between the measured variables and/or shape, is not taken into account in neither of them. The variables could be easily reordered and the same dissimilarity value is obtained.

In [6], the authors propose to compute the Manhattan measure on the first Gaussian derivatives (See Eq. 1) of the curves (Shape measure). Thereby, the shape information that can be obtained from the derivatives is taken into account:

$$d(x_1, x_2) = \sum_{j=1}^{m} |x_{1j}^{\sigma} - x_{2j}^{\sigma}|, \quad x^{\sigma} = \frac{\mathrm{d}}{\mathrm{d}_j} G(j, \sigma) * x \tag{1}$$

The expression of x^{σ} corresponds to the computation of the first Gaussian (that is what G stands for) derivatives of spectra. A smoothing (blurring) is done by a convolution process ($*$) with a gaussian filter and σ stands for the smoothing parameter. Good performances have been obtained for chemical spectral data with this measure [6, 9].

For the 2D representation of objects, generalizations of the Manhattan and Euclidean distances have also been proposed. Assume that two objects y_a and $y_b \in \mathbb{R}^{m \times l}$, where m and l are the number of variables in each of the two directions respectively; $\forall j = 1, 2, \ldots, m$ and $k = 1, 2, \ldots, l$. Then, the AMD measure [10] is defined as:

$$d_{AMD}(y_a, y_b) = \left(\sum_{k=1}^{l} \left(\sum_{j=1}^{m} (y_{a,j,k} - y_{b,j,k})^2 \right)^{p/2} \right)^{1/p} \tag{2}$$

The power p is used to emphasize either small or large differences between the elements, depending on the problem at hand. If $p < 1$, all the differences are reduced, thus the larger ones do not interfere much in the measure. On the other hand, if $p > 1$, the larger differences will be more pronounced, resulting in a heavy influence on the measure. This measure is a generalization of the Frobenius [11] and Yang [12] distance measures. When $p = 1$ in AMD, it is the same as the Yang distance, and for $p = 2$ is then the Frobenius distance.

These measures could be a good option when the spectral (functional) information can be assumed to be present in the data representation. However, this is not the case. Recently, considering the results obtained with the Shape measure for simple spectra, a new version for 2D spectral data (2Dshape measure) was introduced [8]:

1. Compute the matrix D^1

$$D_{a,b}^1 = \left(\sum_{k=1}^{l} \left(\sum_{j=1}^{m} (y_{a,j,k}^{\sigma} - y_{b,j,k}^{\sigma})^2 \right)^{p_1/2} \right)^{1/p_1}, \quad y_{i,j,\cdot}^{\sigma} = \frac{\mathrm{d}}{\mathrm{d}_j} G(j, \sigma) * y_{i,j,\cdot}$$

2. Compute the matrix D^2

$$D^2_{a,b} = \left(\sum_{j=1}^{m}\left(\sum_{k=1}^{l}(y^{\sigma}_{a,j,k} - y^{\sigma}_{b,j,k})^2\right)^{p_2/2}\right)^{1/p_2}, \quad y^{\sigma}_{i,\cdot,k} = \frac{\mathrm{d}}{\mathrm{d}_k}G(k,\sigma) * y_{i,\cdot,k}$$

3. Combine both dissimilarities matrices $D = \alpha_1 D^1 + \alpha_2 D^2$

The variables $y_{i,j,\cdot}$ and $y_{i,\cdot,k}$, stand for the k-th columns and the j-th rows of the i-th matrix (object); $\forall i = 1, 2, \ldots, n$. Their expressions correspond to the computation of the first Gaussian (that is what G stands for) derivatives of spectra, as in the 1D measure. The dissimilarities in step 1 and step 2 correspond to the first and second directions respectively, as indicated by the notation e.g. spectra and time. This measure can also be used in three-way data where there are no variations in shape in one of the directions. In this case, it is enough to use the AMD measure in step 1 or step 2 only, such that only the differences in area are compared. With this measure, the connectivity between the measured points can be taken into account as well as the shape of the spectra.

The previously mentioned measures, which have been used for spectral data, will be used for the purpose of this paper.

3 Experimental Section

For the purpose of this paper, a set of experiments were conducted on small sample size data sets in high-dimensional spaces. Only one of them does not suffer from this problem, but still we want to show how also in this case, with the selection of a suitable dissimilarity measure, a reduced number of training samples can be enough to obtain good classification results with the DR. All of them consist of two-class classification problems. The data sets are described in the following subsection.

3.1 Data sets

The first data set, named Tecator, originates from the food industry [13]. It consists of 215 near infrared absorbance spectra of meat samples, recorded on a Tecator Infratec Food and Feed Analyzer. Each observation consists in a 100 channel absorbance spectrum in the 850-1050 nm wavelength range. It is associated to a content description of meat sample, obtained by analytic chemistry. The classification problem consists in separating 77 meat samples with a high fat content (more than 20%), from 138 samples with a low fat content (less than 20%). Original spectra are preprocessed, each spectrum is reduced to zero mean and unit variance.

The second data set is a real-world data set, which was obtained from a cooperation with the Oil Industry in Cuba. It consists of 31 fuel samples of Fourier Transform Infrared (FT-IR) transmittance spectra in a wavelength range of 600-4000 cm^{-1}. A base line correction and smoothing were performed on the data. The classification problem consists in determining the fuel type of the samples: regular gasoline (16 samples) and especial gasoline (15 samples).

The third data set is another fuel real-world data set of 44 samples measured at 127 wavelengths in a range of 275-220 nm, but this time measures have been taken by a Ultra-Violet Visible (UV) spectrofotometer. The classification problem consists also in determining the fuel type of the samples: regular gasoline (23 samples) and especial gasoline (21 samples).

The fourth and last data set is a three-dimensional array, composed of objects naturally represented by 2D arrays. It is a public domain data set and the description has been taken from the website [14, 15] for a better understanding of this paper. It consists of samples of red wine belonging to different geographical areas and producers. They were analyzed by means of HS-GC-MS (headspace gas chromatography/mass spectrometry). Separation of aroma compounds was carried out on a gas chromatography system (2700 columns from the scans of chromatographic profile). For each sample, a mass spectrum scan (m/z: 5-204) measured at the 2700 elution time-points was obtained, providing a data cube of size $44 \times 2700 \times 200$ i.e. samples (objects) in first direction, elution time points in second direction and mass spectrum in third direction. The data set is composed of samples from 2 different geographical areas: South America (21 samples) and Australia (12 samples).

3.2 Experiments and Discussion

A set of experiments are conducted on the four data sets. A Fisher classifier is built on the dissimilarity space obtained for the two dissimilarity measures which do no take shape information into account (Manhattan and Euclidean) and also for the Shape measure. For the later, several experiments are shown, with different values for parameter σ. In the figures, learning curves are shown for various sizes of training and representation sets. The main idea of this experimental set up is to show how the use of a suitable measure e.g. measures shape in spectral data, can influence not only in the classifiers accuracy, but on the sample size problem.

Training and test objects were randomly chosen from the total data sets in a 10-fold cross-validation process, when the size of the training set allowed it. When the sizes of the training set was too small, a leave-one-out cross-validation was done. Experiments were repeated 10 times. For the training set of different sizes, a random selection of $[25, 30, 40, 50, 60, 70, 80$ and $90\%]$ is done from the total dissimilarity matrix. Different sizes for the representation set were also randomly selected $[10, 30, 50, 70$ and $80\%]$ of the total data set. When using the Shape measure on the one-dimensional spectral data, the following values of σ were applied $[0.5, 1, 2, 3, 5, 7]$.

In the case of the Wine 2D spectral data, in the mass direction the classes only differ because they have different components. Therefore, the only thing we will see is the absence/presence of the peak or some differences in the concentration of the mass fragments. The other difference that we can find between these classes is related to the shape changes between the eluded components in the chromatogram i.e. how the concentration of one of the peaks varies with respect to the others, for the several classes. Thus, for the Wine data set we will use the 2Dshape measure. The D1 matrix will be computed for the chromatography direction. The Gaussian derivatives are applied to take into account the shape in the changes of concentration in the neighboring components. In this case, the following values of σ were applied [1, 2, 5 and 8]. However, for the D2 matrix from the mass spectra mode, we will only compute the overall sum of the differences between the concentration of the mass fragments. The use of derivatives is meaningless, because there is no continuity between the mass fragments.

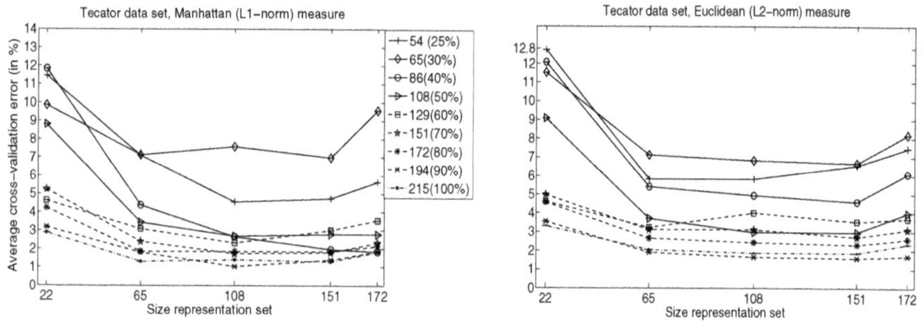

(a) (b)

Fig. 1. Average cross-validation error (in %) for Tecator data set with (a) Manhattan and (b) Euclidean measures. The classifiers accuracy is analyzed for nine training set sizes and five representation set sizes.

In Figure 1 we can observe the same behavior for both measures: Manhattan(1(a)) and Euclidean (1(b)). Classifiers may perform better sometimes in one or the other. However, for both of them the classification error decreases as the training set and representation sets increase. When the training sets are too small, the errors are far higher that for larger training sets. On the other side, for larger training sets, the classification accuracy does not differ that much for different sizes (taking the standard deviation into account). There is even a point, where results are better or the same with 90% of the data, that with the full data set. Nevertheless, due to the so-called peaking phenomenon, when the number of prototypes starts reaching the size of the training set, the errors will increase.

Let us take a look at the results with the Shape measure (See Figure 2). Results have improved with respect to the dissimilarity measures which do not take the shape information into account. Of course, this is not for all values of σ. the optimization of the parameter does influence the results. From Figures 2(a) to 2(d), we can see that results are pretty much stable for all sizes of the training set. Although for $\sigma = 2$ and $\sigma = 3$, the classification errors start increasing. It seems that the parameter σ is better fixed to the data in the first two. Here, if we take the standard deviation of the ten repetitions (around 0.5 the highest) into account, there is

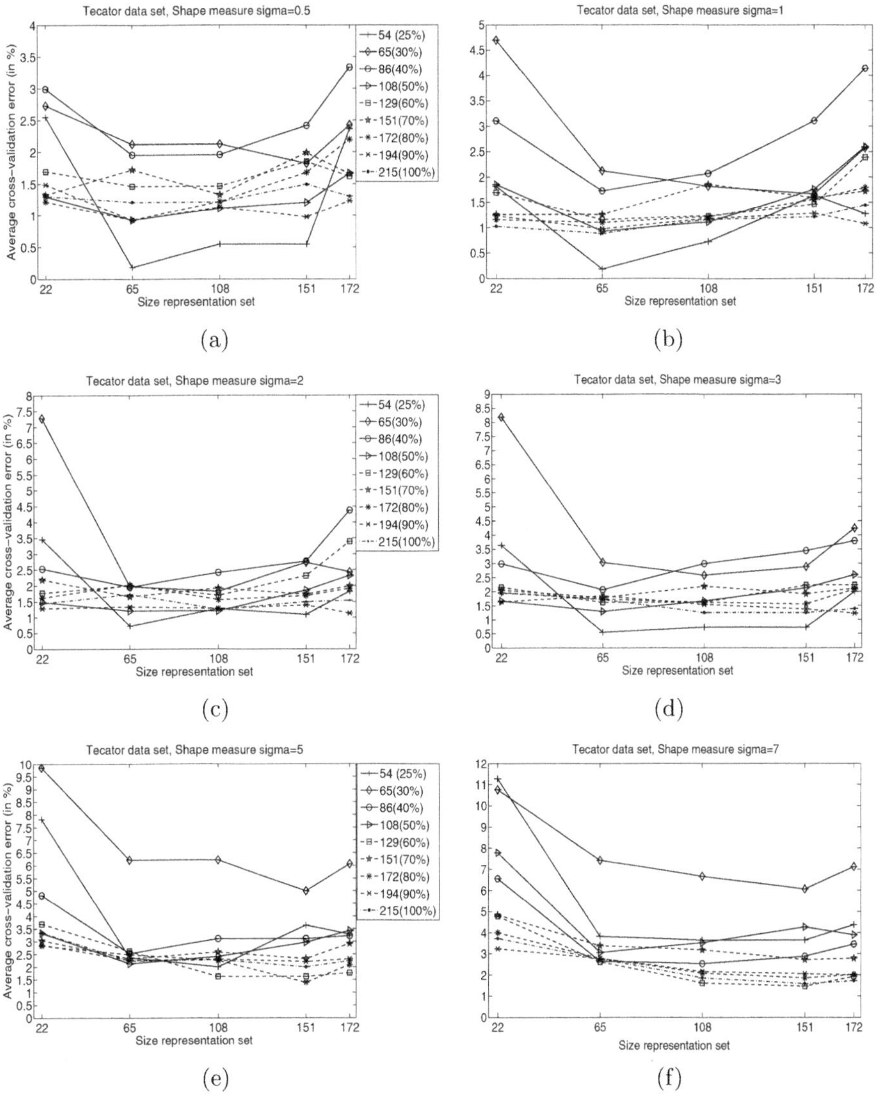

Fig. 2. Average cross-validation error (in %) for Tecator data set with Shape distance and different values of sigma for (a) sigma=0.5, (b) sigma=1, (c) sigma=2, (d) sigma=3, (e) sigma=5 and (f) sigma=7. The classifiers accuracy is analyzed for nine training set sizes and five representation set sizes.

not much difference between using the smallest and the largest sample size. Thus, it seems that with this measure, a small training set is enough to reach even better results than with the other measures. In fact, in this case, the best results are always achieved with the smallest size of the training set. However, the results with 30% of the data are the highest, which could be influenced by the random selection of

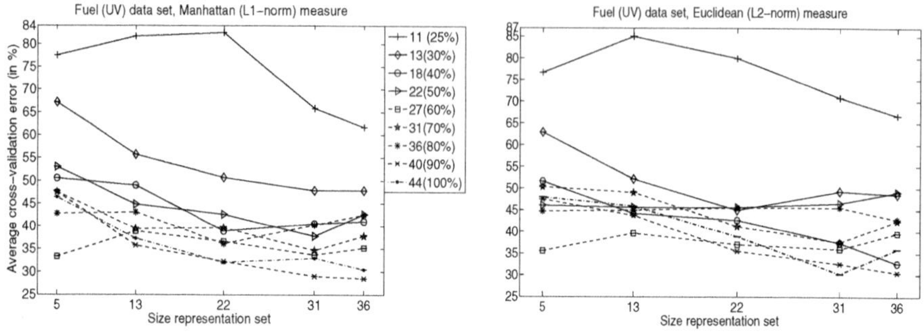

(a) (b)

Fig. 3. Average cross-validation error (in %) for Fuel (UV) data set with (a) Manhattan and (b) Euclidean measures. The classifiers accuracy is analyzed for nine training set sizes and five representation set sizes.

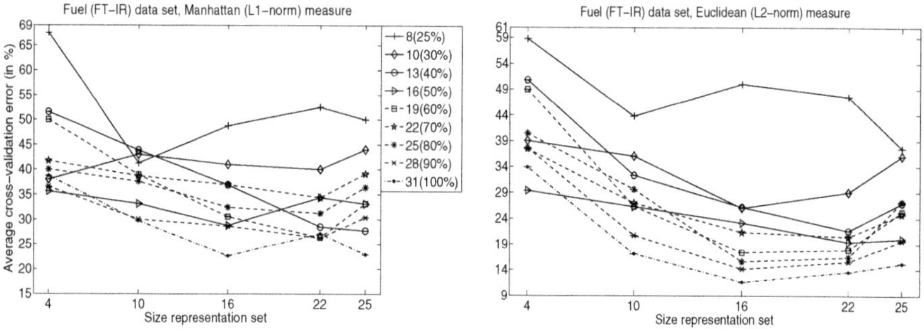

(a) (b)

Fig. 4. Average cross-validation error (in %) for Fuel (FT-IR) data set with (a) Manhattan and (b) Euclidean measures. The classifiers accuracy is analyzed for nine training set sizes and five representation set sizes.

the samples. For the last two values of σ, the results keep increasing a lot, it can be due to the data is so smooth, that the measure starts failing. Thus, the importance of the optimization of the parameter.

With respect to the representation set, for all values of σ, the error always increases while the training set decreases, with the smallest representation set. It seems that the representation set is not representative enough. However, from that point on, the errors always start decreasing, until reaching the size of the training set, where they start increasing again due to the peaking phenomena.

With the two fuel data sets, we are facing a very complicated classification problem: discrimination of special and regular fuel, thereby the classification accuracy is not very good. Moreover, these are both affected by the small sample size problem. In Figures 3 and 4, we can observe the same phenomena as in the first figure. The errors decreasing while the size of the training set increases. In both cases, the results with the smallest sample size are far much higher; in this case the number of samples is really small.

However, if we take a look at Figure 5, we can see that with the Shape measure, for some values of σ parameter, the classifiers perform a lot better than for the Manhattan and Euclidean measures. With respect to the size of the training set, the behavior is a bit different. For the smaller sample sizes, the errors are very high, as in Figure 3. In this case, it can be explained by the fact that the original data suffers already from the small sample size problem. Thus, it would be too much to expect an improvement with so little samples. Nevertheless, from 60% of the data on, if we take the standard deviation into account, the results are very similar (for the σ with which the better results are obtained).

For the Fuel data set from FT-IR, we can see a bigger improvement by using the Shape measure than with the UV. This could be determined by the characteristics of the instrumental technique. It seems that the information obtained from the FT-IR spectra is more discriminative than that of UV-VIS. However, due to the small sample size problem, with the smallest training sets the results are still high. There is no sufficient data. Again, for the best σ values, the errors for the larger training sets, start behave very similar (taking standard deviation). It can also be noticed that for 40% of the whole data set, the best results are always achieved. It could be due to in the selection process, noisy data that could be affecting the results are no included.

The next data set is the three-way Wine data, where samples are represented by high-dimensional 2D matrices. In this case, we also compared the measures which take the shape information into account with does which do not. This is also a small sample size problem, in a very high-dimensional space. When analyzing the AMD measure with different values of p, which are the homologous for the Manhattan and Euclidean measures for one-dimensional data, the behavior is similar(See Figure 7). Although in this case the learning curve are a bit rough, we can see how the error decreases meanwhile the size of the training set increases.

In this case, although there is no shape information in both directions, it can be seen that the results also improve (See Figure 8) when taking this information into account (in the needed direction). If we take a look at the learning curve for all training set sizes, the best results are for $\sigma = 5$, so it seems to be the best value for this parameter, in the range experimented. For this type of data, we can also observe, how by including certain discriminative knowledge in the measure i.e. shape, the results improve. With very small sample sizes the errors are still high (the available data is not enough to learn well). But, when the size of the training sets start increasing, the errors are similar for most sizes (taking standard deviation into account). In which seems to be the best value for σ, the best results are achieved again, with only 50% of the total data set. Maybe, some noisy data which are influencing the results, are removed.

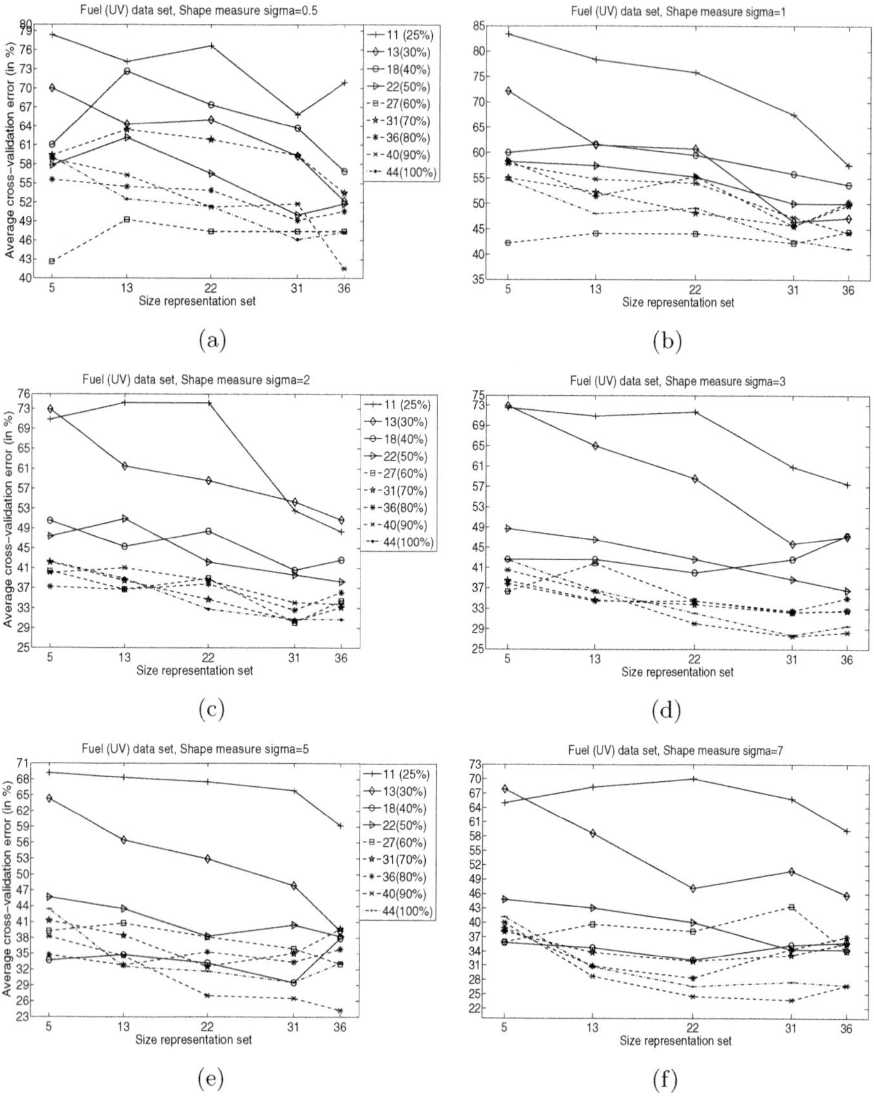

Fig. 5. Average cross-validation error (in %) for Fuel (UV) data set with Shape distance and different values of sigma for (a) sigma=0.5, (b) sigma=1, (c) sigma=2, (d) sigma=3, (e) sigma=5 and (f) sigma=7. The classifiers accuracy is analyzed for nine training set sizes and five representation set sizes.

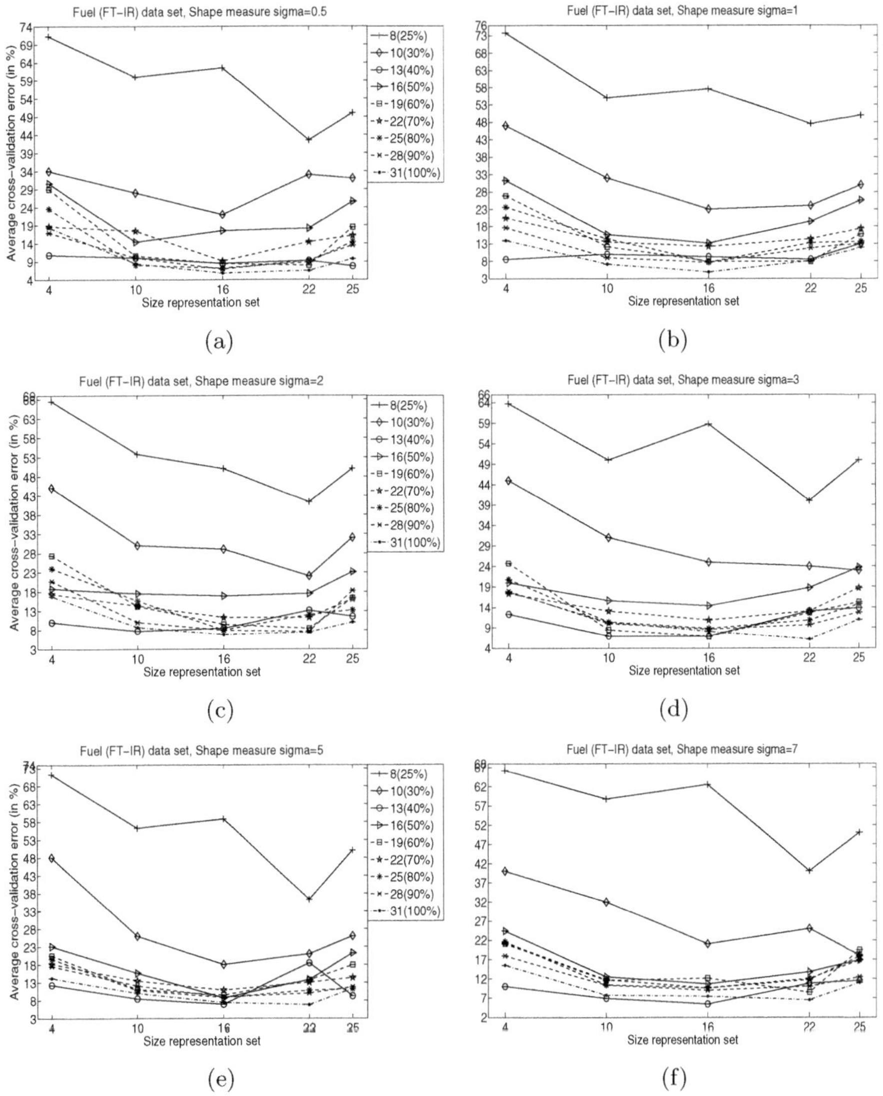

Fig. 6. Average cross-validation error (in %) for Fuel (FT-IR) data set with Shape distance and different values of sigma for (a) sigma=0.5, (b) sigma=1, (c) sigma=2, (d) sigma=3, (e) sigma=5 and (f) sigma=7. The classifiers accuracy is analyzed for nine training set sizes and five representation set sizes.

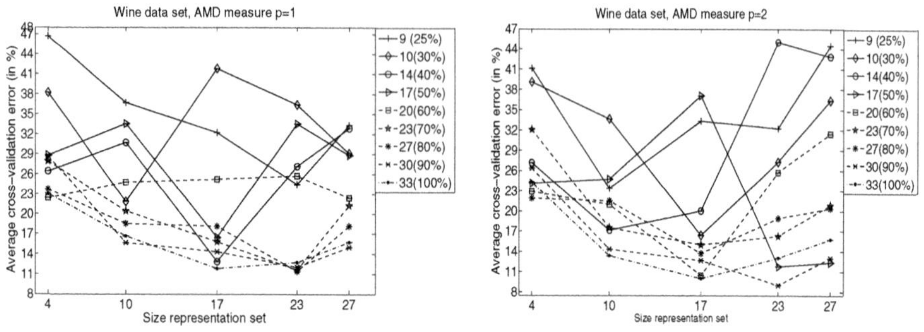

(a) (b)

Fig. 7. Average cross-validation error (in %) for Wine three-way data set with (a) Yang (AMD p=1) and (b) Frobenius (AMD p=2) measures. The classifiers accuracy is analyzed for nine training set sizes and five representation set sizes.

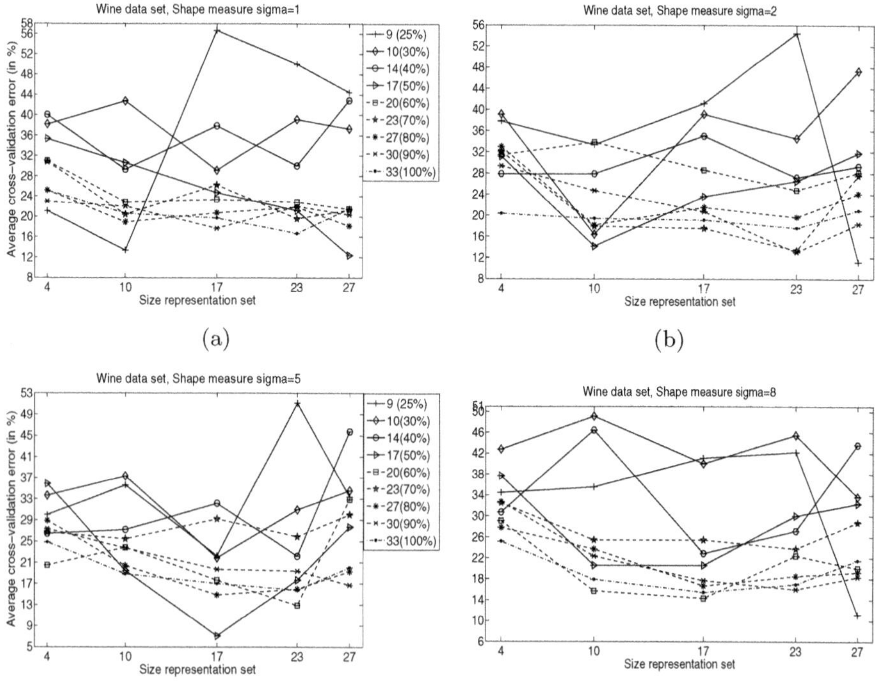

(a) (b)

(c) (d)

Fig. 8. Average cross-validation error (in %) for Wine three-way data set with Shape distance and different values of sigma for (a) sigma=1, (b) sigma=2, (c) sigma=5, (d) sigma=8, (e) sigma=10 and (f) sigma=15. The classifiers accuracy is analyzed for nine training set sizes and five representation set sizes.

4 Discussion and Conclusions

The small sample size problem in high-dimensional spaces is very common in spectral data. Many statistical methods and classifiers fail with this type of data. Alternative representations for such data, to improve classification accuracy, have been explored. Such is the case of the Dissimilarity Representation. However, the key issue of this approach relies on the selection of a suitable dissimilarity measure for the problem at hand. In the case of spectral data, a discriminative feature is the knowledge about the connection between the neighboring points and shape.

In our experimental study, we showed the importance of taking the shape of the curve into account for the success of the DR. Even when we are facing small sample size problems, if we use the shape information, a few samples are enough for classifiers to learn better. For all data sets, there is some size for the training set (usually smaller than the original data size), from which adding new objects will not make much of a difference. This was also experimented, in a not so small data set, and we reached the same conclusions. In this case, we also benefit from lowering the computational complexity of the classifier. This behavior is not the same for measures which do not take discriminative information into account i.e. Manhattan, Euclidean or AMD for 2D data. In this case, the errors are smaller the larger the training set, so we are not solving a small sample size problem, as we would need more samples for the classifiers to learn better.

From the experiments with the measures which take shape into account i.e. Shape and 2Dshape, we can also observe the influence of the optimization of the Gaussian filter parameter. There is always a value of σ for which the classification results are better than without measuring shape. It also stabilizes the learning curves of the different sizes of training set, which are around the same performance.

The representation set is also very important. In all experiments we can observe that even with the large data set (Tecator) the error always increases while the training set decreases, with the smallest representation set. It seems that the representation set is not representative enough. However, from that point on, the errors always start decreasing, until reaching the size of the training set, where they start increasing again due to the peaking phenomena. However, these experiments are all based on two-class classification problems; for multi-class problems, further studies should be done.

In conclusion, the incorporation of shape information in the dissimilarity representation is important for the discrimination of spectral data. It helps avoiding the curse of dimensionality problem, allowing classifiers to perform well in small sample size situations.

Acknowledgment. We acknowledge financial support from the FET programme within the EU FP7, under the project "Similarity-based Pattern Analysis and Recognition - SIMBAD" (contract 213250). We would also like to thank to the project Cálculo científico para caracterización e identificación en problemas dinámicos (code Hermes 10722) granted by Universidad Nacional de Colombia.

References

[1] Fukunaga, K., Hayes, R.: Effects of sample size in classifier design. IEEE Transactions on Pattern Analysis and Machine Intelligence 11(8), 873–885 (1991)
[2] Raudys, S.J., Jain, A.K.: Small sample size effects in statistical pattern recognition: Recommendations for practitioners. IEEE Transactions on Pattern Analysis and Machine Intelligence 3(3), 252–264 (1991)
[3] Classifiers in almost empty spaces. In: 15th International Conference on Pattern Recognition, Barcelona, Spain, vol. 2. IEEE Computer Society, Los Alamitos (2000)
[4] Pekalska, E., Duin, R.P.W.: The Dissimilarity Representation For Pattern Recognition. Foundations and Applications. World Scientific, Singapore (2005)
[5] Orozco-Alzate, M., García, M.E., Duin, R.P.W., Castellanos, C.G.: Dissimilarity-based classification of seismic signals at Nevado del Ruiz Volcano. Earth Sci. Res. J. 10(2), 57–65 (2006)
[6] Paclik, P., Duin, R.P.W.: Dissimilarity-based classification of spectra: computational issues. Real Time Imaging 9(4), 237–244 (2003)
[7] Porro-Muñoz, D., Talavera, I., Duin, R.P.W., Hernández, N., Orozco-Alzate, M.: Dissimilarity representation on functional spectral data for classification. Journal of Chemometrics Early View (2011)
[8] Porro-Muñoz, D., Duin, R.P.W., Orozco-Alzate, M., Talavera, I., Londoño-Bonilla, J.M.: The dissimilarity representation as a tool for three-way data classification: A 2D measure. In: Hancock, E.R., Wilson, R.C., Windeatt, T., Ulusoy, I., Escolano, F. (eds.) SSPR&SPR 2010. LNCS, vol. 6218, pp. 569–578. Springer, Heidelberg (2010)
[9] Porro-Muñoz, D., Talavera, I., Duin, R.P.W., Hernández, N.: The representation of chemical spectral data for classification. In: Bayro-Corrochano, E., Eklundh, J.-O. (eds.) CIARP 2009. LNCS, vol. 5856, pp. 513–520. Springer, Heidelberg (2009)
[10] Zuo, W., Zhang, D., Wang, K.: An assembled matrix distance metric for 2DPCA-based image recognition. Pattern Recognition Letters 27, 210–216 (2006)
[11] Yang, J., Yang, J.Y.: From image vector to matrix: A straightforward image projection technique-IMPCA vs. PCA. Pattern Recognition 35, 1997–1999 (2002)
[12] Yang, J., Zhang, D., Frangi, A., Yang, J.Y.: Two-dimensional PCA: A new approach to appearance-based face representation and recognition. IEEE Trans. Pattern Anal. Machine Intell 26(1), 131–137 (2004)
[13] Thodberg, H.H.: Tecator dataset, Danish Meat Research Institute (1995), `http://www.lib.stat.cmu.edu/datasets/tecator`
[14] Skov, T.: Wine dataset (2008), `http://www.models.kvl.dk/datasets.html`
[15] Skov, T., Ballabio, D., Bro, R.: Multiblock variance partitioning. A new approach for comparing variation in multiple data blocks. Analytica Chimica Acta 615(1), 18–29 (2008)

Feature Point Matching Using a Hermitian Property Matrix

Muhammad Haseeb and Edwin R. Hancock

Department of Computer Science, The University of York, UK

Abstract. This paper describes the computation of feature point correspondences using the spectra of a Hermitian property matrix. Firstly, a complex Laplacian (Hermitian) matrix is constructed from the Gaussian-weighted distances and the difference of SIFT [10] angles between each pair of points in the two images to be matched. Matches are computed by comparing the complex eigenvectors of the Hermitian property matrices for the two point sets acquired from the two images. Secondly, we embed the complex modal structure within Carcassoni's [12] iterative alignment method to render it more robust to rotation. Our method has been evaluated on both synthetic and real-world data.

Keywords: Graph matching, Feature point correspondence, Complex Laplacian, Hermitian matrix, EM algorithm.

1 Introduction

Feature-point matching is one of the most important tasks in computer vision. The problem of feature correspondence matching is to find a one-to-one correspondence between feature points in a pair of images. Graph spectral techniques solve the problem using the eigenvectors and eigenvalues based on the adjacency matrix or the Laplacian matrix (degree minus adjacency) for the point set arrangement. Correspondence matchings are computed by embedding the graphs into a common eigenspace using an eigen-decomposition of the point-proximity matrices, where correspondences are computed by closest point matching in this eigenspace.

Recently, there have been many attempts to use spectral graph theory both in graph matching and point-set matching problems. The work of Umeyama [13] is one of the earliest to use eigen-decomposition of the adjacency matrix for graphs of the same size to locate the correspondence matching. The optimum matching between two weighted graphs is found by locating the least-square permutation matrix. Scott and Longuet-Higgins [6] developed an algorithm to match $2D$ feature-points in two images. They used singular value decomposition on a Gaussian-weighted point association matrix between points from two different images. This method copes with $2D$ translations, expansion and shears. (i.e. affine distortions). However, since this algorithm does not include the structural information within the image and gives equal importance to all the feature points, it fails to correctly match the points especially, where there is a large inter-image rotation. Pilu [4] improved Scott and Longuet-Higgins method by adding the similarity information to compute the point association matrix. Similarity information is computed as the normalized correlation between each pair of point neighborhoods. To overcome the problems of Scott and Longuet-Higgins method, Shapiro

M. Pelillo and E.R. Hancock (Eds.): SIMBAD 2011, LNCS 7005, pp. 321–332, 2011.

and Brady [9] developed a method, which uses the intra-image point proximity matrix rather than the inter-image point association matrix. The eigenvectors of the proximity matrices are compared to calculate the correspondence across a pair of images. Caelli and Kosibov [3] have improved Shapiro's method by re-normalizing the eigenvectors and locating the correspondences by maximizing the inner-product of the normalized eigenvectors. Tang et al. [11] have used Gaussian weighted Laplacian property matrix to calculate correspondence matching from the eigenvectors of the Laplacian matrix.

Several authors have attempted to extend the utility of graph spectral methods using the complex property matrices. This is a natural way of incorporating angular or directional information with the proximity representation. Wilson, Hancock and Luo [5] extended the Laplacian matrix to the complex domain. Veltkamp et al. [8] developed a shape retrieval method using a complex Fielder vector of a Hermitian property matrix.

Although spectral methods are robust they are sensitive to noise and structural errors. To cope with this problem several researchers have used the statistical framework of EM algorithm. One of the earliest examples of using EM algorithm for feature correspondence matching is the work of Cross and Hancock [1]. They extend the standard EM algorithm by introducing structural consistency constraints to the correspondence matches. This is done by gating contributions to the expected log-likelihood function according to their structural consistency. This so-called dual step EM algorithm simultaneously locates point correspondence and parameters of the affine or perspective transformation matrix underlying the motion. Since this method uses a dictionary based approach to compute the correspondence probabilities, it is very time consuming. Carcassoni and Hancock [12] later improved the efficiency of the dual step EM algorithm by using the eigenvalues of the point proximity matrix to compute the gating weights.

In this paper we aim to perform the correspondence matching of point-sets by using a Hermitian property matrix. First, we compute the SIFT angles at the extracted feature points from the two images to be matched, we use the point locations and their angles to construct a complex Laplacian (Hermitian) matrix. Then we compute the complex eigenvectors of the Hermitian property matrix. Correspondence matching is calculated by comparing the complex eigenvectors. We show how to use the Hermitian matrix to render Carcassoni's EM algorithm more robust to noise and point jitter. We compare our results with Shaprio-Brady's and Carcassoni's original alignment methods.

2 Complex Laplacian (Hermitian) Matrix

A Hermitian matrix H (or self-adjoint matrix) is a square matrix with complex elements that remains unchanged under the joint operation of transposition and complex conjugation of the elements. That is, the element in the ith row and j^{th} column is equal to the complex conjugate of the element in the jth row and i^{th} column, for all indices i and j, i.e. $a_{i,j} = \overline{a}_{j,i}$. Complex conjugation is denoted by the dagger operator † i.e. $H^\dagger = H$. Hermitian matrices can be viewed as the complex number extension of the symmetric matrix for real numbers. The on-diagonal elements of a Hermitian matrix are necessarily real quantities. Each off-diagonal element is a complex number which has two components, and can therefore represent a 2-component measurement.

To create a positive semi-definite Hermitian matrix of a graph, there should be some constraints applied on the measurement representations. Let $\{x_1, x_2, ..., x_n\}$ be a set of measurements for the node-set $\mathcal{V}$ and $\{y_{1,2}, y_{1,2}, ..., y_{n,n}\}$ be the set of measurements associated with the edges of the graph, in addition to the graph weights. Each edge then has a pair of observations $(\mathcal{W}_{a,b}, y_{a,b})$ associated with it. There are a number of ways in which the complex number $H_{a,b}$ could represent this information, for example with the real part as $\mathcal{W}$ and the imaginary part as y. However, here we follow Wilson, Hancock and Luo [5] and construct the complex property matrix so as to reflect the Laplacian. As a result the off-diagonal elements of H are chosen to be $H_{a,b} = -\mathcal{W}_{a,b}e^{\iota y_{a,b}}$. The edge weights are encoded by the magnitude of the complex number $H_{a,b}$ and the additional measurement by its phase. By using this encoding, the magnitude of the number is the same as the original Laplacian matrix. This encoding is suitable when measurements are angles, satisfying the conditions $-\pi \leq y_{a,b} < \pi$ and $y_{a,b} = -y_{a,b}$ to produce a Hermitian matrix. To ensure a positive definite matrix, H_{aa} should be greater than $-\Sigma_{b \neq a}|H_{ab}|$. This condition is satisfied if $H_{aa} = x_a + \Sigma_{b \neq a}\mathcal{W}_{a,b}$ and $x_a \geq 0$. When defined in this way the property matrix is a complex analogue of the weighted Laplacian matrix for the graph.

For a Hermitian matrix there is an orthogonal complete basis set of eigenvectors and eigenvalues i.e. $H\phi = \lambda\phi$. The eigenvalues λ_i of Hermitian matrix are real while the eigenvectors ϕ_i are complex. There is a potential ambiguity in the eigenvectors, in that any multiple of an eigenvector is a solution of the the eigenvector equation $H\phi = \lambda\phi$. i.e. $H\alpha\phi = \lambda\alpha\phi$. Therefore, we need two constraints for them. Firstly, make each eigenvector of unit length vector i.e. $|\phi_i| = 1$, and secondly impose the condition $\arg \sum_i \phi_{ij} = 0$.

Given two images I and I' with m and n feature points respectivly. We commence by creating complex proximity matrices H and H' for both set of feature points. Besides the (x, y) coordinates of the feature points in the input images, we also calculate the angles at each of the feature points. We use SIFT [10] feature extraction algorithm to acquire angles at these points. The diagonal elements of H are calculated using a Gaussian-weighting function as:

$$H_{ij} = -e^{-r_{ij}^2/2\sigma^2} e^{\iota(\theta_i - \theta_j)} \tag{1}$$

where $r_{ij}^2 = \|x_i - x_j\|^2$ is the squared Euclidian distance between each pair of feature points. The parameter σ^2 controls the interaction between features and $(\theta_i - \theta_j)$ is the difference between each pair of angles within the same image. The on-diagonal elements are given by the sum of the real parts of the elements in the same row or in the same column of the matrix and hence are real numbers.

$$H_{ii} = \sum_{i \neq j} e^{-r_{ij}^2/2\sigma^2} \tag{2}$$

Once we have H and H' to hand we perform the eigen decomposition, i.e. $H = V\Lambda V^T$ and $H' = V'\Lambda'V'^T$ where V and V' are the modal matrices of the images I and I' respectively, with complex eigenvectors in its columns, Λ and Λ' are the diagonal matrices with real eigenvalues along their principal diagonals. Each row of the modal matrix V is a *feature vector* F_i, while each row of the modal matrix V' is a *feature vector* F'_j.

$$V = \begin{bmatrix} F_1 \\ F_2 \\ \vdots \\ F_m \end{bmatrix}, V' = \begin{bmatrix} F'_1 \\ F'_2 \\ \vdots \\ F'_n \end{bmatrix}$$

The least significant $|m - n|$ eigenvectors and feature vectors are removed from the larger modal matrix, in the case where V and V' are of different sizes.

The next step is to calculate the correspondence probabilities matrix ζ from the $feature\ vectors$ F_i of the image I and F'_j of the image I' by taking the Euclidian distances between each pair of feature vectors of both images using the following binary decision.

$$\zeta_{ij} = \begin{cases} 1, & \text{if } j = \arg min_{j'} \|F_i - F'_{j'}\|^2 \\ 0, & \text{otherwise} \end{cases}$$

$i = 1...|m - n|$, $j = 1...|m - n|$. However, the permutation of feature points in the input images changes the direction of the eigenvectors. Therefore, until the eigenvector direction for both modal matrices are not consistent, a direct comparison of the eigenvectors causes an error in the correspondence matching. If we take the matrix V as a reference matrix and correct the signs of the column in matrix V' as

$$\phi'_i := \begin{cases} \phi'_i, & \text{if } \|\phi_i + \phi'_i\| > \|\phi_i - \phi'_i\| \\ -\phi'_i, & \text{otherwise} \end{cases}$$

where ϕ_i are the columns of V and ϕ'_i are the columns of V'. Matches between the pair of points are given by the elements of association matrix Z which are maximum in their respective row and column.

3 Expectation Maximization

Suppose $\Phi^{(n)}$ is the geometric transformation that best aligns a set of image feature points $\overrightarrow{w}$ with the feature points $\overrightarrow{z}$ in a model. Each point is encoded in homogeneous co-ordinates. i.e. $\overrightarrow{w}_i = (x_i, y_i, 1)^T$ and $\overrightarrow{z}_j = (x_j, y_j, 1)^T$. Carcassoni and Hancock [12] EM algorithm matches point-features across a pair of images. They have shown how structural constraints can be embedded in an EM algorithm for point alignment under affine and perspective distortion. Graph-spectra are used to compute the required correspondence probabilities. Point correspondence matching and the parameters of the affine transformation matrix underlying the motion are simultaneously computed, so as to maximize the expected log-likelihood function:

$$Q(\Phi^{(n+1)}|\Phi^{(n)}) = \sum_{i \in D} \sum_{j \in M} P(\overrightarrow{z}_j|\overrightarrow{w}_i, \Phi^{(n)})\zeta_{i,j}^{(n)} \times \ln p(\overrightarrow{w}_i|\overrightarrow{z}_j, \Phi^{(n+1)}) \quad (3)$$

where D is the set of data feature points $\overrightarrow{w}_i$, M is the set of data feature points $\overrightarrow{z}_j$. The measurement densities $p(\overrightarrow{w}_i|\overrightarrow{z}_j, \Phi^{(n+1)})$ model the distribution of error-residuals between the two point sets. The log-likelihood contributions at iteration $n+1$ are weighted by the a posteriori measurement probabilities $P(\overrightarrow{z}_j|\overrightarrow{w}_i, \Phi^{(n)})$ computed at the previous iteration. The individual contributions to the expected log-likelihood function are gated by the structural matching probabilities $\zeta_{i,j}^{(n)}$. Under the assignment of Gaussian alignment errors, in the point positions, the correspondence probability matrix is give as

$$\zeta_{i,j}^{(n)} = \frac{\sum_{l=1}^{o} \exp[-\mu \parallel V_D^{(n)}(i,l) - V_M(j,l) \parallel^2]}{\sum_{j' \in M} \sum_{l=1}^{o} \exp[-\mu \parallel V_D^{(n)}(i,l) - V_M(j',l) \parallel^2]} \tag{4}$$

where $o = \min(|D|, |M|)$

3.1 E-Step

In the E step of the algorithm the a posteriori probabilities of the points $\overrightarrow{z}_j$ are updated. The a posteriori probabilities can be written in terms of the conditional measurement densities.

$$P(\overrightarrow{z}_j|\overrightarrow{w}_i, \Phi^{(n)}) = \frac{\alpha_j^{(n)} p(\overrightarrow{w}_i|\overrightarrow{z}_j, \Phi^{(n+1)})}{\sum_{j' \in M} \alpha_{j'}^{(n)} p(\overrightarrow{w}_i|\overrightarrow{z}_{j'}, \Phi^{(n+1)})} \tag{5}$$

where the mixing proportions are calculated as $\alpha_j^{(n+1)} = \frac{1}{|D|} \Sigma_{i \in D} P(\overrightarrow{z}_j|\overrightarrow{w}_i, \Phi^{(n)})$ The conditional measurement densities $p(\overrightarrow{w}_i|\overrightarrow{z}_j, \Phi^{(n)})$ can be defined in terms of a multivariate Gaussian distribution.

$$p(\overrightarrow{w}_i|\overrightarrow{z}_j, \Phi^{(n)}) = \frac{1}{2\pi\sqrt{|\Sigma|}} \times \exp\left[-\frac{1}{2}(\overrightarrow{z}_j - \Phi^{(n)}\overrightarrow{w}_i)^T \Sigma^{-1} (\overrightarrow{z}_j - \Phi^{(n)}\overrightarrow{w}_i)\right] \tag{6}$$

3.2 M-Step

The dual step EM algorithm iterates between the two interleaved maximization steps. The first step maximizes the a posteriori probability correspondence estimating correspondence assignments. The second one locates maximum likelihood for alignment parameters estimation. The update formula to maximize the a posteriori probability of the structural match is

$$f^{n+1}(i) = \arg\max_{j \in M} P(\overrightarrow{z}_j|\overrightarrow{w}_i, \Phi^{(n)}) \zeta_{i,j}^{(n)} \tag{7}$$

The maximum-likelihood affine transformation parameters $\phi_{k,l}^{(n+1)}$ for k=1,2 and l=1,2,3 are found by solving the following saddle-point equations, which can be solved using matrix inversion.

$$\frac{\partial Q(\Phi^{(n+1)}|\Phi^{(n)})}{\partial \phi_{k,l}^{(n+1)}} = 0 \tag{8}$$

$$\begin{aligned} \Phi^{(n+1)} = & \left[\sum_{i \in D} \sum_{j \in M} P(\overrightarrow{z}_j|\overrightarrow{w}_i, \Phi^{(n)}) \zeta_{i,j}^{(n)} \overrightarrow{w}_i U^T \overrightarrow{w}_i^T \Sigma^{-1} \right]^{-1} \\ & \times \left[\sum_{i \in D} \sum_{j \in M} P(\overrightarrow{z}_j|\overrightarrow{w}_i, \Phi^{(n)}) \zeta_{i,j}^{(n)} \overrightarrow{z}_j U^T \overrightarrow{w}_i^T \Sigma^{-1} \right] \end{aligned} \tag{9}$$

where Σ is the variance-covariance matrix for the position errors. The element of the matrix U are the partial derivatives of the affine transformation matrix with respect to the individual parameters, i.e.

$$U = \begin{pmatrix} 1\,1\,1 \\ 1\,1\,1 \\ 0\,0\,0 \end{pmatrix} \tag{10}$$

4 Experimental Results

In this section, we provide some experimental investigation of the correspondence matching using the complex Laplacian. We focus on its use in two different settings. The first is an investigation of using the standard proximity matrix and its Hermitian counterpart in the Shapiro-Brady [9] algorithm. The second is a similar investigation for the Carcassoni-Hancock [12] algorithm. In both settings, we experiment with synthetic and real world data.

Table 1. Performance on the CMU/VASC house sequence. The first image frame has been matched against the $20^{th}, 40^{th}, 60^{th}, 80^{th}$ and 100th frame.

	Number of incorrect matches				
Frame	1-20	1-40	1-60	1-80	1-100
Scott	0	0	4	7	18
Carcassoni	0	1	3	5	8
Hermitian	0	0	1	3	5

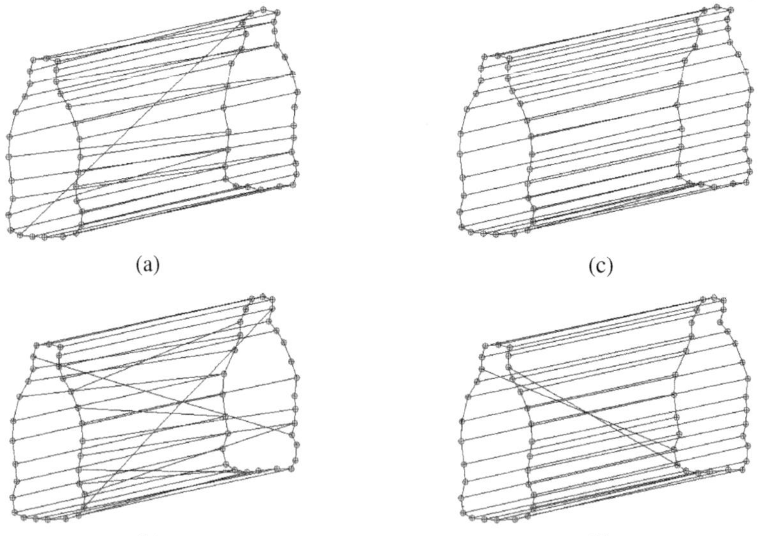

(a) (c) (b) (d)

Fig. 1. Correspondence matching with Gaussian noise added in point positions using (a)Shapiro-Brady method $\sigma = 0.1$ (b)Shapiro-Brady method $\sigma = 0.2$ (c)Hermitian matrix $\sigma = 0.1$ (d)Hermitian matrix $\sigma = 0.2$,

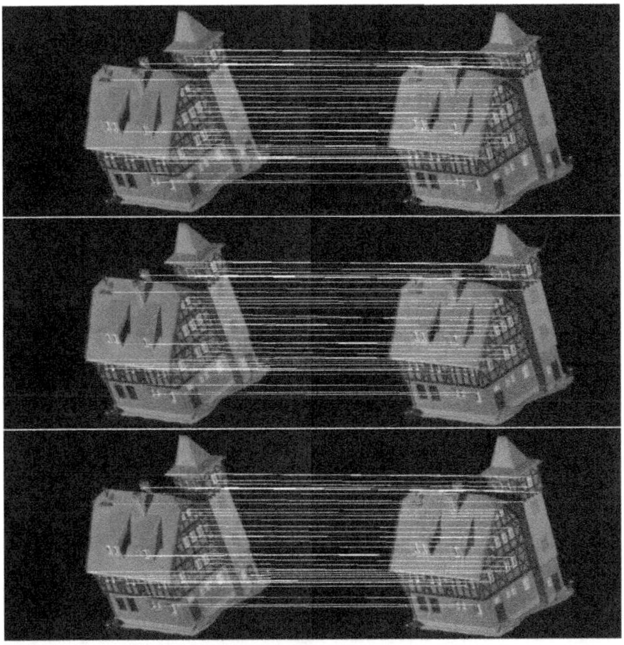

(a) Matching the 1st and 20th frame

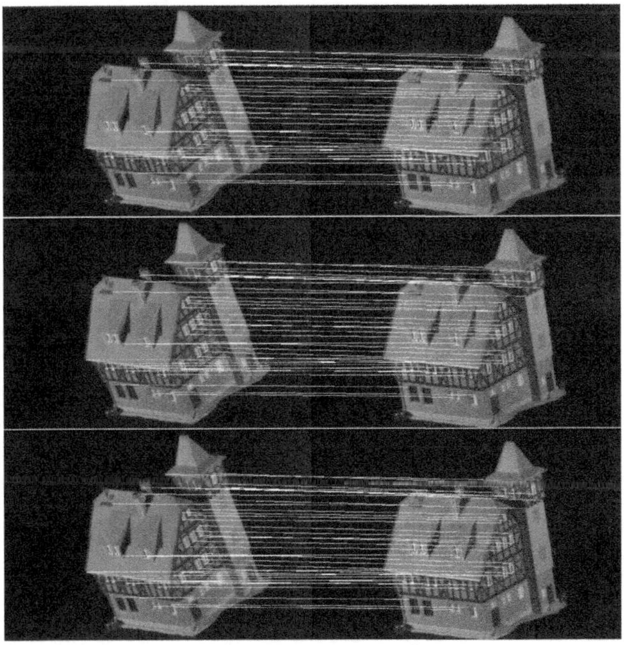

(b) Matching the 1st and 40th frame

Fig. 2. Comparisons between Carassoni, Scott and Longuet-Higgins and Our approach

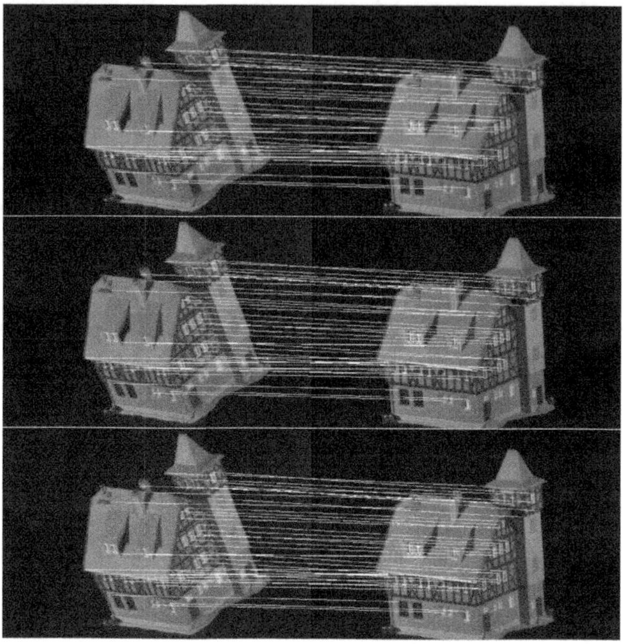

(c) Matching the 1st and 60th frame

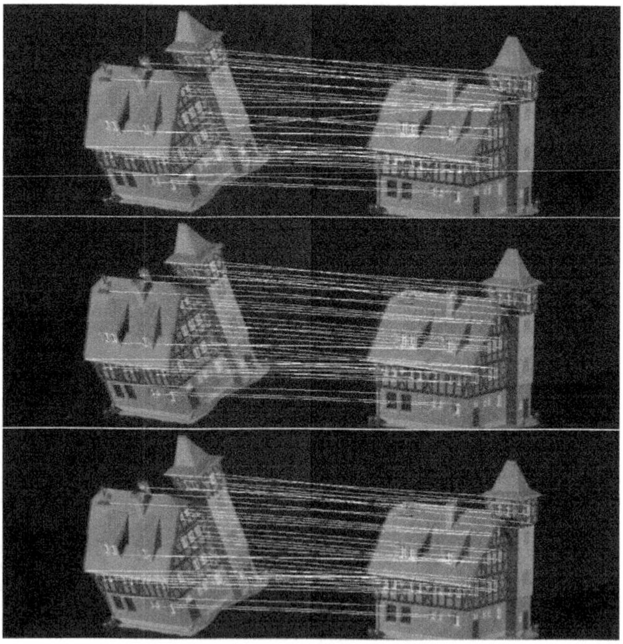

(d) Matching the 1st and 80th frame

Fig. 2. (*Continued*)

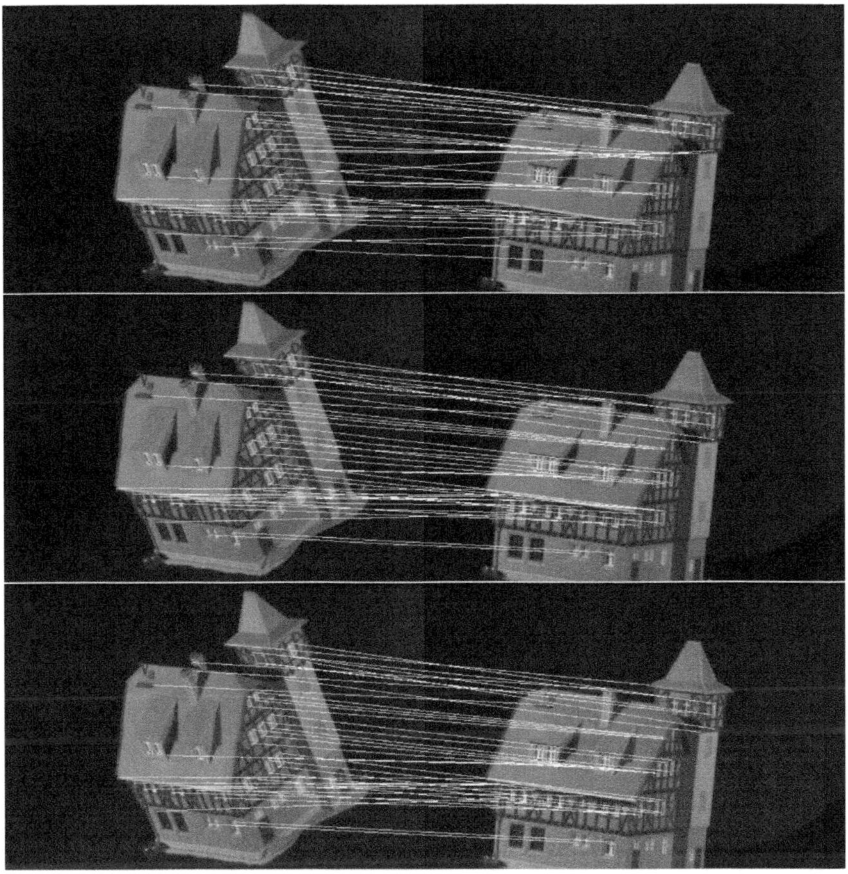

(e) Matching the 1st frame and 100th frame

Fig. 2. *(Continued)*

Our synthetic data is generated as follows. We took 30 equally spaced points along the silhouette of a bottle. We then generated noise corrupted images by adding Gaussian noise to the original point set. Correspondence results of both Shapiro-Brady algorithm and its Hermitian counterpart are shown in Fig. 1. The left column of (Fig 1(a) and Fig1(c)) shows the point matchings using the Hermitian matrix. The right column of (1(a) and 1(c)) shows the matching using Shapiro-Brady method. The upper and lower rows has noise of $\sigma = 0.1$ and $\sigma = 0.2$ added respectively. For real-world data we evaluate our approach on images from the CMU/VASC model-house sequence.

We have compared our method (referred to as Hermitian) with other spectral point matching methods i.e. Scott and Longuet-Higgins (referred to as Scott). and Carcassoni's EM point alignment algorithm. Forty feature points are extracted using KTL [7] feature point extractor from each image. Correspondences are calculated between the 1st frame and the 20th, 40th, 60th, 80th and 100th frames. Fig 4 compares the three different methods. The correspondences are shown in Fig. 4. In Fig. 2(a), 2(b), 2(c), 2(d) and 2(e) the

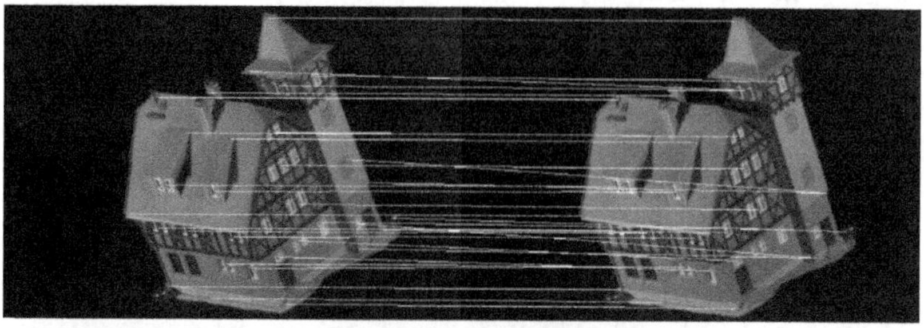

(a)

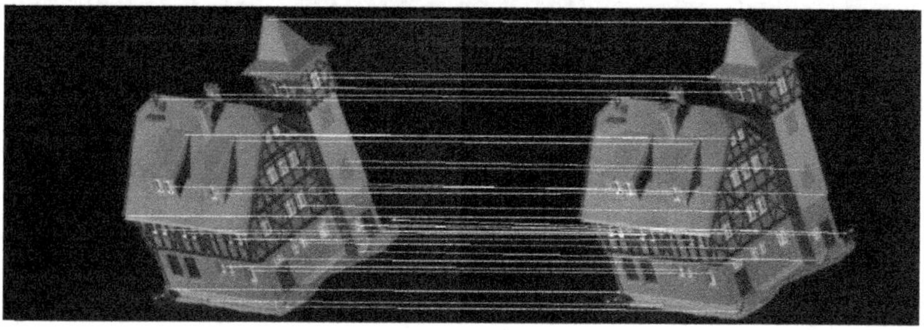

(b)

Fig. 3. Experimental results: Correspondence matching of the 1st and 10th frame (a)using spectral information only (b)using EM alignment along with spectral information

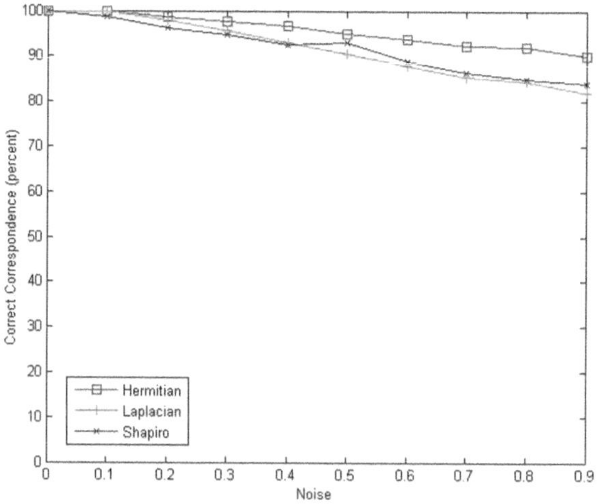

Fig. 4. Effect of noise in point positions

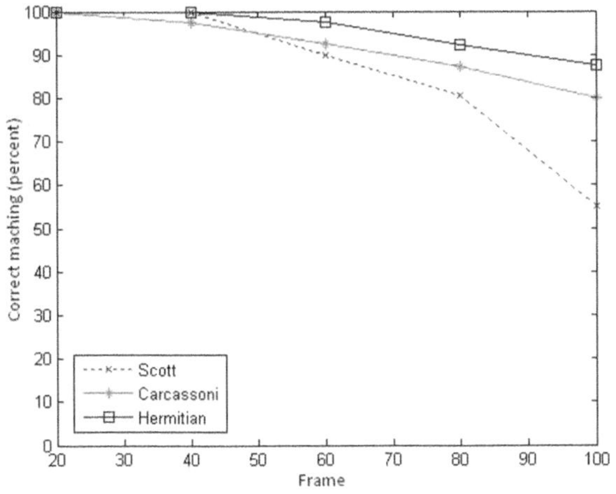

Fig. 5. Effect of viewing angle on correspondence matching

first pair of frames (top) are the results of Scott and Longuet-Higgins[6]. The second pair(middle) are the results of the Carcassoni and Hancock's EM algorithm and the third pair (bottom) are the results obtained when the Hermitian matrix is embedded in Carcassoni and Hancock's algorithm. The same results have been summarized in Table.1 also. Fig. 3 shows the matching between the 1st frame and the 10th frame of the CMU/VASC sequence. There are 6 incorrect matches using only spectral information. However, there is not any wrong matches when EM alignment algorithm is incorporated along with the complex spectral information.

Fig. 4 shows the fraction of correct correspondence against the level of noise added to a randomly generated set of 50 points. We compare the results of Shapiro-Brady's method, the Hermitian method (our approach) and Tang et al. [11] method (referred to as Laplacian), show that our method is more robust to the noise added in point positions.

5 Conclusions

In this paper we have investigated how the correspondence method of Shapiro and Barady [9] can be improved using complex eigenvector coefficients of a Hermitian property matrix. Secondly, we used the complex eigenvectors to calculate the correspondence probabilities matrix to render Carcassoni's EM algorithm more robust to large viewing angle change between the images being matched. Synthetic data and real world data both indicate that our approach works with a relatively higher accuracy.

Acknowledgement. We acknowledge the support form the EU FET project SIMBAD. Edwin R. Hancock is supported by a Royal Society Wolfson Research Merit Award.

References

1. Cross, A.D.J., Hancock, E.R.: Graph matching with a dual step EM algorithm. IEEE Trans. Pattern Anal. Mach. Intell. 20, 1236–1253 (1998)
2. Luo, B., Hancock, E.R.: Structural matching using EM algorithm and singular value decomposition. IEEE Transactions on Pattern Analysis and Machine Intelligence 23, 1120–1136 (2001)
3. Caelli, T., Kosinov, S.: An eigenspace projection clustering method for inexact graph matching. IEEE Trasactions on Pattern Analysis and Machine Intelligence 26(4), 515–519 (2004)
4. Pilu, M.: A direct method for stereo correspondence based on singular value decomposition. In: Proc. CVPR, pp. 261–266 (1997)
5. Wilson, R.C., Hancock, E.R., Luo, B.: Pattern Vectors from Algebraic Graph Theory. IEEE Trans. Pattern Anal. Mach. Intell. 27, 1112–1124 (2005)
6. Scott, G., Longuet-Higgins, H.: An algorithm for associating the features of two patterns. Proc. Royal Society of London, 21–26 (1991)
7. Shi, J., Tomasi, C.: Good features to track. In: CVPR, pp. 593–600 (1994)
8. van Leuken, R.H., Symonova, O., Veltkamp, R.C., De Amicis, R.: Complex Fiedler Vectors for Shape Retrieval. In: da Vitoria Lobo, N., Kasparis, T., Roli, F., Kwok, J.T., Georgiopoulos, M., Anagnostopoulos, G.C., Loog, M. (eds.) S+SSPR 2008. LNCS, vol. 5342, pp. 167–176. Springer, Heidelberg (2008)
9. Shapairo, L.S., Brady, J.M.: A modal approach to feature-based correspondence. Image and Vision Computing 10, 283–288 (1992)
10. Lowe, D.G.: Distinctive image features from scale-invariant keypoints. IJCV 99(2), 91–110 (2004)
11. Tang, J., Liang, D., Wang, N., Fan, Y.: A Laplacian spectral method for stereo correspondence. Pattern Recognition Letters 28, 1391–1399 (2007)
12. Carcassoni, M., Hancock, E.R.: Spectral correspondence for point pattern matching. Pattern Recognition 36(1), 193–204 (2003)
13. Umeyama, S.: An eigendecomposition approach to weighted graph matching problem. IEEE Transactions on Pattern Analysis and Maching Intelligence 13(4), 376–380 (1988)

Author Index

GPSR Compliance

The European Union's (EU) General Product Safety Regulation (GPSR) is a set of rules that requires consumer products to be safe and our obligations to ensure this.

If you have any concerns about our products, you can contact us on ProductSafety@springernature.com

In case Publisher is established outside the EU, the EU authorized representative is:

Springer Nature Customer Service Center GmbH
Europaplatz 3
69115 Heidelberg, Germany

Batch number: 10844619

Printed by Printforce, the Netherlands